Jobs and Careers Abroad

Guy Hobbs

Distributed in the USA by
The Globe Pequot Press, Guilford, Connecticut

VACATION WORK
PUBLICATIONS

Published by Vacation Work, 9 Park End Street, Oxford
www.vacationwork.co.uk

First published in 1971
edited by Alison Garthwaite
Second edition 1975
Third edition 1977
Fourth edition 1979
Fifth edition 1982
Sixth edition 1985
Seventh edition 1989
Eighth edition 1993
Ninth edition 1997
Tenth edition 2000
Eleventh edition 2002
Twelfth edition 2005

Thirteenth Edition 2006
edited by Guy Hobbs

THE DIRECTORY OF JOBS & CAREERS ABROAD

Copyright © Vacation Work 2006

ISBN 13: 978-1-85458-353-6
ISBN 10: 1-85458-353-0

ISSN 0143-3482

Cover design by mccdesign.
Typeset by Vacation Work

Printed and bound in Italy by Legoprint SpA, Trento

Contents

SPECIFIC CAREERS

WORLDWIDE EMPLOYMENT

Introduction

In both Britain and America, the desire amongst ordinary people to emigrate abroad has never been greater. A survey conducted in August 2006 found that in the UK, the number of people hoping to leave Britain in search of a better standard of living had doubled to 13% in just three years. This view was particularly prevalent in the younger generation aged 18-25. In contrast to the picture thirty-five years ago, when this book was first published, people are emigrating for positive reasons. They are not jumping ship or being pushed out by poor quality of life and a lack of opportunities. Cheaper travel and better communications have given people more mobility and greater choice within their careers. Put simply, emigration is now a far more viable option for far more people.

Increasing globalisation and the free access to labour markets has made the world a smaller place for jobseekers. The global economy has become increasingly integrated and people are on the move: however working abroad, although exciting and full of adventure, can be a complicated business. Preparation is the key if you want to make the most of any experience of living and working abroad. People who are likely to find the information in this book useful fall into every possible category, from students contemplating a working holiday to company executives looking for an overseas posting. *The Directory of Jobs and Careers Abroad* is specifically designed to help remove some of those frustrations, by providing its readers with the essential information they will need to find their way to suitable employment.

In order to address a very broad readership, it covers an extensive vocational and geographical spectrum, ranging from annual expeditions to arctic or tropical regions, to five-year engineering contracts in Saudi Arabia, or permanent emigration to New Zealand, Australia, or Canada. Whether you already work for a multinational company or have chosen a more informal career path, or whether you are a new graduate taking time out to travel, or a consultant in a specialised field, there will be a range of information to help you find something exactly suited to your needs.

This thirteenth edition of *The Directory* takes into account the many rapid changes involved in finding work abroad. It takes into account the constantly changing political situation and the new European Union member states; provides updated country-specific information; includes an expanded chapter on the environment; gives extensive new information on jobseeking using the internet; and revises and updates specific information about jobs in different sectors. It also provides current cultural and economic information as a general background to life and work in many different countries.

The world of work is changing. Interest in working abroad has now spread across all social and career boundaries and opportunities for employment mobility have never been better. Educational qualifications and linguistic competence are the two obvious requirements for the international jobseeker. However, flexibility and career 'ownership' – in which the responsibility for pursuing and developing a career lies firmly in the hands of the individual – are also important, whether you are a high-flyer in banking or engineering, a voluntary worker, or a graduate taking your first step on the employment ladder.

Your own decisions will affect, as never before, the outcome of your job search and your future career. This spirit of self-reliance – as well as a readiness to accept new challenges and experiences – is the cornerstone of building a future in a career abroad. Less hampered by rigid corporate structures of promotion and career advancement, we can use these changes in the world of work to our own advantage.

One key change in the modern job market is the demand for 'multi-skilling'. Jobs themselves are no longer immutable in modern, efficient organisations, but are flexible, with responsibilities and requirements changing according to the work that needs to be done. They are not as easily categorised into career structures as they once were. Another trend is globalisation. The beginning of the 21st century has seen the growth of an international market in many fields of employment, especially in specialised areas such as information technology and telecommunications. Developments in electronic communications are constantly pushing this process forward.

All of this can be good news for the creative jobseeker. Where there are few opportunities in your own country, there may be many abroad where the same qualifications and experience may be in short supply. Voluntary work is one area where the market (if this is the right term) is increasingly global; and a period as a volunteer or intern abroad may also lead to more permanent employment in a related field.

In this new career marketplace, CVs now need to be 'functional', so that the individual components of your work and experience are emphasised, and not just your chronological work history. Careers are now 'targeted', and organisational structures are 'flatter'. Recruitment agencies are still looking for the same result as previously – the right person for the right vacancy, procured as efficiently as possible – but increasingly they are doing so in new ways. Scanning technology for CV analysis and short-listing of candidates is now widely used, for instance, so that a portfolio of individual attributes on a CV – the right 'profile' – is more useful than a conventional account of your career to date.

Although the new market for jobs is international, it is not necessarily free. The restrictions of language remain, as do all the difficulties of relocating to another country – magnified many times over if you plan to move with your partner and children. Immigration restrictions also mean that the qualified jobseeker will always be favoured over those who wish to work in unskilled areas of employment. When weighing up the pros and cons of such an undertaking, you should consider your educational background and your aspirations for the future. What experience do you hope to gain? And how do you envisage that your time spent abroad will advance your aspirations?

The problem of large-scale unemployment is one that, although fluctuating, remains intractable even in the most prosperous first-world countries. Governments are always under pressure to keep barriers to international employment in place to guard against the oversupply of labour, even when other trading restrictions have been lifted. When hard times strike, the easiest rallying cry is often 'foreigners are taking our jobs'. Conversely, these same pressures are pushing ever more workers to market their skills abroad, in the expectation of enhanced career prospects, higher earnings and a better lifestyle.

INTERNATIONAL EMPLOYMENT

The rapid transformation of the economies of Central and Eastern Europe, including the former CIS, is one of the most important of recent change in the world economy, opening up a whole new range of employment possibilities for consultants and skilled workers. Free market ideas appear to have won the day in all but a few countries (notably North Korea or Cuba) where the future also looks likely to be one of gradual, or occasionally abrupt, integration into the global economy.

In the English-speaking world, the emergence of a multi-racial democracy in South Africa has had important ramifications for international job opportunities. In other countries, slow growth and unemployment still places some practical limits on the prospects for labour mobility, and in the USA, Canada, New Zealand, Australia, and the

UK, strict controls continue to apply, with immigration encouraged only in certain areas of labour or skills shortage.

In Asia, the handover of Hong Kong to China has not yet noticeably affected the job market, despite early fears of a slowdown, and China itself, with its huge economic potential, is emerging (alongside countries like Burma and Vietnam) as a major force in the 'second wave' of Asian economies to modernise.

Within the European Union (EU) working abroad is far less of a novelty than it used to be and for some, if not all, of its member states, the only real barriers to labour mobility will be cultural and linguistic.

In Latin America one of the major disincentives for British or US citizens seeking employment is cultural. There are stronger historical ties in this region with Spain and Portugal and greater employment and trading links with the USA than with Britain. In Africa, on the other hand, where there are still relatively few opportunities, the main barrier is economic. Voluntary and consultancy work in the field of development are the likeliest sources of employment in these under-developed or developing countries. The oil-producing countries of North Africa and especially the Middle East are, however, an exception to this rule. Some, like Libya, tend to award large-scale contracts to individual companies, which will then advertise the vacancies themselves or employ recruitment agencies. Sanctions against some states may also affect those looking for work. The market for jobs in development, construction, engineering and the petrochemical industry in general remains strong, and is one of the most fruitful areas for specialist professionals.

USING THIS DIRECTORY

This new edition retains the format of previous ones. The first and introductory section is practical, with chapters on *Discovering Your Employment Potential; Getting the Job; The Creative Job Search; Rules and Regulations; Learning the Language*; and *Preparation and Follow-up*. If you want to find out about rules governing employment in the EU, for instance, or about a creative approach to jobseeking, social security or taxation issues, or how to prepare for your stay in another country, you will find the relevant information here, along with some pointers for future research and steps to take. This introductory section is called *The General Approach*.

If a particular career or category of work is your starting-point, the second section on *Specific Careers* is the place to look. There are contacts for recruitment agencies and potential employers, as well as an introduction to each chapter on a particular aspect of the employment market.

The focus of this book is on opportunities across a broad spectrum of careers. Professions and fields covered include banking and accountancy; computer services and information technology; engineering; education; journalism; the law; medicine; secretarial and interpreting work; transport; hospitality; teaching; and tourism. International organisations are separately treated, as are the armed forces and the police. There is also a separate chapter on voluntary work.

The third section of *The Directory* is called *Worldwide Employment*. A general introduction to the country or region is followed by some facts and figures, a guide to conditions of work and work available, and specific contacts for jobseekers. Most people who consider emigrating still choose one of the more affluent countries of Western Europe, the Middle East, Asia, North America or Australasia, and the amount of space devoted to these countries reflects the greater prospects, for English-speakers, of finding work there. Some countries which are in the process of transformation into developed economies, such as Russia, are given greater space, reflecting the potential for opportunities, and their growing importance in the international jobs market.

As in previous editions, in each of these three main sections specific information is provided for North American as well as for British citizens, reflecting the readership of this book in these countries. The approach is open-ended; and each address, specific contact, or suggestion for further research should not be considered to be the end of the story, but as an invitation to research further – one link in a chain of opportunity that could lead to a job or career abroad.

THE CREATIVE JOB SEARCH

The section entitled *The General Approach* also includes techniques for finding work which may be unfamiliar to many readers, and requires some preliminary remarks here. The method is called 'the creative job search'. It is founded on the idea that there are a large number of 'invisible' vacancies and opportunities for employment of which jobseekers using more conventional approaches may be unaware. It is estimated that up to 75 per cent of vacancies in the USA, and about 65 per cent of those in the UK, fall into this category. These 'invisible' vacancies are not publicly advertised through jobcentres, employment agencies or in the press. The reality of recruitment is that jobs are most often found through alternative means such as word-of-mouth, or through a network of contacts who are closely connected with the particular field of employment in which you are interested.

Jobseekers will find their local careers service or business library a useful starting-point for information and advice, however, it is important to bear in mind the other possible routes to finding work. You can establish contacts in your chosen field by visiting the relevant trade fairs, for instance, or by working on a job placement scheme or as a volunteer. In addition, consider all the informal opportunities and encounters you have – the contacts you can make when travelling abroad, for instance, or through the internet.

The 'creative approach' will be more suited to some areas than others. Many vacancies are classified by recruitment professionals as 'low-risk', and these are more likely to be dealt with by the familiar methods of a job application and interview process. Middle management positions are usually 'medium-risk' (or more 'creative'), while 'high-risk' appointments are those that attract high-flyers or short-term workers. These are often in smaller companies where other considerations are foremost, such as time constraints and deadlines. In these high-risk areas a more creative approach will bear fruit.

These days it is said that employees, even of large companies should regard themselves as self-employed (in many cases this may also be how the company itself sees them) and they should actively market their expertise and ability, even when in employment. This frame of mind will benefit all international jobseekers. A positive and enthusiastic approach to career development is the reverse side of the trend towards downsizing and job insecurity, which are features of the jobs market today.

Those who don't move up in their career may be moved sideways, or even into unemployment and the widespread interest in working abroad itself may be a response to the more temporary and uncertain nature of work in a competitive global economy.

The aim of this job search, for those who are willing to take a more creative and positive approach (which will usually run alongside the more conventional methods) is to become a link in the 'chain of informal vacancy notification' (which is discussed more fully in the chapter, *The Creative Job Search*). Consistent preparation and perseverance are also necessary ingredients of your success (as they are also the preconditions for living and working in a country where the way of life and living conditions may be very different).

More than ever, individuals need to take responsibility for their career choices, and this applies most especially to jobs and careers abroad.

VACATION WORK PUBLICATIONS

For over thirty years, Vacation Work has been developing a range of publications for international jobseekers in different countries and fields of employment (and not just for those on vacation). Once you have decided on your career destination, you will find the

Live and Work series indispensable. Countries covered in this invaluable series of books include Australia and New Zealand; Belgium, The Netherlands and Luxembourg; China; Ireland; France; Germany; Italy; Japan; Scotland; Scandinavia; Spain; Portugal; USA and Canada; and Saudi and the Gulf. *Work Your Way Around the World* and *The Directory of Summer Jobs Abroad* are also useful sources of information for those seeking shorter-term jobs in other countries.

In addition, there are a number of more specialised, career-oriented publications providing extensive detail on finding a job in your chosen field. *Teaching English Abroad; Working in Tourism; Working on Cruise Ships; Working on Yachts and Superyachts; The Au Pair & Nanny's Guide to Working Abroad; Working in Ski Resorts; Working in Aviation; The International Directory of Voluntary Work; Working with Animals;* and *Working with the Environment* will put you on the right track. You will find a list of all available titles at the end of this book.

Guy Hobbs
Oxford
September 2006

The General Approach

Discovering Your Employment Potential

Exploring your employment potential is the first step to job-hunting success. Whether you are still at school or university, or have just left school or graduated; whether you are considering a change of employment, or are thinking about working abroad for the first time, the time taken to consider your aims and objectives both in life and career terms will be time well spent.

In the professional arena, some jobs may be ideal while others will simply 'do'. For many, just working and surviving in another country, with its attendant opportunities, may be sufficient challenge. On the other hand, however much you may love a culture or way of life, dreams can fade quickly when confronted with the mundanities of making ends meet. The more career-orientated traveller may have a longer-term goal in mind; but whatever the case, your own perception of your achievements will be your yardstick of success. Think clearly and realistically about your goals. What do you hope to get out of your stay abroad? What kind of work really appeals to you? And how will you match up to its requirements?

One question that careers advisers often ask is: what do you consider to be of importance or value? Look back on your experiences to date, in both work and education, and ask yourself which achievements have given you most satisfaction; which have filled you with a sense of pride and success? These questions are useful for anyone embarking on a career or life change, but they are especially helpful to those considering living and working abroad.

There are many invaluable works of reference now available to anyone thinking of making a significant change in their working life. Among those easily available in larger bookshops or libraries are: the *Careers Encyclopaedia* edited by Audrey Segal; *Equal Opportunities: A Career Guide* by Anna Alston (particularly useful for women); *What Color is your Parachute?* by Richard Nelson Bolles, one of the best-known 'how to' books in the job-search market, published both in the UK and the USA; and *Build Your own Rainbow: A Workbook for Career and Life Management* by Barrie Hopson and Mike Scally, which explores many of the same issues.

For graduates hoping to find work in Europe, *The European Graduate Career Guide* (www.eurograduate.com), published by Setform Ltd (Europa House, 13-17 Ironmonger Row, London EC1V 3QG; ☎ 020-7253 2545; e-mail mail@setform.com; www.setform. com), has articles and information on European recruiters in the fields of banking and finance, retail, engineering, healthcare, IT and Telecommunications. *Europgraduate Live* has a careers database which features thousands of graduate careers across Europe. You can search by any combination of qualification, industry, occupation or country of employment. The *Association of Graduate Careers Advisory Services* (AGCAS Administration Office, Millennium House, 30 Junction Road, Sheffield S11 8XB; ☎ 0114-251 5750; fax 0114-251 5751; www.agcas.org.uk) publishes a wide range of reasonably priced booklets on all kinds of occupations and careers, from jobseeking after graduation to working abroad. For a catalogue, write to CSU Ltd (Prospects House, Booth Street East, Manchester M13 9EP; ☎ 0161-277 5200; www.prospects.ac.uk). Among many other guides, CSU publishes *Where Next*, a self-help pack with a 50-minute video on career planning and making career choices and, for graduates, the *Prospects Directory* (also available from the address above, online and in most libraries) which features profiles and listings from more than 450 employers with Graduate vacancies.

Most universities and colleges in Britain and the USA also provide advice, information centres and libraries for new jobseekers. One leader in the field is the *The Careers Group, University of London* (Stewart House, 32 Russell Square, London WC1B 5DN; ☎020-7863 6066; e-mail careers@careers.lon.ac.uk; www.careers.lon.ac.uk). It is one of the sponsors of the annual London Graduate Recruitment Fair. If you are uncertain about your choice of future employment, or if you want to find out more about working abroad, a visit to the careers advice service in your university or locality is an essential first step.

CAREERS ADVISORY SERVICES

In Britain, Local Education Authorities (LEAs) – which will generally be the responsibility of your local authority or council – are required by law to provide a careers service to schools and some colleges, as well as to young people who are no longer in full-time education. Students at higher education institutions, which have their own careers services, thus have the additional option of consulting their local Careers Advisory Service.

Vocational interest guides, which are frequently linked with one of the growing number of computer databases providing occupational information, are widely used by both higher education and LEA Careers Services. Training and Enterprise Councils (TECS) – known as LECS in Scotland – often maintain similar information centres, holding publications relating to careers, qualifications and work abroad, as well as offering advice services for those considering self-employment.

Access to a careers advisory service, both in Britain and the USA, usually follows a consultation with a careers adviser or guidance practitioner. The easiest way to find state and college-run careers services or your nearest TEC or LEC is to consult your local yellow pages telephone directory or run a search on the internet.

CAREERS EUROPE

Careers Europe is the UK centre for international careers information. It is based in Bradford and provides advice to professionals within the guidance community on education, employment and training opportunities for each of the EU member states, and worldwide. If you are seeking general information about employment prospects in the EU, or if have you an enquiry about a specific career you wish to follow, then Careers Europe is the place to start. You can access Careers Europe's information materials at careers and Connexions centres, public libraries and schools.

Careers Europe produces a database called '*Exodus*' and a wide range of general '*Eurofact*' and '*Globalfact*' information sheets (which are generally available in Connexions, and Careers Service centres, as well as public libraries). These cover many different aspects of working, training and studying in various EU countries and more information about these topics can be found under the different country headings in the *Worldwide Employment* section of this book. Careers Europe also publishes a magazine, *EuroExpress* in both printed and electronic formats, aimed at professionals in the recruitment and advisory field as well as those seeking employment.

Careers Europe cannot respond to enquiries, but provides extensive information through the organisations listed above. The Careers Europe resource centre is based at *Careers Europe*, 72-74 Godwin Street, Bradford, West Yorkshire BD1 3PT; ☎01274-829600; fax 01274-829610; e-mail europe@careersb.co.uk; www.careerseurope.co.uk.

CAREER COUNSELLORS AND CV SERVICES

In addition to publicly funded careers advice services, private career counsellors are also available to those able and willing to pay for them. Independent career counsellors are similar to management recruitment consultants insofar as they deal mainly with more senior and executive-level positions. Their service is, however, aimed at the individual who is considering the whole course of a career, and will usually combine an analysis of his or her capabilities with recommendations for future action.

Career counsellors do not place people in specific jobs, but merely provide general guidelines based on the applicant's personality, achievements, qualifications, ambitions, and personal circumstances, by making use of personality profiles, 'psychometric testing', questionnaires, and other methods of assessment. One positive outcome of such counselling may be a re-evaluation by the individual of his or her employment potential. Crucially, this could help in assessing the applicant's suitability for work abroad.

As well as providing advice on the applicant's future career, much emphasis is placed on matters which should interest all jobseekers, such as how best to present oneself when applying for vacancies, submitting job applications and CVs, and interview and selection techniques. Fees for these services vary widely, but will usually start at around £250. Below is a brief list of professional career counsellors; others may be located through the local yellow pages:

Career Analysts, Career House, 120 Crawford Street, London, W1U 6BD; ☎020-7935 5452; e-mail info@careeranalysts.co.uk; www.careeranalysts.co.uk, a professional group of consultant psychologists offering career assessments and advice to applicants of all ages, including GAP year activities overseas. The service provides a complete career 'check-up' and all assessments include completion of a personal history form, tests of aptitudes, interests, personality and needs, an in-depth consultation, followed by a full report. The services range from young people aged 15 and upwards to senior executives. Advice given on career direction, courses and qualifications, as well as on the best career opportunities abroad. Free brochure available on request.

Career Psychology Ltd., Berkely Square House, Berkely Square, London, W1J 6BD; ☎020-7887 4585; e-mail info@career-psychology.com; www.career-psychology.com. Expert individual counselling on career direction at all levels, including psychometric testing.

Cressing Templar, 42 New Broad Street, London EC2M 1SB; ☎020-7562 4330; fax 020-7496 9449; 6 Chester Street, Edinburgh EH3 7RA; ☎0131-226 7203; fax 0131-225 9972; Allan House, Bothwell Street, Glasgow G2 6NL; ☎0141-204 1686; fax 0141-221 2882; www.cressingtemplar.com. A human resource management consultancy specialising in career management and outplacement for senior managers and board level executives; salary and career change advice for graduates.

CVServices, Dolphin House, Woodgreen, Witney, Oxford OX8 6DH; ☎01993-702040; fax 01993-702100; e-mail s-holmes@btclick.com; www.cvservices.net. Managing consultant Steven Holmes provides CV and letter advice, following an in-depth interview. Additional services can include briefing before job interviews, strategic mailshots in Britain and abroad, advice on careers and training, and appraisal of current approach and CV or résumé-style. The website offers advice on how to write a good CV and provides high-level discussion of job search issues and career management, and a free initial online CV evaluation service.

Résumé Resource Center, PO Box 477, Dover, Delaware 19901, USA; www.resumestore.com. Specialises in writing detailed CVs for international employment. They will also send your details to over 3,000 recruiters and companies worldwide. Free web page. Cost from US$99 for a full CV and $25 for a covering letter.

Getting the Job

OVERVIEW

There are probably almost as many possible ways of finding a job abroad as there are individual jobseekers. In general terms, speaking the local language will, without doubt, be an advantage as will possessing a degree of 'cultural awareness' (see *Preparation and Follow-up* below). An understanding of the application procedures used in different countries can also be vital to your success.

Many jobseekers may already be working in a profession which has potential in the international job market (accountancy, engineering, and nursing are generally considered highly mobile fields), while others will find that working for an international company or organisation in their home country may provide an opening abroad. Many local companies' recruitment activities do not include publicising opportunities for overseas postings, and it can be useful to be aware of this. Companies will want to focus on your suitability for the job itself as their main reason for employing you, and *not* on your interest in foreign travel. On the other hand, in fields such as voluntary work, travel and tourism, or English-language teaching, your readiness and ability to adapt to another culture can be a key 'selling point' in the job search.

Many international jobseekers are looking to start a new career by taking advantage of opportunities that might not be available at home. For some, the impulse will be entrepreneurial (and those economies which are in the process of transformation, in Eastern Europe and elsewhere, are likely destinations for this more adventurous kind of jobseeker). A temporary job in a foreign country may, however, become a permanent one, and you should not fail to consider the possibility of long-term change when making important career and life choices of this kind.

The 'lower' end of the international jobs market largely caters for those with a desire to travel and to see the world. In many cases you will be doing the jobs that locals prefer not to do (working as an au pair for example, or doing seasonal harvest work), and pay will often be poor and the work sporadic. The inspirational book, *Work Your Way Around the World*, is a very useful source here, as are most of Vacation Work's many publications.

For any jobseeker with higher aspirations, qualifications are vital (and may be required before you can even get a visa, as in Japan), however, younger travellers may be able to use a stay abroad to gain the qualifications, as well as the experience, which will give them better leverage in the job market. In some countries shortages of skilled tradespeople mean that there are many profitable opportunities where work is plentiful and well paid, and skilled applicants may have an advantage in the visa application process. This is not only the case in developing areas; Australia, for example, currently requires electricians and other construction professionals. Skilled engineers, electronics and IT and communications professionals, consultants, and those with a specialist knowledge or training will find that their skills are generally in demand around the world.

So, where to begin? Many carry out their job search independently, by using the contact addresses in this directory or other publications; others like to take a chance and save their job search until they arrive at their chosen destination or country. Sometimes your company or organisation will take the decision to send you on an overseas posting (in which case you can 'fast-forward' to the specific country information later in this book, and the chapters on *Rules and Regulations, Learning the Language*, and *Preparation and Follow-up*). In other cases, the decision to work abroad may arise from an opportunity which is simply 'too good to miss', although you can, of course, work to maximise such unexpected opportunities by adopting a more creative approach to your job search.

WHERE TO START

The pages of 'jobs abroad' publications and magazines, at home and overseas, are always full of vacancies. English-language advertisements appear regularly in the main newspapers of every country (see the individual country chapters for these), even where English is not the mother tongue. The development of the internet means that many specialised jobs are now directly accessible, and therefore available, to applicants everywhere in the world. This unprecedented expansion of job availability is leading to greater specialisation in the types of job that are on offer, and in the applicants required. With this in mind you should aim to meet these specialised criteria when you send off that all-important letter of application and CV.

Fluency or even a basic knowledge of another language can be an enormous asset both professionally and personally when looking for work abroad. Major companies in the UK and North America often seek qualified staff with one or more foreign languages or a multicultural background, whether or not there is an immediate opening in an overseas office or subsidiary. Companies in other countries (which have their own language deficit in English) also look to the UK and the English-speaking world as an important source of recruitment and advertise widely in the UK and USA, both through newspapers and recruitment agencies.

Whatever your intended career path, it is vital to do your homework and some preparation beforehand. Daunting though this project may seem, remember that every year large numbers of Britons, North Americans and Australians, Kiwis and South Africans successfully make the transition from merely dreaming of a new lifestyle to actually living and working abroad. There is every reason to feel optimistic!

INTERNATIONAL VACANCIES

Although subject to regular fluctuations unemployment is a worldwide problem. Nonetheless, the number of vacancies and job opportunities around the world remains enormous: in the UK, for example, although there are currently around 1.6 million people unemployed and seeking work, the other side of the coin shows that there are almost 29 million in employment, and that up to 20 per cent of these jobs will change their incumbent over the course of a year. This means that more than four million jobs become vacant every year. The number of advertised vacancies is also high at present, with approximately 600,000 new vacancies registered at local UK Jobcentres each month. It is estimated, however, that only one-third of all jobs are advertised publicly, and thus, allowing for the percentage of jobs which are re-advertised, it is calculated that there are around five million vacancies advertised every year in the UK alone; in Jobcentres, newspapers and magazines, or through recruitment agencies. When you consider that most developed countries are currently operating with the same ballpark figure, you can begin to appreciate just how extensive the international availability of work can be and, as will become clear in the following sections, publicly advertised vacancies are by no means the only source available to those seeking work, either at home or abroad.

Of course, while the magnitude of job opportunities is clear, finding just the right one to suit you will require energy, initiative, and often a willingness to take risks. Competition for jobs across the whole spectrum of careers is greater than ever before, so much so that a reappraisal of traditional methods of job hunting has become necessary. The most successful applicants today are actively marketing their expertise and constantly updating their skills and knowledge of the market. Even those on long-term employment contracts keep their eyes on the market, looking for new opportunities and even freelance sidelines.

Anybody who has ever been unemployed will be familiar with the old adage that looking for a job is a job in itself, and in today's fragmented job market this remains true for many categories of jobseeker. It is no longer enough to rely solely on time-honoured methods of replying to job advertisements, or sending out speculative letters and CVs. Imagination and lateral thinking are now very often the keys to success.

FINDING THE JOB

Apart from responding to advertised vacancies and applying directly to firms, there are two other main methods of finding a long-term job. Either you use a recruitment consultancy of some kind, or you use your own initiative and enterprise and set about finding the job yourself by other means.

A recruitment consultant or jobs database can be very effective, particularly when you have appropriate qualifications. However, you should remember that it is not the function of recruitment agencies to find specific jobs for *the candidates* that come to them. Their role is to find the right applicants for the *employers* who have commissioned their services, as well as to fill any vacancies that remain on their books.

There are many international jobseekers who expect government organisations such as foreign embassies to help them find work in another country. Unfortunately, very few foreign embassies are actively involved in recruitment (there are a few exceptions – see the embassies mentioned below under *Government Agencies*), although they may be able to send useful information and advice on immigration and employment conditions in the country of interest.

A more dynamic approach to jobseeking is very often the most successful – remember that employers are likely to be impressed by initiative and self-reliance, putting you one step ahead in the race to land that perfect job. There are 'conventional' and 'creative' approaches to finding a job, and a combination of the two approaches, involving thoroughness and imagination, consistency and lateral thinking, will achieve the best results.

INTERVIEWS AND CVS

These days there is a surfeit of advice available on all aspects of interview technique and CV preparation, and the diligent job seeker should ensure that he or she keeps up to date with currently favoured recruitment strategies. In essence however, it is important that your CV be carefully laid out and that it includes details about yourself, your employment history and your education. Most CVs take a chronological approach, beginning with the most recent work or educational experience; however, skills-based CVs are now becoming popular and can be useful for applicants who lack a significant work history. When applying, do not forget to mention exactly which position you are interested in. Large firms deal with many applicants every week, and are unlikely to spend time working with incomplete forms.

Always state your qualifications clearly, giving detail where necessary. You may know what your particular qualification means, but an employer who deals with applicants from many countries may not. It can be helpful to contact the embassy of the country involved and enquire whether there is an equivalent qualification that you can mention as a yardstick by which the prospective employer can measure your own qualification(s).

Try to include a self-addressed envelope and International Reply Coupons to the correct value; it shows consideration and will ensure you a reply, even if it turns out to be a negative one. It is becoming increasingly common to apply for jobs by fax or e-mail and in many cases application forms are downloadable over the internet using software such as Adobe Acrobat. Whatever your method of application, a covering letter is always important – use it to make yourself stand out from the crowd.

Many careers counsellors and consultants offer help with CV preparation (see *Career Counsellors*). The *Careers* Group at the University of London recommends the following guides to preparing a good CV and job applications: *And A Good Job Too*, by David

Mackintosh (Orion); *How to Write a Curriculum Vitae* (ULCS); *How to Complete a Job Application Form* (ULCS); *Succeed at Your Job Interview*, by George Heaviside (BBC Books); *Great Answers to Tough Interview Questions*, by Martin John Yate (Kogan Page); and *Test Your Own Aptitude*, by J. Barrett and G. Williams (Kogan Page).

It is important to know what *sort* of CV to prepare for a prospective employer abroad. A German banker will be used to receiving CVs in a format that may differ greatly from that expected by a US banker. You should therefore be aware of the different work cultures of countries and be prepared to adapt your CV to the style of the country in which you wish to find work. A useful book that explores this procedure is *Breaking Through Culture Shock* by Dr Elisabeth Marx (published by Nicholas Brealey Publishing).

Your initial research into recruitment opportunities in your chosen country should include the language requirements and qualifications necessary for the hoped for job, and any likely contacts and networking possibilities that exist. It is also important to develop a feeling for the country and its culture in order to be sure that it is the right environment for you. Good local knowledge will enhance your enjoyment of a new lifestyle immeasurably and will help minimise the problems of culture shock. The *Lonely Planet* and *Rough Guide* series, available in all large bookstores, are useful for both off-the-beaten-track towns and street-wise information.

THE CONVENTIONAL JOB SEARCH

The vast majority of people looking for a job follow the traditional method of jobseeking – the conventional job search. In order to get the best results from this, you must still put time and effort into this approach, but combine it with other more creative ways of seeking work. By doing so you will create a competitive advantage for yourself. Identify your own strengths and weaknesses and take the necessary steps to remedy your areas of inexperience or lack of knowledge. Always play to your strengths and play down your weaknesses.

ADVERTISEMENTS

Advertisements in the press work in two ways. There will certainly be 'situations vacant' and 'situations wanted' columns in the newspaper you read everyday (and its equivalent in the country where you are seeking work). For specialist trades and professions, you will find a greater concentration of suitable vacancies in professional journals and magazines. You should seek out the foreign language equivalents of these specialist publications for the country or countries in which you are considering employment. Sometimes foreign-language newspapers will carry English-language advertising. A full list of general and specialist newspapers and magazines published in the UK is given in *British Rates and Data* (known as 'BRAD'), available in public reference libraries.

The major US newspapers carrying international recruitment advertising (and generally easily available in large cities abroad such as London) are: the *Chicago Tribune* (www.chicagotribune.com); the *Los Angeles Times* (www.latimes.com); the *New York Times* (www.nytimes.com); and the *Wall Street Journal* (www.wsj.com). The *International Herald Tribune* (www.iht.com) also contains high-flying vacancies, as does the *Financial Times* (www.ft.com). International recruitment advertisements appear in the *Financial Times* and the *International Herald Tribune* on Thursdays, and in the *Wall Street Journal* on Tuesdays.

In Britain the four major national broadsheet newspapers are *The Times* (www.timesonline. co.uk), *The Daily Telegraph* (www.telegraph.co.uk), *The Guardian* (www.guardian.co.uk), and *The Independent* (www.independent.co.uk). They all carry extensive advertisements for jobs throughout the UK, as well as a scattering of international appointments, as do their Sunday counterparts *The Sunday Times, The Sunday Telegraph, The Observer* (observer. guardian.co.uk) and the *Independent on Sunday*. Different employment sectors are covered each day of the week.

Canada Employment Weekly (21 New Street, Toronto, Ontario M5R 1P7, Canada; ☎416-964 6069; www.mediacorp.com) advertises professional job vacancies in Canada, as does the national *Globe and Mail* newspaper (444 Front Street West, Toronto, Ontario M5V 2S9; ☎416-585 5000; www.theglobeandmail.com). In Britain, *Outbound Publishing* (1 Commercial Road, Eastbourne, East Sussex BN21 3XQ; ☎01323-726040; www.outboundpublishing.com) publishes newspapers aimed at jobseekers whose intended destinations are New Zealand, Australia, Canada, Europe, South Africa, or the USA; with useful news and information about emigration to these countries. There is more about the various national newspapers in the relevant country section in the *Worldwide Employment* section of this book.

The main UK trade publications carrying overseas recruitment advertising are: *Architects' Journal; Caterer and Hotelkeeper; Certified Accountant; Computing* and *Computing Weekly; Construction News* and *Contract Journal* (for the building and construction trades); *The Engineer, Flight International; The Lancet* (medical); *Nature* (science); *New Scientist; Nursery World; Nursing Times; The Stage; Surveyor* and *Press Gazette*.

The publications of foreign professional and trade associations produced for circulation 'in-house' among their members can be another useful source of possible job opportunities. Your own national trade association or union may also be able to provide other international contacts.

In many ways the best and most direct contacts are found in the foreign press, especially if your focus is on a particular place or country. The better-known foreign papers are available in most newsagents or libraries. One useful contact, *Factiva* (Commodity Quay (6), East Smithfield, London E1W 1AZ; www.factiva.com), a joint venture between Dow Jones and Reuters, is an online service which gives access both to news and to 2,000 business publications from around the world, including newspapers and trade journals. Information can be retrieved by word search or selection lists for companies, countries and topics.

Most major international newspapers now also have online access and will usually place their recruitment classifieds on the internet every week. You can access a complete international list of such publications by using one of the indexed search engines on the internet, such as *Google*. Click on *Newspapers* and navigate downwards to locate particular sites and general newspaper lists for every country. Embassies and cultural organisations also have reading rooms where the general public can access up-to-date issues of newspapers and journals from that country. An excellent selection of international newspapers can also be found at the *City Business Library* in London (1 Brewers' Hall Garden, London EC2V 5BX; ☎020-7332 1812). Most newspapers can also be ordered on subscription through their UK or US agents (see the various countries in the *Worldwide Employment* section). Single copies of foreign newspapers are most easily obtained by contacting the head office (usually the advertising department) of the paper concerned.

In Europe, the *European Media Directory* covers 26 countries, listing specialist publications organised by category and country. 'Situations Wanted' ads can be placed in newspapers indirectly through agencies, which will assist you in your choice of newspaper or journal, even helping with wording if this is necessary. *Benn's Media Directory* (UK, Europe and World volumes) is a useful source of agencies providing this service. It gives the addresses of the main newspapers and a classified list of periodicals and specialist journals with cross-coded references to the UK agents, or to the UK branch office of the newspaper itself. *Willings Press Guide* (www.willingspress.com) provides similar information. You will also find UK and US representatives of the most important newspapers listed in the separate chapters of *Worldwide Employment*. It has to be stressed that these newspaper agents do not arrange jobs abroad, and that they require advance payment.

The 'international' volume lists each country's newspapers and journals in alphabetical order (along with any relevant agents) and the lists are generally more detailed than in *Benn's*. Addresses of major foreign newspapers and UK agents can also be obtained from the *Advertisers Annual* (Hollis Publishing Ltd, Harlequin House, 7 High Street, Teddington, Middlesex TW11 8EL; ☎020-8977 7711; fax 020-8977 1133; www.hollis-pr.com), which details some international recruiters. All these books should be available in public or business libraries. American readers can consult the *Editor & Publisher International Yearbook* (Editor & Publisher, 770 Broadway, New York, NY 10003; ☎1-800-336-4380; www.editorandpublisher.com) or *Ulrich's International Periodicals Directory* (RR Bowker, 630 Central Avenue, New Providence, NJ 07974, USA; ☎1-800-526-9537; www.ulrichsweb.com). In addition, there are also numerous advertising consultancies that act independently of newspapers and can advise you on your choice of medium; they will help you compose your advertisement and place it on your behalf. These consultancies are listed in the *Advertisers' Annual*.

DIRECT APPLICATION

When looking for a job abroad, the most obvious initial approach is to write directly to specific companies or organisations in the country where you are hoping to work. Targeting your letters and including full details of the type of work that you are looking for will obtain the best results. The main challenge, however, is to find the right names and addresses of contacts and companies. Use a library or information centre as a starting point, as well as any other information which may be available to you, including your own personal contacts (see *The Creative Job Search*). You could also consult the international trade yearbooks such as the *Advertisers' Annual, Bankers' Almanac and Yearbook, Flight International Directory, Insurance Directory and Yearbook, Oil and Gas World*, which list companies worldwide. Other publications with contact addresses include the *Europa Yearbook,* which lists international organisations as well as each country's principal banks, universities, radio and TV stations, and trade associations; *The World of Learning* (also published by Europa), which includes information on scholarly societies, research institutes and universities. National or regional guidebooks will also contain some useful addresses for those wishing to work in hospitality and tourism.

Foreign telephone directories and 'yellow pages' naturally offer the widest range of contact details although these will be unfiltered; that is, it is often difficult to tell exactly what kind of organisation you are dealing with, especially in terms of size. Embassies stock their own national directories and an appointment will usually be necessary for access. A large selection of directories are also available at the *City Business Library* in London, however, it does not hold every directory as some are very difficult to obtain, so always telephone in advance. International telephone directories are usually also available at the major reference libraries such as *Westminster Reference Library* in London (35 St Martin's Street, London WC2H 7HP, ☎020-7641 1300; www.westminster.gov.uk/libraries. Open 10am-8pm Monday to Friday, 10am-5pm on Saturday), or those situated in other major cities. In the US, these major libraries include the *Library of Congress* (101 Independence Avenue, South East, Washington, DC 20540; ☎202-707 5000; www.loc.gov. Open 8.30am-9.30pm Monday to Friday, 8.30am-6.30pm Saturday) which provides a reference service on subjects including business, economics, and employment; and the *Federal Trade Commission Library* (600 Pennsylvania Avenue N.W., Washington, DC 20580; ☎202-326 2395; www.ftc.gov. Open 8.30am-5pm Monday to Friday) which also contains 120,000 volumes on legal, economic and business subjects, and 1,000 periodicals. The *Los Angeles Public Library* (630 West 5th Street, Los Angeles, CA90071; ☎213-228 7000; www.lapl.org. Open 10am-8pm Monday to Thursday, 10am-6pm Friday to Saturday, and 1pm-5pm Sunday) has a large business and economics section, and an online computer search service. The Australian telephone directories are available online at www.yellowpages.com.au and www.whitepages.com.au.

Many reference and business libraries also hold a selection of the *Kompass Directories* (www.kompass.com) which contain lists of the major commercial enterprises across the world. They are classified by country and type of product and are now available online, on CD-ROM, as well as in book form. Another valuable collection of international trade and telephone directories is held at the *UK Trade and Investment Information Centre* (Level 1, Kingsgate House, 66-74 Victoria Street, London SW1E 6SW; ☎020-7215 8000; fax 020-7215 4231; www.uktradeinvest.gov.uk). This organisation provides a self-help reference library for exporters and is open from 9am-5.30pm Monday to Friday. It holds market research reports, trade fair catalogues, and country profiles. Students require an appointment. The *British Library Business Information Service* operates the British Library-Lloyds TSB Bank Business Line (open 9am to 5pm; Monday to Friday) which provides useful information on international employment and trade to researchers and companies. The service can be contacted on ☎020-7412 7454.

OVERSEAS SUBSIDIARIES

BRITISH SUBSIDIARIES

The overseas branches or subsidiaries of British firms provide the opportunity to work abroad in one of two ways. Direct application is one method, but the other, more usual way, is to begin working for a company with international branches in Britain and then ask to be transferred abroad. In some cases it may be possible to discuss overseas work opportunities at the interview stage, and some companies will take on workers because they can offer a particular foreign language or cultural background in addition to possessing other qualifications. Of course, being sent on a posting abroad will usually depend on how successful you have been as an employee in your home country, and working for an international company in Britain cannot be counted on as a sure-fire way of moving abroad.

Lists of some of the major British enterprises in European countries are included at the end of the respective chapters in the *Worldwide Employment* section, but more complete and up-to-date information can sometimes be obtained from the British Chambers of Commerce in those countries. The *British Chambers of Commerce Directory* has details of 150 such organisations around the world as well as trade associations in the UK (which often have links abroad). It is available in public libraries and from The *British Chambers of Commerce* (65 Petty France, St James Park, London SW1H 9EU; ☎020-7654 5800; e-mail info@britishchambers.org.uk; www.britishchambers.org.uk). Where such lists of affiliates or subsidiaries of UK or US companies exist separately or as part of Chamber of Commerce yearbooks, details are also given at the end of the individual chapters of the *Worldwide Employment* section.

If you are unwilling to part with your money for all these lists and information services then consult *Who Owns Whom* (Dun & Bradstreet; http://dbuk.dnb.com), which is available in many reference or business libraries. Chambers of Commerce yearbooks are also sometimes found on general reference library shelves. In London, the Science *Reference and Information Services Library* (25 Southampton Buildings, London WC2A 1AW; ☎020-7412 7473) has several CD-ROMs, including *Fame*, *Disclosure World Scope* and *Disclosure*, which give details of UK companies and their subsidiaries worldwide. Increasingly, these specialised electronic resources are also available in County reference libraries, especially those with a Business Information Point.

AMERICAN SUBSIDIARIES

The overseas subsidiaries of American parent companies can also offer work. UK jobseekers can begin with those with a large presence in the UK. However, in some areas only those trained in the USA are likely to be considered. Because of the vast scale of US business enterprise abroad, subsidiaries have not been listed here, but some American Chambers of Commerce publish lists, about which details are given in the *Worldwide Employment* section, where relevant. Directories of American parent and subsidiary companies are also available from *Uniworld Business Publications Inc* (3 Clark Road, Millis, Massachusetts 02054-1213; ☎508-376 6006; e-mail info@uniworldbp.com; www.uniworldbp.com) publish the 4,200-page *Directory of American Firms Operating in Foreign Countries* which contains an extensive list for each country and a short description of the main areas of operation of each company. They also publish the *Directory of Foreign Firms Operating in the United States*. Their pricelist gives the latest prices and postage charges – expect to pay several hundred dollars for these publications, both of which are also available on CD-ROM. Addresses of American parent and subsidiary companies are also included in *Who Owns Whom* (see above).

INTERNATIONAL COMPANIES

There are other international companies that may be contacted by jobseekers with a specialist skill or suitable experience. The *European Handbook* (New Europe Business Publications) is regularly updated and lists leading companies throughout Europe, with detailed information on areas of operation of each. *Europa* (published by Dun & Bradstreet) features around 250,000 companies across Europe and gives useful contact information and details about company size, turnover and fields of operation. The *Directory of Corporate Affiliations* (LexisNexis, PO Box 933, Dayton, Ohio 45401; ☎800-227-4908; e-mail bookstore-support@lexisnexis.com; www.lexisnexis.com) is a directory of international companies, subsidiaries and non-US holdings, classified according to the sectors in which they operate, and is a good sourcebook for companies in a particular area or industry. For information on multinational companies it is worth looking at *Worldwide Branch Locations of Multinational Companies*, edited by David S. Hooper (Thomson Gale, www.galegroup.com). Another directory with profiles of major international companies which can be found in most business libraries is *Hoover's Handbook of World Business*, edited by Patrick J. Spavin and James R. Talbot (Hoover's Inc., www.hoovers.com). This publication also has a comprehensive country-by-country guide. Hoover's also produce MasterLists (directories) of *International Companies* and *US Companies*.

FOREIGN SUBSIDIARIES IN BRITAIN

The British branches, subsidiaries and affiliates of foreign-based firms may also be worth approaching. Addresses of these British-based foreign firms are available through the Commercial Section of the relevant Embassy in London or through the relevant foreign trade centres and associations whose addresses may be found in the Central London Yellow Pages.

TRADE UNIONS AND PROFESSIONAL ASSOCIATIONS

Most unions will be able to advise their members on employment prospects and conditions abroad and in some cases may be able to put you in touch with foreign employers, international associations of trade unions or sister unions in other countries.

Similarly, most professional associations can also offer some kind of help in the search for work abroad. Such help may include an appointments service which includes vacancies abroad, advice on foreign registration requirements or further examinations that have to be passed; an in-house publication that contains advertisements for vacancies overseas; an information service on working conditions; providing introductory letters to sister associations or even direct introductions to potential employers abroad. Most professional associations will offer at least some of these services to their members.

For a comprehensive list of British professional associations readers can consult the book *Trade Associations and Professional Bodies of the United Kingdom,* edited by Patricia Millard, (Graham & Whiteside Ltd). An equally useful source is *Trade Associations and Professional Bodies of the Continental European Union* (Graham & Whiteside Ltd). In Europe, the *European Directory of Trade and Business Associations,* is a directory of professional and trade associations. The *Business Organizations, Agencies, and Publications Directory,* edited by Holly M. Selden (Gale) details trade and business associations in the US and internationally, with a listing of boards of trade and American chambers of commerce worldwide. These books are generally available in the larger public reference libraries. Information on some professional associations appears at the end of relevant chapters in the *Specific Careers* section.

EURES

EURES (the acronym of the European Employment Service) is a computerised, pan-European job information network which brings together the European Commission and the public employment services of the countries belonging to the European Economic Area (EEA) and Switzerland. Its services include the exchange of vacancies, usually for hard to fill posts, or where knowledge of other European languages is required. Another service allows jobseekers to place their CVs on the website (europa.eu.int/eures/) allowing employers to access these as a further tool for recruitment.

Jobcentre Plus produces a series of leaflets of fact sheets about each of the countries in the EEA entitled, *"Working in ..."* followed by the name of the country. They provide the jobseeker with general information and are available to be downloaded from the Jobcentre Plus website (www.jobcentreplus.gov.uk). They are also available in hard copy from the *Jobcentre Plus International Jobsearch Advice (IJA) Team,* Jobcentre Plus Regional Office, 6th Floor Whitehall II, Whitehall Quay, Leeds LS1 4HR; ☎0113-307 8090; fax 0113-307 8213). The EURES job mobility portal is at www.europa.eu.int/eures.

GOVERNMENT AGENCIES

Given that many countries are experiencing high levels of unemployment within their own workforce, it is hardly surprising that few governments wish to promote immigrant labour opportunities. Embassies and diplomatic missions in the UK and USA can do no more than give general background information on their respective countries. Some embassies do, however, act as intermediaries between employers and potential immigrants, or at least run information services and occasional recruitment drives. These include the Canadian, Australian and New Zealand High Commissions (for details, see the separate country chapters). Most vacancies for the consultants and specialists required by individual states, and the programmes run by them, are advertised through the relevant US, EU, or UK agency. The embassies of some Commonwealth states also occasionally place advertisements in the national and trade press. Below are some missions active in the field of recruitment in Britain:

Brunei High Commission: 19-20 Belgrave Square, London SW1X 8PG; ☎020-7581 0521

The Gambia High Commission: 57 Kensington Court, London W8 5DG; ☎020-7937 6316

Sierra Leone High Commission: 41 Eagle Street, Holborn, London WC1R 4TL; ☎020-404 0140; www.slhc-uk.org.uk

Zambia High Commission: Zambia House, 2 Palace Gate, Kensington, London W8 5NG, ☎020-7589 6655; www.zhcl.org.uk

Although needs obviously change from year to year, the most common personnel requirements are for experienced professionals for administrative and advisory positions in government departments and in the various nationally or locally run industries, such as railways or public utilities.

Other governments that promote imported expertise are almost exclusively those of the developing and former communist countries (where the need is for expertise in restructuring or privatisation). The work is usually on fixed-term contracts on particular projects where the ultimate goal is to train local staff to administer and carry on the project after inception. Much of this recruitment activity lies, therefore, in training and consultancy fields and is usually channelled through suitable third parties or bodies concerned mainly with teaching and voluntary work.

Those staff who are chosen by their government or its agencies for consultancy positions or assignments abroad are usually assured of adequate terms and employment conditions, through to arrangements for financial supplementation – a usual part of these contracts.

Department for International Development (DFID), (1 Palace Street, London SW1E 5HE and Abercrombie House Eaglesham Road East Kilbride G75 8EA plus 25 overseas offices; ☎01355 844000; fax 01355 844099; www.dfid.gov.uk). DFID runs the British Government's programme of aid to developing countries. Vacancies occur on an ad hoc basis and are advertised as appropriate in the national or local press, professional journals, overseas publications and the DFID website under Recruitment, Current Vacancies. Skills are required in a wide range of areas from professionals in Governance, Social Development, Conflict, Infrastructure and Urban Development, Education, Enterprise, Health and HIV/AIDS, Environment, Rural Livelihoods, Statistics and Economists to specialists in IT or Procurement to general management and administrative roles. For graduate trainee advisers in the 11 professional cadres, details and application procedures for the DFID Technical Development Faststream can be found on the website: www. fastream.gov.uk. Applicants should have a Masters degree and at least 12 months work experience, preferably in a developing country context, in a relevant subject area. Candidates must be nationals of member states of the European Economic Area (EEA), Swiss Nationals or Commonwealth citizens with the right to work and live in the United Kingdom. DFID is an equal opportunities employer. Applications are welcomed from all parts of the community and DFID actively encourages interest from women, ethnic minority groups and those with a disability. Selection is on merit.

Crown Agents for Oversea Governments and Administration (St Nicholas House, St Nicholas Road, Sutton, Surrey SM1 1EL; ☎020-8643 3311; fax 020-8643 8232; e-mail enquiries@crownagents.co.uk; www.crownagents.com). This is a long-established, self-funding body providing a recruitment service to more than 100 governments, public authorities and international aid agencies. Personnel-related opportunities are greatest in the Middle East and the emerging economies of Eastern Europe and countries of the former Soviet Union, with some programmes in Africa. All overseas positions are for senior level, experienced staff, educated to degree standard and holding relevant professional qualifications. Recent assignments have included human resources development and training, oil/gas industry engineering, development economists, government financial management and logisticians. Vacancies are filled as far as possible from the large CV database held by Crown Agents, for which applications are always welcome. Vacancies may also be advertised in the national, technical or overseas recruitment press.

Overseas Development Institute (111 Westminster Bridge Road, London SE1 7JD;

☎020-7922 0300; fax 020-7922 0399; e-mail d.evans@odi.org.uk; www.odi.org.uk) runs the ODI Fellowship Scheme which enables recent young economists to work for two years in the public sectors of developing countries in Africa, the Caribbean and the Pacific. Candidates may be of any nationality but must have (or be studying for) a postgraduate qualification in economics or a related field. The Fellowship Scheme provides some practical work experience in developing countries and around 35 Fellowships are awarded annually. Application forms and a booklet are available each November from the website at http://www.odi.org.uk/fellows/index/html.

The Natural Resources Institute (University of Greenwich at Medway, Central Avenue, Chatham Maritime, Chatham, Kent ME4 4TB; ☎01634-880088; fax 01634-880077; e-mail nri@greenwich.ac.uk; www.nri.org) was formerly a government agency but is now a part of the University of Greenwich. It is an internationally recognised centre of excellence in the fields of environmental studies and natural resources and provides support to development assistance programmes funded by international donor agencies. The Institute's website includes information on current jobs and recruitment opportunities.

CONSULTANTS AND AGENCIES

For many applicants, the most successful international job search strategy is likely to be the use of management recruitment consultants (MRCs) and employment agencies. This method is particularly effective for well-qualified and experienced candidates who can clearly demonstrate that they have something to offer in the international sector.

In many cases, it is not entirely clear in what ways a management recruitment consultancy might differ from an employment agency. Usually, however, the difference lies in the type of personnel in which they are primarily interested. Management recruitment consultants generally target high-flyers – executives, senior management and professionals, particularly engineers and those with specialised job skills and professional qualifications. Recruitment or employment agencies, on the other hand, find work for a wide range of staff, at the 'low-risk' and 'medium-risk' levels as well as for those seeking temporary employment. Personal assistants, domestic staff and au pairs, as well as clerical staff, translators and workers across commerce and industry can use the services of this kind of employment agency. The current trend towards more flexible employment practices in many industries has also eroded the distinction between temporary and permanent work, and qualifications and training are increasingly important at all levels of employment. There is an important difference in the methods of recruitment used by the two types of agency. Management consultants will spend far more time finding exactly the right person for the right job, matching the supply with the more specialised demand at the 'high-risk' end of the market, while employment agencies deal with more general applications.

In the UK, agencies and consultancies are brought together under the Employment Agencies Act (1976). What this means in practice (with some exceptions, see the *Au Pair and Domestic* chapter) is that agencies and consultants may not charge a fee for finding you a job. However, this law does not apply to agencies which are based abroad and there are regular complaints about some international recruitment agencies – in the construction industry for instance – who charge a fee but fail, in due course, to provide the claimed service, leaving the jobseeker without employment and out of pocket. Agencies earn their money by providing their client companies with a service; and it is worth remembering that they are principally working for their clients, and not for you the jobseeker.

Most recruitment agencies around the world are governed by rules similar to those in the UK. In Germany, however, you should note that it is illegal for agencies that are not in possession of a German Labour Leasing Licence, or companies not registered there, to offer work to British or American jobseekers. Workers must be employed directly by the German company, which will then deduct the individual's tax and insurance. In some other countries the rules are less strict. Generally speaking, prospective employees should be vigilant, particularly when a foreign employment agency offers jobs in a third country.

MANAGEMENT RECRUITMENT CONSULTANTS

There are a number of management recruitment consultants whose remit covers a broad range of employment fields, and which cannot therefore be easily categorised in a particular chapter in the *Specific Careers* section. A brief list of such agencies, which is intended merely as a starting point and is not exhaustive, is given below. Many employment agencies are more career-specific than those detailed here, and are listed in such chapters as *Au Pair and Domestic, Medicine and Nursing*, and *Secretarial, Translating and Interpreting*. Some of the larger foreign-based agencies and consultants are located under the individual country chapters in the *Worldwide Employment* section, along with some relevant British and US employment agencies and consultancies.

Some management recruitment consultants offer a general, international headhunting service while others concentrate on a particular area of recruitment such as information technology or sales. Since consultants have a steady stream of vacancies on their books, many also have a permanent register of job applicants and seek to match up the applicants on file with new vacancies as they arise.

Apart from these in-house databases and other services providing 'portfolios of clients' or 'access to unadvertised vacancies', it is a general rule that very few MRCs will operate actively on behalf of an applicant looking to find a job. Like all employment agencies, their main task is to find people for the jobs on their books, as required by their clients. Typically, some 70 per cent of the business of recruitment consultants lies in jobsearch or headhunting; most will already have a large number of applicants already on their books. For this reason, candidates should target those consultancies that are really suited to their own particular qualifications and experience.

In Britain, the *Institute of Management Consultancy* (3rd Floor, 17-18 Hayward's Place, London EC1R 0EQ; ☎020-7566 5220; fax 020-7566 5230; e-mail consult@imc.co.uk; www.imc.co.uk) provides clients with guidance on their consultancy needs, and will draw up a short-list of appropriate consultants from among its members. Its Client Support Service freephone number is ☎0800-318030. The *Management Consultancies Association* (60 Trafalgar Square, London WC2N 5DS; ☎020-7321 3990; fax 020-7321 3991; www.mca. org.uk) provides similar services and can also advise on appropriate member consultancies. *CEPEC Recruitment* has, in previous years, published an invaluable guide to more than 400 recruitment agencies and search consultants in the UK, about half of who will undertake assignments abroad. This guide also includes useful advice on how to get the most out of recruitment agencies, and on job-search techniques generally. Unfortunately, CEPEC no longer produces this directory, but past editions are often available in libraries and will, in many cases, still provide up-to-date information. More useful advice on effective jobseeking is contained in *Executive Grapevine's Head Hunter*, aimed at executive and professional staff. Internationally, *The International Directory of Executive Recruitment Consultants* (Executive Grapevine International, New Barnes Mill, Cottonmill Lane, St Albans AL1 2HA; ☎01727-844335; www.askgrapevine.com) has more than 900 UK consultants in its first volume and profiles consultants from more than 80 countries in the second.

The Management Recruitment Consultancies below will usually accept applications for a broad range of overseas management or professional positions. Consultancies that advertise regularly in the Press should also be added to your list of useful contacts.

Useful Addresses

Alexander Hughes International (57 Bd. De Montmorency, 75016 Paris; ☎1-44302200; fax 1-42883395; e-mail company@alexanderhughes.co.uk; www.alexander-hughes. co.uk). Recruits management level personnel across all areas of business. Offices throughout Europe and associates worldwide.

Antal International Recruitment (64 Baker Street, London W1U 7GB; ☎0870-770 0020; fax 0870-770 0021; e-mail UK@antal.com; www.antal.com). One of the leading international recruiters within the middle-income market with 37 offices in 20 countries from Russia through to Beijing. It views the candidate/client relationship as paramount to achieving both parties' best interests. In order to supply the best-fit candidates to clients, Antal uses its own proven four-way methodology that incorporates all nuances of the inter-relational recruitment processes.

Anthony Moss & Associates Ltd (Suite 350, Princess House, 50-60 Eastcastle Street, London W1W 8EA; ☎020 7323 2330; fax 020 7323 3340; e-mail recruit@amoss.com; www.amoss.com). Recruits international experts in banking, training, transportation, water, waste, agriculture, construction, manufacturing, and oil and gas at middle and senior management level in Europe, the Middle East and Africa. Candidates must be experienced and qualified to degree or chartered level.

Berenschot EuroManagement (Dutch Office: Postbus 8039, 3503 RA Utrecht, The Netherlands; ☎30-291 6916; fax 30-294 7090; Belgian Office: Marcel Thirylaan 81 B3, B-1200 Brussels; ☎2-777 0645; fax 2-777 0646; www.berenschot.nl) manages and implements large international projects; consults on European affairs and public procurement; and recruits professional consultants and experts from all disciplines, with an emphasis on administration reform, privatisation and regional development for the European Commission and other international agencies. Applicants should have experience of project work in Central and Eastern Europe, the former Soviet Union, and/or the Mediterranean countries, as well as a knowledge of the process of European integration.

Grafton Recruitment Ltd (35-37 Queens Square, Belfast BT1 3FG; ☎028-9024 2824; fax 028-9024 2897; www.grafton-group.com) is Ireland's leading consultancy group, with 33 branches covering nine countries in Central Europe, Africa, South America and Australasia. The International Division recruits experienced and qualified personnel mainly for the Czech Republic, Germany, Hungary, Malaysia, Saudi Arabia and the USA. Sectors handled include accountancy, catering, construction, electronics, IT, nursing, sales and management. Grafton Recruitment also has a very comprehensive website containing current vacancies and a CV database.

Management Resources International B.V. (Fortuna Villa, Frans Erenslaan 2, NL-6164 JH Geleen, The Netherlands; ☎46-423 0800; fax 46-423 0823; e-mail info@mribv.com; www.mribv.com) is an international recruitment consultancy placing candidates in positions in the Netherlands, Belgium, France, Germany, Italy and the UK. It has an online vacancy list.

Further information on recruitment consultants and agencies operating in the UK and dealing with overseas recruitment can be obtained from the *Recruitment & Employment Confederation* (36-38 Mortimer Street, London W1W 7RG; ☎020-7462 3260; fax 020-7255 2878; www.rec.uk.com) – by post only. It also publishes an annual *Yearbook of Recruitment and Employment Services*, and represents both management consultancies and employment agencies.

STUDENT WORKING EXCHANGES

Generally student exchange schemes are either cultural or vocational in nature, however, cultural exchanges can often lead on to educational, employment and career opportunities as well.

The following section deals with a number of vocationally orientated student exchange schemes that provide opportunities for interested students to gain practical experience of living and working abroad. Details of the *British Universities North America Club (BUNAC), Camp America,* and other voluntary exchange schemes are given in the chapter on *Voluntary Work*. Details of farming work exchange schemes appear in the chapter on *Agriculture and the Environment*.

AIESEC (French acronym for *International Association for Students of Economics and Management*) (UK Office: 2nd Floor, 29-31 Cowper Street, London EC2A 4AT; ☎020-7549 1800; fax 020-7336 7971; e-mail national@uk.aiesec.org; www.uk.aiesec.org; US Office: 10th Floor, 127 West 26th Street, New York, NY 10001; ☎212-757 4062; fax 212-757 3774) offers placements in diverse working environments through its *Work Abroad* programme to students and recent graduates in accountancy, business administration, computing, marketing, economics and finance. Placements last between six and seventy-two weeks in any one of AIESEC's 84 member countries at any time of the year. These exchanges are for students and recent graduates with a business-related degree, with languages if they wish to work outside the English-speaking world. The headquarters of AIESEC International is in Brussels. Applications to the *Work Abroad* programme should be made to the addresses above. AIESEC wishes to stress that very few placements are currently available because of an imbalance in the numbers of outgoing and incoming students.

American-Scandinavian Foundation (Scandinavia House, 58 Park Avenue, New York, New York 10016; ☎212-879 9779; e-mail info@amscan.org; www.amscan.org) enables Americans between the ages of 21 and 30 to live and work in Scandinavia on a temporary basis. The exchange programme emphasises the cultural and educational benefits of the exchange. The trainee receives sufficient income to cover living expenses but is expected to meet the cost of the return airfare. A non-refundable application fee of $50 is required; deadline for technical placements is 1 January, and for TEFOL positions 1 February.

Association for International Practical Training (AIPT) (10400 Little Patuxent Parkway, Suite 250, Columbia, Maryland 21044-3510; ☎410-997 2200; fax 410-992 3924; e-mail aipt@aipt.org; www.aipt.org) is a non-profit organisation which promotes international understanding through cross-cultural, on-the-job, practical training exchanges for students and professionals. It places around 250 US citizens in about 25 countries every year and helps around 2,000 people from 70 other countries to train with US employers. Around half of these exchange schemes are with other member countries of IAESTE, of which it is the American branch (like the *British Council Education and Training Group* in Britain, see below). AIPT's major scheme is the *Career Development Exchanges Program* for recent graduates and young professionals and businesses in many career fields. It offers opportunities in Austria, Finland, France, Germany, Ireland, Japan, Malaysia, Switzerland, the Slovak Republic, Hungary, and other countries including the UK. Most vocations and professions can be catered for as long as the foreign placement includes some practical training. Training periods range from eight weeks to 18 months. AIPT's other major scheme, the *Hospitality/Tourism Exchange Programme* is dealt with later in this book in the chapter, *Transport, Tourism and Hospitality*. For more detailed information see AIPT's comprehensive website.

British Council Education and Training Group (10 Spring Gardens, London SW1A 2BN; ☎020-7930 8466; fax 020-7389 6347; e-mail general.enquiries@britishcouncil. org; www.britishcouncil.org/learning) runs the Language Assistants programme which enables students and recent graduates from the UK and more than 20 other countries to spend a year abroad teaching their chosen language in a school or college. It is open to undergraduates doing language degrees and recent graduates of any discipline. Places are also available for gap year students to work as 'Helpers' in boarding schools in Germany. The British Council also the UK National Agency for the European Union programmes Comenius, Minerva, Lingua, Grundtvig, and Arion, and the Education and Training Group manages several other programmes for international experience. The British Council has offices in 110 countries around the world. Other offices in the UK are at: The Tun, 3rd Floor, 4 Jackson's Entry, Holyrood Road, Edinburgh EH8 8PJ, ☎0131-524 5700; fax

0131-524 5701; e-mail britishcouncilscotland@britishcouncil.org; 28 Park Place, Cardiff CF10 3QE; ☎029-2039 7346; fax 029-2023 7494; and Norwich Union House, 7 Fountain Street, Belfast BT1 5EG; ☎028-9024 8220; fax 028-9023 7592; e-mail nireland. enquiries@britishcouncil.org. The British Council does not accept CVs and cannot hold individual details on file. Job vacancies are advertised through the national press (mainly *The Guardian* newspaper) and international journals such as the *Economist*. For more information check the website at www.britishcouncil.org, or contact the British Council Information Centre, ☎0161-957 7755; fax 0161-957 7762; e-mail general.enquiries@ britishcouncil.org.

Council on International Educational Exchange (CIEE), (3 Copley Place, 2nd Floor, Boston MA 02116; ☎617-247 0350; fax 617-247 2911; e-mail info@councilexchanges. org; www.ciee.org) The Council is the largest organisation of its kind in the world with more than 50 years' experience in exchange programmes. CIEE sponsors two- to four-week volunteer projects in the USA and abroad during the summer months, with more than 600 projects worldwide. Participants join an international team of 10-20 volunteers to work on an environmental or community service project alongside local residents. Volunteers (aged 18 and over) have planted grass and trees to protect endangered coastlines and forests, restored historical sites, renovated low-income housing and cared for the disabled while learning the benefits of international co-operation. The cost of participating is $250-$750 plus travel to and from the project site. Room and board is provided. The Council recruits only US residents directly and receives international volunteers on projects in the USA through its partner organisations in other countries. For further country-by-country details write to the above address. Further information is also given in the country chapters further on in this book.

GAP Activity Projects Limited, (GAP House, 44 Queen's Road, Reading, Berkshire RG1 4BB; ☎0118-9594914; fax 0118-9576634; e-mail volunteer@gap.org.uk; www. gap.org.uk). GAP is a registered charity based in Reading which organises voluntary work opportunities for 17-25 year-olds who wish to take a 'year out' between school and higher education, employment or training. Successful volunteers undertake full-time work for between three and twelve months in return for which they receive food, accommodation and (usually) a living allowance. Currently opportunities exist in Argentina, Australia, Brazil, Canada, China, Ecuador, Fiji & the South Pacific, Germany, Ghana, India, Japan, Malawi, Malaysia, Mexico, New Zealand, Paraguay, Russia, South Africa, Thailand, the USA and Vietnam. A wide variety of projects is on offer including teaching English as a foreign language, general duties in schools, assisting on community projects or caring for the sick and people with disabilities, outdoor activities and sports coaching, conservation work and scientific surveys. GAP has no closing date for applications, although you stand a better chance of being placed on your first choice project, if you apply early. GAP welcomes applications at any time from year 12 onwards. Every applicant is invited to interview with interviews taking place from the middle of October onwards in Reading, Leeds, Dublin, Belfast, Glasgow and other regional locations. Brochures are available each year from August onwards for placements starting a year later. To receive a copy of the GAP brochure and application form students should contact the GAP office or visit www.gap.org.uk .

International Association for the Exchange of Students for Technical Experience (IAESTE UK) (c/o British Council Education & Training Group, 10 Spring Gardens, London SW1A 2BN; ☎020-7389 4774, fax 020-7389 4426; e-mail iaeste@britishcouncil.org; www. iaeste.org.uk) arranges an exchange scheme whereby penultimate year students from scientific and technical backgrounds can spend eight to 12 weeks, mainly in the summer vacation, gaining practical experience abroad in more than 60 countries worldwide. Students should apply to the programme in the autumn for placements beginning the following summer.

IST Plus (Rosedale House, Rosedale Road, Richmond, Surrey TW9 2SZ; ☎020-8939 9057; fax 020-8332 7858; e-mail info@istplus.com. www.istplus.com). CIEE's UK partners. IST Plus specialises in cultural exchange programmes for British students, graduates and young professionals. The Internship USA and Internship Canada programmes enable students and recent graduates to complete a period of course-related work experience/training for a period of up to 18 months. Minimum age 18. Applicants must be enrolled in full-time, further, or higher education (HND level or above) and for the US programme the participant must be returning to full-time education. Students may participate after graduation as long as the application is submitted while still studying. Participants must find their own training placements, related to their course of study, and either through payment from their employer or through other means, finance their own visit to the USA. Professional Career Training in the USA gives non-students an opportunity to undertake a traineeship of up to 18 months. IST Plus offers casual work opportunities to Britain for those between the ages of 18 and 30 years on the Work and Travel Australia and Work and Travel New Zealand Programmes. These programmes allow participants to travel for up to one year, taking up work along the way to support themselves. IST Plus and CIEE offer assistance at every stage, from obtaining the visa, to helping find work and accommodation. Ongoing services include mail receiving and holding, 24-hour emergency support, and access to office facilities and free internet access.

SOCRATES is the general name for the European Union Actions on languages, education (at pre-university level) and study visits. The *Erasmus* programme is co-ordinated in the UK by the UK Socrates-Erasmus Council (Rothford, Giles Lane, Canterbury, Kent CT2 7LR; ☎01227-762712; fax 01227-762711; email info@erasmus.ac.uk; www.erasmus.ac.uk). This programme or action covers transnational co-operation and projects between universities. The other schemes are co-ordinated by the *British Council* and comprise: Action 1 is called *Lingua* and provides for exchanges and in-service training in other EU and EEA countries (see the chapter on *Teaching*); Action 2 is *Comenius*, for education at pre-university level and projects organised between schools, and makes provisions for preparatory visits and exchange or study-visits for teachers/managers; Action 3, known as *Arion*, involves more specialist visits and exchanges for education professionals. The similar *Leonardo da Vinci Programme* is in place at university and vocational level and has some strands which support short- and long-term work placements for young people of up to a period of three years, as well as student exchange programmes, vocational training, and language study for work purposes. These EU education and training programmes have recently been extended. Information on contact details for exchange schemes and education within the EU is available in a useful booklet called *The European Union – A Guide for Students and Teachers*, available from the *European Parliament Office (UK)*, 2 Queen Anne's Gate, London SW1H 9AA; ☎020-7227 4300; fax 020-7227 4302; e-mail eplondon@europarl.eu.int; www.europarl.org.uk. Full information is also available on the Socrates website at http://europa.eu.int/comm/education/index_en.html.

OTHER SOURCES

Nexus Expatriate Magazine is a specialist publication containing many international job vacancies, as well as providing other valuable information for expatriates. It can be obtained from *Expat Network* (19 Bartlett Street, Croydon CR2 6TB; ☎020-8256 0311; fax 020-8256 0312; e-mail nexus@expatnetwork.com; www.expatnetwork.com).

International Staffing Consultants Inc. (17310 Redhill Avenue #140, Irvine, CA 92614; ☎949-255 5857; fax 949-767 5959; e-mail iscinc@iscworld.com; www.iscworld.com) runs a weekly research and advertising clippings service via the internet. You can subscribe to this service via their website, after which you will receive weekly updates on the latest job opportunities.

The Creative Job Search

The tried and tested, traditional, methods of going about finding the job that suits your purposes are all well and good but they aren't likely to make you stand out from the scrabbling crowd of other jobseekers. You need to find a way to push yourself to the front of the queue. The 'creative' approach to finding your ideal job will help you to do just that. It is an approach that requires considerable skill, flexibility and self-confidence; the technique originated (unsurprisingly) in North America and can be particularly productive for those searching for work abroad.

The creative job search is premised on the fact that there are thousands of jobs available that are never advertised or made available to the general public. Recruitment for these jobs takes place on an informal basis through a network of contacts who pass information to each other by word of mouth. The objective, for the creative jobseeker, is to become a part of that network – making the most of existing contacts while simultaneously building up useful new ones, any one of which may lead to the possibility of employment. Of course, the 'creative' method is not an entirely new one, and ambitious people have always made the most of their contacts. There is, however, some difference both in approach and in emphasis.

Firstly, to be successful you will need to gain insight into yourself, your aptitudes and interests. Analysing your own employment potential is the first step (see the chapter on *Discovering your Employment Potential*), and requires an introspective realism that takes effort and is something that most of us shy away from most of the time. However, the end result should make the effort worthwhile.

You should also become very well informed about the particular job area that you are interested in and if you intend to concentrate your search on a particular country you should find out more about its politics, economy and culture. In particular, you need to know what the overseas work that you are seeking involves, the experience and qualifications needed and how recruitment in that particular sphere takes place. Who is responsible for recruitment in a particular company or organisation? Who are the decision-makers? Having established answers to these and other similar questions, you will then need to be prepared to place yourself among the network of contacts in which most of this invisible (unadvertised) recruiting takes place. As you are seeking a job abroad, this will be an international network. Your contacts will need to be persuaded that you possess the necessary skills and experience required by that particular kind of work. These are the general objectives of the creative job search.

Such objectives are not necessarily easy to achieve, of course, but then living and working abroad is always going to be a challenge. You should certainly not assume that all the jobs which are available are already public knowledge, and you should not overlook the possibility of the right job being created especially *for* you. Publicly advertised vacancies (including positions circulated through consultants and agencies) are the tip of the proverbial iceberg.

The way in which you go about your job search, and your frame of mind, is vitally important. If you carry out your job search effectively, your chances of finding the right job abroad will be greatly increased. Discovering your own employment potential, and acquiring detailed knowledge about the particular field of work that interests you, are the first steps on the road to landing that plum job.

UNADVERTISED JOB VACANCIES

Every month, thousands of job opportunities occur which are never made public. They do not appear in the Press or in employment service and recruitment agencies. Some of these vacancies may appear in internal newsletters and in-house magazines, on company notice boards, and in the vacancy lists of professional or trade associations such as trade unions. Vacancies created due to promotions being made within companies, especially in large organisations such as the United Nations or the BBC, are frequently first offered in-house. Many vacancies, however, do not receive even this restricted level of publicity, but are circulated instead through a system of well-established (and therefore more reliable) contacts known to the employer. In many small and medium-sized companies advertising is seen as unnecessarily bureaucratic, taking time and money away from more important tasks. Word-of-mouth represents a quicker and more cost-effective approach.

Many employers consider even the standard job interview as being a somewhat haphazard and ineffectual means of recruiting new staff. Such employers will often, therefore, by-pass conventional methods of selection, and this is especially true where a likely candidate is already known to them through other sources. Creative job searching will put you in the picture in circumstances such as these.

'CREATED' POSITIONS

In many cases unadvertised positions are in fact newly created positions – they do not exist before they are filled by the selected candidate. Employers or managers are often prepared to consider constructive ideas, and then take on someone to carry them out, provided that they can be persuaded that they have found the right person for the job. The potential here for the creative jobseeker is enormous. How do you tap this rich vein of opportunity?

In the international jobs market an obvious starting point might be to convince a targeted employer of the great advantages of taking on an English-speaker to deal with their contacts in the English-speaking world. English is already a widely spoken language, but in many countries there are insufficient linguists of a high enough calibre. This kind of opportunity exists in Europe, but more especially throughout the rest of the non English-speaking world, and most notably in developing economies. Even accent can be a deciding factor – an advertising firm in the USA might be persuaded of the value of having someone with an English accent to deal with clients, for example; alternatively, a satellite television station in Europe might consider that it is better to have an announcer who speaks American English. Schools and universities, where the regulations allow, can also often be persuaded to take on a native British or American teacher of English. Companies which trade with others abroad frequently see the advantage of having an English-speaker on the staff, and there are few companies which do not wish to expand their sales or trading activities and in the world of business English is the *lingua franca*. A knowledge of local language and culture, as well as relevant work experience, will also set you apart from the competition. For many case histories where a creative approach resulted in work abroad, sometimes in a surprising or unusual way, see *Work Your Way Around the World* by Susan Griffith (Vacation Work Publications). You can increase your options by many different means; try, for example, joining a club with international connections or sending speculative letters to all the contacts you have in your country of choice. Most importantly, keep your ear to the ground – simply being friendly and chatty with a wide variety of people is likely to bring many ideas and opportunities into view.

THE INTERNET

The internet has revolutionised not just electronic communications but the whole manner in which business is now conducted around the world. In a matter of just a few years, it has expanded from a peripheral, even eccentric, preoccupation, to become the defining force in contemporary commerce. The opportunities it offers the job seeker therefore are enormous.

The advantages that the internet offers recruiters are obvious, especially in high-tech industries and universities where access to computers is commonplace. In many cases, the internet can be the most effective way of advertising vacancies which call for specialist knowledge, especially in the IT field. However, more and more individuals who have no such expertise are also finding that they can access jobs and promote themselves through the medium. Inevitably, as ever-increasing numbers of people have access to the infinite range of information available electronically, so more and more employers and employer-intermediaries will take advantage of the global market it encompasses.

E-mail can also aid your creative job search. There are thousands of discussion groups, forums and newsgroups active on the internet. Many of these can bring you into contact with potential employers or sources of employment, either directly or indirectly. With so many options available, it helps to be fairly precise about your goal, which should be to extend your personal network to include those decision-makers who can aid you in your job search (although, naturally, this will not always be the topic of your discussions). Participating in a newsgroup essentially entails communicating with others who share the same interest. Some newsgroups veer rapidly off into the arcane, weird, or even abusive, and it is sensible to start by looking at the FAQ (frequently asked question) pages, which will give a clearer indication of the nature of the group. If you decide to join a particular group, it is often a good idea to 'lurk' for a short while, reading posts but not engaging in discussion. You will soon become aware of the flavour of a group or list in this way, and will be more confident when you yourself start to post messages. Remember that you should try to contribute information and your own point of view, as well as seeking advice.

Bulletin boards offer another effective method of online networking. Such sites are usually run by individuals, not organisations, and cater effectively to the local community. They are the equivalent of local newsletters and will give you instant access to people who live in the country or locality in which you are hoping to live and work (see the *Preparation and Follow-up* chapter). Some bulletin boards offer jobs, nationally and internationally, as well as business or company listings, and in some cases provide the equivalent of a 'Situation Wanted' advertisement, the chance to post your own CV. Some sites deal with specific sectors such as computing, construction or insurance, while others have detailed information about particular countries.

The internet can be a source of direct employment opportunities too, and recruitment websites now abound. Many such sites have searchable databases of current vacancies that can be accessed by keywords or by employment category, and most also offer the opportunity to post your CV on the site. Often, recruitment sites are aimed primarily at an audience in the constituency of the employer (for example, a Sydney temp agency may post clerical positions online in the likely expectation that they will interest local residents), however, if you are both methodical and persistent in your use of employment resources on the web your chances of succeeding in the international job market will increase daily.

The easiest way to commence your online job search is by using a search engine or directory site such as *Yahoo!* (www.yahoo.com). *Yahoo! HotJobs*, which you can find listed on the front page of the site, will take you through to pages which will help you locate recruiters and develop your CV, as well as providing employment advice and salary information. The list of employment resources listed is enormous and you will need to spend some considerable time navigating through them to find the ones which are likely to be of use to you. A very brief selection of useful employment websites is given at the end of this section. Note that a URL (internet address) ending in the letters 'com' or 'co' means that the site is a commercial one; 'edu' or 'ac' signifies an academic institution; 'gov' denotes a government organisation and 'org' refers to other organisations such as charities.

The publication, *Net That Job!* by Irene Krechowiecka (Kogan Page, £8.99, ISBN 0749433140) has detailed advice on using the internet to find employment, a guide to internet recruiters and companies online, as well as chapters on getting connected and creating your own Home Page and website. Numerous other books with a similar focus are also available in bookshops, and from e-bookshops such as Amazon (www.amazon.com).

USEFUL INTERNATIONAL EMPLOYMENT WEBSITES

Banking and Finance Jobs, www.gaapweb.com.

Healthcare and Medical Employment, http://members.aol.com/pjpohly/links.htm.

SustainableBusiness.com,www.sustainablebusiness.com. Jobs in the field of sustainable development in the USA.

CareerBuilder.com, www.careerbuilder.com. An internet job awareness business in the USA.

Netjobs, www.netjobs.com. Site with jobs in the US and Canada.

New Boss, www.myboss.com/newbosseo. Good general recruitment gateway.

Escape Artist, www.escapeartist.com. Another excellent international site that will lead you to the best recruitment sites for the country in which you are interested. Also provides other wide-ranging information.

Diversity Directory, www.mindexchange.com. International employment, HR and diversity web directory for Asia, Europe, and Latin America.

America's Job Bank, www.ajb.dni.us. The largest database of US jobs on the Net.

Stepstone, www.stepstone.co.uk. Job opportunities across Europe published daily.

Monster, www.monster.co.uk. Good for jobs, careers information and networking in the UK and globally.

PayAway, www.payaway.co.uk. Aimed at the working traveller and gap year students, including job lists, a country index, and links to working holiday schemes.

THE HUMAN FACE OF NETWORKING

The internet can be an invaluable research tool and will help you establish contacts in your prospective area of employment or target country. The process of cultivating contacts is often slow, however, and it may be difficult, if you are looking for a job in a foreign land or culture, to find employment just by using the internet. At some point you will probably need to fall back on the tried and trusted method of networking – personal communication – and your search for international employment is likely to end up in a face-to-face interview (even if your initial contact is by letter, fax, telephone or the web).

The process of widening your range of contacts and meeting the decision-makers always involves three general stages. First, you have to develop a network of intermediaries or 'referees' who can put you in touch with your target contacts; then you must arrange to go and see these contacts (or to get in contact with them online). Finally, you will have to know how to handle the face-to-face meeting (or 'creative job search interview') and how to follow it up most effectively.

INTERMEDIARIES AND REFEREES

Draw up a select list of the people, or the kinds of people, whom you wish to contact; in addition, list the 'referees' you can approach (these will be people who are known both to you and to those you wish to contact). If you direct your speculative job approaches to a specific person – the right person – and mention your connection or referee, your request for information or a meeting is more likely be taken seriously and given due consideration. The age of letters of recommendation may be over (at least in our culture – in Japan they remain essential), but the principle remains the same. You will meet your contact on more equal terms if you can say 'Mr X suggested I contact you....' Naturally, the normal rules of courtesy apply in these circumstances (and when using the internet mind your 'netiquette'); remember, too, that your new contact can be a useful source of future contacts, even if your meeting does not immediately result in a new job. The creative job search is also about planning for the future.

How then do you go about finding referees or intermediaries for jobs overseas? Remember, the conventional jobseeker is unlikely to be exploiting this aspect of their search to the full. The more creative jobseeker will gain a head start by actively exploit existing connections and by using a degree of lateral thinking. You may wish to draw up a general list of suitable newsgroups on the internet or a list of others in your profession who might be able to help. Think about others in your position who might be interested in sharing useful leads and contacts, or people who already live where you wish to work. Possible intermediaries who are already known to you are:

- parents and relations
- friends and their parents and relations
- past or present school or university teachers
- past or present school or university friends and acquaintances
- members of your church, political party, club or society
- your family doctor or solicitor
- your bank or building society manager
- work colleagues – past and present
- people you have met through your work

It can be useful to ask: 'Can you offer me any advice about working abroad?'; 'Do you know anybody who lives in X country or Y city?'; 'Do you know anyone who works in this particular profession or field?'; 'Do you know anyone who knows anyone who does?' There will, of course, be frequent blind alleys, but also some valuable leads; and in the end, these intermediaries may be able to put you in touch with those who can provide you with work. Some other intermediaries who can help you in your creative job search are:

- members of foreign trade associations
- members of your local Chamber of Commerce who have contacts abroad (for instance, many local Chambers of Commerce in the UK are members of the Franco-British Chamber of Commerce and Industry in Paris)
- members of foreign nationals' associations in your country, or the equivalent expatriate associations in the place you wish to work
- managers and employees of international companies, or British or US-based firms with branches abroad
- those working for firms in your chosen field in your own country
- those you have met while travelling abroad

VISITING CONTACTS

The first thing to note when planning a visit to a potential employer or contact (whose organisation does not advertise the vacancy you are ultimately seeking) is that you should not sell yourself too much (except maybe in a field where selling is important). There is no reason at this stage to ask for a job. Such visits are mainly to find out about the work that you are interested in, what it involves, and what jobs are available in that particular sphere of employment. Remember that you may in turn be able to help your contact, and this can lead to other useful contacts in itself. Your eventual aim should be to obtain an interview with someone who can offer you work, or knows someone who can. If you are simply asking for advice, then you are more likely to be able to arrange a meeting; it is easier to refuse a specific request than a general one. If you can't arrange a suitable meeting straightaway then there will normally be somebody else with whom your contact can put you in touch, if he or she feels you are a person worth helping.

Nonetheless, the creative jobseeker needs to bear in mind that making contact is not the aim of the exercise. You have to get that job! So the all-important personal visit is the logical next step; and if, as is often the case, your letter of enquiry is not answered in a reasonable time, telephoning to arrange a visit is often a useful alternative. If you make your first contact by phone or e-mail, it is always advisable to follow this up with a letter – following up your enquiry means that your potential contact is not so likely to have forgotten who you are when you arrive on the doorstep. And don't forget to say thank you!

THE CREATIVE JOB SEARCH INTERVIEW

Unlike a straightforward job interview, the creative job search interview should be seen as a general discussion about the possibilities of obtaining work. You may see your meetings with your target contacts as a means of showing that you are a professional and serious-minded person and it is certainly reasonable to discuss employment possibilities (in a field which, after all, is of interest to you both); or you may use them to find out more about your chosen career or destination. The initial approach is of the greatest importance; every step you take is one closer to achieving your goal.

Some persistence will be needed. The job you can just walk into is probably not the one you are really after, and you need confidence in your own ability to be able to demonstrate this to your potential employer. You could ask him or her about practical details: how they got *their* job, for example and what kind of qualifications or expertise are useful. What do you need to do to integrate into an international environment, and how do you deal with colleagues in countries where working practices may vary from those you are used to? What is living in that country like? Remember that your contact needs to see your approach in a positive light, as an opportunity and not a problem.

The right approach will depend on the person, but the message you are trying to get across is always the same. You need to demonstrate the seriousness of your enquiry, and your genuine interest in the job. Only when you have made this impression, or got this message across, is it worth asking a more direct question. If someone from your background and with your experience were to apply for a job with this organisation, how would it be viewed? From the answer to this question, you may be able to gather how closely you should keep in touch with this contact in future. It is also a good idea to find out all you can about other target contacts in your field of interest. From these, you will quickly create a network of contacts and this will give you the greatest chance of success.

If you follow these general principles, you will soon know – and become known by – a large number of key people; this applies to your participation in newsgroups on the internet too. If you are working effectively, you will have managed in a very short time what most people take years to achieve. You will become a link in the chain of notification through which non-publicly advertised or 'invisible' vacancies are circulated.

The approach outline here represents a précis of the many informal methods of finding work which are actually used by jobseekers. More detailed information about the methods of the creative job search is available in the invaluable book on career guidance *What Color is Your Parachute?* by Richard Nelson Bolles (advertised as 'The Best Selling Job Hunting Book in the World').

SHORT TERM WORK ABROAD

The determined jobseeker will be able to exploit the methods outlined above in both a conventional and a creative sense. There is no creative job search that does not have specific goals and objectives, and conversely, no conventional method that doesn't also involve some creativity and imagination. But there is also a third, albeit riskier, way of finding work abroad for those who enjoy travel and are prepared to spend some time in their chosen country; that is, to apply the techniques of both conventional and creative job searches on the spot and look for work once in the country concerned.

Such a method will naturally be more suited to some careers and professions than others. For example, English language teaching, agricultural work and tourism. One way of following this approach may be to take on short-term work in the country in which you are interested in order to support yourself while you continue your search for a longer-term career. Being on the spot is often advantageous and many employers prefer to take on someone who is based locally and who is already familiar with the country and its customs.

Taking a temporary job in another country can bring you closer to the more permanent career you are seeking. This approach, for British and Irish citizens, can be easier in the EU than elsewhere, though not so easy for Americans. The implementation of the European Economic Area Treaty in 1993 has abolished the need for work permits for EU citizens in any member state, as well as in Iceland, Norway, Liechtenstein, and Switzerland. Very few other countries will allow foreigners to enter a country for the sole purpose of finding work and in most cases you will need to establish entitlement to residence. A holiday in your chosen destination can, however, provide you with a way of checking out job opportunities and familiarising yourself with the local environment. At the same time, you can find out how to get a work permit, which is, as often as not, a practical rather than a legal matter. Educational or exchange visits to another country can also provide a route into the world of work. (See *Working Exchanges* above).

Once in your chosen country you should aim to make friends, meet people, keep an eye on vacancies in newspapers, and visit at least a few employment agencies or companies. It is best to go armed with a potential list of contacts and to make the right preparations before you go; time will be at a premium. Spending a short time abroad will give you an opportunity to improve your understanding of the local culture, way of life and language and will also put you one step ahead in your search. In addition, you are likely to discover something about yourself and about how you would cope living abroad for a longer time.

Most short-term jobs available to foreigners, in whatever country, do not require any specific qualifications, apart from a willingness to work at the bottom end of the jobs market (and some knowledge of the native language). Such jobs are largely found in agriculture, the tourist industry, labouring and voluntary work. There are many regions which call for large numbers of unskilled workers for a short time each year, while in others, jobs may exist because of a local labour shortage, or a need for English-speakers. In practice, there is no such thing as total labour mobility, and enthusiastic workers from abroad may be more adaptable (or exploitable) than many of the locals.

This book gives brief details of the temporary work opportunities to be found in each country and mentions some of the main organisations that can help you to find work abroad. Other books available from Vacation Work Publications, particularly the *Live and Work* series, can provide you with more detailed information including useful contact points. The *Specific Careers* section of this book covers those approaches to finding work which are more widely applicable, for example, writing to national tourist offices to obtain lists of hotels, or reading guide-books (in the *Transport, Tourism and Hospitality* chapter). The chapters in the *Worldwide Employment* section cover those aspects of temporary work which are unique to that country, and describe exactly what and where the opportunities are.

Rules and Regulations

There are few countries in the world that actively encourage immigration, and most have very strict entry regulations that have to be dealt with in advance. Most commonly, if you are looking to live and work in a particular country, you will be required to have a positive job offer, be able to speak the language and have pre-arranged accommodation. Anyone seeking work abroad is advised to request up-to-date information on the current requirements from the appropriate embassy. Addresses of embassies and high commissions are given in the individual country chapters of this book. If you are working in a sponsored programme or for an international company, the immigration requirements will usually be taken care of for you; if not, the usual requirement is for an employer to apply on your behalf to the immigration authorities some months in advance of you taking up employment. Those travelling abroad on holiday or for business will have different requirements to fulfil.

THE EUROPEAN UNION

The Treaty of Rome, which established the European Economic Community (EEC), was signed by its original six members – France, West Germany, Italy, the Netherlands, Belgium and Luxembourg – in 1957. In 1967, this core group merged with the European Coal and Steel Community (ECSC) (the forerunner of the EEC) to form the European Community or EC. The Maastricht Treaty, when it came into force in 1993, changed the name and vocation of the EC and it is now known as the European Union (EU). The EC is one of the constituent parts or 'pillars' of the EU, which has a common European citizenship and a timetable for European Monetary Union. The UK, Eire and Denmark joined the EC in January 1973, Greece entered in January 1981, Spain and Portugal in January 1986, and the former East Germany became a part of the EU when Germany was reunified in 1990. Austria, Finland and Sweden (members of the 'rival' European Free Trade Area) joined the EU in 1995. In 2004, Poland, Hungary, the Czech Republic, Latvia, Lithuania, Estonia, Slovakia, Slovenia, Southern Cyprus, and Malta became members. Romania and Bulgaria have signed agreements which should lead to their membership being granted in January 2007. At the time of writing this looked very likely, although both countries still had to meet certain targets before their entry became certain. Turkey has an association agreement (and has previously tried to join and failed). Partnership agreements, which exclude membership, have been signed with Ukraine, Russia, Moldova, Kyrgyzstan, and Belarus. There is close co-operation between the EU and those European Free Trade Area (EFTA) countries that have not become members of the EU (currently Iceland, Liechtenstein, Norway and Switzerland). EFTA was originally a free trade area that was set up in response to the creation of the EEC, and this joint grouping is known as the European Economic Area (EEA).

The aims of the EU are varied. Its remit extends to areas like education, culture and the law, as well as economics. The most important aim is the creation of a federal or decentralised union of all member states – in effect the creation of a single state, or union. This aim is of great significance for businesses wishing to operate in the European market, as well as for international companies investing in EU countries. Most importantly for the purposes of this book, however, is the policy of free movement of labour, which makes travelling within its borders and working abroad easier for EU citizens; as has the abolition of work permits (which are no longer required) and the development of the European Monetary Union and the creation of a single currency. A federal union is the logical consequence of the harmonisation of tax and labour law, progress towards a level playing field for competition between EU companies and the establishment of a common European citizenship.

At present, it seems likely that a core group of European countries, notably France, Germany, the Benelux countries and Italy, will lead the way in the creation of a federal Europe, with later entry for countries such as Britain. The abolition of work permits and a single or common currency does not necessarily create new jobs, of course, and employers will always tend to recruit local labour on purely practical grounds. Such changes will, however, create more favourable conditions for international jobseekers in some areas, such as teaching, where restrictions to mobility between EU countries will in the course of time be lifted. The removal of passport and frontier controls between the countries covered by the 1995 Schengen Agreement (currently Austria, France, Germany, Belgium, Luxembourg, Norway, the Netherlands, Spain, Portugal, Austria, Italy, Greece, Denmark, Finland and Sweden) has already made travel between these countries a lot easier for everyone.

EUROPEAN MONETARY UNION (EMU)

In December 1991, the Treaty of European Union was signed in Maastricht in the Netherlands. The Maastricht Treaty set out the plans for a European economic, monetary and political union. It established the European Union, comprising the previously existing European Community and all its laws; the European Political Co-operation framework dealing with foreign and security policy; and justice and interior affairs, including immigration and conditions of entry.

Despite opposition in some countries, and the reservations of many economists, progress towards EMU has been swift and fairly painless. Already, EU businesses have unrestricted access to a market that is larger than that of the United States or Japan. The Single Market – which came into being in 1 January 1993 – was meant to create jobs, but the need to bring the widely differing economies of member states together (a process known as 'convergence') has, in fact, led to a slowdown in economic growth which is gradually being reversed.

Immigration and Residence

As far as the British jobseeker is concerned, EMU should make it easier to live and work in other European countries. The EURES scheme (see the *Getting There* section) already allows well-qualified and multilingual applicants in Britain to visit any Jobcentre and fill in a form, which can then be sent to the relevant Employment Service in other EU countries for linking with suitable posts. The Single Market means that you are entitled to exactly the same rights, rates of pay, healthcare and unemployment provision in the EU country where you are working as nationals of that country (leading to the anomaly of greater employment rights in some countries than exist for workers in the UK, which presently has secured an 'opt-out' from some EU labour laws). You must also pay the same taxes and Social Security contributions as nationals of the country where you are working and you may claim the local equivalent of Unemployment Benefit (see *Social Security* below).

Those who are not working also have some new rights. After the Maastricht Treaty it became possible for students, pensioners and persons of independent means to move to another EU country without applying for a residence permit in their home country; instead, it is now possible to make an application on arrival. The implication of this is that UK or Irish citizens can apply for a residence permit after they have arrived in another EU country, provided that they have found a job, are actually or potentially self-employed or are looking for work (evidence of which may be required, for example, copies of job applications). EU Nationals do not require a work permit for any EU country but will usually need a residence permit and sometimes a national identity card. An identity card (without a passport) is itself sufficient for travel between many EU countries. ID cards are granted automatically to those who fulfil the criteria above, last for five years and are automatically renewable. Authorities in some EU countries can, however, still deport an EU citizen who has no means of support.

These changes do not benefit US citizens or those from the Commonwealth countries who do not have a right to UK or EU citizenship. Immigration regulations for EU and US citizens are given in the *Immigration* sections under each country chapter.

The current regulations for EU members can be broadly summarised as follows. EU nationals are permitted to stay in any member state for up to three months without obtaining a residence permit. Once you find work and decide to stay longer than this period, you will usually need to apply for a residence permit (although in both France and Spain these need only be applied for on a voluntary basis) at the local police station or town hall. You will need to take your passport, photos, proof of local address and a copy of your employment contract. This procedure may vary slightly from country to country. A temporary residence permit is usually issued if the contract of employment lasts for between three months and a year. Completing these formalities means you will have some protection and rights. It is generally not advisable to work for employers who cut corners and are not willing to provide you with a suitable letter or contract.

The abolition of internal frontier controls between the signatories to the Schengen Agreement (see above) means that these conditions also apply to British and Irish citizens when they move between these countries. An ID card or residence permit of one country is enough to obtain entry to another. Thus, it is more difficult for the authorities in each country to know how long you have been in their territory since your passport is unlikely to be stamped or checked.

THE EUROPEAN ECONOMIC AREA

Of great significance to EU workers is the implementation of the European Economic Area (EEA) Treaty in January 1993. Agreement on the EEA Treaty was reached in April 1992 between the EC member states and the seven members of the European Free Trade Association (EFTA). In broad terms it guarantees the free movement of labour, goods, services and capital within the EU countries and those which are still in EFTA, meaning that the abolition of work permits for EU citizens also applies in Iceland, Norway, Liechtenstein and Switzerland. The need for residence permits remains.

RECOGNITION OF QUALIFICATIONS

Many EU directives have appeared over the years concerning mutual recognition of professional qualifications, such as those of doctors, veterinarians and nurses. In many other professions EU citizens are eligible to join a counterpart professional association in another EU country without having to retrain. Some professions, such as teaching, have aptitude tests or exams in the language of the country concerned, although many of these discriminatory restrictions are being challenged at present.

The basic directive on training and qualifications which recognises three-year training courses has been expanded so that qualifications gained through any post-secondary course of more than one year, as well as work experience, are now taken into account where entry to a job is regulated on the basis of specific national qualifications. This means that National and Scottish Vocational Qualifications (NVQs/SVQs) and GNVQs and their equivalents are now recognised in the EU. You can check the acceptability of your UK qualifications by contacting the Comparability Co-ordinator at the Employment Department, QS1, Room E603, Moorfoot, Sheffield S1 4PQ, ☎0114-259 4144; fax 0114 259 3167.

If you have on the job experience but no formal qualifications in a particular field, it is also possible to obtain a European Community Certificate of Experience. For EU citizens in the UK, this is issued by the Department of Trade and Industry (DTI). You should first make sure that your type of work experience is covered by an EU directive by asking your trade union or professional organisation. If you are in doubt, the DTI will send you a copy of the relevant directive. You can write to them at the *Department of Trade and Industry*, Enquiry Unit, 1 Victoria Street, London SW1H 0ET; ☎020-7215 5000; e-mail dti.enquiries@dti. gsi.gov.uk; www.dti.gov.uk. The DTI also supplies the application form for the Certificate of

Experience, with explanations attached.

Further useful information on qualifications, and other aspects of working in the EU, can be found in the *Eurofacts* leaflets published by Careers Europe to be found in Careers Advice Offices and TECS (training and enterprise councils). *First Steps to Working in Europe* (CSU Ltd, Prospects House, Booth Street East, Manchester M13 9EP; ☎0161-277 5200; e-mail enquiries@prospects.ac.uk; www.prospects.ac.uk) is a guide for higher education students and recent graduates in Britain and Ireland who wish to work in another European country (other guides in their 'special interest series' include *Using Languages* and *Work and Study Abroad*). The *European Commission (UK)* (8 Storey's Gate, London SW1P 3AT; ☎020-7973 1992; fax 020-7973 1900; www.cec.org.uk) can give useful information about the EU and its institutions. *Comparability of Vocational Training Qualifications*, published by the Office for Official Publications of the European Communities, is a directory of EU qualifications and their equivalents. This office also publishes *Working in the European Union: A Guide for Graduate Recruiters and Jobseekers*, by W. H. Archer and J. C. Raban.

SELF-EMPLOYMENT

Many work contracts, especially in the construction industry, are issued on a self-employed basis. A prospective employee must normally be self-employed in the United Kingdom before he or she can apply for the certificate E101, issued by the Inland Revenue (National Insurance Contributions Office, International Services, Benton Park View, Longbenton, Newcastle-upon-Tyne NE98 1ZZ; ☎0845-915 4811; fax 0845-915 7800; www.inlandrevenue.gov.uk). The E101 exempts the holder from paying social security contributions in another EU country for up to 12 months. It can only be issued on the basis of a definite job offer from a named employer and can take several weeks to process. This can lead to problems, as many employers will not offer you a job unless you already have an E101. The Department for Work and Pensions (www.dwp.gov.uk/) issues a leaflet, SA 29, which gives more about the position of the self-employed in Europe.

Under EU law a person registered for VAT in the UK may recover certain VAT costs suffered in another EU country, provided that the expenditure is incurred for business purposes and that the person is not already registered, or liable to be registered, for VAT in that country. A claim form (UK version – VAT65) must be completed in the language of the country against which the claim is to be made and handed to the tax authorities.

Anyone thinking of setting up in the EU in a non-salaried or independent profession (e.g. carpenter, plumber, plasterer, restaurateur) will have to register their qualifications or a Certificate of Experience with the relevant local regulatory body. Proof of ability to manage one's own business is also needed. This is not a discriminatory practice but rather a requirement to conform to those regulations that govern local people who provide services to the public.

BRITISH CITIZENSHIP

The 1981 British Nationality Act complicated the issue of citizenship somewhat by replacing the old category of 'citizen of the United Kingdom and colonies' with three new categories of citizenship:

CATEGORIES OF BRITISH CITIZENSHIP

o   *British Citizenship*, for people closely connected (i.e. by birth, registration/ naturalisation, or descent) with the United Kingdom, the Channel Islands and the Isle of Man.

o   *British Dependent Territories Citizenship*, people connected with the dependencies.

o   *British Overseas Citizenship*, for those citizens of the United Kingdom and Colonies who do not have these connections with either the United Kingdom or the dependencies.

The Home Office advises that free movement of labour within the EU and the EEA is granted only to those with British Citizenship (Class 1) who have the right of abode in the UK. The only exception to this is for British Dependent Territories Citizens (Class 2) connected with Gibraltar.

In order to work within the EU or EEA you must have a valid British passport. This must be either endorsed *Holder has the right of abode in the United Kingdom* or show the holder's national status as a British citizen. Any queries on nationality from people living in the United Kingdom should be addressed to the *Nationality Division,* 3rd floor, India Buildings, Water Street, Liverpool L2 0QN; ☎0151-236 4723. People resident abroad should contact their nearest British consulate or embassy.

Among the entitlements of a UK citizen in Europe is the right for his spouse and dependants to join him and enjoy the same privileges, including the right to take up employment.

SOCIAL SECURITY

Working in a foreign country normally means joining that country's social security scheme. There are many exceptions to this rule, however, and in certain cases contributions are still payable in Britain. Claims for national insurance benefits can also be complicated where more than one country's scheme is involved. The Department of Social Security publishes a series of leaflets (described below) that are available from the Inland Revenue, National Insurance Contributions Office, Benton Park View, Longbenton, Newcastle-upon-Tyne NE98 1ZZ. Leaflets CH 5 and CH 6, relating to Child Benefit, can also be obtained from any local Social Security office, Inland Revenue Enquiry Centre, Citizens Advice Bureau and main libraries.

The leaflet, *Social Security Abroad,* explains in general terms those cases where there are no reciprocal agreements involved. If you are claiming child benefit, ask for leaflets CH 5 *Child Benefit for People Entering Britain,* and CH 6 *Child Benefit for People Leaving Britain.* Note, however, that child benefit is only affected if the child will be abroad for more than eight weeks.

European Union Regulations

The rules concerning the EU Social Security Regulations are complex, and you will need to obtain proper advice from the Contributions Agency of the Department for Work and Pensiones International Services should you decide to live or work in another EU country. Leaflet SA 29 explains your social security, insurance benefits, and health-care rights in the EU, Iceland, Liechtenstein and Norway. The European Commission also issues a useful guide which explain in basic terms the Social Security arrangements of each EU country: *The Community Provisions on Social Security.* Copies are available on application to the Contributions Agency, International Services (EU), at the address above.

Other Reciprocal Agreements

In addition to the leaflets mentioned above, the following leaflets outline social security agreements between Britain and *Australia* (SA 5); *Barbados* (SA 43); *Bermuda* (SA 23); *Canada* (SA 20); *Cyprus* (SA 12); *Israel* (SA 14); *Jamaica* (SA 27); *Jersey and Guernsey* (SA 4); *Malta* (SA 11); *Mauritius* (SA 38); *New Zealand* (SA 8); *The Philippines* (SA 42); *Turkey* (SA 22); *USA* (SA 33); and the states of the *former Yugoslavia* (SA 17).

HEALTHCARE

No matter what country you are heading for, you should obtain the Department of Health leaflet T7.1 *Health Advice for Travellers* (updated May 2006). This leaflet should be available from any post office or doctor's surgery. Alternatively you can request a free copy on the Health Literature Line ☎0870 155 5455 or read it online at www.dh.gov.uk, which also has country-by-country details.

The old E111 certificate of entitlement to medical treatment within Europe has been superseded by the European Health Insurance Card (EHIC). In the first phase of introduction, the new card will cover health care for short stays. By 2008, the electronic card will take the place of the current E128 and E119 which cover longer stays. At present this reciprocal cover is extended only to emergency treatment, so private insurance is also highly recommended. Among the leading providers of medical cover is *BUPA International* (Russell Mews, Brighton, East Sussex BN1 2NR; ☎01273-718406; www.bupa-intl.com).

UNEMPLOYMENT BENEFIT IN EU COUNTRIES

Those who have been registered as unemployed (but not if in receipt of jobseekers allowance) in Britain for four weeks can go abroad to other EU countries to look for work, and still receive the UK benefit (see Leaflet JSAL 22 *Unemployment benefit for people going abroad or coming from abroad*). There is an application form for transferring benefit: E303, and this should be completed before your departure. It should be noted that transfer of benefits is only possible in the case of benefit subsidised by your National Insurance contributions, and does not apply to income support.

Those wishing to transfer their unemployment benefit abroad should first select the town where they intend to look for work and notify their local unemployment benefit office of their plans. The unemployment benefit office will inform the Pensions and Overseas Benefits Directorate of the Department for Work and Pensions (Tyneview Park, Whitley Road, Benton, Newcastle-upon-Tyne, NE98 1BA; ☎0191-218 7777; fax 0191-218 7293; e-mail pod-customer-care-ba@ms04.dwp.gsi.gov.uk) who will consider the issuing of form E303. This form authorises the other state to pay your UK unemployment benefit/ Jobseeker's Allowance. It may be issued to you before departure from the UK if time allows, and you are going to Austria, Belgium, Finland, France, Germany, Greece, Iceland, Italy, Norway, Portugal, Spain or Sweden. Otherwise, the E303 form will be sent to a liaison officer in the country concerned and your unemployment benefit office can supply you with a letter of introduction to the foreign employment service. It is important that you put these arrangements in place before your departure.

This system involves the exporting of UK unemployment benefit, and also works in the other direction. Benefit is paid at the standard UK rate, which may not go far in a country like Sweden with its high cost of living. It is also possible for people who have worked in another EU country, and have paid enough contributions into its unemployment benefit insurance scheme, to claim unemployment benefit there at that country's rate, which is likely to be higher than in Britain. The exact details, such as who administers the system and the length of time for which contributions must have been paid, vary from country to country.

Time spent working and paying contributions in one EU country can be credited towards your entitlement to unemployment benefit if you move on to another EU country. Thus, someone might work first in Britain and then in Germany, where he might lose his job and begin claiming German unemployment benefit. His UK insurance may be used first to satisfy the rules for payment of German unemployment benefit. If he then moves on to France he can continue to claim unemployment benefit there for up to three months, at the German rate.

TAXATION

The extent of the liability to United Kingdom tax of a person who is temporarily abroad depends on several factors, the principal one being whether the person is classed as resident in the UK for tax purposes. In the simplest of cases, where a UK citizen works abroad full-time during an entire tax year (i.e. 6 April to 5 April), there will be no liability for UK tax as long as that person does not spend more than 62 days in the UK on average in one tax year. Anyone who spends more than 182 days in the UK during a particular year will be treated as a UK resident for tax purposes, with no exceptions. An outline of residence and its effect on tax liability is given in the Inland Revenue's leaflet IR 20, *Residents' and Non-Residents' Liability to Tax in the United Kingdom*; leaflet IR 139, *Income from Abroad? A Guide to Tax on Overseas Income*, may also be helpful.

Where a person who is abroad remains resident in the UK for tax purposes, they may in some circumstances be liable to tax both in the UK and in the country they are visiting. If this happens, however, they can normally claim relief from either one tax or the other under a Double Taxation Agreement made between the two countries. Details are given in the Inland Revenue's leaflet IR 58, *Going to Work Abroad*. Inland Revenue leaflets are available from any local office of the Inspector of Taxes. Other general enquiries, claims and problems (including enquiries about claims to exemption under a Double Taxation Agreement) should be addressed to the *Inland Revenue Enquiry Line* on ☎ 020-7667 4001.

Many EU countries operate a 'pay as you earn' system similar to that in Britain. This means you are taxed a certain amount on the assumption that your monthly income is representative of your annual income. However, if your job is seasonal, or temporary, or varies from month to month, this often isn't the case, and thus you will have a right to claim back tax. It doesn't mean you can get around the system by moving from country to country, however, and this is the reason for the 'double taxation' agreements mentioned above. It is a good idea – especially when you work abroad – to keep all payslips and other financial information in case you need to plead your case at a later date; and you should be vigilant when your employer sets out your tax position at the beginning of your employment. There are rules, which vary from country to country, but generally you do not want to end up on the local equivalent of emergency or higher-rate tax.

US CITIZENS IN THE EU

Economic and Monetary Union will not improve the chances of Americans wishing to work in EU countries, and those countries which have previously been willing to tolerate some illegal non-EU workers are increasingly taking steps to stop such practices. It is also important to bear in mind that the EU and EEA also have to deal with large numbers of migrant workers, many from Eastern Europe, where political change has also opened up a new source of potential labour.

US citizens can, of course, be legally employed where no suitable EU worker can be found and a work permit has been issued; there is, however, no equivalent of the Green Card. To obtain a work permit, you will need a letter or authorisation from the company that intends to employ you; and it should be noted that you must have the relevant documentation with you when you arrive to take up employment.

Details of programmes which allow American citizens to work abroad legally are given in many of the chapters in *Specific Careers* – in particular under *Agriculture and the Environment; Au Pair and Domestic; Transport and Tourism*; and *Voluntary Work*. Further information is also given in the individual country chapters.

US citizens should ascertain their tax liability on overseas earnings before heading abroad. Even where overseas residence is established there is a ceiling on the amount that can be earned free of US tax (currently US$80,000). The Inland Revenue Service issues a helpful leaflet, *Tax Guide for US Citizens and Resident Aliens Abroad (Publication 54)*, which is available from the *Forms Distribution Centre* (PO Box 25866, Richmond, Virginia 23260; www.irs.gov). As far as social security is concerned, US citizens working for US companies abroad can continue to pay US social security contributions for several years, and claim exemption from local social security payments so long as a reciprocal agreement exists with the other country.

Learning the Language

Living and working abroad usually means having to learn another language. Even in those countries where English is widely and fluently spoken (in Scandinavia or the Netherlands for example), the ability to communicate effectively in the local tongue will have a significant impact on the success of your transition into a new culture, lifestyle and working environment. As an international jobseeker, some skills in the language of your target destination will usefully demonstrate both the seriousness of your career intentions and your suitability as an employee. If you already have a rusty school-standard grounding in a 'world' language like French, German or Spanish, consider the preliminary step of lifting your fluency in the language. Or it might be more appropriate to develop specific language skills on that basis of your desired career destination.

Native speakers of 'minority' languages, like Finnish or Flemish understand very well the importance of mastering other languages and we can learn something from their attitudes to language learning. Fluency in a second, third, or even fourth foreign language is commonplace in the Netherlands, a country which has itself started exporting English language teachers around the world and where it is accepted that language learning is not a difficult or academic subject, but rather a skill involving mastering the phonology – or system of sounds – of a language, as well as its grammar and written form. These skills can be quickly mastered, at least at a functional level, with just a little application.

As barriers to the free movement of labour in Europe come down, those with a good knowledge of other languages will inevitably have the widest range of job opportunities open to them; in fields such as translation and interpreting for instance, but also in administration, sales and marketing and other areas. If Britons and Americans do not learn French, or Russian, or Japanese then we can be sure that many speakers of these other languages are already busy learning ours and will be competing against English-speakers in the multilingual marketplace.

In your daily life abroad, even if English is spoken in your work environment, you will be disadvantaged in your ability to interact with the local community and may be crucially out of step when it comes to recognising opportunities for career advancement. Fluency in the language of the country in which you have settled will help you to integrate both socially and professionally and is likely to be a decisive factor in the success (or otherwise) of your stay. As native speakers of the worldwide language of commerce the British and Irish still lag behind the other EU nations as far as language learning is concerned, but economic necessity and an increased emphasis on languages in schools means that this is now changing.

Where, though, should you start? Certainly, you should adopt the position that learning another language is not a kind of grim necessity, but rather a positive opportunity. Readers of this book may choose to visit their local library or bookshop where they will find self-directed language courses ranging from the basic *Teach Yourself...* books published by Hodder Headline (best used in combination with other material or even a teacher), through to more interactive courses such as the Routledge *Colloquial...* series which include cassettes. One of the best-known language learning methods, now with many imitators, is the *Linguaphone* concept, in which you 'listen, speak, and understand'. Linguaphone (UK freephone ☎0800-136 973; www.linguaphone.co.uk) courses do require a certain amount of dedication, and sometimes a high boredom threshold, but are highly regarded for the results that can be achieved.

If you choose the self-study approach, remember that the simple repetition of phrases – although useful to an extent – will not be enough to guarantee you any degree of fluency. Instead, you should, in addition, gain an understanding of the basic grammatical structures of your new language, and of its phonetics. One useful companion book which explains some of these issues (and which is an indispensable reference book for those who intend to teach English as a foreign language) is *A Mouthful of Air* by Anthony Burgess (Hutchinson), which gives a practical insight into successful methods of learning a foreign language.

There are, of course, many phrase books on the market but these are generally less than useful as most transcribe phrases into English with little explanation of how a word or phrase sounds. Berlitz publish some phrase books, as do *Lonely Planet* and *Rough Guides*. In the USA and Canada the *Cortina Institute of Languages* (7 Hollyhock Rd, Wilton Connecticut 06897; ☎1800-245 2145; e-mail info@cortina-languages.com; www.cortina-languages.com) publishes a series of *Traveller's Dictionaries*, as well as interactive courses comprising books and cassettes.

CD-ROM multi-media language learning is the latest addition to the self-study market. *Eurotalk* (315-317 New Kings Road, London SW6 4RF; ☎020-7371 7711; fax 020-7371 7781; e-mail info@eurotalf.co.uk; www.eurotalk.co.uk) has a range of learning materials in this format, as do an ever-increasing number of new media publishers. There are also a growing number of internet language study sites, as well as language interest groups and bulletin boards. If you are interested in Japanese for example, you could try www.japanese-online.com. Use a search engine such as *Google* to locate sites of interest to you.

Private or home tuition, study in your local college or university, or a combination of these will probably get you the desired results most quickly. The importance of communicating with real, live human beings, even if their efforts are as stumbling as your own, should not be underestimated. Contact with native speakers of the target language is also invaluable (and could be a part of your creative job search and preparation too). Some countries, such as Norway and Belgium, provide special language classes for foreign workers and their families and some companies in the USA and UK include language courses as part of their training programmes. In many countries language courses for the locals are even subsidised by the state, and may lead to employment for English language teachers (see the chapter on *Teaching*). After arrival in your destination country, you will, of course, find many language schools and colleges providing general or specialist courses on the spot (see below). Whatever approach you decide upon, it is advisable to start your study before you depart and some ideas on where to begin are given below.

LOCAL COURSES

Most universities and colleges of further education, as well as workers' educational associations and adult education centres, run part-time or evening classes in a number of foreign languages. These are often very good value. You may wish to combine them with some more intensive study, private tuition, a home study or distance-learning course or a short intensive or 'immersion' course abroad. In Britain, most county and city councils publish information about forthcoming courses in local newspapers before the start of each new term; keep a look out for these around August, December and March. In London *Floodlight* (www.floodlight.co.uk), available in all newsagents and public libraries, gives details of every conceivable course taking place in the Greater London Area.

THE OPEN UNIVERSITY

The *Open University (OU)* (Walton Hall, Milton Keynes MK7 6AA; ☎01908-274066; fax 01908-653744; e-mail general-enquiries@open.ac.uk; www.open.ac.uk) provides distance or 'open-learning' courses in French, German and Spanish. Those who have learnt these languages on an *ad hoc* basis, or who have no formal qualifications, are encouraged to apply. Course fees include books, audio CDs, and videos. Students have the use of centres where they can 'drop in' for tuition (between 18 and 21 hours of individual tuition over a 32-week period). The OU course can lead towards a degree-level qualification. To join you will need an entry level approximately equivalent to GCSE standard and by the third year of study will be expected to have attained a level approximately equivalent to that of a second-year undergraduate course at a conventional university.

CILT

CILT, the *National Centre for Languages* (20 Bedfordbury, London WC2N 4LB; ☎020-7379 5101; fax 020-7379 5082; e-mail info@cilt.org.uk; www.cilt.org.uk) is the UK's primary resource for information on the range of study materials available for many languages. Their database caters for many exotic languages, as well as the more usual choices, including those for which information is often difficult to obtain. If you are heading for Ulan Bator and pondering which language might be of most use, then the *CILT Library* is probably the place to visit. CILT holds a certain amount of documentation on language courses, especially in London, and a list of their publications can be obtained from the above address.

PRIVATE LANGUAGE SCHOOLS

There are many private language schools offering everything from correspondence courses with cassettes to total immersion courses abroad. A brief list of some of the better-known language schools is given below. More detailed information can be obtained from *The Earls Guide to Language Schools in Europe* (Cassell), which lists more than 1,000 schools in Europe – from Poland to Portugal, including many in France, Germany, Italy and Spain. The book is cross-referenced by subject and contains useful information on many of the schools listed.

Alliance Française (1 Dorset Square, London NW1 6PU; ☎020-7723 6439; e-mail info@alliancefrancaise.org.uk; www.alliancefrancaise.org.uk; and 1,135 other centres in 138 countries). The Alliance Française is unquestionably the best of the world's established French language associations, offering courses at branches across the globe. In the UK, there are language teaching centres in Bath, Belfast, Bristol, Cambridge, Exeter, Glasgow, Jersey, London, Milton Keynes, Manchester, Oxford and York, as well as a further 53 French clubs where you can practice your language skills in congenial company.

Berlitz (UK) Ltd (Lincoln House, 296-302 High Holborn, London WC1 7JH; ☎020-7611 9640; fax 020-7611 9656; www.berlitz.co.uk). Berlitz has more than 400 branches and schools in more than 60 countries across Europe and the US, all of which use native-speakers to teach almost any language you could wish to learn. The Berlitz method was one of the first to combine the study of grammar with speaking, and will be suited to those who prefer a rather more formal approach to learning. Courses range from group tuition (up to eight students) to the 'total immersion' course. Private tuition can be arranged at times to suit the individual student, as can crash courses of six hours a day, five days a week. In-company language training can be given to groups of up to 12 people in the same firm and executive crash courses can be arranged. Addresses of some other Berlitz schools are: 38 Avenue de l'Opera, Paris 75002, France; ☎1-4494 5000, fax 1-4494 5005; Oxfordstrasse 24, Bonn 53111, Germany, ☎228-655005, fax 228-63 6238; Via Larga 8, 20122 Milan, Italy, ☎02-869 0814; fax 02-809395; and Gran Via 80/4, E-28013 Madrid, Spain, ☎91-541 6103; fax 91-541 2765. Applications should be directed to individual schools.

Italian Cultural Institute (39 Belgrave Square, London SW1X 8NX; ☎020-7235 1461; fax 020-7235 4618; e-mail icilondon@esteri.it; www.icilondon.esteri.it. The Italian Cultural Institute is the official Italian government agency for the promotion of cultural exchanges between Great Britain and Italy. The Institute promotes collaboration between Universities, academies and learned societies in the two countries and assists in the organisation of major Italian cultural events in Britain. It organises and promotes lectures, exhibitions, symposia and concerts, both at the Institute and elsewhere and can give information on all aspects of Italian cultural and social life. General Italian courses on all levels are conducted at the Institute, in Italian, and provide training in all basic communication skills – listening, speaking, reading and writing – with a systematic study of grammar. Teachers are university-qualified and native speakers.

EF Language Travel (114A Cromwell Road, London. SW7 4ES; ☎ 020-7341 8612; fax 020-7341 8501; e-mail louisa.cliff@ef.com; www.ef.com) provides foreign language courses in France, Germany, Italy, Spain, Ecuador, Russia, and China. Courses are from two-52 weeks and run year-round. All teaching is in the target language, with special interest classes on the country's culture. Short term courses from £300 per week including accommodation and half board; nine-month fluency courses from £200 per week including accommodation, half board and return flight.

ENFOREX Spanish Language School (26 Alberto Aguillera, Madrid, E-28015, Spain; ☎91-594 3776; fax 91-594 5159; e-mail info@enforex.es; www.enforex.es) is a widely recognised language school with a series of courses adapted to every need: general Spanish, business and legal Spanish, teaching Spanish, study tours, and one-to-one tuition. Family, residential and hotel accommodation can be provided. Classes are small and cultural activities organised. More than 17 centres in Spain and Latin America.

Eurocentres (56 Eccleston Square, London SW1V 1PH; ☎020-7963 8450; fax 020-7963 8479; e-mail info@eurocentres.com; www.eurocentres.com is a non profit-making organisation which provides language courses in 29 schools on five continents for periods of up to six months. The minimum age for students is 16. Besides 16 centres for English in the UK, Ireland, Malta, Australia, New Zealand, South Africa, Canada and the USA, there are centres for French in Paris, La Rochelle, Amboise and Lausanne; German in Cologne; Spanish in Valencia and Barcelona; Italian in Florence; and Japanese in Kanazawa. All teaching is conducted in the language concerned, with extensive use of language laboratories, computer-assisted language learning and audio-visual materials. Excursions are organised and all schools have facilities for independent study to complement class work. Accommodation is arranged in private households, residences and shared flats.

The Eurolingua Institute (5 rue Henri Guinier, 34000 Montpellier, France, tel/fax +33 467 15 04 73; e-mail info@eurolingua.com; www.eurolingua.com) is the largest organisation of its kind, offering study abroad language and work experience programmes throughout Europe, Scandinavia, North America, Latin America, South Africa, Japan, New Zealand, Australia and the Caribbean. Learn to speak: Chinese, Dutch, English, French, German, Italian, Japanese, Portuguese, Russian, Spanish or Swedish like a native, living and studying in a country where your target language is spoken.

Goethe-Institut (50 Princes Gate, Exhibition Road, London SW7 2PH; ☎020-7596 4000; fax 020-7594 0240; e-mail mail@london.goethe.org; www.goethe.de) offers language courses at its centres in London, Manchester (☎0161-275 8041) and Glasgow (☎0141-332 2555). It also has 16 language centres in major German cities, including Munich, Berlin, Dresden, Düsseldorf, Hamburg, Frankfurt, and Weimar. The Goethe-

Institut runs a series of intensive business and commercial German courses for the international business community, as well as specialised courses in German for lawyers and the hospitality industries.

inlingua International (Belpstrasse 11, CH-3007 Bern, Switzerland; ☎31-388 7777; fax 31-388 7766; e-mail service@inlingua.com; www.inlingua.com) offers a wide variety of courses in all the major western European languages, as well as many rarer ones, at centres in Austria, France, Germany, Italy, Spain, Bangkok, Saõ Paolo, and Tokyo. There is an extensive range of courses and prospective participants should, in the first instance, contact the information centre at the above address or check the website.

McGill Centre for Continuing Education (688 Sherbrooke Street West, 11th Floor, Montreal, H3A 3R1, Canada; ☎514-398 6200; fax 514-398 4448; e-mail info.conted@mcgill.ca; www.mcgill.ca) offers intensive language programmes in both English and French at levels ranging from beginners to advanced intermediates. Special Intensive Programmes run for nine weeks, five days a week in small classes of about 15 students work with an emphasis on communication and the personal attention of experienced lecturers. Students who complete level five of the Certificate of Proficiency in French may go on to take an advanced programme aimed at people who wish to practise in an entirely or partially French-speaking professional environment. There are also a variety of other professional and business programmes available.

SOUFFLE (Espace Charlotte, 83260 La Crau, France; ☎04-9400 9465; fax 04-9400 9230; e-mail coumier@souffle.asso.fr; www.souffle.asso.fr) is an association of 17 language centres in France which offers a charter of quality and can send you a list of its member schools which offer a variety of French business and vacation courses.

Twin Languages Abroad (67-71 Lewisham High Street, Lewisham, London SE13 5JX; ☎020-8297 0505; fax 020-8297 0984; e-mail languagesabroad@twinuk.com; www.twinlanguagesabroad.com) offers a number of courses in French, German, Italian, Portuguese and Spanish in attractive locations across Europe. There is also a school in Ecuador. These courses will suit both young people and adults. Intensive executive courses are also available at all levels (beginning on any Monday of the year).

Preparation and Follow-up

It is terribly easy to fall into lazy generalisations about other countries, about their people, customs and way of life. While it is true that stereotyping is one of the ways in which we come to understand another country or culture – and many people have an interest in another country which developed from initial stereotypes: the French and food, the Italians and fashion, the Aussies and their barbies – it is important to be open to the wider picture.

Many cultural stereotypes are negative, but sometimes even the positive ones can be misleading. If you treasure a vision of French hedonism you may, for example, be disappointed to find yourself working in a serious-minded and hierarchical French company. Or perhaps you may be surprised to discover that the Japanese are not always as devoted to their work as you had expected, and that they throw themselves with equal devotion into the drunken *enkai*. On the other hand, you may hold fast to notions of the innate superiority of your own country and way of life, and this, too, will limit you. It can be as well to remember that your hosts may be equally convinced of their own unmatchable sophistication and cultivation.

As well as learning the language of the country in which you will be working, it is always worthwhile finding out something about the local culture. This is especially true if your destination is one in which the cultural and social climate is very different from your own. Even if you work and socialise mainly with other expatriates some understanding of the cultural background will help you settle in and, in due course, to feel at home. Many companies and government bodies believe that it is worthwhile investing in briefings for employees who are about to serve terms overseas, in the expectation that these employees can then operate more efficiently and acclimatise themselves more rapidly to their new environment. If you are not attached to such an organisation remember that you can always brief yourself, and that understanding the culture of your new home is bound to pay significant personal dividends.

GETTING THERE

The arrangements for your trip should be made as far in advance as possible. Shopping around, whether for a removal company or for airline tickets, will help keep costs down; never take the first deal you find, even if it is tempting to take the easiest way out. Specialist removal companies advertise in the international employment press and can also easily be found through your local Yellow Pages. Air ticket and travel agencies advertise widely in the travel sections of all major newspapers, as well as in backpackers' magazines such as *TNT* available at mainline stations and other major tourist spots in London. The travel agencies listed below all operate at the budget end of the market and provide highly competitive fares with reputable carriers.

Useful Addresses
STA Travel, ☎0870-1 630 026 for national sales; e-mail help@statravel.co.uk; www. statravel.co.uk; STA Travel specialises in student travel and discount fares for the under-35 market. It has 65 branches in the UK and 450 worldwide. The company is particularly helpful in arranging independent and non-standard travel and has offices around the

world, particularly in cities with large student populations, such as Oxford, Cambridge, Bristol, and Edinburgh in the UK.

Airline Network, ☎0870-700 0543 (9am-9pm Monday to Sunday); www.airnet.co.uk. An independent travel company with up-to-the-minute discount deals.

Trailfinders, ☎0845-058 5858; www.trailfinders.com. Trailfinders also has offices in Belfast, Birmingham, Bristol, Cambridge, Dublin, Glasgow, Leeds, Manchester, Newcastle, and Oxford. The Kensington office is open seven days a week.

Travelbag, ☎0800-082 5000; www.travelbag.co.uk. Tailor-made travel service.

Internet Ticket Discounters

Bucketshop.com: Digital travel portal.

www.cheapflights.com: Products and prices from over 300 companies in the travel industry.

www.deckchair.com: Cheap deals on flights.

www.discountfares.com: Discounted international farer with main destinations being Mexico, Central America, South America, and Europe.

www.ebookers.com: Last minute deals and cheap flights.

www.expedia.com: Great all purpose travel website with bargains on planes, car hire, and hotels.

www.flightsdirect.com: Bargain flights worldwide.

www.opodo.com: Great all purpose travel website with bargains on planes, car hire, and hotels.

www.travelocity.co.uk: Great all purpose travel website with bargains on planes, car hire, and hotels.

www.skyscanner.net: Search engine for cheap flights in Europe and Australiasia.

CULTURE SHOCK

Everyone who moves to another country will experience, to a greater or lesser extent, a phenomenon known to psychologists as culture shock. It is as well to be aware of this before you go and to be prepared for its effects – ranging from elation to disappointment, depending on the individual, the environment and the experiences he or she has. You should understand that living abroad has its highs and lows and that such changes are entirely to be expected.

There are several stages in the process of acclimatisation which you can expect to experience beginning with a 'honeymoon stage' when, in a state of general excitement, you are prepared to accept and enthuse about every aspect of your new environment. The next stage in the process will, however, strike no matter how euphoric your initial impressions are. Be prepared for a period of crisis and disintegration as you become more aware of differences in values and behaviour. At this time you may experience feelings of intense isolation. Next follows a period of re-adjustment or re-integration, in which you look for a return to the values and beliefs of your own culture, and may even reject the new culture, preferring to keep company with those with a similar cultural background to your own – American expatriates start finding things in common with their British colleagues and so on. You may cling to stereotypes about your own country that you find reassuring and your own prejudices may be reinforced. Nonetheless, you will begin to find your own space in a new and unfamiliar world and with time and growing self-esteem you will move towards a state of 'autonomy'. From this position, you will find yourself enjoying the positive aspects of the new culture and being prepared to forgive the negative ones. The more self-confident and well-travelled an individual is, the easier the transition is to living in a new country; others less flexible or accommodating are likely to eventually return home sooner.

Like any mild disorder, culture shock can be combated with some simple coping strategies. Awareness of the symptoms, which can include physical and psychological effects ranging from headaches and tiredness to sleep problems and irritability helps, as does good preparation. Prior contact with local people and a good (theoretical) knowledge of the local way of life are immensely useful. It is a good idea to avoid mixing only with expatriates and other foreigners, and you should try to reduce stress during the 'crisis' stage by keeping fit and healthy. Try keeping a journal, or seeing if you can change or influence those aspects of the new way of life that you find you dislike. Finally, on your return home, be aware that some of the symptoms of culture shock can be repeated in reverse as you re-integrate back into your native environment.

PREPARATION

There are some practical steps that you can take to make it easier to settle in to a foreign country. There is not the space here for an exhaustive plan of action, but it is essential that you do take the time to sit down and write out a checklist of things to do. Such a list will include travel arrangements, financial arrangements (both at home and for when you arrive at your destination), packing and shipping, accommodation, and visas. The *Equitable Guide to Working Abroad*, by William Essex (Bloomsbury) has useful chapters on financial planning for UK citizens, as well as on dealing with family-related issues such as international schooling.

If you are being posted abroad with your partner and children you will face additional decisions and challenges – and so will they. More than 90 per cent of international postings involve male employees, and in many cases women who accompany their partners abroad leave behind fulfilling careers of their own, resulting in frustration and boredom in their new environment. A large proportion of those who accompany their spouse abroad fail to find employment, and very few corporate relocation policies offer spousal jobsearch assistance. In response to these challenges the human resources consultancy, ECA International, has launched *Together on Assignment*, a self-help tool to guide expatriate families through the difficulties they are likely to face. The three-part package includes a *Partner's Guide*, containing case studies, a checklist, information on children and work issues and an activity planner. *Together on Assignment* is available from ECA International (Anchor House, 15 Britten Street, London SW3 3TY; ☎020-7351 5000; fax 020-7351 9396; e-mail eca@eca-international.com; www.eca-international.com).

Below are listed a few of the organisations which might be useful in preparing for your new life abroad. However, you should note that none of them are in any way involved in recruitment.

Farnham Castle International Briefing and Conference Centre (Farnham Castle, Farnham, Surrey GU9 0AG; ☎01252-720416; fax 01252-719277; e-mail info@farhamcastle.com; www.farnhamcastle.com) is the market leader in international effectiveness training. The Centre runs hundreds of different programmes every year, which aim to assist people going overseas or coming to the UK to work more effectively in their new environment. Strands include business briefings, country briefings, repatriation, working with the British, intensive language tuition, cross-cultural awareness and management of international personnel. Programmes can be provided on any country, and include a survey of the region's history, geography, politics and economics, as well as a study of the people and their culture. The Centre is an independent non-profit organisation, founded in 1953.

Corona Worldwide (South Bank House, Black Prince Road, London SE1 7SJ; ☎020-7793 4020; fax 020-7793 4042; www.coronaworldwide.org) is a voluntary organisation with branches in the UK and overseas providing, among other services, postal and personal briefing for women and men about to live or work abroad. The postal briefing is in the form of a series of booklets containing all the practical and domestic details needed to prepare for setting up home in a new country, such as climate, clothing, educational and medical facilities, housing, household requirements, food, leisure activities. The society also runs day-long and telephone briefings on how to adapt to a new lifestyle and culture. Lectures, medical advice and a chance to meet a briefer who has recently returned from the target country are also available. Membership of the society is free to any woman who has attended a meeting; men can join as associate members. An annual magazine lists contacts and addresses in addition to reports from people who are already working abroad.

Global Integration Limited, (75 Nine Mile Ride, Finchampstead, Berkshire RG40 4ND; ☎0118-932 8912; fax 0118-932 8870; e-mail us@global-integration.com; www.global-integration.com) provides individually tailored cross-cultural training programmes for senior managers and executives, and has offices in the USA.

SOURCES OF INFORMATION

BBC World Service (Bush House, Strand, London W12 0ZY; ☎020-7240 3456; www.bbc.co.uk/worldservice) can keep you in touch with events in Britain through quality English-language broadcasting wherever you are in the world. To be sure of receiving its programmes the World Service recommends a short-wave radio covering the frequency ranges 5950-6200, 7100-7600, 9400-9900, 11500-12100, 13600-13900, 15000-156000, 17700-17900, 21400-21800 kHz. A monthly listings guide, *BBC On Air*, provides comprehensive programme information, advice on frequencies, and background features. You can obtain information and subscribe to *BBC On Air* online via the BBC website. BBC radio programmes are also relayed through many local stations abroad, and there is a worldwide television service, *BBC World*, available on satellite or cable.

Foreign & Commonwealth Office (Travel Advice Unit, Consular Directorate, Old Admiralty Building, London SW1A 2PA; ☎0870-850 2829; fax 020-7008 0155; e-mail consular.fco@gtnet.gov.uk; www.fco.gov.uk) can send copies of Consular Department publications with details of those services Consuls abroad can and cannot provide. Their website contains recent travel advice, and information on diplomatic missions and foreign policy issues.

Transitions Abroad (PO Box 745, Bennington, VT 05201; ☎802-442 4827; e-mail info@transitionsabroad.com; www.transitionsabroad.com) is a bi-monthly magazine with excellent articles on living and working in foreign countries and letters from readers abroad. It also contains addresses of organisations that can arrange work abroad and promotes 'active involvement as a guest rather than as a tourist' in the host community. The company also publishes the *Alternative Travel Directory* with country-by-country listings including study programmes and volunteer opportunities, and can send back issues and country planning guides.

Specific
Careers

Agriculture, Fisheries and the Environment

Agriculture and the fishing industry have always been popular sources of seasonal and temporary work abroad. There are, however, also numerous longer-term opportunities for those with the right experience and qualifications in these fields, as well as in the allied area of forestry. In addition, conservation and the environment are now key areas of international concern and consequently a growth area in international employment. This chapter deals with some of the opportunities available for both professionals and volunteers.

While many developing countries have progressed towards self-sufficiency in food production, much of the developed world is now struggling with problems caused by over-production and the concomitant damage to the environment. Genetically modified crops have also recently altered the balance of the equation, and there are increased opportunities in this area of agricultural research and development, as well as in its polar opposite, organic farming. The organic sector of agriculture is expanding in all OECD countries to meet increasing demand and has been growing at 15 to 30 per cent a year, albeit from a low base.

Intensive farming methods and an over-reliance on monoculture in Third World countries (and former Soviet economies like the 'new' republics of Central Asia) have had disastrous environmental consequences. In these regions, there is an international aid and development emphasis on diversification and self-sufficiency, and many people are now employed in this field helping communities and countries to develop more stable production and distribution systems. Technological progress has already enabled many countries to be free of food shortages and there is now a need to implement the small-scale technologies, and the larger-scale infrastructure, which will lead to sustainable development.

Environmental protection is often allied with both agricultural and voluntary work. Disasters like Chernobyl, and the wrecking of oil tankers, have focused attention on the international scale of the problem, as well as on the necessity of developing 'joined-up' solutions. The same companies which are involved in large-scale 'clear-cutting' and permanent degradation of the forests in Siberia and South America may also be operating in the same way in Cambodia or Zaire. The habitats of widely differing species can come under the same threat, and global agreements are needed to preserve species as diverse as the Siberian tiger or Asian orang-utans.

It is widely recognised that action in the environmental field must be international and this is why it is a growing field for international workers, who may often pursue a career in many countries. There are several international organisations, such as Friends of the Earth and Greenpeace, which exist to promote conservation and sustainable development in both the developing and the developed worlds. While it is true to say that conservationists and ecologists are generally most concerned with helping developing countries preserve their varied wildlife and natural habitats, many of the same issues also apply in the developed economies of Europe and North America. Agriculturalists, the international fisheries industry, economists, and environmentalists are all faced with the problem of developing systems for sustainable development.

Agriculture and its allied industries offer a wide range of career opportunities abroad, whether or not you posses a relevant degree qualification. However, the more specialised careers do require either a degree or experience (whether paid or unpaid), and increasingly, competition for jobs means that more applicants now have a postgraduate qualification too. Limited opportunities occur with government and non-government organisations and in private consultancy groups. Much of the work is of a short-term nature, usually on contract, working on specific projects for third-world governments. Above all, experience is vital in this sector, and voluntary work on international projects is one highly effective way of staying a step ahead of the competition. If you choose to work on a voluntary project you will need, in addition to being suitably qualified and experienced, to be resourceful and highly committed to overseas service. Conditions are often harsh. Many voluntary organisations are also religiously affiliated, and many will expect you to be a committed Christian; most also require you to serve for at least one year.

AGRICULTURE, FISHERIES AND FORESTRY

Agriculturalists, acquaculturalists and foresters with recognised professional qualifications and experience are in steady demand throughout the developing world – in research and development, education, and rural administration. Appointments vary: from consultancy appointments of only a few weeks duration through to contracts lasting several years. A degree in agriculture or forestry is usually the minimum requirement; applicants with post-graduate training and experience in a specialised field relevant to the work being offered are generally preferred.

Most work of this kind is handled by foreign governments whose recruitment programmes are often administered in collaboration with voluntary organisations (see the chapter on Voluntary Work), United Nations specialised agencies and development programmes (see *United Nations*), other official and international bodies (see *International Organisations* later in this section and also *Working Exchanges* in the chapter *Getting the Job*), and occasionally by management recruitment consultants (see *The Conventional Job Search*).

Opportunities in industrialised nations are more limited, not because such work is scarce, but because most developed countries can supply their own suitably qualified workers.

Useful Addresses

AgriVenture, Speedwell Farm Bungalow, Nettle Bank, Wisbech, Cambridgeshire PE14 0SA ☎01945 450999; e-mail uk@agriventure.com; www.agriventure.com, arranges working visits to Australia, New Zealand, Canada, the USA and many other countries for those with a background or an interest in farming or horticulture. Applicants must be single and aged between 18 and 30. Participants receive a wage in accordance with local rates. AgriVenture arranges group air travel, full insurance cover and work permits. There is an information meeting before departure, and an orientation seminar and supervision in the host country. AgriVenture's website is informative and includes a FAQ page. AgriVenture also has servicing offices in Australia, Canada, Denmark and New Zealand that can arrange placements and exchanges from these countries (conditions of acceptance are the same as above).

Servicing offices can only deal with applications from citizens of that country, with the exception of the European office, which arranges placements for applicants from Austria, Belgium, Czech Republic, Denmark, Finland, France, Germany, Iceland, Luxembourg, the Netherlands, Norway, Sweden and Switzerland. Agriventure's international servicing office addresses are as follows: *Australia*: Office 2, Level 1, 208 Victoria Road, Drummoyne, NSW 2047; ☎+61 2 9181 3122; fax+61 2 9181 4299; *Canada and US*: 202A, 300 Merganser Drive, Chestermere, Alberta, T1X 1L6; ☎+1   403 255 7799; fax +1 403 255 6024; *New Zealand*: PO Box 134, 55 Victoria Street, Cambridge 2351, North Island; ☎+64 7 823 5700; fax +64 7 823 5701. All AgriVenture offices can also be contacted by email, using the format canada@agriventure.com, inserting the appropriate country name as the first part of the e-mail address.

MESA: Multinational Exchange for Sustainable Agriculture, (2002 Addison Street, Suite 202, Berkeley, CA 94704, USA; ☎+1 510 654 8858; fax +1 603 699 2459; e-mail mesa@mesaprogram.org; www.mesaprogram.org), is a non-profit organisation dedicated to advancing organic and sustainable farming practices around the world. MESA co-ordinates hands-on training programmes for young international farmers, enabling them to learn about ecological training systems at host farms in the USA. Selected 'farm interns' are given eight or 12-month on-the-farm programmes. To qualify, you will need to be nominated by a MESA Global Partner organisation, have genuine agricultural experience, basic conversational English and be aged between 21 and 35 years.

Overseas Development Institute, 111 Westminster Bridge Road, London SE1 7JD; ☎020-7922 0300; fax 020-7922 0399; www.odi.org.uk, runs the ODI Fellowship Scheme where recent young economists and those in related fields, from Britain and the EU countries, and occasionally from the USA, can work for up to two years in the public sectors of developing countries in Africa, the Caribbean and the Pacific. Candidates must have (or be studying for) a postgraduate qualification. The Fellowship Scheme provides some practical work experience in developing countries and around 25 Fellowships are awarded annually. A new scheme run by the ODI and funded by the Commonwealth, the ODI-Commonwealth Fellowship Scheme, has recently been established with the aim of placing postgraduate economists from Commonwealth countries in international trade posts, initially in the Pacific. Application forms and a booklet are available each October from the Fellowship Scheme Administrator and from University Careers Advisory Offices.

Tearfund, International Personnel Team, 100 Church Road, Teddington, Middlesex TW11 8QE; ☎020-8943 9144; e-mail enquiry@tearfund.org; www.tearfund.org, a Christian action charity offering short-term volunteer and salaried posts in the UK and abroad.

CONSERVATION AND THE ENVIRONMENT

The field of conservation includes agriculture and forestry and encompasses the whole area of ecology and the environment. Opportunities range from research work to practical participation in international projects. While agriculture and forestry are traditionally aimed at the most practical and economical use of land resources, conservation seeks to protect and improve habitats and the environment. In many countries around the world, ecological or 'green' movements have had a considerable influence on governments, although it remains to be seen whether developed nations will ultimately be willing to sacrifice their increasingly affluent lifestyles for the sake of the environment.

Many developing countries now insist that environmental programmes should be paid for by the wealthy industrialised nations, which initially caused environmental problems through their exploitation of natural resources. Increasingly, however, these countries are now taking on such responsibilities themselves, and their principle demand is for a more equitable economic order. The pressures of population growth and industrialisation still make environmental protection a low priority for the very poorest nations.

The numbers of vacancies, and the scope for an international career in conservation and the environment, continue to increase, as major programmes are undertaken and international agreements implemented. A substantial amount of international consultancy work is now being funded by the European Community, for example through its LIFE programme and others which aim to implement habitat directives; and through the PHARE and TACIS programmes of aid to Central and Eastern Europe and the former CIS.

Generally speaking, the intervention of outside agencies is seen as a means of promoting sustainable development or preserving wildlife habitats, and the help of outside experts in the short- or medium-term is often needed, as schemes are implemented and local staff trained. Working for an international organisation or pressure group is one way into a career in conservation. Those who are seeking salaried work in another country usually require qualifications in agriculture, forestry and biology, or allied areas. Knowledge of at least one other language is also generally required.

Useful Addresses

Asian Development Bank, HQ: PO Box 789, 0980 Manila, Philippines; e-mail information@ adb.org; ☎+632 632 4444; fax +632 636 2444; www.adb.org; European Representative Office: Rahmhofstrasse 2-4, 60313 Frankfurt am Main, Germany ☎+49 69 2193 6400; fax +49 69 2193 6444; e-mail adbero@adb.org; North American Representative Office: 815 Connecticut Avenue, NW, Suite 325, Washington DC 20006; ☎+1 202 728 1500; +1 202 728 1505; e-mail naro@adb.org. Administers a portfolio of developments loans in Asia and the Pacific and occasionally seeks staff with post-graduate qualifications and experience (at least part of which should have been in Asia). Knowledge of the concepts and practices relating to sustainable development is required. Job opportunities are listed on the ADB website, as well as opportunities for consulting work for businesses.

BTCV International Conservation Holidays, Sedum House, Mallard Way, Potteric Carr, Doncaster DN4 8DB; ☎01302-572200; e-mail information@btcv.org; www.btcv. org. Conservation holidays in 26 countries around the world focusing on supporting and developing its partner organisations and enabling local people to improve their environment. The cost of these holidays does not usually include transport to the pick-up point and prices for international destinations start from around £290. It is not necessary to have done conservation work before, but some more experienced volunteers are always needed. Conservation holidays in the UK are also available. Contact BTCV for an up-to-date brochure.

Conservation Volunteers Australia, PO Box 423, Ballarat Vic 3353, Australia; ☎+61 3 5330 2600; fax +61 3 5330 2922; e-mail bookings@conservationvolunteers.com.au; www.conservationvolunteers.com.au, offers opportunities for international volunteers in Australia and New Zealand. Typical projects include tree-planting, erosion and salinity control, seed collecting, restoring damaged habitats, monitoring endangered fauna, creating wetlands, and constructing walking-tracks. Volunteers must be at least 18 years old. Experience and qualifications relating to the environment are welcome but not essential. Conservation Volunteers Australia projects cost from A$30 (including GST) a night. This includes all meals, accommodation and project related travel.

Department for International Development (DFID), 1 Palace Street, London SW1E 5HE and Abercrombie House Eaglesham Road East Kilbride G75 8EA plus 25 overseas offices; ☎01355 844000; fax 01355 844099; www.dfid.gov.uk. DFID runs the British Government's programme of aid to developing countries. Vacancies occur on an ad hoc basis and are advertised as appropriate in the national or local press, professional journals, overseas publications and the DFID website under Recruitment, Current Vacancies. Skills are required in a wide range of areas from professionals in Governance, Social Development, Conflict, Infrastructure and Urban Development, Education, Enterprise, Health and HIV/AIDS, Environment, Rural Livelihoods, Statistics and Economists to specialists in IT or Procurement to general management and administrative roles. For graduate trainee advisers in the 11 professional cadres, details and application procedures for the DFID Technical Development Faststream can be found on the website (www. fastream.gov.uk). Applicants should have a Masters degree and at least 12 months work experience, preferably in a developing country context, in a relevant subject area. Candidates must be nationals of member states of the European Economic Area (EEA), Swiss Nationals or Commonwealth citizens with the right to work and live in the United Kingdom. DFID is an equal opportunities employer. Applications are welcomed from all parts of the community and DFID actively encourages interest from women, ethnic minority groups and those with a disability. Selection is on merit.

Frontier, 50-52 Rivington Street, Shoreditch, London EC2A 3QP; ☎020-7613 2422; fax 020-7613 2992; e-mail info@frontier.ac.uk; www.frontier.ac.uk, conducts conservation research into threatened wildlife and habitats around the world. Projects are currently focused on biodiversity conservation and management issues in tropical forests (Cambodia), game reserves (Tanzania), and coral reefs (Tanzania, Madagascar and Fiji). Projects are operated in conjunction with host country institutions such as a university or resource management authorities. Volunteer research assistants are required to carry out biological surveys during 10- or 20-week projects. There are also 28-day expeditions available. No previous experience is necessary and training is provided in the field. Many Frontier volunteers go on to careers in natural resource conservation and development. Volunteers are required to raise a certain amount of money to cover flights, insurance, local travel, food and accommodation. Details of projects and fees can be found on the Frontier website.

Greenforce, 11-15 Betterton Street, Covent Garden, London WC2H 9BP; ☎020-7470 8888; fax 020-7470 8889; e-mail info@greenforce.org; www.greenforce.org. Volunteers needed to work throughout the world on conservation and humanitarian projects. Teams of volunteers are sent out every three months to work on Greenforce projects to help international NGOs such as WWF, Wildlife Conservation Society and Red Cross. Full training is included, so no experience is required. Expeditions available from two weeks to one year.

International Primate Protection League, PO Box 766, Summerville, SC 29484, USA; ☎+1 843 871 2280; fax +1 843 871 7988; e-mail ippl@bellsouth.net; www.ippl. org, provides sanctuaries and other measures to protect endangered primates. Long-term volunteers are taken on to assist with general administration and animal care. There are also opportunities to assist on some field projects. Suitable practical experience and a proven commitment to animal welfare is required. The International Primate Protection League has a UK office at: IPPL (UK), Gilmore House, 166 Gilmore Road, London SE13 5AE; 020-8297 2129; fax 020-8297 2099; e-mail enquiries@ippl-uk.org; www.ippl-uk.org.

National Wildlife Federation, 11100 Wildlife Center Drive, Reston, VA 20190-5362, Canada; ☎+1-800 822 9919; e-mail info@nwf.org; www.nwf.org, publishes the annual *Conservation Directory*, which lists American and Canadian organisations concerned with conservation and also gives the addresses of some conservation and environment departments of foreign governments. Job opportunities are listed on the website.

Rainforest Foundation, 32 Broadway, Suite 1614, New York, NY 10004, USA; ☎+1 212 431 9098; fax +1 212 431 9197; e-mail rffny@rffny.org; www.rainforestfoundation. org. *Rainforest Foundation UK,* Suite A5 City Cloisters, 196 Old Street, London EC1V 9FR; ☎020-7251 6345; fax 020-7251 4969; e-mail rainforestuk@rainforestuk.com; www.rainforestfoundation.org.uk, works to conserve the world's rainforests and protect the rights of indigenous people. Environmental and human rights campaigning, multicultural management and communications skills, as well as at least one other language, are the attributes they look for in potential volunteers and recruits. It has an international network with projects in 18 rainforest countries in Asia, Africa, Central and South America.

Willing Workers on Organic Farms (WWOOF), PO Box 2675, Lewes, Sussex BN7 1RB; ☎01273-476286; e-mail hello@wwoof.org.uk; www.wwoof.org.uk; http://www. wwoofinternational.org/home/. WWOOF is a worldwide movement providing voluntary help to organic farmers and smallholders. There are 23 WWOOF groups throughout the world completely independent of each other. Details of opportunities are available on each WWOOF website; links will be found on the international website.

World Wide Fund for Nature (WWF), Avenue du Mont-Blanc1196, Gland, Switzerland; ☎+41 22 364 9111; fax +41 22 364 8836; e-mail ajungius@wwfint.org; www.panda.org, is one of the largest independent conservation organisations supporting programmes and campaigns around the world. Staff directly employed in conservation work are generally qualified to post-graduate level in areas such as biology, ecology and natural resources management and will have several years experience of working in these fields. The international office in Switzerland does not take on volunteers or interns but the Human Resources Department there is a useful point of contact. A complete list of WWF offices around the world can be found on the website. In the US, the WWF provides information on internships and summer jobs (Human Resources Department, 1250 24th Street, NW Washington, DC 20037-1175; www.worldwildlife.org).

OTHER SOURCES OF JOBS AND INFORMATION

PUBLICATIONS

AGCAS Careers Information Booklets. One booklet worth getting hold of is *Environment Management, Protection and Conservation*, available from Direct Mailing Service, Graduate Prospects, Prospects House, Booth Street East, Manchester M13 9EP; www. prospects.ac.uk, and from higher education careers offices. Further information is also available on www.prospects.ac.uk under 'explore Job sector' and 'explore types of jobs.'

Environment Post, ADC Environment, PO Box 2138, Wickford SS12 0WB; ☎01268-468000; e-mail jobs@environmentpost.co.uk; www.environmentpost.co.uk). A twice-monthly publication containing both voluntary and paid opportunities.

Fish Farming International, Heighway/Informa, Albert House, 1-4 Singer Street, London EC2A 4BQ; ☎020-7017 4513; www.fishfarminginternational.co.uk. Monthly trade newspaper for food-fish and shellfish farmers worldwide.

Green Volunteers, by Fabio Ausenda distributed in the UK by Vacation Work Publications, www.vacationwork.co.uk. A world-wide guide to voluntary work in nature conservation

Working with the Environment by Tim Ryder & Deborah Penrith (published by Vacation Work Publications, 9 Park End Street, Oxford OX1 1HH.

ONLINE RECRUITMENT

Agriculture:

AgJobs, www.agcenter.com. Agricultural jobs, mainly in Texas.

Agricultural Labour Pool, www.agri-labourpool.com. Seasonal and permanent agricultural jobs in the USA and Canada.

Cyber-Sierra's Natural Resources Job Search, www.cyber-sierra.com/nrjobs. Lists jobs in agriculture, forestry and the environment in the US. Contains links to other websites.

Fisheries:

Alaska Fishing Jobs Clearing House, www.fishingjobs.com. Work opportunities on Alaskan fishing boats.

Aquaculture Network Information Center, www.agnic.org. Internet gateway to international agriculture and fisheries opportunities.

Forestry:

Global Association of Online Foresters, www.foresters.org. Lists forestry vacancies.

Canadian Forestry Employment Bulletin, www.canadian-forests.com/job.html. Lists job openings in every branch of Canada's forestry sector.

Earthworks-jobs.com, www.earthworks-jobs.com. Worldwide forestry, agriculture, and agronomy job listings.

University of British Columbia Faculty of Forestry, www.forestry.ubc.ca. Provides links to worldwide organisations offering volunteer positions in conservation, environmental education, community development, agriculture and organic farming, and forestry.

Environment:

SustainableBusiness.com, www.sustainablebusiness.com/jobs/. Environmental jobs in the US.

EnvironmentalCareer, http://environmentalcareer.com. Lists vacancies in environmental sector in the US for experienced applicants.

Environmentjob, www.environmentjob.co.uk. A UK based website for job and volunteering opportunities in the environmental sector, with vacancies from recycling in Essex to coral reef conservation in Madagascar. Sectors covered by the site include conservation, environmental education and renewable energy.

The Green Directory, www.greendirectory.net/jobs/. Online search facility for jobs.

Au Pair and Domestic

There are many employment agencies specialising in the recruitment of au pairs, nannies and mothers' helps, and these are generally the best sources of finding such employment. In this chapter you will find a brief list of some of the best known of these agencies but many more can be located through the Yellow Pages and on the internet. The classifieds section of the UK-based weekly magazine *The Lady* is another excellent source for British and international nanny positions and jobseekers from abroad will also find this magazine useful and can subscribe by contacting *The Lady* at 39-40 Bedford Street, London WC2E 9ER; ☎020-7379 4717; fax 020-7497 2137; e-mail editors@lady.co.uk; www.lady.co.uk. The classified section includes an 'overseas situations vacant' section. Various national newspapers also carry advertisements for nanny and au pair agencies. *The Recruitment & Employment Confederation* (36-38 Mortimer Street, London W1W 7RG; ☎020-7462 3260; fax 020-7255 2878; e-mail info@rec.uk.com; www.rec. uk.com) publishes a list of their member agencies offering this kind of work, which you can obtain from the above address.

Some au pair agencies charge a fee for their overseas job placement service (usually around £55), payable when a job has been confirmed. Prospective au pairs are advised to check any such financial obligations with the agency concerned before registering.

It is important to be aware when considering this type of work that au pairs, mothers' helps and nannies are not considered to be the same thing for legal and employment purposes. According to the definition agreed upon by the Council of Europe an au pair is a young person whose primary purpose in living abroad is to improve their language skills while living with a family; any child-minding work is secondary to this intention. In the UK, the Home Office Guidelines set by the government states that au pairs work 25 hours a week for five days a week (which may include up to three evenings of babysitting), in return for which they receive pocket money (£55 per week) or living expenses. They are (or should be) treated more like a member of the family than as paid help. In theory, an au pair has less responsibility for the welfare of the children than a nanny. Au pairing is a good way to live and work in another country but, unsurprisingly, the financial rewards are not great.

An au pair who finds work in response to a privately placed advertisement will be taking more of a risk than one who goes through an agency that vets its clients; sometimes conditions will be good but in other cases they might not. Given the recent legal problems which have befallen au pairs and nannies abroad, it may be reassuring to have the back-up of an agency and their insurance in the unlikely but nonetheless real possibility of disaster. The support of family and friends is also important and you will benefit greatly from gaining some prior knowledge and understanding of the country in which you intend to work. The normal minimum age for au pair and other private domestic work is 18, but in some countries (such as Italy, Spain and Belgium) responsible girls of 17 are accepted.

Mothers' helps often work full-time doing general domestic duties in exchange for a wage, while nannies work only with children and usually require some formal qualification in this field such as the NNEB (Nursery Nurses Examination Board) Diploma, or an NVQ (National Vocational Qualification) in Child Care and Education. Further information may be obtained from the *Council for Awards in Children's Care and Education (CACHE)* (Beaufort House, Grosvenor Road, St Albans, Hertfordshire, AL1 3AW; ☎01727-818616; fax 01727-818618; e-mail info@cache.org.uk; www.cache.org.uk). Like governesses, who are usually engaged to teach children, nannies should expect a salary.

Private domestic positions for men are nowadays quite rare (although there are some opportunities for authentically British butlers in the United States and some other countries). Male au pairs must have previous childcare experience and relevant qualifications and are generally exempt from the usual sex discrimination laws – in other words, families can usually legally reject male applicants for childcare positions simply on the grounds that they are male. Some of the agencies below can occasionally offer work for male as well as female staff.

The idea of professionally trained nannies has been slow to catch on in the USA and there is no qualification comparable to the NNEB Diploma. The *International Nanny Association* (2020 Southwest Freeway, Suite 208, Houston, Texas 77098; ☎+1 713 526 2670; +1 713 526 2667; www.nanny.org) is a non-profit educational organisation for nannies, nanny employers, educators and placement agencies. Its website provides useful information for nannies, including links and contacts to member agencies and educational resources.

IMMIGRATION PROCEDURES

A word of warning concerning immigration regulations: while work permits are unnecessary for EU citizens going to another EU country, in most other cases residence and work permits will be needed and there may be special immigration arrangements which govern au pair and domestic work. It is also important to have adequate health insurance (especially if you are applying direct and not through an agency). These arrangements all need to be put in place before you go abroad.

As noted above, au pairs are officially associated with language learning, at least in Europe, and some European countries require non-EU au pairs to be registered on language courses or to show basic proficiency in the language before a work-permit is granted. It is possible for au pairs to go to the USA on a one-year approved au pair scheme or on exchange programmes available through agencies such as *Au Pair in America* (see below). In such cases you will be given an Exchange Visitor visa (J1) and need to be between 18 and 25, have UK or other western European nationality, and hold a driving licence or learner's permit. Entry on a J1 visa is currently the only legal way to work as an au pair in the USA.

Those interested in opportunities in North America should note that the Canadian Immigration authorities have introduced measures enabling people to apply for permanent residence after the completion of two years as a nanny or mother's help. A work permit must be obtained before taking up employment and there are a number of rules to follow. Prospective domestic carers must have an approved job offer, the equivalent of a Grade 12 (A-level) education, and at least one year's relevant experience. Under the 'Live-In Caregiver Program' candidates must have at least six months' training in some aspect of caregiving, such as childhood education, geriatric care, paediatric nursing, first aid, or one year's full-time employment, six months of which has been with the same employer. There is also a stringent medical examination. Information can be obtained from the *Canadian High Commission*, Immigration Division (38 Grosvenor Street, London W1K 4AA. All enquiries via mail or fax only, fax 020-7258 6506; www.canada.org.uk), although agencies dealing with that country should be well informed about these regulations. On completion of your second year you will be free to undertake any type of employment in Canada for which you are qualified. There is a $150 processing fee for the initial Employment Authorisation and a $490 fee for a permanent residency application. Further information is also available from agencies such as *Childcare in Canada*. Americans seeking work in Europe may contact such organisations as *AIFS*.

More detailed information on au pair and nanny work can be found in *The Au Pair and Nanny's Guide to Working Abroad*, edited by Susan Griffith (Vacation Work Publications, www.vacationwork.co.uk), which contains a country-by-country guide to au pair and nanny regulations as well as listing the names and addresses of many other employment agencies.

AGENCIES

When making enquiries to agencies it is helpful to enclose a large stamped addressed envelope (SAE), or International Reply Coupons to the correct value (normally this is approximately the same as the cost of postage to the country in question).

Useful Addresses

The Au Pair Agency, 231 Hale Lane, Edgware, Middlesex HA8 9QF; ☎020-8958 1750; fax 020-8958 5261; e-mail elaine@aupairagency.com; www.aupairagency.com. Places au pairs in France, Spain, Germany and Italy.

Au Pair Agency Bournemouth, 45 Strouden Road, Bournemouth BH9 1QL; ☎01202-532600; fax 01202-532600; e-mail andrea.rose@virgin.net. Offers placements for British applicants throughout Western and Eastern Europe. Au pairs are expected to work 25 hours per week, 5 days a week. Wages are £55 per week (overtime is paid extra). Applicants must love children and have experience in childcare (e.g. babysitting) and basic knowledge of cleaning. Applicants must speak English. British applicants are charged £40 on departure. 24-hour emergency mobile phone number is provided for au pairs during placement. Applications to Andrea Rose (see above for contact details).

Au Pair in America, 37 Queen's Gate, London SW7 5HR; ☎020-7581 7322; fax 020-7581 7345/55; e-mail info@aupairamerica.co.uk; www.aupairamerica.co.uk; and River Plaza, 9 West Broad Street, Stamford CT 06902; ☎203-399 5000; e-mail aupair.info@ aifs.com; www.aupairinamerica.com. The largest and most experienced legal childcare programme to the United States. Au pairs and nannies are placed with a carefully screened family for a 12-month placement providing 45 hours childcare per week. Benefits include free return flights between major European cities and New York plus onward travel to the host family, free board and lodging, a weekly payment, four-day orientation programme, Exchange Visa, $500 study allowance, medical insurance, two weeks' paid holiday, an optional 13th month to travel, and year-long support. For qualified and experienced childcare providers there is also *Au Pair Extraordinaire*. There is also *Educare in America*, a new programme for 18-26 year old students who wish to broaden their education through study in the USA while living in a family environment for 10-12 months and providing pre- and after-school care for children aged six and over. For details of these schemes, contact the *Au Pair in America* address.

A-One Au Pairs and Nannies, Court Lodge House, 9 Rookes Lane, Lymington, Hants SO41 8FP; ☎01590-689496; fax by arrangement only; e-mail info@aupairsetc. co.uk; www.aupairsetc.co.uk.Au Pairs/Au Pairs Plus required for light housework and childcare 5 days a week. Wages, board and accommodation vary according to hours worked. Placements available throughout America and Europe. Applicants should be 18-27 years old.

ABC Au Pairs, 42 Underhill Road, London SE22 0QT; ☎020-8299 3052; fax 020-8299 6086; e-mail vivienne@abc-aupairs.co.uk; www.abc-aupairs.co.uk. Sends au pairs to most European countries and provides services to families and au pairs in the UK.

Au Pair Connections, 39 Tamarisk Road, Wildern Gate, Hedge End, Southampton SO30 4TN; ☎01489-780438; fax 01489-692656; e-mail info@aupair-connections.co.uk; www.

aupair-connnections.co.uk. Placements in England, France, Spain, and Italy.

AuPairCare Inc, 600 California Street, 10th Floor, San Francisco, CA 94108, USA; ☎+1 415 434 8788; fax +1 415 434 5415; e-mail hwoehl@aupaircare.com; www.aupaircare. com. Has placed 25,000 au pairs with families in the US. They provide au pair support throughout the year, sponsor visas, and organise travel. One-year placements with an opportunity to extend for a second year.

Au-Pair International, Cherry Gardens, Nouds Lane, Lynsted, Sittingbourne, Kent ME9 0ES; ☎01795-522544; fax 01795-522878; e-mail info@aupairinternational.co.uk; www. au-pairinternational.co.uk. Places overseas applicants (aged 17-27) in the UK. Applicants intending to work with under-twos must have over 200 hours' previous childcare experience. Offers jobs for au-pairs and nannies.

Au Pair Network International, 118 Cromwell Road, London SW7 4ET; ☎020-7370 3798; fax 020-7370 4718; e-mail admin@apni.co.uk; www.apni.co.uk. Placements for nannies, au pairs and mother's helps.

Camp America, 37a Queen's Gate, London SW7 5HR; ☎020-7581 7373; fax 020-7581 7377; email enquiries@campamerica.co.uk; www.campamerica.co.uk. A leading summer camp programme with 40 years experience in placing people from Europe, Asia, Africa, Australia, and New Zealand on American summer camps. Camp America recruits skilled people for a variety of jobs from Camp Counsellors to Camp Power or Resort America positions. Camp Counsellor work (minimum nine weeks) consists of childcare, teaching sports activities, music, arts, drama and dance. Camp Power (nine weeks minimum) involves assisting in kitchen/laundry duties, administration and general camp maintenance. Resort America (minimum 12 weeks) duties consist mainly of providing catering and administration support at holiday resorts and hotels. All programmes offer free return flights from London and other selected international airports to New York, transfer to camp/resort, free accommodation and meals, medical insurance and pocket money ranging from $700 to $1600 depending on age and experience. Office in the US, Australia, Germany, Poland, and South Africa.

Childcare International, Trafalgar House, Grenville Place, London NW7 3SA; ☎020-8906 3611; fax 020-8906 3461; e-mail office@childint.co.uk; www.childint.co.uk. Places au pairs, mothers' helps and nannies wanting to work in Europe, the US, Canada, and Australia. Length of contract is six-12 months starting at any time of the year. Also short-term summer placements and winter ski au pair positions available. Childcare International works in co-operation with *Au Pair in America,* 36 South State, Suite 3000, Salt Lake City, UT 84111-1410; ☎801-943 7788; fax 801-943 5527.

The Edgware and Solihull Au-Pair Agency, PO Box 147, Radlett, Herts WD7 8WX; ☎01923-289737; fax 01923-289739; e-mail info@the-aupair-shop.com, or 5 Parklands, Blossomfield Road, Solihull, B91 1NG; e-mail aupairs1@btconnect.com; www.100s-aupairs.co.uk. Places au pairs in the UK, Europe, and the US and can also arrange work for non-UK European citizens within Europe. Charge a placement fee. Positions are usually of between two and 12 months duration.

Europair Services, 13 rue Vavin, 75006 Paris, France; ☎+33 1 4329 8001; fax +33 1 4329 8037; e-mail contact@europairservices.com; www.europairservices.com.

InterExchange Inc., 161 6th Avenue, New York, NY 10013; ☎+1 212 924 0446; fax +1 212 924 0575; e-mail info@interexchange.org; www.interexchange.org. InterExchange is a non-profit organisation dedicated to promoting cultural awareness through work and travel, language school, volunteer, professional training, internship and au pair programmes within the United States and around the world. In the USA they offer J-1 Visa programmes and an H-2B Visa programme. InterExchange offers placements in the USA, Australia, Costa Rica, France, Germany, England, India, Italy, Kenya, Mexico, Namibia, the Netherlands, Norway, Peru, South Africa, Spain and Zimbabwe.

Kensington Nannies, 3 Hornton Place, Kensington, London W8 4LZ; ☎020-7937

2333; ☎020-7937 1027; e-mail nannies@easynet.co.uk; www.kensington-nannies.com. London's longest established nanny agency.

Nurse Au Pair Placement, 16 rue le Sueur, 75116 Paris, France; ☎+33 1 4500 3388; fax +33 1 4500 3399; e-mail nappsarl@aoal.com; www.napp.fr. French or English-speaking nannies and au pairs. Placements in France and worldwide.

Petite Pumpkin Au Pair Agency, 45 Nelson Street, Buckingham, Buckinghamshire, MK18 1BT; ☎01280-824745; e-mail susan@petitepumpkin.co.uk; www.petitepumpkin. co.uk, places au pairs in the UK, Germany, Spain and Switzerland. Applicants must be single and at least 18. The service is free to the au pair, the fee for finding an au pair is charged to the family.

Séjours Internationaux Linguistiques et Culturels (SILC), 32 Rempart de l'Est, 16022 Angoulême Cedex, France; ☎+33 5 4597 4190; fax +33 5 4594 2063; e-mail france@ silc.fr; www.silc-france.com. Organises educational, cultural, and language programmes around the world.

Select Au-Pairs, Crosbie House, Moredun Road, Paisley, Renfrewshire PA2 9LJ; ☎0141-884 8361; fax 0141-884 1566; e-mail selectaupairs@aol.com; www.select-aupairs.com. Pre- and after-placement service in Scotland and northern England.

OTHER EUROPEAN AGENCIES:

Allianssi Youth Exchanges, Asemapäällikönkatu, Helsinki 00520, Finland; ☎+358 2075 52603; fax +358 2075 52627; e-mail vaihto@alli.fi; www.nuorisovaihto.fi.

INWOX - International Workexperience, Zum Oberfeld 17, 55286 Wörrstadt, Germany; ☎+49 67 3293 7735; fax +49 67 3293 7641; e-mail info@inwox.com; www.inwox. com. Placements in Africa, Australia, New Zealand, Germany, Europe and the USA.

World Wide Au Pair & Nanny, Burg. Hogguerstraat 785, 1064 EB Amsterdam, Netherlands; ☎+31 20 411 6010; fax +31 20 611 0330; e-mail info@worldwideaupair-nanny.com; www.worldwideaupair-nanny.com.

ONLINE AU PAIR SITES

There are literally hundreds of au pair and nanny employment sites now available on the internet, which can easily be found by searching under 'au pair', 'childcare', 'nanny', or similar. *Au Pair Wizard* (www.au-pair.com) will allow you to post an application online and is particularly good for jobs in Germany. In the UK, *Au Pair Job Match* (www. aupairs.co.uk/aup20uk.html) provides an excellent service which includes information, jobs, advertisements and a discussion forum. The US site, *NannyJobs,* (www.nannyjobs. com) has hundreds of jobs which are constantly updated, as well as information about agencies, taxes and nanny pay. This site also allows you to post your résumé online. *The International Au Pair Association (IAPA)* (Bregade 25H, 1260 Copenhagen K, Denmark; ☎+45 3317 0066; fax +45 3393 9675; www.iapa.org) is a global trade association for au pair agencies. IAPA's website contains contacts to its 143 members in 39 countries.

Banking and Accountancy

The financial arena offers career possibilities in four major areas, all of which can be divided into specialist subsidiary fields. Broadly, these are:

o **Retail Banking** – Private and company bank accounts
o **Investment Banking** – Corporate finance and investment management
o **Accountancy** – Auditing service, taxation and financial management
o **Insurance/Actuarial** – Pension, insurance and investment funds

Most recruitment for personnel working in these fields is carried out directly by banks and other financial organisations. However, recruitment consultants specialising in banking and accountancy positions are also increasingly active in this field. International banking organisations, such as the World Bank and International Monetary Fund are discussed in more detail in the chapter *United Nations*.

RETAIL BANKS

The retail banking sector deals with personal bank accounts and domestic financial products, such as loans and mortgages. Most high street banks are also engaged in some of the same activities as merchant bankers, for example, handling company profits, investments and credit facilities, and offering advisory services on taxation, insurance and unit trusts.

Retail banking is at present a rapidly changing environment, which is experiencing new pressure from competitors in the emerging electronic banking sector. Most high street banks are now actively establishing themselves in the e-commerce market, offering a large number of their services online, as well as moving into home banking via interactive digital television. As a result, many local branches are closing or amalgamating as banks discover that they no longer need the same degree of shop-front presence. There are likely to be increasing redundancies in over-the-counter banking jobs and increased opportunities in technical and call-centre banking personnel.

Retail banks are the largest recruiters of banking personnel but in most cases overseas opportunities are limited, as foreign branches of the major banks are generally run and staffed by local workers and managers. On the other hand, monetary union in Europe and the general globalisation of banking services, mean that banking trainees who want to spend some time abroad have a better chance of doing so than previously. The major banks are always actively recruiting new graduates and there are openings in the financial services sector for consultants and staff in the rapidly developing eastern European economies and Russia. The best chance of working abroad early on in a financial career still lies with the investment banks (see below). Language skills are always an advantage all those wishing to work in international banking or financial services.

THE CLEARING BANKS

The major high street clearing banks in the UK, especially Barclays, Lloyds TSB, NatWest and HSBC (previously Midland Bank), are the ones most likely to offer overseas opportunities. The recruitment activities of their respective international divisions are detailed below.

Barclays PLC, 1 Churchill Place, London E14 5HP; brochure hotline ☎0870 607 0781; e-mail candidate.support@PeopleBank.com; www. barclays.co.uk/careers/, is one of the largest international banking organisations in the world, operating in more than 60 countries. The company has five major divisions: UK Banking, Barclaycard (global credit card company), Barclays Wealth Management (incorporating Barclays Capital, a global investment bank), International Retail and Commercial Banking and Central Support functions (including Finance, IT, HR and Marketing). They offer a Business Leadership Programme, which combines intensive formal training with business attachments over a period of two and a half years. Once graduates achieve a managerial role there are opportunities for overseas postings. Enquiries should be directed to 'Graduate Recruitment' at the address above. Applications should be submitted online.

Lloyds TSB Bank plc, Recruitment Centre, 4, 1st Floor, High Street, Mold, Flintshire CH17 1ZL; www.lloydstsb.com, offers a series of two-year Management Development Programmes in retail management, marketing, human resources, finance, corporate banking, international banking, operations, business development and distribution. There are approximately 100 vacancies on their training programme per year. Further details can be found on the website at www.lloydstsbgraduate.co.uk.

HSBC, Group Head Office, 8 Canada Square, London E14 5HQ; ☎020-7991 8888; www.hsbc.com. HSBC Bank incorporated the Midland Bank into its global brand several years ago. The company is a diverse banking and financial services organisation offering a wide range of career opportunities in the UK and in a network of more than 9,500 offices across the world (HSBC stands for Hong Kong and Shanghai Banking Corporation). There are many opportunities available to graduates with good honours degrees, and the bank is particularly strong in IT training for the financial sector. Further details can be found at www.hsbc.com/hsbc/careers.

NatWest, Recruitment: ☎0800 328 6593; www.natwestrecruitment.com; e-mail graduate. recruit@rbs.co.uk. Natwest ranks as the fifth largest bank in the world with extensive operations worldwide. It was incorporated into the Royal Bank of Scotland group in 2000. The bank runs a number of Graduate Programmes in retail banking, operations management, human resources, insurance and corporate banking. There are usually 25 graduate openings per sector.

OTHER BRITISH AND COMMONWEALTH BANKS

A number of overseas banks with close connections to the UK recruit locally for staff and offer opportunities for transfer internationally. These include:

Australia and New Zealand Banking Group Ltd. (ANZ), Minerva House, Montague Close, London SE1 9DH; ☎020-7378 2121; fax 020-7378 2378 www.anz.com. Originated in the UK in 1835. Concentrates on Investment Banking and International Network Services.

Bank of Cyprus (London) Ltd., Human Resources, 87/93 Chase Side, Southgate, London N14 5BU; ☎020-8267 7320; fax 020-8886 3047; e-mail hr@bankofcyprus.co.uk; www. bankofcyprus.co.uk. The Bank of Cyprus was established in the UK in 1955 and provides banking services mainly to the Hellenic and Cypriot communities in the UK.

Commonwealth Bank of Australia, Senator House, 85 Queen Victoria Street, London EC4V 4HA; ☎020-7710 3990; www.commbank.com.au. Providers of integrated financial services.

Westpac Banking Corporation, 2nd Floor, 63 St Mary Axe, London EC3A 8LE; ☎020-7621 7036; fax 020-7621 7027; www.westpac.com.au. Personal, business, and corporate banking services.

Standard Chartered Bank, 1 Aldermanbury Square, London EC2V 7SB; ☎020-7280 7500; fax 020-7280 7791; www.standardchartered.com. Represented in Asia, the Middles East, Africa, and the UK.

FOREIGN BANKS

Those who have already gained several years' banking experience at home, and who have the necessary languages and cultural adaptability, may wish to consider working abroad for a foreign bank. Working in the London or New York branch of a foreign bank can offer the possibility of an eventual transfer abroad. A more direct approach, for experienced staff, is to apply direct to banks abroad, to use the services of a recruitment consultant, or to use the methods of the creative job search to keep in touch with international vacancies.

Apart from the City of London, the main financial centres of the world are Zurich, New York and Tokyo. Swiss immigration laws mean that the opportunities for working in Switzerland are restricted only to the most senior personnel. In recent years there has been a strong growth in the number of Japanese banks represented internationally, and a scaling down of the presence of American banks abroad. Eight out of ten of the world's largest banks, in terms of capital, are now Japanese, while American banks are no longer represented in the top ten at all.

In spite of the slow down in the Japanese economy there is still some demand for personnel bilingual in English and Japanese in the major Japanese banks. The addresses of the most important of these are listed below.

Bank of Japan, Basildon House, 7-11 Moorgate, London EC2R 6AF, ☎020-7606 2454; fax 020-7726-4819; e-mail prd@info.boj.or.jp; www.boj.or.jp.
Bank of Tokyo-Mitsubishi Ltd., Finsbury Circus House, 12-15 Finsbury Circus, London EC2M 7BT; ☎020-7588 1111; www.btm.co.uk.
Daiwa Banking Europe, 5 King William Street, London EC4N 7AX; ☎020-7597 8000; fax 020-7597 8600; e-mail info@daiwasmbc.co.uk; www.daiwasmbc.co.uk.
Sumitomo Mitsui Banking Corporation Europe, Temple Court, 11 Queen Victoria Street, London EC4N 4TA; ☎020-7786 1000; fax 020-7236 0049; www.smbc.co.jp/global.

The *Japan Information and Cultural Centre*, Embassy of Japan, 101-104 Piccadilly, London W1J 7JT; ☎020-7465 6543/6544; fax 020-7491 9347; e-mail info@jpembassy. org.uk; www.uk.emb-japan.go.jp, can provide a comprehensive list of Japanese banks in the UK.

INVESTMENT BANKS

Investment banking was established as a profession when traders in medieval Italian city states such as Venice began to expand their international markets by providing financial services to other traders; and this remains the essence of their work today. Investment banking services are offered not only to international traders, but also to industry, insurance companies, transport companies, and anyone with large financing needs. In the UK, the term 'merchant banking' is still occasionally used.

The services provided in this sector may be conveniently grouped into banking, corporate finance, investment management and securities trading. They include project finance, advisory services to governments and international corporations, and dealing in financial derivatives. The investment banks all have offices in the City of London and, being international businesses, they are strongly represented overseas through subsidiaries, affiliates and representative offices.

In terms of numbers employed, investment banks are small in comparison with clearing banks. The best opportunities are for graduates, usually, though not necessarily, with degrees in economics, law, or business studies. In addition to qualified banking staff there are also occasional vacancies for experienced specialist staff such as accountants.

Recruitment is carried out by the banks themselves, all of which offer graduate training programmes lasting from six months to two years, sometimes including an overseas posting. The number of vacancies per year is low and entry is highly competitive. Following the initial training period, the early part of a career is likely to be spent in London (or New York) but at the senior level opportunities should arise for promotion, secondment or transfer to branches or agents abroad.

The most prominent investment banks are those that are members of the Securities and Futures Authority. Key players in the industry include:

Deutsche Bank, 6-8 Bishopsgate, London, EC2N 4DA; ☎020-7545 3033; http://careers. db.com.

Goldman Sachs, Peterborough Court, 133 Fleet Street, London EC4A 2BB; ☎020-7774- 1000; www.gs.com/recruiting.

JPMorgan Chase, 125 London Wall, London EC2Y 5AJ; ☎020-7742 7000; www. jpmorganchase.com.

Kleinwort Benson Private Bank, 30 Gresham Street, London EC2V 7PG; ☎020-3207 7000; www.kbpb.co.uk.

Lazard & Co. Ltd., 50 Stratton Street, London W1J 8LL; ☎020-7187 2000; fax 020-7072 6000; www.lazard.com.

Merrill Lynch, 2 King Edward Street, London EC1A 1HQ; ☎020-7628 1000; www. ml.com/careers/.

Schroders, 31 Gresham Street, London, EC2V 7QA; ☎020-7658 6000; www.schroders. com/graduaterecruitment.

Further information regarding career prospects in investment banking can be obtained from the *London Investment Banking Association (LIBA)*, 6 Frederick's Place, London EC2R 8BT; ☎020-7796 3606; fax 020-7796 4345; e-mail liba@liba.org.uk; www.liba. org.uk.

Accountancy

Accountancy is a relatively secure profession with good prospects in the international career marketplace – which are growing as financial markets and companies themselves become more global. British and US accountants are in demand in many countries throughout the world. Some 15,000 members of the *Institute of Chartered Accountants in England & Wales* (ICAEW) are based overseas. School leavers, and more particularly graduates intending to take up accountancy as a career, are faced with a confusing array of qualifications in Britain from which to choose and some preparatory research – for example, consulting the AGCAS booklet, *Financial Services* (published by Graduate Prospects, Prospects House, Booth Street East, Manchester M13 9EP; ☎0161-277 5274; www.prospects.ac.uk) – is useful. Further information is also available on www.prospects.ac.uk under 'explore Job sectors' and 'explore types of jobs.' Trade magazines are also a useful source of comparative information. The *Institute of Company Accountants* publishes *Company Accountant* and the *Student Digest* while the *Chartered Association of Certified Accountants* publishes *Certified Accountant*; and in Canada, *CGA Magazine* is published by the *Certified General Accountants Association of Canada*. These associations also publish vacancies updates or lists. All accountancy qualifications involve a period of practical experience (usually a minimum of three years), as well as a preliminary or foundation exam (for non-graduates) followed by a professional examination.

Qualified accountants in Great Britain and Northern Ireland fall into four main groups: chartered accountants, certified accountants, management accountants, and accountants in public services. The qualifications are recognised by the Consultative Committee of Accounting Bodies (CCAB) and are offered by the following associations:

The Institute of Chartered Accountants in England and Wales, PO Box 433, Chartered
   Accountants' Hall, London EC2P 2BJ; ☎020-7920 8100; fax 020-7920 0547; www.
   icaew.co.uk
The Association of Chartered Certified Accountants, 29 Lincoln's Inn Fields, London
   WC2A 3EE; ☎020-7059 5000; fax 020-7059 5050; e-mail info@accaglobal.com;
   www.acca.co.uk
The Association of International Accountants, South Bank Building, Kingsway, Team Valley,
   Newcastle-upon-Tyne NE11 0JS; ☎0191-482 4409; fax 0191-482 5578; e-mail aia@aia.org.
   uk; www.aia.org.uk
The Institute of Chartered Accountants of Scotland, CA House, 21 Haymarket Yards,
   Edinburgh EH12 5BH; ☎0131-347 0100; fax 0131-347 0105; e-mail enquiries@icas.
   org.uk; www.icas.org.uk
The Chartered Institute of Management Accountants, 26 Chapter Street
   London SW1P 4NP; ☎020-8849 2251; fax 020-8849 2450; e-mail cima.contact@
   cimaglobal.com; www.cimaglobal.com
The Chartered Institute of Taxation, 12 Upper Belgrave Street, London SW1X 8BB;
   ☎020-7235 9381; fax 020-7235 2562; e-mail post@tax.org.uk; www.tax.org.uk

TRAINING

To qualify as a Chartered Accountant, training must be undertaken in an authorised training office. The majority of students train with firms of chartered accountants, but training is now also available in a growing number of industrial, commercial and public sector organisations under the Training Outside Public Practice (TOPP) scheme. The training contract combines work experience with preparation for the Professional Examinations and students train for three or four years depending on their educational background. Chartered Management Accountants, Certified Accountants, and Company Accountants train within a specific company and are able to determine their training schedule as they study towards obtaining their professional qualifications.

Once qualified there are many openings abroad for Chartered Accountants but Certified Management Accountants are slightly more restricted as their qualifications are more UK-specific. It is now becoming common practice for recently qualified accountants to go abroad on a short-term assignment (up to two years) immediately after qualifying. An international posting is seen as a way to make rapid progress to the top of the profession in the major international accountancy firms, and Australasia and the Far East are popular destinations. There are also postings in the EU and Eastern Europe. British accountants are also in demand in Canada, South Africa and the Middle East. The largest British firms with overseas associated offices are:

Tohmatsui Deloitte Touche, Stonecutter Court, 1 Stonecutter Street, London EC4A 4TR;
   ☎020-7936 3000; fax 020-7583 1198; e-mail gradrec@deloitte.co.uk; www.deloitte.
   co.uk
Ernst & Young, Becket House, 1 Lambeth Palace Road, London SE1 7EU; ☎020-7951
   2000; fax 020-7951 1345; www.ey.com/careers/
KPMG, 8 Salisbury Square, London EC4Y 8BB; ☎020-7311 1000; fax 020-7311 3311;
   www.kpmgcareers.co.uk
PriceWaterhouseCoopers, Southwark Towers, 32 London Bridge Street, London SE1
   9SY; ☎020-7583 5000; fax 020-7822 4652; www.pwcglobal.com

ACCOUNTANTS IN THE SINGLE EUROPEAN MARKET

EU member countries are currently working towards harmonisation of their auditing practices, and accountancy organisations in each country are now obliged to have schemes whereby accountants can transfer their skills abroad. To facilitate this requirement, it is now required that accountants who wish to practise in Europe must pass an aptitude test in the relevant language of their destination country.

While European accountants tend to concern themselves with auditing a firm's books once a year (an auditor is known as a *commissaire aux comptes* in French and a *Wirtschaftsprüfer* in German), British accountants are more likely to be involved in advising firms on how best to manage their finances from day to day (management accountancy). British qualifications are well respected in Europe and there is considerable scope for Britons to work abroad advising UK, US and European businesses. The EU countries most open to foreign accountants are Belgium, the Netherlands and France.

ACCOUNTANCY IN THE USA AND CANADA

Accountancy in the US is regulated by 54 State Boards of Accountancy (the 50 States plus Washington DC, Guam, Puerto Rico, and the US Virgin Islands), the *American Institute of Certified Public Accountants (AICPA)*, 1211 Avenue of the Americas, New York, NY 10036-8775; ☎212-596 6200; fax 212-596 6213; www.aicpa.org, and the 54 *State Societies of Certified Public Accountants*. The AICPA is responsible for the Uniform Final Examination, which is the accepted final qualifying examination throughout the USA. Only 35 State Boards will consider applications from those holding overseas qualifications. Most British accountants are to be found in New York, New Jersey, Connecticut and California.

Certified accountants face fewer problems. There are no restrictions on British certified accountants working in industry and commerce but you can improve your chances of finding employment if you hold local qualifications. The *Institute of Management Accountants* (IMA, 10 Paragon Drive, Montvale, NJ 07645; ☎201-573 9000; www. imanet.org) administers the Certified Management Accountant and Certified in Financial Management examinations.

Canada is more accessible to British accountants than the USA but it is still advisable to gain Canadian qualifications. The three main associations listed below can give information on qualifications:

Certified General Accountants Association of Canada (CGA), 800-1188 West Georgia Street, Vancouver, British Columbia V6E 4A2; ☎604-6693555; fax 604-689 5845; e-mail public@cga-canada.org; www.cga-canada.org.

Canadian Institute of Chartered Accountants (CICA), 277 Wellington Street West, Toronto, ON M5V 3H2; ☎416-977 3222; fax 416-977 8585; www.cica.ca.

Chartered Institute of Management Accountants, 36 Toronto Street, Suite 850, Toronto, ON M5C 2C5, Canada; ☎+1 905 773 7858; www.cimacanada.org.

ACTUARIES

Actuaries are key employees of insurance companies, working in management, forecasting and risk analysis at the highest levels of business. Within a life insurance company, areas of responsibility can include marketing, product development, risk assessment and investment. Actuarial consultants provide advice to clients on all aspects of pension schemes – from establishment to contributions. Salaries are high, and an experienced actuary can earn over £130,000 per year. A high level of mathematical ability is a prerequisite for training as an actuary, and most enter the profession with a degree in mathematics or statistics.

To qualify as an actuary you must pass the professional examinations of the Faculty of *and Institute of Actuaries* (Napier House, 4 Worcester Street, Oxford OX1 2AW; ☎01865-268228; fax 01865-268222; e-mail careers@actuaries.org.uk; www.actuaries.org.uk). The Faculty and Institute of Actuaries can provide a *List of Actuarial Employers*, which includes opportunities overseas. They also publish a useful pamphlet, *Information for those considering an Actuarial Career*, containing information on international actuarial science degrees and diplomas. The relevant Scottish body is the *Faculty of Actuaries* (Maclaurin House, 18 Dublin Street, Edinburgh EH1 3PP; ☎0131-240 1300; fax 0131-240 1313; e-mail faculty@actuaries.org.uk). There are a number of associations in the USA, including the *American Academy of Actuaries* (1100 17th Street NW, 7th Floor, Washington DC 20036; ☎202-223 8196; fax 202-872 1948; www.actuary.org) which can provide information about training.

FINANCIAL RECRUITMENT SPECIALISTS

The following recruitment consultants are specialists in banking and finance, including recruitment for overseas appointments:

ASA International, Head Office: 6 Coates Crescent, Edinburgh EH3 7AL; ☎0131-226 6222; fax 0131-226 5110; e-mail burgh@asainternational.co.uk; www.asainternational. co.uk. ASA International is Scotland's largest independent recruitment organisation. It has offices in Edinburgh, Aberdeen, Glasgow and Kirkcaldy. It also has overseas division. ASA provides a wide-ranging service through specialist divisions (including financial services), which recruit permanent, temporary and contract staff from junior to management level. ASA consultants ensure that the candidate is best prepared for any interview or position.

Badenoch & Clark, Overseas Division, UK; ☎020 7429 5136; fax 020 7429 5003; e-mail overseas@badenochandclark.com; www.badenochandclark.com. Recruitment consultancy for experienced accountancy & finance, financial services, legal, public sector, HR, IT and marketing professionals. Badenoch & Clark operates 17 offices across the UK and offers a growing European presence (Luxembourg, Budapest, Frankfurt, Brussels). Also take advantage of its affiliate relationships in Australia and New Zealand. Search and apply for vacancies at www.badenochandclark.com, or e-mail overseas@ badenochandclark.com with details of your relocation plans.

Think Global Recruitment, 93 George Street, Edinburgh EH2 3ES; ☎0131-240 1291; fax 0131-240 1275; e-mail mail@thinkgr.com; www.thinkgr.com. One of the UK's leading specialist accountancy and financial recruitment consultancies. Places qualified accountants in locations throughout the world. Its database system automatically matches candidates to client requirements as they are registered and vice-versa and has a large international network of contacts. Offices in Edinburgh, London , Glasgow, New Zealand and Sydney.

ONLINE RECRUITMENT

A brief selection of the many Internet recruitment sites operating in the field of banking and finance is given below:

http://accounting.smartpros.com/. Accountancy links in the USA.

www.careerbank.com. Career centre for the accounting, finance, mortgage, insurance and banking community in the US. Offers news, articles and newsletters on the career development.

www.cityjobs.com. Banking, accounting, insurance, financial services, finance related IT and marketing vacancies.

www.chadwicknott.co.uk. Legal and accountancy jobs.

www.hays.com. Accouncancy & finance and banking jobs worldwide.

www.jobs.efinancialcareers.co.uk. Lists jobs in various sectors of the international financial markets (Australia, Belgium, France, Germany, Hong Kong, Ireland, Italy, Luxembourg, Netherlands, Singapore, Switzerland, the UK, the US); also offers careers information and advice.

www.huntswood.co.uk. Senior positions in financial management around the world.

PROFESSIONAL ASSOCIATIONS

BANKING

Career prospects in commercial banking, both domestically and internationally, are greatly enhanced by passing the Chartered Institute of Banker's examinations, which include papers on law, accountancy, economic and monetary theory and practice of banking. Successful candidates also receive a BSc (Hons) from Manchester University. The qualification is an integral part of special management trainee programmes offered by the major British banks. Details of the qualification, the Associateship of the Chartered Institute of Bankers (ACIB), are available from the *Institute of Financial Services* (Ifs House, 4-9 Burgate Lane, Canterbury, Kent, CT1 2XJ; ☎01227-818609; fax 01227-818631; e-mail customerservices@ifslearning.com; www.ifslearning.com).

The *American Bankers Association* (1120 Connecticut Avenue, NW, Washington DC 20036; www.aba.com) runs various programmes to encourage high school and college graduates to train for careers in banking. Unfortunately it does not hold specific information on working abroad.

ACCOUNTANCY

The Institute of Chartered Accountants in England and Wales (PO Box 433, Chartered Accountants' Hall, Moorgate Place, London EC2P 2BJ; ☎020-7920 8100; fax 020-7920 0547; www.icaew.co.uk) runs a recruitment service for its members which covers all countries and publishes an annual vacancy list.

The *Chartered Institute of Public Finance and Accountancy* (3 Robert Street, London WC2N 6RL; ☎020-7543 5600; fax 020-7543 5700; www.cipfa.org.uk) publishes other useful booklets. A list of vacancies can be found on their website.

In the USA, the *American Institute of Certified Public Accountants (AICPA)* (1211 Avenue of the Americas, New York, NY 10036-8775, USA; ☎+1 212 596 6200; fax +1 212 596 6213; www.aicpa.org) is the oldest and largest professional organisation for CPAs. The Institute produces a number of publications including the *Journal of Accountancy*, the *CPA Letter*, and *The Practising CPA*.

Information Technology

THE COMPUTER INDUSTRY

Information Technology and computing has become the driving force of contemporary society. Its role in our lives has grown as personal computers have become widely available for home and business use. Software systems are now in use in ways almost too numerous to mention throughout industry, commerce, the media, science and medicine, administration, management, distribution, manufacturing, sales, human resources, and a host of other applications. Banking transactions, ticket reservations, research and international communications, financial services, academic and scientific work, and even medical diagnosis, can all now be carried out more efficiently as computers have come to dominate our everyday lives.

This global revolution in information processing and communications has meant the growth of new industries and careers. It is also changing the nature of work itself, which can now be 'international' even when you work from home. Giant corporations like Microsoft have grown up, bringing a level of power and flexibility in home and desktop computing which would have been inconceivable just ten years ago. In addition, there are myriad small, new companies working at the cutting edge of software and website development and providing mass market IT services.

We now live in an information-based, post-industrial society in which the relationship between producer and consumer has changed dramatically. The successful employee of today understands that work is now knowledge-based and that it is the ability to manipulate this information, rather than extensive knowledge of computer hardware itself, which is the key to success.

As computers 'replace' people in many sectors of industry, there have inevitably been losses in traditional job sectors; this has been offset, however, by newly created job specifications and IT related industries. New staff are required in many companies and organisations to design software and to operate systems. The recruitment market for IT specialists has become truly international and the internet is a powerful recruiting tool in the industry. There are job opportunities around the globe, the most highly paid work being available in the USA, the strong EU economies such as Germany, Holland, Belgium and France, and in South-East Asia. The Central and Eastern European region is a new and expanding market for IT specialists and there are technical, training and specialist openings in Russia and neighbouring states. Computer skills are easily transferable as their general principles – the computer languages for instance – can be understood internationally. A knowledge of a foreign language (especially French or German) will open many doors; a degree is sometimes called for but is not always required.

CAREERS IN IT

The rapid growth in applications for information technology means that the prospects for advancement for suitably qualified people are good. Recent surveys have predicted continued employment growth across the sector as a whole, and opportunities are available to graduates of almost any discipline. To work in information technology, the basic requirement is not so much dependent a background in mathematics or science, as on the possession of a flexible mind and a certain level of analytical intelligence.

Working professionally with computers in a particular field or application essentially requires a knowledge of that field or application; and is more a practical than a theoretical matter. The complexity of the software systems themselves will often not be an issue as most applications involve adapting an existing system or software package to a particular use. Someone already experienced in that field will be best placed to carry this out. A methodical approach must be combined with a knowledge of the application. This, a good track record together with an appropriate qualification, will mean that you are well placed to look for work in the IT field.

> Although the range of IT opportunities is enormous, there are currently three main groups of employers:
>
> o *Technology Creators* provide hardware and software, and range from major corporations, such as IBM and Microsoft, to boutique software firms specialising in one product or market segment.
> o *Technology Enhancers* include software firms and consultancies which provide advice to client companies and, as outsourcers, take responsibility for a client's total IT needs.
> o *End-users* are the organisations which use IT to support their core activities.

JOBS IN THE IT SECTOR

The IT industry tends not to have clearly defined and differentiated job titles, and it is quite usual for one individual to undertake a variety of tasks.

> **THE MOST COMMON JOB TITLES IN IT**
>
> o *IT Consultant.* This term can apply across the IT spectrum but is most often found in management consultancy firms, software and systems houses, and some large manufacturers of computing equipment offering related consulting services. The role varies widely between employers.
> o *Systems Analysts* analyse existing systems before drawing up specific proposals for modified or replacement systems.
> o *Systems Designers (builders/architects)* work in the components side of the industry, ensuring that hardware and software will meet the specific needs of the client.
> o *Software Engineers/Application Developers* write or code new software.
> o *Multimedia Programmers.* Multimedia is the most important emerging sector of the IT industry, and involves the control of a range of elements, which include: text, graphics, data, sound, still pictures, animation, and moving pictures. These are brought together through sophisticated computer programmes. The industry is dominated by artists, graphic designers, event producers, filmmakers and animators – all of whom ultimately depend on the expertise of the programmer or software engineer. Multimedia is an extremely fast growing industry, with enormous employment potential.
> o *Technical Authors* prepare the documentation, manuals and online help facilities for new systems. If you are looking for work in this field, your CV will literally be your selling document and should reflect the abilities that you can bring to design and content organisation.
> o *Software Trainers* provide training on an individual or group basis for users of new and existing systems.
> o *Computer Sales and Support Staff* provide technical advice on all aspects of the installation and use of computer systems.

Many consultancies and end-users recruit graduates with degrees in any discipline and provide the appropriate technical training. Newcomers to the consultancy profession usually begin in programming and testing before moving into systems analysis and design work. The attributes most commonly sought by employers include good communications skills, problem solving ability, the ability to work well as part of a team, and an enthusiasm for the industry.

Many UK-based employers offer opportunities to work abroad. The skills gap in IT has created the need for qualified computer specialists to work across Europe, the Middle East, the USA, and Australia. The more unusual your field of expertise, the greater your opportunities are likely to be. Currently Oracle, IBM mainframe experience, Unix, and real time development skills are in high demand worldwide.

USEFUL PUBLICATIONS

The *Computer User's Yearbook*, available in most libraries, is a valuable source of information and contains useful lists and addresses of recruitment agencies throughout Britain, in addition to extensive lists of the various training courses available at all levels, plus salary surveys for each job area. In Britain, the weekly journals *Computing* (VNU Business Publications, VNU House, 32-34 Broadwick Street, London W1A 2HG; ☎020-7316 9000; fax 020-7316 9160; www.computing.co.uk) and *Computer Weekly* (Quadrant House, The Quadrant, Sutton Surrey SM2 5AS; ☎020-8652 8642; fax 020-8652 8979; www.computerweekly.com) are the reference points for vacancies in the computer industry, including many vacancies abroad. A complete list of trade magazines is available in the *Computer User's Yearbook* and a number of IT journals are available online from VNU Publications on the Internet (www.vnu.co.uk).

IT RECRUITMENT AGENCIES

The following organisations recruit staff for both local and overseas jobs. It must be strongly emphasised, however, that only those with relevant experience should apply for work through these agencies.

Abraxas, UK office: United Kingdom House, 180 Oxford Street, London W1D 1NN; ☎020-7255 5555; fax 020-7636 0333; e-mail corporate@abraxas.com; www.abraxas. co.uk. Abraxas recruits for permanent and contract positions in the UK and Europe. Offices in Australia (Abraxas Technologies (Pty) Ltd., Suite 204, O'Connell House, 15-19 Ben Street, Sydney, NSW 2000; ☎+612 9222 1224; fax +612 9222 1137; e-mail sydney@ abraxas.com; www. abraxastechnologies.com.au) and in Germany and Switzerland. For undergraduate and graudate recruitment visit www.ragtime.com.

Aquent, 60 Parker Street, London WC2B 5PZ; ☎020-7404 0077; fax 020-7404 0088; e-mail london@aquent.com; www.aquent.com; and HQ: 711 Boylston Street, Boston, MA 02116, USA; ☎+1 617 535 5000; fax +1 617 535 5005. Aquent has been operating for 20 years, and with 95 offices in 20 countries, It provides services in the fields of design, new media, creative and marketing as well as in recruitment, outsourcing and technology.

ASA International, Head Office: 6 Coates Crescent, Edinburgh EH3 7AL; ☎0131-226 6222; fax 0131-226 5110; e-mail edinburgh@asainternational.co.uk; www.asainternational. co.uk. ASA International is Scotland's largest independent recruitment organization. It has offices in Edinburgh, Aberdeen, Glasgow and Kirkcaldy. It also has overseas division. ASA provides a wide-ranging service through specialist divisions (including IT), which recruit permanent, temporary and contract staff from junior to management level. ASA consultants ensure that the candidate is best prepared for any interview or position.

Computer Futures Solutions, 2 Foubert's Place, 5th Floor, Regent Street, London W1F 7AD; ☎020-7446 6666; fax 020-7446 6600; e-mail contract@computerfutures.com;

www.compfutures.com, are market leaders in the provision of SAP Personnel and IT managers internationally with many opportunities in the UK, United States, Australia and Europe; they can arrange visas, accommodation, and flights.

Computer International Consultants Inc, 109 5th Street East, St Petersburg, Florida 33715; ☎+1 727 865 9701; e-mail jobs@cictampa.com; www.cictampa.com. International and US jobs in all areas of IT.

Computer People, 1A New Street, London EC2M 4TP; ☎020-7015 2495; fax 020-7015 2496; e-mail city@computerpeople.com; www.computerpeople.com, places staff with at least one year's experience in computer systems or software across the UK. Computer People is part of Ajilon, a global recruitment company with offices in 17 countries across North America, Europe and Asia Pacific.

Eclectic International Consulting B.V., Sprundelsebaan 47, 4838 GM Breda, Netherlands; ☎+31 76 531 6647; fax +31 76 514 2394; www.eclectic.nl. Specialises in ERP software, e-commerce solutions, and customer relationship management solutions, with jobs in Europe, the Americas and the Pacific Rim. Also has offices in Germany.

EuroTechnique Consulting, 61 The London Fruit & Wool Exchange, Old Spitalfields Fruit Market, Brushfield Street, London E1 6EX; ☎0870-744 3383; fax 0871-277 2773; e-mail info@eurotechnique.co.uk; www.eurotechnique.co.uk. Eurotechnique provides IT consultants to financial institutions throughout the UK and Europe, as well as occasionally in the USA.

Grafton Recruitment Ltd., 1 Wellington Quay, Dublin 2; ☎+353 1 648 9800; fax +353 1 648 9999; www.graftonrecruitment.com. Grafton has 55 branches spanning nine different countries including the United Kingdom, Republic of Ireland, Chile, Dubai, Poland, the Czech Republic and Slovakia. The company recruits for the Private & Public sector with specialist divisions in Banking& Finance, IT, Industrial, office services, HR consulting and managed services.

Harvey Nash Plc., 13 Bruton Street, London W1J 6QA; ☎020-7333 0033; fax 020-7333 0032; e-mail info@harveynash.com; www.harveynash.com, offers wide range of senior and other IT appointments in most areas for international companies.

InterConnect Communications, Merlin House, Station Road, Chepstow, Monmouthshire NP16 5PB; ☎01291-638400; fax 01291-638401; e-mail info@icc-uk.com; www.icc-uk.com, is an independent telecommunications and postal consulting company. It requires skilled consultants to work throughout Europe, the Middle East, and Africa for short periods of time across a broad range of regulatory, technical, and commercial activities including regulatory capacity building, radio spectrum management, and network interconnection.

IT Career International, Room 1006 10/F., World-Wide House, 19 Des Voeux Road, Central, Hong Kong; ☎+852 2561 0333; fax +852 3012 1688; e-mail jobs@itcareer.com; www.itcareer.com. IT jobs in Hong Kong, China, and South East Asia.

Marshall Wilkins, Eastgate House, The Gates, Ancells Business Park, Fleet, Hampshire GU51 2UN; ☎01252-773200; fax 01252-773201; e-mail perm@marshallwilkins. com; www.marshallwilkins.com, is an IT recruitment company specialising in Oracle. They provide permanent and contract resources to leading UK, European and overseas companies. You can register via their website to receive current vacancies information.

Octagon Support BV, Laan Copes van Cattenburch 62, 2585 GC The Hague, Netherlands; ☎+31 70 324 9300; fax +31 70 326 4712; e-mail octagon@octagon.nl; www.octagon.nl. Suppliers of IT personnel to local and international businesses for more than 10 years.

Spring, 4th Floor, Alliance House, 29-30 High Holborn, London WC1V 6AZ; ☎020-7400 5910; fax 020-7400 5919; e-mail personnel-city@spring.com, specialises in contract and permanent IT, technology and telecom recruitment and staffing services.

TMP Worldwide eResourcing, Chancery House, 53-64 Chancery Lane, London WC2A 1QS; ☎020-7406 5000; fax 020-7406 3501; www.tmpw.co.uk. Recruitment advertising agency, a division of Monster Worldwide.

ONLINE RECRUITMENT

The Internet should be one of the first ports of call for IT professionals looking for work internationally. The nature of the business has meant that virtually every IT firm now has a presence on the web and that there are vast numbers of jobs in the field advertised online. *IT Jobs* (www.internet-solutions.com/itjobs.htm), for example, provides links to large numbers of recruitment agencies in the UK, the USA and Europe. Other useful sites are:

Computer People, www.computerpeople.co.uk. Recruits for IT professionals.

eFinancial Careers, http://technology.efinancialcareers.co.uk. Lists IT jobs in finance and banking in international markets.

Fairfax IT Jobs Australia, http://itjobs.mycareer.com.au/. IT recruitment site run by one of Australia's biggest media corporations. Updated daily.

Hays, www.hays.com/it. Lists IT jobs opportunities worldwide.

IT Opportunities, www.it-opportunities.co.uk.

Job Universe, www.jobuniverse.co.nz. IT jobs in New Zealand.

totaljobs.com, www.totaljobs.com/jobseekers/itinternet.asp. IT jobs worldwide.

Tech-centric, www.tech-centric.net. Jobs for technology professionals. Can be searched locally or internationally.

PROFESSIONAL ASSOCIATIONS

Association for Computing Machinery (ACM), One Astor Plaza, 1515 Broadway, 17th Floor, New York, NY, 10036, USA; ☎+1 212 869 7440; fax +1 212 944 1818; e-mail ACMHELP@acm.org; www.acm.org sets qualifying examinations for the computer industry in the USA, and can also supply information on careers in computing.

British Computer Society, 1st Floor, Block D, North Star House, North Star Avenue, Swindon SN2 1FA, ☎01793-417417; fax 01793-417444; e-mail bcshq@hq.bcs.org. uk; www.bcs.org, produces a useful *Careers in IT leaflets* available on its website and sets qualifying examinations.

Canadian Information Processing Society, 2800 Skymark Avenue, Suite 402, Mississauga, ON L4W 5A6, Canada; ☎+1 905 602 1370; fax +1 905 602 7884; e-mail info@cips.ca; www.cips.ca. Provides leadership in information systems and technologies.

Institution of Analysts and Programmers, Charles House, 36 Culmington Road, London W13 9NH; ☎020-8567 2118; fax 020-8567 4379; e-mail dg@iap.org.uk; www.iap. org.uk, can help members and potential members with general advice on careers in computer programming and systems analysis.

ICPA (International Computer Professional Association), 1388 Sutter Street, Suite 1210, San Francisco, CA 94109, USA; ☎+1 415 835 0280; fax +1 415 835 0286; e-mail mail1@icpa.com; www.icpa.com, offers services to software professionals in all countries looking for work in Japan. No charge to applicants sending résumés. Also has an office in Japan.

The Institute of Scientific and Technical Communicators, PO Box 522, Peterborough PE2 5WX, Cambridgeshire; ☎01733-390141; fax 01733-390126; e-mail istc@istc.org.uk; www.istc.org.uk.

Journalism

Although there are large numbers of freelance journalists successfully earning a living, permanent openings in the profession are few, and the industry is fiercely competitive. A journalist will usually spend several years working on a regional newspaper or specialist magazine before progressing on to a national daily – where opportunities for international postings are most likely to occur.

The official entry criterion for the professional is a GCSE-level education (Year 12 in the USA), however, 70 per cent of new entrants are, in fact, university graduates. Most will also undertake post-university training through the NCTJ (National Council for the Training of Journalists) or on post-graduate journalism diploma courses. In addition to relevant training, journalists in any area of the media need to have a wide knowledge of current affairs, a lively interest in people, places and events, the ability to write well and concisely, and a willingness to work under pressure to meet deadlines. Potential employers like to see evidence of a commitment to journalism in the form of a file of published work, as well as a CV or résumé and most serious applicants will have worked without pay on university publications and local freesheets to gain this experience. In freelance journalism, a great deal of work is found by word of mouth and through a network of personal contacts; but this is of course only possible if you are already on the inside track. Submitting articles on spec is possible (always include a covering letter and SAE). Increasingly, foreign language magazines and newspapers are accepting English language articles.

PRINT JOURNALISM

THE UK PRESS

Working for a UK newspaper will only bring an overseas appointment if you are employed by one of the national daily or Sunday papers. Several years' experience on a national paper are usually necessary before being sent abroad and full-time staff positions abroad are few and far between. Very few staff are posted permanently abroad, and those that are will generally be specialists. This is also true of the working practices of newspapers in the US and other countries.

If you have specialist local knowledge (particularly of the language) and are sufficiently determined, it is possible to work at least part-time as a freelance foreign correspondent, although it is advisable to have some solid journalistic experience before you start and to develop contacts among editors and commissioning editors. The section on *Stringers*, below, discusses this in more detail.

It is common for journalists to gain experience on local newspapers or specialist or trade magazines before moving on to a national or international career. However, this is by no means the only way in which to enter the profession. Many journalists have a recognised qualification such as the National Certificate, a National Vocational Qualification in Newspaper Journalism (Writing), or equivalent. Details of training programmes are available from *The Newspaper Society* (Training Department, Bloomsbury House, 74-77 Great Russell Street, London WC1B 3DA; ☎020-7636 7014; fax 020-7631 5119; e-mail ns@newspapersoc.org.uk; www.newspapersoc.org.uk) which represents and promotes 1,300 titles. For most international jobseekers a more creative approach will be required, which will involve identifying a market for your articles, finding out what editors want, and then working to supply it. If you already live abroad, US or UK newspapers may be interested in a wide variety of articles and approaches to the country concerned, and there will always be local English-language publications that you could approach.

Journalists who wish to write for UK newspapers should apply to the appropriate editors, giving a strong reason or unique selling point to encourage them to consider your work.

Useful Addresses

Daily Express/Daily Star/Sunday Express, The Northern & Shell Building, 10 Lower Thames Street, London EC3R 6EN; ☎08714-341010; www.express.co.uk

Daily Mail/Mail on Sunday, Northcliffe House, 2 Derry Street, London W8 5TT; ☎020-7938 6000; fax 020-7937 3251; www.dailymail.co.uk

Daily Mirror/Sunday Mirror/The People, 1 Canada Square, Canary Wharf, London E14 5AP; ☎020-7293 3000; fax 020-7293 3409; www.mirror.co.uk

Daily Telegraph/Sunday Telegraph, 1 Canada Square, Canary Wharf, London E14 5DT; ☎020-7538 5000; fax 020-7538 6242; www.telegraph.co.uk

Financial Times, 1 Southwark Bridge, London SE1 9HL; ☎020-7873 3000; fax 020-7873 3076; www.ft.com

Guardian/Observer, 119 Farringdon Road, London EC1R 3ER; ☎020-7278 2332; fax 020-7837 2114; www.guardian.co.uk

The Independent/The Independent on Sunday, Independent House, 191 Marsh Wall, London E14 9RS; ☎020-7005 2000; www.independent.co.uk

Sun/News of the World, 1 Virginia Street, Wapping, London E98 1SN; ☎020-7782 4000; www.thesun.co.uk

The Times/Sunday Times, Times House, 1 Pennington Street, London E98 1TT; ☎020-7782 5000; fax 020-7488 3242 www.timesonline.co.uk

THE US PRESS

Becoming a foreign correspondent for an American newspaper is not essentially different from the career path described above. Editors will generally consider a wide knowledge of politics, international affairs and history as more important than a degree in journalism. Taking a course in journalism is of course always useful, but it is practical experience, as well as useful contacts acquired through internships on newspapers, which will have most influence on the course of your intended career. The major American papers employ numerous foreign correspondents (*The New York Times* and *The Washington Post* have the most).

Useful Addresses

Christian Science Monitor, One Norway Street, Boston, MA 02115; ☎+1 617 450 2000; USA; www.csmonitor.com

Los Angeles Times, 202 West 1st Street, Los Angeles, CA 90012; ☎+1 213 237 5000; www.latimes.com

New York Times, 229 West 43rd Street, New York, NY 10036; ☎+1 212 556 1234; www.nytimes.com. Job opportunities can be found on www.nytco.com/job-search.html

Newsweek Magazine Inc., 251 West 57th Street, New York, NY 10019; ☎+1 212 4454000; www.msnbc.com

Time, Inc., 1271 Avenue of the Americas, New York, NY 10020; ☎+1 212 5221212; www.time.com

The Wall Street Journal, 200 Liberty Street, New York NY 10281; ☎+1 2124162000; www.wsj.com. The Wall Street Journal also has a mid-west and a south-western edition

Washington Post, 1150 15th Street NW, Washington DC 20071; ☎+1 202 3346000; www.washingtonpost.com

INTERNATIONAL ENGLISH-LANGUAGE PRESS

British Commonwealth countries all have a well-established English-language press and there are opportunities not only for field reporters and photographers, but also for editorial and management staff. Needless to say, a high level of professionalism and training is expected.

The most practical way of finding work on a foreign paper is by direct application. Addresses of newspapers can be found in *Willings Press Guide* (Chess House, 34 Germain Street, Chesham, Bucks HP5 1SJ, ☎0870-736 0100; fax 0870-736 0011; e-mail enquiries@willingpress.com; www.willingspress.com) the international volume of *Benn's Media Directory*, or the blue pages of the *Advertisers Annual* (Hollis Publishing, Harlequin House, 7 High Street, Teddington, Middlesex TW11 8EL; ☎020-8977 7711; fax 020-8977 1133; www.hollis-pr.com). All three directories can be obtained in local reference libraries. In addition, the *Writers' and Artists' Yearbook* (A&C Black, 38 Soho Square, London W1D 3HB; ☎020-7758 0200; www.acblack.com) lists the addresses of newspapers and magazines throughout the English-speaking world (excluding the USA).

If you already live abroad, or are intending to move, there is always a possibility of finding work on a local English-language newspaper or magazine where enthusiasm and a direct approach may count for more than experience. A personal visit to these publications should be on your itinerary. Such publications are found in most countries where there are English-speaking expatriates, for example in Europe, the Middle East and Asia, as well as Eastern Europe. Large multinationals with overseas offices also usually have in-house magazines and these provide another useful route into a career in journalism.

BROADCAST JOURNALISM

BRITISH RADIO AND TELEVISION

The BBC is perhaps the single most important producer of television and radio programmes in the UK, however, changes in the broadcasting industry in recent years mean that there has been a big expansion in the number of small independent production companies.

Competition to enter the industry at any level is extremely intense, with positions at the BBC still carrying particular status. The BBC offers a wide range of entry possibilities and the range of skills and experience required is broad. Most media jobs open to external applicants are advertised in the UK national press and prospective applicants should keep a close eye on the appointments pages (*The Guardian* on Monday is the best source of media jobs). There are limited opportunities to work abroad, and it is rare that such responsibility would be given very quickly to a newcomer to the industry. Trainee jobs, when advertised, require enthusiasm and involvement in activities relevant to the job. Many positions now require bi-media skills (the ability to work across television, radio and new media) and you should try and gain as much crossover experience as possible. These days a great many people find positions in journalism and the media by working first in a company as unpaid labour. If you can afford to fund yourself over the initial period of a few months this can be the best way to get a foot in the door. You will have shown willing, will begin to make contacts, and get your face known by the people that make decisions when it comes to hiring and firing. Competition for places being as fierce as it is, just getting some work experience can be a challenge. Journalism is a profession where contacts and personality are all important. Getting your big break depends on talking to people and persuading them to give you a chance.

Employment in independent television is handled by the individual companies whose addresses can be obtained from *Ofcom*, Riverside House, 2a Southwark Bridge Road, London SE1 9HA; ☎020-7981 3000; fax 020-7981 3333; www.ofcom.org.uk. Information on independent radio is also available from *Ofcom*.

Useful Addresses

BBC Recruitment, PO Box 48305, London W12 6YE; e-mail recruitment@bbc.co.uk; www.bbc.co.uk/jobs/index.shtml

BBC World Service, Bush House, Strand, London WC2B 4PH; ☎020-7240 3456; fax 020-7557 1258; e-mail worldservice@bbc.co.uk; www.bbc.co.uk/worldservice/. The BBC also has overseas offices in New York, Washington, Cairo, Singapore, Buenos Aires, Sydney, New Delhi, Paris, Berlin and Brussels

BskyB, Grant Way, Isleworth, Middlesex TW7 5QD; ☎08702-403000; www.sky.co.uk

Channel 4, 124 Horseferry Road, London SW1P 2TX; ☎020-7306 8333;; www.channel4. com

Five, 22 Long Acre Avenue, London WC2E 9LY; ☎020-7421 7270; fax 020-7497 5222; www.five.tv

Independent Television News (ITN) Ltd., 200 Grays Inn Road, London WC1X 8XZ; ☎020-7833 3000; fax 020-7430 4868; e-mail editor@itn.co.uk; www.itn.co.uk

The Broadcast Journalist Training Council (BJTC), Secretary, 18 Miller's Close, Rippingale, Lincolnshire PE10 0TH; ☎01778-440025; e-mail sec@bjtc.org.uk; www. bjtc.org.uk

AMERICAN RADIO AND TELEVISION

The US broadcasting media maintain considerable numbers of staff overseas though jobs are not easy to come by, especially in desirable foreign locations. Satellite broadcasters such as CNN (Cable News Network) offer some of the best opportunities for entry into the profession at an international level.

Useful Addresses

ABC News, 47 West 66th Street, New York, NY 10023; ☎+1 212 4561571; www.abcnews. go.com

Cable News Network, 100 International Blvd NW, Atlanta, GA 30303; ☎+1 404 8271500; fax +1 404 878 0891; www.cnn.com

CBS Inc., 51 West 52nd Avenue, New York, NY 10019; ☎+1 212 975 4321; www.cbs.com

HBO, 1100 Avenue of the Americas, New York, NY 10036-6712; ☎ +1 212 512 1000; www. hbo.com

NBC, 30 Rockefeller Plaza, Floor 2, New York, NY 10112; ☎+1 212 3147100; www.nbc.com

Turner Broadcasting System, 1 CNN Center; Atlanta, GA 30303; ☎+1 404 827 1700; www. turner.com

OVERSEAS RADIO AND TELEVISION

The chance of vacancies occurring in overseas broadcasting companies is less common than such a thing occurring in the foreign press. The major companies in the English-speaking world can usually fill their own needs internally; other specialised vacancies are sometimes advertised in the British and American press. Addresses of individual companies are to be found in the *World Radio TV Handbook* (WRTH Publications, PO Box 290, Oxford OX2 7FT; ☎01865-514405; e-mail sales@wrth.com; www.wrth.com), available online through their secure website for £22.00 inc. post & packing as well as from bookshops.

There are many non English-speaking countries that have English language broadcasts, usually as part of their external services and rather similar to the BBC World Service or Voice of America. There are occasional openings for native English-speaking personnel to produce, direct and broadcast these services. Full details of English language broadcasts are also given in the *World Radio and TV Handbook*.

STRINGERS

The international news system is structured in such a way that most of the foreign news in the British and American media originates either from news agencies, or from individuals known as stringers, rather than from permanently based expatriate reporters. Stringers are journalists already based overseas who, for a retainer and/or commission, will feed stories from their part of the world back to Britain. Stringers thus function on a part-time, freelance basis, and their work, while providing a valuable source of extra income, is usually secondary to a full-time career (often as a reporter or editor for a locally-based paper). If you have journalistic experience and are going abroad to another job, you should consider offering your services as a stringer to one of the national papers.

There are considerable opportunities for the dedicated foreign stringer, which do not fall into any of the conventional categories discussed so far. A stringer need not be restricted to finding the occasional news story for the national and international press. If he or she really knows the market, opportunities for writing travel, sociological, or current affairs features for national and specialist magazines and newspapers are plentiful. To ensure the best chances of success you should contact likely sources of publication before setting off abroad. The *Writers' and Artists' Yearbook* contains useful information on newspapers and magazines across the world, while the *Press Gazette* (19 Scarbrook Road, Croydon, Surrey CR9 1LX; ☎020-8565 4200; fax 020-8565 4462; www.pressgazette.co.uk), the weekly newspaper for journalists, sometimes contains advertisements from sources looking for foreign freelance contributions and prospective foreign stringers would also do well to advertise their availability for occasional or one-off contributions in those columns.

NEWS AGENCIES

The many news agencies (also known as wire services) offer good opportunities for journalists based abroad. In recent times international newsgathering has come to be dominated by European companies, particularly *Reuters* (The Reuters Building, 30 South Colonnade, Canary Wharf, London E14 5EP; ☎020-7250 1122; e-mail candidate. support@reuters.com; www.reuters.com) and *Agence France Presse* (13 Place de la Bourse, 75002, Paris, ☎+33 1 4041 4646; fax +33 1 4041 4632; www.afp.com). Reuters' main competitor in supplying global news services is now the American-owned *Associated Press (AP)* (450 West 33rd Street, New York, NY 10001; ☎+1 212 621 1500; e-mail info@ap.org; www.ap.org).

A list of the news agencies in Britain, and the services they provide, is given in *Benn's Media Directory* under the heading *Agencies and Services for the Media Industry*. As many of these agencies operate mainly within the UK or US, a career in one of the larger agencies is unlikely to include more than the occasional trip or tour of duty overseas. The major exception to this rule, however, is *Reuters,* which is an international news organisation that supplies news of political, economic, financial, general and sports interest to the media and business communities in most countries of the world. It also produces a wide range of computerised data retrieval services, combining both news and statistical data, and uses the latest technology to supply banks, brokers, financial institutions and major corporations worldwide with up-to-the-minute information on international money rates, securities, commodities and all factors affecting these markets.

Reuters has one of the largest private communication systems in the world and services over 330,000 professional users in some 150 countries. Its extensive real-time data retrieval networks are among the most sophisticated and reliable in operation, interfacing with high-speed communication links and making use of satellites, cables and high-frequency radio. They employ a number of graduates each year for training in a wide range of disciplines including marketing, finance, journalism and information technology. Successful candidates will be expected to have at least a second-class honours degree.

In addition, applicants for the journalist training-scheme will be required to speak two languages, one of which should be English. All their schemes offer opportunities for posts at home and abroad. Applications should submitted online on www.about.reuters.com/ careers/graduate/ before 30 December each year.

Associated Press (AP) provides many of the same services as Reuters, but is less heavily involved in supplying financial data. AP employs 200 correspondents around the world. AP correspondents seeking an international posting would normally be expected to begin their career in one of AP's smaller offices in the USA, moving on to a foreign desk in New York, before being sent abroad. In some exceptional cases, however, AP will hire locally based reporters when the need arises.

NEW MEDIA

Both the print and broadcast media have recently moved strongly into electronic publication, offering a new range of opportunities for journalists with good IT skills. The BBC website (www.bbc.co.uk), for example, has several thousands of pages, many updated minute-by-minute, relating to their broadcast output. A whole new range of IT-literate employees have been hired to launch and service this operation, and opportunities are listed on their website. Similarly, all major newspapers now have parallel websites, and in many cases specialist journalists are employed to write for these services. New media, with its strong relationship to the international IT market, now offers some of the best (and best paid) opportunities in international journalism. Entrants to the fields will require the usual journalistic skills, experience, and training, as well as skills in HTML and web design. A number of colleges and universities now offer vocational diploma courses in the new media field and these can be found through the *Universities and Colleges Admissions Service* (UCAS), Rosehill, New Barn Lane, Cheltenham, Gloucestershire GL52 3LZ; ☎0870-112 2211; e-mail enquiries@ucas.ac.uk; www.ucas.com.

USEFUL CONTACTS

Association of British Science Writers, Wellcome Wolfson Building, 165 Queen's Gate, London SW7 5HD; ☎0870-770 3361; e-mail absw@absw.org.uk; www.absw.org.uk
The *Media Centre*, 29 Crescent Road, Reigate, Surrey RH2 8HT; ☎07932-065767; fax 01737-212287; www.mediamasters.co.uk, is an excellent online media jobs source, which also carries other related information, advice and links.
National Union of Journalists (NUJ), Headland House, 308-312 Gray's Inn Road, London WC1X 8DP; ☎020-7278 7916; e-mail info@nuj.org.uk; www.nuj.org.uk
National Council for the Training of Journalists (NCTJ), Station Road, Newport, Saffron Walden, Essex CB11 3PL; ☎01799-544014; fax 01799-544015; e-mail info@nctj.com; www.nctj.com
Periodicals Training Council, Queens House, 28 Kingsway, London WC2B 6JR; ☎020-7400 7509; fax 020-7404 4167; www.ppa.co.uk.

ONLINE RECRUITMENT

www.iwantmedia.com/jobs/, links to other media job sites.
www.journalismjobs.com. Jobs in media in the US.
www.journalism.co.uk. Jobs in media throughout the world; a selection of newsletters.
http://www.broadcastfreelancer.com/broadcast/Home.do
http://www.jobsword.co.uk/media.html
http://www.dmgtopportunities.com/
http://www.recruitmedia.co.uk/jobs_list.asp?division=editorial
http://www.tmn.co.uk/vacancies.asp
http://www.mediaweek.co.uk/jobs/
http://www.pressgazette.co.uk/template/jobs/

The Law

As in banking and accountancy, British-trained lawyers are well respected internationally and career opportunities exist for them in many countries throughout the world.

SOLICITORS

Despite the wide differences between legal systems in countries across the world, which might be thought to restrict career mobility, a variety of opportunities exist for solicitors to practise abroad. Many of the larger London solicitors' firms have offices abroad – particularly in Europe, the USA and the Middle East – and it is now a common practice to send trainees abroad for six months to gain overseas experience in Paris or Brussels, or other European cities.

International commercial law is not in itself a separate category of law, but refers rather to the practice of law across national boundaries. Only those who already hold a high level of expertise in the legal system of their own country can expect to move into this area. Good language skills are essential, and the ability to adapt to another culture is also an asset. Cases involving the laws of other countries are generally handled by the most experienced partners in any firm, and trainees who are sent abroad will generally work in a low-level supporting role.

A number of UK solicitors hold advisory posts with international legal firms or in the in-house legal departments of industrial and commercial concerns. Needless to say, mastering a legal system in a foreign language is intellectually highly demanding and therefore, because of the common law roots of their legal systems, as well as a common language, many UK solicitors seek admission to the United States, Canada, Australia and New Zealand, although immigration restrictions and the need for further training can often be a barrier to such endeavours.

Solicitors are also found on the staffs of various international organisations, such as the institutions of the European Union, the European Patent Office, the Council of Europe, and the United Nations, where they undertake legal and administrative work or act as translators and interpreters. Others may work as legal draftsmen or in other capacities in various Commonwealth countries under schemes run by the Commonwealth Fund for Technical Co-operation and other Commonwealth institutions.

In addition, there are a number of professional exchange opportunities for those solicitors interested in gaining practical experience of other legal systems for short periods. Details of the Young Lawyers' International Associations Scheme and other national schemes are available from The Law Society's International Relations Department (address below).

The training required in order to qualify as a solicitor is lengthy and exacting. A would-be solicitor must normally either obtain a law degree (details of these are available from the Law Society) or a degree in a subject other than law, and then take the conversion course leading to the Common Professional Examination or its equivalent (details available from the Law Society). They must then successfully complete the Legal Practice Course at a validated institution. Full details of how to qualify, including information about the non-graduate route into the profession, are included in the booklet *Careers in the International Legal Field* available from the Law Society's Recruitment Office, 113 Chancery Lane, London WC2A 1PL; ☎ 020-7242 1222.

BARRISTERS

To qualify as a barrister in Britain, a student must first be admitted to an Inn of Court; second, satisfy the educational and training requirements of the Bar Council, including pupilage, and finally, be called to the Bar. He or she should hold a degree from a British or Irish university.

The Bar Council, 289-293 High Holborn, London WC1V 7HZ; ☎ 020-7242 0082; fax 020-7831 9217; www.barcouncil.org.uk, advises that, in many countries, the distinction between the work done in the UK by a barrister and that performed by a solicitor does not exist, since the professions are merged. It follows that much of the information describing opportunities for solicitors can also, therefore, be applied to professional prospects for barristers abroad. There are, however, no official professional exchange schemes for barristers.

Overseas vacancies for British barristers are more common in the Commonwealth and North America than other countries. Intending overseas barristers are advised to contact the Bar Association of the country in which they are interested (addresses are available on request from the Bar Council or from the information offices of the relevant embassy in London).

Further information is available from the Bar Council (address above), www.barcouncil.org.uk and www.legaleducation.org.uk.

US LAWYERS

American lawyers generally find it difficult to practise abroad, unless employed by an American company where they are required to deal mainly with US law. If this is not the case, US-qualified lawyers will need to pass the examinations of the country in which they wish to practise, usually after completing a recognised course of study. As noted above, international law is generally the preserve of the most experienced partners in any firm. Some law schools offer courses in international law and also have international law societies for students. Further information can be obtained from the *American Bar Association* (740 15th Street, N.W., Washington, DC 20005; ☎ +1 202 662 1000; e-mail careers@abanet.org; www.abanet.org).

RECRUITMENT CONSULTANTS AND OTHER JOB SOURCES

The following firms deal with legal appointments abroad:

Coudert Brothers, 1114 Avenue of the America, New York, NY 10036; ☎ +1 212 626 4400; fax +1 212 626 4120; www.coudert.com. Coudert Brothers has offices in Paris, London, Brussels, Antwerp, Stockholm, Ghent, Berlin, Frankfurt, Milan, Rome, Moscow, St. Petersburg, Almaty, Jakarta, Mexico City, Bangkok, Beijing, Hong Kong, Shanghai, Singapore, Tokyo, and Sydney. In Budapest, Coudert Brothers is associated with the law firm of Nagy és Trócsányi, in Prague with the law firm of Giese and Partner, and in Stockholm with Schürmann & Grönberg.

Garfield Robbins International, 30 Farringdon Street, London EC4A 4EA; ☎ 020-7417 1400; fax 020-7417 1445; e-mail info@garfieldrobbins.com; www.garfieldrobbins.co.uk, recruits at all levels. Associated offices in Hong Kong, Australia and New York.

Law Staff Legal Recruitment, 1 Munro House, Trafalgar Way, Bar Hill, Cambridge CB3 8SQ; ☎ 0845-230 1664; fax 0870-350 1664; e-mail admin@law-staff.co.uk; www.law-staff.co.uk. Offers legal jobs across the UK. It also offers online recruitment on www.law-staff-online.co.uk.

INTERNET RESOURCES

The best source of legal jobs and information on the Internet is the *Legal Employment Search Site* at www.legalemploy.com, with a huge linked list of recruitment firms, associations and information sources. You can also use this site to post your CV online with the *National Lawyers Association Résumé Forum*.

You can access the *Washburn University School of Law's* law library at www. washburnlaw.edu/library/. There are also a number of newsgroups and legal profession forums on the web, which may be useful in networking when looking for international jobs. These include: misc.legal, misc.legal.moderated, aus.legal (an Australian group), uk.legal (British) and us.legal (American). Additionally, *The Lawyer's Guide to Jobsurfing on the Internet* by William T. Barrett (published by Career Education Institutes, PO Box 11171, Winston-Salem, WC 27116, USA; ☎+1 336768 2999) is a useful guide to finding international work via the web. Some of the websites listing law jobs are:

Law Recruiter, www.lawrecruiter.co.uk. Legal jobs within the UK.

Legal Prospects, www.legalprospects.co.uk. Law jobs positions across the UK.

LegalWeekJobs, www.legalweekjobs.com. Vacancies for assistant solicitors, partners, in-house lawyers, paralegals, legal secretaries and support staff within the UK.

Ten-Percent Legal Recruitment, www.ten-percent.co.uk. Concentrated on the recruitment of solicitors but offers vacancies for legal executives as well. The website also contains links to legal resources, such as career websites, legal information portals and other legal recruitment websites.

PROFESSIONAL ASSOCIATION

The Professional Association for solicitors in England and Wales is the *Law Society*, 113 Chancery Lane, London WC2V 1PL; ☎020-7242 1222; fax 020-7320 5955; www. lawsociety.org.uk. The Law Society's *Careers and Recruitment Service* does not have vacancies for solicitors abroad and can only give general advice in this area.

Medicine and Nursing

There is always a demand for people with medical, paramedical and nursing qualifications who are willing to work abroad. Many countries including Germany, South Africa, France, Denmark, and Britain are suffering from a shortage of nurses. Due to the relatively low pay awarded to nursing staff in Britain many are leaving the UK to seek work abroad – especially in the USA where salaries can often be double that paid back home. British and US qualifications are highly respected around the world and it is now far easier for UK and Irish personnel to work in other EU countries due to the mutual recognition of qualifications between member states. The UK, North America, Australia, New Zealand and the Middle East are popular destinations for travelling health professionals, although the demand is uneven and it is advisable to research where the opportunities currently lie before taking your chances abroad. In countries such as Saudi Arabia and the USA, there are often generous salaries and benefits packages available, especially through some of the recruitment agencies listed below. Although there is an urgent need for doctors and nurses in Eastern Europe, most of the work is done on a voluntary basis and usually involves training local personnel

English-speaking medical personnel, in particular doctors and dentists, usually restrict themselves to working in hospitals and other institutions overseas where they can communicate in English. Those who can speak other languages will find a great many more opportunities open to them. The *Nursing Standard* (The Heights, 59-65 Lowlands Road, Harrow, Middlesex HA1 3AW; ☎020-8423 1066; e-mail nursing.standard@ rcnpublishing.co.uk; www.nursing-standard.co.uk), which is on sale through subscriptions and newsagents weekly, carries international vacancies, as does *Nursing Standard Online*, accessible on its website.

This chapter sets out the major employment possibilities in a wide range of medical and hospital careers. Further substantial references to this type of work will be found in many of the chapters in *Worldwide Employment*, and also in the chapters on *Voluntary Work*, *United Nations* and *Military Service*.

Agencies dealing with nursery nurses for domestic positions are dealt with in the chapter *Au Pair and Domestic*. Other employers and recruitment agencies can also be found in the chapter *Getting the Job*.

AGENCIES

There are a huge number of recruitment agencies dealing with international employment opportunities for doctors, nurses, dentists, occupational and physiotherapists, pharmacists and many other categories of health professional. The following list includes a selection offering a range of appointments.

Arabian Careers Ltd., e-mail recruiter@arabiancareers.com; www.arabiancareers.com. Wide range of medical and nursing appointments in Saudi Arabia and other regions in the Middle East.

ASA International, Head Office: 6 Coates Crescent, Edinburgh EH3 7AL; ☎0131-226 6222; fax 0131-226 5110; e-mail edinburgh@asainternational.co.uk; www.asainternational.co.uk. ASA International is Scotland's largest independent recruitment organisation. It has offices in Edinburgh, Aberdeen, Glasgow and Kirkcaldy. It also has overseas division. ASA provides a wide-ranging service through specialist divisions (including health care), which recruit permanent, temporary and contract staff from junior to management level. ASA consultants ensure that the candidate is best prepared for any interview or position.

Catto International, 75 Lynwood Drive, Camberley, Surrey GU16 6BU; ☎01276 500 522; fax 01256-500 529; www.nurses.uk.com. Places all types of medical and ancillary personnel around the world.

Centennial Nurses Agency, 34 Queens Park Road, Bondi Junction, Sydney, NSW 2022, Australia; ☎+61 2 9369 4325; fax +61 2 8905 9385; e-mail joy@centennialnurses.com. au; www.centennialnurses.com.au. Supply registered nurses to hospitals in Sydney and NSW.

EHL Services Inc, Edmonton Office, 206, 3132 97 Street, Edmonton, Alberta T6N 1L6, Canada; ☎+1 780 907 6354; fax +1 604 504 3906; e-mail info@e-h-l.com; www. e-h-l.com. Professional medical search and placement services, with an emphasis on international relocation. Clients mainly in Canada and USA..

Harrison Jones Associates, Talbot House, 204-226 Imperial Drive, Rayners Lane, Middlesex HA2 7HH; ☎0845-644 6894; fax 0845-644 6892; e-mail info@hjajobs.net; www.hjajobs.net, recruits British and non-British passport holders to medical and nursing positions in Saudi Arabia.

Health Professionals, 67 Knightsbridge, London SW1X 7RA; ☎020-7201 1140; fax 020-7935 8883; e-mail team@healthprofessionals.com; www.healthprofessionals. info. Specialist nursing recruitment company for nurses seeking to work in the UK and Ireland.

International Medical Placement, 100 Sylvan Pkwy, Suite 300, Amherst, NY 14228, USA; ☎+1 716 689 6000; fax +1 716 689 6187; e-mail info@intlmedicalplacement. com www.intlmedicalplacement.com. Industry leader in physician recruitment to the USA across all specialties.

O'Grady Peyton International, 1/3 Norton Folgate, London EC1 6DB; ☎0870-700 0140; fax 0870-700 0141; e-mail routeeurope@ogradypeyton.com; www.ogradypeyton. com. Specialist in nursing recruitment to the USA with offices in Australia, India, Ireland, Singapore, South Africa, the UK and the USA.

TeamStaff RX Inc., 1545 Peachtree St NE, Suite 340, Atlanta, GA 30309, USA; ☎+1 866 352 5304; www.teamstaffrx.com. Nursing, physical and speech therapy, medical clerical, cardiac cath lab and diagnostic imaging placements throughout the USA.

Worldwide Healthcare Exchange, 2nd Floor, Culpitt House, 74-78 Town Centre, Hatfield, Hertfordshire, AL10 0JW; ☎0845-6080454; fax 0845-6080455; international callers: +44 1707 282915; e-mail info@whe.co.uk; www.whe.co.uk. Appointments are available for short and long-term contracts in Australia, New Zealand, Dubai, Saudi Arabia, USA, Canada and Bermuda.

WorldWide Healthstaff Associates Ltd., 3rd Floor, 691 Wolseley Avenue, Winnipeg, Manitoba R3G 1C3, Canada; ☎+1 204 958 7023; fax +1 204 488 7121; e-mail info@ healthstaff.org; www.nursejobs.ca; US office: 6000 Fairview Road, Suite 1200, Charlotte, North Carolina 28210, USA; ☎+1 704 552 3699; fax +1 704 552 3705. International recruitment company specialising in placing nurses, pharmacists, diagnostic imaging technologists, physical therapists, and occupational therapists.

INTERNET RESOURCES

There are a large number of recruiters in medical and allied professions working solely via the Internet. Some sites worth looking at are:

Hays, www.hays.com/healthcare. International job opportunities in healthcare.
Hospital Jobs Online, www.hospitaljobsonline.com. A US based healthcare job board.
Jobs in Health, www.jobsinhealth.co.uk. The only UK Internet recruitment site that
   covers all jobs in the health industry: nursing, medical, administrative, managerial, and
   support positions, across the acute, community, mental and independent health sectors;
   represents the major employers in both the public and private health sectors.
NurseFindersUK, www.nursefindersuk.com. Lists nursing and medical jobs in the UK and
   across the world.
Nurse Options USA, www.nurseoptions.com. Offers free information on employment to
   registered nurse and nursing management candidates seeking employment throughout
   the US.
Nurserve, www.nurserve.co.uk. Specialist nursing site, including jobs in the UK.
Phyjob, www.docjob.com. Physician employment in the USA.
Queensland Health, www.health.qld.gov.au. Run by Queensland Health, the Australian
   state health department. A list of hospitals offering graduate positions can be found on
   the website as part of Graduate Nurse Online Recruitment.

HOSPITAL MANAGEMENT ORGANISATIONS

In many countries, including the USA and the Middle East, commercial organisations take
responsibility for the entire management and staffing of hospitals or chains of hospitals.
Qualified medical and health care staff are often recruited from overseas, sometimes
through agencies specifically set up to meet a particular hospital's – or group of hospitals'
– needs. The following agencies service this need:

Arabian Careers Ltd., e-mail recruiter@arabiancareers.com; www.arabiancareers.com.
Wide range of medical and nursing appointments in Saudi Arabia and other regions in the
Middle East.

Bridgewater International Recruitment Direct, 109 Bodmin Road, Astley, Tyldesley,
Manchester M29 7PE; ☎01942-873158; fax 01942-896946; e-mail birdrecruit@
blueyonder.co.uk; www.bridgewaterinternational.co.uk. Recruits healthcare personnel
for countries in the Middle East.

HCCA International, Mountainview House, 151 High Street, Southgate, London N14
6PQ; ☎020-8882 6363; fax 020-8882 5266; e-mail london@hccaintl.com; www.hccaintl.
com. International healthcare management and recruitment company specialising in the
recruitment of nurses to the USA.

The major professional journal in the field, which includes advertisements, is the *Health
Service Journal*, available online at www.hsj.co.uk.

PROFESSIONAL ASSOCIATIONS

Professional associations are most useful for their advisory and information services,
which in some cases are also available to non-members. Some associations are also active
in helping their members to find work abroad. The associations below are amongst the
most helpful.

The *British Dental Association*, 64 Wimpole Street, London W1G 8YS; ☎020-
7563 0875; fax 020-7487 5232; e-mail enquiries@bda.org; www.bda-dentistry.org.uk,
publishes a number of advice factsheets listing manpower statistics, education, licensing
and legislation information on oral health care systems.
The *British Medical Association*, BMA House, Tavistock Square, London WC1H 9JP;

☎020-7387 4499; fax 020-7383 6400; e-mail info.web@bma.org.uk; www.bma.org.uk. The International Department of this trade union gives advice and information to members wishing to work abroad.

The *Medical Women's Federation*, Tavistock House South, Tavistock Square, London WC1H 9HX; tel/fax 020-7387 7765; www.medicalwomensfederation.org.uk. The appointments service circulates information on vacancies in Britain and overseas to interested members.

The *Royal College of Midwives*, 15 Mansfield Street, London W1G 9NH; ☎020-7312 3535; fax 020-7312 3536; e-mail info@rcm.org.uk; www.rcm.org.uk, is able to advise members who are interested in practising midwifery overseas or making study visits for short periods. It also welcomes applications from overseas for its courses and will design a specific programme for an individual or group of midwives visiting the UK.

The *Royal College of Nursing*, 20 Cavendish Square, London W1G 0PQ; ☎020-7927 7220; fax 020-7927 7221; e-mail london.region@rcn.org.uk; www.rcn.org.uk, has an international office that provides an advisory service for members seeking employment overseas, planning electives or professional visits outside the UK. The International Office does not arrange employment but can provide information and contacts for most countries.

The *Royal Pharmaceutical Society of Great Britain*, 1 Lambeth High Street, London SE1 7JN; ☎020-7735 9141; e-mail enquiries@rpsgb.org; www.rpsgb.org, cannot help in finding employment, but overseas vacancies are advertised in their publication, the weekly *Pharmaceutical Journal*. Registered pharmaceutical chemists applying for a position abroad are advised to contact the Society for information on pharmaceutical practice in the country concerned. This is particularly important for those seeking work in countries where no reciprocal recognition of qualifications exists.

The *British Association of Social Workers*, 16 Kent Street, Birmingham B5 6RD; ☎0121-622 3911; fax 0121-622 4860; e-mail info@basw.co.uk; www.basw.co.uk, can put its members in touch with other member associations of the International Federation of Social Workers.

The *Society of Chiropodists and Podiatrists*, 1 Fellmonger's Path, Tower Bridge Road, London SE1 3LY; ☎020-7234 8620; fax 0845-450 3721; www.feetforlife.org, can advise state-registered members on working abroad and on international recognition of qualifications.

FURTHER INFORMATION

The best sources of information on work prospects abroad are the professional associations (see above), which will also be able to give advice on the acceptability of British qualifications in foreign countries. Specific advertisements for posts abroad as well as background information can be found in the *British Medical Journal*, *Nursing Standard* and other professional journals.

Information on training and careers in nursing and midwifery is offered by *NHS Careers*, PO Box 376, Bristol BS99 3EY; ☎0845-606 0655; e-mail advice@nhscareers.nhs.uk; www.nhscareers.nhs.uk.

The *Nursing and Midwifery Council(NMC)*, 23 Portland Place, London W1B 1PZ; ☎020-7637 7181; fax 020-7436 2924; e-mail advice@nmc-uk.org; www.nmc-uk.org; the NMC sets the standards for pre-registration nursing and midwifery programmes, post registration courses leading to registration as a specialist community public health nurse and those for the recordable qualifications as a specialist practitioner and nurse prescriber. They provide transcripts of training and verification of registration.

Individuals seeking places on pre-registration courses should contact the Nursing and Midwifery Admissions Service. Registered nurses are advised to contact individual universities for information on availability of courses leading to either a registerable or recordable qualification. Approved programme providers can be found on the NMC website.

Nurses who obtained their qualifications overseas are advised to contact the overseas call center on ☎020-7333 6600 to request the requisite information on registering with the NMC, or to visit the overseas pages of the website.

INTERNATIONAL CHARITIES AND ORGANISATIONS

British Red Cross Society (BRCS), 44 Moorfields, London EC2Y 9AL; ☎020-7877 7477; fax 020-7562 2000; e-mail information@redcross.org.uk; www.redcross.org.uk, works as part of the International Red Cross and Red Crescent Movement, protecting and assisting victims of conflicts and natural disasters, with neutrality and impartiality, in the UK and overseas. BRCS volunteers in the UK not only provide a trained and skilled response to emergencies, but also care for people in crisis, by offering vital services in the local community. The BRCS maintains a register of suitably qualified doctors and nurses who are available for work overseas. The BRCS does not send volunteers overseas.

CARE International UK, 10-13 Rushworth Street, London SE1 0RB; ☎020-7934 9334; fax 020-7934 9335; www.careinternational.org.uk. CARE is one of the world's largest relief and development charities, working in Africa, Asia, Latin America and Eastern Europe. It employs health professionals with extensive experience in their field, preferably gained with an organisation similar to CARE.

International Health Exchange/RedR, 1 Great George Street, London SW1P 3AA; ☎020-7233 3116; fax 020-7233 3590; e-mail info@redr.org.uk www.redr.org. International Health Exchange merged with RedR London in 2003. It is a is a registered charity that helps humanitarian organisations improve the effectiveness of their aid programmes by recruiting humanitarian and development professionals for certain positions, and providing generic and tailored training courses in the UK and overseas to those already involved in, or wishing to be a part of the, humanitarian and development sector. Its website lists job vacancies in international health, as well as provides a good source of information regarding health-related issues affecting the work of those in the sector today.

International Medical Corps, 1919 Santa Monica Boulevard, Suite 300, Santa Monica, CA 90404, USA; ☎+1 310 826 7800; fax +1 310 442 6622; e-mail imc@imcworldwide.org; www.imcworldwide.com. IMC is a non-profit humanitarian relief organisation that aims to relieve suffering through healthcare intervention around the world.

Médecins Sans Frontières (MSF), 67-74 Saffron Hill, London EC1N 8QX; ☎020-7404 6600; fax 020-7404 4466; e-mail office-ldn@london.msf.org; www.uk.msf.org; and *MSF International,* Rue de la Lausanne 78, CP 116, 1211 Geneva 21, Switzerland; ☎+41 22 849 8400; fax +41 22 849 8404. MSF is a leading non-governmental organisation for emergency medical aid, providing independent medical relief to victims of war, disasters and epidemics in more than 75 countries around the world. MSF strives to provide assistance to those who need it most, regardless of ethnic origin, religion or political affiliation. In 1999 MSF won the Nobel Peace Prize.

MSF is a voluntary organisation. Each year, approximately 2,500 medical, paramedical and non-medical professionals from around the world leave on field assignments where they work closely with thousands of national staff. Volunteers are usually contracted for a minimum of nine months. All jobs require at least two years professional experience post qualification, previous travel experience in a developing country as well as fluency in English (other languages are desirable). Visit their website for details of the specific requirements and person specification for each profession.

MERLIN, 12th Floor, 207 Old Street, London EC1V 9NR; ☎020-7014 1600; fax

020-7014 1601; e-mail hq@merlin.org.uk; www.merlin.org.uk. MERLIN is the only specialist UK agency which responds worldwide with vital healthcare and medical relief for vulnerable people caught up in natural disasters, conflict, disease and health system collapse. Medical professionals: doctors and nurses. Non-medical professionals: logisticians, project managers and finance managers. Must be flexible, motivated, committed, have overseas experience and be receptive and responsive to local cultures. Contracts are for six to 24 months.

Tearfund, 100 Church Road, Teddington, Middlesex TW11 8QE; ☎020-8943 9144 fax 020-8943 3594; e-mail enquiry@tearfund.org; www.tearfund.org, is an evangelical Christian and relief organisation which provides personnel for church and Christian groups. Skilled and experienced medical and ancillary staff are needed for community development programmes. Contracts are mostly for two or three years.

Many other charitable organisations with a medical or nursing brief are cited in the chapter *Voluntary Work*.

COMPLEMENTARY THERAPIES

Complementary or alternative medicine is one of the fastest growing fields in the healthcare profession. While some therapies are regarded as distinctly borderline, or even quackery, by mainstream medical professionals, others have gained a wide reputation for their effectiveness and it is not uncommon now for GPs to refer patients to acupuncturists or chiropractors, for example, for additional treatment. In most cases, complementary practitioners will be self-employed or work for a small alternative practise and there is not, therefore, the same large scale recruitment network in this branch of healthcare. Nonetheless, opportunities are available for practice abroad, particularly in chiropractics, and the various professional organisations are the best source of information for opportunities in other countries. Remember, though, that there is no point taking coals to Newcastle: China already has plenty of acupuncturists and Japan has no shortage of shiatsu therapists, although in such countries there may be good opportunities to gain work experience.

Useful Addresses
British Complementary Medicine Association, PO Box 5122, Bournemouth BH8 0WG; ☎0845-345 5977; fax 0845-345 5978; e-mail info@bcma.co.uk; www.bcma.co.uk
Institute for Complementary Medicine, PO Box 194, London SE16 7QZ; ☎020-7237 5165; fax 020-7237 5175; e-mail info@icmedicine.co.uk; www.icmedicine.co.uk
British Medical Acupuncture Society, BMAS House, 3 Winnington Court, Northwich, Cheshire CW8 1AQ; ☎01606-786782; fax 01606-786783; e-mail Admin@medical-acupuncture.org.uk; www.medical-acupuncture.co.uk
British Chiropractic Association, 59 Castle Street, Reading, Berkshire RG1 7SN; ☎0118-950 5950; fax 0118-958 8946; e-mail enquiries@chiropractic-uk.co.uk; www. chiropractic-uk.co.uk
British Homeopathic Association, Hahnemann House, 29 Park Street West, Luton LU1 3BE; ☎0870-444 3950; fax 0870-444 3960; www.trusthomeopathy.org
General Council and Register of Naturopaths, Goswell House, 2 Goswell Road, Street, Somerset BA16 0JG; ☎0870-745 6984; fax 0870-745 6985; e-mail admin@naturopathy. org.uk; www.naturopathy.org.uk
General Osteopathic Council, Osteopathy House, 176 Tower Bridge Road, London SE1 3LU; ☎020-7357 6655; fax 020-7357 0011; e-mail info@osteopathy.org.uk; www. osteopathy.org.uk

Oil and Gas, Mining and Engineering

A career in engineering offers outstanding job mobility, with good opportunities for involvement in major international construction and development projects. Engineers can qualify in a great variety of disciplines, and it is scarcely possible to explore each area in detail in a chapter of this length. Almost without exception engineers, whether civil, mechanical, electrical, petrochemical or marine, will have directly relevant degrees or other university-level training and professional qualifications.

Many major construction projects around the world are in the hands of British and North American companies, all needing engineers both for project management and to supervise day-to-day work on the ground. The recession of the early 1990s hit the engineering industry less hard than most, however, employment rates remain volatile and are directly dependent on companies success in tendering for projects. There are, nevertheless, major infrastructure projects in progress or under tender in most Middle Eastern countries, in China, Hong Kong, Australia and in much of Eastern Europe. The war in Kosovo and Yugoslavia has lead to large scale rebuilding projects in the region to replace bridges, roads, and power stations destroyed by the conflict.

Many opportunities exist for qualified engineers in the oil and petrochemical industries. Engineers experienced in the use of information technology are in demand across every sector of industry. In general, however, numbers employed in the profession are not expected to rise over the next few years, and the Institution of Civil Engineers is in the process of raising the requirements for admission to chartered membership. Competition for contracts both in the UK and overseas has intensified, and work abroad has become more difficult to obtain.

THE OIL AND GAS INDUSTRY

Oil and gas companies require a wide range of scientists, engineers and other types of personnel – from the earliest exploration stages (pilots, aerial photographers, divers, geologists, geophysicists and cartographers) through to production (drilling engineers, geochemists, petrochemists), refining and manufacturing. Opportunities also exist in research and development, marketing and distribution, and other commercial services (for example, financial management, trading, logistics, marketing, and human resources). Recruitment requirements vary in these various areas, but overall large transnational companies, most of which are household names, dominate the industry. On any particular exploration and production project, the approximate staff breakdown will generally be as follows: engineers – 30%; geotechnical staff – 25%; IT specialists – 10%; financial management – 10%; R&D staff – 20%; lawyers, doctors, nurses and others – 5%. A typical offshore oilrig will have around 100 people on board, the vast majority of whom will be employed by contractors.

Graduate recruitment is buoyant in the oil industry, and international job prospects are strong. Many major oil companies have developed relations with universities in the UK and US, and have annual recruitment programmes. Details are available through campus careers services and in the yearly *Prospects Directory* (CSU Ltd., Prospects House, Booth Street East, Manchester M13 9EP; ☎ 0161-277 5200; e-mail enquiries@prospects.ac.uk; www. prospects.ac.uk). There are also openings for graduates from non-scientific backgrounds in administrative and financial operations. Oil companies also employ many non-graduate workers, in particular on oilrigs, where drilling positions range from roustabout through to roughneck and derrickmen, up to drillers and toolpushers. For such positions it is essential to take an 'Offshore Survival Course' and then to be available for work in one of the main centres of offshore drilling activity, which in the UK means Yarmouth, Lowestoft and Aberdeen. Experience of onshore operations is also advantageous. To be considered for overseas assignments by UK companies, workers will be expected to have at least two years' experience on North Sea oilrigs. Working conditions on oilrigs are not easy, but the work is highly paid and the intense periods of life offshore are balanced by long periods of leave. Workers under the age of 21 are rarely taken on, and applicants over 28 are unlikely to be successful unless they have transferable skills. There are also positions for deep-sea divers with specialist exploration skills. Deep-sea diving is a highly specialised, high-risk profession, with large financial rewards but the career span is generally short.

The main overseas opportunities in the oil and gas industries lie in the Middle East, North Africa, North America, Venezuela, Mexico, Brazil, Australia, Brunei, Indonesia, and several European countries. The Netherlands has recently become a major producer of natural gas, and both China and Japan are competing for the untold resources of oil and gas in Russia. A multi-billion pipeline will open up the eastern Siberian oilfields for exporters. Russia is the world's largest oil producer after Saudi Arabia. China also has signed agreements with several foreign companies to develop its petrochemicals industry. The North Sea oil industry is continuing to attract new investment and it is possible that new reserves will soon be exploited on the west coast of the UK – from the Shetlands to the Irish Sea. One of the new gas exploration regions is off the Mauritanian coast in West Africa where drilling is under way and huge reservoirs are being mooted.

Some companies offer various trainee opportunities for school-leavers, for those with three acceptable GCSE passes or equivalent GNVQs. Entry level appointments for graduates are often in the field, where working conditions can be very harsh, and applicants will need to be fit and geographically mobile. Employers look for people who are not only prepared to go anywhere, but also who have no significant ties, such as dependent relatives, which might make repatriation mid-project necessary. International oil companies usually recruit local staff wherever possible, and posts abroad are often filled by internal transfer or through promotion. Competition for vacancies is, therefore, fierce and often only those with good scientific, engineering, mathematics, or other qualifications will be considered.

Details of the world's oil and gas companies and their activities can be found on the *Subsea Oil and Gas Directory* website (www.subsea.org) and the *Oil and Gas International Yearbook*, available in public reference and business libraries. *The UK Offshore Oil and Gas Yearbook* has detailed information on the production and exploration licensees in the British, Norwegian, German and Dutch sectors of the North Sea, as well as lists of the contractors and companies actively involved in providing services to the North Sea oil and gas industries. For the latest information it is worth consulting the weekly *Oil & Gas Journal* (PennWell Publishing, PO Box 1260, 1421 South Sheridan Road, Tulsa, Oklahoma 74112, USA; ☎ +1 918 8353161; fax +1 918 832 9290; www.pennwell.com). *World Oil* (PO Box 2608, Houston, TX 77252, USA; ☎ +1 713 529 4301; fax +1 713 520 4433; www.worldoil.com), is a specialist 'downhole' magazine, dealing with exploration, drilling and production. *Hydrocarbon Processing* (available from *World Oil* address; www.hydrocarbonprocessing.com) deals with downstream management and technical issues in the international Hydrocarbon Processing Industry (HPI) including refining, gas processing, synfuels and chemical/petrochemical manufacturing.

PIPELINES

One area where personnel are constantly required is pipeline work – there is a large turnover of staff in this field and although your prospects will be improved if you have some kind of specialist skill (digger, driver, welder or crane operator for example), there is also work available for the unskilled in fencing and general labouring.

Finding employment abroad in this particular line of work is very much a matter of knocking on the right door at the right time, and you are unlikely to be successful if you rely solely on sending in your CV to various personnel departments. Instead, you should equip yourself with up-to-date knowledge of recently awarded contracts and contact the successful bidding firms directly. The leading trade publication *Pipeline Digest*, (PO Box 1917, Denver, Colorado 80201-1917, USA) contains lists of all the major contracts planned throughout the world, including the name of the main contractor with telephone number and the start-up and completion dates. Armed with such information it is a simple matter to locate the main contractor and to find out from that source the firms involved in sub-contracted work. *Hydrocarbon Processing* (PO Box 2608, Houston, TX 77252, USA; ☎+1 713 529 4301; www.hydrocarbonprocessing.com) is another good source for industry news, technical information and markets trends.

SOURCES OF EMPLOYMENT IN OIL AND GAS

Recruitment in the petrochemical industry is often handled by management recruitment companies, some of which are listed under *Consultants and Agencies* in the chapter *Getting the Job*. The personnel or human resources departments of major national and multinational oil companies can supply details of their current recruitment programmes. The UK offices handling recruitment for some of the principal operating companies are:

BP plc, International Headquarters, 1 St James's Square, London SW1Y 4PD; 020-7496 4000; fax 020-7496 4630; www.bp.com

ExxonMobil, Ermyn Way, Leatherhead, Surrey KT 22 8UX; ☎1372-222000; www. exxonmobil.com

Shell Services International Ltd., Shell Centre, London SE1 7NA; ☎020-7934 1234; fax 020-7934 8060; www.shell.com

Some of the major US oil companies can be contacted at the following addresses:

ChevronTexaco Corporation, 6001 Bollinger Canyon Road, San Ramon CA 94583; ☎+1 925 842 1000; www.texaco.com

Conoco Phillips, 600 North Dairy Ashford (77079-1175), PO Box 2197, Houston, TX 77252-2197; ☎+1 281 2931000; www.conocophillips.com

ExxonMobil Corporation, applications should be completed online on www.exxonmobil. com/careers/usa

Marathon Oil Corporation, 5555 San Felipe Road, Houston, TX 77056; ☎+1 713 629 6600; www.marathon.com

Occidental Petroleum Corporation, 10889 Wilshire Boulevard, Los Angeles, CA 90024; ☎+1 310 208 8800; www.oxy.com

SchlumbergerLimited, 300 Schlumberger Drive, Sugar Land, TX 77478, USA; ☎+1 281 285 8500; fax +1 281 285 8548; www.slb.com. The company recruits graduates mainly as Field Engineers, but also as researchers, scientists and engineers. Applicants must have a good degree in engineering, physics, geology or geophysics and need to be single, physically fit and under 28 years old.

The following companies offer other career opportunities in oil industry:
Oilfield Production Consultants (OPC) Ltd., 1-2 Apollo Studios, Charlton Kings Road,

London NW5 2SB; ☎020-7428 1111; fax 020-7428 1122; e-mail london@opc.co.uk; www.opc.co.uk

ASC International; PO Box 24038, 2490 AA The Hague, Netherlands; ☎+31 70 317 8400; fax +31 70 320 4760; e-mail asc@nl.asc.net; www.asc.net, provides manpower services to the upstream oil and gas, petrochemical and power industries

RECRUITMENT CONSULTANTS

ABB Lutech Resources Ltd., Aquila House, 35 London Road, Redhill, Surrey, RH1 1NJ; ☎01737-236500; fax 01737-236546; e-mail lutech@gb.abb.com; www.lutech. lummusonline.com, recruits multi-disciplined engineers and technical staff for both upstream (oil and gas exploration and production) and downstream (petrochemicals and refineries) within the UK and overseas.

Ably Resource, 1 Buchanan Court, Stepps, Glasgow G33 6HZ; ☎0141-565 1270; fax 0141-565 1275; e-mail Jacqueline@ablyresource.com; www.ablyresource.com, provides engineering personnel to the oil and gas, construction and defence industries worldwide.

Air Resources Ltd., Bank House, 9 Charlotte Street, Manchester M1 4ET; 0870-112 9444; fax 0870-112 9445; e-mail resources@group-air.com; www.group-air.com. Supplier of global project services in the international process and energy, telecoms, banking and infrastructures markets. Recruits specialists in technical disciplines including oil and gas exploration and production, pipelines and petrochemicals to work on offshore and onshore sites in Europe, the Americas, West Africa, Middle East and former Soviet Union.

Al Wazan, PO Box 3994, Abu Dhabi, UAE; ☎+971 2 622 3400; fax +971 2 622 3334; e-mail alwazan@emirates.net.ae; www.alwazanuae.com, is one of the leading oil and gas recruitment agencies in the Gulf, covering Abu Dhabi, Dubai, Bahrain, Saudi Arabia, Qatar, Oman and Kuwait.

Anthony Moss and Associates Ltd., AMA Energy Management, Suite 350, Princess House, 50-60 Eastcastle Street, London W1W 8EA; ☎0207-323 2330; fax 0207-323 3340; www.amoss.com. Specialises in the recruitment of a wide range of senior management and professionals, specifically with up-stream oil and gas companies, in Europe, Africa, the Middle East and the Far East.

Aus Mining Personnel, Suite 16, 29 Grafton Street, Cairns, QLD 4870, Australia; ☎+61 7 4041 1377; fax +61 7 4051 0880; e-mail admin@ausmining.com.au; www.ausmining. com.au, recruits for the oil, gas, mining and construction industries in Australia, Papua New Guinea and Indonesia.

AustCorp Recruitment, PO Box 0969, QVB Post Office, Sydney NSW 1230, Australia; ☎+61 2 9290 2266; fax +61 2 9290 3828; e-mail enquiries@acrworld.com; www. acrworld.com. An Australian recruitment company specialising in national and international engineering markets and oil, gas and energy industry.

Carlton Resources Solutions, 21 Conduit Street, London W1S 2XP; ☎020-7499 4573; e-mail cvlondon@carltonrs.com; www.carltonrs.com; a local, national and international recruitment company operating in technical engineering, oil and gas, petrochemical, construction, building services and pharmaceutical industries.

Contracts Consultancy Ltd (CCL), 162-164 Upper Richmond Road, Putney, London SW15 2SL; ☎020-8333 4141; fax 020-8333 4151; e-mail ccl@cclglobal.com; www. cclglobal.com; and 11490 Westheimer, Suite 850, Houston, Texas TX 77077; ☎713-425 6304; fax 713-783 0067; e-mail ccl@ccl.us.com; www.cclglobal.com, recruits high calibre, qualified engineers and professionals with recent experience of offshore and onshore oil, gas, power and infrastructure projects in and for the UK, Europe, the Americas, Africa, the Middle East and the Far East.

The Delton Group, Ribblesdale House, 14 Ribblesdale Place, Preston PR1 3NA, Lancashire; ☎0177-2884 4545; fax 0117-2885 5005; e-mail recruitment@deltongroup. com; www.deltongroup.com. A technical recruitment and training consultancy providing services to the worldwide oil, gas and petrochemical industry.

Executech International, 3rd Floor, Suite 202B, Tokai Village, Vans Road, Tokai 7945, Cape Town, South Africa; ☎+27 21 712 0663; fax +27 21 712 0599; e-mail info@ medixmatch.com; www.executechintl.net. Provides personnel in the South African and Middle East oil and gas industries.

JMT Consultancy, 64 Stafford Road, Wallington, Surrey SM6 9AY; ☎020-8669 1518; fax 020-8669 2834; e-mail info@jmt.co.uk; www.jmt.co.uk, specialises in supplying technical and engineering personnel to the building services, oil and gas, onshore/offshore petrochemical, pharmaceutical and power industries.

L.A. Recruitment, 173 Union Street, Aberdeen AB11 6BB;   ☎01224-212929; fax 01224-573845; e-mail jacquie@larecruitment.co.uk; www.larecruitment.co.uk. A privately owned company providing recruitment to engineering, and oil and gas industries for clients in the UK, Norway, Middle East, Far East, Australia and the US.

NES Overseas, Station House, Stamford New Road, Altrincham, Cheshire, WA14 1EP; ☎0161-942 7100; fax 0161-926 9867; e-mail admin@nesoverseas.com; www. nesoverseas.com, is a global staffing services provider. It operates across a range of sectors including oil and gas, construction, infrastructure, rail power generation and IT in the Middle East, Asia, Africa, the Americas and Europe.

Onstream European Consultancy, Nijverheidsweg 9, 1785 AA Den Helder, Nertherlands; ☎+31 2 2366 9679; fax +31 2 2366 9668; e-mail jobs@onstreamgroup.com; www. onstreamgroup.com, employs worldwide management personnel, discipline engineers and construction management for both offshore and onshore oil and gas and petrochemical industries.

Petro-Canada, PO Box 2844, Calgary, Alberta T2P 3E3, Canada; ☎+1 403 296 8000; fax +1 403 296 3030; www.petro-canada.ca, is one of Canada's largest oil and gas companies, operating in both the upstream and the downstream sectors of the industry in Canada and internationally. Petro-Canada develops energy resources and provides petroleum products and services. The company employs approximately 5,000 professional, technical, clerical and secretarial staff. New graduates, co-op, internship and summer students can view and apply for current opportunities at their campus career centre.

Petroplan, 77-83 Walnut Tree Close, Guildford, Surrey GU1 4UH; ☎01483-881500; fax 01483-881501; e-mail info@petroplan.com; www.petroplan.com; recruits engineers in industries including chemicals, oil and gas and civil construction.

Professional Management Resources (PMR) Ltd, PO Box 23, Wadhurst, East Sussex TN5 6XL; ☎01892-784226; fax 01892-784228; e-mail info@pmr-worldjobs.co.uk; www.pmr-worldjobs.co.uk, recruits expatriate manpower for clients and projects in the Middle East, Far East and Africa. They deal in all engineering disciplines and provide support personnel to the civil construction, oil, gas, power and water industries.

Recruitment Services Ltd. (RSL), Penthouse Suite, Worthing House, 2-6 South Street, Worthing, West Sussex, BN11 3AE; ☎01903-820303; fax 01903-821414; e-mail jobs@ rsljobs.com; www.rsljobs.com. Recruits for jobs within the oil, gas and petrochemical industries for both on and offshore in the UK and overseas.

Search Consultants International, 4545 Post Oak Place, Suite 208, Houston, TX 77027, USA; ☎713 622 9188; fax +1 713 622 9186; e-mail info@searchconsultants.com; www. searchconsultants.com. Specialises in the placement of mid to senior level engineers and managers in the chemical, petrochemical, oil and gas; environmental, health and safety; and independent power fields. Also places power marketers and power traders for independent power and energy companies. Additional employment in finance, accounting, and sales.

Senit Associates, Victoria House, East Blackhall Street, Greenock PA15 1HD; ☎01475-806807; e-mail info@senit.co.uk; www.senit.co.uk. Supplies a list of UK and overseas job opportunities in areas such as power, oil and gas, petrochemical and engineering.

Umm Al-Jawaby Oil Service Company Limited, Recruitment Department, 15-17

Lodge Road, London NW8 7JA; ☎020-7314 6000; fax 020-7314 6136; e-mail mdean@ jawaby.co.uk, pnicholls@jawaby.co.uk; www.jawaby.co.uk. Overseas recruitment for the oil and petrochemical industries.

PROFESSIONAL ASSOCIATIONS

The American Petroleum Institute, 1220 L Street NW, Washington DC 20005, USA; ☎+1 202 6828000; www.api.org, is a regulatory and research organisation representing more than 400 companies in the oil and gas industry. The institute can provide information on employment prospects in the industry.

The Energy Institute, 61 New Cavendish Street, London W1G 7AR; ☎020-7467 7100; fax 020 7255 1472; info@energyinst.org.uk www.energyinst.org.uk. This organisation gives advice to those intending to work in the oil industry in the UK in the upstream and downstream sectors, onshore and offshore. The Institute produces a wide range of useful publications, career information booklets, and oil data sheets, which are available to the public. *Energy – Careers in the Oil and Gas Industry* outlines careers opportunities for graduates and the different fields of work in the oil industry (the list is available online). *Working Offshore* is a useful information pack which is regularly updated, outlining training courses, jobs available in North Sea operating companies, drilling companies and construction yards, and a list of recruitment agencies handling such work. Both are available online or printed copies can be obtained from Energy Institute, Library and Information Services (address above).

Other professional bodies offering advice and information in the industry include:
The *Petroleum Exploration Society of Great Britain*, 5th Floor, 9 Berkeley Street, London W1J 8DW; ☎020-7408 2000; fax 020-7408 2050; e-mail pesgb@pesgb.org.uk; www. pesgb.org.uk
UK Offshore Operators' Association, 2nd Floor, 232-242 Vauxhall Bridge Road, London SW1V 1AU; ☎020-7802 2400; fax 020-7802 2401; e-mail info@ukooa.co.uk; www. ukooa.co.uk
UK Petroleum Industry Association (UKPIA), 9 Kingsway, London WC2B 6XF; ☎020-7240 0289; www.ukpia.com

Offshore Technology is the website for the offshore oil and gas industry, and can be found on the Internet at www.offshore-technology.com.

MINING

Like the oil industry, mining is dominated by large multinationals, which means that there are very good prospects for working all around the world. The main areas for recruitment are the former Soviet Union, Canada, Australia and South Africa. Other countries such as Brazil, Thailand and Malaysia employ experienced international workers in their mining industries, particularly in training and engineering, as well as in administration and other areas. All mining companies employ geologists, metallurgists, geophysicists and surveyors, and employment prospects abroad in these professions are good.

SOURCES OF EMPLOYMENT

ARA (Applied Research Associates), 4300 San Mateo Boulevard NE, Suite A-220 Albuquerque NM87110, US; ☎+1 505 881 8074; fax +1 505 883 3679; e-mail info@ ara.com; www.ara.com, provides research, engineering and technical support services in the US. Recruits specialists in categories including construction, mining, information technology and engineering.

Aus Mining Personnel, Suite 16, 29 Grafton Street, Cairns, QLD 4870, Australia; ☎+61 7 4041 1377; fax +61 7 4051 0880; e-mail admin@ausmining.comau; www.ausmining.

com.au. Recruit for the oil, gas, mining and construction industries in Australia, Papua New Guinea and Indonesia.

Earthworks-jobs, www.earthworks-jobs.com. Jobs in oil, energy and mining.

P.W. Overseas Mining Ltd., Leabeg, Newcastle Road, Kilcoole, Co. Wicklow, Ireland; ☎1-287 2400; fax 1-287 1717; e-mail pwm@pw-limited.com; www.pw-limited.net; specialises in construction and mining operations in Africa.

Rio Tinto plc, Human Resources Department, 6 St. James's Square, London SW1Y 4LD; ☎020-7930 2399; fax 020-7930 3249; www.riotinto.com. Rio Tinto is one of the world's leading mining companies whose operations are highly diverse, both geographically and by commodity.

PROFESSIONAL ASSOCIATIONS

Institute of Materials, Minerals and Mining, 1 Carlton House Terrace, London SW1Y 5DB; ☎020-7451 7300; fax 020-7839 1702; www.iom3.org

Institute of Quarrying, 7 Regent Street, Nottingham NG1 5BS; ☎0115-945 3880; fax 0115-948 4035; e-mail mail@quarrying.org; www.quarrying.org

RICS (Royal Institution of Chartered Surveyors), 12 Great George Street, Parliament Square, London SW1P 3AD; ☎0870-333 1600; e-mail contactrics@rics.org; www.rics.org./careers

Association for Mineral Exploration British Columbia (AME BC), 800-889 West Pender Street, Vancouver, British Columbia, V6C 3B2, Canada; ☎+1 604 689 5271; fax +1 604 681 2363; www.amebc.ca

USEFUL PUBLICATIONS

The Directory of Quarries and Pits, published by the Institute of Quarrying.

The Geologist's Directory, published annually by the Geological Society Publishing House.

Minerals Industry International. Journal of the Institute of Materials, Minerals and Mining.

Mining Journal. London-based, monthly publication (www.mining-journal.com).

CIVIL ENGINEERING

There are numerous specialisations within civil engineering; these include structural, water and waste management, coastal and transport engineering, as well as geotechnics and water resource planning. This diversity of skills means that appropriate recruitment organisations may also be found listed in other chapters of this book for example in, among others, *International Organisations* and *Agriculture and the Environment*.

RECRUITMENT CONSULTANTS

Below is a selection of the many management recruitment consultancies involved principally in engineering recruitment. Those with a broader field of interest are otherwise listed in the *Getting the Job* chapter.

The AIM Group, Suite 300, 400 5th Avenue SW, Calgary, AB, T2P 0L6, Canada; ☎+1 403 303 2881; fax +1 403 303 2883; e-mail calgary@theaimgroup.ca; www.theaimgroup. ca, is an international recruitment company offering placements in design, engineering, procurement and construction management.

AndersElite, Capital House, 1 Houndwell Place, Southampton SO14 1HU; ☎023-8021 9209; fax 023-8021 9176; e-mail contactus@anderselite.com; www.anderselite.com. AndersElite are marketing-leading consultants serving fourteen professional sectors across the Built Environment, providing total recruitment solutions for a widespread private and public portfolio. With a network of regional offices throughout the country, they provide a traditional consultancy service and an e-recruitment website.

ASA International, Head Office: 6 Coates Crescent, Edinburgh EH3 7AL; ☎0131-226 6222; fax 0131-226 5110; e-mail edinburgh@asainternational.co.uk; www.asainternational. co.uk. ASA International is Scotland's largest independent recruitment organization. It has offices in Edinburgh, Aberdeen, Glasgow and Kirkcaldy. It also has overseas division. ASA provides a wide-ranging service through specialist divisions (including construction and building, and engineering), which recruit permanent, temporary and contract staff from junior to management level. ASA consultants ensure that the candidate is best prepared for any interview or position.

Beresford Blake Thomas (BBT), PO Box 500362, Dubai, UAE; ☎+971 4 390 0375; e-mail etwaite@bbtworldwide.com; www.bbtuae.com, is a human resources and recruitment consultancy covering the technical engineering and healthcare markets worldwide. Its website lists vacancies grouped according to regional offices throughout the world, with main focus on Middle East.

Daulton Construction Personnel, 2 Greycoat Place, London SW1P 1SB; ☎020-7222 0817; fax 020-7233 0734; e-mail info@daultonpersonnel.co.uk; www.daultonpersonnel. co.uk. Specialise in architecture, construction and engineering, with vacancies for civil, mechanical, and project engineers worldwide.

Desurvey PLC, Old Harbour Office, Embankment Road, St. Helens, Ryde, Isle of Wight PO33 1YS; ☎01983-875999; fax 01983-874933; e-mail jim@desurvey.com; www. desurvey.com, places design, engineering and IT personnel in the process and energy industries.

Fircroft, Trinity House, 114 Northenden Road, Sale, Cheshire M33 3FZ; ☎0161-905 2020; fax 0161-969 1743; hq@fircroft.co.uk. Recruitment specialists with a global network of offices. Recruits for a broad spectrum of industry sectors including chemical, oil and gas, mining and engineering.

Heads Recruitment, Thornley House, Carrington Business Park, Carrington, Manchester M31 4SG; ☎0161-746 7575; fax 0161-777 9431; e-mail engineering@heads-uk.com; www.heads-uk.com, recruits for engineering, construction and associated industries.

International Staffing Consultants Inc, 17310 Redhill Avenue #140, Irvine CA92614, USA; ☎+1 949-255 5857; fax +1 949 767 5959; e-mail iscinc@iscworld.com; www. iscworld.com, are members of the largest and oldest network of employment agencies in the world, the NPA. They recruit experienced and qualified engineers, as well as managers, sales, marketing and IT professionals for the USA, Europe and the Middle East.

Premier PersonnelLtd., 25-29 High Street, Leatherhead, Surrey KT22 8AB; ☎01372-379183; fax 01372-372301; e-mail candidate@prem-per.demon.co.uk; www. premierpersonnel.co.uk, recruits for jobs in civil, electrical and mechanical engineering and oil and gas industries throughout the world.

Professional Management Resources Ltd. (PMR), PO Box 23, Wadhurst, East Sussex TN5 6XL; ☎01892-784226; fax 01892-784228; e-mail info@pmr-worldjobs.co.uk; www.pmr-worldjobs.co.uk, recruits for international engineering primarily to its clients in the UK, European Community, Middle East, Far East and Africa.

SEPAM Specialist, 41-44 Upper Irishtown, Clonmel, Co. Tipperary, Republic of Ireland, ☎+353 52 83600; fax +353 52 22674; e-mail info@sepam.com; www.sepam.com. A privately owned Irish based international engineering, procurement, management and construction company. It operates in the US, Europe, Middle East, Asia and former Soviet Union.

Taylor Recruitment Ltd., 1 St John's Court, Farncombe Street, Godalming, Surrey GU7 3BA; ☎01483-418383; fax 01483-418989; e-mail jobs@taylorrecruitment.com; www. taylorrecruitment.com. A specialist supplier in sectors including oil, gas and petrochemical industry and civil and structural engineering.

TechStaff Recruitment Ltd., 11 Strand Road, Bray, Co. Wocklow, Republic of Ireland;

☎+353 1 276 3030; fax +353 1 286 1522; e-mail Elaine@techstaff.ie; www.techstaff.ie, recruits engineers and designers for large industrial, commercial and residential projects in Ireland and Australia.

Wadi Jobs & Consultancy Dubai, PO Box 37103, Dubai, UAE; ☎+971 4 398 3540; fax +971 4 398 9051; e-mail info@wadijobs.com; www.wadijobs.com; a privately owned company specialising in recruitment in Middle East in sectors including engineering.

PROFESSIONAL ASSOCIATIONS

Royal Institute of British Architects (66 Portland Place, London W1B 1AD; ☎020-7580 5533; fax 020-7255 1541; www.architecture.com). RIBA Appointments and RIBA Classified (www.riba-jobs.com) handles UK and overseas appointments (often in the Middle East) for experienced architects and architectural technicians. Its *International Directory of Practices* gives details of British firms with overseas offices.

Royal Institute of Chartered Surveyors (RICS Contact Centre, Surveyor Court, Westwood Way, Coventry CV4 8JE; ☎0870-333 1600; e-mail contracts@rics.org; www.rics.org.uk) has a recruitment consultancy which can advise on overseas employment. More than 7,000 of its qualified members are serving overseas in 100 countries.

Institution of Engineers and Technology (Savoy Place, London WC2R 0BL; ☎020-7240 1871; fax 020-7240 7735; e-mail postmaster@theiet.org; www.theiet.org) provides a professional brief for its members called *Working Abroad* which contains general information on living and working abroad. Its fortnightly newspaper *IEE Recruitment* is included as a supplement with *IEE News* and *IEE Review* and contains classified advertisements which sometimes include overseas positions. Vacancies are also carried on the IET website.

Other professional bodies that may be able to offer advice on overseas employment are:
Association of Consulting Engineers, Alliance House, 12 Caxton Street, London SW1H 0QL; ☎020-7222 6557; fax 020-7222 0750; e-mail consult@acenet.co.uk; www.acenet.co.uk
British Geotechnical Society, at The Institution of Civil Engineers, 1 Great George Street, London SW1P 3AA; ☎020-7665 2233; fax 020-7799 1325; e-mail bga@britishgeotech.org.uk; www.britishgeotech.org.uk
The Institution of Structural Engineers, 11 Upper Belgrave Street, London SW1X 8BH; ☎020-7235 4535; fax 020-7235 4294; www.istructe.org.uk

TRADE JOURNALS

Engineers from all sectors will find trade journals useful sources of employment information. The following are key industry publications:
Building Engineer (monthly), *Building Services and Environmental Engineering* (monthly), *Construction News* (weekly), *Contract Journal* (weekly), *Electronic News*, *New Civil Engineer* (weekly), *Surveyor* (weekly), *The Engineer*.

ONLINE RECRUITMENT

The Career Engineer, www.thecareerengineer.com. Engineering and construction jobs for graduates.
Hays, www.hays.com/engineering. International job opportunities in engineering.
Red Goldfish, http://engineering.redgoldfish.co.uk/jobs.asp. Engineering jobs across the UK.
UK Civil Engineering, www.ukcivilengineering.com. Civil ngineering and construction jobs in the UK.
Utility Job Search, www.utilityjobsearch.com/engineer-jobs. Lists engineering jobs in the UK utilities industry.

Secretarial, Translating and Interpreting

SECRETARIAL AND ADMINISTRATIVE WORK

Even though English is now the commercial language of the world, opportunities for properly trained secretaries with language skills abound in many organisations abroad. Apart from the employment agencies listed below, those interested in secretarial work should consult the chapters on *International Organisations, United Nations, Voluntary Work* and *British Government Departments*. Agencies that specialise in secretarial vacancies in particular countries may also be found in the relevant country chapters of this book. Branches, affiliates and subsidiaries of British- or US-based companies abroad listed in these country chapters may also be worth contacting. It should be noted that a 'bilingual secretary' is one who is fluent in both writing and speaking another language.

Anyone interested in a career as an international secretary may do well to attend one of the courses that cater especially for business linguists. These courses differ from straight language courses in that they teach the participant office management, computer and business skills as well as a fair degree of fluency in one or more languages. Courses last a year and will put attendees ahead of the rest in the search for jobs abroad.

Other training opportunities for this type of work include the scheme run by the Foreign and Commonwealth Office (contact the recruitment team of the Overseas Undergraduate Attachment Scheme at Foreign and Commonwealth Office, ☎020-7008 1500) which offers 50 places on unpaid work experience in consulates worldwide for those in their penultimate year at university. *Interspeak Placements and Homestays* (Stretton Lower Hall, Stretton, Malpas, Cheshire SY14 7HS; ☎01829-250973; fax 01829-250596; www. interspeak.co.uk) can arrange short (one to three weeks) and long (four to 24 weeks) work placements in the UK, France, Germany, and Spain at any time of the year. All placements are tailored individually to the requirements and abilities of each client.

A very brief list of agencies dealing with secretarial and bilingual administrative positions is given below; many more can be found by consulting the Yellow Pages under 'Employment Agencies', or through a search on the internet using a search engine such as *Google*. Several of the companies listed in the section *Management Recruitment Consultants*, in the *Getting the Job* chapter also recruit senior secretarial and administrative staff. Other agencies such as *Manpower* (13-15 Brompton Road, Knightsbridge, London SW3 1ED; ☎020-7589 2446; fax 020-7584 9244; www. manpower.co.uk) and *Drake International* (☎ 020-7484 0800; fax 020-7484 0808 e-mail info@drakeintl.co.uk; www.drakeintl.com) have offices throughout the UK and worldwide. After you have found work with them once (you should register with as many agencies as possible at first) and proven yourself to be a conscientious employee you may be able to find work through their offices abroad. The *Recruitment & Employment Confederation* (36-38 Mortimer Street, London W1W 7RG; ☎020-7462 3260; fax 020-7255 2878; e-mail info@rec.uk.com; www.rec.uk.com) produces a list of agencies that specialise in overseas placements.

RECRUITMENT AGENCIES

Appointments Bi-language, 143 Long Acre, London WC2E 9AD; ☎020-7836 7878; fax 020-7836 7615; e-mail info@appointmentsbilanguage.co.uk; www. appointmentsbilanguage.co.uk, recruit bilingual secretaries, translators, interpreters and other office staff.

ASA International, Head Office: 6 Coates Crescent, Edinburgh EH3 7AL; ☎0131-226 6222; fax 0131-226 5110; e-mail edinburgh@asainternational.co.uk; www. asainternational.co.uk. ASA International is Scotland's largest independent recruitment organisation. It has offices in Edinburgh, Aberdeen, Glasgow and Kirkcaldy. It also has overseas division. ASA provides a wide-ranging service through specialist divisions (including office personnel), which recruit permanent, temporary and contract staff from junior to management level. ASA consultants ensure that the candidate is best prepared for any interview or position.

Bilingual People Ltd, Bloomsbury House, 4 Bloomsbury Square, London WC1A 2RP; ☎020-7405 5005; fax 020-7405 5003; e-mail admin@bilingualpeople.com; www.bilingualpeople.com. Contract and temporary staff: secretaries, PAs, executives, translators and interpreters with two or more languages, recruited for the UK and overseas.

Boyce Recruitment, 43 Eagle Street, London WC1R 4AP; ☎020-7306 6800; fax 020-7306 6801; e-mail info@boycerecruitment.co.uk; www.boycerecruitment.co.uk. International language recruitment specialists; contract, permanent and temporary personnel in a wide range of fields and languages, including all European languages, Russian, Japanese, Chinese and Arabic.

CLC Language Services, 73 New Bond Street, London W1; ☎020-7499 3365. Specialises in placing staff with languages in EU countries in a variety of sectors, including translating, interpreting and secretarial. Opportunities open to EU citizens and North Americans with valid work permits. Relevant experience is preferred.

Crone Corkill, Stratton House, 1 Stratton Street, London W1J 8LA; ☎020-7636 0800; fax 020-7499 4300; www.cronecorkill.co.uk. Crone Corkill recruits bilingual personnel in London, Paris, Brussels and other European capitals. Candidates wishing to work abroad should ideally possess a language degree plus a minimum of six months' secretarial training, or a bilingual secretarial diploma. Minimum typing speed of 50 wpm and some word processing knowledge are essential.

Euro London Appointments, Three Kings Court, 150 Fleet Street, London EC4A 2DQ; ☎020-7583 0180; fax 020-7583 7800; e-mail city@eurolondon.com; www.eurolondon. com. Multilingual positions across all sectors, including banking and finance, IT and telecommunications, sales and marketing, call centre/customer services, as well as executive and secretarial appointments. Offices in Frankfurt and Paris.

Merrow Language Recruitment, 100 New Kings Road, London SW6 4LX; ☎0845-226 4748; fax 020-7348 6038; e-mail recruit@merrow.co.uk; www.merrow.co.uk. Recruits across the board – for customer services, helpdesks, administration, accounting, secretarial, IT and commerce – for clients in the UK and abroad.

Pasona Europe Ltd, 12 Nicholas Lane, London EC4N 7BN; ☎020-7621 0055; fax 020-7621 1001; e-mail info@pasona-eu.com; www.pasona-eu.com. Japanese specialists with positions in the UK, Europe and Japan.

Sheila Burgess International, 62 rue Saint-Lazare, 75009 Paris, France; ☎+33 1 4463 0257; fax +33 1 4463 0259; e-mail sbi@sheilaburgessint.fr; www.sheilaburgessint. fr. Established for more than 20 years, a recruitment consultancy which specialises in providing international companies in Paris, Switzerland and Germany with qualified multilingual secretarial, PA and administrative staff. Regular interviews organised in London (☎020-7584 6446).

TRANSLATING AND INTERPRETING

Overseas work for translators and interpreters is open to properly qualified personnel and work is often assigned to locally available people as the need arises. Getting started in the translation and interpreting industries can be tough as competition for work is fierce. Apart from fluency in languages and a university language degree, candidates usually need to have some post-graduate training. Translating needs a high level of expertise both linguistically and in terms of the subject matter and potential customers, whether they are agencies or direct clients, will naturally expect proof of this. Both degree level qualifications and practical working experience in relevant fields are important. Universities offer Diplomas in Translation and Interpreting, and details of these can be obtained from *UCAS* (Rosehill, New Barn Lane, Cheltenham, Gloucestershire, GL52 3LZ; ☎0870-112 2211; e-mail enquiries@ucas.ac.uk; www.ucas.ac.uk). Advice on which courses to take is available from the *Institute of Translating and Interpreting* or the *Institute of Linguists* (see below). Although there is no legal obligation for translators to join a professional body, potential customers will normally prefer to work with translators who are members of recognised professional organisations.

Translators and interpreters generally specialise in certain technical, scientific or commercial fields and may have degrees in other subjects in addition to their linguistic abilities. At present, the greatest demand in the translating industry is for technical translation from German to English, followed by French to English. Opportunities for translators with Eastern European languages are currently increasing rapidly.

Translators are employed by all the various institutions of the EU; at the Commission, the Parliament, the Court of Justice and the Court of Auditors. The European Patent Office also employs translators. Each division recruits independently and some offer in-service traineeships (*stagiaires*). The United Nations and its agencies also employ British translators, mostly based in New York and Geneva. UN translators are needed in the six official languages of the organisations, namely English, French, Spanish, Russian, Chinese and Arabic.

The interpreting industry is increasingly dominated by freelancers – even within organisations such as the EU and the UN (although these two bodies do constitute the largest employers of staff interpreters). Those who wish to work as freelance interpreters will have to prove their ability to potential employers before they can expect a steady flow of work, and most freelancers do a considerable amount of written translation work as well. Successful freelancers are usually members of a professional association, such as the IL, ITI, AIIC (see below). Potential employers are listed in the chapters, *International Organisations* and *United Nations* and can also be found in the Yellow Pages of major cities under 'Translating and Interpreting'. Other work opportunities open to those with fluency in at least one language are film dubbing and voice-overs, simultaneous translations at conferences and events, and working with local English-language radio stations and news agencies.

There are several useful books that give an in-depth look at careers in translating and interpreting: *A Practical Guide for Translators* by Samuelsson-Brown, *Careers Using Languages* by Edda Ostarhild (Kogan Page) and *A Dictionary of Translation Studies*, by Mark Shuttleworth and Moira Cowie (St Jerome Publishing).

RECRUITMENT AGENCIES

Bilinguagroup, 4th Floor East, 79/80 Margaret Street, London W1W 8TA; ☎020-7580 4441; fax 020-7580 1909; www.bilinguagroup.com. Also has offices in Paris and Frankfurt.

Accent Multilingual Services, 9-11 Mansell Street, St Peter Port, Guernsey GY1 1HP, Channel Islands; ☎01481-714 909; fax 01481-715880; www.accent.guernsey.net.

Specialists in legal and financial translations.

Admark Translations, PO Box 2034, 8900 Randers, Denmark; ☎+45 22 342030; fax +45 87770181; www.admark.dk. Specialists in translations into and from English.

BBC Languages Ltd, Balfour House, 39 Brooklands Road, Weybridge, Surrey KT13 0RU; ☎01932-348 800; www.bbclang.co.uk. Has subsidiary operations in Scandinavia, France, Germany, Austria, Italy and Spain. Translation, interpreting, localisation, proofreading, film dubbing.

English Services, Winterdijk 55a, 5142 EA Waalwijk, Netherlands; ☎+31 416 340777; fax +31 416 335642; www.englishservices.nl. Specialises in English-Dutch-English translations.

Kien International Networking, Via B Gigli 22, 20090 Trezzano, S/N Milan, Italy; ☎+39 02 445 0057; fax +39 02 445 2667; e-mail info@internationalnetwording.it; www. internationalnetwording.it; and 401 North Michigan Avenue, Suite 3030, Chicago, IL 60611, USA; ☎+1 312 329 9400; fax +1 312 670 5147. Offers multilingual communication, translation and interpretation. Subsidiaries in Amsterdam, Barcelona, Buenos Aires, Frankfurt, Hong Kong, Lisbon, London, Los Angeles, Mexico City, Moscow, Paris, Prague, Tokyo, Tripoli and Zurich.

The Language Business, Hiltongrove Business Centre, Hatherley Mews, London E17 4QP; 020-8503 7766; fax 020-8503 7950; e-mail admin@languagebusiness.co.uk; www. languagebusiness.co.uk, specialises in permanent and temporary language vacancies. The majority of their jobs are based in London with some overseas opportunities. Applications and enquiries should be made via e-mail or telephone.

Office Team, Ground Floor, 3 Shortlands, Hammersmith, London W6 8DD; ☎020-8752 6330; fax 020-8748 6222; hammersmith@officeteamuk.com; www.roberthalf.co.uk. A multinational company specialising in administrative recruitment.

RWS Translations Ltd., Europa House, Marsham Way, Gerrards Cross, Bucks SL9 8BQ; ☎01753-480 200; fax 01753-480 280; e-mail rwstrans@rws.com; www.rws-group. com. A patent translation and search company. It also provides translation, documentation and localisation services to a variety of industries. Its offices are located across the UK, in Benelux, France, Germany and the US.

Tate, 16 St Helen's Place, London EC3A 6DP; ☎020-7562 1650; fax 020-7562 1651; www.tate.co.uk; specialises in secretarial recruitment. CVs and covering letters should be submitted online.

TDR srl, Via Feltre, 11 - 20132Milan, Italy; ☎+39 2 2159 7210; fax +39 2 2159 7509; e-mail job@tdrtraduzioni.com; www.tdrtraduzioni.com. Translation, interpreting and conference specialists.

thebigword, 59 Charlotte Street, London W1T 4PE; ☎0870-748 8000; fax 0870-748 8001/8002; e-mail enquiries@thebigword.com; www.thebigword.com. Translation services company translating into and out of 140 languages and multilingual recruitment division. Offices in the UK, US, Germany, Belgium, Denmark, and Japan.

Tongue Tied (UK) Ltd, Waterside House, Basin Road North, Hove, East Sussex BN41 1UY; ☎01273-419999; fax 01273-415111; e-mail sales@tongue-tied.co.uk; www. tongue-tied.co.uk. Also have offices in Bristol, Kent, Manchester, Scotland, and US.

UPS Translations, 111 Baker Street, London W1U 6RR; ☎020-7837 8300; fax 020-7486 3272; e-mail info@upstranslations.com; www.upstranslations.com. Mother tongue translations of the written, spoken, digital, scripted, and creative word. Associated offices in 21 European countries, including France, Germany, Italy, Spain, the Netherlands, Scandinavian countries and the Baltic States.

USEFUL ADDRESSES

Association Internationale des Interprètes de Conférence (AIIC), 10 Avenue de Sécheron, CH-1202 Geneva, Switzerland; ☎+41 22 908 1540; fax +41 22732 4151; e-mail info@

aiic.net; www.aiic.net, is the only worldwide association of conference interpreters. AIIC negotiates and concludes agreements with inter-governmental organisations and generally fosters high standards in the profession.

Association of Translation Companies, 5th Floor, Greener House, 66-68 Haymarket, London SW1Y 4RF; ☎020-7930 2200; fax 020-7451 7051; e-mail info@atc.org.uk; www.atc.org.uk, is a professional organisation looking after the interests of those working in the field of translation and interpreting. They publish a members' directory.

Chartered Institute of Linguists, Saxon House, 48 Southwark Street, London SE1 1UN; ☎020-7940 3100; fax 020-7940 3101; e-mail info@iol.org.uk; www.iol.org.uk. Offers general advice on careers with languages, how to make use of qualifications already held and details of qualifications required for specific jobs connected with languages.

Institute of Translating and Interpreting (ITI), Fortuna House, South Fifth Street, Milton Keynes MK9 2EU; ☎01908-325250; fax 01908-325259; www.iti.org.uk. The Institute is the only independent professional association of practising translators and interpreters in the UK. It provides an information service for members and the general public, including a referral service for translation and interpreting work, which is available on its website. The website also gives details of events across the ITI regions as well as training courses and job vacancies. ITI's journal, *bulletin,* is published bi-monthly and carries features on new publications, reviews, articles on industry topics and new IT software. The *bulletin* also lists events and publishes letters and job vacancies; it is free to all members and available by subscription to non-members.

SDL International, Globe House, Clivemont Road, Maidenhead, Berkshire SL6 7DY8AA; ☎01628-410100; fax 01628-410150; www.sdl.com. SDL is one of the world's leading full-service localisation companies, focused on meeting the translation and localisation needs of software, multimedia and web publishers around the globe. SDL has 40 offices throughout the world. The USA Headquarters are located at 5700 Granite Parkway, Suite 410, Plano, Texas 75024; ☎214-387 8500; fax 214-387 9120.

OPPORTUNITIES FOR US CITIZENS

Major employers of translators and interpreters in the USA include the Federal Government, CIA, FBI, the National Security Agency and Voice of America Radio. American citizens interested in working in this field can obtain a free publication, *Special Career Opportunities for Linguists/Translators/Interpreters* from: US Department of State, Language Services Division, Room 1405 SA1 (Interpreting), 1400 SA1 (Translating), 2401 E Street NW, Suite 518 H, Washington DC 20520, USA; ☎202-+1 261 8800, +1 202 261 8777.

Teaching

There are good opportunities for teachers wishing to work abroad, although this will depend on the subject that you teach and your qualifications. In Britain and the USA there are too few trained teachers in some subjects and too many in others; and the uncertain jobs situation leads many to consider moving to another country, where the salaries can be higher and the lifestyle may be less stressful. Teaching overseas provides a realistic opportunity for career development, particularly in higher education and specialist training. In the EU, recent rulings by the European Court mean that member countries can no longer prevent non-nationals working in public-sector jobs, including education, and this should allow UK and Irish teachers greater freedom to move to other European Union countries. In the developing world there is a general shortage of qualified teachers and, if you are prepared to work under rather different conditions from those at home, there are plenty of opportunities for volunteers. Vacancies are widely advertised in the national press, particularly in *The Times Educational* and *Higher Education Supplements*.

One disadvantage of moving abroad is that you will not have any guarantee of employment when you return. Teachers already employed by their Local Education Authority or, in other countries the state education sector, should check on their right to return to a position at an equivalent level and in an equivalent school. Those employed in the private sector will almost certainly have to job hunt from scratch on returning home but may well find their international experience makes their CV stand out from the crowd.

Working abroad can have an adverse effect on your social security rights (enquire at your DSS office) and on your state and private pension arrangements. *Teachers' Pensions* (Capita Teachers' Pensions, Mowden Hall, Darlington DL3 9EE; ☎0845-606 6166; www.teacherspensions.co.uk) can offer advice on your likely position. The TPS (Teachers' Pension Scheme) issues free leaflets that explain the options to those who wish to leave their contributory scheme early. One possible arrangement allows teachers to contribute to the scheme during a period of absence if they pay both the employers and employees contribution for a limited time, which is usually six years if you are employed outside the British isles. The arrangement is known as Current Added Years and you must apply for it within six months of leaving pensionable employment (see *The General Approach* section for more about social security issues).

When looking for teaching work abroad, whether in the developing or developed world, some sort of qualification is usually necessary. For those who wish to teach but are currently unqualified, English as a Foreign Language teaching offers the quickest route into the classroom. The two most useful qualifications in this field are the Certificate in English Language Teaching to Adults (CELTA) and the Diploma in English Language Teaching to Adults (DELTA) offered by the University of Cambridge ESOL Examinations (English for Speakers of Other Languages), a part of the Cambridge Assessment group and the Trinity College TESOL diploma. Both are equally well regarded and widely accepted. Cambridge ESOL can be contacted at 1 Hills Road, Cambridge CB1 2EU; ☎01223-553355; fax 01223-460278; e-mail ESOLhelpdesk@CambridgeESOL.org; www.CambridgeESOL.org, and *Trinity College London* at 89 Albert Embankment, London SE1 7TP; ☎020-7820 6100; fax 020-7820 6161; e-mail info@trinitycollege.co.uk; www.trinitycollege.co.uk. These organisations will send details of their accredited national and international training centres.

Graduates looking for a more advanced initial qualification can also qualify to teach

English abroad through a one-year Postgraduate Certificate in Education (PGCE) course in teaching English as a Foreign Language. Many English language schools, however, are more concerned with practical teaching ability than with advanced qualifications and training courses without a classroom practice component are viewed with scepticism. Far Eastern employers and those in Russia and its neighbouring countries still attach the traditional importance to degrees; and some of the communicative teaching methods currently taught to TEFL trainees may be less appropriate in these countries, although the qualifications are often necessary. In Japan, a degree is essential to acquire a visa, however, language schools do not always require TEFL qualifications as well. In many cases school directors are more interested in a bright and enthusiastic personality, and will employ a vibrant, unqualified teacher in preference to a dull and bookish one, regardless of how many letters they have after their name.

The British Council Information Centre (Bridgewater House, 58 Whitworth Street, Manchester, M1 6BB; ☎0161-957 7755; fax 0161-957 7762; e-mail general.enquiries@ britishcouncil.org) is the place to find information about embarking on a career as a TEFL teacher. The British Council website also carries information about recruitment procedures and vacancies (www.britishcouncil.org/teacherrecruitment).

Apart from the prospects outlined on the following pages, teaching posts are also featured in the chapters on *Voluntary Work* and *British Government Departments*, and under the separate country chapters.

TRAINING IN THE UNITED STATES, CANADA, AND AUSTRALIA

In the USA most TESL (the American acronym for Teaching English as a Second Language) training is integrated into college degree courses. The most popular postgraduate qualification is the one-year MA in TESOL (Teachers of English to Speakers of Other Languages), which requires a considerable financial investment; alternatively it is also possible to take a BA in Education or TESOL/Applied Linguistics. The one-month RSA/UCLES CELTA qualification (see above) is, however, now gaining popularity and credibility in the United States and there are currently eight Cambridge/RSA centres in the USA.

The most comprehensive listing of TESL courses in the USA is the *Directory of Teacher Education Programs in TESOL in the United States and Canada*. The current edition costs US$39.95 plus p&p, and is available from *TESOL* (700 South Washington Street, Suite 200, Alexandria, Virginia 22314, USA; ☎+1 703 836 0774; fax +1 703 836 7864; e-mail info@tesol.org; www.tesol.org). In Australia, ACTA (Australian Council of TESOL Associations) can help with finding courses and work. ACTA has offices throughout Australia; their website can be found at www.tesol.org.au.

TEACHER EXCHANGE SCHEMES AND ASSISTANTSHIPS

The British Council, Bridgewater House 58 Whitworth Street, Manchetser, M1 6BB; ☎0161-957 7755; fax 0161 957 7762; e-mail general.enquiries@britishcouncil.org; www. britishcouncil.org/learning; manages a range of programmes for professional development for teachers, headteachers, and other educational practitioners in primary, secondary, and special schools in the UK.

The Teachers' International Professional Development (TIPD) programme offers international theme-based study visits for teachers (from England) in all subject areas to experience good practice in countries around the world. The Fulbright UK/US Teacher Exchange programme offers UK teachers of all subjects the opportunity to swap places with an American teacher for six weeks, the autumn term, or a full academic year.

Teachers can also apply to spend 1-2 weeks in a school in France, Germany or Spain, either as a part of a group study visit or in an individual capacity on a teacher fellowship or teacher shadowing project. For secondary teachers of modern foreign languages, the British Council administers exchange programmes in France, Germany and Spain, and enables teachers with experience of teaching German to act as group leaders on two-week German Pupil Courses in Germany. Those interested in visiting a partner school overseas can apply to further develop the link by applying for a School Linking Visit.

Together with the National College of School Leadership, British Council has developed the International Placements for Headteachers (IPH) programme, which offers international theme-based study visits for groups of headteachers (from England) to examine and reflect on their own practice in the light of the leadership practices of other principals worldwide. The British Council also administers European Union Socrates education programmes, including Comenius 2.2, Council of Europe in-service training courses, and Arion study visits for teachers, headteachers, and other educational practitioners. For more information see www.britishcouncil.org/learning, or contact the British Council Information Centre (☎0161-957 7755; fax 0161-957 7762; e-mail general.enquiries@britishcouncil.org).

IST Plus, Rosedale House, Rosedale Road, Richmond, Surrey TW9 2SZ; ☎020-8939 9057; fax 020-8332 7858; e-mail info@istplus.com; www.istplus.com, promotes cultural awareness through a wide variety of exciting and life changing work, travel, teaching, and language study programmes. Schemes include teaching English in China and Thailand. American applicants apply to CIEE (Council on International Educational Exchange), Three Copley Place, 3rd Floor, Boston MA 02116, USA; ☎+1617 247 0350; fax +1212 247 2911; e-mail wat@ciee.org; www.ciee.org.

League for the Exchange of Commonwealth Teachers (LECT), 7 Lion Yard, Tremadoc Road, Clapham, London SW4 7NQ; ☎0870-770 2636; fax 0870-770 2637; e-mail info@ lect.org.uk; www.lect.org.uk. LECT supports and promotes a wide range of international professional development programmes for teachers and educators throughout the 54 developed and developing nations of the Commonwealth. UK teachers are invited to join LECT study visits where they can study a particular theme in education, such as *Immersion French teaching* and *Teaching and Learning Strategies*, through visiting schools, and meeting overseas teachers and educational officials during holidays and half-terms. Other programmes include long-term teacher exchange programmes (one year). LECT's newsletters will keep you up-to-date with teacher exchange news.

Office of English Language Programs, US Department of State, SA44, Room 304, 301 4th Street, SW, Washington, DC 20547, USA; ☎+1 202 453 8859; fax +1 202 453 8858; e-mail english@state.gov . Formerly run by the US Information Agency (USIA) and now part of the US Department of State, this office runs a network of overseas field offices based in United States Embassies known as the Public Affairs Section of American Embassies. They promote US culture and are therefore (broadly speaking) the counterpart of the British Council. Select Public Affairs Sections have English Teaching Programs which provide English language instruction as do binational centres (which are locally run). These English Teaching Programs and binational centres are located in about 100 countries, mainly in the developing world. Most teachers for binational centres are hired directly by the centre in question (addresses are listed on the website). The English Language Fellow Program places TEFL/TESL and Applied Linguistics for short term (two to six weeks) assignments abroad. Qualified candidates who want to teach in binational centres should contact the centres directly. Information on applying for the EL Fellow and Specialist programs is on the website.

THE BRITISH COUNCIL

The British Council is one of the largest and most prestigious suppliers of English language teachers to the international community. In addition to recruiting for their own schools, the British Council also acts as a recruiting agency for teaching and educational advisory posts within foreign governments and institutions. Most vacancies are for senior English language positions at all levels of education and require a degree or diploma in education, or a TEFL qualification at Diploma or PGCE level. Teaching experience is always required except for lectureships and assistantships in some less popular destinations. The scope of appointments is international but is concentrated mainly in non English-speaking countries. Contracts are from one to three years and although terms and conditions are not standardised, all teachers employed through London receive their airfares and a baggage allowance.

Further details can be obtained from: Teacher Recruitment Unit, British Council, 10 Spring Gardens, London SW1A 2BN; ☎020-7389 4931; fax 020-7389 4140; e-mail teacher.vacancies@britishcouncil.org; www.britishcouncil.org/teacherrecruitment. The many British Council offices and resource centres around the world (and their notice boards) can be a useful source of vacancies and contacts for private tutors.

INTERNATIONAL BACCALAUREATE ORGANIZATION

The International Baccalaureate Organization (IBO) is a leading non-profit educational foundation working with over 1,800 schools in 124 countries. The IBO works with both state and privately funded schools. The IBO offers three programmes for students aged 3 to 19: Primary Years Programme, Middle Years Programme and Diploma Programme. The three official languages of the IBO are English, French and Spanish.

The IBO website (www.ibo.org) lists job opportunities advertised by its member schools. The IBO also recruits its own specialist staff, as well as subject examiners whose positions are available at certain times of the year (there are two examination sessions per year).

Further details can be obtained from regional offices or schools. Contacts can be found on the IBO website. Applications for IBO staff jobs should be made to International Baccalaureate Organization, Human Resources Department, Peterson House, Malthouse Avenue, Cardiff Gate, Cardiff, Wales CF23 8GL (☎029-2054 7777; fax 029-2054 6062; e-mail recruit@ibo.org).

PRIVATE SCHOOLS

The *Council of International Schools (CIS)*, UK office: European Council of International Schools, 21B Lavant Street, Petersfield, Hampshire GU32 3EL; ☎01730-268244; fax 01730-267914; e-mail ecis@ecis.org; www.ecis.org. CIS is an organisation of more than 570 independent international schools around the world from Japan to the United States. It has associate and affiliate members among other education-related organisations, and assists in staffing member schools. CIS publishes the *International Schools Directory*, providing information on around 960 independent and international schools, which can also be searched on www.cis.org; they also publish a newsletter and the annual *International Schools Journal*, concerned specifically with education in international schools. Applications for positions are welcome from candidates who are suitably qualified and who have a minimum of two years' recent full-time experience in teaching in the age range of 3-18 years. Individual members of CIS can also make use of the Council's placement service, which matches applications to current vacancies, circulating professional dossiers to appropriate schools. Members can also be considered for the twice-yearly London Recruitment Centres, which are attended by school representatives from all over the world. ECIS North American Office is at: 401 E. State Street, Suite 405, Ithaca, New York 14850, USA; ☎+1 607272 6758; fax +1 607 272 5051; e-mail paulamitchell@cois.org. There are also offices in Spain and Australia.

Gabbitas Educational Consultants Ltd., Carrington House,126-130 Regent St, London W1B 5EE; ☎020-7734 0161; fax 020-7437 1764; www.gabbitas.co.uk. Gabbitas supply full time teachers to independent schools in both the UK and overseas. These posts are normally for a minimum of 2 years; they do not recruit TEFL teachers.

International Schools Service, 15 Roszel Road, PO Box 5910, Princeton, New Jersey 08543, USA; ☎+1 609 452 0990; fax +1 609 452 2690; e-mail edustaffing@iss.edu; www.iss.edu, places experienced K-12 teachers in American international schools following an American or IB curriculum. Most of the recruitment meetings are held in January/February/March when interviews are conducted from approximately 200 schools worldwide. Recruitment for unanticipated vacancies takes place in the early summer.

WES World-wide Education Service of CfBT Education Trust, East Devon Business Centre, Heathpark Way, Heathpark, Honiton, Devon EX14 1SF; ☎01404-47301; e-mail wes@wesworldwide.com; www.wesworldwide.com and www.cftb.com, Educational consultancy which recruits fully qualified teachers for full-time posts with British and International schools worldwide. WES maintains a register of qualified teachers and consultants to act as advisers/mentors on overseas projects. As part of the CfTB Education Trust, WES is also associated with major EFL projects in Brunei, Malaysia, Oman, Abu Dhabi and other countries.

LANGUAGE SCHOOLS

TEFL and TESOL teachers are now widely employed in the many language schools around the world, and increasingly in schools and universities. Although methods based on role-plays and communication are widely used (which mean that teaching is usually entirely in English) a knowledge of the country's language, and the experience of learning it, is always an asset and occasionally a requirement. Prospective teachers should be aware of the general principles of classroom management, especially if teaching large groups; and many of the wide range of EFL or ELT textbooks available have a teacher's manual that advises on such practical matters.

As a rule, punctuality, courtesy and a professional appearance will count for a great deal in the world of Teaching English as a Foreign Language. In Japan such professionalism is one of the most desired qualities in a teacher, and may offset any inadequacies in experience or qualification. Many language schools hire native speakers who simply turn up in person at the school, or who are known to someone already teaching there and it is often easier to find work on the spot, than by making applications in advance. Many EFL teachers work freelance or have several jobs, building up a regular clientele. Creative jobsearching is vital in this profession, and once you have a job you should stay alert to future opportunities.

Ideally, prospective teachers should try to arrange employment before departure but as this often means going through a formal and time-consuming process, in many instances a trip to the country concerned may be the most fruitful method of obtaining work. Some international chains of language schools run four-week or eight-week training courses in the UK and other countries, providing a formalised entry route into the profession and such courses have generally become indispensable if you want to pursue a longer-term career or increase your earning power. In some cases, in addition to any qualifications they already hold, teachers are also required to take a short induction course in the school's own particular teaching methods before they start work.

With the enormous demand for English teachers throughout the world, opportunities for EFL teachers wishing to work abroad have never been better. However, the profession is becoming more regulated and numbers entering the field are increasing. The number of English language teachers trained to Certificate level has increased enormously and there is stiff competition for the more prestigious and better-paid jobs. It can be easy to find work but difficult to develop a longer-term career in TEFL.

The weekly *Times Educational Supplement (TES)* carries a strong overseas TEFL vacancies section in its newspaper (available every Friday), as well as at www.tes.co.uk. These jobs generally require qualifications and/or experience. Annual subscriptions to the TES can be purchased either by phone ☎01858-438805 or via the website.

USEFUL ADDRESSES

AEON Corporation, www.aeonet.com, AEON has the largest chain of English conversation schools in Japan with 300 branch schools and 800 foreign teachers. It has five full-time recruiting offices outside Japan including 3 in the US (Los Angeles, New York, Chicago), 1 in Australia (Sydney) and 1 in Canada (Toronto). Group and personal interviews held on a regular basis in the US, Canada, and Australia and 2-3 times a year in London, UK and Auckland, New Zealand. Positions start every month. Rolling deadlines. A Bachelor's degree in any subject and a perfect command of the English language is required. AEON hires new teachers to fill one-year contracts, which are renewable. Teachers work 5 days a week, 29.5 hours. Salary is 255,000 yen per month. They provide a single occupancy apartment furnished to Japanese standards, at a subsidized monthly rent of 42,000 yen. Accident and sickness insurance is also provided. 3 weeks of paid vacation and paid training included. Initial applicants should send resumé and 500-word essay entitled 'Why I Want to Live and Work in Japan.' For up-to-date information regarding recruiting trips and application instructions see the website.

The Boland School T.E.F.L. Training Centre, Stefanikova 1, 60200 Brno, Czech Republic; tel/fax +420 541 241 674; e-mail info@boland-czech.com. www.boland-czech.com; China location: 195 Fengmen Road, Suzhou, Jiangsu province, 215006 China; ☎+86 512 6741 3422; e-mail info@boland-china.com; www.boland-china.com. The Boland School was founded in 1992 and has TEFL teacher training centres in both the Czech Republic and China offering the International TEFL Diploma on a 4 and a half-week residential programme. Courses are held every month, all year round. Job placement service is available to all programme graduates. For details of opportunities check the websites.

ELS Language Centers, Director of Franchise Operations and Curriculum Support, ELS Language Centres, 400 Alexander Park, Princeton, NJ 08540, USA; ☎+1 609-750-3512; fax +1 609-750 3596; e-mail smatson@els.com; www.els.com. ELS has language schools in Australia, Canada, China, Colombia, Egypt, Indonesia, Kuwait, Malaysia, Oman, Panama, Qatar, Saudi Arabia, South Korea, Taiwan, United Arab Emirates and Vietnam. Centres in Australia, Canada, Japan, and Panama generally hire from within the local pool of candidates. Enquiries should be accompanied by your CV and made through direct contact with the country centre. Candidates must have a minimum of a bachelor's degree and a TEFL Certificate and preferably one or two years' experience.

Embassy CES, Recruitment Department, Lorna House, 103 Lorna Road, Hove BN3 3EL; ☎01273-322353; www.embassyces.com. Embassy CES is one of the largest British Council accredited summer school providers in the UK with more than 25 locations in the summer months all over the south of England, Wales, and also in Ireland. They also have year-round language schools for adults in the UK, USA, Australia, New Zealand and Canada. Embassy CES are well-known for their International Teacher Training Institute where potential TEFL teachers can pick up the qualifications they need to begin or continue their EFL careers, such as the Cambridge CELTA and DELTA, available in their centres in Brighton, Cambridge, Hastings in the UK, and in New York in the USA. There are numerous course start dates throughout the year. Most teachers qualifying from the Institute can get a job offer from Embassy CES for work in their summer centres.

inlingua Cheltenham, Teacher Training and Recruitment, Rodney Lodge, Rodney Road, Cheltenham GL50 1HX; ☎01242-250493; fax 01242-250495; e-mail info@ inlingua-cheltenham.co.uk; www.inlingua-cheltenham.co.uk. inlingua runs more than 300 schools on five continents and recruits approximately 200 teachers of English as a Foreign Language each year to work in both inlingua's own, and other, schools abroad. Vacancies occur mainly in Western and Eastern Europe with some positions in Asia. Minimum qualifications are TESOL or CELTA certificates, or the inlingua Introduction to TEFL qualification. A degree is often required.

International House World Organisation (IHWO), London; e-mail worldrecruit@ ihworld.co.uk; www.ihworld.com. IHWO is a network of 135 affiliated schools in more than 40 countries in Europe, Asia, the Middle East, Central and South America. Over the last 50 years it has been providing teacher training and language programmes to people from all over the world. Recruitment Services at IHWO helps to recruit both teachers and senior staff for the affiliate schools overseas. The minimum requirement for teaching posts is CELTA, Trinity TESOL Certificate or IHCTL. Most recruiting is carried out in spring or early summer in preparation for the beginning of the next academic year; however, some posts are available at other times of the year. Contracts in Europe are normally for nine months, while those further afield tend to be for two years. Positions are normally renewable by mutual consent. All schools provide educational support and are well resourced. A transfer system is operated whereby teachers can move from country to country, and solid career routes exist with opportunities to move up within the organisation. For further information on teaching and senior posts abroad visit their website.

Language Link, Teacher Training, 181 Earl's Court Road, London SW5 9RB; ☎020-7370 4755; fax 020-7370 1123; e-mail teachertraining@languagelink.co.uk; www.languagelink.co.uk. A teacher training and recruitment agency that places about 200 qualified (including newly qualified) teachers in its network of affiliated schools in Slovakia, Poland, Russia, Czech Republic, the Ukraine, Vietnam, and China.

Saxoncourt Training & Recruitment, 59 South Molton Street, London W1K 5SN; ☎020-7491 1911; fax 020-7493 3657; e-mail applications@saxoncourt.com; www.saxoncourt.com. Saxoncourt is a specialist EFL recruitment service placing more than 600 English instructors annually for schools in Asia (Japan, Taiwan, China, Vietnam), Western Europe

(Spain, Italy), Eastern Europe (Poland, Russia) and South America (Peru). Candidates must have either CELTA or Trinity College TESOL certificate. Some positions (in Japan, Taiwan and China) provide free TEFL training.

OTHER OPPORTUNITIES

Berlitz (UK) Limited, Lincoln House, 296-302 High Holborn, London WC1 7JH; ☎020-7611 9640; fax 020-7611 9656; www.berlitz.com, holds a list of Berlitz schools around the world.

Christians Abroad, Room 233 Bon Marché Centre, 241-251 Ferndale Road, London SW9 8BJ; ☎0870-770 7990; fax 0870-770 7991; e-mail director@cabroad.org.uk; www.cabroad.org.uk, recruits professional staff and volunteers with Christian commitment for teaching posts, mainly in East and West Africa but also in Asia. Some paid but mostly volunteer posts and opportunities in health and community activities too. Christians Abroad also gives general advice on career and volunteering opportunities through World Service Enquiry (www.wse.org.uk).

The Japanese Embassy, JET Desk, 101-104 Piccadilly, London W1J 7JT; ☎020-7465 6668; e-mail info@jet-uk.org; www.uk.emb-japan.go.jp and www.jet-uk.org. The Japanese Embassy runs the Japan Exchange and Teaching (JET) programme for the Government of Japan. This programme recruits Assistant Language Teachers from Great Britain, Ireland, the USA, Canada, Australia and New Zealand on one to three year contracts in Japan. See the chapter on *Japan* for further information.

Teaching & Projects Abroad, Aldsworth Parade, Goring, Sussex BN12 4TX; ☎01903-708300; fax 01903-501026; e-mail info@teaching-abroad.co.uk; www.teaching-abroad.co.uk, requires teachers to work in Bolivia, Chile, Peru, India, Mongolia, Nepal, Sri Lanka, Mexico, Toga, China, Thailand, Romania, Russia, Ghana, and South Africa. No TEFL or teaching qualifications required. Placements range in length from one month to a year. Teachers must pay to join the programme with food, accommodation, and insurance included. Prices start from £845.

Office of English Language Programs, US Department of State, SA44, Room 304, 301 4th Street, SW, Washington, DC 20547; ☎202-453 8859; fax 202-453 8858; e-mail english@state.gov; http://englishprograms.state.gov, offers programmes overseas through the Public Affairs Section of United States Embassies, known as the Public Affairs Section of American Embassies. They promote US culture and are similar in their remit to the British Council, with many English teaching programmes. A list of programmes is listed on the website. Also see entry under *Teacher Exchange Schemes and Assistantships*.

WorldTeach, c/o Center for International Development, Harvard University, 79 John F. Kennedy Street, Cambridge MA 02138, USA; ☎+1 617 495 5527; fax +1 617 495 1599; e-mail info@worldteach.org; www.worldteach.org. WorldTeach is a private non-profit organisation that sends English-speaking volunteers abroad primarily to teach English. There are programmes in Chile, China, Costa Rica, Ecuador, Guyana, the Marshall Islands, Namibia, Pohnpei, Poland, and South Africa. A fee is paid to cover transportation and other costs; teachers receive a stipend equivalent to local teaching rates. Some programmes are fully funded by their in-country partners.

POSITIONS IN HIGHER EDUCATION

Association of Commonwealth Universities (20-24 Tavistock Square, London WC1H 9HF; ☎020-7380 6700; fax 020-7387 2655; e-mail info@acu.ac.uk; www.acu.ac.uk) advertises academic and some non-teaching posts in a wide range of Commonwealth countries. A twice-monthly publication *Appointments in Commonwealth Universities* lists the latest vacancies and is available free of charge.

SOURCES OF INFORMATION

All the organisations above provide brochures and information on their services. If you want to apply directly to schools abroad, local telephone or business directories are a good starting point and some cultural institutes can provide lists of possible employers. A number of relevant reference sources will be found in the various chapters in the *Worldwide Employment* section.

Those who wish to make direct applications to foreign universities, colleges, schools of art and music, and research institutes will find a very comprehensive listing of addresses and contact names in the *The Europa World of Learning*, published by Routledge (Haines House, 21 John Street, London WC1N 2BP; ☎020-7017-6600; fax 020-7017-6700; e-mail wol@informa.com; www.worldoflearning.com) and available in public reference libraries. Detailed information about universities in all Commonwealth countries is contained in the *Commonwealth Universities Yearbook*, published by the Association of Commonwealth Universities (see above). These books are available for consultation in academic and public reference libraries and in many British Council offices.

JOBS ON THE INTERNET

There are many EFL-related websites on the Internet, with a good number offering jobs or the opportunity to post your CV. Some of the best are:

Axcis, www.axcis.co.uk. Lists international teaching positions.

O-hayo Sensei, www.ohayosensei.com. Free twice-monthly electronic newsletter with over 100 positions of teaching jobs in Japan.

Dave's ESL Cafe, www.eslcafe.com. A well-known site for EFL and ESL teachers and students around the world. Extensive information on all aspects of teaching English.

ESL Jobs Centre, www.jobs.edufind.com. A general English language teaching job website.

EFLWeb, www.eflweb.com. Useful site for prospective EFL/ESL teachers.

Hays, www.hays.com/education. Lists jobs in education across the world.

TeacherNet, www.teachernet.gov.uk. Offers links to other websites with teaching vacancies.

USEFUL PUBLICATIONS

EL Gazette, Unit 3, Constantine Court, 6 Fairclough Street, London E1 1PW; ☎020-7481 6700; fax 020-7488 9240; e-mail info@elgazette.com; www.elgazette.com. This monthly newspaper deals with all aspects of English language teaching and includes country reports, information on training and qualifications, and job advertisements. It is available from specialist language-teaching bookshops or by subscription.

Teaching English Abroad, by Susan Griffith (Vacation Work Publications, 9 Park End Street, Oxford OX1 1HH; www.vacationwork.co.uk) is the indispensable guide to training and working in TEFL around the world. It carries extensive lists of language schools and agencies in many countries.

TESOL Placement E-Bulletin, published by Teachers of English to Speakers of Other Languages, 700 South Washington Street, Suite 200, Alexandria, Virginia 22314, USA; ☎+1 703 836 0774; fax +1 703 836 7864; e-mail info@tesol.org; www.tesol.org. TESOL members may subscribe to the *Placement E-Bulletin* via the website.

Transport and Tourism

Tourism and transport are growth industries throughout the developed world. Many of the jobs described in this chapter will enable you to travel around the world in the course of your career and daily work. However, aspiring globetrotters should be aware that there are also many jobs in the industry that will often require you to be based at home, or in one place, sometimes for extended periods. Not every job in the travel industry is a whirlwind of glamour in exotic locations. If you are employed as an airline pilot or a long-distance driver or in the merchant navy, it is likely that you will not need to relocate abroad and that in fact the time you spend in other lands will be quite limited – or that once you are there you will be too tired to enjoy it. On the other hand, many of the seasonal and permanent staff of international tour operators will spend much of their time abroad. For such employees, working in the tourist industry can be the ideal way to subsidise their own travels and see the world. *Work Your Way Around the World* and *Working in Tourism* (both published by Vacation Work Publications) detail the many opportunities for seasonal and permanent staff across the world in this industry.

THE MERCHANT NAVY

In recent years there has been a steady decline in the British Merchant Navy, nonetheless, there is still a good demand for qualified deck officers, engineers and ratings in the merchant fleet. Furthermore, opportunities in the cruise line industry are booming. Enquiries regarding positions in all types of shipping should be made direct to the individual companies listed in Lloyd's *Register of Ships* (available online) and *Register of International Ship Owning Groups* (Lloyd's Register – Fairplay, Lombard House, 3 Princess Way, Redhill, Surrey RH1 1UP; ☎01737-379000; fax 01737-379001; e-mail info@lrfairplay.com; www.lrfairplay.com). Both of these publications can also be found in reference and business libraries, or ordered online. Addresses are also listed in the *World Shipping Directory*, and in the Yellow Pages (or equivalent) of major seaport areas, usually under *Shipping Companies and Agents*. The *Department for Transport* (www.dft.gov.uk) is involved in the training of Merchant Navy officers, and further details are available from: The Merchant Navy Training Board, Carthusian Court, 12 Carthusian Street, London EC1M 6EZ; ☎020-7417 2800; fax 020-7726 2080; e-mail enquiry@mntb.org.uk; www.mntb.org.

OFFICERS

Junior Deck, Engine-room and Catering Ratings. Pre-sea training takes place at *The National Sea Training Centre*, North West Kent College, Dering Way, Gravesend, Kent DA12 2JJ; ☎01322-629600; fax 01322-629687; www.nwkcollege.ac.uk. Applicants should have a minimum of Maths and English GCSE and must be in good health (including good eyesight). Training usually begins at age 16 with a normal maximum entry age of around 18 years old.

Deck and Engineer Cadets. Officer cadetships involve integrated programmes of college-based education and shipboard training, leading to various National and Higher National awards, as well as the statutory qualifications issued by the Department of Transport. Applicants must apply directly to a shipping company, which will then sponsor them through their studies, usually paying a weekly salary. To be considered, you will need four GCSE passes (or equivalent) including English, Maths and a science subject, or two A Levels (for a shortened cadetship). Again, candidates for the deck department must have excellent eyesight and good physical health. There is an upper age-limit of 22 years on entry. The average cadetship lasts four years, with a leaving qualification of the Class III Certificate. Further progression is possible after a period of practical experience at sea followed by further study. The highest level of qualification is the Class I (Master Mariner) Certificate, or Master's Ticket, usually acquired after around ten years training and experience.

Radio and Electronics Officers. Candidates for these positions must complete a course of training for the GMDSS Certificate at a college affiliated to the Association of Marine Electronic Radio Colleges (AMERC) before engagement. A minimum of six months' experience at sea is needed to validate the Certificate and permit the new officer to operate ships' radio equipment without supervision. Employment opportunities for sea-going radio officers are restricted. Enquiries should be addressed to one of the colleges listed below.

Pursers (including Nurses, Stewards). These administrative and other posts are normally only found on passenger ships. Such posts are keenly sought after and there is no system of on-board traineeships. Applicants will normally have had experience of similar positions on land (for example, in hotel management, accounting or reception work) and are likely, therefore, to be at least 21 years of age. The ability to speak at least one foreign language is desirable, as is a qualification, such as a Higher National Diploma (HND) in a related field.

Adult Entry. Vacancies for adult entrants/re-entrants do occur from time to time, especially for those with specialist skills or with engineering qualifications. Those interested should make enquiries to individual shipping companies.

Information on specialist courses and career opportunities in the Merchant Navy can be obtained from the following colleges:

Blackpool and the Fylde College, School of Maritime Operations, Fleetwood Nautical Campus, Broadwater, Fleetwood, Lancashire FY7 8JZ; ☎01253-779123; fax 01253-773014; e-mail maritime@blackpool.ac.uk; www.blackpool.ac.uk/fosc.

Clyde Marine Recruitment Ltd, Clyde House, 209 Govan Road, Glasgow G51 1HJ; ☎0141-427-5100; fax 0141-427-6878; e-mail recruitment-glasgow@clydemarine.com; www.clydemarine.com. This company has the capacity to place cadets with shipping companies.

Glasgow College of Nautical Studies, Faculty of Maritime Studies, 21 Thistle Street, Glasgow G5 9XB; ☎0141-565 2500; fax 0141-565 2599; e-mail enquiries@gcns.ac.uk; www.glasgow-nautical.ac.uk.

Liverpool John Moores University, Maritime Faculty, Roscoe Court, 4 Rodney Street, Liverpool L1 2TZ; ☎0151-231 5090; fax 0151-231 3462; e-mail recruitment@ljmu.ac.uk; www.livjm.ac.uk.

Lowestoft College, Maritime and Offshore Centre, St Peters Street, Lowestoft, Suffolk NR32 2NB; ☎01502-583521; fax 01502-500031; e-mail courseenquiries@lowestoft.ac.uk; www.lowestoft.ac.uk.

School of Maritime and Coastal Studies, Southampton Institute, East Park Terrace, Southampton, Hampshire SO14 0YN; ☎023-8031 9975; fax 023-8031 9739; e-mail ft.admissions@solent.ac.uk; www.solent.ac.uk/technology/maritime_and_coastal.aspx.

South Tyneside College, Nautical Science Faculty, St. George's Avenue, South Shields, Tyne & Wear NE34 6ET; ☎0191-427 3772; fax 0191-427 3918; www.stc.ac.uk.

Trinity House, Tower Hill, London EC3N 4DH; ☎020-7481 6900; www.trinityhouse.co.uk. Awards scholarships; cadet training scheme.

Warsash Maritime Centre, Newtown Road, Warsash, Southampton, Hampshire, SO31 9ZL; ☎01489-576161; fax 01489-573988; e-mail wmc@solent.ac.uk; www.warsashcentre.co.uk.

In the US, further information can be obtained from:

Great Lakes Maritime Academy, Northwestern Michigan College, 715 East Front Street, Traverse City, Michigan 49686, USA; ☎+1 800 748 0566 ext.1200; e-mail jjohnson@nmc.edu; www. nmc.edu/maritime/.

Maine Maritime Academy, 66 Pleasant Street, Castine, ME 04420; ☎800-464 6565 (in Maine), +1 800 227 8465 (out of Maine); e-mail admissions@mma.edu; www. mainemaritime.edu.

United States Merchant Marine Academy, 300 Steamboat Road, Kings Point, New York NY11024-1699; ☎+1 516 773 5391; fax +1 516 773 5390; www.usmma.edu.

RATINGS

Ratings are technical, engineering and other staff of non-officer rank. In the Merchant Navy low-wage staff from third-world countries often fill these positions. Entry as a junior deck or catering rating is generally restricted to young persons aged 16-17. Able Seaman (AB) certificates are issued to deck ratings who have passed the qualifying exam and complied with regulations regarding periods of service and pre-sea training. Details of the certificates that can be gained by Merchant Navy ratings are given in the relevant Merchant Shipping Notices issued by the Department for Transport (see under *Useful Addresses,* below). Deckhands with company sponsorship normally attend a course at the *National Sea Training College* in Kent (see below), obtaining the Efficient Deck Hand examination (EDH).

Useful Addresses

The *Department for Transport,* Great Minster House, 76 Marsham Street, London SW1P 4DR; ☎020-7944 8300; fax 020-7944 9643; www.dft.gov.uk, issues a wide variety of Merchant Shipping Notices, including regulations regarding examinations, qualifications, periods of service, required for attaining different ranks and information about relevant publications.

Maritime Operations Centre, Warsash Maritime Centre, Southampton Institute, Newtown Road, Warsash, Southampton, Hampshire SO31 9ZL; ☎01489-576161; fax 01489-573988; www.warsashcentre.com, can supply information, training and examination facilities for the GMDSS General Operator Certificate.

The National Sea Training Centre, North West Kent College, Dering Way, Gravesend, Kent DA12 2JJ; ☎01322-629600; fax 01322-629687; www.nwkcollege.ac.uk, can provide further information about recruitment opportunities for ratings. Information is also available from local careers advice services.

PASSENGER AND CRUISE SHIPS

The openings described above are available on both passenger and freight vessels, although promotion will generally be quicker on vessels such as tankers and container ships. There are, additionally, a number of other types of vacancy available on passenger and cruise ships. However, competition for such positions is very keen and there are generally no training schemes (other than those in tourism, hospitality and catering) for this kind of work. Direct application should be made to those shipping companies operating large passenger vessels (lists available in the *Journal of Commerce,* Commonwealth Business Media, 400 Windsor Corporate Center, 50 Millstone Road, Suite 200, East Windsor, NJ08520-1415, USA; ☎+1 973 848 7000; fax +1 609 371 7879; www.joc.com) or to the major cruise lines (Carnival, Princess Cruises, Royal Caribbean, Cunard, Costa, Holland America Line, Norwegian Cruise Line, Regal Cruises, P&O Cruises, and Disney). There are also a number of specialist recruitment agencies, and in many cases shipping companies will refer you to their standard recruiter. *Caterer and Hotelkeeper* magazine (Reed Business Information, Quadrant House, The Quadrant, Sutton, Surrey SM2 5AS;

☎020-8652 3500; www.reedbusiness.com) occasionally advertises vacancies on cruise ships in its appointments section. The following is a guide to some specialist staff areas and their requirements:

Assistant Purser – secretarial, clerical and reception work. Candidates should be 21-30, with GCSEs in English and maths, shorthand at 120 wpm, typing at 55 wpm, and have a pleasant manner.

Children's Host/Hostess – responsible to the purser for children on board (organising games, entertainment). Candidates, aged 25-35, should possess the relevant qualifications and experience for working with children under 12. Some ships also take on Nursery Stewards/Stewardesses, who may be younger but must have an NNEB Certificate or equivalent.

Social Host/Hostess – plays host to passengers, especially the old and lonely, and organises general passenger entertainment. Candidates, aged 26-34, should combine a high educational standard with a sympathetic manner and good organisational ability.

Telephonist – maintains a 24-hour service based on a duty rota. Candidates should be aged 24-35 with professional training and experience. Knowledge of at least one European language is preferred.

Hairdresser – must hold a recognised hairdressing diploma and be fully trained and qualified in styling, beauty culture and manicure. Experience (as with all posts) is an advantage.

Retail Assistant – must have several years retail experience.

Security Officer – responsible for all aspects of security from identity papers to fire and safety regulation enforcement. On high-profile ships, the Chief Security Officer may be from a military background and trained in bomb disposal. Security offers good opportunities for mature applicants with an appropriate career background.

There is a wide range of jobs available on cruise and passenger ships. *Working on Cruise Ships* by Sandra Bow (£10.99; Vacation Work Publications; www.vacationwork.co.uk) is an indispensable guide to the industry and describes such vacancies in detail, as well as providing useful background information. In addition to the positions mentioned above, jobs are also advertised from time to time in the following areas: shore excursion guides; casino staff; professional entertainment (musicians, dancers); sports and fitness instructors; medical and photography.

SOURCES OF JOBS

The following cruise lines and recruitment agencies employ staff in the UK and the USA:

Apollo Ship Chandlers Inc., 1775 NW 70th Avenue, Miami, FL 33126, USA; ☎+1 305 592 8790; fax +1 305 593 8335; e-mail services@apolloships.com; www.apolloships.com.

BlueSeas International Cruise Services Inc., 1033 Tyler Street, Hollywood, Florida 33019, USA. Vacancies registered throughout the hotel department, including beauty salons and gift shops. Their new International Seafarers Exchange (www.jobxchange.com) undertakes to match cruise ship vacancies with qualified staff who pay a membership fee.

Carnival Cruise Lines Inc., 3655 NW. 87th Avenue, Miami, FL 33178, USA; ☎ +1 305 599 2600; fax +1 305 406 4700; www.carnival.com.

Costa Cruise Lines, Venture Corporate Center 11, 200 South Park Road, Suite 200, Hollywood, FL 33021-8541, USA; ☎+1 305 358 7325; fax +1 305 375 0676; e-mail onboard@costa.it, shoreside@costa.it; www.costacruises.com.

CTI Group, 3696 N. Federal Highway, Suite 303, Fort Lauderdale, FL 33308-6262, USA; ☎+1 954 568 5900; fax +1 954 568 5888; e-mail CTI-USA@cti-usa.com; www.cti-usa.com.

Cruise Service Centre, Palme & Associates, 9 Crown Lofts, Marsh Street, Walsall WS2 9LB; ☎01922-722356; e-mail office@cruiseservicecenter.com; www.cruiseservicecenter.com.

Cunard Line (UK), Fleet Personnel Department, Mountbatten House, Grosvenor Square, Southampton, Hampshire SO15 2BF; ☎0845-071 0300; fax 023-8022 5843; www. cunard.com.

Harding Brothers Duty Free, Avonmouth Way, Avonmouth, Bristol BS11 8DD; ☎0117-982 5961; fax 0117-982 7276; e-mail sc@hardingbros.co.uk; www.hardingbrothers.co.uk.

Holland America Line, 300 Elliott Avenue. West Seattle, WA 98119, USA; ☎+1 206 281 3535; fax +1 206 281 7110; www.hollandamerica.com.

International Cruise Management Agency A/S, Jembanetorget 4B, PO Box 95, Sentrum, N-0101 Oslo, Norway; ☎+47 2335 7900; fax +47 2335 7901; e-mail employment@ icma.no; www.icma.no.

Norwegian Cruise Line (NCL), recruit direct through their website www.ncl.com/news/ employment.htm.

Openwide International, 24/26 Arcadia Avenue, Finchley Central, London N3 2JU; ☎020-8349 7195; fax 020-8349 7197; e-mail contact@openwideinternational.com; www.openwideinternational.com. Recruits entertainers and performers to work on cruise ships in the Mediterranean and Caribbean.

P&O Cruises (Head Office), Richmond House, Terminus Terrace, Southampton SO14 3PN; ☎0845-355 5333; fax 023-8065 7030; www.pocruises.com.

Princess Cruises, Fleet Personnel Department, 24844 Avenue Rockefeller, Santa Clarita, CA 91355-4999, USA; www.princess.com. Princess Cruises will only take enquiries through the Internet or by mail.

Royal Caribbean International, Crown & Anchor Society, PO Box 026053, Miami, FL 33102-6053, USA; ☎+1 316 –554 5951; fax +1 305 –373 4394; e-mail crownandanchor@rccl.com; www.royalcaribbean.com.

Seefar Associates, 7 Berkley Crescent, Gravesend, Kent DA12 2AH; ☎01474-329990; fax 01474-329995; e-mail seefarassociates@btclick.com; www.seefarassociates.co.uk. Seefar recruit all grades of shipboard personnel for the world's top cruise lines.

Steiner Leisure (UK office), The Lodge, 92 Uxbridge Road, Harrow Weald, Middlesex HA3 6DQ; ☎020-8909 5016; fax 020-8909 5040; e-mail info@str.co.uk; www.str.co.uk. Recruits hairdressers, beauty therapists, nail technicians, acupunturists and aerobic instructors for their health spas on more than 100 cruise ships around the world.

VIP International, 17 Charing Cross Road, London WC2H 0QW; ☎087-0033 0014; fax 020-7930 2860; e-mail vip@vipinternational.co.uk; www.vipinternational.co.uk.

CIVIL AVIATION

Civil Aviation is an expanding industry that each year offers a growing number of career possibilities. Generally, air traffic controllers, airport staff and other ground crew personnel, with the exception of a few top-flight managers and administrators, are recruited locally and foreign airlines prefer to recruit their own nationals in their home country. Even the developing countries, which in the past have relied on experienced personnel from Britain and the USA, are now training their own staff and becoming more self-reliant. Expertise in management and administration is required by many airlines in former Eastern bloc countries that are currently upgrading their services and systems; specialists in the fields of aircraft maintenance, telecommunications and information technology are also required.

PILOTS

Airline pilots are qualified at the highest level and must undergo years of rigorous (and expensive) training on the ground and in the air. The minimum qualification required in the UK is the Civil Aviation Authority Commercial Pilot's Licence and Instrument Rating; to fly as an airline captain it is necessary to hold the senior CAA professional pilot's licence, the Airline Transport Pilot's Licence. At present only the major British airlines have any form of sponsorship scheme, and many enter the profession after gaining their Wings in military service and serving out their commission.

An applicant for a pilot training scheme with British Airways will require, at a minimum, five GCSEs at Grade 'C' or above (which must include English Language, Mathematics and a Science subject, preferably Physics) as well as two A levels, preferably in Mathematics and Physics. The pilot cadet must be at least 18 years old on entry and a high standard of physical fitness is required. Pilots are subjected to stringent annual medical examinations and can expect to lose their licence if their health falls below the required standard.

There are many schools in the UK that run CAA approved courses (including flight training) for the Airline Transport Pilot's Licence, Commercial Pilot's Licence and Helicopter Instrument Rating. These are:

Bristow Helicopters, Aberdeen Airport, Dyce, Aberdeen AB21 0NT, Scotland; ☎01224-723151; fax 01224-775570; e-mail training@bristow.co.uk; www.bristowgroup.com.

Cabair College of Air Training, Cranfield Airfield, Bedford MK43 0RJ; ☎01234-751243; fax 01234-751363; e-mail keren-caird@cabair.com; www.ccat.org.uk.

Oxford Aviation Training, Oxford Airport, Kidlington, Oxford OX5 1QX; ☎01865-378797; fax 01865-841207; www.oxfordaviation.net.

The BHAB (British Helicopter Advisory Board) www.bhab.org. is a useful website which lists CAA/JAA approved Flight Training Organisations (FTO's) who provide Helicopter licence and Instrument Rating courses.

In addition, *London Metropolitan University* (100, Minories, London EC3N 1JY; ☎020-7320 1757; fax 020-7320 1759; e-mail aviation@londonmet.ac.uk; www.londonmet.ac.uk) offers courses in Civil Aviation Studies (comprising the theoretical components of the various qualifications) at its Centre for Civil Aviation. Their informative website contains details of their programmes as well as general industry information. Aspiring British pilots may be interested to know that the practical component of flight training (the hours spent in the air) is considerably cheaper in the USA and Canada, and that it is possible to undertake the theoretical studies in the UK and complete the flying requirements elsewhere. Further information can be obtained from the *Civil Aviation Authority*, CAA House, 45-59 Kingsway, London WC2B 6TE; ☎020-7379 7311; www.caa.co.uk.

CABIN CREW

The work of air stewards and air stewardesses (or hostesses) is very demanding: during one flight they can expect to fulfil the roles of receptionist, clerk, nurse, waiter, nanny, guide and companion. While experience in any of these occupations is obviously an advantage, a more important qualification is the ability to discharge all these duties while retaining an unruffled appearance and a pleasant humour throughout. Cabin crew increasingly face the phenomenon of air rage and are frequently called upon to restrain and manage disruptive, drunken and violent passengers. Cabin crew require skill, diplomacy and thorough training in order to contain such occupational hazards.

Although applicants are normally required to have reached a GCSE standard of education (and a fluency in at least one foreign language is also preferred), the selection procedure is based far more on the applicant's disposition and ability to converse pleasantly, freely and reassuringly in English. An above average intelligence and general awareness are essential.

Good health is another key factor, and for practical reasons there are also height and weight limitations. An attractive appearance and good grooming is also required. The minimum entry age is 18, but most successful candidates are in their early to mid-twenties.

GENERAL PUBLICATIONS

Leaflets on careers in Civil Aviation can be found in your local careers offices. The Civil Aviation Authority also publishes a number of books and pamphlets, including some that are of interest to prospective air and ground crew members. A catalogue is available from *Documedia*, 37 Windsor Street, Cheltenham, Gloucestershire GL52 2DG; ☎01242-283100; www.documedia.co.uk.

Careers advice is provided by the *Royal Aeronautical Society*, 4 Hamilton Place, London W1J 7BQ; ☎020-7670 4326/325; www.aerosociety.com/careers.

ROAD TRANSPORT

There are opportunities for drivers with HGV licences and several years' experience in the UK to drive vehicles on international routes, mainly within Europe (a few companies operate on routes into Asia and North Africa). Knowledge of foreign languages is obviously helpful although far from essential. Most international road haulage companies prefer to employ drivers for a trial period of several months in Britain before sending them abroad.

Since most only employ a few drivers for their foreign routes, applicants should enquire about prospects for international work with more than one company. A wide variety of companies, both removal and freight, are listed in the Yellow Pages and in other business telephone directories under *Road Haulage*.

If you are employed as an international trucker, or if you are running a haulage firm that operates on international routes, you are advised to obtain the *Guidance Notes – A Guide to Taking Your Lorry Abroad* from the Department for Transport, Logistics Policy Division, Great Minster House, 76 Marsham Street, London SW1P 4DR; ☎020-7944 8300; fax 020-7944 2928.

Business directories and Yellow Pages for listings of employers in the industry can be consulted in public libraries. The website *TruckNet* (www.trucknetuk.com) is a very comprehensive database, containing everything you always wanted to know about trucking but were afraid to ask. As well as a wealth of other information, it contains an online job application service.

Other useful road haulage recruitment websites are at www.truckdriver.com; www.truckersjobbank.com; www.truckinfo.net; and www.layover.com.

TRAVEL AND TOURISM

TOUR OPERATORS

The overseas requirements of conventional tour operators usually involve couriers and representatives posts are mainly seasonal. Recent market trends, however, have seen increasing specialisation in the tourist industry and a growing diversity in the kinds of staff who are needed. Some companies seek guides with specialised skills, knowledge or experience while others need campsite couriers and resort representatives, entertainment or administrative staff and instructors in sports such as skiing, windsurfing, and scuba diving. Tour companies also require coach drivers.

Although coach drivers and couriers work from a home base, reps are based in towns and resorts abroad, and are sometimes recruited locally or selected from among the permanent staff at home. A PSV licence and coach driving experience is essential for aspiring coach drivers. Couriers and reps must have the ability to organise their tour groups, liaise with hotels, and generally be efficient, organised, and able to put people at their ease. Knowledge of the language of the country where you'll be working is obviously advantageous but not always necessary. Often tour companies will arrange short training courses for their reps, which aim to develop these and other skills. Couriers and guides also need to be able to cope with any emergencies that might arise and like resort reps, they need a good knowledge of the area in which they are located.

Recruitment for the summer season usually takes place in the period beginning in the September prior to the next high season, and is usually completed by February. Advertisements for skiing and winter holiday reps and staff begin to appear in the summer, sometimes even earlier – after Easter when the skiing season ends. Many ski companies do not advertise, as plenty of prospective employees can be expected to approach them directly. If you are interested in work of this kind, you should research the market and make your first contact to companies as early as possible. Forward planning (including recruitment and training) is an all-year activity for travel companies, and this means that you should start planning early too. Although the jobs themselves may be short-term, it does not mean you should leave your application to the last minute.

Word of mouth and the techniques of the creative job search are also important in an industry that involves meeting and getting on with people. In many cases networking is the primary source of jobs. Tourism trade fairs can be a productive source of information and will also put you directly in touch with prospective employers. The various national tourist offices are another useful source of information and there is a list of these offices in the UK in the Vacation Work publication *Working in Tourism*. Details can also be found in the Yellow Pages of major cities.

Working in travel and tourism can often provide you with the opportunity to travel abroad, and the work experience gained may often be useful to gaining entry into other areas of the job market. Administration in tourism is a good preparation for administration in other fields, for example. It is now estimated that this global industry employs one in every 15 workers worldwide, directly or indirectly, and it is an increasingly popular career choice. Applying on the spot or in advance from your own country are both options but some previous experience, or at least some of the skills mentioned above, will help. A list of general tour operators who carry out regular (but mostly seasonal) recruitment is given below. More detailed information can be found in the books *Summer Jobs Abroad, Summer Jobs in Britain, Summer Jobs in the USA, Working in Ski Resorts* and *Working in Tourism* (which also has UK, European and US training courses and a guide to some more permanent jobs), all published by Vacation Work Publications. When contacting travel and tour companies, do enclose a large SAE as well as a CV and covering letter.

Canvas Holidays, 12 East Port, Dunfermline, Fife KY12 7JG; ☎01383-629012; fax 01383-629071; e-mail recruitment@vrgcampingrecruitment.co.uk; www. vrgcampingrecruitment.co.uk. Recruits hardworking, enthusiastic, flexible, level-headed individuals for their overseas team to work on one of their campsites across Europe during summer. For further information or to apply for a position call the recruitment team or visit their website.

Club Cantabrica Holidays Ltd., Holiday House,146-148 London Road, St Albans, AL1 1PQ; ☎01727-866177; fax 01727-843766; www.cantabrica.co.uk. Family run travel company operating in Europe for both winter and summer seasons. Summer (May-October) requires hotel staff (managers, receptionists, chefs, general reps) for their Club Hotels in France and Austria. Also require campsite couriers, resort managers, maintenance staff and Kids Klub Reps (NNEB or equivalent) for campsite resorts in Costa Brava, Spain, Southern France and Northern Italy. Winter (December-April) requires hotel and chalet staff for Club Properties - managers, receptionist, bar manager, Kids Klub Reps (NNEB or equivalent), ski explorers and technicians, chefs and general reps. Knowledge of languages in an advantage and customer service experience preferable. Peak season positions are available. Applications via website or by posting CV in an envelope marked 'Recruitment.'

CLUB MED, Recruitment Department, 132 rue Bossuet, 69458 Lyon Cedex 06, France; ☎+33 8453-676767; e-mail recruit.uk@clubmed.com; www.clubmed-jobs.com. Club Méditeranée specialises in all-inclusive holidays. It has 80 Villages in 40 countries and the cruise liner club Med 2. Club Med require qualified and experienced instructors in golf, scuba-diving, sailing, water-skiing, riding and tennis, as well as hosts/hostesses, cashiers, nurses, beauty therapists, playgroup leaders and restaurant, boutique and administrative personnel. Applicants must be aged between 20 and 30, and be fluent in both French and English (for some positions a third language is required); sports instructors must have appropriate instructing qualifications.

Eurocamp and Keycamp, Hartford Manor, Greenbank Lane, Northwich, Cheshire CW8 1HW; ☎01606-787000; www.holidaybreakjobs.com. Eurocamp is a leading camping and mobile home tour operator, recruiting staff for operations in 10 countries throughout Europe on more than 200 campsites. Applicants should be over 18 and have a good working knowledge of a European language. Children's Couriers organise activities for groups of children and must have experience of this kind of work. Telephone (☎01606-787525) and online applications are preferred, from October, with interviews held up to April each year.

Free Radicals (Employment Agency), www.freeradicals.co.uk. Arranges winter jobs in Alpine ski resorts with UK chalet companies. Free Radicals look for a variety of staff to run chalets; managers, chalet cooks, chalet hosts, nannies, and drivers. Winter jobs last from December to April. All applicants must be EU nationals, hardworking, and flexible, with good relevant work experience. Wages are about £300 to £400 a month plus free board, lodging, travel to/from the UK, lift pass, and ski equipment.

Inghams Travel, Gemini House, 10-18 Putney Hill, London SW15 6AX; ☎020-8780 4400; e-mail (for representative and resort managers positions) travel@inghams.com, (for chalet positions) joanne.rolliston@inghams.co.uk; www.inghams.co.uk. Inghams are well known for their Chalet Skiing holidays, but also operate a summer Alps programme popular with an older clientele. In winter they employ around 300 staff for resorts in Switzerland, Austria, Italy, France and Andorra, including hotel managers, chefs, cooks/chalet girls/boys, nannies, and waitresses/chambermaids. Applicants for Rep work must speak French, German, or Italian; chalet staff need cooking qualifications and experience.

Jobs in the Alps (Employment Agency), 17 High Street, Gretton, Northamptonshire NN17 3DE; ☎01536-771150; fax 01536 771914; e-mail enquiries@jobs-in-the-alps.co.uk; www.jobs-in-the-alps.co.uk. Arranges jobs in Alpine resorts in France and Switzerland with locally based hotels and restaurants. Winter jobs last from December to April; summer jobs are generally two to three months including July and August. Applicants must be EU nationals, intelligent, hardworking and responsible, with good French and/or German language skills. Hotel and hospitality experience is preferred but not essential. Wages are approximately £450-£500 per month plus free board and lodging.

Mark Warner Recruitment, George House, 61-65 Kensington Church Street, London W8 4BA; ☎08700-330 750; www.markwarner.co.uk/recruitment. Recruits hotel managers, chefs, kitchen porters, water sports instructors, tennis instructors, ski hosts, chambermaids, waitresses, nannies, bar staff, security staff, handymen, accountants, aerobics instructors, pool attendants, nurses/first aid officers and customer services officers for their summer water sports holidays in Turkey, Greece, and Corsica, Sardinia, Red Sea and Indian Ocean and for their winter ski holidays in France, Austria, and Italy. A seasonal package is provided including return travel, accommodation, all meals, uniform, medical insurance, use of all watersports and activities or ski pass and ski hire.

MyTravel UK, Holiday House, Sandbrook Park, Sandbrook Way, Rochdale, Lancashire OL11 1SA; ☎0870-241 2642; fax 01706-232328; overseasjobs@mytravel.co.uk; www.

mytravelcareers.co.uk. UK tour operator operating under Airtours Holidays, Aspro, Direct Holidays, Panorama, and Manos Holidays. Recruits Overseas Representatives to work long and unsociable hours to ensure a high standard of customer service to clients on holiday in Europe. Applicants must be a minimum of 20 years of age, well groomed, with good communication and administration skills, and able to work on their own initiative. Experience of working in a customer service or sales environment is essential. Children's Representatives are responsible for organising and running daily activities for groups of up to 15 children aged from three to 15 years, as well as guiding evening excursions and accompanying guests to and from the airport. Children's reps must be at least 18 years of age and have both a strong desire to work with children, and relevant experience. Nursery Nurses are responsible for the safety, welfare and enjoyment of the children in the day to day run nurseries. Applicants must be a minimum of 18 years of age with relevant experience and a 3 level CACHE/NNEB, BTEC, NVQ or equivalent qualification. Positions also available for Transfer Representatives and Overseas Administrators.

PGL Travel Ltd, PGL Recruitment Team, Alton Court, Penyard Lane, Ross-on-Wye, Herefordshire HR9 5GL; ☎0870-401 4411; fax 0870-401 4444; e-mail recruitment@pgl. co.uk; www.pgl.co.uk/recruitment. PGL run residential adventure holidays for children in the UK, France, and Spain and require canoe and sailing instructors, group leaders, kitchen, site and store assistants, drivers, and administrative assistants from February to October. More than 2,000 positions available each year.

Skiworld, Overseas Personnel Department, 3 Vencourt Place, London W6 9NU; ☎0870-420 5912; fax 020-8741 1131; e-mail recruitment@skiworld.ltd.uk; www. skiworld.ltd.uk. Recruits overseas staff for the winter season. Vacancies exist in 16 top resorts within France, Switzerland, the USA and Canada. They require resort managers and resort representatives who have relevant language experience, related experience, and good skiing ability; head chefs to run the kitchens of chalet hotels (50-70 covers)and chalet hosts/couples to run their chalets, catering for up to 12 people; and nannies (NNEB or equivalent) to run crèche facilities. All applicants need to have a friendly, outgoing personality and there is a minimum age of 21 years. All staff are given a weekly wage, travel, accommodation, ski equipment and a lift pass will be provided. Applicants need to be available from early December to mid/end April. Check the Skiworld website for application procedure.

Thomson Holidays, a divison of TUI UK Ltd., Wigmore House, Wigmore Place, Luton LU2 9TN; ☎0845-055 0255/8; overseas_careers@Thomson.co.uk; www.thomson.co.uk. Britain's largest tour operator, recruits staff for positions with duties including meeting guests, organising social events and giving advice and information on hotel and resort facilities. Applicants need to be flexible, be over 21 and fluent in English and at least one of the following: Spanish, German, Greek, Italian, French, Portuguese. You must also have at least one year's experience working with the public in a customer service or quality sales role, be in good health and be particularly well-groomed. Salary is paid monthly in the UK, with commission on excursion sales.

Children's representatives are also required, to organise a varied programme of activities for children aged four-11. Applicants should be aged 18-30 and must have a childcare, infant teaching or nursing qualification, with a minimum of six months practical experience working independently with large groups of children. Accommodation, meals and uniform are provided. For all jobs, applicants must have a friendly, outgoing nature, lots of enthusiasm, tact, diplomacy and a strong sense of purpose. Applicants must be available to work from the beginning of April to the end of October and hold a UK or EU passport.

Travelsphere, Human Resources Department, Compass House, Rockingham Road, Market Harborough, Leicestershire LE16 7QD; e-mail human-resources@travelsphere. co.uk; www.travelsphere.co.uk. Travelsphere requires tour managers (aged 20 to 55) to accompany groups of 40-50 people on European tours, giving commentaries on places of interest, and looking after the general well being of the group. Minimum period of work six weeks between April and October; daily wage plus commission on excursions sold, board and accommodation free of charge. Applicants must have a friendly outgoing personality, be hardworking and have a thorough knowledge of a European language, preferably German, Italian, or French. Applications should be sent to the above address from January to March enclosing a full CV and a recent photograph.

Vigvatten Klubb, Apartado 3253, E-01002 Vitoria-Gasteiz, Spain; tel/fax +34 945 281794. Organises camps that run in sessions of two weeks over the summer to help Spanish children and teenagers (aged eight-18) to improve their knowledge of the English language and to provide a balanced programme of leisure activities and adventure holidays. The first language of the camps is English. Monitors, support staff, cooks and nurses are required, and all staff are required to take part in a training programme a few days before the start of each summer camp.

Village Camps, Recruitment Office, 14 rue de la Morâche, 1260 Nyon, Switzerland; ☎+41 22 990 9405; fax +41 22 990 9494; e-mail personnel@villagecamps.ch; www. villagecamps.com. Recruits monitors, counsellors, and medical staff to work for the summer or winter seasons at international children's activity camps in Switzerland, France, Holland, UK and Austria. Applicants must be over 21, possess a working knowledge of a second European language , and have experience in working with children and must hold a basic first aid and CPR certificate.

ONLINE RECRUITMENT

The following websites are a good source of jobs in the tourism and hospitality industry worldwide:

www.traveljobs.com.au: Travel jobs in Australia.

www.nationjob.com/hotel: Jobs in the hospitality, food and travel industries in the USA.

www.jobsinparadise.com: Tips and advice on finding jobs on cruise lines and in ski resorts, hotels and the travel industry generally.

www.jobsonships.com: Recruitment services and seminars for cruise ships, run by Five Star Cruises.

www.escapeartist.com: Detailed information about ways and means of living and working abroad.

www.transitionsabroad.com: Online guide to work, travel and study abroad.

www.wanderlust.co.uk/jobshop: Travel industry recruitment section of *Wanderlust* magazine.

OVERLANDERS AND SPECIALIST OPERATORS

Overland tour companies differ from other tour operators and travel agencies in two main ways, that is, in the places they go and in the way that they do it. Overlanders travel through difficult terrain to reach some of the world's most remote regions, most of which have not yet been developed as destinations for mass tourism. Some companies organise such trips all year round while others operate only in the summer months. Overlanding is not an expedition (an overland tour is promoted and marketed in much the same way as other forms of tourism). It is, however, one kind of special interest tour where the main motivation is adventure and self-discovery rather than 'leisure' travel. Other special interest holidays include health and spa resorts; travel for the disabled; leisure complexes and campsite holidays; senior citizen travel; ski and other sporting holidays (see above); language and youth travel; the cruise industry (see above); cultural tourism; and eco-tourism (see *Agriculture and the Environment*).

In all of these areas the experience and qualifications called for in potential employees will also be of a more specialised nature. A background outside the tourist industry, in everything from sales and marketing to vehicle maintenance, can be an advantage. The type of work involved on overland tours is rigorous and usually all the travellers will be expected to participate and pull their weight in some way. Many tours are run by one leader/driver, who is in charge of route planning, the itinerary, driving, fixing mechanical problems and any other difficulties (of a legal or medical nature, for instance) that may arise on a long-distance trip in unfamiliar surroundings. For insurance purposes, drivers must be aged 25 or over and have an HGV or PCV licence, depending on the type of vehicle used. They also need linguistic, mechanical and organisational abilities. Most companies prefer their drivers to work for two years (or two summers) as a minimum. Training is always given and the first tour of duty might be as an unpaid assistant driver. Some of the less arduous tours are staffed by more than one person, however, a driver, a leader and a cook, is likely to be the outside limit on staff quotas an overland tour.

The list of overland and specialist tour operators given below is by no means exhaustive (the number of companies in this category probably runs into hundreds) but is intended to give an idea of the scope of operations and recruitment policies. Other companies can be found by looking through the advertisements in *Trailfinder*, published three times yearly by Trailfinders (194 Kensington High Street, London W8 7RG; www.trailfinders.com). *TNT* and *Southern Cross* magazines, available free at mainline stations, backpacker hostels and other locations in central London, contain advertisements for some of the main overlander companies in Britain. A useful website giving details of overlanding companies is *The Adventure Directory* (www.adventuredirectory.com). If you have the necessary skills, it is worth noting that it is possible to find work with overland tour operators on the spot. In Africa, almost all the overland companies are usually on the look out for mechanics to work as drivers. Some of the main overland tour companies are:

Contiki Holidays, Wells House, 15 Elmfield Road, Bromley BR1 1LS; ☎020-8290 6777; fax 020-8225 4246; e-mail travel@contiki.co.uk; www.contiki.com. Specialises in coach tours holidays for 18 to 35 year olds throughout Europe, Australia, the USA, New Zealand, and the UK. In Europe, tour managers and drivers are employed on a seasonal basis from March to October. All successful trainees receive thorough training in the form of a seven-week road trip in Europe. Recruitment starts in September for the following year's season. Applicants must hold an EU passport or be able to obtain a valid visa which gives them the legal right to work in the UK.

Explore!, Nelson House, 55 Victoria Road, Farnborough, Hampshire GU14 7PA; ☎01252-379553, fax 01252-379554; e-mail ops@exploreworldwide.com; www. exploreworldwide.com. Recruits annually for leaders for a comprehensive worldwide programme of small group adventure/exploratory holidays. Tour Leaders to work 7 days per week for 3-6 months leading tour groups of 16-24 clients per group, to over 100 countries around the world. Fees start at £25 a day. Full training given. Preference will be given to those who can demonstrate previous travel experience, particularly in the Third World, as well as linguistic ability and experience of working with groups. For some trekking tours, mountain leadership qualifications are essential. Tour leaders are on duty 24/7. You must be available to leave the UK for certain set periods of time. Work is available throughout the year, with the minimum period of work being 3 weeks, although the peak periods of Christmas, summer holidays and Easter are the most popular times. Applications to the above address are accepted all year round and must be on an application form, which can be downloaded from the website.

The Imaginative Traveller, TL Jobs, 1 Betts Avenue, Martlesham Heath, Suffolk IP5 7RH; e-mail tljobs@imtrav.net. Leading adventure travel specialist in the Middle East, Turkey, India, Nepal, China, Europe, Africa, and South-East Asia. The Imaginative Traveller employs tour leaders for small groups who live in various destinations for a minimum of 13 months. No specific skills are required, although the company emphasises sound experience in people management and having the capacity to handle a crisis. Applicants will also need to be knowledgeable about the company's destinations. Successful applicants go through an extensive training period.

Journey Latin America Ltd., 12-13 Heathfield Terrace, Chiswick, London W4 4JE; ☎020-8747 8315; fax 020-8742 1312; www.journeylatinamerica.co.uk. Overland tour operator to South and Central America. The main requirements for tour leaders are a good working knowledge of Spanish or Portuguese, experience of the region, and experience with groups or organising people. Tour leaders do not need to be drivers since transport is organised locally. Journey Latin America cannot offer general advice on employment in Latin America.

Roxtons, 25 High Street, Hungerford, Berks RG17 0NF; ☎01488-683222; fax 01488-682977; e-mail shooting@roxtons.com; www.roxtons.com. Fishing camps in Russia, Norway, Cuba and Iceland; shooting lodges in the UK, Spain, and Africa. Safaris in Africa.

EXPEDITIONS

Taking part in an expedition is one way to travel abroad and gain the experience and understanding that may lead to a job in another country. It may seem misleading to include expeditions in a directory of jobs and careers as almost without exception participation in expeditions involves no financial reward and no employer-employee relationship. But travel experience is important if you are considering living and working abroad, and there are always opportunities in tourism, as in voluntary work, some of which are paid and some for which you pay. These opportunities can be considered to lie somewhere on the fringes of work and education, much like work placements or volunteer work. Taking part in an expedition can be a valuable life experience, but is also good training for some of the jobs covered in this and the following chapters. Many employers who are seeking leadership and planning skills will consider expedition experience an asset.

Below is a list of a few of the organisations that run or sponsor expeditions, as well as some self-help organisations that offer advice, assistance and even financial aid for independent expeditions. Many such organisations have branches affiliated to schools, universities and associations or clubs, and most have a scientific, educational or environmental brief. Paid employment, where available, is generally for science graduates with relevant degrees in geology, biology, or conservation (depending on the expedition), and for photographers and leaders who will also be required to take part. Having a wide range of skills, or a willingness to learn, is a key factor in joining an expedition, as duties such as cooking or driving will often be shared. On school expeditions the staff and leaders will usually include qualified teachers.

It must be emphasised that the organisations below do not offer employment in the conventional sense of the word, but an interchange of ideas and information which will be useful for those thinking of planning or participating in an expedition.

BSES Expeditions, at the Royal Geographical Society, 1 Kensington Gore, London SW7 2AR; ☎020-7591 3141; fax 020-7591 3140; e-mail info@bses.org.uk; www.bses.org.uk. Organises annual expeditions (between 4 and 12 weeks in duration) to arctic, sub-arctic or tropical regions, between July and September. Expeditions of up to 100 people (aged 16-20) from schools and colleges are led by experts in the field from universities, the services and industry – preferably with past expedition experience, and a register of experienced personnel is maintained. Other three-four month expeditions are also mounted for those between school and university. Application forms can be downloaded from the website and should be sent to BSES.

Expedition Advisory Centre, at the Royal Geographical Society, 1 Kensington Gore, London SW7 2AR; ☎020-7591 3030; fax 020-7591 3031; e-mail eac@rgs.org; www. rgs.org. Aims to advise and assist individuals and groups in planning expeditions and fieldwork overseas. The Centre provides information, training, and advice through a range of training seminars and workshops, publications, and information resources. *Explore*, the annual expedition and fieldwork planning seminar, for example, is the starting point for many hundreds of projects. Popular publications include *The Expedition Handbook* and *Expedition Medicine*. For those wanting to join an expedition the centre publishes a *Bulletin of Expedition Vacancies* and a directory of recruiting organisations on its website. Further information is available on www.rgs.org/je/.

Raleigh International, Raleigh House, 27 Parsons Green Lane, London SW6 4HZ; ☎020-7371 8585; fax 020-7371 5116; www.raleigh.org.uk, aims to develop the potential of young people by sending them on environmental and community projects around the world. For more information see the *Voluntary Work* chapter.

WEXAS (World Expeditionary Association), 45-49 Brompton Road, Knightsbridge, London SW3 1DE; ☎020-7589 3315; fax 020-7371 5852; e-mail mship@wexas.com; www.wexas.com. WEXAS provides members with advice and information through *Traveller*, a magazine which is published quarterly. Its website is also a fund of useful information. WEXAS offers financial assistance to selected expeditions through its annual award programme administered by the Royal Geographical Society. Annual membership of WEXAS costs £59 (£72 for couples and families).

USEFUL PUBLICATIONS

ABTA's Guide to Working in Travel, Currently out of print but available in libraries.
Careers in Travel and Tourism, (£7.99; Trotman). Overview of the main career opportunities throughout the industry.
Travel and Hospitality Career Directory by Bradley Morgan, 1993 (Gale). Useful for Americans wishing to work in the US tourist industry.
Working in Tourism by Verité Reily Collins, 3rd edition 2004 (£11.95; Vacation Work Publications, 9 Park End Street, Oxford; www.vacationwork.co.uk).

Hospitality and Catering

The hospitality industry encompasses hotel and restaurant work, institutional catering, (staff canteens, hospitals, schools) and work in tourism. In the UK, it is the second largest employer in the country and there are plenty of career opportunities for hospitality staff to work abroad, especially those who speak a second language. Currently, over ten per cent of the members of the Hotel Catering and Institutional Management Association (HCIMA) work overseas, in more than 90 countries around the world.

Hotel and restaurant work is partly seasonal. Many hotels and restaurants need large numbers of extra workers to look after clients at the height of their tourist seasons, often for as little as a few weeks. Such seasonal workers need not always have previous experience or even knowledge of the local language, although this will help. Such jobs represent just a small part of the picture, however, and a temporary job can easily become a full-time one – most restaurants and hotels need staff all the year round.

Hospitality and catering work can be either short- or long-term and you can begin your job search in your own country, or at your chosen destination. The various travel guides available in all good bookshops and libraries are useful sources of names and addresses of potential employers: those published by *Lonely Planet* and *Rough Guides* are particularly useful in this respect.

If you hope to follow an international career in hospitality, and especially in catering, you will benefit from gaining qualifications, experience and skills, and knowledge of languages (which in part you can acquire through living and working abroad). Although work on cruise ships, in tourist complexes and in the more up-market hotels is now largely limited to qualified and experienced personnel, there are still numerous freelance opportunities in the catering field. These will always require experience but may be had with fewer 'paper' qualifications.

International vacancies are advertised in the trade journal *Caterer and Hotelkeeper* (Reed Business Information, Quadrant House, The Quadrant, Sutton, Surrey SM2 5AS; ☎020-8652 3500; www.reedbusiness.com). It is published weekly on Thursdays and is the best-known journal of the British hospitality trade. It has a large jobs section, including jobs abroad. *The Lady* (39-40 Bedford Street, London, WC2E 9ER; ☎020-7379 4717; fax 020-7497 2137; e-mail editors@lady.co.uk; www.lady.co.uk) is a prime source for catering jobs in private homes and estates around Britain, as well as in ski chalets, on yachts, and in villas abroad. North American readers can also try *Catering Magazine* (GP Publishing, 609 E. Oregon Avenue, Suite #100, Phoenix, AZ 85012, USA; ☎+1 602 265 7778; fax +1 602 265 7771; www.cateringmagazine.com). Published six times a year, this magazine occupies a similar market niche to *Caterer and Hotelkeeper* and is a useful guide to the industry in the USA.

The *Hotel & Catering International Management Association (HCIMA)* (Trinity Court, 34 West Street, Sutton, Surrey SM1 1SH; ☎020-8661 4900; fax 020-8661 4901; e-mail commdept@hcima.co.uk; www.hcima.org.uk) can supply useful brochures on the various career paths in the industry. Their website includes membership information and professional development services.

TRAINING AND QUALIFICATIONS

In Britain, the *Hotel and Catering Training Company* (2nd Floor, South Wing, 26-28 Hammersmith, Grove, London W6 7HT; ☎020-8735 9700; e-mail hctc@hctc.co.uk; www. hctc.co.uk) is the leading industry training provider. They publish a *Careers Guide,* available free of charge, which explains, in detail, the qualifications needed and lists recognised colleges and training centres. Information about advanced qualifications is available from the *Hotel, Catering and Institutional Management Association* (address above).

If you wish to work in Europe you should obtain the booklet *Living, Working, Studying in another EU country: an overview of you EU rights,* available from the Europe Direct website http://europa.eu/int/europedirect/ or by phone ☎00 800 6789 1011. The range of cookery courses available is wide. Most reputable and well-established schools will offer a selection of short certificate courses (up to three months, usually intended for keen amateurs or for those looking for a gap year qualification) through to advanced diploma courses (intended for aspiring professional chefs). The cost of a year-long diploma course is likely to be around £10,000, although this can usually be broken down into term-long unit courses.

One leading school is the *Edinburgh School of Food and Wine,* The Coach House, Newliston, Edinburgh EH29 9EB; ☎0131-333 5001; info@esfw.com; www.esfw.com. Courses for cooks of all levels from basic to 'cordon bleu' standard cookery. Their six-month Diploma in Food and Wine is ideal for those wishing to start a career in the catering industry or embark on a change in career. Of particular interest to chalet cooks is the Certificate Course four-week intensive which is geared towards chalet work. Other courses include the one-Week Survival Certificated Course for those living away from home for the first time, and one-day cookery courses for the enthusiastic amateur. Prices range from £475 (one week to £8,800 (six months). The school is located in an idyllic situation, just 12 miles west of Edinburgh City centre.

In addition to privately owned schools, there are many colleges offering training in hospitality, usually combined with a degree in management. These courses are generally less expensive than those offered by private schools, and lead to nationally recognised qualifications, such as NVQs, BTECs and City and Guilds. A complete list of colleges appears on the *Hotel Catering and Institutional Management Association* website (www. hcima.org.uk).

Another training option is the 'modern apprenticeship' – a system of work-based programmes for chefs and food service staff established in 1998. The apprenticeship provides paid placements combined with college study, and leads to a level 3 NVQ.

INTERNATIONAL WORK EXCHANGE SCHEME

Association for International Practical Training (AIPT), Hospitality/Tourism Exchanges, Suite 250, 10400 Little Patuxent Parkway, Columbia, Maryland 21044, USA; ☎+1 410 997 2200; fax +1 410 992 3924; e-mail aipt@aipt.org; www.aipt.org. AIPT arranges work experience and exchanges abroad for US citizens in the hospitality industry. The training period varies from six to 18 months, and the age limit is from 18 to 35 depending on the country. Countries covered include Austria, Finland, France, Germany, Malaysia, Switzerland, and the UK. Applicants should be either students or graduates in Hotel Management or Culinary Arts and some countries will only accept graduates.

FREELANCE COOKING OPPORTUNITIES

Qualified chefs are sought after and often well rewarded all around the world. Cooking is a highly mobile profession and the opportunities for freelance work are particularly good – with the right training, experience and a little research, the world can be your oyster.

STATELY HOMES AND SHOOTING LODGES

These are two of the staples of the cooking profession in Britain with agencies discreetly fielding work for some of the oldest and most distinguished society names (including royal households). This kind of work is rarely publicly advertised as clients place a premium on their privacy and generally prefer to put such matters into the hands of a reputable agency. Agencies seek chefs who are flexible and reliable, well-presented, articulate, and prepared to put up with occasional eccentricities. In this kind of job, you need to be able to balance your sense of self as a highly trained professional with your clients' sense of you as a servant; the mix is not always an easy one.

If you have no principled objections to hunting for sport, working in hunting, shooting and fishing lodges offers another unique cultural experience. The isolated rural atmosphere can be particularly bracing and the nature of the endeavour means that you have the opportunity to cook with the freshest possible ingredients. Country pursuits of this kind are very expensive for the participants and high standards will be expected at the table.

These opportunities may be of special interest to North American and Australian-trained chefs who are looking for something completely different.

YACHT CHARTERS

There are few opportunities to compare with working on a yacht as it island-hops around the beauty spots of the seven seas. The typical yacht chef is easy-going by nature (and not bothered by the severe limitations of a galley kitchen) with a passion for good food and for the sea. Yachting experience is not usually essential but extensive cooking experience and, increasingly, good qualifications are. If you get as far as an interview for a yacht job, expect to have to cook a test meal before any contract is forthcoming. Wages can be as high as $5,000 per month, with all expenses met, and few crewmembers pay any taxes as they are officially working abroad (except for US citizens, who will pay tax in all circumstances). Most yacht work comes through specialist agencies but some may also be picked up on the spot, using the age-old method of hanging around the docks and marinas.

SKI CHALETS

Chalet work has got itself rather a hooray-Henry image over the years, with many people perceiving it solely as the domain of Sloanes working/playing away during their gap year between school and university. In fact, working as a chalet-girl (or boy) can be demanding and you will need to be a competent cook with some experience and preferably some short-course training, to be successful. Once you have the daily routine down to a tee, however, you can expect to have your share of fun on the slopes. Efficient and experienced chalet hosts get their day's work out of the way by mid-morning and have plenty of time to ski and socialise whilst being paid for the privilege of doing so. Most chalet work is found by approaching ski tour operators directly.

LOCATION CATERING

This is the glamorous end of the industry, with opportunities to work internationally on films, behind the scenes at major music events, or on the Grand Prix circuit. However, be under no illusions – this sector of the market is for the real professionals. The work is extremely arduous, with long hours, incessant travel and high levels of stress, and at all times you will be expected to prepare food to restaurant standards. Agencies are not interested in inexperienced chefs at any level and there is no room for the star-struck. These positions are almost never advertised and chefs interested in breaking into this sector need to show their motivation by seeking out the right people in both the catering and production side of the industry. *Eat to the Beat* is the largest location caterer in the UK, and there are a number of specialist agencies which deal with international sports catering (see below).

RECRUITMENT AGENCIES

A brief selection of the many specialist agencies working in this field is given below.

Abbey Recruitment, 18 James Street, London W1U 3EQ; ☎020-7495 4342; fax 020-7495 4345; e-mail paul@abbeyrecruitment.co.uk; www.abbeyrecruitment.co.uk. Specialist chef and hospitality agency. Permanent positions for chefs (commis to Head Chef) in top class restaurants and hotels; also event, hospitality, corporate, and exhibition work.

Absolute Taste Ltd., 14 Edgel Street, London SW18 1SR; ☎020-8870 5151; fax 020-8970 9191; e-mail info@absolutetaste.com; www.absolutetaste.com. Jobs all over the world for prestigious private and corporate events and also on the Formula One Circuit.

Berkeley Scott Recruitment, Sutherland House, 5-6 Argyll Street, London W1F 7TE; ☎020-7025 1400; fax 020-7025 1442; e-mail pbr.london@bsgplc.com; www.berkeley-scott.co.uk. Offices countrywide, recruiting chefs and employees for the hospitality and leisure market.

Blues Agency, Brighton House, 19 Oxberry Avenue, London SW6 5SP; ☎020-7381 4747; fax 020-7736 8132; e-mail blues@bluesagency.co.uk; www.bluesagency.co.uk. Cooks for short- and long-term summer and winter jobs in private villas, house, chalets. Extensive freelance work available internationally and in the UK. Very high standard of personnel.

Book-a-Cook, Throop House, Throop, Dorchester, Dorset DT2 7JD; ☎01929-471505; fax 01929-472398; e-mail viviaarmitage@ntlworld.com. An Agency that finds cooks to help clients with dinner parties, short breaks and holidays, weekends, holidays and freezers. Contact Mrs Vivienne Armitage.

CIP Recruitment Ltd., 116 Lumley Road, Horley, Surrey RH6 9AB; ☎01293-778000; fax 01293-821825; head.office@ciprecruitment.com; www.ciprecruitment.com. Short- and long-term jobs around the UK, including estates and castles in Scotland.

Eat to the Beat, Studio 4 & 5, Garnet Close, Watford, Hertfordshire WD24 7GN; ☎01923-211703; fax 01923-211704; e-mail catering@eattothebeat.com; www.eattothebeat.com. Leading location catering contractor. Offices in the UK and US.

Hospitality Search International, 8-10 West Bar, Banbury, Oxfordshire OX16 9RR; ☎01295-279696; fax 01295-279697; e-mail recruit@hospitalitysearch.co.uk; www. hospitalitysearch.co.uk. International recruitment for all areas of the hotel and hospitality industry for some of the world's best-known operators.

Leith's List, 21 St. Alban's Grove, London W8 5BP; ☎020-7229 0177; fax 020-7937 5257; e-mail list@leiths.com; www.leiths.com/LeithsList.asp. Employment division of the famous Leith's School of Food and Wine. Placements in the UK and internationally for both private and restaurant chefs.

Letheby and Christopher, Wembley Conference and Exhibition Centre, Empire Way, Wembley HA9 0DW; ☎020-8795 8103; e-mail zena.eastburn@compass-group.co.uk; www.wembley.co.uk. One of the UK's leading sporting, social and corporate caterers for racing, stadiums, the media and large conference and exhibition venues.

Lumley's, Lumley Employment Company, 85 Charlwood Street, London SW1V 4QB; ☎020-7630 0545; fax 020-976 6000; admin@lumleycooks.co.uk; www.lumleyscooks. co.uk. Large database of jobs in Britain, Europe and beyond for cooks, assistants, waitresses, butlers, or a pair of hands. Also has a branch in Scotland (Kingscroft, Jedburgh, Scotland TD8 6SJ; ☎01835-864268) .

Voluntary Work

Voluntary work can be not only highly rewarding in itself, but in many cases can provide valuable work experience abroad. While voluntary work is generally associated with the poorer nations of Africa, Asia and Latin America, there is a great demand for volunteer labour even in developed countries and in regions with transitional economies, such as Eastern Europe and Russia. Volunteers are generally unpaid, but there is in fact a variety of ways in which volunteers are involved with voluntary and charitable organisations. In some cases, the worker pays a contribution to take part in a particular project – and some organisations making this kind of stipulation are themselves more commercial than charitable – while other volunteers are required to raise funds for their charity before participating in a project. There are also many full-time and paid opportunities in fundraising, administration, or development, and it is not unusual for a volunteer to eventually find paid employment within their charitable organisation, or a similar one. Typically, longer-term volunteers receive free board and accommodation and an adequate local salary or allowance.

A volunteer might best be described as someone who works without the primary motive of financial or material gain. Many more enlightened charities and non-governmental organisations (NGOs) see voluntary work as a way to educate and inform the volunteer, as well as a means of assisting the local people they may be helping. These charity or aid projects are about working with people and encouraging autonomy and self-reliance. It is essential that you consider your own motivation and outlook before committing yourself to charitable or voluntary work abroad.

Potential volunteers should be sceptical of those voluntary organisations that charge an excessive fee or on-charge another organisation for their (your) services. Organisations of this type do exist, and are not dissimilar to employment agencies. Nonetheless, if you are aware of their method of doing business, and are prepared to participate in it, for many volunteers who wish to work overseas they still offer a useful service.

This chapter caters not only for volunteers driven by altruistic, missionary or humanitarian zeal, but also for those who seek to broaden their experience and cultural awareness in order to benefit their future life and career.

The Developing World

Attitudes to development have changed radically over recent years. The emphasis of international aid programmes has shifted towards assisting developing countries to help themselves through the provision of expert guidance, rather than through the supply of voluntary labour (which itself may be in plentiful supply in that country). Developing countries, as a general rule, need expertise and education, and may not welcome volunteers who work without reference to local communities, and to their own assessment of their needs. Particular importance is now attached to appropriate technologies that can be operated and maintained in the country concerned, as well as to the protection of the environment, and to economic development that will benefit the whole community. The demand in the voluntary sector is, therefore, essentially for skilled professionals, especially in the fields of administration, agriculture, education, engineering, finance and medicine. Volunteers are usually recruited for at least a year (with the exception of short-term emergency relief). Longer contract periods give volunteers time to acclimatise to their new physical and cultural environment, thereby enabling them to make a more meaningful contribution than they might on a short-term placement. It is, of course, also more cost-effective for the charities to employ volunteer staff who are prepared to work for longer periods in the field, reducing resettlement costs.

It must be emphasised that in the developing world, most voluntary or professional work requires the training, qualifications or skills in demand in the country concerned. Even then, the selection process can be rigorous, with no guarantee of a job. There are other obstacles, too, not the least of which is getting a work permit, as well as restrictions on foreign workers (which are imposed by many governments even in areas where skilled workers are desperately needed). However, once accepted as a volunteer by a reputable charitable organisation you can expect, at the very least, assistance with such practicalities.

Recruitment is mainly carried out by organisations based in Europe and North America, classified here under the two broad categories of 'religious' and 'secular'.

CHRISTIAN ORGANISATIONS AND CHARITIES

There are hundreds of denominational missionary societies in the UK and many more in the United States; so a complete listing is not possible in this chapter. A useful guide to Christian and other volunteering, *Opportunities Abroad*, is published by *World Service Enquiry* (see below). This publication lists agencies and organisations (both religious and secular) involved in development and volunteer work, as well as summer placements and exchanges.

A selection of the larger recruiters of volunteers and other personnel in the fields of agriculture, engineering, education and medicine are listed below. Although membership of the religious denomination in question is not always specified, applicants with a Christian background are generally preferred and you will be required to have a positive attitude towards the ethos of the organisation in question. Regions and countries in which these organisations and societies operate vary but most work primarily in Africa and Asia, although British charities also have strong links with come of the Commonwealth countries.

Associate Missionaries of the Assumption, 11 Old English Road Worcester, MA 01609, USA; ☎+1 508 767 1356; e-mail ama-usa@juno.com; www.assumption.edu. Projects in Europe, Africa, the Americas, and Asia and requires 15 volunteers a year. Applicants must be single Catholics aged 22 and older, with a college degree, who speak the local language. Benefits include room, board, stipend, and health insurance in some cases. Volunteers pay their own travel and visa expenses.

Catholic Medical Mission Board (CMMB), 10 West 17th Street, New York, NY 10011-5765, USA; ☎+1 212 242 7757; fax +1 212 807 9161; e-mail info@cmmb.org; www. cmmb.org. The Medical Volunteer Program of the CMMB facilitates the placement of health care volunteers in independent medical missions in Latin America, the Caribbean, Africa, the Middle East and Asia. Each mission/country has its own requirements, however, most prefer one or more years' service commitment. There are a limited number of short-term (one week to three months) opportunities. Missions provide room and board, medical and evacuation insurance and life insurance, For long-term volunteers assistance is also provided for travel, visas and medical licences. Applicants should fill in the preliminary application available form from the website, fax it to +1 212 242 0930 or send it to Rosemary DeCostanzo at the above address.

Catholic Network of Volunteer Service, 6930 Carroll Avenue, Suite 506, Takoma Park, MD20912, USA; ☎+1 301 270 0900; fax +1 301 270 0901; e-mail cnvsinfo@ cnvs.org; www.cnvs.org, is the national network for more than 200 voluntary lay mission programmes. They publish a free directory of volunteer opportunities, short and long-term, domestic and international, called *Response* (available online).

Church Mission Society, Partnership House, 157 Waterloo Road, London SE1 8UU; ☎020-7928 8681; fax 020-7401 3215; e-mail info@cms-uk.org; www.cms-uk.org. Offers opportunities to qualified and experienced people in a range of areas, including medical and pastoral, in partnership with churches in Europe, Middle East, Africa and Asia. Mission Partner openings are for a minimum of three years. Overseas Experience Placements are available for those aged over 21. These individual placements provide opportunities for young people to gain experience of the Church in a different culture. Placements are self-financing and vary in length from six months to two years.

Church of Scotland, Board of World Mission, 121 George Street, Edinburgh EH2 4YN; ☎0131-225 5722; www.churchofscotland.org.uk. Places professionals with a Christian outlook, including accountants, agriculturalists, ministers, teachers, technical staff and all kinds of medical and paramedical staff in Africa and Asia, usually for a minimum of four years.

Council for World Mission, Ipalo House, 32-34 Great Peter Street, London SW1P 2DB; ☎020-7222 4214; fax 020-7233 1747; e-mail council@cwmission.org.uk; www. cwmission.org.uk. An international organisation serving different churches which recruit Missionaries for specialised ministries, teaching, medical and administrative work in Zambia, Papua New Guinea, Samoa, Kiribati, Taiwan, and many other countries. Offers of service should be made through the member churches in the United Kingdom: the Congregational Federation; the Presbyterian Church of Wales; the Union of Welsh Independents and the United Reformed Church in the UK.

Methodist Church in Britain, Methodist Church House, 25 Marylebone Road, London NW1 5JR; ☎020-7486 5502; fax 020-7467 5283; e-mail WCO.Personnel@methodistchurch. org.uk; www.methodist.org.uk. Sends Christians who are professionally qualified and experienced teachers, doctors, midwives, nursing tutors, accountants, and others to work at the invitation of partner churches in Africa, Asia, Latin America, the Pacific, and Europe. Secondments usually last three years and are renewable.

Volunteer opportunities in the UK: QVA organises summer volunteer projects lasting two to four weeks in Britain and Northern Ireland. Typical projects include play schemes and work with people with mental and physical disabilities, manual projects such as decorating homeless shelters, youth work, community arts projects, and more. The minimum age for volunteers is 18 years; volunteers with disabilities are welcome to apply. No special skills or qualifications are needed, but motivation, enthusiasm and commitment are.

Volunteer opportunities in other countries: QVA's projects abroad are similar in scope and are arranged through exchange agreements with volunteer organisations abroad, including Eastern Europe, Turkey, and the USA. Projects run in the summer months and last from one to four weeks. The minimum age is 18. Simple food and accommodation are provided on all projects but volunteers pay a registration fee of between £45 and £80, depending on location and ability to pay. Applicants outside the UK should apply through organisations in their own country.

Short Term Experience Projects (Step) Latin Link, 175 Tower Bridge Road, London SE1 2AB; ☎020-7939 9000; fax 020-7939 9015; info@latinlink.org; www.stepteams.org, sends around 150 young Christians to help with community-based tasks in support of the Latin American Church in Brazil, Peru, Bolivia, Argentina, Ecuador, Mexico, and Cuba, and also Spain and Portugal. Tasks are varied and periods of work range from three weeks to six months. Specific skills are not necessary. Applicants should over 17 and committed Christians. Those aged 35 and above can take part in Step 35 plus Teams projects, which last for three to four weeks during August.Travel expenses are not paid.

WEC International, Bulstrode, Oxford Road, Gerrards Cross, Bucks SL9 8SZ; ☎01753-278103; fax 01753-278166; e-mail info@uk.wec-int.org; www.wec-int.org.uk. Founded in 1913, WEC has more than 1,800 full-time workers of varying ages and qualifications and of 48 different nationalities. Their aim is to create fellowships of local believers who would meet together in cities, towns and villages. They offer both long and short term vacancies worldwide for people with all kinds of skills and abilities. Salaries are not paid; workers share in the offerings of supporters of sending bases around the world. In addition to evangelical work, there are special ministries, such as medical, educational, and rural development programmes where this is deemed to advance the primary objective of evangelisation. More information is available on their website, via e-mail of phonecall.

World Exchange, St. Colm's International House, 23 Inverleith Terrace, Edinburgh EH3 5NS; ☎0131-315 4444; e-mail we@stcolms.org; www.worldexchange.org.uk recruits around 25 volunteers a year for the Scottish churches and from the United Reformed Church across the UK. Projects last from 4 weeks to 12 months.

World Service Enquiry, 237 Bon Marché Centre, 241-251 Ferndale Road, London SW9 8BJ; ☎0870-770 3274; fax 0870-770 7991; e-mail wse@wse.org.uk; www.wse.org. uk, has a number of services for people wanting to work or volunteer in international development, including a *Guide to Volunteering for Development* (free on the website), the monthly *Opportunities Abroad* job magazine from about 40 voluntary and development agencies, and career guidance through an on-line coaching service *Evolve,* and face-to-face interviews. Practical help is offered to people volunteering and working overseas (from briefings to travel insurance). World Service Enquiry is the information and advice arm of Christians Abroad.

NON-DENOMINATIONAL CHRISTIAN ORGANISATIONS

The following societies are non-denominational, but they recruit mainly for overseas churches and Christian institutions and therefore prefer applicants with a Christian background.

Eirene, International Christian Service for Peace, Engerser Strasse 81, 56564 Neuwied, Germany; ☎+49 2631 83790; e-mail eirene-int@eirene.org; www.eirene.org. Organises programmes in Nicaragua, Niger and Chad, as well as in Europe and the USA. Thirty volunteers are required each year, most recruited from Germany. Applicants must know the language of the local country. Costs are paid but volunteers are asked to find a support group to give some financial contribution. The minimum duration of service is one year.

HealthServe, Christian Medical Fellowship, Partnership House, 157 Waterloo Road, London SE1 8XN; ☎020-7928 4694; fax 020-7620 2453; e-mail healthserve@cmf.org. uk; www.healthserve.org. Exists to mobilise healthcare professionals to serve in mission and church-related hospitals overseas. They can advise on student elective training periods, and overseas and long-term service, but do not recruit. Overseas opportunities are regularly updated on the website.

Tearfund, 100 Church Road, Teddington, Middlesex TW11 8QE; ☎020-8977 9144; fax 020-8943 3594; e-mail enquiry@tearfund.org; www.tearfund.org. An evangelical Christian relief and development agency which provides personnel and other assistance to churches and Christian groups throughout the developing world. Skilled and experienced personnel are needed for community development programmes, mainly in the following areas: doctors, nurses, midwives, community health advisors, physiotherapists, agriculturalists, technical trainers, programme managers and community development advisors. Appointments are generally for two years. For further details contact the Overseas Service Advisor. Volunteering opportunities for young people are also available: *Transform* is Tearfund's short-term volunteer programme which offers placements in the UK and overseas for 4-6 weeks from early July to the end of August, in teams of 8-12 people. Assignments include practical work, renovation and work with children. Applicants should be over 18 and committed Christians. Details are available from the Enquiry Unit (☎020-8943 7777; e-mail transform@tearfund.org; http://youth.tearfund.org/transform) and applications should be received by mid-February. Tearfund's *Year Team* offers full-time volunteering opportunities (from September to August). Applicants should be aged between 20 and 30. Volunteers spend two days a week working as a regional and student coordinator, two days working in a local church or community project and one day a week studying. More information can be found on http://youth.tearfund.org/students/uk+year+team/ (☎020-8943 7859; e-mail yearteam@tearfund.org).

OTHER ORGANISATIONS

ATD Fourth World, 48 Addington Square, London SE5 7LB; ☎020-7703 3231; e-mail atd@atd-uk.org; www.atd-uk.org. An international organisation working in Europe, the USA, Canada, Asia, Africa and Central America, which is involved in long-term projects working with the most disadvantaged. Practical projects show 'the will and the capacity of the very poorest individuals and families to fulfil their roles as parents and citizens'. International volunteers undergo a three-month training programme in London. The induction programme is free and accommodation is provided. Participants live at the UK National Centre. The minimum age is 18. Good health and references are required, as is the ability to work in a team and enthusiasm for working with the poorest most excluded members of society otherwise no specific qualifications are needed. For more information, and details of introductory weekends and summer camps in the UK, contact the above address. For summer camps in Europe check www.atd-fourthworld.org.

Bharat Sevak Samaj (BSS), Nehru Seva Kendra, Gurgoan Bypass Road, Mehrauli, New Delhi, India; ☎+91 11 657 609. The Samaj was founded by Shri Jawaharlal Nehru, the first Prime Minister of India, as a non-political national platform for mobilising people to assist in national reconstruction. It has a network of branches all over India, with around 10,000 members working on projects at any one time. It takes around 50 foreign volunteers every year. The normal programme of the Samaj includes the organisation of urban community centres in slum areas, night shelters, child welfare centres and nursery schools. Both skilled and unskilled workers are welcome. Foreign volunteers can serve from between 15 days and three months, and should be prepared to live in simple accommodation and respect local customs and traditions. They must finance their own stay, and it is preferred that they speak English. Applicants should contact the General Secretary at the above address, enclosing international reply coupons.

British Executive Service Overseas (BESO), 317 Putney Bridge Road, London SW15 2PN; ☎020-8780 7200; e-mail enquiry@vso.org.uk; www.beso.org, recruits retired volunteer business executives with professional, technical or specialised management skills to advise on projects overseas. Short-term placements on an expenses only basis.Volunteer jobs are also available for qualified and experienced professionals, aged between 20 and 75.

British Red Cross Society (BRCS), 44 Moorfields, London EC2Y 9AL; ☎020-7877 7477; fax 020-7562 2000; e-mail information@redcross.org.uk; www.redcross.org.uk. Keeps a register of doctors, nurses, administrators, mechanics, engineers, agriculturalists, programme managers, telecommunications specialists, development advisers and others with relevant professional experience who are willing to go abroad on short-term assignments to assist victims of disasters. Longer-term development projects are occasionally undertaken. Age 25+; airfares and allowances are provided.

Comhlamh Volunteering Options, Comhlámh, 10 Upper Camden Street, Dublin 2, Ireland; ☎+353 1 478 3490; fax +353 1 478 3738; e-mail info@volunteeringoptions. org; www.volunteeringoptions.org. Part of the programme set up by Irish Government and funded by Irish Aid, the state programme of assistance to developing countries. The Volunteering Options offers support to volunteers in both short and long-term projects. Its database contains information on over 100 organisations which offer volunteer placements overseas (Africa, Asia, Europe and Latin America). It publishes *Working for a Better World*, a guide to volunteering in global development, which can be purchased on the website or ordered by phone (☎+353 1 478 3490).

CUSO, 500 – 2255 Carling Avenue, Ottawa, ON K2B 1A6, Canada; (☎613-829-

7445; fax 613-829-7996; e-mail info@cuso.ca; www.cuso.org. A non-profit organisation committed to social justice around the globe. CUSO shares specific skills through the placement of Canadian volunteers overseas. It also provides funds for locally-controlled development projects and programmes, promotes awareness of the developing world, and helps forge links between similar groups with common concerns in Canada and overseas. Volunteers are expected to provide specialised technical assistance and administrative and organisational support. The annual intake of volunteers is about 200 and contracts are for two years. Applicants must be Canadian citizens or landed immigrants. Experience and/or qualifications are always required.

Experiment in International Living (EIL), 287 Worcester Road, Malvern, Worcs., WR14 1AB; ☎01684-562577; fax 01684-562212; e-mail info@eiluk.org; www.eiluk.org. Primarily a cultural organisation, EIL also runs an au pair homestay programme that offers 12-month placements with two weeks' paid vacation included.

Global Volunteers, 375 East Little Canada Road, St. Paul, MN 55117-1628, USA; ☎+1 800 487 1074; fax +1 651 482 0915; e-mail email@globalvolunteers.org; www. globalvolunteers.org, offers international volunteer programmes, which include nurturing orphaned or abused children, teaching conversational English, helping to construct new schools, providing direct patient healthcare and helping to develop a community to self-sufficiency, allowing you to experience another culture as locals. Typical programmes are one to three weeks (with extended stays up to 43 weeks available at some sites). Discounts available for students, families and groups. No special skills are required. Global Volunteers has more than 250 scheduled teams annually working in more than 100 host communities across the world. Inquiries for additional information may be submitted through their website.

The *Institute of Cultural Affairs UK (ICA UK)*, Voluntary Service Programme Co-ordinator, PO Box 171, Manchester M15 5BE; ☎0845-450 0305; e-mail ica@ica-uk.org. uk; www.icaworld.org.uk, is a registered charity involved with community development projects and training programmes in many countries worldwide. Volunteers may be taken through the volunteer programme of ICA in The Netherlands (www.icanederland.nl) for a minimum of six months. No specific requirements are necessary.

Institute for International Cooperation and Development, PO Box 520, Williamstown MA 01267, USA; ☎+1 413 441 5126; fax +1 413 458 3323; e-mail info@iicd-volunteer. org; www.iicd-volunteer.org. Volunteers take part in development and community work in Africa, Central America and Brazil. The projects last between 6 and 20 months, including the training. The programme fee covers food, accommodation, transportation, training costs, international travel, travel vaccinations and health insurance. Non-American applicants need B1/B2 visa.

International Medical Corps, 1919 Santa Monica Boulevard, Suite 300, Santa Monica, CA 90404, USA; ☎+1 310 826 7800; fax +1 310 442 6622; e-mail imc@imcworldwide. org; www.imcworldwide.org. A private, non-profit, humanitarian organisation which provides health care and training to devastated areas worldwide, often where few other relief organisations operate. The philosophy is not to help people merely with a handout, but to give them the knowledge to rebuild their lives and healthcare systems. Qualified applicants should send a résumé indicating international experience and foreign language skills.

Peace Corps, 1111 20th Street NW, Washington DC 20526, USA; ☎+1 800 425 8580; www.peacecorps.gov. Is the official agency for the US government which sends some 150,000 US citizens each year to work on two-year assignments in Africa, Asia and Latin America. Most opportunities arise in the following areas: teaching, health and nutrition, energy projects, forestry and fisheries, water sanitation, vocational skills and agriculture.

Project Trust, The Hebridean Centre, Isle of Coll, Scotland PA78 6TE; ☎01879-230444; fax 01879-230357; e-mail info@projecttrust.org.uk; www.projecttrust.org.uk. Sends around 200 GAP year school leavers each year on one-year voluntary placements overseas. Volunteers must be aged between 17 and 19 and hold an EU citizenship. Environmental, social service, or teaching projects take place throughout the world, and volunteers must raise £4,190, which covers nearly all costs of a year overseas.

Save the Children, 1 St John's Lane, London EC1M 4AR; ☎020-7012 6400; fax 020-7012 6963; www.savethechildren.org.uk, is the UK's largest international voluntary agency concerned with child health and welfare. The principal emphasis of overseas work is on long-term programmes concerned with health, nutrition, community development, and welfare; and recruitment is generally within each country (where there is some scope for volunteers). In addition, there are paid posts for qualified and experienced project co-ordinators, medical officers, nurses, midwives, tutors, health visitors, nutritionists, engineers, social workers, disability specialists, and others.

Skillshare International, 126 New Walk Street, Leicester LE1 7JA; ☎0116-254 1862; fax 0116-254 2614; e-mail recruitment@skillshare.org; www.skillshare.org. recruits professionals to share their skills and experience with local communities for further economic and social development in Botswana, Kenya, Lesotho, Mozambique, Namibia, South Africa, Swaziland, Tanzanaia, Uganda, India and Nepal. It is committed to the promotion of self-reliance and so volunteers are placed only where there is a real need for outside help and where the transfer of skills accords with the ideas and ideals of the people of Africa and Asia. Projects cover a wide range of activities and general management, agricultural, technical, educational and medical skills are all required. Applicants should be aged over 21, have relevant qualifications and experience, particularly in training others. Placements are usually for two years. Skillshare offers a modest living allowance, flights/travel to the placement and return, medical cover, pre and post placement grants to assist with relocation. The living allowance is adequate to cover your living costs whilst in the country of placement but not adequate for savings or meeting other costs you may have in your country of residence. An information pack is available from the above address.

SPW (Students Partnership Worldwide), 2nd Floor, Faith House, 7 Tufton Street, London, SW1P 3QB; ☎020-7222 0138; fax 020-7233 0088; e-mail info@spw.org; www.spw.org. Placements available on Health Education and Community Resource Programmes for 4-11 months in Nepal, India, Uganda, South Africa, Zambia, and Tanzania. International volunteers aged 18-28 live and work in partnership with young African and Asian volunteers, sharing knowledge, experience, and ideas to support rural communities in their response to health and environmental issues that affect their lives. Volunteer also have a minimum funraising target of £3600. All costs associated with the programme are covered (include flights, visa, insurance, accommodation and training).

Teaching & Projects Abroad, Aldsworth Parade, Goring, Rustington, West Sussex BN12 4TX; ☎01903-708300; fax 01903-501026; e-mail info@projects-abroad.co.uk; www. projects-abroad.co.uk, offers opportunities in teaching, care & community, medicine, journalism/media, conservation, veterinary medicine, archaeology, sport, business, law and nomad projects in various countries including Argentina, Bolivia, Cambodia, China, India, Mexico, Moldova, Mongolia, Nepal, Peru, Romania, Senegal, South Africa, Sri Lanka, Swaziland and Thailand. Summer and long-term work (for up to a year) available. Volunteers pay for their participation in the scheme, with a package, including comfortable accommodation, insurance and food, travel can be arranged, starting at around £895.

United Nations Volunteers (UNV), Postfach 260 111, D-53153 Bonn, Germany; ☎+49 228 815 2000; fax +49 228 815 2001; e-mail information@unvolunteers.org; www. unvolunteers.org. Is 40 years old and recruits highly qualified and experienced volunteers from all UN countries to work in 140 countries for UN-sponsored development projects (average length of initial assignments two years, renewable) and shorter term humanitarian relief work or electoral assistance. Travel to and from the country is provided for volunteers and dependants are authorised to accompany them. A modest monthly allowance is provided at either single or dependency rates, along with a settling in grant. Appropriate academic or trade qualifications in a particular profession are required. The average person has worked in his/her field for 10 years. UK applicants should contact VSO at the address below for an application form. More information on the UN and its agencies is available in the chapter *United Nations*.

Voluntary Service Overseas (VSO), 317 Putney Bridge Road, London SW15 2PN; ☎020-8780 7200; fax 020-8780 7300; e-mail enquiry@vso.org.uk; www.vso.org.uk, an international development charity that works through volunteers. They enable people age 18-75 to share their skills and experience with local communities in the developing world. Placements are offered in a whole range of skill areas including education, business and management, health, natural resources, and technical trades. Around 900 volunteers are sent overseas each year to 34 countries in Africa and Asia.. Flights, health insurance and national insurance contributions, plus grants towards equipment and resettlement are paid. The local employer provides accommodation and a modest living allowance. VSO currently recruits volunteers of any nationality living in the EU, Canada, and the USA. In addition, they are currently running programmes recruiting volunteers from Kenya, Uganda, India and the Philippines.

Projects in the Developed World

WORK CAMPS

Voluntary work in the developed world is as varied as the social and environmental problems such projects serve. Programmes requiring volunteers exist throughout Europe, North America and East Asia (as well as Australasia). Work camps or summer camps, which accept short-term labour and often unskilled help, also provide an opportunity for international volunteering. These are popular with young people interested in working holidays. The work itself is often demanding, involving physical labour in construction or agriculture and general maintenance, cleaning and cooking, or activities with a more social bias (play schemes for deprived or disabled children, hospital work, development work, teaching and environmental protection). Financial arrangements vary considerably. In some cases, volunteers are provided with board, lodging and pocket money; in others, volunteers may have to make a substantial contribution towards costs. Travel expenses are usually (although not always) the responsibility of the volunteer.

Applicants should normally apply for work camps through an organisation's representatives in their own country, however, there are some organisations abroad to which applications must be made direct, and these may suit those who prefer independent travel. An enormous number of associations recruit for work camps at a local or national level in the UK and USA, so only a brief selection has been included here. A creative job search will turn up many more, and some are included under the country headings of the *Worldwide Employment section*. Lists of these organisations will also be found in the publications cited under *Sources of Information* below.

Within Western Europe and North America major efforts have been made to co-ordinate work camp programmes, so volunteers should contact the appropriate body in their own country where possible, or the international head offices abroad. When writing to an organisation which deals with many countries, or one which offers exchange programmes, the applicant should state their preferred destinations and type of work, and include dates of availability and other relevant information (such as childcare qualifications and previous experience).

Those wishing to work in the less developed regions of Eastern European or former CIS countries are advised to check with a work camp organisation in their own country if they are applying direct. Usually this means going through one of the members of *Service Civil International (SCI)* in countries that send volunteers to work camps. These include: *International Voluntary Service (IVS)* in the UK and *SCI-USA* or *Volunteers for Peace (VFP)* in the USA (see below).

American Hiking Society, 1422 Fenwick Lane, Silver Spring, MD 20910, USA; ☎+1 301 565 6704; fax +1 301 565 6714; www.americanhiking.org. Has more than 120 trips annually and they include Alaska, Hawaii, Puerto Rico and the Virgin Islands. Volunteers work on trails conserving a legacy in America's most remote wild places. Also crew leader training opportunities. Volunteers should be over 18 years of age, able to hike five miles in a day, supply all their own backpacking equipment (backpack, tent, sleeping bag, personal items), and pay a registration fee to American Hiking Society upon application. The American Hiking Society also publishes the Hiker's Information Center, an online resource for volunteer opportunities.

Concordia, 19 North Street, Portslade, Brighton BN41 1DH; ☎01273-422218; fax 01273-421182; e-mail info@concordia-iye.org.uk; www.concordia-iye.org.uk, Their International Volunteer Programme offers 16-30 year olds the opportunity to join international teams of volunteers working on short-term projects in more than 50 countries worldwide. Projects can include conservation, restoration, archaeology, construction, the arts, work with people with special needs, children playschemes, and teaching. Volunteers pay their own travel costs and a registration fee of £100. Applicants must be UK citizens.

International Voluntary Service (IVS) Britain, Old Hall, East Bergholt, Colchester CO7 6TQ; ☎01206-298215; e-mail ivssouth@ivs-gb.org.uk; www.ivs-gborg.uk. A peace organisation working for the sustainable development of local and global communities around the world. It runs programmes of international projects consisting of six to 15 volunteers from several countries working and living together for one to four weeks. IVS co-ordinates approximately 30 short-term camps a year in Britain and sends British volunteers to take part in projects in about 50 countries in Europe (west and east), North Africa, and North America plus some 'North/South' programmes in Africa/Asia/Latin America. In some countries the projects take place with branches of SCI (*Service Civil International*), the movement of which IVS is a part. In others, IVS co-operates with other work camp organisations. Most projects last two to three weeks and take place between June and September. A list of summer projects abroad is available from late March. Contact the above address for information. There are also offices in other parts of the UK – details can be obtained from the website. Applicants must be over 18 and pay a registration fee/ membership to IVS and their own costs. The projects are not holidays and the work can be hard and demands commitment.

Involvement Volunteers Association Inc (IVI), PO Box 218, Port Melbourne, Victoria 3207, Australia; ☎+61 3 9646 5504; e-mail ivworldwide@volunteering.org.au; www. volunteering.org.au. IV volunteers from any country can participate as individual volunteers or groups of individual volunteers in Networked International Volunteering Programs, as unpaid participants. The aim of Involvement Volunteering is to enable volunteers to assist non-profit projects related to the natural environment (at farms, national or zoological parks, animal reserves, or historic places) or social service in the community (at homes, camps or schools for disadvantaged people, orphanages, village schools) teaching spoken English. Placements of two to 12 weeks available in Argentina, Australia, Austria, Bangladesh, Botswana, Brazil, Cambodia, China, Ecuador, East Timor, Estonia, Fiji, Finland, France, Ghana, Greece, Guatemala, Guinea-Bissau, Iceland, India, Israel, Italy, Kenya, Korea, Kosovo, Latvia, Lebanon, Lithuania, Mexico, Mongolia, Namibia, Nepal, New Zealand, Palestine, Panama, Peru, Philippines, Poland, Sabah (Malaysia), Samoa, South Africa, Spain, Tanzania, Thailand, Togo, Turkey, UK, Ukraine, USA, Vietnam, and Zambia. Single

Placement Programs or Multiple Placement Programs (as many placements as can be fitted in a 12-month period travelling the world) can provide valuable practical experience related to potential tertiary education, completed degree courses, or completed careers (for early retirees). Some placements have food and accommodation provided while some can cost up to £35 per week for food and accommodation. IV programmes are developed for the individual person to cost from £303 ($437) for one placement, £515 ($743) for two placements and £682 ($983) for three placements, plus any Placement costs that may apply, etc.

SCI International Voluntary Service (SCI-IVS), 5505 Walnut Level Road, Crozet, VA 22932, USA; ☎+1 206 350 6585; e-mail sciinfo@sci-ivs.org; www.sci-ivs.org. Is the US branch of Service Civil International/International Voluntary Service and one of the major co-ordinating centres for US citizens who wish to organise voluntary work in Europe; there are particularly close links with Eastern European organisations. Volunteers for Europe should be aged at least 18 and may be required to speak a foreign language. Volunteers applying to workcamps in Africa, Asia or Latin America need to be at least 21 and speak the language of the chosen country.

UNA Exchange, Temple of Peace and Health, Cathays Park, Cardiff CF10 3AP; ☎029-2022 3088; fax 029-2022 2540; e-mail info@unaexchange.org; www.unaexchange.org. Recruits young people who live in Britain to work for two to three weeks on international voluntary projects run by sister organisations in Europe, the USA, some African countries, South East Asia, Latin America and India. There are also longer-term voluntary projects available.

Volunteers for Peace (VFP), 1034 Tiffany Road, Belmont, Vermont 05730, USA; ☎+1 802 259 2759; fax +1 802 259 2922; e-mail vfp@vfp.org; www.vfp.org. Co-ordinates international work camps in over 100 countries in Europe, North and West Africa, and North and Central America. VFP is strongly represented in the countries of Eastern Europe and the former Soviet Union (the Czech Republic, Slovakia, Poland, Lithuania, Estonia, the Ukraine, Belarus, Hungary, Romania, Bulgaria, Armenia, Slovenia, and Croatia). Work involved includes construction, environmental, agricultural, and social work. There is an emphasis on learning and recreation. Camps last two to three weeks. Minimum age in most cases is 18; upper age limit variable. Volunteers pay travel expenses. Phone, write or check the website for a newsletter and information on available work camps.

Youth Action for Peace UK (YAPUK), PO Box 43670, London SE22 0XX; ☎0870-165 7927; e-mail action@yap-uk.org; www.yap-uk.org. Volunteers needed to take part in voluntary work projects (workcamps) organized by YAP in the UK and its sister organisations in 80 countries in Europe, the Americas, Africa and Asia. The work undertaken may consist of tasks such as restoration, entertaining children in need or environmental, social or artistic work. Projects generally last for two to three weeks each, and take place all year round, but mainly in the summer. There are possibilities of longer term projects (3-12 months). Participants will usually be working for around 30-35 hours a week with volunteers from different countries and local people; food, accommodation and leisure activities are provided. No particular qualifications are necessary, but applicants must normally be aged at least 18. There is an extra fee (in average US$200) payable on arrival for projects taking place in Africa, Asia and Latin America. Volunteers must organise their own travel. For further details, check the website.

KIBBUTZIM AND MOSHAVIM

Kibbutzim are unique to Israel. They began in 1909 as agriculturally based collective villages and today are rural communal settlements whose members share work, income and property. They are essentially communes: the means of production are owned by the community as a whole, and working visitors are expected to participate in the alternative lifestyle. Division of labour is decided according to ability and the division of wealth according to need. Long-term members of a Kibbutz must undergo a trial period of a year, but temporary workers from abroad are accepted and can apply through specialist agencies. Visits should be arranged in advance. Vacancies occur throughout the year although these are more limited in July and August. Visitors are expected to work eight hours a day, six days a week, with a few days' holiday each month. The minimum period of work is usually one month, and board and lodging are provided, together with other allowances.

Moshavim are family-based settlements which, like Kibbutzim, were originally agricultural but are now involved in other work as well. Unlike the Kibbutz, the Moshav allows for private enterprise and members have their own land and property. Volunteers are given accommodation and a small wage by the family for whom they work. Visitors are expected to share in the social and cultural activities of the village, and the wage which volunteers receive, the longer working hours and the greater personal involvement with the family all make life on a Moshav somewhat different to that on a Kibbutz.

Kibbutz Program Center (Volunteer Department, Takam-Artzi, 18 Frishman Str./cr. Ben Yehuda, Tel-Aviv 61030, Israel; ☎+972 3 527 8874; fax +972 3 523 9966; email kpc@volunteer.co.il; www.kibbutz.org.il) represents all Kibbutzim in Israel. KPC can provide information on kibbutz stays, Hebrew-study, cultural and other programmes in the kibbutzim. Participants in programmes serve as kibbutz volunteers, and while resident in the kibbutz are a part of the community, sharing in all its social and material benefits. Volunteers do not choose their work independently, however, no volunteer is forced to stay at a workplace against his or her will. The minimum programme length is two months, the maximum, six months.

ARCHAEOLOGICAL DIGS

Archaeological work is often hard but can be extremely satisfying for those with an interest in the subject, or who are keen to learn. Archaeological digs are generally a rather expensive form of voluntary work, as there are usually significant budgetary restraints on such projects. Fares are seldom paid except to qualified specialists, however, food and accommodation are usually provided on site. Some digs will pay pocket money to volunteers. The minimum stay required is usually two weeks but may be longer. Volunteers are advised to gain some experience on one or two local digs before applying for a position abroad.

Archaeology Abroad, c/o Institute of Archaeology, 31-34 Gordon Square, London WC1H 0PY; tel/fax 020-8537 0849; e-mail arch.abroad@ucl.ac.uk; www.britarch.ac.uk/archabroad/, provides twice yearly bulletins (available by subscription) listing opportunities to join archaeological excavations and field schools outside the UK. Bulletins are published on CD ROM and include fully illustrated feature articles and reports and illustration on wealth of other useful organisations, publications and societies. Subscribers are eligible to apply for Fieldwork Awards to help meet their dig expenses. An annual subscription costs £20 (UK), £22 (Europe), and £24 (worldwide). Cheque with details of address for posting and e-mail address should be sent to the above address. Subscriptions can also be paid securely online at www.britarch.ac/uk/shop.

Information on digs to be carried out in Britain is given in the alternate-monthly *British Archaeology*, available from the *Council for British Archaeology*, St Mary's House, 66 Bootham, York YO30 7BZ; ☎01904-671417; fax 01904-671384; e-mail info@britarch. ac.uk; www.britarch.ac.uk. The CBA is an educational charity working throughout the UK to involve people in archaeology and to promote the appreciation and care of the historic environment for the benefit of present and future generations. The magazine is published six times a year. An annual subscription costs £25 (£19 for the first year); however, it also forms part of an individual membership package which is available for £32 per year and brings extra benefits.In the USA, a list of more than 250 digs worldwide needing volunteers is given in the *Archaeological Fieldwork Opportunities Bulletin* (Archaeological Institute of America, Boston University, 656 Beacon Street, Boston, MA 02215-2006, USA; ☎+1 617 353 9361; e-mail aia@aia.bu.edu; www.archaeological.org) available online.

Archaeology (36-33ʳᵈ Street, Long Island City, New York, NY 11106, USA; ☎+1 718 472 3050; e-mail general@archaeology.org; www.archaeology.org), a richly illustrated magazine covering worldwide archaeology, is available by subscription (US$21.95 a year, ☎+1 815 734 4151; e-mail subscription@archaeology.org).

CONSERVATION

Unpaid and paid work in conservation has become a popular choice for short- and long-term placements in the developing and developed countries. Many of the voluntary organisations listed in the various sections above offer programmes that include in their aims a remit to protect the environment and to conserve habitats and ecosystems. Opportunities exist in such organisations for scientists and others with training in biology, zoology and environmental disciplines, as well as for untrained volunteers (also see the *Agriculture and the Environment* chapter).

BTCV, Conservation Centre, Sedum House, Mallard Way, Potteric Carr, Doncaster DN4 8DB; ☎01302-572244; fax 01302-310167; e-mail information@btcv.org.uk; www.btcv. org.uk, is the country's leading charity protecting the environment through practical action. A network of affiliated offices allows some 130,000 volunteers of all ages and from all sections of the community to train and take part in a wide range of environmental projects, including tree-planting, repairing footpaths and dry stone walls, creating community gardens and involvement with recycling projects. No experience is needed for participation in BTCV's conservation projects – just energy and enthusiasm.

Concordia, 19 North Street, Portslade, Brighton BN41 1DH; ☎01273-422218; fax 01273-421182; e-mail info@concordia-iye.org.uk; www.concordia-iye.org.uk, Their International Volunteer Programme offers 16-30 years oldsthe opportunity to join international teams of volunteers working on short-term projects in over 50 countries worldwide. Projects can include conservation, restoration, archaeology, construction, the arts, work with people with special needs, children playschemes and teaching. Volunteers pay their own travel costs and a registration fee of £110. Applicants must be UK citizens.

Coral Cay Conservation, 40-42 Osnaburgh Street, London NW1 3ND; ☎0870-750 0668; fax 0870-750 0667; e-mail info@coralcay.org; www.coralcay.org. Sends teams of volunteers to assist with tropical forest and coral reef conservation. Volunteers are trained to collect scientific data which is used to help establish marine reserves and wildlife parks. Expeditions depart monthly to Fiji, Trynidad and Tobago, and the Philippines. Costs start from £600 for forest and £700 for marine expeditions. No experience is required as full scientific and scuba training are provided. Qualified staff are also recruited to help manage expeditions.

Earthwatch Institute (Europe), 267 Banbury Road, Oxford OX2 7HT; ☎01865-318838; fax 01865-311383; e-mail info@earthwatch.org.uk; www. earthwatch.org. Earthwatch is an international environmental charity which places conservation volunteers on scientific research expeditions around the world. Eathwatch currently supports 130 expeditions in about 50 countries, from looking at the impacts of climate change in the Arctic, to the protection of cheetah in Namibia. Volunteer field assistants are needed throughout the UK and worldwide. Earthwatch volunteers range in age from 16 to 85 - there is no maximum age limit. No special qualifications are needed and projects vary in length from three days to three weeks. Volunteers' contribution towards the cost of projects varies from £150 to £2,450.

Raleigh International, Raleigh House, 27 Parsons Green Lane, London SW6 4HZ; ☎020-7371 8585; fax 020-7371 5852; e-mail volunteer@raleigh.org.uk; www.raleigh. org.uk. Recruits 17-25 year olds (skilled staff must be over 26) to work on community and conservation programmes abroad. Volunteers must be able to swim but no other special qualifications are required. Candidates are selected during an Assessment Weekend. Past expeditions have included work in Guyana, Belize and Alaska, among others.

LONG-TERM OPPORTUNITIES

Those doing long-term voluntary work are increasingly required to bring specific skills in areas such as project management and training, in addition to the physical fitness, enthusiasm, and a willingness to learn from your hosts, which are the features of all voluntary work abroad. Long-term volunteers will need a greater dedication and willingness to adapt, as well as a realistic idea of their own expectations and objectives. In-depth preparation (which may include learning another language) will also be required (see the chapter *Preparation and Follow-up*). These postings often involve a complete break from a secure job at home. You will have to be prepared to work with others and show self-reliance. Culture shock, and all the practical problems involved in living and working abroad, is also an issue that will need to be faced before your departure.

The International Directory of Voluntary Work (Vacation Work Publications, £11.95) is a comprehensive guide to all aspects of volunteering abroad with many useful contacts.

Organisations offering long-term opportunities include:

Association of Camphill Communities in the UK and Ireland, 55 Cainscross Road, Stroud, Glos. GL5 4EX; ☎01453-753142; fax 01453-767469; e-mail coworker@ camphill.org.uk; www.camphill.org.uk. Runs schools, colleges and adult communities on Rudolf Steiner principles with children, adolescents and adults with learning disabilities in Austria, Brazil, Finland, France, Germany, The Netherlands, Norway, South Africa, Switzerland, and the USA. Volunteers work for a minimum of six months. More details can be obtained from the website.

Brethren Volunteer Service, BVS Recruitment, 1451 Dundee Avenue, Elgin, IL 60120, USA; ☎+1 847 742 5100; fax +1 847 742 0278; e-mail bvs_gb@brethren.org; www. brethrenvolunteerservice.org. Runs a programme, the aims of which include peacemaking, advocating social justice, meeting human needs, and caring for the environment. Volunteers help in many different positions, including community development, social work, children and youth work, and administrative support. Minimum period of work is one year in the USA or two years abroad. The minimum age for applicants is 20; specific requirements may apply to some placements. The more skills an applicant has the better, but none are essential. Applicants need not be Christian but must be motivated by humanitarian concern. Knowledge of a foreign language will improve your chances of a placement.

OTHER SOURCES OF INFORMATION

Catholic Network of Volunteer Service, 6930 Carroll Avenue, Suite 506, Takoma Park, MD 20912, USA; ☎+1 301 270 0900; fax +1 301 270 0901; e-mail cnvsinfo@cnvs.org; www.cnvs.org, is a resource centre for more than 200 faith-based volunteer programmes. It publishes *Response Volunteer Opportunities Directory*, which lists contacts and other useful information about the member programmes and the opportunities they offer. People interested in volunteering can submit their profile online and it will be sent to the affiliated organisations. A free printed copy of *Response* may be ordered via e-mail of by contacting the office directly.

CR Search and Selection, 40 Roseberry Avenue, London EC1R 4RX; ☎020-7833 0770; fax 020-7833 0188; e-mail info@crsearchandselection.com; www.crsearch. co.ukRecruiting mid to senior and board level appointments to the not-for-profit sector for the past 20 years.

Christians Abroad, 233 Bon Marché Centre, 241-251 Ferndale Road, London SW9 8BJ;

☎0870-770 7990; fax 0870-770 7991; e-mail director@cabroad.org.uk; www.cabroad. org.uk. Recruits professional staff and volunteers with Christian commitment for general, medical, and educational opportunities, mainly in sub-Saharan Africa, including some paid posts (such as English teachers in China). Through its *World Service Enquiry* (☎0870-770 3274; www.wse.org.uk) there are a number of services for people of all faiths, or none, including an *Annual Guide to Volunteering for Development* (free on the website), the monthly *Opportunities Abroad* listing vacancies from around 400 voluntary and development agencies, career guidance through an online coaching service *Evolve* (a booklet *Working in Development* to help entry into jobs), and face-to-face interviews. Practical help is offered to people volunteering and working overseas (from briefings to travel insurance).

Commission on Voluntary Service and Action, 1 Union Square West, Suite 902, New York, NY 10003, USA; ☎+1 646 486 2446; e-mail cvsa@bway.net, publishes the excellent *Invest Yourself – A Guide to Action* catalogue which provides a comprehensive list of openings (full-time, long-term and short-term) in voluntary work with non-government organisations serving people in need in America and internationally. CVSA also provides additional consultation and services to volunteer organisations, and produces the quarterly newsletter, *Items,* from CVSA, dealing with the non-governmental voluntary service movement.

Co-ordinating Committee for International Voluntary Service (CCIVS), UNESCO House, 31 rue François Bonvin, 75732 Paris Cedex 15, France; ☎+33 1 4568 4936; fax +33 1 4273 0521; e-mail ccivs@unesco.org; www.unesco.org/ccivs/. Issues lists of work camp/long-term voluntary service organisers by country and publishes on a regular basis directories of short-term and long-term voluntary service throughout the world. A list of CCIVS publications and their costs is also available on the website.

International Health Exchange/RedR, 1 Great George Street, London SW1P 3AA; ☎020-7233 3116; fax 020-72333590; e-mail info@redr.org.uk; www.redr.org. A registered charity helping humanitarian organisations improve the effectiveness of their aid programmes. It also runs training courses and produces a magazine exploring issues in health care in developing countries, as well as carrying job and course information.

The National Council for Voluntary Organisations (NCVO), Regents Wharf, 8 All Saints Street, London N1 9RL; ☎020-7713 6161; fax 020-7713 6300; e-mail ncvo@ncvo-vol. org.uk; www.ncvo-vol.org.uk. Provides high quality information and advice on voluntary organisations, through its HelpDesk, publications, *VoluntarySector* magazine, events, and information networks. They do not provide guidance on volunteering opportunities.

Returned Volunteer Action, 76 Wentworth Street, London E1 7SA; ☎020-7247 6406; e-mail retvolact@lineone.net. An independent organisation for prospective, serving, and returned overseas development workers, as well as people interested or active in development work. It does not send people overseas, but provides advice and information. It also supports returning volunteers in adjusting to life back in Britain. RVA publishes a several booklets, including: *Thinking About Volunteering Overseas, Overseas Development: A Guide to Opportunities,* and the *Handbook for Development Workers Overseas.*

Vacation Work Publications, 9 Park End Street, Oxford OX1 1HH; ☎01865-241978; fax 01865-790885; e-mail info@vacationwork.co.uk; www.vacationwork.co.uk. Publish *The International Directory of Voluntary Work,* a comprehensive, worldwide guide which lists more than 600 organisations and covers all types of work; and *Summer Jobs Abroad,* with details of voluntary projects from conservation to care of the elderly.

ONLINE INFORMATION

Voluntary sector information, with good links, is available at www.ncvo-vol.org.uk; another site with good links is www.volunteering.org.uk. Charitynet, at www.charitynet. org, includes relevant fortnightly articles from *The Observer* newspaper and is a good source of general information.

International Organisations

Employment opportunities in the United Nations, the largest of all international bodies, are treated separately in the next chapter. The international organisations included in this chapter recruit on a smaller scale, but have a steady intake of UK and international personnel, particularly at the professional and senior administrative levels. The European Union and its agencies are major employers of international staff at all levels. It should be noted that British citizens are under-represented in European Union institutions, and that open competitions are organised for entry to the secretarial and clerical grades (see below).

The organisations listed below provide an example of the scope of work available, but are only a few of the international bodies that may be recruiting at any particular time. A more complete list of the world's major international organisations and associations is given in Volume I of the *Europa Yearbook* and a comprehensive list is found in the *Yearbook of International Organisations* (published by the Union of International Associations in Brussels). Both of these publications are available in all good public reference libraries.

THE EUROPEAN UNION

CONSTITUTION

The European Union is set apart from other international organisations by its unique institutional structure. In becoming signatories to the treaties of Rome, Paris and Maastricht, member states of the EU effectively agree to surrender a measure of their sovereignty, which is invested in some of the institutions below. These various agencies and institutions work together, and all subscribe to the same recruitment procedures. Further information on the background of the European Union and its relation to the European Economic Area can be found in the chapter *Rules and Regulations* earlier in this book. A useful source of information on the general structure of the EU, including details of all its operations and representatives, is *The European Companion*, published by The Stationary Office and available in most reference libraries. The European Union has a website at http://europa.eu.int.

The *European Commission*, Rue de la Loi 200, B-1049 Brussels, Belgium; ☎+32 2 299 1111; fax +32 2 299 4609; http://europa.eu.int/comm/, was created by the merger of the EEC (European Economic Community), ECSC (European Coal and Steel Community), and Euratom in 1967, and is the forerunner of today's EU. It enjoys a great deal of independence in its duties and represents the Community interest, rather than that of the individual member states. The European Commission is responsible for the implementation of regulations and directives of the European Council and can bring a case before the European Court of Justice to ensure that Community law is enforced. It is the guardian of the various Treaties that established the EU and its institutions, and can intervene in the legislative process to facilitate agreement between the European Council and Parliament. It also has powers in respect of research and technology, development aid within the EU and regional cohesion, and the conduct of common policies. The Commission is organised into 23 Directorates-General, each administering different areas of policy, and departments including the Legal Service, Joint Interpretation and Conference Service, Statistical Office, Informatics Directorate and Translation Service, located mainly in Brussels and Luxembourg. In contrast to many other international organisations it controls its own financial affairs, and is seen by some as the embryo of a future pan-European government accountable to a two-chamber parliament that might evolve from the present European Parliament (see below). The European Commission employs around 17,000 administrative staff, the majority of whom work in Brussels.

Council of the European Union, Rue de la Loi 175, B-1048 Brussels, Belgium; ☎+32 2 281 6589; fax +32 2 281 7397; e-mail public.info@consilium.europa.eu; www.consilium.europa.eu, is a body which has characteristics of both a supranational and an intergovernmental organisation. The heads of state of EU Member Countries meet (along with the President of the European Commission) under the auspices of the Council of the EU twice a year; and there are other ministerial meetings in areas such as foreign affairs, agriculture, transport and the environment. The Council legislates for the European Union (along with the Parliament and Commission, whose proposals it must ratify) and is primarily a decision making body, setting political and practical objectives for the Union. The Council also deals with current international issues through the common foreign and security policy (CFSP), which allows the Member States to align their diplomatic positions. Each state has a national delegation of civil servants, diplomats and administrative staff. The Council is supported by a secretariat of around 2,500 staff based in Brussels, about of whom 450 are administrative (A grade) and a further 600, translation staff (LA grade).

European Parliament, Secretariat-General of the European Parliament, European Centre, Plateau du Kirchberg, BP 1601, 2929 Luxembourg; ☎+352 43001; fax +352-4300 29494; www.europarl.europa.eu., has legislatory, budgetary and supervisory roles within the EU. Elections to the European Parliament are held every five years and its plenary sessions are normally in Strasbourg. Brussels is the usual venue for meetings of its various committees, which prepare the ground for full sittings of the Parliament. The Maastricht Treaty strengthened the European Parliament's legislative role by extending its powers of decision to specific areas such as the free movement of workers, education, research, the environment, health, culture and consumer protection. It also approves the European Union's budget each year.

European Court of Auditors, 12 rue Alcide De Gasperi, L-1615 Luxembourg; ☎+352 4398 45410; fax +352 4398 46430; e-mail euraud@eca.europa.eu; www.eca.europa.eu, audits the accounts of the European Union and its various institutions and agencies. Its members are appointed by the member states of the Union.

The Court of Justice, L-2925, Luxembourg; ☎352-43031; fax 352-4303 2600; e-mail ECJ.Registry@curia.eu.eu; http://curia.eu.int/. The Court of Justice comprise twenty five judges and eight advocates-general who work to ensure that Community law is interpreted and implemented in line with the Treaties. The Courts of First Instance were established in 1989 to speed the work of the Courts of Justice by taking on cases relating to competition, damages and staff claims.

European Economic and Social Committee, 99 rue Belliard, B-1040 Brussels, Belgium; ☎+32 2 546 9011; fax +32 2 513 4893; www.eesc.europa.eu. ECOSOC represents the interests of employers and employees (via trade unions), as well as various interest groups such as farmers and consumers.

Committee of the Regions, 101 rue Belliard, B-1040 Brussels, Belgium, ☎+32 2 282 2211, fax +32 2 282 2325; www.cor.europa.eu, was set up by the Maastricht Treaty and is consulted by the Council, the European Parliament or the Commission on matters of regional policy.

European Central Bank, Kaiserstrasse 29, D-60311 Frankfurt am Main, Germany; ☎+49 –69 13440; fax +49 69 134460; e-mail info@ecb.int; www.ecb.int, is the central bank for Europe's single currency, the euro. The ECB's main task is to maintain the euro's purchasing power and thus price stability in the euro area. The euro area comprises the 12 European Union countries that have introduced the euro since 1999.

OTHER INSTITUTIONS OF THE EU

In recent years a number of new institutions have been set up by the EU, all of which recruit via the same process as the other bodies mentioned above. These agencies, their remit, and locations are as follows:

European Agency of Health and Safety at Work, Spain; http://europe.osha.eu.int. Improving work conditions.

European Centre for the Development of Vocational Training, Greece; www.cedefop. europa.eu.

European Agency for Reconstruction, Greece; www.ear.eu.int.

European Monitoring Centre for Drugs and Drug Addiction (EMCDDA), Lisbon; www. emcdda.europa.eu. Analysing data and trends in drugs.

European Environment Agency, Copenhagen; www.eea.eu.int. Evaluating and monitoring of environmental statistics.

European Training Foundation, Turin; www.etf.eu. Harmonising training procedures.

European Medicines Agency (EMEA); www.emea.eu.int. Evaluation and supervision of medicines.

European Community Plant Variety Office, France; www.cpvo.fr.

European Monitoring Centre on Racism and Xenophobia, Vienna; www.eumc.eu.int.

Office of the European Union Trade Marks and Design, Spain; http://oami.europa.eu. Registration of trademarks.

Europol, The Hague; www.europol.eu.int. EU law enforcement organisation.

European Foundation for the Improvement of Living and Working Conditions, Ireland; www.eurofound.ie.

Translation Centre for the Bodies of the European Union, Luxembourg; www.cdt.europa.eu.

RECRUITMENT

The European Union currently employs over 27,000 permanent and 2,000 temporary staff and opportunities exist for EU citizens to work in these institutions at all grades. In theory positions are open to all nationals, however, in practice an unofficial quota system exists to ensure that jobs are equally distributed among citizens of the various member states. Personnel for all EU institutions are recruited in the following categories:

- Grade A – Senior administrative staff (graduate level)
- Grade LA – Linguists/translators/interpreters (graduate level)
- Grade B – Administrative assistant staff (secondary education level)
- Grade C – Clerical officers, secretaries, shorthand/typists
- Grade D – Skilled workers

The Commission, Council, Parliament, Committee of the Regions and the Economic and Social Committee all share the same method of recruitment: vacancies are filled by open competition following published notices. These competitions comprise three stages and the process usually takes some months. Advertisements of notices are published in the national press; and for more detailed information you can see the *Official Journal of the European Communities*, (see under *Information* below). Candidates who are selected in the open competitions form a reserve recruitment list and may be offered positions as they become vacant. Success in a competition is not, therefore, a guarantee of getting a job; and it may be several years before a post is offered. Entry-level posts are usually restricted to those under

35 years of age. For entry to higher-level posts, the usual age limit may be raised to 50 years. In addition to permanent staff, the Commission sometimes advertises for administrators and specialists for temporary contracts of three to five years. For these short-term posts, recruitment procedures may differ from the competition process.

Enquiries concerning competitions should be addressed to the Personnel Division or General Administration of the institution concerned. You can also subscribe directly to the *Official Journal of the European Communities* by contacting the various national government bookshops (UK addresses below); this publication is also available in all good reference libraries. Details on recruitment into the European Commission are available from http://europa.eu/epso/.

Those interested in interpreting and translating for the Commission can obtain further information from the *Joint Interpreting and Conference Service*, Translation Service and Recruitment Unit, European Commission, Wetstraat 200, rue de la Loi, B-1049 Brussels, Belgium, by fax from +32 2 296 4306, or visit http://ec.europa.eu/dgs_ en.htm, which lists all the directorates-general including Interpretation and Translation. Applications to participate in the intensive six-month training course this service offers should be addressed to *Head of Training*, SCIC, 200 Rue de la Loi, B-1049 Brussels (which is also the contact address for freelance interpreters). There are strict eligibility criteria. The Council of Ministers also employs translators but not interpreters, as they use the Commission's interpreters. Details are published in the *Official Journal of the European Unions* in the C series (containing information and notices), which can be obtained through a network of sales agents all around the EU and the rest of the world. Further information is available on the European Union's publisher's website (http://publications.europa.eu).

Information concerning scientific posts can be obtained from the *Directorate-General for Science Research and Development*, Joint Research Centre, European Commission, Public Relations Unit, SDME 10/78, B-1049 Brussels, Belgium; ☎+32 2 295 7624; fax +32 2 299 6322; e-mail jrc-info@ec.europa.eu; www.jrc.cec.eu.int.

SPECIAL ENTRY SCHEMES

Robert Schuman Scholarships

In addition to the normal recruitment channels outlined, there are a number of special entry schemes. The European Parliament offers following training schemes: Robert Schuman Scholarships (general and journalism options) for graduates of universities or equivalent institutions Translation Traineeships for linguists, which allows qualified applicants to spend periods of three months in the translating departments. Participation in these schemes in no way guarantees permanent employment. Applications should be completed online. For further information on Robert Schuman scholarships contact: The *European Parliament*, Traineeships Office (Robert Schuman Scholarships), KAD 02C008, L-2929, Luxembourg; ☎+352 4300 24882; e-mail stages@europarl.eu.int, and for details about translation traineeships contact: European Parliament,Translation Traineeships Office, TOB 04B022, L-2929 Luxembourg; ☎+352 4300 27777; e-mail translationtraineeships@ eurparl.eu.int, or visit the European Parliament website www.europarl.europa.eu and see 'Traineeships' under 'Parliament and you'.

Stagiaires

The European Commission, the Committee of the Regions, and the Economic and Social Committee run a *stagiaire* training course for graduates (the age limit is 30) which lasts between three and five months. A stagiaire can be helpful in preparing for the competitive examinations for Grade A (administrative) posts. Enquiries should be made to the Traineeships Office, *European Commission*, B-1049 Brussels, Belgium; ☎+32

2 299 2339; fax +32 2 299 0871; e-mail eac-stages@ec.europa.eu; http://ec.europa.eu/stages/. Approximately 200 stagiaire positions are offered annually. Applicants should register online.

Undergraduates and recent graduates wishing to find out about *stages* (or work placements) for administrative trainees should visit the website of *European Commission Office* in London http://ec.europa.eu/unitedkingdom under 'How to work with the EU'. Further information and an application form for *stagiaire* opportunities in the *Translation Service*, can be obtained from the Translation Service address above.

The Court of Justice and The Court of First Instance

The Court of Justice and First Instance recruit independently of the other institutions of the European Communities, although their procedures are similar. All vacant posts are advertised in the national press as and when they arise. The list is also available at http://curia.europa.eu.

The Court of Justice offers a limited number of stages ever year (maximum duration 5 months). Applicants must be holders of a degree in law or in political sciences. For traineeships in the Interpreting Division, a diploma in conference interpreting and a postgraduate qualification are required. Application forms should be downloaded from http://curia.eu.int/en/infosprat/formulaire_stage.htm and posted with requested documents to: The Court of Justice, Division du personnel de la cour de justice des Communautés europénes, L-2925 Luxembourg.

FURTHER INFORMATION

The Personnel and Administration Department of the European Commission produces a free booklet entitled *Opportunities in the European Commission*, explaining its recruitment procedures and employment conditions. Detailed information about careers in the Commission may be obtained from the Recruitment Unit – Info-Recruitment, European Personnel Selection Office, Office C80 4/11, B-1049 Brussels, Belgium, ☎+32 2 299 3131; fax +32 2 295 7488; http://europa.eu.int/en/epso/.

In addition to the separate institutions themselves, information can be obtained from the Representative Offices of the European Commission in all member states. In the UK, there are Representations at the following addresses:

○ 8 Storey's Gate, London SW1P 3AT; ☎020-7973 1992; http://ec.europa.eu/unitedkingdom/.
○ 9 Alva Street, Edinburgh EH2 4PH; ☎0131-225 2058.
○ 2 Caspian Point, Cardiff CF10 4QQ; ☎029-2089 5020.
○ Windsor House, 9-15 Bedford Street, Belfast; ☎028-9024 0708.

The Irish Representation of the *European Commission* is at European House, Dawson Street, Dublin 2; ☎1- 662 5113; fax 1-662 5118; e-mail eu-ie-info-request@cec.eu.int; www.euireland.ie. There are also regional European Information Centres in many cities, which can be contacted for information about funding and regional development. The London office of the *European Parliament* is at 2 Queen Anne's Gate, London SW1H 9AA; ☎020-7227 4300; fax 020-7227 4302; e-mail eplondon@europarl.europa.eu; www.europarl.org.uk; and in Ireland at 43 Molesworth Street, Dublin 2; ☎+353 1-605 7900; fax +353 1 605 7999; e-mail epdublin@europarl.eu.int; www.europarl.ie.

The *Official Journal of the European Communities* can be consulted at these offices, as can copies of all EU documents and publications. These can also be found at many public, university and specialist libraries (some of which are designated as *European Documentation Centres*).

OTHER ORGANISATIONS

Consultative Group on International Agricultural Research (CGIAR), Secretariat, MSN G6-601, 1818 H Street NW, Washington DC, 20433; ☎202-473 8951; fax 202-473 8110. www.cgiar.org, is an informal association of 64 members which supports a network of 15 international agricultural research centres. The Group, co-sponsored by FAO, UNDP, UNEP and the World Bank, consists of 37 governments, 11 multilateral development agencies, and four non-government foundations. CGIAR centres conduct research into food crops that provide 75 per cent of food energy and a similar share of protein requirements in developing countries.

Council of Europe, Avenue de l'Europe, F-67075 Strasbourg, France; ☎+33 3 8841 2033; fax +33 3 8841 2475; e-mail infopoint@coe.int; www.coe.int, periodically recruits graduates for general administrative posts at the secretariat in Strasbourg, with an initial contract of two years. The essential requirements are a good university degree, excellent drafting ability in English and a very good reading knowledge of French. Two years' administrative experience is usually required. Recruitment is by competitive written examination and interview of short listed candidates. Specialist vacancies also occur, notably for practising lawyers. In addition, experienced English-language secretaries with good GCSEs and some A levels (with good grades in English and French) and 50 wpm minimum typing are regularly recruited. A copy of the current list of competitions and up-to-date information on career opportunities are available via the website www.coe-recruitment.com. Occasional freelance work for fully qualified conference interpreters with bilingual English/French, capable of translating from German, Italian, Russian or other major Slavonic languages. Postgraduate translation diploma and experience essential. There are also traineeships offered by the Council of Europe. The Trainee Scheme consists of three three-month periods per year: January to March, April to June and October to December.

European Organisation for Nuclear Research (CERN), Recruitment Service, Human Resources Department, CH-1211 Geneva 23, Switzerland; ☎+41 22 767 2735; fax +41 22 767 2750; www.humanresources.web.cern.ch, accepts applications from nationals of member states (including the UK) for their fellowships. Most appointments are in the field of experimental and theoretical subnuclear physics. However, there are some openings in applied physics, electronics, computing and engineering for recent graduates at Bachelor level or above. One year CERN Fellowship Programme (extending for a second year) has two sub-programmes: the Senior Fellowship for people with a PhD or at least four years of experience after the degree, and the Junior Fellowship for those with a Technical Engineer degree (or equivalent) and at most a MSc degree with not more than four years of experience.

Associateships in the fields listed above are available for research scientists of any nationality, who will normally be on leave of absence from their parent institute during the tenancy of the associateship (maximum duration one year). Scientific associateships for collaboration in CERN laboratory work are usually supported financially by parent institutes, but there are a number of paid associateships to enable scientists to join an existing project.

Applications should be made electronically via the e-recruitment system https://ert.cern.ch/.

International Organization for Migration (IOM), 17 Route des Morillons, CH-1211 Geneva 19, Switzerland; ☎+41 22 717 9111; fax +41 22 798 6150; e-mail info@iom. int; www.iom.ch, has 118 member governments, including the UK and USA, and 20 observer governments. Since 1951, IOM has assisted migratory movements of refugees and nationals on a worldwide scale; since its foundation it has processed and moved more than 11 million migrants to resettlement countries.

In addition to providing services and assistance to refugees, the Organisation's task is to assist qualified technicians and professionals to ensure transfer of technology in order to promote the economic, social and cultural advancement of developing countries. In this connection IOM carries out Migration for Development programmes such as Return of Talent, Selective Migration, Integrated Experts, and Intra-regional Co-operation among Latin American countries in close co-operation with the national labour authorities.

North Atlantic Treaty Organisation (NATO), Recruitment Service, NATO Headquarters, 1110 Brussels, Belgium; ☎+32 2 707 3677; e-mail recruitment.a@hq.nato.int (for Grades A), or recruitment.lbc@hq.nato.int (for grades L, B, C); www.nato.int, has vacancies for professional and administrative posts, which are filled either by secondment from member nations' civil service and diplomatic service staff or directly by NATO. These posts generally require several years' graduate experience together with a good knowledge of the two NATO official languages, English and French. There is also a need for secretarial and linguistic staff; examinations are held regularly for the recruitment of translators and interpreters. NATO employs citizens of all 26 NATO nations. Candidates wishing to apply for the International Staff of NATO in Brussels should use the NATO application form, which can be downloaded from the website, and send it to the NATO HQ Recruitment Office (address above). Applications for vacancies in any of the NATO Agencies should be sent to the body concerned.

Organisation for Economic Co-operation and Development (OECD), 2 rue André Pascal, F-75775 Paris 16, France; ☎+33 1 4524 8200; www.oecd.org. Its mission is to improve public policy-making and enhance international cooperation in a wide range of disciplines dealing with the functioning of economies, societies and their core institutions. Joining the OECD Secretariat means working with 2,300 colleagues in collaboration with more than 30,000 senior national policy-makers who each year participate in the OECD technical and policy meetings. It is a highly stimulating multicultural team environment. The OECD offers challenging and rewarding opportunities to motivated professionals interested mainly in applied economic policy analysis and international policy dialogue, but also in other areas like statistics or IT. Applicants should have an advanced university degree in economics or related OECD field and relevant experience in applied policy analysis in one of the organisation's spheres of activity; social affairs, labour, education, environment, science, industry, agriculture and fisheries, energy, finance and public management. Excellent knowledge of one of the two official languages of the Organisation (English and French) and good working knowledge of the other is required. Its headquarters are located in Paris, France, and offers excellent tax-free salary plus a benefits package including expatriation allowance and family allowance, depending on individual situation. Appointments are initially made for a fixed two or three year term.

The *Secretariat of the Pacific Community*, BP D5, 95 Promenade Roger, Laroque, Anse Vata, 8848 Noumea Cedex, New Caledonia; ☎+687 262000; fax +687 263818; e-mail spc@spc.int; www.spc.int, employs two main categories of staff: specialists and support staff. Most of the latter are recruited, whenever possible, locally. Occasionally, support service vacancies arise which cannot be filled locally.

The Secretariat of the Pacific Community is a technical and developmental organisation providing training and assistance in social, economic and cultural fields, with particular emphasis on rural development. The Secretariat has staff members based at SPC headquarters in Noumea, New Caledonia and in Suva. The official languages of the Commission are French and English.

Fields of activity include Land Resources (Forestry, Crop Improvement, Animal Health and Production, Plant Protection); Marine Resources (Coastal and Oceanic Fisheries); Public Health Programme (Public Health Surveillance and Communicable Disease Control, HIV/STI Prevention, Tuberclosis Control, Prevention/Lifestyle Health, Tobacco and Alcohol Control, Adolescent Reproductive Health), Socio-Economic Activities (Population and Demography, Statistics, Women Affairs, Youth Affairs, Cultural Affairs, Consultancy Education).

United Nations Populations Fund (UNFPA), Staffing & Recruitment Branch, Division of Human Resources,220 East 42nd Street, 17th Floor, New York, NY 10017, USA; ☎+1 212 297 5000; fax +1 212 297 4908; www.unfpa.org, is an initiative wholly funded by voluntary contributions which are not part of the regular United Nations budget. It was set up by 10 developing countries with the aim of promoting co-operation in the field of reproductive health and family planning. Technical advisers with excellent communications skills (and, in the Middle East, Arabic) are required. Applicants must hold a post-graduate degree in public or business administration, social sciences, or health science. They should be fluent in English. Knowledge of one other UN language, preferably French or Spanish is desirable. UNFPA also offers Junior Professional Officer Programme and Internship programme.

Universal Esperanto Association, Head Office, Nieuwe Binnenweg 176, NL-3015 BJ Rotterdam, Netherlands; ☎+31 10 436 1044; fax +31 10 436 1751; e-mail info@uea.org, www.uea.org, collects and files information on opportunities for paid and voluntary work, which is mainly clerical, at the head office. Fluent knowledge of Esperanto is essential.

The United Nations

The United Nations organisation has a variety of agencies, all of which offer employment opportunities for qualified personnel. A wide variety of employment is available at the UN Secretariat headquarters in New York, in overseas offices and missions directly subordinate to the Secretariat, as well as in the specialised agencies of the UN, which are independent in most activities, including personnel recruitment. Vacancies are open to nationals of all member countries, and at the professional level attempts are made to maintain a proportional geographical distribution of personnel. Britain and the USA are members of the UN and its main agencies, however, as both are heavily over-represented, prospects for employment from these countries may be limited.

The best opportunities exist for specialised professional staff, although clerical and administrative staff are also recruited. The UN is a major employer of linguists as translators and interpreters; however, competition is extremely intense for these positions. Preference is always given to applicants with knowledge of both English and French, the official working languages of the UN, and knowledge of one of the other four official languages (Arabic, Chinese, Russian and Spanish) can also be an advantage.

The *United Nations Information Centre,* Residence Palace, 155 rue de la Loi, 1040 Brussels, Belgium; ☎+32 2 788 8484; fax +32 2 788 8485; e-mail info@runic-europe. org; www.runic-europe.org; and U*nited Nations Information Centre*, 1775 K Street NW, Suite 400, Washington DC 20006, USA; ☎+1 202 331 8670; fax +1 202 331 9191; e-mail unicdc@unicwash.org; www.unicwash.org, can supply a list of recruitment office addresses of the United Nations and its specialised agencies, and any other information on request. This information is also available on the UN website at www.un.org.

Details of opportunities in the international organisations of the UN are available from the UN Employment home page http://jobs.un.org. All those interested in employment with the UN or its associated organisations may also contact: United Nations Staffing Support Section Office of Human Resources Management, Room S-2475, New York, NY 10017, USA; fax +1 212 963 3134; e-mail staffing@un.org, alternatively enquiries may be made to the separate organisations below.

THE SECRETARIAT

The United Nations Secretariat includes the United Nations Headquarters in New York, the United Nations Offices in Geneva and Vienna, the United Nations Conference on Trade and Development (UNCTAD), the Office of the United Nations High Commissioner for Refugees (UNHCR) in Geneva, the United Nations Population Fund (UNFPA) in New York, the peace-keeping missions, information centres throughout the world and various economic commissions of the UN.

The United Nations has a steady need for competent staff in various fields. It is impossible to list in detail here the different types of positions for which the Organisation recruits, however, the major categories are given below. The majority of professional posts in the Secretariat are closely related to the nature of the work required by the resolutions of the General Assembly and its principal bodies. As a result, the need is largely for specialists in the fields of administration, economics, information technology and science; and in providing technical assistance to developing countries in the areas of economic and social development.

The United Nations is particularly interested in those candidates with international experience in more than one of these major areas which will enable them to follow an integrated and interdisciplinary approach to problems in development planning, econometrics, financial and industrial planning and administration of economic programmes. In statistical work, vacancies may arise in census and demography, industrial labour and trade statistics, national accounts and training of personnel in statistical methodology. In the fields of energy and natural resources, experts are needed in geothermal, petroleum and mineral exploration, energy systems planning, solar energy development and water management. In the field of housing and planning, professionals in construction, environmental planning and urban, rural and regional planning are sought.

There is always a requirement for *stenographic and clerical staff* and for high-speed conference typists in the six official languages of the United Nations (Arabic, Chinese, English, French, Russian and Spanish).

The United Nations *field service staff* are responsible for servicing various United Nations field missions and comprises security officers, vehicle mechanics, radio technicians, radio officers and secretaries.

Guides are recruited, usually once a year, for a period of two years; service as a Guide does not carry any expectation of career employment with the organisation.

Recruitment of *translators/précis writers* and *interpreters* is by competitive examinations. Apart from their own native language, which must be one of the six official languages of the UN, candidates should be fluent in at least two of the other languages.

Librarians should have an advanced degree or equivalent professional qualification, and a working knowledge of at least two of the official languages, together with several years' practical library experience.

The United Nations is especially interested in recruiting women with a combination of skills and experiences acquired in an international setting, which will enable them to assume administrative responsibilities.

Grade levels are circumscribed by certain age limits, and these are taken into consideration when evaluating candidates for professional posts. Applicants for professional posts require an advanced university degree (Master's or Doctoral level) and the ability to work easily in either English or French. Knowledge of one of the other official languages of the United Nations may also be desirable, as indicated above.

Staff may be expected to work at United Nations Headquarters in New York or in any of its other offices around the world (see below).

Requests for further information about posts in any of the above job areas should be addressed to the United Nations Staffing Support Section Office of Human Resources Management, Room S-2475, New York, NY 10017, USA; fax +1 212 963 3134; e-mail staffing@un.org.

OTHER OFFICES AND MISSIONS

The United Nations Office in Geneva is the largest United Nations office outside UN Headquarters in New York. The work done in Geneva is primarily concerned with conference and other international meetings, specialised economic activities, administrative and related functions. The United Nations at Geneva always gives careful consideration to applications from persons well qualified for employment. Secretarial staff are recruited locally and priority is normally given to candidates who already have familiarity with the function of the Organisation, and to those whose names have been put on a waiting list. Applications for all types of work should be addressed to the *Secretariat Recruitment Section*, Personnel Service, Palais des Nations, CH-1211 Geneva 10, Switzerland; ☎+41 22 917 1234; fax +41 22 917 0123; www.unog.ch. Due to on-going financial restrictions, vacancies that do arise are in the first instance filled through internal redeployment.

The International Trade Centre (ITC), Chief of Personnel, International Trade Centre

(ITC), 54-56 rue de Montbrillant, 1211, Geneva 10, Switzerland; fax 22 730 0803; www. intracen.org. The International Trade Centre is the joint technical co-operation agency of the United Nations Conference on Trade and Development (UNCTAD) and the World Trade Organization (WTO) for business aspects of trade development. ITC assists technical co-operation activities with developing countries involved in trade promotion. ITC recruits approximately 700 consultants each year for its various projects in developing countries. Such consultants work in the areas of institutional infrastructure for trade promotion, export marketing, specialised trade promotion services, import techniques and training.

United Nations Conference on Trade and Development (UNCTAD), Palais des Nations, 8-14 Avenue de la Paix, 1211 Geneva 10, Switzerland; ☎+41 22 917 5809; fax +41 22 917 0051; e-mail info@unctad.org; www.unctad.org. UNCTAD deals with international trade and related issues such as protectionism. Contact Human Resources Management for information on vacancies.

United Nations Industrial Development Organization (UNIDO): Director Human Resource Management Branch, Vienna International Centre, PO Box 300, A-1400 Vienna, Austria; ☎+43 1 260260; fax +43 1 2134 63157; e-mail recruitment@unido.org; www.unido.org, is the specialist agency of the United Nations dedicated to promoting sustainable industrial development in countries with developing and transitional economies. It harnesses the joint forces of government and the private sector to foster competitive industrial economies, develop international industrial partnerships and promote socially equitable and environmentally friendly industrial development. UNIDO is the only worldwide organisation dealing exclusively with industry from a development perspective. Its services are non-profit, neutral and specialised. UNIDO staff are highly qualified, with a wide range and depth of industrial expertise. The Organisation acts as a catalyst to help generate national economic wealth and raise industrial capacity through its roles as a worldwide forum for industrial development, and as a provider of technical co-operation services. UNIDO's ultimate goal is to create a better life for people by laying the industrial foundations for long-term prosperity.

The recruitment for posts at UNIDO headquarters is carried out by UNIDO's recruitment section, the Personnel Services Division; and for technical assistance field assignments, by UNIDO'S Project Personnel Recruitment Branch. The main professional need in this area of activity is for highly qualified experts with at least five years' professional experience who have specialised in problems related to industrial development. UNIDO'S secretarial staff are normally recruited locally and candidates who are in Vienna, even on a temporary basis, are allowed to sit for the qualifying tests. Enquiries about these posts should be addressed to UNIDO'S Recruitment Section.

United Nations Development Programmes (UNDP), One United Nations Plaza, New York, NY 10017, USA; ☎+1 212 906 5000 fax +1 212 906 5364; e-mail ohr.recruitment. hq@undp.org; www.undp.org. UNDP is the largest provider of UN technical co-operation grants, and the main co-ordinator of UN development assistance. The goal of UNDP is to help countries build a capacity for sustainable human development combining economic growth, an equitable distribution of benefits and careful management of natural resources.

Through a network of 136 offices worldwide, UNDP works with people and governments in 166 countries and territories, focusing on the eradication of poverty, environmental regeneration, job creation and the advancement of women. In support of these objectives it is frequently asked to assist in promoting sound governance and market development, and to help in rebuilding societies in the aftermath of war and humanitarian emergencies.

UNDP employs around 7,000 people, and requires applicants to hold postgraduate qualifications, preferably in the social sciences (economics, public administration, sociology). Candidates should have reached a high professional standing in their fields, after long experience – usually at least 15 years. There is also a Junior Professional Officer programme and a graduate internship programme.

United Nations Environment Programme (UNEP), Recruitment Section, Human Resources Management Service (HRMS), United Nations Office at Nairobi (UNON), United Nations Avenue, Gigiri, PO Box 30552, Nairobi, Kenya; ☎+254 20 7621 234; fax +254 20 7623 927/692; www.unep.org/Vac/. UNEP, like UNCTAD and UNIDO, is a part of the Secretariat, but carries out its own recruitment. The Programme's work is based on environmental problems, and experts in this field are occasionally needed. Job vacancies and other current information can be viewed online.

United Nations Economic Commission for Europe, Palais des Nations, CH-1211 Geneva 10, Switzerland; ☎+41 22 917 1234; fax +41 22 917 0505 e-mail info.ece@unece. org, is one of the five regional economic commissions maintained by the UN which are concerned with the economic and social development of the areas they represent. The other four commissions are the ESCAP (for Asia and the Pacific), in Bangkok, Thailand, with a sub-regional office in Suva; ECLAC (for Latin America and the Caribbean) in Santiago, Chile, with sub-regional offices in Mexico City, Mexico, and Port of Spain, Trinidad and Tobago; ECA (for Africa) in Addis Ababa, Ethiopia, with sub-regional offices (Multinational Programming and Operational Centres, MULPOCS) for North Africa in Tangier, Morocco; for West Africa in Niamey, Niger; for East Africa in Kigali, Rwanda; for Southern Africa in Lusaka, Zambia; for Central Africa in Yaounde, Cameroon. ESCWA (for Western Asia) has regional offices in Beirut, Lebanon. Staff recruitment in all these offices is primarily for specialists experienced in economics, statistics, sociology, public administration and related fields. Details of vacancies can be found on the UN Human Resources webpages (http://jobs.un.org)

There are several projects under way in the developing countries, which began under the auspices of the UN or one or more of its agencies, and which are now largely autonomous. Such a project is the Interim Mekong Committee, whose headquarters are in Bangkok. It is partially (five per cent) funded by UNDP.

Information Centres and Field Missions: The UN maintains small information centres around the world, as well as a number of field missions. These offices have no vacancies to speak of, since administrative posts are filled by internal reassignment, and secretarial staff are recruited locally.

Military Personnel: Military observers and UN peace-keeping forces are not recruited by the UN, but are selected from the armed forces of member countries.

Associated Projects: There are several projects which are now largely autonomous for recruitment purposes. The varied associated agencies of the UN include the *Centro Internacional de Agricultura Tropical (CIAT)*, Apartado Aereo 6713, Cali, Colombia; ☎+87 2 445 0000; fax +87 2 445 0073; e-mail ciat@cgiar.org; www.ciat.cgiar.org.

Voluntary Work: The opportunities for voluntary service under UN schemes are covered in the chapter on *Voluntary Work*.

Internships: The *United Nations Internship Programme* is offered to graduate students who may find sponsors or provide financial support themselves. It consists of three two-month programmes through the year, January to March, June to August, and September to

November. Interested candidates should contact *Internship Co-ordinator*, United Nations, Room S-2500F, New York, NY 10017, USA; fax +1 212 963 9514; e-mail OHRM_ interns@un.org; www.un.org/Depts/OHRM/sds/internsh/index.htm.

SPECIALISED AGENCIES

The United Nations specialised agencies recruit their own staff, both for work in their head offices, and also on projects and development programmes abroad, especially in the developing countries. Secretarial and clerical staff are invariably recruited from local sources, and the only vacancies to be filled internationally are for fully qualified and well experienced professionals in the fields with which the agencies are concerned. Details of only a few agencies are given below, on the understanding that agencies' recruitment programmes differ only in the type of professional staff they employ; further information can always be obtained from the agencies themselves.

In general, unsolicited applications to any of the agencies below are unlikely to be considered; nor do many agencies maintain files on candidates. Instead, details of vacancies are forwarded to the appropriate departments in member states, who are invited to advertise the vacancies, hold interviews, and return a short list of suitable candidates. These departments in turn are responsible for recruitment, and many of them maintain selective files of candidates already screened, who would be likely to fill the type of vacancies that might arise.

Food and Agriculture Organization (FAO), Viale delle Terme di Caracalla, I-00100 Rome, Italy; ☎+39 6 57051; fax +39 6 5705 3152; e-mail FAO-HQ@fao.org; www.fao. org, employs around 2,500 staff at headquarters and more than 1,500 staff in the field, the vast majority of whom work in developing countries. Most of the FAO's professional staff work at Headquarters, effecting FAO's development mandate in agriculture, fisheries and forestry, and in related areas such as soil and water resources, nutrition, economics, marketing, statistics, and project evaluation. Most positions require a minimum of five years' professional experience after university; there are, however, a limited number of junior level openings for candidates with less experience. Young candidates (under 30 or 32) usually join FAO as an Associate Professional Officer – a two or three year post financed by the officer's national government. Enquiries can be made to the Foreign Affairs Ministry, International Organizations Branch or equivalent in your own country. Experienced candidates can enquire about vacancies on the FAO website.

International Atomic Energy Agency (IAEA), Wagramer strasse 5, PO Box 100, A-1400 Vienna, Austria; ☎+43 1 –2600 0; fax +43 1 –2600 7; e-mail official.mail@iaea.org; www.iaea.org. Recruitment is usually for professionals with experience in nuclear sciences, reactor physics and engineering, spectrometry, and the application of radioisotopes in agriculture, biology, industry and medicine, in addition to management areas. Applicants are strongly encouraged to apply online at www.iaea.org/About/Jobs/index.html.

World Bank, 1818 H Street NW, Washington DC 20433, USA; ☎+1 202 473 1000; fax +1 202 477 6391; www.worldbank.org, comprises the *International Development Association (IDA)*, the *International Finance Corporation (IFC)*, the *Multilateral Investment Guarantee Agency (MIGA)*, the *International Centre for the Settlement of Investment Disputes (ICSID)* and the *International Bank for Reconstruction and Development (IBRD)* (all based at the above address). Recruitment is carried out both separately, by the agencies, and jointly, under the auspices of the World Bank. The World Bank employs 10,000 development professionals in Washington or in their 109 Country Offices. These are economists, educators, environmental scientists, financial analysts, anthropologists, engineers and others. Qualified, experienced economists are most in demand, in the preferred age range of 30-55. Applied experience is required in one of the fields in which the Bank operates, such as development economics, transport, agriculture, industrial problems, commodities, international trade, or fiscal affairs. The Bank's predominant concern with loans and the investigation of schemes put forward for loan approval, leads to the employment of two further categories of staff: those with specialised knowledge or experience of the various aspects of investments and loans; and those experts who can investigate schemes requiring loans – including agriculturalists, agricultural and irrigation engineers; power, telecommunications and water supply engineers; road, port and railway engineers; architects, planners and educationalists. Candidates aged under 32 years old with a recognised masters degree or equivalent in economics, management, public administration, law, or related fields, can apply for employment under the Junior Professional Officer Programme, which involves two or three years of duty. Selection is on a competitive basis.

International Labour Organisation (ILO), 4 Route des Morillons, CH-1211 Geneva 22, Switzerland; ☎+41 22 799 6111; fax +41 22 798 8685; e-mail ilo@ilo.org; www.ilo. org. The experts employed by ILO need long experience in employment and development (manpower planning, alleviation of poverty, small scale industry development); vocational training; sectoral activities (development of co-operatives); working conditions; and industrial relations.

International Monetary Fund (IMF), 700 19th Street NW, Washington DC 20431, USA; ☎+1 202 623 7000; fax +1 202 623 4661; www.imf.org, employs qualified economists, as well as accountants, administrators, computer systems officers, language specialists and lawyers. Nearly all staff members are based in Washington although the Fund also maintains small offices in Paris and Geneva. A few staff members are also stationed for varying periods in member countries as resident representatives. In addition, work assignments frequently require travel to member countries to study economic problems and lend technical assistance. Recruitment is either through direct appointment to the regular staff (or by appointment for a fixed term, usually 2-3 years), or through the Fund's Economist Programme, which is open to well-educated graduates below 33 years of age, who may not have previous relevant work experience; enquiries should be made to the Recruitment Division. For direct or fixed term appointments, applicants are expected to have significant prior experience in a government department or academic or financial institution.

International Telecommunication Union (ITU), Place des Nations, 1211 Geneva 20, Switzerland; ☎+41 22 730 5111; fax +41 22 733 7256; e-mail itumail@itu.int; www. itu.int. Vacancies at headquarters (which are rare and very competitive) and in the developing countries are advertised internationally and on the ITU webpages. Specialist posts are open to qualified engineers with several years' experience in one of the fields of telecommunications.

United Nations Educational, Scientific and Cultural Organization (UNESCO), UNESCO House, 7 Place de Fontenoy 07 SP, F-75352 Paris, France; ☎+33 1 4568 1000; fax +33 1 4567 1690; www.unesco.org, frequently needs specialists to work on projects in the UNESCO Field Programme in the developing countries. Most field appointments are for one to two years, but some may be even shorter. The Field Programme requires highly qualified people already established in a specific field of education (particularly in the areas of science, engineering and technology), and with a substantial amount of teaching experience at university, college of education or technical college level; experience in curriculum development, teacher-training and educational organisation, administration and research are common prerequisites. Vacancies also arise for experts in educational broadcasting, audio-visual aids, mass media, librarianship and documentation. Details of vacancies are carried on the UNESCO webpages, through the National Commissions for UNESCO of the Member States (professional posts), through posting at Headquarters and at field offices (professional and local general service posts) and through the United Nations offices (professional posts).

World Health Organization (WHO), Central Human Resources Services (HRC), 20

Avenue Appia, CH-1211 Geneva 27, Switzerland; fax +41 22 791 4773; www.who.int, mainly requires highly qualified and experienced medical personnel to work on health projects in developing countries. Such staff include: senior medical officers, nursing administrators and sanitary engineers, who act as advisers to governments on broad health programmes; nurse educators, sanitary engineers and other medical personnel to teach or supervise teams of instructors in schools and institutes; specialists in paediatrics and child health, serology, entomology, bacteriology, biochemistry and epidemiology; hospital administrators, radiologists, X-ray technicians and dieticians; and fully qualified doctors with experience in malaria, tuberculosis, nutrition, leprology, venereal diseases and treponematoses. Vacancies at WHO head office are rare, but the Geneva headquarters also recruits on behalf of the regional head offices in Brazzaville (covering Africa), New Delhi (Asia), Copenhagen (Europe), Alexandria (Eastern Mediterranean), Manila (Western Pacific) and Washington DC (Americas).

Other specialised agencies include:
International Fund for Agricultural Development (IFAD), 107 Via del Serafico, 00142 Rome, Italy; ☎+39 6 54591; fax +39 6 504 3463; e-mail ifad@ifad.org; www.ifad.org.
International Maritime Organization (IMO), 55 Victoria Street, London SW1H 0EU; ☎020-7735 7611; fax 020-7587 3210; www.imo.org.
United Nations Children's Fund (UNICEF), 3 United Nations Plaza, New York, NY 10017, USA; ☎+1 212 326 7000; fax +1 212 887 7465; www.unicef.org.
Universal Postal Union (UPU), International Bureau, PO Box 13, CH-3000 Berne 15, Switzerland; ☎+41 31 350 3111; fax +41 31 350 3110; e-mail info@upu.int; www.upu.int.
World Intellectual Property Organization (WIPO), PO Box 18, 34 chemin des Colombettes, CH-1211 Geneva 20, Switzerland; ☎+41 22 338 9111; fax +1 22 733 5428; e-mail wipo.mail@wipo.int; www.wipo.org.
World Meteorological Organization (WMO), 7 bis, Avenue de la Paix, PO Box 2300, Geneva 2, Switzerland; ☎+41 22 730 8111; fax +41 22 730 8181; e-mail wmo@wmo.int; www.wmo.int.

INFORMATION ON THE INTERNET

The website of the United Nations is at www.un.org. This very large site contains links to all the international agencies of the UN, as well as to the various member states. It includes extensive recruitment information and current vacancies. The Institute of Development Studies at Sussex University has a good source of reference materials at www.sussex.ac.uk/Units/CDU/cideve.html.

SUB-CONTRACTS

In many cases, the work of the United Nations and its specialised agencies consists of providing financial assistance to enable countries and bodies to complete a particular project. The money allocated is used to procure relevant services through international bidding for contracts. Sometimes a contract may only be for supplies and equipment, but in some cases a complete project, including personnel, is involved. In these cases opportunities to work for successful contractors will arise, and such work will usually be advertised in the international press. Details of contracts currently being offered are published in the fortnightly newspaper *UN Development Business*, issued by the UN. Information on subscriptions is available from Subscription Department, UN Development Business, 1 UN Plaza, United Nations, New York, NY 10017, USA; fax +1 212 963 1381; e-mail dbsubscribe@un.org; www.devbusiness.com.

British Government and Related Agencies

THE DIPLOMATIC SERVICE

Members of the Diplomatic Service staff British Embassies, High Commissions, Consulates, and other missions worldwide. They must serve overseas wherever and whenever they are required. In practice, officers spend half to two thirds of their career in diplomatic missions overseas, and the remainder in the Foreign and Commonwealth Office (FCO) in London. The work is demanding, calling for adaptability, resourcefulness, resilience, and the ability to mix with all types of people. Applicants for entry to the Diplomatic Service must be British citizens and be able to show a close affiliation with the United Kingdom, taking into account such considerations as upbringing and residence.

CAREER OPPORTUNITIES

New entrants to the Diplomatic Service join as Policy Entrants, whose role is to advise and support ministers in formulating foreign policy, and to review information relevant to particular countries. You can expect to be posted overseas within two years of joining the diplomatic service, and this posting will normally be for between three and four years (and almost certainly to a less-than-popular destination). Competition is fierce for entry into this branch of the civil service, with more than 100 applicants for every available position. You will need at least a second-class degree, a quick and analytical mind, and the ability to master complex issues effectively. Recruitment takes place via the general fast stream competition (described below). Further information and advice can be obtained from the Recruitment Section, Personnel Command, Room 2/98, Foreign and Commonwealth Office, Old Admiralty Building, Whitehall, London SW1A 2AH; ☎0870-606 0290; e-mail Recruitment.Public@fco.gov.uk; www.fco.gov.uk.

Fast Stream Entry

Fast Stream offers an accelerated training and development programme for graduates with the potential to reach the heights of the Civil Service, employing them in a myriad of departments and areas. Careers are developed within three career groups: corporate services, operational delivery and policy delivery. There is a choice of Fast Stream schemes: the Graduate Fast Stream, Economist Fast Stream, Statisticians Fast Stream and Technology in Business Fast Stream. Whichever scheme you choose you will be providing excellent customer focused, public services and have the opportunity to make a difference. To apply or find out more visit their website at www.faststream.gov.uk for further details and eligibility requirements. During the application period you will need to take online tests - there is a self-assessment test to check out whether you are likely to enjoy and be suited to Fast Stream work and some practice tests. If successful you will be invited to an invigilated e-Tray exercise at a regional centre for half a day. Pass and you will be asked to their assessment centre in London for a day. To order a brochure e-mail faststream@parity. net or telephone ☎01276-400300.

Other Opportunities

Legal Advisers: There are a small number of legal advisers in the Diplomatic Service, most of whom are based in London, although there are a few opportunities for work abroad. Applicants must be barristers or admitted solicitors. Vacancies are advertised as they occur.

Research Analysts: Officers compile information on the history, politics and current affairs of certain foreign countries, and prepare reports. Candidates must have a good honours degree, an aptitude for foreign languages and special qualifications in a relevant field, e.g. history, economics, and political studies. The Department is based in London, although there are occasional opportunities for work abroad. Vacancies are advertised as they occur.

Further information on Civil Service recruitment is available from *Capita RAS (Recruitment & Assessment Services)*, Innovation Court, New Street, Basingstoke, Hampshire RG21 7JB; ☎01256-383900; www.capitaras.co.uk. Capita RAS can supply interested applicants with a comprehensive preparation package containing sample tests and other detailed information.

THE BRITISH COUNCIL

The British Council promotes Britain abroad, providing access to British ideas, talents and experience through education and training, books and periodicals, the English language, the arts, sciences and technology. It is an independent, non-political body managed by a Director General working to a Board of Management. With a presence in 111 countries, it provides a network of contacts between government departments, universities and professional and business organisations in Britain and around the world. Its work helps to promote a climate for international co-operation in all its fields of activity, and its range of contacts enables it to act as a catalyst for British interests abroad. Most staff are employed overseas. The five principle activities of the British Council are:

o *Helping people to study, train or make professional contacts in Britain; and to enable British specialists to teach, advise or establish joint projects abroad.* Thousands of people visit the UK every year under Council auspices, on individual study visits, attachments to educational institutions, courses or international conferences. Many are involved in the government's Technical Co-operation Training Programme, which the Council administers on contract for the Overseas Development Administration. Other programmes are handled on behalf of the Foreign and Commonwealth Office, UN agencies, the World Bank, the European Union and other funding bodies. The Council also sends teaching and other staff to work overseas. For information on these appointments, contact the *British Council*, Bridgewater House, 58 Whitworth Street, Manchester M1 6BB; ☎0161-957 7000; fax 0161-957 7111; e-mail general.enquiries@britishcouncil.org; www.britishcouncil.org.

o *Teaching English and promoting its use.* The Council manages its own network of English language teaching and resource centres throughout the non-English-speaking world. Teachers are recruited on fixed-term contracts and are encouraged to move periodically around the network. A Certificate level TEFL qualification is essential for all British Council EFL teachers, and some posts require futher qualifications such as TEFL Diploma. For information contact the Teacher Recruitment Unit, *British Council*, 10 Spring Gardens, London SW1A 2BN; ☎020-7389 4931; fax 020-7389 4140; e-mail teacher.vacancies@britishcouncil.org; www.britishcouncil.org/teacherrecruitment.

o   *Providing library and information services.* Working overseas in close co-operation with the local British Diplomatic Mission, the Council provides an information service that handles enquiries about British education and English language teaching, books, culture and qualifications. The service is provided from the network of libraries and resource centres mentioned above, in the major centres of population in the countries in which the Council has a presence.

o   *Promoting British education, science and technology.* Through its network of contacts in higher education, research institutions and government ministries, the Council enables co-operation between individuals and institutions and, working with relevant sections of HM Mission, encourages and promotes the use of British services and products.

o   *Promoting British arts and literature.* Council assistance enables the promotion of high-quality British drama, dance and music, as well as a range of exhibitions that regularly tour the world, with significant and growing amounts of sponsorship from the business world both in the United Kingdom and abroad.

RECRUITMENT FOR POSTS OVERSEAS

Recruitment campaigns are publicised in the UK national press, notably *The Guardian*, as well as in relevant specialist journals such as the *Library Association Record* and *New Scientist*. Essential criteria are a good first degree and at least three years' work experience; a further degree plus experience of working overseas for an extended period are highly desirable. Ability and interest in foreign language learning is essential, though language training is provided when necessary. The British Council is an equal opportunity employer.

Further details can be obtained from Development and Training Services, *British Council*, Bridgewater House, 58 Whitworth Street, Manchester M1 6BB; ☎0161-957 7000; fax 0161-957 7111; e-mail general.enquiries@britishcouncicl.org; www.britishcouncil.org.

BRITISH GEOLOGICAL SURVEY

The British Geological Survey is concerned with geological mapping and resource investigations in Great Britain and its continental shelf, and in developing countries overseas. Scientific staff of the British Geological Survey have the opportunity of serving overseas either as members of geological teams working on specific projects or on secondment as members of geological survey departments overseas.

Much of the work overseas involves specialists in the fields of hydrogeology, geophysics, geochemistry, engineering and geology, and other related fields.

Further details on employment and career prospects can be obtained from Personnel, *British Geological Survey*, Kingsley Dunham Centre, Keyworth, Nottingham NG12 5GG; ☎0115-936 3100; fax 0115-936 3200; www.bgs.ac.uk.

The Armed Forces

THE BRITISH ARMY

Europe has been transformed since the pulling down of the Berlin Wall in 1989: the Warsaw Pact has been dismantled and Germany has been united. These factors have in turn had an effect on the shape, function and size of the British Army. The new Army is smaller, even more highly trained, flexible, more mobile and better prepared to operate as part of a multinational force – a role it is increasingly having to fulfil, with participation in conflict resolution from Kosovo to East Timor.

Every year, the British Army seeks new officers, of which approximately three-quarters are graduates. New officers, both male and female, are always needed to bring youthful drive, enthusiasm and energy into the Army, as well as contemporary educational and technical skills. British Army officers are employed in more than 80 countries worldwide, including Germany, Belize, Kosovo, Kenya, Cyprus, the Falkland Islands and Gibraltar.

ELIGIBILITY

The following eligibility criteria should be noted before an application is made:

○ *Marital Status* – Women and men, both single and married, are eligible to apply. Employment within or in support of the Armed Forces is in accordance with the conditions of the Equal Opportunities Act.

○ *Nationality* – An applicant joining from the UK must be a resident of the UK or the Irish Republic, and preferably have lived there for a minimum of five years immediately prior to making the application to join the Army, The applicant must hold UK, Commonwealth or Irish citizenship. A candidate, whether or not of UK origin, must have resided in the UK for a period of at least five years prior to the Commissioning Course.

○ *Political Bias* – No one, while a member of the Armed Forces, may take part in any political activity.

○ *Age* – The minimum age for entry into the Armed Forces is 16. Parents' consent is needed for entrants under 18. The upper age limit is 30. Age limits vary depending on the Corps.

○ *Health* – All applicants must pass a strict health examination. Applicants for some branches may be refused on the grounds of their height, hearing or eyesight.

OBTAINING A COMMISSION

Officers are commissioned at the Royal Military Academy, Sandhurst. All officers, graduates, non-graduates, men and women, those hoping for a Regular Commission, and those hoping for a Short Service Commission, undertake the same Commissioning Course, which lasts 11 months. The two types of commission in the British Army are:

1. *The Regular Commission* – open to both graduates and non-graduates and to both male and female applicants. All applicants must be aged over 17 years nine months and under 29 on entry to the Royal Military Academy, Sandhurst for officer training. In the case of the Technical Corps an upper age limit of 27 may be considered. Passes are required in five separate approved GCSE examinations (A-C grades), including English Language and Mathematics, as well as either a science subject or a foreign language. Passes are also required in two A-levels at grades A-E. Regular Commission officers have the opportunity to serve up to the age of 55.

2. *The Short Service Commission* – open to graduates and non-graduates and to male and female applicants. All applicants must be aged over 17 years 9 months and under 29 on entry to the Royal Military Academy, Sandhurst for officer training. In the case of the technical corps an upper age limit of 27 may be considered. Passes are required in five separate approved GCSE examinations (A-C grades), including English language and Mathematics. The Short Service Commission officer serves a minimum of three and up to a maximum of eight years.

GAP Year Commission

In addition to the two long-term types of commission, there is a temporary commission, known as the Short Service Limited Commission (GYC). The GAP Year Commission is open to school leavers before they take up a firm place at university to read for a degree. They must first pass the Regular Commissions Board selection. Successful candidates complete a four-week course at the Royal Military Academy, Sandhurst. Then they serve for between four to 18 months. They are required to give six weeks' notice if they wish to terminate their service. They have no reserve liability and no subsequent obligation to serve in the Army.

PROFESSIONAL BRANCHES

Short Service and Regular commissions are granted to appropriately qualified personnel to serve in the Royal Army Chaplains' Department, Royal Army Medical Corps, Royal Army Veterinary Corps, Royal Army Dental Corps, the Queen Alexandra's Royal Army Nursing Corps and the Army Legal Corps. Commissioned entry into these departments is via a four-week course at Sandhurst. Medical, legal and dental cadetships are also available.

ARMY SPONSORSHIP

The Army has several Army Education Grants (also called Army Vocational Bursaries) to sponsor young people while at school, sixth form college and university. These are:

o *Undergraduate Medical Cadetships* – open to undergraduate medical or dental students. Cadets agree to serve for six years on completion of their Pre-Registration House Officer year. Dental Cadets serve for seven years after graduation.

o *Undergraduate Bursaries* – open to men and women who are at or about to go to university or college of higher education. A bursary holder is not commissioned but does sign an agreement to serve for three years on completion of training at Sandhurst, where he or she must take up a place after graduating and before 29th birthday.

o *Sixth Form Scholarship Scheme*– Army scholarships are awarded to boys and girls aged 16-16½, to enable them to take the A-levels necessary for Sandhurst entrance. Scholarphi holders must complete three years of commissioned service.

o *Welbeck College* – boys and girls aged 15-17½ with GCSEs in Maths, Physics, and preferably Further Maths or another science subjects, can take science A-levels at the Army Sixth Form College, Welbeck, to qualify to enter Sandhurst. They will mainly be commissioned into one of the technical corps.

NON-COMMISSIONED SERVICE

In addition to officer posts, the Army has openings for entry into the ranks. The following opportunities are available:

o   *Technical, Arms and Corps Apprenticeships* – various technical apprentice colleges offer one-year courses for boys and girls aged 16 years to 17 years 6 months on entry. Basic military and leadership training, general subjects, and many specialist occupations are taught. Applicants for apprenticeships should expect to obtain GCSEs in Maths and English at Grade C or above, and in one other craft or technical subject. Training in technical and artisan trades is aimed at achieving NVQ 3 awards, and can lead to further training opportunities.

o   *Adult Entry* – unqualified men and women aged 17-25 (sometimes up to age 30) may enter one of the 135 occupations in the Army.

Length of Service

Entry into the ranks is on the terms of an open engagement. Enlistment is for a minimum period of four years. Apprentices serve for a minimum of four years from their 18th birthday. Entrants under the age of 17½ are allowed to leave the Army within the first 6 months if they find themselves unsuited to Army life. A full career in the ranks is reckoned as 22 years, but 12 months' notice can be given at any time once the initial period of enlistment has been served.

WOMEN IN THE BRITISH ARMY

The Women's Royal Army Corps (WRAC) was disbanded in 1992, and today women who serve as commissioned officers or as non-commissioned soldiers are employed in all Regiments and Corps of the British Army on an equal basis with men. The only exception to the foregoing is that women cannot at present be commissioned into the Household Cavalry, the Royal Armoured Corps or the Infantry; however, women may be attached to these Units for up to three years at a time. Men and women are trained together at all stages, including officer training at Sandhurst.

Women apply for commissioned service, both Short Service and Regular Commissions, and for non-commissioned service, in the same way as men. All terms of service, training, pay and promotion rules are identical. Likewise, entry requirements are identical to those for male applicants.

FURTHER DETAILS

Further details on both commissioned and non-commissioned entry is available from one of the 123 Army Recruitment Offices. The addresses can be found on www.armygrants.mod.uk/contact. The Army also has a good website at www.army.mod.uk.

THE ROYAL NAVY

The Royal Navy provides extensive opportunities to serve both in ships and shore establishments situated all over the world. After a period of reduction, the Navy currently recruits about 500 officers and 4,500 ratings every year.

COMMISSIONED SERVICE

Scholarships and reserved places in the warfare, supply and aircrew branches are available to young men and women aged 15-17 with five GCSE passes or equivalent. All branches of the Navy are open to graduate entry and university sponsorships are also offered, including an engineering sponsorship scheme at Southampton University.

All new commissioned officers join the Royal Navy on a 12-year initial commission with opportunities to transfer to longer periods of service at a later stage. The age limits on entry differ depending on branch and commission, but range between 17 and 40. Doctors and dentists all enter the Navy on Short Career Commissions, and age limits vary. All Naval officers go to the Britannia Royal Naval College, Dartmouth, for basic officer training. Both men and women are recruited into all branches of the naval service except for the Submarine Branch and the Royal Marines, which remain male only.

NON-COMMISSIONED SERVICE

Educational qualifications are not required for entry into most branches in the Royal Navy, but all applicants must pass a recruiting test and medical. Male and female applicants for Junior and Adult Entry in non-technical branches and for Artificer Apprentice entry must be between the ages of 16 and 32. Artificer Apprentice applicants must possess acceptable grades at GCSE or equivalent in Maths, English Language, and Physics (or a suitable physics-based science subject).

Applicants for entry as a Medical Technician must have acceptable grades at GCSE or equivalent in at least five subjects. For some Medical Technician specialisations, A levels or SCE passes at Higher Grades are required. Applicants must be between the ages of $17\frac{1}{2}$ and 32, and pass a selection board process. Entry is also open to fully qualified Medical Technicians subject to Service requirements.

Applicants for entry as a Communication Technician must have acceptable grades at GCSE in at least two subjects, one of which must be English Language, and must pass aptitude tests and a selection board.

For further information and how to apply to the Royal Navy and the Royal Marines see *Methods of Application* below.

THE ROYAL MARINE COMMANDOS

The Royal Marines are an autonomous military corps within the Royal Navy, and provide Britain's commando forces. Special training for jungle, desert, snow and mountain warfare is given in Malaysia, Borneo, the Arctic, Norway, Canada and Scotland. The Royal Marines comprises around 7,000 officers and men.

Commissioned Service in the Marines

Royal Marines officers undergo their initial training at the Commando Training Centre for Royal Marines near Exeter; the course includes a period at the Brittania Royal Naval College. A limited number of sponsorships for undergraduates are available. Entry age depends on commission and whether the candidate is a graduate but ages range from 17-26. Training lasts three years and minimum periods of service are comparable with those of the RN. The Royal Marines is open to males only.

Non-Commissioned Service

Applicants for entry to Royal Marines General Duties (other ranks) do not require educational qualifications, but must be male and between the ages of 16 and 27. They must pass a recruiting test (reasoning, numeracy, literacy, and mechanical comprehension), a medical and the Potential Royal Marines Course.

Applicants for the position of Royal Marines Musician and Bugler do not require educational qualifications but must be between the ages of 16 and 27, male or female. They must pass a recruiting test, medical, and music assessment and audition. Selected candidates may apply for a bursary to attend an approved college music course.

METHODS OF APPLICATION – ROYAL NAVY AND ROYAL MARINES

For further information, enquirers should contact the nearest Armed Forces Careers Office, Jobcentre or Careers Service. Those wishing to apply for a Royal Navy or Royal Marines commission should contact *Officer Career Liaison Centres*, St George's Court, 2-12 Bloomsbury Way, London WC1A 2SH; ☎020-7305 2214; fax 020-7305 4310; e-mail oclc.london@dnr.mod.uk. There are Officer Career Liaison Centres in Bristol, Birmingham, Manchester, Rosyth and Belfast. The Royal Navy websites are www.royal-navy.mod.uk and www.royal-marines.mod.uk.

THE ROYAL AIR FORCE

Although the number of RAF bases abroad has been reduced, there are still opportunities for overseas service. The Women's Royal Air Force is not a separate force and so is not listed separately. The RAF is an equal opportunities employer and male and female applicants are recruited for all branches except the RAF Regiment, which remains male only.

Commissioned Service

University cadetships are available to applicants aged under 23 years of age who have a university place or at least good prospects of gaining one. The scheme is designed to help entrants obtain a degree and provides generous sponsorship.

Direct Entry into commissioned service is via the RAF College at Cranwell. There are 15 Officer specialisations, including Pilot, Navigator, ATC and Fighter Control. Men and women aged over 17½, with two A-levels and five GCSE level passes can be considered for Officer Training. The upper age limit varies according to the branch and can be up to 39 (for medical officers); however, applicants for Pilot training must be under 24 at start of training.

Professionally qualified men and women up to age 30 may enter via a shortened course at RAF College Cranwell into the Medical, Dental, Chaplains and Legal branches.

The brochure *Officer & Aircrew* contains detailed information about conditions of entry at officer level in the Royal Air Force, and is available from your local Armed Forces Careers Office (call 020-7305 4278 to find location or check the webpage www.rafcareers. com). It also details sponsorship arrangements and scholarships available.

Non-Commissioned Service

The RAF recruits other personnel in the following roles:

o *Non-Commissioned Aircrew* – opportunities exist for NCO aircrew in the positions of Air Loadmaster and Air Electronics Operator. Applicants must usually be under 31 with 5 GCSEs at grade C, including mathematics, English Language and a science subject.

o *Royal Air Force Trades* – men and women aged between 16 and 30 may apply for entry to various trade positions. No GCSEs are required in certain areas of operations support, engineering and logistics, communications, for training as a medical assistant and dental nurse, or in administration. For entry to trades in intelligence and cartography, technical engineering, nursing, radiography, catering (qualified chef) and other roles, between two and five GCSEs are required. Requirements change from time to time and detailed information is available from your RAF careers office.

Length of Service

There are two types of commission – Regular and Short. Regular commissions can last until the age of 55 but may be terminated at the age of 38 or after 16 years service if you enter after the age of 21, whichever is the later. Short service commissions are for three to six years for ground branches, and 12 years, with an option of leaving earlier, for aircrew. Fixed engagements for non-commissioned service are normally for nine years.

Further details can be obtained from your nearest Armed Forces Careers Office or from the RAF website at www.rafcareers.com.

ANCILLARY SERVICES

Positions are available for nursing and welfare staff in all three armed force services, all of which offer good prospects for overseas posting. There are service hospitals wherever large numbers of servicemen and their families are based and nurses are constantly in demand.

Queen Alexandra's Royal Army Nursing Corps

Nursing Officers: Men and women aged 21–39 years with 2 years experience with the NMC as a RN (Adult or Mental Health). A 6 year commission is offered following selection with opportunities to serve until the age of 55 years. Applicants must thrive in a team, enjoy a challenge, be hard working, reliable, adaptable and able to lead by example.

Registered Nurse – soldier (Adult or Mental Health): Men and women aged 21–33 years can join following selection as soon as qualified and registered with the NMC as a RN (Adult or Mental Health). A 4 year engagement is offered with opportunities to extend to have a full career including commissioning. Applicants must be reliable, adaptable and have some leadership potential.

Student Nurses: Men and women aged 17 years, 10 months up to 33 years. A 7 year engagement is initially offered including 3 years student nurse training. Opportunities exist to extend to a full career including commissioning. Applicants need to have a real desire to care for people and to work as part of a team in a variety of situations. They should be keen to learn, self-motivated and enjoy a challenge.

Health Care Assistants: Men and Women aged 17 years and 6 months up to 33 years. A 4 year engagement is offered including 2 years training at NVQ level 2. Opportunities exist to extend for a full career. Applicants should have a real interest in caring for people and the desire to work as part of a team in a variety of situations. They should be flexible and enjoy challenges.

Princess Mary's Royal Air Force Nursing Service

Registered General Nurses aged 21-27 may apply for a Staff Nurse post in the PMRAFNS. If you are aged between 23 and 34 with a minimum of two years' post-registration experience, preferably with some experience of ward management and normally a second nursing certificate, you are eligible to apply for a four year short service commission as a Nursing Officer. Limited opportunities for further service are open to suitable candidates.

Soldiers', Sailors' and Airmen's Families Association Forces Help

The SSAFA Forces Help provides health care for Service families posted overseas. SSAFA recruits experienced United Kingdom-based civilian Health Visitors, Midwives, Community Psychiatric Nurses, Pharmacists, Practice Managers, and Practice Nurses to work with Service families. There are well established Health Promotion and In-service Training Departments.

SSAFA Forces Help employs qualified and experienced Social Workers to work with Servicemen and their families both overseas and in the United Kingdom. For further details contact *SSAFA Forces Help*, 19 Queen Elizabeth Street, London SE1 2LP; ☎0845-1300975; e-mail info@ssafa.org.uk; www.ssafa.org.uk.

FOREIGN ARMED FORCES

National armed forces are usually open only to citizens of that country. However, some countries welcome other nationals into their ranks. Some countries may, in fact, insist that foreign permanent residents are prepared to do military service. The Arabian Gulf states are among those countries prominent in recruiting trained foreign personnel for their armed forces.

THE FRENCH FOREIGN LEGION

The French Foreign Legion, immortalised in the book *Beau Geste*, was created in 1831 and is a semi-autonomous unit under the control of the French Ministry of Defence. Although the life of the legionnaire is idealised in fiction and the recruitment leaflets, it can in fact be lonely and austere. The chances of getting out before the end of the five-year contract are slim.

Entry Requirements

Applicants must be aged between 17 and 40 (with the average age being 24). Seventeen year olds must get written consent from their parents. All applicants must be physically fit. Beyond this, the only requirement is complete loyalty to the legion, whose motto *legio patria nostra* (the legion is our country) demands that soldiers should renounce their loyalties to family, friends and home country. Intellectual ability and knowledge of the French language are not required; colour, creed, nationality and social class have no bearing; and few questions are asked about identity or background.

Enlistment can only take place in France at one of the 17 Foreign Legion information centres. Any gendarmerie in France can direct you to the nearest centre. The obligatory medical, psychological and professional tests are held at Aubagne, near Marseille.

Service

Contracts are initially for five years, starting with 16 weeks' training at Castelnaudary. Following the training course, soldiers are classified as specialist combatant, technician or corporal, with promotion prospects to officer status. Service is in one of the parachute, infantry, cavalry or mixed regiments in Corsica or the south of France. During the first five years it is also possible to serve for two years in one of the regiments stationed in Tahiti, Mayotte, Djibouti and French Guyana. Special training can be given in a variety of trades, including telecommunications, mechanics and building.

At the end of five years, contracts can be renewed for up to three years at a time, and you will become pensionable after a total of 15 years' service.

Further Details

Further details of recruitment procedure and recruitment centres in France are available from the *Légion Etrangère Bureau du Recrutement*, Quartier Viénot BP 38, 13998 Marseilles Armée, France; ☎+33 442 188 257; www.legion-recrute.com. Enquiries can be accepted in English.

OTHER SERVICES

THE POLICE

Opportunities for British policemen and women occasionally arise in a few Commonwealth member states, although these have been reduced in recent years. There are no formal foreign exchange schemes available to police officers, but a small number of officers are seconded abroad each year from the Metropolitan and other constabularies. Police positions overseas are sometimes advertised in the *Police Review*, available on subscription from *Jane's Information Group*, Sentinel House, 163 Brighton Road, Coulsdon, Surrey CR5 2YH; ☎020-8700 3700; fax 020-8763 1006; e-mail janes@ subs@qss-uk.com; www. janes.com.

The Service Recruitment and Selection Centre of the Metropolitan Police (address below) advises that at any one time some 20 fairly senior officers will be seconded abroad from this country. The Metropolitan Police Force also advise that much of this recruitment takes place by word of mouth. General information about joining the police force can be obtained by calling ☎0845-608 3000 or checking the Police Recruitment Service website at www.policecouldyou.co.uk.

The Metropolitan Police Force

All officers recruited to the Metropolitan Police Force must meet certain minimum entry standards. They must be a British or Commonwealth citizen permanently resident in the UK, physically fit, 18½ or older, and have good eyesight. They must have experience of living or working in London, possess excellent communication skills and be of good character.

Prospective police officers take a series of written tests and must also pass a rigorous physical fitness test and appear in front of a selection board. If appointed, they will begin their careers with a two-year probationary period. The first 16 weeks of this are spent on integrated training, based at the Metropolitan Police Training Centre at the Peel Centre, Hendon, North London.

General correspondence and enquiries to the *Metropolitan Police Force*, Police Recruitment Centre, Simpson House, Peel Centre, Aerodrome Road, London NW9 5RF; ☎020-7230 1212, 0845-727 2212; www.metcareers.co.uk.

Worldwide Employment

WESTERN EUROPE

The following section provides general information on living and working in those countries of western, southern and northern Europe belonging to the EU and European Economic Area. The significance of these political alliances for jobseekers is explained in detail in the earlier chapter on Rules and Regulations. Switzerland, although not a part of the European Union, is also included for both geographical and cultural reasons: its location and history means that Switzerland has close links with its neighbours, even though the regulations for those seeking work are not the same. The institutions and agencies of the European Union are detailed, with particular reference to employment opportunities, at the beginning of the *International Organisations* chapter.

The countries of central and Eastern Europe are treated in a later section. Many of these are now EU members but, in those countries that are not yet EU members there has been a rapid process of economic change, and it is only recently that significant numbers of international workers have gained employment in the region. Expatriate workers are generally employed in specialised areas arising from the transition from centrally planned to free market economy, as well as to a more open society, which has brought both problems and opportunities in its wake. In general, however, the opportunities for foreign nationals to live and work elsewhere in Europe are largely concentrated in the countries of Western Europe detailed in this first section, and it is for this reason that the two regions are treated separately.

THE EURO €

On 1 January 2002, twelve member states of the European Union replaced their national currency with a new, single currency known as the 'euro'(€). The euro has been created as a keystone in the transition towards Economic and Monetary Union (EMU), with participating countries forming a 'eurozone'. The twelve countries of the euro-zone are Austria, Belgium, Finland, France, Germany, Greece, the Republic of Ireland, Italy, Luxembourg, the Netherlands, Portugal and Spain. The UK, Denmark and Sweden have decided not to join EMU at this stage, although the topic is hotly debated in the United Kingdom, and many see it as inevitable that Britain will join within the next half-decade. The 10 new member states (see *Rules and Regulations*) that joined the EU on 1 May 2004 will adopt the euro once they have fulfilled the necessary conditions: achieving the high degree of sustainable economic convergence with the euro area.

In the twelve countries of the 'euro-zone' the *only* notes and coins used are now euros. All non-cash transactions – for example bank transfers and cheques – which were formerly in the existing national currencies, must be in euro.

The value of the euro fluctuates like that of any other currency, but euro-zone countries now share a single foreign-exchange rate policy and a single interest rate. There are 100 cents in every euro, and there are seven bank notes in denominations of 5, 10, 20, 50, 100, 200, and 500 euro. Coinage consists of 1, 2, 5, 10, 20, and 50 cent coins and 1 and 2 euro. At the time of writing, the euro is very approximately equivalent to 67 pence (UK) and 81 cents (US).

Any payments you receive in euro when working in euro-zone countries can be converted to your national currency (such as pounds sterling), and it is also possible to open a euro bank account. The British government has a euro information website at www.euro.gov.uk.

Austria

- o **Year of EU accession:** 1995
- o **Austrian Embassy,** 18 Belgrave Mews West, London SW1X 8HU; ☎020-7344 3250; fax 020-7344 0292; e-mail embassy@austria.org.uk; www.austria.org.uk
- o **Austrian Embassy,** 3524 International Court NW, Washington, DC 20008; ☎202-895 6711; fax 202-895 6773; www.austria.org
- o **Currency:** 1 Euro (€) = 100 cents
- o **Rate of Exchange:** £1 = €1.44; $1 = €0.78
- o **Country Code:** +43

Austria has been a full member of the EU since 1995, which means that no work permit is required for citizens of other EU member states. More information on immigration and employment in EU countries is given in the chapter on *Rules and Regulations*, and these general rules hold true for Austria. Austria's entry into the EU has been particularly good news for its tourist industry, which now recruits significant numbers of English-speaking staff, above all in ski resorts. The main competition for jobs in hotel and tourism work is from East Europeans who are usually prepared to accept low pay and less satisfactory conditions than Western Europeans.

Like Poland, the Czech Republic or Hungary, Austria regards itself as a Central European country, at the crossroads of east and west. It is a small economy, but has strong trading and cultural links with its neighbours. Austria enjoys a low inflation rate, currently just more than one per cent, and relatively low unemployment (under four per cent). It is experiencing economic growth at a rate of 3.1 per cent per annum.

Austria is, in fact, one of the wealthiest and most stable of the EU member states. It is a highly developed industrialised nation with an important services sector. The most important industries are foods, luxury commodities, mechanical engineering and steel construction, chemicals and vehicle manufacturing. Manufacturing, including mining, accounts for nearly 31 per cent of Austria's Gross Domestic Product (GDP). The country has a strong agricultural industry, which meets around 90 per cent of the country's food needs. Currently the service sector, including banking, commerce, transport and tourism, accounts for around 67 per cent of GDP. Austria is an export-orientated country with a wide-ranging foreign trade system. It has trade links with some 150 countries around the world, with other EU countries accounting for two-thirds of its foreign trade.

In Austria coffee shops are a national (if rather expensive) institution and the nightlife is somewhat quiet. 'Early to bed, early to rise' could equally be an Austrian saying. Winter sports and other alpine pursuits are a way of life. Work relations are generally formal, and as elsewhere a smart appearance is important if you want to make a good impression. A working knowledge of German will greatly improve your chances of finding employment.

GENERAL FACTS

POPULATION AND GEOGRAPHY

Austria has a population of 8.2 million. Population density is low and currently stands at around 97 people per square kilometre. The landscape is famously scenic, with the high Alpine mountains of the Tyrol, the lakes of Carinthia, the River Danube (which flows through the capital Vienna), and the forests of Styria. Vienna has a population of 1.6 million. Austria is a landlocked country bordered by Switzerland, Liechtenstein, Germany, the Czech Republic, the Slovak Republic, Hungary, Slovenia and Italy, and is predominantly Alpine. Its geographical location means that both historically and economically it has strong links with Eastern Europe.

CLIMATE

Be prepared for cold weather in winter. This is a moderate continental climate, and summers can be hot.

GOVERNMENT

Austria is a democratic republic. 'Legislative power is in the hands of the people.' So begins the Federal Constitution, which has its origins in the anti-fascist parties, which proclaimed Austria's independence after its liberation in 1945. The head of state is the President; and there is a bicameral parliament, known as the federal assembly, made up of the *Nationalrat* and *Bundesrat*. The former is elected every four years and to the latter, Austria's nine provinces and their parliaments send representatives.

RELIGION, SPORT AND CULTURE

Austria is 73 per cent Roman Catholic and five per cent Protestant. Soccer, motor sports and cycling are important, but Austria leads the way in Alpine skiing and the various other winter sports, particularly tobogganing, for which it often hosts international competitions. Three million Austrians belong to sports or health and fitness clubs. Architecture, painting and music are Austria's great cultural achievements; the annual Salzburg festival focuses mainly on work by Mozart and Richard Strauss. The ornate baroque architecture to be found in Salzburg and Vienna is regarded as representative of the Austrian national character. The end of the Austro-Hungarian Empire was also a time of great artistic and cultural activity, with writers like Robert Musil, the composer Arnold Schönberg, and psychologist Sigmund Freud among the leading lights.

FACTORS INFLUENCING EMPLOYMENT

IMMIGRATION

Visas are not required by US citizens for stays of up to 90 days, however, all non-EU nationals will require a work permit. The Austrian Embassy states that, for non-EU citizens, a work permit must be applied for by the future employer in Austria, prior to the prospective employee's intended departure from their home country. Once an offer of work is secured, the employer obtains the work permit from the *Arbeitmarktservice* (employment agency – see below) which then forwards it to the *Austrian Consulate-General* in the employee's country of residence. The employee then sends the work permit application together with his or her passport, a completed application form for the issuing of a visa and the fee, to the Consulate-General. The special visa will then be issued upon approval. For non-EU citizens it is virtually impossible to obtain a work permit for casual and seasonal work. Au pairs from outside the EU must obtain both a work and residence permit (*Beschäftigungsbewilligung*), however, this can also be applied for inside Austria, for a fee. At present there is a quota on foreign workers from outside the EU, and when the annual quota is filled no further permits are granted.

EU and EEA nationals do not require a work permit and are not subject to these restrictions. You have six months to find an employer, who will then support your application for a residence permit. *EURES* (see *Getting the Job*) is the best contact in the UK, and you should approach your local Jobcentre. The equivalent employment services in Austria are the state-run *Arbeitmarktservice-Geschäftsstelle* (Austrian Employment Service) offices (which will expect you to speak German). To find the address of the nearest jobcentre in Austria either look in the local telephone directory or contact the head office of the *Austrian Employment Service* (Bundesgeschäftsstelle, Arbeitmarktservice Österreich, Weihburggasse 30, A-1011, Wien; ☎ 1-515250; www.ams.or.at). They also have an online job search and can provide a list of companies looking for employees.

Foreign nationals (and Austrians as well) who intend to set up in business require both a work permit and a permit from the head of the provincial government (*Landeshauptmann*) and for certain trades and professions a licence, or proof of qualifications given.

All foreign nationals intending to reside in Austria are required to register with the police at their local aliens administration office within three days of arrival. After ten years' residence in Austria, immigrants may apply for Austrian nationality. Detailed information on the Austrian labour market as well as living and working conditions in Austria (i.e. accommodation, taxes, health and social issues, legislation, etc.) are available on the EURES Job Mobility Portal-site (http://europa.eu/).

LANGUAGE

The official language of Austria is German, though Slovenian, Croatian and Hungarian are also spoken in some provinces. The ability to read and write German will be a requirement for almost all jobs in Austria.

EDUCATION

Compulsory schooling lasts nine years. Primary school (ages 6 to 10) is followed by secondary education (ages 10 to 14) and grammar school (ages 10 to 18) in either a *Hauptschule* or the lower classes of an *allgemein bildende höch Schule*. Pupils who leave school at 14 can enrol at a *Polytechnikum* to prepare for working life. Apprentices attend vocational school. Upper secondary education is required for entry to university. All Austria's schools are covered by the same regulations. No fees are charged at state-run schools, and school textbooks and travel to and from school are also free. Further information is available at www.bmbwk.gv.at.

CONDITIONS OF EMPLOYMENT

Every employee in Austria has a legal right to at least five weeks' paid holiday leave per year. If an employee falls ill, he or she will either continue to be paid in full, or will receive sick pay from the social insurance scheme. Parents are entitled to two years' maternity leave from the date of birth, during which time they receive maternity benefits.

The official working day is eight hours, and the working week, a maximum of forty hours, spread over five days wherever possible. Higher wage rates apply to overtime. Young people, women and mothers enjoy special protection as employees, and high safety standards are applied in the workplace and carefully monitored.

SOCIAL SECURITY

Austria has a full cradle-to-grave social security system. Its legislation includes extensive national insurance coverage for accident, illness (including surgery), childbirth, unemployment, pensions, and even spa treatments. People officially resident in Austria who provide for a child are also eligible to receive various children's allowances.

All employees (with the exception of au pairs) have around 16 per cent of their wages deducted to contribute to the compulsory Health and Social Security Scheme which also comprises a pension scheme, covering most medical expenses, including hospital treatment. Minimum income workers are not obliged to pay sickness and pension insurance contributions.

EMBASSIES AND CONSULATES

British Embassy, Jaurèsgasse 12, A-1030 Vienna; ☎1-716130; fax 1-71613 2999; www. britishembassy.at.
Consular Section, Jaurèsgasse 10, A-1030 Vienna; ☎1- 71613-5151; fax 1-71613 5900.
American Embassy, Boltzmanngasse 16, A-1091 Vienna; ☎1-31339; http://vienna.usembassy.gov.
US Consulate, Parkring 12, A-1010 Vienna; ☎1-512 5835.

TOURIST OFFICES

Austrian National Tourist Office, 13-14 Cork Street, London W1A 2QB; ☎0845-101 8181; www.austria.info.
Austrian National Tourist Office, PO Box 1142, Times Square, New York, NY 10108-1142, USA; ☎212-944-6880; www.austria.info.

NEWSPAPERS

Austrian newspapers can be consulted in the reading room of the Austrian Cultural Forum, 28 Rutland Gate, London SW7 1PQ; ☎020-7584 8653; www.austria.org.uk. Advertisements can be placed in the daily *Die Presse* through *The Powers Turner Group*, Gordon House, Greencoat Place, London SW1P 1PH; ☎020-7592 8300; fax 020-7592 8301; e-mail ppn-london@publicitas.com; www.publicitas.com (which represents a wide range of newspapers and magazines worldwide). Many of the Austrian national and regional newspapers carry job advertisements on Saturdays.

INTERNET JOBSEARCH SITES

www.jobpilot.at
www.bueroring.at
www.eurojobs.at
www.jobboerse.at
www.jobbox.at

www.jobsearch.at
www.job-direct.at
www.jobcenter.at
www.jobfinder.at

SPECIFIC CONTACTS

EMPLOYMENT SERVICES

The Austrian Embassy cannot help in finding employment. Information can be obtained from Jobcentres in Britain or from the relevant regional employment office (*Arbeitmarktservice*) in Austria. These *Arbeitmarktservice* addresses are:

Permayerstrasse 10, A-7001 Eisenstadt; ☎2682 692	Burgenland
Rudolfsbahngértel 42, A-9020 Klagenfurt; ☎463-38310	Carinthia
Hohenstaufengasse 2, A-1013 Vienna; ☎1-53136	Lower Austria
Europaplatz 9, A-4020 Linz; ☎70-32 6963-0	Upper Austria
Auerpergstrasse 67a, A-5020 Salzburg; ☎662-8883	Salzburg
Bahnhofgértel 85, A-8021 Graz; ☎316-9081	Styria
Schöpfstrasse 5, A-6010 Innsbruck; ☎512-5903	Tyrol
Rheinstrasse 32, A-6903 Bregenz; ☎5574-691	Vorarlberg
Weihburggasse 30, A-1010 Vienna; ☎1-51525	Vienna

Enquiries and applications may be addressed to any one of these offices as Austria has a nationwide computerised system of vacancy notification. These should be typed in German and contain the following details: name and address; date of birth; education; profession; nature of present employment; knowledge of foreign languages; length of intended stay; type of job and location required. In Britain, EURES can advise on the procedure. However, the employment service may not help enquiries from outside the EU or EEA. For US and other non-EU citizens, permission to work in Austria can be hard to obtain, and immigration is not encouraged.

AU PAIRS

If you are looking for au pair work you are advised to contact the Vienna agency Au-Pair4You (formerly *Auslands-Sozialdienst*), Hasnerstrasse 31/22, 1160 Vienna; ☎1-990 1574; fax 1-990 157412; e-mail office@au-pair4you.at; www.aupair4you.at. A number of private agents based in cities around Austria offer a service for incoming au pairs. Most are accustomed to dealing with direct applications from abroad, though almost all expect to communicate in German. Here are some to try:

Au Pair Austria, Mariahilferstrasse 99/2/37, 1060 Vienna; tel/fax 1-920 3842; e-mail office@aupairaustria.com; www.aupairaustria.com.

Au-Pair Agentur Calimer, Stelzhamerstr.2/2/9, 4020 Linz ☎732-666233; fax 732/666244; e-mail office@calimero.co.at; www.calimero.co.at. Contact Katerina Unterluggauer.

Au Pair-Agentur Lederle Brigitte, Kaufmännen 40, 6850 Dornbirn; ☎5572-36 809; fax 5572-36 809 – 11; e-mail brigitte.lederle@vol.at.

Au-Pair & Family, Blindengasse 52/1/3, 1080 Vienna; tel/fax 1-405 405 0; e-mail office@ aupair-family.at; www.aupair-family.at.

Au-pair Corner, Josef Buchinger Straße 3, 3100 St. Pölten; ☎2742-25 85 36; fax 2742-21080; e-mail monika.essenhofer@essenhofer.at; www.au-pair-corner.at.

Family Business, Hessstrasse 2.2, 3100 St. Pölten; ☎2742-79 990; fax 2742-79 990 20; e-mail info@kinderbetreuung.at; www.kinderbetreuung.at.

Friends Au-Pair Vermittlungsagentur, Napoleongasse 7/18, 2301 Gross-Enzersdorf; ☎2249-4650; e-mail office@aupairvermittlung.at; www.aupairvermittlung.at.

Au pairs in Austria must be aged 18-28. The agency requirements are not usually very strenuous when it comes to childcare, and many inexperienced 18-year-olds are placed, especially if they have done German at GCSE or A level.

Au pairs from EU countries will have no trouble sorting out the paperwork in Austria. Officially au pairs from outside the EU must obtain both a work and residence permit *(Beschäftigungsbewilligung).* Although this can be applied for inside Austria, the process is expensive and time-consuming and some avoid it. Alien au pairs are allowed to stay in Austria for no more then a year and must renew their permit a month before the first six months is up.

If a host family wants to try to obtain a *Beschäftigungsbewilligung* for their non-EU au pair from the US, Canada, Australia, New Zealand, Japan and a few others, they should apply to the local employment office *(Arbeitsmarktservice)* at least two weeks before the au pair is due to arrive. Before the permit can be approved and an *Anzeigebestätigung* issued, the authorities must see an agreement or contract (Ref: 10 Abs 3 FrG, signed by the employer and the au pair) and proof that health and accident insurance cover has been obtained by the au pair. A template of the contract is available on the Austrian Employment Service website (www.ams.or.at/download/aupair-vertrag. pdf). The agency should help with this process and tell the au pair where to take the documents to be stamped (for a fee).

INTERNATIONAL ORGANISATIONS

An exception to the rigid work permit and visa requirements for non-EU citizens is made in the case of the international agencies in the Vienna city area. The Consular Section of the British Embassy (see above) advises that these organisations may employ foreign staff, accountants and computer programmers from abroad. Details can be obtained direct from *The Division of Personnel, UNIDO (United Nations Industrial Development Organization),*

Vienna International Centre, PO Box 300, A-1400 Vienna; ☎1-26026; fax 1-2692669; e-mail unido@unido.org; www.unido.org, or the *United Nations* office in Vienna (see *United Nations* chapter).

TEACHERS

Teachers in the Austrian State School System have civil servant status and therefore have to be Austrian citizens. A limited programme for the exchange of teachers is run by the *British Council English Language Assistants programme* (see the *Teaching* chapter).

American language students can spend eight months (October-May) working as English-teaching assistants in Austrian schools. Applications should be sent before March to the *Austrian-American Educational Commission (Fulbright Commission)*, Schmidgasse 14, A-1082 Vienna; ☎1-313 5685; fax 1-408 7765; www.fulbright.at.

The English-teaching market in Austria is relatively small and the emphasis is on business English and in-house company teaching. The *Austrian Cultural Forum*, 28 Rutland Gate, London SW7 1PQ can supply information on language schools in Austria. *Berlitz* and *inlingua* both have schools in Austria (see the *Teaching* chapter). *SPIDI (Spracheninstitut der Industrie)*, Mariahilfer Strasse 32, 1070 Vienna; 1-524 1717-11; fax 1-524 1717-100; e-mail office@mdi.at; www.spidi.at, hires part-time staff with a BA and several years' TEFL experience. A local interview is essential.

OTHER OPPORTUNITIES

The following international management recruitment and search consultancies are active in Austria. Many others can be found in the Yellow Pages, including multinational firms such as Manpower and Adecco. A list of private recruitment companies can be found on the Austrian Employment Service website at www.ams.or.at/sfa/txt1100.htm.

Catro, A-1080 Vienna, Trautsongasse 6; ☎1-408 2511-0; fax 1- 408 3008; e-mail office@ catro.com; www.catro.com. Management consultancy recruitment.

Preng and Associates, 42 Brook Street, London W1K 5DB; ☎020-7958 9043; fax 020-7958 9090; and 2925 Briarpark, Suite 1111, Houston, Texas 77042; ☎713-266 2600; fax 713-266 3070; www.preng.com. Specialising in recruitment for the energy and natural resources industries with placements in Austria.

SHORT TERM WORK

Although the Austrian authorities have made it very difficult for foreign temporary workers to work legally, EU citizens will have no trouble in obtaining casual and seasonal work in Austria.

SEASONAL WORK

Austria's hotels need extra staff to cover both the summer and winter tourist seasons. For hotel work the best single area is the Tyrol, particularly in resorts around Innsbruck. Names of individual hotels can be found in the Vacation Work book *Summer Jobs Abroad*. Campsite companies such as *Canvas Holidays* and *Eurocamp* can also offer jobs over the summer (see *Transport, Tourism and Hospitality* chapter for details).

SKI RESORTS

Austria ranks second to France as the most popular destination for British skiers, and there are good chances of finding work for English-speakers. Competent ski instructors with some German may find work at the height of the season when there is a shortage of instructors. Others can try hotel, restaurant and chalet work.

VOLUNTARY WORK

Organisations offering work camps are to be found in *Voluntary Work*. Austrian organisations who may be contacted directly include *Service Civil International, Österreichischer Zweig*, Schottengasse 3a/1/4/59, 1010 Vienna; ☎ 1-535 9108; fax 1-532 7416; e-mail office@sci. or.at; www.sci.or.at (general work camps); and *Young Austria Sommercamps*, Alpenstrasse 108a, A-5020 Salzburg; ☎ 662-625 758-0; e-mail gudrun@youngaustria.at; www.camps. at (summer language and sports camps).

INTERNATIONAL COMPANIES IN AUSTRIA

BP Austria AG **35** Schwarzenbergplatz 13/3 A-1041 Vienna	GlaxoSmithKline **8** Albert-Schweitzer-Gasse 6 A-1140 Vienna
British Airways **3** Kärntner Ring 10 A-1010 Vienna	Candy Hoover Austria GmbH **18** Mariahilferstrasse 176/2/6 A-1150 Vienna
British Bookshop **38** Blackwell & Hadwiger GmbH Weihburggasse 24-26 A-1010 Vienna	ICI Austria GmbH **10** Schwarzenbergplatz 7 A-1037 Vienna
Castrol Austria GmbH **35** IZ-NÖ-Séd Strasse 6 2355 Neudorf	Johnson Matthey & Co **28** Steckhovengasse 12 1132 Vienna
EMI Austria GmbH **10** Webgasse 43 A-1060 Vienna	Österreichische Unilever GmbH **8** Wienerbergstrasse 7 A-1103 Vienna
Ernst & Young **14** Praterstrasse 70 A-1020 Vienna	Reuters Ltd **38** Zweigniederlassung Wien 1 Börsegasse 11 A-1010 Vienna
Fujitsu Services GesmbH **10** Griessgasse 10/11 A-8020 Graz	Shell Austria AG **35** 3 Rennweg 12 1030 Vienna
Gestetner GmbH **30** Siemensstrasse 160 A-1211 Vienna	Thorn Licht GmbH **10** 22 Erzherzog-Karlstrasse 57 A-1220 Vienna

Further information on British companies with Austrian links may be obtained from the *Austrian Trade Commission*, 45 Princes Gate, Exhibition Road, London SW7 2QA; ☎ 020-7584 4411; fax 020-7584 2565; www.austriatrade.org. American companies operating in Austria are comprehensively listed in the annual *US List*, published by the *American Chamber of Commerce in Austria (AmCham)*, Porzellangasse 35, A-1090 Vienna; ☎ 1-319 5751; fax 1-319 5151; e-mail office@amcham.or.at; www.amcham.or.at.

Belgium

o **Year of EU Accession:** 1952
o **Belgian Embassy,** 17 Grosvenor Crescent, London SW1X 7EE; ☎020-7470 3700; fax 020-7470 3795; e-mail london@diplobel.be; www.diplobel.org/uk.
o **Belgian Embassy,** 3330 Garfield Street, NW, Washington DC 20008; ☎202-333 6900; fax 202-333 5457; e-mail washington@diplobel.org; www.diplobel.us.
o **Currency:** 1 Euro (€) = 100 cents
o **Rate of exchange:** £1 = €1.44; $1 = €0.78
o **Country Code:** +32

Belgium is the seat of the EU, NATO, and more than 1,000 other international organisations, which regularly recruit English-speaking personnel. Short-term, au pair and seasonal work is also available. For long-term workers from the UK a weekend at home presents little problem. Brussels has a large and diverse expatriate community. Although there is still a shortage of skilled labour in some economic sectors, high unemployment means considerable competition for jobs that do not require specialist expertise. Knowledge of French or Dutch may be required. Belgium is an 'international' country at a major European crossroads proud of its affiliation with the EU. English is quite widely spoken, especially in the Flemish-speaking north and west. The economy is especially dependent on export earnings, and wages fall somewhere between the high salaries in Holland and the more moderate levels of France.

Employment legislation is strictly enforced in Belgium with minimum wage levels; compulsory bonuses, and sickness and holiday pay for all legal workers. The demand for temporary workers is high, but there is little agricultural seasonal work of the kind found in other European countries.

GENERAL FACTS

POPULATION

Belgium has a population of 10.4 million. With a total area of 11,783 square miles (30,517 sq km), Belgium has, after the Netherlands, the second highest population density in Europe – 858 per square mile.

Belgium is a little larger than the American state of Maryland, making it the second smallest country in the EU after Luxembourg. The landscape is mainly flat and rolling, rising above 300m only in the Ardennes in the east of the country. Over half the land area is farmland; industry accounts for a considerable part of land use.

CLIMATE

The climate of most of Belgium is similar to that in the southeast of England. A more continental climate (with colder winters and drier summers) is found in the Ardennes and Luxembourg.

GOVERNMENT

Belgium is a constitutional monarchy and has been since 1830. The central legislative system consists of two chambers: the Chamber of Representatives, and the Senate.

Members of the Chamber of Representatives are elected every four years. Senators also serve four-year terms. Belgium is also a federal state, with largely autonomous regions in Flanders, Wallonia, and Brussels controlling over half of the national budget. This federal structure may in part explain the enthusiasm for a European federal state in this linguistically divided country.

There are two lower tiers of government: ten provinces which are administratively divided into 589 *communes* or communal councils. The constitutional revisions that came into effect in 1995 allowed representation for its main language communities for the first time.

CITIES

Belgium is more urbanised than most European countries. More than 30 per cent of the population is concentrated in five main urban areas: Brussels (which has a population of nearly one million); Antwerp (480,000); Ghent (230,000); Charleroi (210,000); and Liège (200,000). Antwerp at the mouth of the Schelde River is one of the world's major ports.

RURAL LIFE

Farmland accounts for over half of the total land area, but less than three per cent of the labour force is employed in agriculture. This figure also covers employees in forestry (a further 20 per cent of the land area) and the fisheries on the North Sea Coast. There is minimum demand for seasonal workers in harvesting and processing.

RELIGION, SPORT AND CULTURE

Belgium is overwhelmingly Roman Catholic, although religious freedom is observed. Traditionally, the country's most popular sport has been cycling, with football a close second. Many clubs are still semi-professional. Golf, tennis, and basketball are also played, and there is the Belgian Grand Prix every year for Formula 1 fans. The national Belgian football team is known as the Red Devils.

The history of Belgian art is long, and some of its best-known names include Van Eyck, Breughel, Rubens and Magritte, many of whose paintings can be seen in the Brussels Museum of Ancient Arts. While the major cultural institutions are concentrated in Brussels, all the larger Belgian cities have art galleries, theatres and concert halls. Jazz and avant-garde theatre are popular, and the Belgian National Tourist office can be contacted for details of the many festivals. Antwerp was a European Cultural capital in 1993. Other cultural and historic centres like Bruges as well as battlefield sites and spas are popular tourist attractions.

FACTORS INFLUENCING EMPLOYMENT

IMMIGRATION

The Belgian Embassy, although unable to assist in finding work, issues some general information for those wishing to settle in Belgium.

Although work permits are no longer required for EU citizens, all Britons intending to take up employment in Belgium must register their address within eight days of arrival at the town hall (French *maison communale*/Dutch *stadhuis*) of the district in which they are staying. The *maison communale* can issue a temporary residence permit, but a permanent residence permit can only be issued later on approval by the Aliens Police. Belgium is part of the 'borderless' region in the EU created by the Schengen Agreement.

US citizens may remain in Belgium for a three-month period without a visa. However, work permits must be obtained before arriving in Belgium if this is the reason for your travel. People wishing to take up temporary residence should apply to the Belgian Embassy.

LANGUAGE

The main linguistic division in Belgium is between the 'Flemings' and the Walloons, who speak Dutch and French respectively. For its first 164 years Belgium was a highly centralised state but in 1971 legislation created a federal structure which could embrace Flemish, French and German speakers. The division between these language communities is one of the main political issues in the country. The Dutch-speaking part in the north and west of Belgium contains 58 per cent of the total population, compared with only 33 per cent in the French-speaking area. Brussels has nine per cent of the total population, the majority of whom are bilingual. The fourth area is the small German-speaking Eupen-Malmédy region on the German frontier.

COST AND STANDARD OF LIVING

Thanks to an improved economic situation Belgium now has a small budget surplus and is planning to reduce taxes over the coming years to make the country more of an entrepreneurial society. It is highly integrated into the EU and more than three-quarters of trade is with other EU states. Together with its strategic position in Europe, this important trading role gives Belgium an economic and diplomatic profile in world affairs, which is out of proportion to its size and population. The cost of living is a little less than in the UK but about 25 per cent more than in the US. Brussels is one of Europe's cheapest capitals; rents are about half those in London.

WAY OF LIFE

Belgian cuisine is similar to that of France, but each region has its own specialities and traditions. Local beers are renowned throughout the world and the majority of cafés have a licence to serve spirits. There are no licensing hours and there is a lively restaurant scene and nightlife in most Belgian towns despite the sometimes dour image of the country. Belgium is one of the few countries in Europe that does not have an accommodation shortage, but prices, especially in Brussels, can be high. Ceramics, chocolate, lace and jewellery are traditional products. Flemish-speakers in the north may prefer you to speak English to them rather than French.

HEALTH AND WELFARE

Belgium has a comprehensive welfare system and workers pay compulsory contributions out of their earnings, which entitle them to sickness, disablement and unemployment benefits, pensions, maternity and family allowances, and almost complete medical insurance. Employees who have completed a trial period are entitled to their full salary for one month in case of illness or accident and are then entitled to disability payments. Any employee's contract is legally suspended during a period of illness and cannot be terminated for six months. After this period, it can be terminated provided the employee is paid an indemnity equivalent to six months' salary. Women are entitled to 15 weeks' maternity leave.

EDUCATION

Education in Belgium is free from the age of 2½. With the latest moves towards federalisation, most of the responsibility for education has been transferred from the central government to the Communities (the tier of government concerned with language and culture). General policy is still decided by the central state, but in other respects there are divergences between the regions. Foreign schools offer education along British and American lines for all ages. School is compulsory for all children between the ages of six and 18; and crèches and nursery schools (from 18 months to two years) are available for working mothers. There are kindergartens for children from 2½ to six. Apart from the state schools there are also a large number of private schools ('free schools'), many of which are linked to the Catholic Church.

Belgium has a university in each of its major cities. These are state-financed or subsidised, and entrance requirements are high. Many now offer courses taught in the English language. Undergraduate courses are generally longer than in British universities, usually lasting four years.

EMBASSIES AND CONSULATES

British Embassy, Rue d'Arlon 85 Aalenstraat, 1040 Brussels; ☎2-287 6211; fax 2-287 6270. Consular Section: ☎2-287 6211; fax 2-287 6320; e-mail consularsection brussels@fco.gov.uk; www.britishembassy.gov.uk/belgium.

British Consulate, Postbox 580, Groenplaats, 2000 Antwerpen; ☎3-213 2125; fax 3-213 2991; e-mail cgantwerp@unicall.be.

British Consulate, c/o Mevvaert Glass Engineering NV, Dok Noord 3, B-9000 Ghent; ☎9-235 7221; fax 9-222 8127.

US Embassy, Regentlaan 27 Boulevard du Régent, B-1000 Brussels; ☎2-508 2111; fax 2-511 2725; www.usembassy.be.

TOURIST OFFICES

Tourism Flanders Brussels, 1a Cavendish Square, London W1G 0LD; ☎ 020 7307 7738; www.visitflanders.co.uk.

Belgian Tourist Office, 217 Marsh Wall, London E14 9FJ; ☎0207-537 1132; fax 020-7531 0393; www.belgiumtheplaceto.be.

Belgian Tourist Office, 220 East 42nd Street, Suite 3402, New York, NY 10017; ☎212-758 8130; fax 212-355 7675; www.visitbelgium.com.

CONDITIONS OF EMPLOYMENT

WAGES

There is a standard legal minimum wage for workers over 21, currently €1,234.21 (£832) per month. Monthly salaries for white-collar workers are determined by negotiation between employers and unions according to age and skills. As already mentioned, wage levels (and the cost of living) in Belgium are relatively high.

HOURS

Standard working hours are limited by law to 39 hours per week, eight hours per day; although within some industries the unions and employers have negotiated a longer working week or shift system. The average Belgian works 38½ hours a week, about two hours less than in the UK. Employees are not obliged to work overtime. If overtime is worked, this has to be paid at an additional 50 per cent. Overtime on Sundays and public holidays is paid at double time.

HOLIDAYS

There are ten public holidays in Belgium. In addition there are a couple of regional holidays: in Flanders 11 July is a holiday commemorating the defeat of the French at the Battle of the Golden Spurs in 1302; on 27 September the Walloons celebrate the anniversary of the defeat of the Dutch in the 1830 revolution. For most workers, the legal minimum holiday is four weeks, and an extra holiday allowance is paid. All workers are entitled to ten days' unpaid leave per year for urgent family reasons.

TRADE UNIONS

Belgium is one of the most heavily unionised countries in the Western world; 50 to 85 per cent of workers are likely to be members of unions in any given industry. Unions are organised by industry, and affiliated to one of three trade union federations, which are split up on linguistic and political/religious lines. Membership is voluntary, and workers will have several unions representing them.

Labour-management relations are highly organised, with permanent delegations representing both sides at local and national levels. Agreements are usually reached without the necessity for drastic action, but there are special Labour Courts to settle tough cases.

TAXATION

The tax system in Belgium is so complicated that tax regulations might be construed as a deliberate ploy to employ more accountants and fiscal experts. If you are based in the country, you will be taxed under the Belgian system (although non-Belgian residents hired by Belgian companies on a temporary basis may escape this). Income tax is deducted from wages at source and is progressive, ranging from 25 per cent to 55 per cent. There are allowances for dependants and many professional expenses.

EMPLOYMENT PROSPECTS

GENERAL

The Belgian economy depends on manufacturing and trade, and there is a high level of foreign investment into the country. Belgium is a world leader in non-ferrous metallurgy, and also in industrial textiles. The food industry has expanded rapidly in recent years and some companies in this sector hire graduates with languages from abroad. Other good prospects are in administration, finance, information technology and manufacturing, as well as English teaching and temporary work. However, a high level of language ability is often necessary in order to be able to compete with the locals. There are numerous American and British subsidiary companies in Belgium (see below) and the EU and NATO are among the major employers of English speakers (see the *International Organisations* chapter).

Further information on all aspects of living and working in Belgium can be found in *Live and Work in Belgium, the Netherlands and Luxembourg*, (www.vacationwork.co.uk).

NEWSPAPERS

The leading French language newspaper, *Le Soir*, is represented by Rossel & Cie SA, Rue Royale 120, 1000 Brussels; ☎2-217 77 50; www.lesoir.be; and in Britain by *The Powers Turner Group*, Gordon House, Greencoat Place, London SW1P 1PH; ☎020-7592 8300; fax 020-7592 8301; e-mail ppn-london@publicitas.com; www.publicitas. com. The Powers Turner Group can also place advertisements in the largest Flemish daily *Het Laatste Nieuws* and other newspapers and specialist magazines. *Le Soir* has a special section on Tuesdays and Saturdays for jobseekers. Advertisements can be placed in the English language magazine *The Bulletin*, Ackroyd Publications, 1038 Chaussée de Waterloo, 1180 Brussels; ☎2-373 9909; fax 2-375 9822; www.ackroyd.be.

SPECIFIC CONTACTS

EMPLOYMENT SERVICE

British citizens, once in Belgium, may use the services of one of the regional employment services which each have sub-regional offices. The main employment office in Brussels is known as ORBEM (*Office Régional Bruxellois de l'Emploi*) or BGDA (*Brusselse*

Gewestelijke Dienst voor Arbeidsbemiddeling). The website is: www.orbem.be. In addition, there are sub-regional employment offices in Wallonia (the *Services Subrégionaux de l'Emploi – SSE)* and in Flanders (the *Subregionale Tewerkstellingsdiensten –* STD). These are listed in the local Yellow Pages. A list of sub-regional employment offices can be obtained from ORBEM, Boulevard Anspach 65, 1000 Brussels; ☎2-505 14 11; fax 2-511 3052; e-mail info@orbem.be; www.orbem.be; or BGDA, Anspachlaan 65, 1000 Brussels; ☎2-505 7777; fax 2-511 3052; e-mail info@bgda.be; www.bgda.be.

CONSULTANTS AND AGENCIES

As well as some organisations listed in the section *Consultants and Agencies*, the following recruit personnel for positions in Belgium – mostly in Brussels. A fee is generally not paid to recruitment agencies.

Focus Career Services, 23 Rue Lesbroussart, B-1050 Brussels; ☎2-646 6530; fax 2-646 9602; e-mail focus@focusbelgium.org; www.focusbelgium.org, is an association providing services to people looking for career opportunities or exploring career alternatives, and is open to women and men of all nationalities. It provides information on education, training and job opportunities; publishes a bi-monthly newsletter; and organises workshops and seminars.

Personnel Management Services (PMS), Rode Kruislaan 75, Avenue des Croix Rouge, 1020 Brussels; ☎2-461 2797; fax 2-461 2810; e-mail info@pms-aims.com; www.pms-aims.com, recruits for a wide range of enterprises in the Brussels, Louvain, Antwerp area. PMS specialises in low and middle management assignments and support staff (secretarial and administrative). Appointments are initially for a fixed term, but may become permanent.

Financial Search & Selection, Av. de Mai 40, 1200 Brussels; ☎2-771 7261; fax 2-772 4018.

Robert Half/Fontaine Archer van de Voorde, Av. Générale de Gaulle 47, 1050 Brussels; ☎2-626 1111; fax 2-646 3038. Finance, accountancy, banking and legal personnel.

TEACHERS

The addresses of Belgian universities and language schools can be obtained from Belgian embassies and local telephone directories. As one of the capitals of the European Union there is a huge demand for English language teaching, however, TEFL teachers may have trouble finding casual work in Belgium, due to the competition from highly qualified expats. The Education Office of the *British Council* in Brussels (Leopold Plaza, Rue de Trône 108, 1050 Brussels; ☎2-227 0840; fax 2-227 0849; e-mail enquiries@britishcouncil. be) distributes a list of 20 private language schools. A good source of information on opportunities is the English language magazine, *The Bulletin* (Ackroyd Publications, 1038 Chaussée de Waterloo, 1180 Brussels; ☎2-373 9909; fax 2-375 9822; www.ackroyd. be), which publishes an annual Schools Guide in April containing a section on language schools. The *Berlitz Language Center* (Avenue Louise 306-310, 1050 Brussels; ☎2-649 6175; fax 2-640 1137; e-mail info@berlitz.com; www.berlitz.com) employs around 50 staff, and the Berlitz organisation has a number of schools throughout Belgium.

SHORT TERM WORK

Belgium offers good prospects for temporary, casual and seasonal work. Hotel and tourism opportunities are listed in *Summer Jobs Abroad* published annually by Vacation Work Publications. Britons are helped both by their right to work here without a work permit and their ability to make use of the Belgian employment service (T-Service/T-Interim) which has branches that specialise in finding short-term work. Some of these are located at:

o   Sint Joacobsmarkt 66, 2000 Antwerp; ☎3-232 9860.
o   24 Rue Général Molitz, 6700 Arlon; ☎63-22 6645.
o   Smedenstraat 4, 8000 Bruges; ☎50-44 2044.
o   Anspachlaan 69, 1000 Brussels; ☎2-511 2385.
o   Rue de Montigny 36B, 6000 Charleroi; ☎71-20 2080.
o   Kortrijksesteenweg 130, 9000 Ghent; ☎9-243 8850.
o   Thonissenlaan 18, bus 1, 3500 Hasselt; ☎11-26 4990.
o   Bvd. de la Sauvernière 60, 4000 Liège; ☎4-230 3080.
o   86 de Merodelei, 2300 Tournhout; ☎14-42 2731.

There are also numerous temporary work agencies. Two of the largest are:
Manpower, Louizalaan 523, 1050 Brussels; ☎02-639 1070; fax 02-639 1071; e-mail info@manpower.be; www.manpower.be, seeks bilingual secretaries (English-French) with any other EU language.
Select HR, 68 Rue Solleveld, 1200 Brussels; ☎2-231 0333; fax 2-230 1210; e-mail www. selectinterim.be. Typists, secretaries and accountants.

Temping appointments generally last a maximum of six months, as after this period employees become eligible for full-time employee benefits and holidays.

SEASONAL WORK

It is possible to find seasonal employment in the hotel, catering and tourism sectors. Those looking for jobs should write directly to individual hotels (a list can be obtained from the Belgium Tourist Office or an up-to-date travel guide). The major tourist centre of Bruges is particularly busy in the summer and is a good place to look. Local employment services will also be able to help. Some voluntary organisations organise work camps in the summer:

Natuur 2000 (Flemish Youth Federation for the Study of Nature and Environmental Conservation), Bervoetsraat 33, 2000 Antwerp; ☎3-231 2604; fax 3-233 6499; e-mail natuur2000@telenet.be; www.natuur2000.be. Organises conservation activities and nature-study and conservation camps in Dutch-speaking parts of Belgium. They are open to all nationalities. There is a membership fee of €12.39, which covers insurance, and a registration fee of about €50 a week depending on costs.

AU PAIRS

Very few agencies in the UK and continental Europe deal with Belgium. A better possibility is to make contact with one of the big Dutch agencies that place au pairs both in the Netherlands and Belgium, namely:
*S- Au Pairs Intermediate,*Hinthamerstraat 34, 5211 MP 's-Hertogenbosch, Netherlands; ☎+31 (0)73-614 9483; fax +31 (0)73-691 0889; e-mail info@saupair.com; www. saupair.com.
House-o-Orange Au Pairs, Oostduinlaan 115, 2596 JJ The Hague, Netherlands; ☎+31 (0)70-324 5903; fax +31 (0)70-324 5913; e-mail house-o-orange@planet.nl; www. house-o-orange.nl.
Juno Au Pairs Bemiddelingsbureau, Weide 37, 3121 XV Schiedam, Netherlands; ☎+31 10-471 5431; fax +31 10-471 7662; www.junoaupairs.com.
In addition to these Dutch agencies, IAPA member Au Pairs Worldwide in the Netherlands places au pairs in Belgium as well as Holland, Germany, etc. (Morgenster 13, Marum, 9363 LH; Postal address: PO Box 36, 9300 AA Roden (tel/fax +31 594-510 801; aupairww@ worldonline.nl; www.aupairsworldwide.com).

Indigenous au pair agencies are placing fewer au pairs in Belgium than they once did, though it might be worth giving one of these a try:

Home From Home, Spillemanstraat 1, 2140 Antwerp (☎+32 3-235 97 20; fax + 3-235 97 19; info@homefromhome.be; www.homefromhome.be). Works in partnership with House-o-Orange Agency in the Netherlands, so that agency's au pairs in Belgium can participate in House-o-Orange Au Pair Club activities. Contact Lut Vereycken or Annemie Delfosse.

Services de la Jeunesse Feminine asbl, rue de Dave 174, 5100 Namur, Belgium (tel/fax +32 81-30 91 35). Belgian branch of Catholic organisation ACISJF/In Via.

Stufam V.Z.W, Vierwindenlaan 7, 1780 Wemmel, Belgium (☎+32 2-460 33 95; fax +32 2-460 00 71; aupair.stufam@scarlet.be; www.aupair-stufam.be). Contact Lieve Deschuymere.

Belgium's English language weekly publication *The Bulletin* carries job adverts such as live-in positions (normally with English-speaking ex-pat families) and language tuition. The classified advertisements can be seen online at www.xpats.com/classifieds_main. shtml (click on 'Children') where some au pair vacancies are listed among the many more 'Jobs Wanted' advertisements. The magazine is published on Thursdays and can be bought from newsstands for €2.70.

INTERNATIONAL COMPANIES IN BELGIUM

Alcatel Bell **45**	Ernst & Young **1**
Francis Wellesplein 1	Avenue Marcel Thiry 204
2018 Antwerp	1200 Brussels
Arthur Anderson & Co. **1**	Exxon Chemical Belgium NV **35**
Montagne du Parc 4	Polderdijk 3
1000 Brussels	Antwerpen
Bank of America **4**	Ford Motor Company (Belgium) **7**
Av. E. Van Nieuwenhuyse 6	Groenenborgerlaan 16
1160 Brussels	2610 Wilrijk
BP Chemicals Belgium **8**	General Accident plc **23**
Niuwe Weg 1	Brusselstr. 59,
2070 Zwijndrecht	2018 Antwerp
BT Worldwide Ltd **45**	Glaxo Wellcome Belgium NV **8**
Excelsiorlaan 48-50	Industrielaan 1,
1930 Zaventem	9320 Aalst
Commercial Union Assurance **23**	Honeywell SA **10**
(Belgium) Ltd	Av. de Schiphol 3
Av. Hermann Debroux 54	1140 Brussels
1160 Brussels	
	ICI (Europe) **46**
Dow Corning Europe **8**	Everslaan 45
Rue Gén. de Gaulle 62	3078 Eversberg
1310 La Hulpe	

ICL Benelux E. Mommaertslaan 16A 1831 Diegem	10	Rank Xerox SA Wezembeekstraat 5 B-1930 Zaventem	30
Johnson Matthey SA Av. de Bâle 8 1140 Brussels	8	Reuters Ltd Rue de Trèves 61 1040 Brussels	38
KPMG SC Av. Bourget 40 1030 Brussels	1	Siemens Nixdorf Information Systems Chaussée de Charleroi 116 1060 Brussels	10
Kraft-Jacobs-Suchard NV Bilkensveld 1 1500 Halle	16	Schweppes Belgium SA Rue du Cerf 127 1332 Genval	16
Lloyds Bank International Avenue de Tervueren 2 1040 Brussels	4	Shell SA Cantersteen 47 1000 Brussels	35
Nestlé Belgilux [sic] SA Rue Birmingham 221, bte 7 1070 Brussels	16	Smithkline Beecham Pharma SA Rue de Tilleul 13 1332 Genval	8
Pilkington-Continental Autoglass SA Heiveldekens 9/B 2550 Kontich	19	Unisys Belgium SA Av. du Bourget 20 1130 Brussels	10
Pricewaterhouse Coopers Av. de Cortenbergh 75 1200 Brussels	1	United Distillers Belgium NV Doornveld 1 bte 19 1731 Zellik	16

A copy of the *Year Book of the British Chamber of Commerce in Belgium* containing the names and addresses of its member firms can be obtained from the secretary of the Chamber at Boulevard Saint- Michel 47 1040 Brussels; ☎2-540 9030; fax 2-512 8363; www.britcham.be.

The *American Chamber of Commerce in Brussels* (Rue du Commerce 39-41 Handelsstraat, 1000 Brussels; ☎2-513 6770; fax 2-513 3590; e-mail gchamber@amcham. be; www.amcham.be) publishes a yearly list of its 1,700 members and all American firms operating in Belgium (€130 for non-members, free for members).

The *Belgian Employers' Federation* issues a free list of member organisations, obtainable from Verbond van Belgische Ondernemingen-Fédération des Entreprises Belges (VBO-FEB), Ravensteinstraat 4, 1000 Brussels, ☎2-515 0811; www.vbo-feb.be.

Denmark

o **Year of EU Accession:** 1973
o **Royal Danish Embassy,** 55 Sloane Street, London SW1X 9SR; ☎020-7333 0200; fax 020-7333 0270; e-mail lonamb@um.dk; www.denmark.org.uk
o **Royal Danish Embassy,** 3200 Whitehaven Street NW, Washington DC 20008; ☎202-234 4300; e-mail wasamb@um.dk; www.denmarkemb.org
o **Currency:** 1 Danish kroner (Dkr) = 100 øre
o **Rate of Exchange:** £1 = Dkr 10.77; $1 = Dkr 5.86; €1 = Dkr 7.46
o **Country Code:** +45

Denmark has the highest average wage of any EU country, but unemployment, previously in rapid decline, has been increasing slowly since the beginning of this century. Denmark is a wealthy country and there are many opportunities for employment, particularly casual work. According to the Gross National Product per head of the population, Denmark ranks as the world's sixth richest country, and second after Luxembourg in the EU. As always, knowledge of the local language will put you ahead of the competition but English is widely and well spoken throughout Scandinavia, and there are fewer language problems in Denmark than elsewhere. Work is available in offices and hotels, and in international companies. A useful booklet called *Short Cuts* is published by *Use It*, a Youth Information Centre at Rädhusstraede 13, 1466 Copenhagen K; ☎3373 0650; fax 3373 0649; e-mail ui@kff.kk.dk; www.ui.dk. *Short Cuts* costs kr40 plus kr20 postage abroad, and contains lots of detailed information about red tape procedures and some good advice on job hunting. The publication encourages newly arrived jobseekers to visit the *Use It* centre to consult their files, newspapers and Yellow Pages directories.

There are no Danish offices operating as employment advisory bureaux for foreigners, but when in Denmark you can try the national labour exchange or *AF* (Arbejdsformidlingen). A list of addresses can be obtained from the State Employment Service *Arbejdsmarkedsstyrelsen*, AMS, Holmens Kanal 20, Postbox 2150, 1016 Copenhagen K; ☎3528 8100; fax 3535 2411; e-mail ams@ams.dk; www.ams.dk. Alternatively, the addresses of local offices can be found under *Arbejdsformidlingen* in the telephone directory.

GENERAL FACTS

POPULATION
Denmark's total population is 5.4 million. It is the smallest of the Scandinavian countries and covers 16,638 square miles (43,093 sq km). In addition to the Jutland peninsula, and its low-lying landscape of beech woods, small lakes and fjords, there are 483 islands, 100 of them inhabited. Population density is 850 per square mile. There are few mineral resources and most of the land is in productive agricultural use.

CLIMATE
Denmark's climate is similar to that of Britain or neighbouring Germany, rather different from the rest of Scandinavia. It is a maritime climate, but there is generally more sunshine in summer than in England, and winter temperatures tend to be lower.

GOVERNMENT

Denmark is a constitutional monarchy and the oldest kingdom in Europe. The present Queen is Margrethe II. The *Folketing* is the legislative assembly, and the government is led by a Prime Minister. Elections are held every four years. Denmark entered the EEC in 1973 and has a reputation (like Britain) as a less than enthusiastic member of the EU. The Danes made history in 1992 by narrowly rejecting, through a national referendum, the Maastrict Treaty although this decision was later overturned. They are also currently holding out against the adoption of the euro.

CITIES

Copenhagen, the capital and the largest port in Scandinavia, has a population of 1.7 million (and is famed for the Little Mermaid statue in the bay). It was a European Cultural Capital in 1996. Other cities (with much smaller populations) are Aarhus, famous for its historic buildings and museum; Aalborg, the chief city of North Jutland, a gourmet's paradise with 120 restaurants; and Odense, the picturesque town made famous by Hans Christian Andersen. Legoland near Esbjerg is a popular tourist attraction.

RURAL LIFE

Farms tend to be small, and the main agricultural products are dairy, cattle and pigs. There is a current trend towards amalgamating smaller farms into larger, more intensive production units. Agriculture and fishing are the basis of Denmark's large food-processing industry but even today only 16 per cent of farms have any full-time employees, the rest being family-run. Forestry is also important to the Danish economy (forests cover 10 per cent of the country's land area), as is the production of fruit and vegetables. The country is almost entirely surrounded by water and fishing plays an important part in Danish life and culture, and is organised on a co-operative basis.

RELIGION, SPORT AND CULTURE

Most Danes belong to the established Evangelical-Lutheran Church. The most popular sport in Denmark (as in most other European countries) is soccer, and soccer players are another of its 'exports' to major European clubs. In 1992, the Danish national team won the European Championship, its first major honour. Walking, cycling, golf, angling, windsurfing and tennis are popular pastimes. The Danes are a self-contained (some might say introverted) people, but are very friendly. There is a lively nightlife in Copenhagen, but the national character is better expressed in small intimate gatherings around a fire or at a picnic, in an atmosphere said to be *hygge*, which means intimate or cosy. A former British ambassador to the country once said that the Danes reminded him of the Ashanti tribe of Ghana, whose society and political system is based on consensus and general agreement. Danes are sociable and are described by most visitors as easy-going and welcoming.

FACTORS INFLUENCING EMPLOYMENT

IMMIGRATION

In Denmark, you must have legal residence (and a work permit before you arrive if you are from outside the EU or EEA). Immigration is not encouraged but the EU agreement on free movement of labour still applies, so Britons and other EU nationals are allowed to look for work.

EU nationals who intend to stay longer than three months should apply for a residence permit (*Opholdsbevis*) from the Copenhagen *Overpraesidium* at Hammerensgade 1, 1267 Copenhagen K; ☎3312 2380. You will need to supply two photos, your passport and, if possible, a contract of employment or proof of means of support. Non-EU nationals should apply to the Danish Immigration Service, *Direktoratet for Udlaendinge* (Aliens' Department), Ryesgade 53, 2100 Copenhagen Ø; ☎3536 6600; 3536 1916; e-mail udlst@ udlst.dk; www.udlst.dk; in other towns, apply to the local police. Only certain categories of entrant (for example, au pairs) will be eligible for residency.

Anyone intending to stay in Denmark for more than three months will also need a *personnummer* (or CPR). The CPR is a personal registration number for which you should apply within five days of arrival. In Copenhagen this can be obtained from the *Folkeregistret*, Dahlerupsgade 6, 1640 Copenhagen V; ☎3366 3366.

Denmark joined the Schengen area, along with the other Nordic countries, in March 2001. US and Canadian citizens landing in Denmark will, under usual circumstances, receive a Schengen visa which allows them to spend up to 90 days out of six months in one of the Schengen countries. This means that if you arrive from another Scandinavian country, your allowed period of stay in Denmark will be limited. If you wish to stay longer than three months, you should make a visa application in the USA before your departure.

LANGUAGE

Not speaking Danish is a problem if you are looking for work on the spot. English is quite widely spoken, but prospective jobseekers are advised to learn some Danish before they leave their home country. Once in Denmark, local education authorities can arrange cheap language classes with an English-speaking teacher when the need arises. The Universities of Copenhagen and Aarhus hold courses in Danish for beginners and intermediate students.

COST AND STANDARD OF LIVING

Almost all fields of work are covered by agreements between employers and the trade unions, so people working in Denmark are assured of a fairly stable standard of living; visitors to the country will find prices high.

HOUSING AND ACCOMMODATION

Housing standards in Denmark are good, but it can be hard to find somewhere to live. One of the conditions for the granting of residence permits, however, is that the applicant has a suitable dwelling, so it is a good idea to try to arrange accommodation before you arrive. Rents are high, even for a single room, and for long-term foreign residents, buying, too, can be a problem. Foreigners wishing to buy a house must apply for permission to the Ministry of Justice, and this is only given if the applicant intends to reside in Denmark permanently.

HEALTH AND WELFARE

Denmark was one of the first countries in the world to introduce a welfare state, and social security today is the largest single item of Danish national expenditure. Sickness and unemployment benefit are as much as 90 per cent of the wage, and because of this there is little incentive for the unemployed to look to other EU countries for work. Foreigners qualify for social security benefits if they have contributed to the system for a year, during which they must have worked for six months. Other benefits, such as maternity and industrial injury compensation are available on similar terms. Maternity leave is granted for four weeks prior to the birth and up to 24 weeks after. Paternity leave of two weeks is available. Hospital treatment is generally provided free of charge to EU visitors. Doctors and dentists are generally paid by the patient for treatment received, and then this money is refunded in part or in full by local municipal offices.

EDUCATION

Most education, including university, is free, although there are some private schools. Kindergartens care for around three quarters of all children aged from three to six and education is compulsory from six to 16. Denmark has five universities (at Copenhagen, Aarhus, Aalborg, Odense and Roskilde). There are also a number of other specialised training institutions and courses for vocational training at secondary and tertiary level. State grants are available to both Danes and foreigners for higher education.

EMBASSIES AND CONSULATES

British Embassy, 36-40 Kastelsvej, 2100 Copenhagen Ø; ☎3544 5200; fax 3544 5253; www.britishembassy.dk.
There are consulates in Aabenraa, Alborg, Arhus, Esbjerg, Fredericia, Herning, Odense, and Tørshavn (Faroe Islands).
US Embassy, Dag Hammerskjöld's Allé 24, DK-2100 Copenhagen Ø; ☎3341 7100; fax 3543 0223; www.usembassy.dk.

NATIONAL TOURIST OFFICES

Danish Tourist Board, 55 Sloane St, London SW1X 9SY; ☎020-7259 5959; fax 020-7259 5955; e-mail london@visitdenmark.com; www.visitdenmark.dk.
Scandinavian Tourist Board, 655 3rd Ave, New York, NY 10017; ☎212-885 9700; e-mail info@goscandinavia.com;www.visitdenmark.dk.

CONDITIONS OF EMPLOYMENT

WAGES

Wages and working conditions are fixed by negotiation between worker and employer organisations. Conditions of work are generally good. The Danes are widely regarded as hardworking and industrious. Danish salaries are generally lower (relative to cost of living) than those in the US, UK, France and Germany, although somewhat higher than those in Sweden and Finland. The greatest single item of expenditure is housing.

HOURS

In Denmark, 37 hours and a five-day working week are the norm. Shops generally close early on Saturdays, except for the first Saturday of the month. Banks are open until 6pm on Thursday, 5pm other weekdays, and closed on Saturday.

HOLIDAYS

All employees in Denmark are entitled to thirty days' paid holiday per year. In addition, the following public holidays are observed: New Year's Day; Maundy Thursday (4 April); Good Friday; Easter Monday; Common Prayer's Day (April or May); Ascension (16 May); Whit Monday (27 May); Constitution Day (5 June, half day); Christmas Eve, Christmas Day, Boxing Day; and New Year's Eve (half day).

TRADE UNIONS

On taking up employment you will be requested to join a trade union, and in most industries wages and conditions are negotiated by these unions with the employer. Union membership, while not obligatory, covers around 80 per cent of the workforce. Most foreigners join a Danish union; the rules then require contributions to the Unemployment Funds (*arbejdsløshedskasser*). To become a member you must have had, or be going to have, five weeks of work. It is also possible to become a member of an unemployment fund (*A-kasser*) without joining a union.

TAXATION

Tax is deducted at source. A foreigner will be subject to unlimited liability upon arrival if he indicates his intention to become a Danish resident, or if his stay exceeds six months. You need a *skattekort* (tax card). Without this document the employer has to deduct 60 per cent of your salary to cover income taxes (but this tax can be claimed back in June of the next calendar year). You can get your *skattekort* at Københavns Skatteforvaltning (Gyldenløvesgade 15, 1639 Copenhagen V; ☎ 33 66 33 66). You will need a *personnummer* in order to apply. Tax is paid according to your income, how long you work in Denmark, and any bilateral agreements with your own country (which you should check on first). Sickness and unemployment insurance contributions are also deducted at source, but are calculated separately. Comprehensive information can be obtained from the Danish Embassy.

EMPLOYMENT PROSPECTS

GENERAL

It is worth emphasising that finding work in Denmark is no easy task, and British jobseekers are advised to check the current situation at a local Jobcentre through the *EURES* scheme (see *Getting the Job*). In fact, few vacancies in Denmark are advertised in Britain or the USA or in the international employment press. Non-EU nationals really need to be posted to Denmark by their company or organisation. Otherwise, your job search will have to be creative and on the spot. The services of *Use It*, once you are there, are very helpful (see above). No foreigner is allowed to take up a post in the Danish Civil Service.

NEWSPAPERS

Advertisements can be placed in *Berlingske Tidende* and national and regional dailies. *The Powers Turner Group* (Gordon House, Greencoat Place, London SW1P 1PH; ☎ 020-7592 8300; fax 020-7592 8301; e-mail ppn-london@publicitas.com; www.publicitas.com) represents the leading daily *Jyllands-Posten*. There is a weekly English newspaper, *The Copenhagen Post*, which comes out on Fridays and costs kr15 (see www.cphpost.dk). In Copenhagen there are plenty of job adverts in the twice-weekly *Den Blå Avis* (www.dba. dk) and the Sunday paper Søndagsavisen (www.son.dk).

THE INTERNET

As everywhere in Scandinavia, the internet has become an important part of the recruitment process. The first site to try is *EURES* (www.eures.dk), where you can access many agricultural jobs. The *British Embassy* site also has advice for jobseekers (www.britishembassy.dk), but the embassy itself does not help people to find jobs. The Copenhagen Jobcentre has a site at www.koebenhavn.af.dk. Other AF sites can be found just by substituting the name of the town for Koebenhavn, or try searching on *Arbejdsformidling*. Many sites have a *job* link. The following is only a small selection of other websites: www.jubii.dk; www.bf.dk/jobs; www.jobindex.dk; www.jobbanken.dk, www.monster.dk. There is a good Danish website explaining all aspects of Danish life at www.workindenmark.dk.

SPECIFIC CONTACTS

LOCAL AGENCIES

There are a number of employment agencies in Copenhagen that may be able to offer jobs in offices and factories to personal callers. The main *Jobcentre* in Copenhagen is at Vesterbrogade 123, 1620 Copenhagen K (☎ 3355 1714; fax 3355 1072; e-mail af@abh.

af.dk; www.koebenhavn.af.dk). There is a special branch which deals just with students who visit in person, the *Studenterformidlingen*, Tøndergade 16, Vesterbro. There is a casual work centre (*Løsarbejderformidling*) at Tøndergade 14, Vesterbro. You will need to have a knowledge of Danish and be an early riser; jobs are allocated between 6 am and 6.30 am.

There are a number of chains of general employment agencies that may have jobs in offices, factories, hotels and so on to offer to personal callers. One of the largest is *Adecco* (Falkoner Allé 1, 2000 Frederiksberg; ☎3888 9400; fax 3888 9401; www.adecco.dk). Other agencies can be found under *vikarbureauer* in the telephone directory, or look on the website: www.jubii.dk under *rekrutteringsfirmaer*.

MEDICAL STAFF

Medical personnel wishing to work in Danish hospitals should consult the weekly journal of *Den Almindelige Danske Lægeforening* (Danish Medical Association, Trondhjemsgade 9, 2100 Copenhagen Ø; ☎3544 8500; fax 3544 8505; e-mail dadl@dadl.uk; www.laeger. dk) in which hospital medical posts are advertised. A list of hospitals and other medical institutions is available from the same source, as is the free booklet *Information for Doctors Migrating to Denmark*.

In order to obtain authorisation to work as a doctor in Denmark, the *National Board of Health* (*Sundhedsstyrelsen*, Islands Brygge 67, Box 1881, 2300 Copenhagen S; ☎7222 7400; fax 7222 7411; e-mail sst@sst.dk; www.sundhedsstyrelsen.dk) should be contacted after employment has been obtained but before work is taken up. A solid knowledge of the Danish language is usually needed. See the Sunday edition of *Berlingske Tidende* for medical and nursing vacancies (cited under *Newspapers* above).

SHORT TERM WORK

SEASONAL WORK

It is worth writing directly to hotels for jobs in the tourist industry. Casual workers are also needed to help harvest tomatoes, strawberries, cherries and apples over the summer. One contact, *Alstrup Frugtplantage* (Alstrupvej 1, Alstrup 8305 Samso; ☎8659 3138; fax 8659 3138), offers strawberry picking between May and July. Note, however, that farmers can only accept workers with EU nationality and an EHIC card, and that this is rigidly adhered to.

Landsbladet, a farming journal published by Vester Farimagsgade 6, 1606 Copenhagen K; ☎3338 2222; www.landsbladet.dk, carries advertisements for farm work and it is also possible to place an 'employment wanted' advert. Students looking for temporary work around Copenhagen can use a special branch of the national employment service known as the *Studenternes Arbejdsformidling*.

AU PAIRS

Conditions for au pairs in Denmark are generally congenial. On top of the monthly pocket money of at least DKK 2,500, you should be given health insurance and are entitled to join free language courses in Danish. The main au pair agencies in Denmark are:
Au Pairs International, Sixtusvej 15, 2300 Copenhagan S, Denmark; ☎+45 32-841002; fax +45 32-843102; e-mail info@aupairsinternational.dk; www.aupairsinternational.dk.
Scandinavian Au Pair Center Denmark, Moelledamsvej 2, 9382 Tylstrup, Denmark; ☎+45 98-261242; e-mail scandinavian@aupaircentre.dk; www.aupaircentre.dk.
If arranging a placement independently, place a free advertisement in English or Danish in the twice-weekly Copenhagen paper *Den Bla Avis* (meaning 'The Blue Paper'), a member of the Free Ads Paper International Association; it comes out on Monday and Thursday. The free Copenhagen paper *Sondagsavisen* carries a good number of ads for casual work

and is distributed on Sundays. If you know a Danish speaker, check adverts in the jobs *(erhvervs)* section of the Sunday and Wednesday editions of *Berlingske Tidende* and *Politiken* newspapers. Advertisements in English are accepted by these papers. There is usually a fair sprinkling of adverts for au pairs and home helps.

The website of the Danish Immigration Service (www.udlst.dk) has a section in English about au pairing in Denmark.

OTHER WORK

Voluntary work can be arranged through some of the international agencies mentioned in *Voluntary Work*. If you are already in the country, *Mellemfolkeligt Samvirke*, (Danish Association of International Co-operation), Studsgade 20, 8000 Aarhus; ☎8619 7766; www.ms.dk, organises work camps during the summer in Denmark as well as Greenland and the Faroe Islands. The object of these programmes is to bring participants into contact with social problems and deprivation. *Mellemfolkeligt Samvirke* organise several camps per year. The work can be hard and don't expect much idle time. *Use It* (see above) is another useful source of information on volunteer work in Denmark.

The Danish Chamber of Commerce, *Det Danske Handelskammer*, Børsen, DK-1217 Copenhagen K; ☎7013 1200; fax 7013 1201; e-mail hts@hts.dk; www.htsi.dk, can provide other useful advice and information about business in Denmark.

INTERNATIONAL COMPANIES IN DENMARK

Albright & Wilson Siestavej 7, 2600 Glostrup	8	Corus Denmark A/S Hans Edvard Teglere Vej 7 2920 Charlottenlund	28
Amersham Pharmacia Biotech Slotsmarken 14 2970 Hørsholm	8	Dansk Shell A/S Kampmannsgade 2 1604 Copenhagen	35
Baxenden Scandinavia A/S Fulbyvej 4 Pedersborg 4180 Sorø	8	Deb Swarfega A/S Teglvaerksvej 6 5620 Glamsbjerg	8
Black & Decker A/S Hegrevang 268 3450 Allerød	26	Deloitte H C Andersons Boulevard 2 1780 Copenhagen V	1
Boeg-Thomsen A/S Nybyvej 11 4390 Vipperod	16	DHL Worldwide Express A/S Jydekrogen 14 2625 Vallensbaek	17
Castrol A/S Esplanaden 7 1263 Copenhagen K	35	Digital Equipment Corporation A/S Olof Palmes Alle 25 8200 Aarhus N	10
Colgate-Palmolive A/S Smedeland 9 2600 Glostrup	11	Dunlop Tyres Rygards Alle 131 2900 Hellerup	42

EMI-Medley A/S Vognmagergade 10 1120 Copenhagen K	10	Minolta Denmark Valhøys Allé 160 2610 Rødovre	30
Ernst & Young Tagensvej 86 2200 Copenhagen N	1	Mortensen & Beierholm Vester Søgade 10/1 1601 Copenhagen V	1
Hewlett Packard Kongevejen 25 3460 Birkerød	10	Nokia Denmark A/S Frederikskaj 5 1790 Copenhagen V	45
Honeywell A/S Klamsergervej 35 8230 Abyhøj	10	PricewaterhouseCoopers Toldbuen 1 4700 Naestved	1
Hoechst Marion Roussel A/S Slotsmarken 14 2970 Hørsholm	8	Reckitt Benckiser Scandinavia A/S Vadstrupvej 22 2880 Bagsvaerd	16
Johnson Matthey A/S Frederikssundsvej 247D Copenhagen	28	Renold A/S Skelmarksvej 6 2600 Glostrup	25
KPMG C Jesperson Borups Allé 177 PO Box 250 Frederiksberg	1	Smithkline Beecham A/S Lautruphøj 1-3 2750 Ballerup	8
Lloyd's Register of Shipping A/S Standgade 4C 1401 Copenhagen K	23	Xerox A/S Borupvang 5c 2750 Ballerup	30

Finland

- **Year of EU Accession:** 1995
- **Finnish Embassy,** 38 Chesham Place, London SW1X 8HW; ☎020-7838 6200; fax 020-7235 3680; www.finemb.org.uk
- **Finnish Embassy,** 3301 Massachusetts Avenue NW, 20008 Washington DC; ☎202-298 5800; fax 202-298 6030; www.finland.org
- **Currency:** 1 Euro (€) = 100 cents
- **Rate of Exchange:** £1 = €1.44; $1 = €0.78
- **Country Code:** +358

Finland is the only EU country to share a border with Russia and is well placed to take advantage of trading links with that country. It has a highly industrialised economy, producing a wide range of industrial goods. Agriculture is also important and Finland is virtually self-sufficient in food production, despite a climate that allows only a very short growing season. Engineering is a major industry; and timber, paper, furniture, and other wood-related products are also manufactured. Tourism is less important to the economy than these other sectors.

Finns tend to be rather reserved and introverted people who appreciate deeds rather than words. Conventions in work and business are rather more formal than in the UK or United States; and if you do not enjoy long periods of silence in a conversation, this may not be the place to be! Finns are also a very pensive people. Finland was the only country to notify the author of its 'Foreigners' Crisis Centres', set up 'to help foreigners in crisis situations'. These are in Helsinki and Turku.

Riding, hiking, fishing and water sports are all popular, as are cross-country skiing, golf (including a variety called snow golf) and tennis. One little-known Finnish leisure activity is gold-panning, however, a much better known institution is the sauna, always the most popular place to relax in the company of friends or family. Food has both western (French) and eastern (Russian) influences and local specialities include smoked reindeer meat. There are ambivalent attitudes towards excessive drinking, which is both common, especially in winter, and strictly licensed. Like Russia, Finland has a certain vodka problem.

The landscape is flat and forested, interspersed with many lakes and rivers. The forests recede to Arctic tundra in the far north. The population of just more than 5.2 million is low, compared to the land area of 338,145 square kilometres, and is concentrated in the capital Helsinki, which has around half a million inhabitants. Other major towns are Turku, Tampere, and Oulu. The religion is mainly Lutheran, with other Protestant churches, Finnish Orthodox and Roman Catholic all represented. Nature, Finnish traditions, and the language, all play an important part in national life.

FACTORS INFLUENCING EMPLOYMENT

IMMIGRATION

US and Canadian citizens may remain in Scandinavia (including Finland) for a total of three months without a visa, although a residence permit will be required if you intend to work in the country, along with a Labour Permit. This will only be granted for a specific job, and a letter of recommendation from the prospective employer must be included with the application. Applications should be addressed to the *Finnish Embassy* (see above), from where they will be forwarded to the relevant authorities in Finland. Processing of applications can take up to six weeks. The Finnish Embassy does not provide assistance finding work, but can supply (along with the National Tourist Board) comprehensive information on residence, working, self-employment, housing, education, recognition of qualifications, social security, and health. They can also provide a list of the twenty-seven or so Employment Offices (*työvoimatoimisto*) which have an international labour adviser or EURES adviser.

EU citizens living or working in Finland for longer than three months will require a residence permit although EU nationals do not require a work permit (with the exception of the member states that gained accession in 2004). The residence permit can be obtained from local police stations on production of a passport, photo and employment contract (*työsopimus*) or similar document.

Immigration enquiries can also be directed to the *Directorate of Immigration* (UVI), Lautatarhaukatu 10, 00581 Helsinki; ☎9-476 5500; fax 9-4765 5858; e-mail ulkomaalaisvirasto@uvi.fi; www.uvi.fi/englanti.

LANGUAGE

Finland has two official languages: Finnish, spoken by 94 per cent of the population and Swedish, spoken by six per cent. A tiny minority speaks the Lapp language, Sami. Finnish is not an Indo-European language, like most of the others spoken in Europe, but Finno-Ugric, like Hungarian. The language has no less than thirteen case endings. Some interest in learning the language by foreign visitors is appreciated (but not expected). English is taught as the first foreign language, and German is also widely understood.

EMBASSIES AND CONSULATES

British Embassy, Itäinen Puistotie 17, 00140 Helsinki; ☎9-2286 5100; fax 9-2286 5262; e-mail info@britishembassy.fi; www.britishembassy.fi.
There are also British Consulates in Jyväskylä, Kotka, Kuopio, Oulu, Rovaniemi, Tampere, Turku, Vaasa, and Aland Islands.
US Embassy, Itäinen Puistotie 14B, 00140 Helsinki; ☎9-616250; www.usembassy.fi.

TOURIST OFFICES

Finnish Tourist Board, PO Box 33213, London W6 8JX; ☎020-7365 2512; fax 020-8600 5681; e-mail finlandinfo.lon@mek.fi; www.visitfinland.com/uk; www.mek.fi.
Finnish Tourist Board, PO Box 4649, Grand Central Station, New York, NY 10163-4649; ☎212-885 9700; e-mail mek.usa@mek.fi; www.gofinland.org.

EMPLOYMENT PROSPECTS

GENERAL

Finland has significant shipbuilding, engineering and textile industries. Scope for foreign workers is limited because of the small size of the economy and the fact that Finnish is an unusually difficult language. A knowledge of Swedish or German is an asset and professionally qualified persons interested in working in Finland should approach appropriate recruitment agencies.

Finland actively encourages trainees to come to Finland for short-term paid work. The International Trainee Exchange programme is administered by *CIMO*, the Centre for International Mobility (PO Box 343, 00531 Helsinki; ☎9-7747 7033; fax 9-7747 7064; www.cimo.fi). Opportunities are available in agriculture, tourism, teaching and other areas. Readers from non-EU countries should write to CIMO for further information, however, it is generally more difficult for non-EU nationals to participate. North Americans can contact the *American-Scandinavian Foundation,* Scandinavia House, 58 Park Avenue, New York, NY 10016; ☎212-879 9779; e-mail info@amscan.org; www.amscan.org, who run trainee schemes in Finland, primarily in technology, horticulture, teaching and forestry.

The following websites are recommended to those seeking work in Finland: www.mol.fi (Ministry of Labour); www.minedu.fi (Ministry of Education); www.monster.fi.

NEWSPAPERS

Crane Media Partners, 20-28 Dalling Road, London W6 0JB; ☎020-8237 8601, represents *Turun Sanomat* (Turku) and *Aamulehti* (Tampere) in Britain.

SPECIFIC CONTACTS

Työmarkkinat, published in Finnish and Swedish and available from employment offices, is a fortnightly publication which gives information on vacancies and adult training opportunities.

Those who do not qualify as international trainees will find it difficult to obtain employment, although there are occasional labour shortages in certain areas, such as language teaching, hospitality, and in the flower nurseries around Helsinki.

TEACHING

There is a reasonable demand for English teachers with degrees and relevant training, and it is possible to obtain a list of language schools from the Finnish Embassy in London or Washington. A key English-teaching organisation in Finland is the *Finnish-British Society*, Puistokatu 1 b A, 00140 Helsinki; ☎9-687 70240; fax 9-687 70210; e-mail finnbrit@ finnbrit.fi; www.finnbrit.fi). Teaching posts are available in Helsinki, Oulu and Pietarsaari. Interviews are held in London in April.

There are also sometimes opportunities for suitably qualified teachers at the summer universities, which are run to help secondary school students prepare for university examinations. The *Summer High School Association in Finland* address is Kesälukioseura, Kruunuvuorenkatu 5 C, PL 115, FIN-00161 Helsinki; ☎9-686 0770; fax 9-666130; e-mail toirnisto@kesalukioseura.fi; www.kesalukioseura.fi, and the *Association of Summer Universities in Finland* is at Rautatienkatu 26 A 4, FIN-33100 Tampere; ☎3-214 7626; fax 3-214 7629; e-mail info@kesayliopistot.fi; www.kesayliopistot.fi.

SHORT TERM WORK

The *Finnish Family Programme,* organised by CIMO (see above), enables young people aged 18-25 whose mother tongue is English, French or German to spend the summer months teaching the language to a Finnish family. The deadline for applications is in January.

Other opportunities for temporary work are available through the organisations mentioned in *Voluntary Work.* WWOOF (Willing Workers on Organic Farms) can be contacted via Anne Konsti, Partala Information Services for Organic Agriculture, Huttulantie 1, 51900 Juva; ☎15-321 2380; fax 15-321 2350; anne.konsti@mtt.fi.

Allianssi, Olympiastadion, Eteläkaarre, Helsinki 00250, Finland; ☎9-3482 4313; fax 9-491290; e-mail vaihto@alli.fi; www.alli.fi, places au pairs in Finland and the USA.

OTHER INFORMATION

The Crisis Prevention Center for Foreigners, Simononkatu 12 B 13, 00100 Helsinki; ☎9-685 2828, has been set up to help foreigners in Finland through crisis situations, especially with social and psychological problems.

Live and Work in Scandinavia (Vacation Work Publications, www.vacationwork.co.uk) contains detailed information on life and employment in Finland.

INTERNATIONAL COMPANIES IN FINLAND

British Airways 3
Aleksanterinkatu 21 A, 4th Floor
00100 Helsinki

Lloyds Register of Shipping 23
Aleksanterinkatu 48A
00100 Helsinki

British Telecom/Telenor AS 45
BT Ignite Oy
Kaisaniemenkatu 1 B a, 4t floor
00100 Helsinki

Pilkington Automotive Finland Oy 7
Huurretie
39160 Julkujävi

Corus Finland Oy 28
Arkadiankatu 21 A5
00100 Helsinki

Reuters Suomi Oy 38
Yrjönkatu 236
00101 Helsinki

EMI Finland Oy 29
Tallberginkatu 2A 5th Floor
00180 Helsinki

Ross and Co 24
Pohj. Makasiinikatu 7A
00130 Helsinki

GlaxoSmithKline Oy 8
Kurjenkellontie 5
02270 Espoo

Scottish and Newcastle/Hartwell Oy 16
Ristipellontie 4
00390 Helsinki

Heath Lambert Finland Oy 8
Laurinmäenkuja 3A
00441 Helsinki

Shell AB 35
Neilikkat 17, PL16
01301 Vantaa

Howden Insurance Brokers Oy 23
Aleksanterinkatu 17 WTC
00101 Helsinki

Suomen Unilever Oy 16
Lönnrotinkatu 20
00120 Helsinki

ICL Invia Oy 8
PL 458 Valimotie 16
00101 Helsinki

Viking Line AS 48
Box 166
22101 Mariehamn

Other commercial information about Finland can be supplied by the *Finnish Foreign Trade Association* (PO Box 908, 00101 Helsinki; ☎9-46951; *Finpro* (an association of international Finnish companies) P.O. Box 358, 00181 Helsinki; ☎204 6951; fax 204 200; e-mail info@finpro.fi; www.finpro..fi; and the *Finnish American Chamber of Commerce* (866 UN Plaza, New York, NY 10017; ☎212-821 0225; fax 212-750 4418; e-mail info@ finlandtrade.com; www.finlandtrade.com).

France

- o **Year of EU Accession:** 1952
- o **French Embassy,** 58 Knightsbridge, London SW1X 7JT; ☎020-7073 1000; fax 020-7073 1004; www.ambafrance-uk.org
- o **French Consulate General,** 21 Cromwell Road, London SW7 2EN; ☎020-7073 1200; fax 020-7073 1201; www.ambafrance.org.uk
- o **French Embassy,** 4101 Reservoir Road NW, Washington DC 20007; ☎202-944 6195; fax 202-944 6148; www.info-france-usa.org
- o **Currency:** 1 Euro (€) = 100 cents
- o **Rate of Exchange:** £1 = €1.44; $1 = €0.78
- o **Country Code:** +33

Although unemployment remains high (about 10%), particularly among the young and unskilled, France is a prime destination for international workers. Opportunities for young professionals are generally good, however, with so many French unemployed, foreigners looking for jobs in France will have most success in areas where there is a demand for bilingualism.

It has never been easier or quicker to get from England to France. Air, road and rail communications are good and the standard of living is generally high. There is a large English-speaking expatriate community in Paris, as well as in the south and east of the country. Although the economy has its problems, the outlook for the medium-term is improving.

France is often a first-choice for young Britons considering short-term or seasonal work abroad for the first time, as there are strong historical ties between the UK and France (even though the relationship has at times been stormy). Au pair and summer work prospects are good; grape picking is the traditional agricultural occupation; and many Britons also choose to retire in France, or buy a second home there, in the region around Calais or Normandy, or in the south (Provence and the Dordogne). English is not always spoken, but most educated people understand more than they are prepared to articulate and French is commonly taught as a second language in British and American schools. Most English-speaking people find that they can get by, although it really is essential (and courteous) to learn to speak French if you are considering staying any length of time. The French have high standards in personal grooming, and you will be considered unprofessional if you do not make the effort to dress well. The French are also more formal in their working relationships than the British or Americans and most offices have a distinctly rigid hierarchy.

GENERAL FACTS

POPULATION

France's population is nearly 60.9 million. Bordered by Italy, Switzerland and Spain in the south, and Germany, Luxembourg and Belgium in the north and east (with the English Channel to the north, and the Atlantic Ocean to the west) France covers 220,668 square miles (571,527 sq km). The only countries in Europe larger are Russia and the Ukraine. The average population density is 262 per square mile.

CLIMATE

France has all three European subdivisions of climate ranging from continental (in the east), to maritime (in the west) and mediterranean (in the south). The wettest parts are the Central Plateau, the Jura, the Alps, the Pyrenees and the coastal Brittany area. The Paris Basin and the Mediterranean coast are the driest. The climate of the southeast of the country along the Mediterranean coast, and in the lee of the Maritime Alps, is probably the most pleasant. Winters in the north can be cold and dreary.

GOVERNMENT

France is a Republic headed by a President elected every seven years. The President is both head of state and, in the influence he wields over the Prime Minister, effectively the head of the government too. The Prime Minister chooses his ministers but this decision is then ratified by the President. The Parliament is bicameral, consisting of the National Assembly and the Senate. Major political groupings are the Socialists and the Gaullists (RPR) with a dwindling and largely unreconstructed Communist party and a regrettably popular racist party, the National Front. Referenda are occasionally used in national decision-making as when, in 1992, France narrowly accepted the Maastricht Treaty on European Union.

Administratively, the country is divided into 22 regions and 96 departments (*départements*), which in turn are divided into 324 local areas, or *arrondissements*. The smallest administrative unit is the *commune*, of which there are about 36,500. The island of Corsica, birthplace of Napoleon, is a region of France, as are the various overseas possessions including Guadeloupe, French Guiana, Réunion, Tahiti and New Caledonia.

RURAL LIFE

For many British people, with an idealised view of its bucolic life, the countryside epitomises the real France. In fact, rural life is increasingly less important in national affairs as the Common Agricultural Policy and intensive farming methods have hit the smaller French farmers and accelerated a drift to the cities. Historically France has always been an agricultural country, to which the Industrial Revolution came relatively late. Her richest natural resources are her fertile farmlands and forests. France is a large wheat producer, with barley, oats, rice, grapes, beef and dairy production. Fisheries are also important.

RELIGION, SPORT AND CULTURE

Most French people are baptised into the Roman Catholic Church but unlike Spain or Ireland for example, France is not a deeply observant country. There is a minority of about 800,000 Protestants, and other evangelical and non-Christian faiths are represented. There are a large number of Jews in France, and two million or so Muslims from the large North African Arab communities (Morocco, Tunisia and Algeria), most of whom were born in the country and are French citizens.

Sport is an important part of national life, with considerable achievements in athletics, soccer and rugby. In 1998, France hosted, and won, the Football World Cup, and came a surprise second in the Rugby World Cup in Wales in 1999. In 2006 France again reached the World Cup finals, but lost out to Italy on penalties. Horseracing and other spectator sports are also popular. Cycling is widely followed, and the annual *Tour de France* is a national preoccupation in summer. Many French people also enjoy hiking, as well as other outdoor sports such as mountaineering and windsurfing. Skiing is another favoured pastime, with an exodus to the Alps and the Pyrenees in winter matching the annual migration to the beaches in the south in August (when much of the country closes down). One traditional activity – more usually played in the south – is *boules* or *pétanque*.

The French are proud of their achievements in culture, philosophy and the arts, and their architectural heritage. There is a tendency to see these not just as great national achievements but also as being of global importance; and the arts in France are strongly supported by the state. Popular and experimental art forms are also encouraged, another consequence of France's self-perception as the international standard-bearer of high culture. The French film industry is internationally renowned.

FACTORS INFLUENCING EMPLOYMENT

IMMIGRATION

France abolished the need for residence permits (*carte de séjour*) for EU nationals in 2003. However, you can still apply for one voluntarily for identification purposes at the local police station (*préfecture*) or town hall (*mairie*), as soon as you have a job. You will need to take your passport, four photos, proof of address, and a contract of employment or proof of funds. The *carte de séjour* is free and should be granted automatically once you present the correct documents.

Non-EU nationals must obtain work documents before they leave their home country in order to work legally. These must be applied for by the employer through the Office des Migrations Internationles (44 rue Bargue, 75732, Paris Cedex 15). Special exemptions exist for certain categories such as au pairs and students. In addition, there is a special scheme by which American students with a working knowledge of French (normally two years' study at university) are allowed to look for a job in France and work for up to three months with an *authorisation provisoire de travail*. Apply to *Council on International Education Exchange (CIEE)* 7 Custom House Street, 3rd Floor, Portland, ME 04101; ☎ 1-207 553 7600; fax 1-207 553 7699).

LANGUAGE

The French are very proud of their language and literature. It is seen as an international language too, and there is some resistance to the idea that English may have superseded it as the main medium of international communication in areas like diplomacy, science and commerce. Written English and grammar are taught in French schools but the spoken language is not taught well, so there are opportunities for English teachers to remedy this situation in the many private schools that exist. Basque is also spoken by some in the Basque region in the southwest of the country, and Breton in Brittany by a few. The dialect of the south of France, Occitan, has its origin in a language different to French and is often difficult to understand.

COST AND STANDARD OF LIVING

France has one of the best economies in the world and its general standard of living is higher than that of Britain (although not of the USA). This relative affluence does not extend to all areas of society, however, and there are areas of exclusion and unemployment that are a major cause of concern in the suburbs of towns and in the countryside. There is almost the same consensus abroad as in France that French food is the best in the world. The way of life in France is relaxed and there is an enjoyment of the good things of life unmatched in Britain or America. As with their work, the French also take their leisure seriously. Consumer goods and services (and eating out) are generally a more important area of expenditure than housing.

HOUSING AND ACCOMMODATION

Many French people do not like to invest money in property, and have a strong preference for rented accommodation. All the same, more than half of French families own their accommodation. All kinds of rented property are available for expatriate workers, and prices vary enormously depending on location. Paris and the Côte d'Azur are the most expensive areas in which to rent property.

HEALTH AND WELFARE

The various social security schemes cover almost everyone in France: wage earners, salaried staff, self-employed people and their families (including those foreign nationals who have paid their contributions).

The system is financed by contributions from both employer and employee. Reciprocal arrangements are also available for British and other EU nationals (see the *Rules and Regulations* chapter in *The General Approach* section), which cover national insurance, pensions (amounts dependent on salary and length of insurance); death, maternity, family and housing allowances; and industrial accident insurance.

Medical treatment and medicines are available to EU citizens under the same conditions as for French nationals. North Americans will need to have paid contributions to receive these benefits.

EDUCATION

The French attach great importance to education, and are leaders in science and knowledge-based industries such as information technology. Schooling is free and compulsory from the age of six to 16 and nursery schools and crèches are widely available. There is only a small private education sector (which includes international schools in areas where there are expatriate communities). State education is prestigious, and private schools are usually the repository for problem children.

Primary education lasts from six to 11. The first stage of secondary education lasts a further four years. Students usually stay on to take the *baccalauréat* exams which are necessary for university entry. French universities only require a modest payment for tuition charges and are open to foreigners with equivalent qualifications but they are sometimes overcrowded and of variable quality. The reform of higher education is a major political problem that no party as yet has been able to solve. There are also the more prestigious *grandes écoles*, which are part of the same system and originally founded by Napoleon as military colleges, for which additional preparatory study is necessary. Entry to these is by annual *concurrence* or competition.

EMBASSIES AND CONSULATES

British Embassy, 35 rue du Faubourg St. Honoré, 75383 Paris, Cedex 08; ☎ 1-4451 3100; fax 1-4451 3127; www.amb-grandebretagne.fr.
British Consulate-Generals in Paris, Bordeaux, Lille, Lyon, and Marseille.
US Embassy, 2 avenue Gabriel, 75382 Paris, Cedex 08; ☎ 1-4312 2222; www.amb-usa. fr.
US Consulates in Bordeaux, Lille, Lyon, Marseille, Rennes, Toulouse, and Strasbourg.

TOURIST OFFICES

French Government Tourist Office – Maison de la France, 178 Piccadilly, 3rd floor, London W1J 9AL; ☎ 09068-244123; fax 020-7493 6594; e-mail info.uk@franceguide.com; www.franceguide.com/uk.
French Government Tourist Office, 444 Madison Avenue, New York, NY 10022; ☎ 212-838 7800; www.francetourism.com.

TELEPHONES

For all calls within France a zero is dialled before the nine-digit number which is now standard, except for Paris numbers beginning with 1. From France, as in Britain, international calls begin 00.

CONDITIONS OF WORK

WAGES

Salaries in Paris are generally higher than in the rest of the country, and overall salaries in France are around 30 per cent higher than those in the UK. The cost of living is also lower. Comparisons with the USA are less favourable, however. The national hourly minimum wage (known as the SMIC – *Salaire Minimum Interprofessionel de Croissance*) is regularly reviewed to keep up with inflation. Currently the SMIC rate is 8.27 euros (about £5.60) per hour. Almost all workers in France are paid monthly. Opening a bank account can be a time-consuming process well decorated with red tape and asking your employer for a recommendation will make things easier.

HOURS

The 35 hour working week was introduced in France in 2000. However, it is slowly becoming more flexible so that people can work longer hours if they wish. More information on working hours can be found at www.35h.travail.gouv.fr. The traditional working day lasts from 8.30 or 9am to 6 or 6.30pm with a long lunch break, although a shorter day is becoming more common. Flexi-time (*horaire mobilé*) is practised in many companies.

HOLIDAYS

There are 11 public holidays annually, and by law all employees are entitled to 30 days annual leave. There have been moves in industry to curtail the annual mass August departure by staggering summer holidays but these have been only partially successful. The public holidays are: New Year's Day; Easter Monday; Labour Day (1 May); Victory in Europe Day (8 May); Ascension (16 May); Whit Monday (May); Bastille Day (14 July); Assumption (15 August); All Saints (1 November); Armistice Day (11 November); Christmas Day. There is an interesting French expression *faire le pont*, which means bridging the time between one of these holidays and the weekend by taking another day or two unofficial holiday.

SAFETY AND COMPENSATION

Hygiene and Security Committees are obligatory in large firms, and there are regular inspections. In addition, those working in France can expect an annual, free medical check-up.

Contributions for sickness and injury benefits come under social security (with the various taxes for social security, unemployment, as well as your social security number, detailed separately on your pay-slip). Compensation for industrial accidents usually covers the full cost of medical expenses, rehabilitation and retraining. Unemployment does not come under this social security heading, but under a separate scheme run by ASSIDEC (*Associations pour l'emploi dans l'industrie et le commerce*).

TRADE UNIONS

The influence of organised labour has declined rapidly since the 70s and 80s, and now lies mainly in the public sector. Membership of the largest and most influential union, the CGT (*Confédération Générale du Travail*) fell by about 50 per cent in the 1990s. Recent legislation has encouraged employers and employees to negotiate directly regarding wages and working conditions, so that traditional problems between workers and management have been reduced. Unions tend to be strongest in the traditional industries and have little influence in new, high technology ones. They usually operate on a regional rather than national basis, with the exception of the notorious French lorry drivers' union.

TAXATION

Personal income tax is known as IRPP (*Impôt sur le Revenue des Personnes Physicques*) and ranges from a minimum of 12 per cent to a maximum of 56.8 per cent, depending on salary. There are, however, a huge number of income tax allowances in France, which for most people will bring the rate down significantly. The highest wage earners will find that they pay more than they would in the UK, while for average earners, the take-home pay will generally be more. Deductions are made for national insurance at around 18 per cent.

Indirect taxes are a main source of French government revenue, and Value Added Tax is levied in some areas that are not taxed in Britain. The tax year runs from January to December; and returns must be filed before 1 March, on the basis of predicted income for the year. Taxes are paid in instalments, either three times per year, or monthly.

EMPLOYMENT PROSPECTS

OVERVIEW

France has a modern, developed economy, and there are few areas where work is not available to qualified experienced personnel. The only fields really restricted are teaching and government service, where exams in the French language mean that only the most linguistically competent can qualify. French employers value training, and generally expect recruits to have specific professional qualifications for whatever job they are taken on to do. The general workplace atmosphere tends to be more formal and sometimes more hierarchical than in Britain or America. There are two definite categories of employee: blue-collar workers (known as *le personnel*) and white-collar staff (known as *cadres*). It is also worth noting that a high standard of presentation in letters and CVs, as well as in personal appearance is expected of prospective new recruits. You should include international reply coupons in your letters of enquiry, or send a fax.

NEWSPAPERS

You can both place adverts in French newspapers as well as use them as a source of possible jobs. Keeping an eye on the jobs advertised in French newspapers could be helpful but obviously the majority of posts are aimed at French nationals. The potential for finding a job increases substantially if you are already in France, speak French and have marketable skills and a track record. For jobs in Paris, the main newspapers to consult are *Le Monde* (especially the monthly supplement called *Campus*, which contains job vacancies and general labour market information); *Le Figaro* (especially the pink Monday supplement) and *France Soir*. *Carrières et Emplois* which comes out on Wednesdays combines the week's job offers from both *France Soir* and *Le Figaro*.

The *International Herald Tribune* newspaper is published in Paris and has a worldwide circulation. Advertisements can be placed through its offices at 40 Marsh Wall, London E14 9TP; ☎020-7836 4802; www.iht.com, or at the New York office, 850 Third Avenue, New York, NY 10022; ☎212-752 3890. The *International Herald Tribune* has a circulation in France of 39,000 and international recruitment appears on Thursdays.

SPECIFIC CONTACTS

EMPLOYMENT SERVICES

The official labour exchange in France is the *Agence Nationale pour l'Emploi (ANPE)* which has branches in the main French towns (41 alone in Paris). They handle all types of work and special engineering departments exist in the offices in Paris, Lyon and Marseille. A list of ANPE's throughout France is available from the main office at *ANPE*, 4 rue Galilée, 93198 Noisy-le-Grand; ☎1-4931 7400; fax 1-4305 6786; www.anpe.fr which also operates EURES (the European Employment Service). You will need to speak French to use the services of ANPE. About 120,000 vacancies are registered daily on ANPE's website.

There is a regional branch of EURES in Britain at *EURES Crossborder HNFK*, South Kent College, Shakespeare Centre, 145-147 Sandgate Road, Folkestone, Kent CT20 2NA; ☎01303-226184, which assists with work in northern France.

Some of the current international and French job sites are: www.overseasjobs.com; www.jobware.net; www.cadresonline.com; www.apec.fr; www.cadremploi.fr; and www.monster.fr.

LOCAL AGENCIES

Legal restrictions mean that private employment agencies are prohibited in France (as they are in Germany) and can only function as temporary employment agencies (*agences de travail temporaire/agence d'intérim*). Most such agencies are chains with branches in several cities.

Employment agencies are required by law to request a social security number (*un séu*), which means that you can only use them to find a job if you have already worked legally in France.

The *Union Nationale des Entreprises de Travail Temporaires (UNETT)* (22 rue de l'Arcade, 75008 Paris; ☎1-4268 0644; fax 1-4265 9031) and *PROMATT* (94 rue St Lazare, 75009 Paris; ☎1-4878 1121), can provide a list of temporary work agencies throughout France, categorised by the sector in which they operate.

Two bilingual recruitment agencies for experienced secretaries are *Sheila Burgess International* (62 rue Saint Lazare, 75009 Paris, France; ☎1-4463 0257; fax 1-4463 0259; e-mail sbi@sheilaburgessint.fr; www.sheilaburgessint.fr). *Boyce Recruitment* (43 Eagle Street, London WC1R 4AT; ☎020-7306 6800; fax 020-7306 6801; e-mail info@boycerecruitment.co.uk; www.boycerecruitment.co.uk) recruits secretaries for Paris and the Paris area.

CENTRES D'INFORMATION JEUNESSE (CIJS)

There are about 30 CIJs in France, which are a useful source of information particularly for foreign students. Although it is by no means their main function, they can help people find jobs, particularly seasonal agricultural work and other part-time and temporary possibilities for the summer and winter. In addition they can provide leaflets on the regulations that affect foreign students. If you wish to have information about these in advance, you should send four International Reply Coupons to their Paris office: *Centre d'Information et de Documentation Jeunesse (CIDJ)*, 101 Quai Branly, 75740 Paris Cedex 15; ☎1-4449 1200; www.cidj.com. They will not, however, deal with job applications by post. For these you must call in person. Some CIJs just display vacancies on notice boards in their offices, while others have a more formal system run in conjunction with the local ANPE. There are CIJs in Amiens, Bastia (Corsica), Besançon, Bordeaux, Caen, Clermond Ferrand, Dijon, Grenoble, Lille, Limoges, Lyon, Marseille, Montpellier, Nancy, Nantes, Nice, Orléans, Poitiers, Reims, Rennes, Rouen, Strasbourg, and Toulouse.

The CIJ in Marseille (96 la Canebière, 13001 Marseille, Cedex 4; ☎4- 9124 3350; www.crijpa.com) is particularly useful for agricultural jobs and for *animateurs* (children's summer camp monitors), while the Nice CIJ has plenty of catering jobs. Mother's help jobs are also available through some CIJs.

AGRICULTURAL AND SEASONAL WORK

Work Your Way Around the World by Susan Griffith (Vacation Work Publications, www. vacationwork.co.uk) contains a definitive guide to finding farm work in France. The *vendange* or grape harvest, which starts around September, offers the best opportunities, but there are many others. You should certainly visit the local ANPE office in the wine-growing and other regions if you are looking for work there. If you have agricultural experience, you may be able to make arrangements in advance to work as an agricultural trainee through *Sésame*, 6 Rue de la Rochefoucauld - 75009 Paris; ☎1-4054 0708; www. agriplanete.com. Sésame does not, however, deal with seasonal work.

AU PAIRS

Apart from agencies listed in the *Au Pair* chapter, au pair positions are arranged throughout France by:

AFJE - Accueil Familial des Jeunes Etrangers, 23 rue du Cherche-Midi, 75006 Paris; ☎1-4222 5034; fax 1-4544 6048; e-mail accueil@afje-paris.org; www.afje-paris.org.
Accueil International Services, 2a rue Ducastel, 78100 St. Germain en Laye; ☎1-3973 0498; fax 1-3973 1525; e-mail au-pair@easyconnect.fr; www.accueil-international.com.
Association Familles & Jeunesse (AFJ), 4 Rue Massena, 06000 Nice; ☎4-9382 2822; fax 4-9388 1286; info@afj-aupair.org; www.afj-aupair.org.
Au Pair Azur, 155 avenue de Cireuil, 06210 Villeneuve Loubet, France; ☎6-6198 8181; e-mail aupairazur@aol.com; www.aupairazur.com.
Butterfly & Papillon, 5 Avenue de Genève, 74000 Annecy; ☎4-5067 0133; fax 4-5067 0351; www.butterfly-papillon.com.
Europair Services, 13 rue Vavin, 75006 Paris; ☎1-4329 8001; fax 1-4329 8037; e-mail contact@europairservices.com; www.europairservices.com.
Fee Revee, 6 Rue de Bellevue, 91250 Suresnes; tel/fax 1-4144 –185; e-mail contact@fee-revee.com; www.fee-revee.com.
France Au Pair Eurojob, B.P. 89, 6 alee des Saules, 14720 Saint-Palais-sur-Mer; ☎5-4623 9988; fax 5-4638 7511; e-mail contact@eurojob.fr; www.eurojob.fr.
Good Morning Europe Ltd., Au Pair in Paris, 38 rue Traversiere, 75012 Paris; ☎1-4487 0122; fax 1-4487 0142; e-mail aupair@good-morning-europe.com; www.good-morning-eruope.com.
Inter-Sejours, 179 rue de Courcelles, 75017 Paris; ☎1-4763 0681; e-mail aideinfo. intersejours@wanadoo.fr; http://asso.intersejours.free.fr.
Nurse Au Pair Placement (NAPP), 16 Rue le Sueur, 75116 Paris; ☎1-4500 3388; 1-4500 3399; e-mail nappsarl@aol.com; www.napp.fr.
Oliver Twist Association, 7 rue Léon Marin, Pessac 33600; ☎5-5726 9326; fax 5-5636 2185; e-mail oliver.twist@wanadoo.fr; www.oliver.twist.org.

MEDICAL STAFF

The Association Médicale Française, 180 Boulevard Haussmann, Paris 75008; ☎1-53 89 32 66; fax 1-53 89 32 27, can provide information on areas where doctors are needed. The nurses' association in France is *ANFIIDE*, 5 Rue Blaise Pascal, 94440 Villecresnes; www.anfiide.com.

There is a very uneven distribution of doctors in France, especially GPs. Departments experiencing shortages are mainly in the north of the country.

TEACHERS

Teachers of English are always needed in every region and *département* of France, if not in every *commune*, as the country struggles to reconcile its own international role in an increasingly English-speaking world with its attachment to French language and culture.

In other words, there is a great desire, as well as a reluctance, to know how to use English, which many may have learnt imperfectly at school. Learners range from children to business executives, at all levels of proficiency in the language. Many companies provide their employees with free language courses and thus business people provide the main source of clients in many language schools.

Most schools prefer staff to work for at least a year on contract, however, some, most notably Berlitz, have a high turnover of staff in their Paris schools. Competition for positions is keen because of the number of people in the market, and to have a realistic chance of finding work you will need a TEFL qualification, a degree, or experience (and often all three).

The best way to find work is by contacting schools directly. You can find them listed under *Enseignements Privé de Langues* or *Ecoles de Langues* in the Yellow Pages. The *British Council* (9 rue de Constantine, 75340 Paris Cedex 07; ☎ 1-4955 7300; fax 1-4705 7702; e-mail information@britishcouncil.fr; www.britishcouncil.fr) publishes a booklet *Teaching English As A Foreign Language in France*, as well as a list of institutions offering English language tuition in the Paris area with an indication of their minimum teaching requirements.

Séjours Internationaux Linguistiques et Culturels (SILC), 32 Rempart de l'Est, 16022 Angoulême; ☎ 5-4597 4100; fax 5-4594 2063; e-mail france@silc.fr; www.silc. fr, organises educational, cultural, and language programmes for juniors, students, and professionals around the world.

TOURISM

As one of the great tourist destinations of Europe, France has no shortage of related temporary work to offer in many categories. This section covers most of them including Euro Disney and the adjacent Parc Walt Disney Studios, hotels and catering, holiday centres and campsites, ski resorts and holiday boats. Of course work in tourism need not be temporary; those interested in making a career in tourism will find that most big companies, such as Club Med, have career development opportunities. Further details on employment opportunities at *Euro Disney* are available from Service de Recruitement-Casting, BP 110, 77777 Marne-la-Vallée, Cedex 4; ☎ 1-6474 6147.

Tour operators offering work opportunities in France are included in the chapter, *Transport, Tourism and Hospitality*. In addition, there is a wide variety of tourism and hotel work that can be found on the spot (see *Work Your Way Around the World*, which also has useful tips for other kinds of seasonal and short-term work).

VOLUNTARY WORK

France has a wide range of opportunities for voluntary work. Projects normally last for two to three weeks during the summer. A great many archaeological digs and building restoration projects are carried out each year. Every May the Ministry of Culture (*Direction de l'Architecture et du Patrimoine, Sous-Direction de l'Archéologie*, 4 rue d'Aboukir, 75002 Paris; ☎ 1-4015 7781; www.culture.fr/fouilles) publishes a list of excavations throughout France requiring up to 5,000 volunteers. Most digs charge unskilled labourers for board and lodgings.

REMPART (1 rue des Guillemites, 75004 Paris; ☎ 1-4271 9655; fax 1-4271 7300; www. rempart.com) is similar to the National Trust organisation in Britain and is in charge of 140 endangered monuments around France. They accept volunteers on their conservation projects and charge around £4 per day for board and lodgings.

USEFUL PUBLICATIONS

Live and Work in France by Victoria Pybus (www.vacationwork.co.uk) provides comprehensive information on all aspects of life in France.

International Jobs (A Guide for UK and Overseas Students) and *Working in Europe*, both from the University of London Careers Service, 49-51 Gordon Square, London WC1H

0PQ; ☎020-7554 4500; e-mail careers@careers.lon.ac.uk; www.careers.lon.ac.uk, provide useful information on multinationals who recruit in Britain. Further information on all sorts of opportunities abroad can be found on the Careers Service website.

INTERNATIONAL COMPANIES IN FRANCE

Automotive Products France 22
177 rue des Fauvelles
92404 Courbevoie

Barclays Bank International 4
45 Blvd. Haussmann
75009 Paris

British Airways 3
Immeuble Kupka A
18 rue Hoche
75009 Paris-la-Défense

BT France SA 45
Immeuble Jean Monnet
11 Place des Vosges
92061 Paris-la-Défense Cedex

British Tourist Authority 48
63 rue Pierre Charron
75008 Paris

Charterhouse SA 4
47 Avenue George V
75008 Paris

CGU Courtage 23
100 re de Courcelles
75017 Paris

Cooper France SA 8
15 rue Sorins
92000 Nanterre

Corus France SA 28
3 allée des Barbanniers
92632 Gennevilliers

Courtaulds Fibres SA 46
Pont de Leu
62231 Coquelles

DHL International 17
BP 50252
241 rue de la Belle Etoile
95957 Roissy

Financial Times Europe Ltd. 38
Centre d'Affaires
Le Louvre
168 rue de Rivoli
75008 Paris

Gestetner SA 30
71 rue Cammille Groult
94400 Vitry-sur-Seine

Guardian Royal Exchange plc 23
42 rue des Mathurins
75008 Paris

Hambros France Ltd 4
16 place Vendôme
75001 Paris

ICI Paints Déco France 26
2 ave Louis Armand
92607 Asnières

ICL France SA 10
24 avenue de l'Europe
78140 Velizy-Villacoublay

International Herald Tribune 38
181 av. Charles de Gaulle
92521 Neuilly

JCB France (Rochester UK) 27
BP 671
3 rue de Vignolle
95200 Sarcelles

Johnson Matthey & CIE 28
13 rue de la Perdrix ZI
93290 Tremblay-en-France

Laboratoires Fisons SA	8	Reckitt Benckiser France	18
Tour PFA, La Défense 10		15 rue Ampère	
92076 Paris-la-Défense Cedex 43		91301 Massy Cedex	
Laboratoires Glaxo Wellcome	8	SAFAD (Alfred Dunhill)	47
43 rue Vineuse		15 rue de la Paix	
BP 166 16		75002 Paris	
75016 Paris			
		Securicor France SA	43
Legal & General Assurance	23	12 avenue des Cocquelicots	
58 rue Victoire		94380 Bonneuil-sur-Marne	
75009 Paris			
		WH Smith & Son SA	13
Lloyds Bank SA	4	248 rue de Rivoli	
15 avenue d'Iéna		75001 Paris	
75783 Paris Cedex 16			
		Standard Chartered Bank Ltd	4
Lucas France SA	26	4 rue Ventadour	
11 rue Lord Byron		F-75001 Paris	
75008 Paris			
		Thorn EMI Computer Software	10
NatWest Markets France	4	101-109 rue Jean Jaurès	
National Westminster Bank SA		92300 Levallois-Perret	
13 rue d'Uzès			
75002 Paris		Trusthouse Hotels	20
		23 Place Vendôme	
Rank Video Services France	36	75001 Paris	
1 rue Edouard Denis Baldus			
71100 Chalon-sur-Saône		Weatherall Green & Smith	40
		64 rue La Boétie	
Rank-Xerox SA	22	75008 Paris	
3 rue Bellini			
F-92806 Puteaux		Wimpey SA	6
		72-78 Grande Rue	
		F-92312 Sèvres	

The *Franco-British Chamber of Commerce & Industry*, 31 rue Boissy d'Anglas, 75008 Paris; ☎1- 5330 8130; www.francobritishchamber.com, publishes a *Year Book* containing a full list of members of the Chamber, many of which are branches, subsidiaries or agents of British-based companies. The *Chambre de Commerce Française de Grande-Bretagne*, 21 Dartmouth Street, Westminster, London SW1H 9BP; ☎020-7304 7071; fax 020-7304 4034; e-mail mail@ccfgb.co.uk; www.ccfgb.co.uk produces useful publications including *Setting up a Business in France* (£20) and *Making Yourself at Home in France* (£20). The series is available for £35 and £25 for members.

The *Guide to Doing Business in France*, compiled by the American Chamber of Commerce and the Commercial Services of the American Embassy in France, is published by the *American Chamber of Commerce in France* (156 boulevard Haussmann, F-75008 Paris; ☎1-5643 4567; fax 1-5643 4560; e-mail amchamfrance@amchamfrance.org; www.amchamfrance.org). This guide includes a complete list of US firms in France; US products and services represented in France; special sections on economic and political trends; investment climate and other useful addresses in France and the United States.

Germany

- **Year of EU Accession:** 1952 (West Germany); 1990 (united Germany)
- **German Embassy,** 23 Belgrave Square, London SW1X 8PZ; ☎020-7824 1300; fax 020-7824 1449; www.London.diplo.de
- **German Embassy,** 4645 Reservoir Road NW, Washington DC 20007; ☎202-298 4000; www.germany.info
- **Currency:** 1 Euro (€) = 100 cents
- **Rate of Exchange:** £1 = €1.44; $1 = €0.78
- **Country Code:** +49

Germany is still in many ways coming to terms with the 1990 reunification of former East and West Germany, with the costs of reunification placing a burden not only on German citizens but also across the entire European Union. Major reconstruction work has taken place in Berlin, which has become, once again, the capital city. Since reunification foreign workers have flocked to Germany from Poland, Portugal, Vietnam, Yugoslavia, the UK and elsewhere – joining the millions of Turkish 'guest workers' who have been in Germany for a generation. Wages were initially high and prospects good, but unemployment is currently quite high at around 11%.

Germany's location in central Europe means that it is well placed to take advantage of commercial and trade opportunities in the East, where its cultural influence is also strong. The country is one of the driving forces in the EU in respect of Economic and Monetary Union and its economy is taken as a baseline standard for EMU. Germany leads the way in industries such as vehicle manufacture and engineering but many enterprises are locating new factories in countries where wage costs are lower. German business is exporting tens of thousands of jobs to places such as Eastern Europe, China and India. More than 30,000 German scientists have moved to work in the USA.

Germans are courteous and friendly, but there is far less 'service with a smile' than can be found in the United States, or even Britain, and their directness is sometimes taken as rudeness. If you want to meet people you have to be proactive and introduce yourself. The work environment can also seem rather formal and bureaucratic at first. Team working is the rule (as in many other countries nowadays), and this can be frustrating for those who prefer to work in a more individualistic way. 'Quiet Time' (1pm to 3pm and 10pm through to 7am) is taken very seriously; during these hours try not to annoy the neighbours, who have the right to call the police if they are bothered by loud noises. In the workplace, a more informal dress code is becoming common but a neat appearance and, most importantly, punctuality are always required. Stereotypes are inevitably inaccurate, but observers note a general difference in atmosphere between the north and south of Germany. In the north, a more serious work ethic is evident, while those in the more Catholic southern part of the country take a more relaxed view of life (and there are more festivals, like the Munich Beer Festival, and the Shrove Tuesday Carnival).

GENERAL FACTS

POPULATION

Germany's population numbers around 82.4 million, of whom 7.2 million are classified as foreigners. The birth rate is 8.25 per 1,000 inhabitants, one of the lowest in the world. Germany covers 137,838 square miles (356,999 sq km) and the average population density throughout the country is 229 inhabitants per square kilometre, a little less than that of Britain.

CLIMATE

Germany's climate is temperate, with warm summers and cold winters. Annual precipitation varies, and is higher in the Alps. Winters can be severe, but in most parts of the country prolonged periods of frost and snow are rare.

GOVERNMENT

Germany is a Federal Republic governed under a parliamentary system. Its Constitution is the 1949 Basic Law. Until 1990, Germany was split into the liberal Federal Republic of Germany (FRG) in the West, and the communist German Democratic Republic (GDR) in the East. East Germany has now been completely absorbed into the Federal Republic's political system. The Federal Republic is headed by a President whose term of office lasts five years. The Chancellor is the head of the government, and may remain in office for a maximum of four years when the new Bundestag (the legislative body) is elected. The Bundesrat is the second chamber, whose members are appointed by the 16 federal states. These states are: Bavaria and Baden-Wérttemberg (the two largest); Berlin; Brandenburg; Bremen; Hamburg; Hesse; Lower Saxony; Mecklenburg-Western Pomerania; North Rhine-Westphalia; Rhineland-Palatinate; Saarland; Saxony; Saxony-Anhalt; Schleswig-Holstein; and Thuringia. Berlin is the national capital city.

CITIES

About one-third of the population lives in the 85 cities with over 100,000 inhabitants. These include Berlin with its rapidly growing population of around 3.5 million; Hamburg (1.7 million); Munich (1.2 million); and Cologne, with around one million. Bonn, the former political and administrative capital of West Germany, has a population of around 300,000.

RURAL LIFE

Germany has diverse landscapes ranging from high mountain ranges to uplands, hilly regions and lakelands as well as wide, open lowlands. Land use is similarly varied. The chief crops are milk, pork and beef, cereals and sugarbeet. The production of wine and the growing of fruit and vegetables are also important in some regions. The number of agricultural workers is decreasing every year and the number of small family farms is also diminishing. The collective farms of the East are now privately owned, or operate as co-operatives. There is also a gradual population shift away from the large towns, particularly in the industrialised and overcrowded Ruhr Valley, which is turning some villages into small towns.

RELIGION, SPORT AND CULTURE

'Freedom of faith and conscience' is guaranteed under the German Constitution. In the western part of the country 42 per cent of Germans are Protestant and 43 per cent Catholic. In the former East, 47 per cent are Protestant and only seven per cent Catholic. In addition, there are churches of immigrant groups (such as the Greek Orthodox church) as well as other faiths present, including Islam, with around 1.7 million adherents (mainly Turkish residents), and Judaism. Before the Nazi genocide about 530,000 Jews lived in Germany. Today this community numbers around 40,000.

Sport is a favourite leisure activity; and football is the most popular. There are more than five million members of the German Football Federation and thousands of amateur clubs. Germany was universally praised for its efficiently organised hosting of the 2006 World Cup and the national team claimed third place. Sports like gymnastics, rifle-shooting, athletics, tennis, golf and swimming are also favoured. Horse riding is also popular, as is motor racing. Winter sports are widely enjoyed and include skiing, ski-jumping, skating, ice-hockey and tobogganing. Travel is also a popular leisure activity.

Germany has a tradition of decentralisation, which is embodied in the modern state. This makes for a wide and rich range of cultural diversity. Nightlife is lively in the major cities, and Germans are fond of joining clubs and participating in team sports.

FACTORS INFLUENCING EMPLOYMENT

IMMIGRATION

EU citizens do not require a visa, residence permit (except Swiss citizens) or a work permit in Germany. They must however register with the local authorities (*Einwohnermeldeamt*) within three months of entering the country. Once registered, they will automatically receive a residence certificate from the *Ausländerberhörde* (Aliens Department). Workers from the 'new' EU member states (i.e. those who gained accession in 2004 or later) are entitled to reside in Germany without a residence permit, but only nationals of Malta and Cyprus may enjoy free access to the German labour market.

US citizens and nationals of the European Free Trade Area (EFTA) non-EU states (Iceland, Liechtenstein, Norway, and Switzerland) can remain in Germany for up to 90 days as tourists and no visa is required, but work permits must be obtained while outside the country. Non-EU nationals who apply for a residence permit must supply a notarised certificate of good conduct, evidence of health insurance, and proof of accommodation and means of support. The permit must specify that employment is permitted before the bearer has any hope of obtaining a work permit (*Arbeitslaubnis*).

German Embassies cannot help in finding employment, but can give information to prospective workers and residents in Germany.

LANGUAGE

English is widely spoken, as is French in certain regions, particularly in the Saarland. Danish is spoken by the small Danish minority in the north of Schleswig-Holstein. Regional dialects often differ markedly from standard German. Most English-speakers find German quite easy to pronounce, but the grammar and word order more difficult to master.

COST AND STANDARD OF LIVING

Incomes have increased constantly in Germany thanks to its 'economic miracle' (*Wirtschaftswunder*) and, as in the United States, a very broad middle class has emerged. Germany has enjoyed low inflation for many years, while salaries and the material standard of living have steadily increased. To an outsider, prices may appear quite high, and there has been a high rate of inflation since the unification of the country.

HOUSING AND ACCOMMODATION

Because of the enormous destruction of old houses during the Second World War, most of the present housing supply was built after 1945. In spite of substantial state subsidies for house building, there is still a severe accommodation shortage at the lower end of the market, and repair and restoration is a major priority in the East of the country. German house prices are very high by comparison with most of Europe. Although owner-occupation has increased, and it is not uncommon for Germans to build their own house, most people in cities live in rented accommodation. Finding this is not easy. Rented flats usually come with some kitchen appliances and efficient central heating.

HEALTH AND WELFARE

Germany's general social policy is to help an individual when in need through no fault of his or her own (through sickness, accident or old age), but not to allow any absolute claim on the state for subsistence. About 30 per cent of the national budget goes on social security. Contributions from employer and employee are high – the contribution for sickness insurance is currently around 12-14 per cent, with an added 1.7 per cent for long-term care. Pension contributions amount to 19.1 per cent and unemployment insurance is another 6.5 per cent – but benefits are also high (up to 100 per cent of earnings in case of sickness). Over 90 per cent of the population are covered.

Insurance distinctions are made between manual workers (*Arbeiter*) and office staff (*Angestellte*). The *Arbeiter* are compulsorily insured, while above a certain (quite high) level of income *Angestellte* may choose whether or not to insure themselves, in which case the employer makes only a limited contribution.

The contributions paid cover maternity and unemployment benefits, death payments, old age and disability pensions, children's allowances, widows' and orphans' pensions, all medical and most dental treatment, and supplementary benefits in all cases of need.

As soon as you commence employment, your employer will take the necessary steps to register you with social security. The first step is to register with the *Krankenkass*, which issues an insurance number used to track your pension and insurance contributions, much the same as the British National Insurance number. The insurance authority will then issue you with a social insurance identity card (*Sozialversicherungsausweis*) and the pensions authority will provide you with an insurance book (*Versicherungsnachweisheft*). If you have previously worked in Germany, you should simply hand your old book to your new employer to reactivate your contributions.

EDUCATION

There are few private schools, and most children go to free state schools, starting with voluntary kindergarten at three or four years of age. About 70 per cent of all three to six year olds attend kindergarten. Education is compulsory from the age of six when children enter primary school (*Grundschule*) for four years before moving on to a *Gymnasium* (grammar school), *Hauptschule* (intermediate school) – which may lead on to a course of vocational training – or a *Realschule* (general secondary school). *Gymnasium* pupils often stay on until they are 18 or 19 and then continue with higher education. Pupils from the *Realschule* generally continue their studies at a *Fachschule* or technical college to learn a skill or trade. This is regarded as a preparation for a medium-level career in business or administration, and around a third of school students achieve this qualification.

NATIONAL SERVICE

All German males have to serve 15 months' military national service, or in an alternative civilian service. Foreigners are exempt.

EMBASSIES AND CONSULATES

British Embassy, Wilhelmstrasse 70, 10117 Berlin; ☎30-20457-0; fax 30-20457 579; www.britischebotschaft.de.
Consulates in Dusseldorf, Frankfurt am Main, Hamburg, Munich, and Stuttgart.
American Embassy, Neustädtische Kirchstr. 4-5, 10117 Berlin; ☎30-2385 174; www.usembassy.de.
Consulates in Berlin, Frankfurt am Main, Dusseldorf, Hamburg, Leipzig, and Munich.

TOURIST OFFICES

German National Tourist Office, PO Box 2695, London W1A 3TN; ☎020-7317 0908; fax 020-7317 0917; e-mail gntolon@d-z-t.com; www.germany-tourism.co.uk.
German National Tourist Office, 52nd Floor, 122 East 42nd Street, New York, NY 10168-0072; ☎212-661 7200; fax 212-661 7174; e-mail gntonyc@d-z-t.com; www. cometogermany.com.

CONDITIONS OF WORK

WAGES

German salaries are among the highest in the world, averaging out at the equivalent of £20 per hour. Taxes and social security deductions are high, however, and the take-home salary is likely to be considerably less than half this amount. There is no statutory minimum wage, although there are widely perceived minimum figures for most types of employment. German workers receive Christmas bonuses and extra pay during holiday periods.

HOURS

Most contracts are now for a five-day, 35-hour week, and in some industries a 29-hour week has been adopted to stave off redundancies. Legislation provides that the regular working time may not exceed eight hours a day. Professionals and the self-employed often work longer hours. Only 14 per cent of the German workforce work a 40-hour week, compared to 47 per cent in Britain.

HOLIDAYS

Employees in Germany receive on average 42 days paid leave per year (including public holidays), with a statutory minimum of 18 days or three weeks. The following days are public holidays: New Year's Day; Epiphany (6 Jan); Good Friday; Easter Monday; Labour Day (1 May); Ascension Day (16 May); Whit Monday; Corpus Christi (not in Protestant areas); German Unity Day (3 October); Reformation Day (31 Oct, in Protestant areas); All Saints' Day (1 November, again not in Protestant areas); Christmas Day and Boxing Day. Immaculate Conception (15 Aug) is also a holiday in some Catholic areas.

SAFETY AND COMPENSATION

Special labour courts protect employees against unfair dismissal, and safeguard holiday rights. Accident insurance is paid by all employers, who contribute to an industrial injury society. This covers retraining and rehabilitation, medical treatment, daily cash allowances and pensions for those totally incapacitated, and compensation for the widows and orphans of men killed at work.

TRADE UNIONS

In Germany there is free collective bargaining between employers and unions. These are known as the 'social partners', each defending their own interests, and with a responsibility for society as a whole. The unions in Germany are 'unitary' in the sense that each represents all the workers in a particular sector of industry, and have no formal political or religious ties. Around nine million German workers are members of trade unions at present, marking a drop of 17 per cent in union membership since 1985.

TAXATION

All German employees are divided into six income tax brackets, based on age, marital status and number of dependants. Single persons with no children (Class 1) are taxed at the highest rate. Very low-income groups pay no tax at all. Tax rates begin around 25 per cent and go up to a maximum of 53 per cent of income. All residents must pay a Church tax (*Kirchensteuer*) of around eight per cent, however, it is possible to claim an exception due to atheism. German income tax is quite moderate in EU terms. However, social security contributions are among the steepest.

EMPLOYMENT PROSPECTS

OVERVIEW

Germany has one of the best-trained workforces in Europe, or possibly even the world, and competition for jobs is high. To gain employment in this market, foreigners will need to offer skills or services which are in demand and which cannot be provided, or which have not yet been exploited, by the Germans themselves. There is a demand for top-flight executives with a knowledge of foreign markets, as well as for experts in fields such as taxation and business law.

Management consultants in Germany advertise their services in the Saturday papers and can be looked up under *Personalberatung* in the Yellow Pages. Your first contact should be with the personnel department of a prospective employer, and sending in a detailed CV with copies of letters of recommendation, references and citations is also recommended.

The Germans are widely acknowledged as the world leaders in engineering, in particular in the automotive field and much of Germany's industrial prowess stems from the excellent education and training of its workers. More junior positions are likely to be filled by local staff; and the more menial jobs tend to be done by guest workers (*Gastarbeiter*), who number in the millions, from former Yugoslavia, Poland, Turkey, Greece and other countries. Skilled office workers may find employment if they speak German. For temporary and seasonal jobs in tourism or agriculture and au pair work, see below. Construction work has traditionally been popular with British and Irish workers, and there are agencies (which advertise in the UK tabloid press, often giving just a telephone number) that deal with this kind of work. Legitimate ones should ask you for your Department of Trade and Industry Certificate of Experience or for the European Union EC2/GN.

NEWSPAPERS

German dailies are published on a regional basis. Many German newspapers, including the leading national *Séddeutsche Zeitung.* and major local dailies *Frankfurter Rundschau, Kölnische Rundschau, Hannoversche Allgemeine Zeitung,* and the *Westdeutsche Allgemeine,* are represented by *The Powers Turner Group*, Gordon House, Greencoat Place, London SW1P 1PH; ☎020-7592 8300; fax 020-7592 8301; e-mail ppn-london@publicitas. com; www.publicitas.com. Most of the major dailies, such as the *Frankfurter Allgemeine Zeitung* carry their jobs supplements on Saturdays, and go on sale on Friday evenings. Anyone wishing to advertise in the widely read *Frankfurter Allgemeine Zeitung* should contact the London office (2nd Floor, West, Bedford Chambers, Covent Garden Piazza, London, WC2E 8HA; ☎020-7836 5540; www.faz.de). Situations wanted usually appear in the Wednesday edition. *BZ* in Berlin has a good selection of vacancies for unskilled workers.

SPECIFIC CONTACTS

EMPLOYMENT SERVICES

The Federal Employment Institute, or *Bundesanstalt fér Arbeit* (D-90327, Nérnberg) has a nationwide network of 181 offices. These employment offices, or *arbeitsämter*, are the main resource in job finding as private agencies are rare, and only operate under certain highly restricted conditions. The Central Placement Office (*Zentralstelle fér Arbeitsvermittlung)* at Villemombler Str. 76, D-53123 Bonn, Germany; ☎228-7130; fax 228-713 1111; www. arbeitsamt.de, can process enquiries for all types of work, sending them out to regional offices. Enquiries should include an international reply coupon and the following detailed information: your full name; address; date and place of birth; marital and family status and whether you intend to enter Germany alone or with other members of your family; professional or vocational training, qualifications and experience; present employer and occupation; degree of proficiency in the German language; type of employment you are seeking and the length of your intended stay in Germany. Non-EU nationals will generally need some special trade or qualification to be considered by this service.

The Federal Employment Institute is currently reviewing its policy of discouraging private employment agencies, and the number of these is likely to increase in the future. International temping agencies such as Manpower (with 75 offices), Adecco, and Ranstad have offices in large cities around Germany. *Euro-London Appointments*, Goethestrasse 23, 60313 Frankfurt; ☎69-219 320; fax 69-2193 2111; e-mail frankfurt@eurolondon.de; www.eurolondon.com, has offices in the UK and France and places multilingual personnel in a wide variety of industries.

AU PAIRS

Among the longest established agencies is the non-profit Roman Catholic agency *IN VIA* whose full title is Katholische Mädchensozialarbeit, Deutscher Verband e.V. with branches throughout Germany and one in England *(German Catholic Social Centre)* and one in Paris (Foyer Porta, 14 Pierre Demours, 75017 Paris; ☎1-45 72 18 66). Its Protestant counterpart is *Verein für Internationale Jugendarbeit* (VIJ) also with offices throughout the country. Both place both male and female au pairs for a preferred minimum stay of one year.

Dozens of secular agents have popped up all over Germany, many of them members of the Aupair-Society e.V. (www.au-pair-society.org) which has three offices in Germany and more than 40 member agencies. Commercial au pair agencies do not charge a placement fee to incoming au pairs. Listed below are German agencies, all of which invite direct applications from individuals abroad to meet the healthy demand for English-speaking au pairs:

A'nF – Au Pair and Family, Argentinische Allee 110, 14163 Berlin-Zehlendorf, Germany;☎+49 30-303 49 722; fax: +49 30-303 49 723; e-mail info@aupairandfamily. de; www.aupairandfamily.de.

Apab Au-Pair Agentur Berger, Lothringer Str. 28, 44805 Bochum, Germany; ☎+49 234-953 6884; fax: +49 234-953 6661; e-mail office@au-pair-berger.de and office@au-pair-berger.com; www.au-pair-berger.com.

Aupair2000, Am Neckarufer 6, 68535 Edingen, Germany; ☎/fax: +49 6203-839427; e-mail ghalasy@t-online.de or info@aupair2000.de.

Au Pair Agentur Sylviane Zürner, Läutenring 1, 85235 Pfaffenhofen (Glonn), Germany; ☎+49 8134-935 565; fax: +49 8134-935 464; e-mail: sylviane@au-pair-zuerner.de; www.au-pair-zuerner.de.

Au-Pair Interconnection, Staufenstrasse 17, 86899 Landsberg am Lech, Germany; ☎+49 8191-941 378; fax: +49 8191-941 379; e-mail: susanne@caudera.de; www.aupair-interconnection.de.

Au Pair Service Silke Sommer, Steindamm 39, 25485 Hemdingen, Germany; ☎+49 4123-7749; fax: 4123-7728; e-mail aps.sommer@t-online.de; www.aupairprofi.de.

CP Au-Pair Agentur, Pilgrimstr. 4, 46053 Duisburg, Germany; ☎/fax: +49 203-3635 901; fax: +49 203-3635 926; e-mail christel.paul@cp-au-pair.com; www.cp-au-pair.com.

Family Au-Pair Service, Gernsheimerstr. 38, 12247 Berlin, Germany; ☎+49 30-75 47 97 93; fax: +49 30-75 47 97 92; e-mail berlin@family-au-pair-service.de; www.family-au-pair-service.de.

GSAP International Exchange Programs, Bgm-Hasberg Str. 41, 25767 Bunsoh, Germany. ☎+49 4835 972790; fax: +49 4835 972791; e-mail greis@gsap.info; www.gsap.info.

INWOX (International Work Experience), Zum Oberfeld 17, 55286 Wörrstadt, Germany; ☎+49 6732-937735; fax: +49 6732-937642; e-mail: info@inwox.com; www.inwox.com.

Munichaupair, Drachenseestr. 13, 81373 Munich, Germany; ☎+49 89-7672 9510; fax +49 89-7672 9511; e-mail patricia@munichaupair.com; www.munichaupair.com.

Perfect Partners, Am Sonnenhügel 2, 97450 Arnstein, Germany; ☎+49 9363-994291; fax: +49 9363-994292; e-mail: info@perfect-partners.de; www.perfect-partners.de.

It is also possible to find a job independently through advertisements, notice boards and so on. The Saturday edition of *Suddeutscher Zeitung* carries plenty of adverts, though many are aimed at German women to work for families abroad. Local English-language papers and websites might prove useful such as www.munichfound.com (click on 'Jobmarket' then 'Private Jobs' Offered).

CONSTRUCTION AND BUILDING

After reunification, the building industry boomed in Germany, as houses, hotels, roads and public buildings were commissioned, mostly in East Berlin and the former GDR. Large numbers of British and Irish construction workers, mostly qualified tradespeople, found work in Germany, usually bypassing statutory wage regulations and the high national insurance contributions. German building workers, however, protested at the loss of their jobs to foreigners and staged mass demonstrations against deregulation.

The boom is now over and the German construction industry is shrinking, with a loss of around 70,000 jobs per year. Those British and Irish workers who remain are generally in more stable employment, earning the same wages as their local counterparts. Inspectors regularly visit sites and issue on-the-spot fines to employers breaking the rules, and this has essentially brought to a halt the operations of agents and sub-contractors who for many years recruited workers from the UK on behalf of German construction companies. The German Building, Agricultural and Environmental Union (*Industriegewerkschaft Bauen-Agrar-Umwelt*) has, together with the GMB in Britain, put together an explanatory bilingual booklet on the terms and conditions which apply to building and construction workers, including details of the minimum wages due to building site workers. The booklet *Fellow Worker, Do You Know Your Rights?,* is available from the GMB by calling freephone ☎ 0800-834690.

DOCTORS

Because of legal restrictions, arrangements for employment for doctors and medical staff can be made only through the *Zentralstelle fér Arbeitsvermittlung* in Bonn (see above). Vacancies are advertised in the weekly *Deutsches Ärzte-Verlag* available from the publishers at Dieselstrasse 2, D-50859 Köln; www.aerzteblatt.de. Further information and advice can be obtained from the German Medical Association (*Bundesärztekammer*), Herbert-Lewin-Platz 1, 10623, Berlin; ☎30-400456-0; fax 30-400456-388; e-mail info@baek.be; www.bundesaerztekammer.de.

TEACHERS

Germany has an excellent state education system, which ensures that a very high proportion of Germans have a good grounding in English. As a result, there is less demand for teachers of English, especially at beginner's level, than in other European countries. The greatest demand is from business people taking courses at language schools, or in-house at their place of work. The best prospects for teachers are in language schools which specialise in commercial English, and a TEFL qualification and even a degree in Economics or Business are important if you intend to approach these companies. The reunification of Germany has created a huge demand for teachers as Germans from the East of the country, many of whom never had the chance to learn English under the communists, want to learn business English.

Organisations which recruit English teachers for Germany from the UK include *International House* (see *Teaching*). The Education and Training Group of the British Council (formerly the Central Bureau) arranges positions for language assistants or teachers in the German school system (see the *Teaching* chapter). Positions as *lektors* in German universities can sometimes be obtained by direct application to the university.

OTHER OPPORTUNITIES

There are good opportunities for bilingual secretaries and administrators in Germany, however, you will need to be genuinely bilingual and have recognised secretarial qualifications and office management skills. *Bilingual People,* Bloomsbury House, 4 Bloomsbury Square, London, WC1A 2RP; ☎020-7405 5005; fax 020-7405 5003; e-mail admin@bilingualpeople.com; www.bilingualpeople.com, is one agency in the UK which provides permanent, contract and temporary staff in these fields to Germany.

In recent years the demand for IT professionals has increased enormously, with employers crying out for skilled staff. *Track International,* ☎01872-573937; fax 01872-571282; www.trackint.com, has regularly updated listings of places available online. Other useful careers websites include: www.jobpilot.de; www.stepstone.de; www.jobware.de; and www.stellen-online.de.

There are regular vacancies for British qualified nurses in Germany, as well as vacancies for laboratory technicians. Attractive packages are usually offered including subsidised accommodation, free flights, free language tuition, and an average nurse to patient ratio of 1:3. *Jenrick Nursing,* Jenrick House, 145-147 Frimley Road, Camberley, Surrey GU15 2PS; ☎01276-676121; e-mail nursing@jenrickmedical.co.uk; www.jenrickmedical. co.uk, can place nurses with a minimum of one year's post-registration experience in positions throughout Germany.

SHORT TERM WORK

SEASONAL WORK

Seasonal opportunities in Germany are mainly in tourism and agriculture. Work can be found in hotels and restaurants in the Bavarian Alps and the Black Forest in the summer and during the winter skiing seasons. Summer jobs can also be found in resorts along the North Sea and Baltic coasts; in spa and health resorts; and in the major cities. The chapter on tourism gives advice on how to obtain this sort of job. Addresses of individual hotels can be found in *Summer Jobs Abroad,* published annually by Vacation Work. In addition the agency *Alpotels,* (e-mail info@jobs-in-the-alps.com, www.jobs-in-the-alps.com), recruits and carries out interviews for employers looking for seasonal hotel staff.

Farm jobs have become difficult to find in recent years because the large numbers of 'guestworkers' who work for very low wages. Grape production is the only branch of agriculture employing casual workers in any great number. The grape harvest begins in October, slightly later than in France, and continues into November. Vineyards can be found along the Rhine, Mosel, Saar, Ruwer, and Nahe valleys. Other kinds of fruit are picked earlier in the summer. There is a particular concentration of fruit farms in the Altland, a region along the south bank of the Elbe to the west of Hamburg. Very few of these types of jobs are advertised with the state employment service, and a direct approach to farmers is likely to be more successful.

OTHER WORK

See the relevant chapters in the *Specific Careers* section for information on how to find temporary, voluntary, domestic and office work. Again, the *Zentralstelle fér Arbeitsvermittlung* in Bonn should be contacted (see above). In Germany, there are relatively few private employment agencies, although branches of *Adia, Echo, Interim* and *Manpower* can be found in larger cities and are worth visiting. Jobseekers who are already in Germany should also look out for the mobile temporary employment offices that are set up where there is a special need for temporary workers, for trade fairs or the wine or beer festivals. These offices are called *Service-Vermittlung.*

Opportunities for US Citizens

A number of working exchanges, like those run by *AIESEC* and *AIPT*, are detailed under the *Working Exchanges* heading in the *Getting the Job* chapter. You may also e-mail *CDS International* (e-mail info@cdsintl.org; www.cdsintl.org), which specialises in arranging career training, fellowships and internships in Germany for young Americans. A knowledge of German, and business or technical experience or training, is required.

USEFUL PUBLICATIONS

Live and Work in Germany (Vacation Work Publications, www.vacationwork.co.uk) provides comprehensive information about all aspects of employment in Germany.

INTERNATIONAL COMPANIES IN GERMANY

Albright and Wilson GMBH   4
Frankfurter Strasse 181
63263 Neu-Isenberg

Alcan Chemicals Europe Ltd   35
Gartenstr.6
D-53894 Mechernich

Barclays Bank plc   4
Niederlassung Frankfurt
Bockenheimer Landstr. 38-40
60323 Frankfurt am Main

Batig Gesellschaft Fur   16
Beteillgungen Gmbh
Alsterufer 4
D-20354 Hamburg

Blackwell Science Ltd.   45
Blackwell Wissenschaft Sverlag
Kurférstendamm 57
10707 Berlin

British Airways plc   48
Wartungesallee 13
D-85356 Ménchen-Flughafen

British Telecommunications plc   45
Viag Interkom Gmbh & Co KG
Georg-Brauchle-Ring 23-25
D-80992 Ménchen

British Tourist Authority   48
Britsche Zentrale fur Fremdenverkehr
Westendsr. 16-22
D-60325 Frankfurt am Main

Boots Healthcare Deutschland Gmbh   8
Scolzstr. 3
D-21465 Reinbek

Cable & Wireless plc   45
Arabellastr. 17
D-81925 Ménchen

The EMI Group   45
EMI Elektrola GmbH
Maarweg 149
50825 Köln

Equitable Life Deutschland   23
Oberlander Ufer 180-182
D-50968 Köln

Ernst & Young GMBH   1
Wirtschaftspréfungesellschaft
Eschersheimer Landstr. 14
60322 Frankfurt am Main

Four Seasons Hotels & Resorts, Regent   20
International Hotels
Oeder Weg 15
D-60318 Frankfurt am Main

General Accident Fire & Life Assurance   4
Neumarkt 15
D-66117 Saarbrucken

Glaxo Wellcome Gmbh & Co   8
Am Trippelsberg 48
D-40589 Désseldorf

Guinness Brewing Worldwide Ltd.   16
Guinness GmbH
Limbecker Str.20-28
D-45127 Essen

ICI Paints Deco Gmbh	8
Ittepartk 2-4	
D-40724 Hilden	
ICL International Computer Ltd.	10
Vogelsanger Weg 91	
40470 Désseldorf	
Johnson Matthey Gmbh	8
Otto-Vogler Str 9b	
D-65843 Sulzbach	
KPMG Deutsche Treuhand-Gesellschaft AG	1
Kurze Méhren 1	
20095 Hamburg	
Linguarama International Group plc	45
Linguarama Spracheninstitut GmbH	
Geotheplatz 2	
60311 Frankfurt am Main	
Lloyd's Register of Shipping	40
Monckebergstr. 27	
D-20095 Hamburg	
Michael Page International	34
Immermannstrasse 40	
D-40210 Désseldorf	
Pilkington Deutschland Gmbh	25
Auf der Reihe 2	
D-45884 Gelsenkirchen	
Reed Exhibition Companies Ltd.	20
Heerdter Sandberg 32	
40549 Désseldorf	
Reebok Deutschland Gmbh	44
Keltenring 14	
D-82041 Oberhaching	

Reuters Holdings plc	45
Friedrich-Ebert-Anlage 49	
60327 Frankfurt am Main	
Rothmans International plc	16
Nordstr. 78	
D-52078 Hamburg	
The Sage Group plc	10
KHK Software GmbH and Co. KG	
Bernerstr. 23	
60437 Frankfurt am Main	
Sotherby's Deutschland Gmbh	15
Mendelssonhnstr. 66	
D-60325 Frankfurt am Main	
Standard Life Assurance Co	23
Lyoner Str. 15	
D-60528 Frankfurt am Main	
The Royal Bank of Scotland	4
Postfach 11 10 51	
D-60045 Frankfurt am Main	
Thomas Cook Group Ltd.	48
Direktion	
Hahnstr.68	
60528 Frankfurt am Main	
Unilever plc	8
Dammtorwall 15	
20355 Hamburg	
Virgin Records Gmbh	29
Herzogstr. 64	
D-80803 Ménchen	
Xerox Gmbh	30
Hellersbergstrasse 2a	
D-40885 Ratingen	

The *British Chamber of Commerce in Germany*, General Office, Brückenstrasse 2, 50667 Köln; ☎221-314458; fax 221-315335; e-mail info@bccg.de; www.bccg.de, can provide further information about British businesses in Germany. The *American Chamber of Commerce in Germany* is at Rossmarkt 12, 60311 Frankfurt am Main; ☎69-929 104-0; fax 69-929 104-11; e-mail info@amcham.de; www.amcham.de.

Greece

- ○ **Year of EU Accession:** 1981
- ○ **Greek Embassy,** 1A Holland Park, London W11 3TP; ☎020-7221 6467; fax 020-7243 3202; www.greekembassy.org.uk
- ○ **Greek Embassy,** 2221 Massachusetts Avenue NW, Washington DC 20008; ☎202-939 1300; fax 202-939 1324; www.greekembassy.org
- ○ **Currency:** 1 Euro (€) = 100 cents
- ○ **Rate of Exchange:** £1 = €1.44; $1 = €0.78
- ○ **Country Code:** +30

Greece is an integral part of the EU, and was its first Balkan member. Its historical links with Britain, and the Greek community in the United States, as well as the congenial climate and scenery which attract countless tourists each year, have made it a popular place for working travellers and those working in industry and commerce. It is a growing, although still relatively small, export market for Britain, and expanding sectors for exports include telecommunications, sound recording equipment, clothing, power generation machinery, and professional and scientific instruments. There is more to the Greek economy than just tourism. Iron and steel, beverages and cars are some of its most important manufacturing industries. Negative factors include high unemployment and inflation. There are opportunities for the jobseeker in tourism, au pair work and English teaching, as well as for consultants in civil engineering, finance and technical areas. The Greek-owned merchant fleet, the largest in the world, is partly run from London and makes heavy use of its financial services. Greece's profile as a tourist destination means that many foreigners who work there have often found employment while holidaying in the country.

GENERAL FACTS

POPULATION, CITIES AND CLIMATE

The population of Greece currently stands at around 10.7 million and, spread over 50,960 square miles (131,833 sq km), is relatively diffuse. Although the metropolitan area of Athens has a total of 3.6 million inhabitants, the country has few large cities – the main ones being Piraeus near Athens (200,000), Patras on the Gulf of Corinth (150,000), and Thessaloniki in the north (400,000 citizens). Greece's myriad islands stretch almost to the coast of Turkey in the east, to Crete in the south, and along the Ionian coast in the west. The mainland is bisected by the Gulf of Corinth. To the south, the Peloponnese has a very stunning coastline; there is a fertile central plain in Thessaly, with mountains to the north, south and west. The northern region of Macedonia has some cultural as well as geographical differences from the rest of Greece. There are pine-covered uplands, craggy, scrub-covered foothills, and farmland; and the landscape is greenest in spring. The climate is Mediterranean, and mild in winter; but summers can be insufferably hot, especially in Athens.

THE GOVERNMENT

Greece has had a rather unstable political history, and there are deeply felt divisions between the Right and the Left, with a majority for the Pasok Socialist Party, which has been whittled away in recent years. Six years after the *coup d'état* of 1967, there was a referendum to decide whether Greece should be a republic: 77.2 per cent voted in favour, but President Papadopoulos's government collapsed in 1974 and elections had to be held in November of that year, leading to the new Constitution of 1975, under which the President became the Head of State. He is elected to a five-year term of office. The Chamber of Deputies is elected by universal suffrage every four years.

RURAL LIFE

Farming remains a vital part of Greece's economy, although increased mechanisation has led to an exodus from the countryside that has left large tracts of land deserted. On many of the islands tourism has replaced agriculture, as it is a more profitable source of income for the locals. In 1960, agriculture accounted for 91 per cent of all exports but by the mid-seventies this had dropped to 36 per cent and continues to fall. The agrarian sector today accounts for only 8.3 per cent of Greece's GDP. Wheat, sugar beet, olives, raisins and figs are the main agricultural products. The principal agriculture-based industries are producing canned fruit, cigarettes, leather, paper and viniculture. Much of the cultivation is still small-scale and traditional, as the landscape often does not favour mechanisation and large-scale cultivation. In some areas peasant life continues as it has always done.

RELIGION, SPORT AND CULTURE

The Greek Orthodox Church, to which about 98 per cent of the population belong, plays an important part in Greek life. There are also Muslim, Roman Catholic and Jewish minorities. Interference with, and proselytising by, the Church is forbidden under the Constitution and complete religious freedom is observed.

Ancient rather than modern Greeks were famous for their athletic achievements. Today there are many tennis clubs and water sports centres and fishing is popular. In 2004, after 108 years the Olympic Games came home when Greece hosted the 28th Olympiad. Football remains the most popular spectator sport enhanced by the national side winning the *Euro 2004* competition in Portugal. Hill walking is enjoyed by Athenians getting away from it all, and residents and visitors alike enjoy the many festivals throughout the country. Greeks enjoy food, especially seafood, and bars are traditionally a male bastion – although this is changing. Tourism means that nightlife on the islands (and in Athens) is lively and international. Nightclubs featuring Greek Bazouki music are also popular.

HOLIDAYS

There are eleven public holidays a year: New Year's Day; Epiphany (6 January); Shrove Monday (26 February); Independence Day (25 March); The Greek Orthodox Easter (two days); May Day; Holy Spirit Day (June); Assumption (15 August); *Ohi* day, celebrating the defiant stand against Italy in 1940 (28 October); Christmas Day; and Boxing Day.

FACTORS INFLUENCING EMPLOYMENT

IMMIGRATION

The Consular Section of the British Embassy in Athens (see below) issues a free leaflet called *Notes on Greece for British Passport Holders*. Although nationals of EU (and EEA) countries do not require work permits to work in Greece, a residence permit is required for stays of over three months. Applications for this must be made within three months of arrival to the Aliens Department Office, 173 Alexandras Avenue, GR-15 522 Athens ☎ 1-641 1746); or to the local police station. In order to obtain a residence permit, you must have found employment or possess sufficient funds to stay in Greece. You should take your passport, a letter from your employer, and a medical certificate issued by the local hospital. If you wish to stay in Greece you will need to find employment within three months of arrival. The residence permit is valid for five years.

US citizens can stay for up to three months without a visa. If a US citizen wishes to remain in Greece for longer, he or she has to obtain a permit by applying to the Aliens Bureau of the Athens Police General Directorate at 175 Alexandras Avenue, Athens (or at other Aliens Centres in Greece) at least 20 days prior to the three-month expiration date. This may involve some communications with the USA – or a trip home – as you should receive a letter of hire in your home country first; and it is necessary to get your passport stamped at the nearest Greek Consulate in your home country showing you have done this. Work permits must be obtained before entering the country to work.

LANGUAGE

Greek is not a difficult language to learn and learning the alphabet is the first step. There are two branches of Modern Greek: *Katharevousa*, a formal revival of the classical language is rapidly losing ground to *Demotiki*, the more usual spoken language. Those connected to tourism or trade will speak at least some English, German, Italian or French.

HEALTH, WELFARE AND EDUCATION

A state social insurance system exists, including voluntary staff insurance for salaried people, and sickness and old age pension benefits for nearly everyone. Nursery, primary and secondary education is free for children between the ages of six and 15. There are six universities, one polytechnic and various other university-level independent institutions.

UK citizens requiring emergency medical treatment should contact the Greek National Health Insurance scheme, known as IKA (*Idrima Kinonikon Asfaliseon*), Tmima Diethnon Scheseon, Kifissias Avenue 178, GR-152 31, Athens; ☎01-647 1140; www.ika.gr, and submit your EHIC (see *Rules and Regulations*). The costs of medical and dental treatment should then be refunded. Local offices of the IKA are called *Ipokatastimata* or *Parartimata*. Contributions are deducted from salary at a rate of about 16 per cent, and after 60 days employment your employer should issue you with an IKA book, after which you will be entitled to free medical treatment. US citizens should certainly be insured, and this is a good idea for British citizens too, as there are often long waits at the public hospitals. Further information about the IKA can be found at http://www.ika.gr/en/english.doc.

TRADE UNIONS

All trade union activity is regulated by the Associations Act of 1914: the Constitution guarantees union liberty. The national body is the Greek General Confederation of Labour.

EMBASSIES AND CONSULATES

British Embassy, 1 Ploutarchou Street, 106 75 Athens; ☎210-727 2600; fax 210-727 2720; www.british-embassy.gr.
Consulates are in Corfu and Thessaloniki.
American Embassy, 91 Vasilissis Sophias Avenue, GR-101 60 Athens; ☎210-721 2951; www.usembassy.gr.
There is a US Consulate in Thessaloniki.

TOURIST OFFICES

Greek National Tourism Organisation, 4 Conduit Street, London W15 2DJ; ☎020-7495 9300; fax 020-7287 1369; e-mail info@gnto.co.uk; www.gnto.co.uk or www.gnto.gr.
Greek National Tourist Organisation, Olympic Tower, 645 5th Avenue, Suite 903, New York, NY 10022; ☎212-421 5777; fax 212-826 6940; e-mail info@greektourism.com; www.greektourism.com.

EMPLOYMENT OPPORTUNITIES

Greece is among the least industrialised countries in the EU, with 20 per cent of the workforce involved in agriculture. Tourism is another major sector of employment. The performance of the Greek economy has been disappointing since the 1980s, with slow growth and inflation often in double figures. In recent years, the influx of Albanians, Serbs, Bulgarians and Georgians has made things difficult for others seeking short-term employment in Greece. Although initially entering the country illegally, migrant workers are now able to apply for a white card that allows them to work legally. They have now monopolised the bulk of the casual work available on farms, building sites, as they are prepared to work for as little as half the regular daily wage. The casual work remaining is largely in teaching, bar-work and au pairing.

The major areas of interest to English-speakers wishing to work in Greece are shipping and financial services, tourism and English teaching. Shipping and shipping-related insurance companies are generally based in Piraeus, with offices in London or New York and a number of these are listed below under *British Companies*. In addition, there are some public sector projects in which British and US companies are involved. These include the Athens and Thessaloniki metros, a natural gas project, modernisation of railway and road communications, mobile phone communications, and power generation projects. There is also an outpost of the EU in Thessaloniki, the *European Centre for the Development of Vocational Training* (see the *International Organisations* chapter). Nationals of the European Economic Area (EEA) have the right to access the services of the Greek Employment Service – the *Organismos Apasholisseos Ergatikou Dynamikou (OAED)*. The address of the local OAED offices can be found in the local telephone directory or by contacting the main office at Ethnikis Antistasis 8 str. GR-17456 Alimos, Greece; ☎2-0-998 9000; fax 210-998 9500; www.oaed.gr. EU Nationals can also take advantage of the EURES network (see the *Getting the Job* chapter and at http://europa.eu.int/jobs/eures).

ENGLISH TEACHING

For the TEFL teacher Greece means teaching classes in the sun and (outside Athens) a relaxed way of life. It is an attractive option for newly qualified English language teachers, and advertisements for TEFL teachers in Greece regularly appear in the Tuesday *Guardian* and the *Times Educational Supplement* in the UK – especially over the summer – as the academic year begins in mid-September. American jobseekers may also wish to refer to these publications. Contracts generally run from September to May or from June to September. Work can also be found by visiting private language schools, known as *frontisteria*, in person (of which there are around 6,000 throughout Greece). Addresses appear in the *Blue Guide* (the Greek equivalent to the Yellow Pages). It is not essential to hold a TEFL qualification but all but the dodgiest of schools will insist that you hold a degree (which is a government requirement for a teacher's licence) and that you are an EU national.

Although wages tend to be modest, you can live well on relatively little money in Greece; and you should check out the conditions of service to see how many hours you will be required to teach, or if time-consuming travelling is involved. Further information can be found in the excellent book *Teaching English Abroad* published by Vacation Work (www.vacationwork.co.uk).

Two of the best-known language schools are listed below.

Anglo-Hellenic Teacher Recruitment, PO Box 263, 20100 Corinth; ☎2-7410 53511; fax 2-7410 85579; e-mail info@anglo-hellenic.com; www.anglo-hellenic.com. Interviews are conducted in London, Corinth, or Athens during the summer.

Cambridge Teachers Recruitment, Metron 17, New Philadelphia, Athens 14342, Greece;

☎1-258 5155; in London tel/fax 020-8686 3733; e-mail Macleod_smith_andrew@ hotmail.com. Recruit TEFL around 70-80 teachers per year for private language schools throughout the Greek mainland and islands.

AU PAIRS

Greece has no representation on the International Au Pair Association (IAPA) and very few agencies elsewhere in Europe claim to be able to make placements in Greece. One Athens agency has received praise from partner agencies and from the au pairs and nannies it has placed. *Nine Muses Au Pair Activities* (Thrakis 39 and Vas. Sofias 2, 17121 Nea Smyrni, Athens; ☎210-931 6588; e-mail ninemuses@ninemuses.gr; www.ninemuses.gr) which has recently moved premises to the Athens suburb of Nea Smyrni (located on a trolley bus route from Syntagma Square) accepts postal applications from young European and North American women and also can place candidates after arrival in Athens.

Trained nannies might consider applying to UK tour operators like Mark Warner (www.markwarner.com) which employs nannies at their resorts in Greece. *Weigan Nannies* (1 Whites Row, London E1 7NF; ☎020-7377 2620; e-mail elizabethelder@ thechildcarecompany.co.uk; www.thechildcarecompany.co.uk) recruits a few nannies for Mediterranean resorts on behalf of a tour operator.

It is sometimes worth checking the Situations Vacant column of the English daily *Athens News* (3 V. Lada str, 102 37 Athens; ☎210-333 3733; an-classified@dolnet.gr). You can check the classified ads on the internet (www.athensnews.gr) which are renewed every Tuesday. Some adverts are for live-in jobs in private households, and range from the distinctly dodgy to the legitimate. You could also try placing your own advertisement in the column 'Situations Wanted'. The minimum charge for placing an advert is €11 for 15 words.

SHORT TERM WORK

There are few 'organised' ways of finding a temporary job in Greece, and certainly none which will guarantee an individual earning enough in a couple of weeks to cover the cost of getting there and back. Jobs tend to be found simply by approaching a potential employer and asking for work.

SEASONAL WORK

The chapter, *Transport, Tourism and Hospitality* lists British travel companies which need staff for the summer (in particular *Eurocamps, Mark Warner* and *Thomson Holidays*), and some large hotels needing staff are listed in the book *Summer Jobs Abroad* (Vacation Work Publications, published annually).

A number of British expatriates manage to live all the year round in Greece by combining fruit-picking with building and bar work or English teaching. Anyone prepared to travel to Greece on the off chance of finding work should go in March or April, when hotel owners are preparing for the annual invasion of tourists. The best time is just after the Greek Orthodox Easter (dates change every year). Jobs can be found cleaning and decorating hotels and bars that have been closed all winter. Boats and cruise ships also need staff. There are yacht agencies around the port of Piraeus, and phone numbers of the agencies for cruise ships can be found under *Krouazieres* in the telephone directory.

Work can also be found picking grapes, olives and oranges, but again it is necessary to ask for such work on the spot. The best regions to look for work are on the Peloponnese (especially around Navplion) and on the islands of Crete and Rhodes. Vineyards in Greece are generally far smaller and more widely dispersed than in, say, France. In practice this means that not many workers are needed, and that the harvest may only offer a few days' work if a job is found. Prospects are better in both the olive harvest, which starts in late October, and the orange harvest, which begins in November and continues until April. You will be competing with migrants from Eastern Europe, particularly Albania, for this work, so wages will not be high.

There are many other harvests, from apricots to potatoes, which may provide work at various times of the year. Greece is a country of personal contacts, and the easiest way of discovering what is being grown locally at any time is to find a sympathetic stallholder at the vegetable market.

OTHER WORK

It is worth checking the Situations Vacant column of the English language daily *Athens News* (3 Christou Lada Street, 10237 Athens; ☎210-333 3700; www.athensnews.gr) and the American published weekly, *Hellenic Times*. You can also view these advertisements on the internet. Most classifieds are for bar work, English teachers and au pairs. You can also place your own Situation Wanted advertisement. The minimum rate for advertising is €10 for the first 15 words.

INTERNATIONAL COMPANIES IN GREECE

Barclays Bank plc 4
15 Voukourestious Street
106 71 Athens

DHL International Hellas Ltd 17
44 Alimou Alinos
174 55 Athens

BP Greece 35
268 Kifissias Ave
152 10 Athens Halandri

Ernst & Young OE 1
Appollo Tower
64 Louise Riencourt St.
115-23 Athens

Commercial Union Assurance Co Ltd 23
2-4 Sina Street
06 72 Athens

The *Athens Chamber of Commerce & Industry*, 7 Academias Street, 106 71 Athens; ☎210-360 4815-9; fax 210-361 6408; e-mail info@acci.gr; www.acci.gr provides a comprehensive list of Greek companies and international businesses operating in Greece on its website.

Ireland

- Year of EU Accession: 1973
- Irish Embassy, 17 Grosvenor Place, London SW1X 7HR; ☎020-7245 2171; fax 020-7245 6961; http://Ireland.embassyhomepage.com
- Irish Embassy, 2234 Massachusetts Ave. NW, Washington DC 20008; ☎202-462 3939; fax 202-232 5993; www.irelandemb.org
- Currency: 1 Euro (€) = 100 cents
- Rate of Exchange: £1 = €1.44; $1 = €0.78
- Country Code: +353

The Republic of Ireland (Eire) is an attractive place to live and work, with the added advantages of a familiar language and culture. Increased prosperity as a result of EU membership has been accompanied by social and political change, and the country is sometimes referred to as 'the Celtic Tiger', so swiftly has it achieved economic prosperity. Emigration is no longer the only route for qualified Irish workers, and there is a reverse trend today as graduates return home, bringing with them new skills. Dublin is now a more cosmopolitan (and also more expensive) city than it was 10 years ago, and social mores are changing, with a decreasing birth rate and more women participating in the workforce. Foreign investment and EU support has enabled the Irish economy to grow three times faster than the EU average in recent years, however, unemployment is still relatively high and this means that job opportunities are comparatively limited. Ireland itself has a highly experienced and qualified workforce from which recruitment usually takes place. There are some opportunities in new growth industries such as information technology, in particular for US staff; and some short-term opportunities are described below.

The main disadvantages of working long-term in Ireland are the high taxes and high cost of living relative to wages, but many people feel that these are more than compensated for by the relaxed lifestyle and the warmth, easygoing nature and friendliness of the Irish.

GENERAL FACTS

POPULATION, CITIES AND CLIMATE

The population of Ireland is currently around 4 million spread over 70,280 sq km. The capital city, Dublin, has approximately 1.2 million inhabitants (in the Greater Dublin area), and the only other large city is Cork, with a population of 800,000. Limerick, Waterford, Galway and Dundalk are the other principal towns.

The landscape of Ireland consists of a central plain surrounded by isolated groups of mountains and rolling hills. The climate is similar to that of Britain, although it is generally wetter and a little warmer in the southwest.

GOVERNMENT

Following seven centuries of English rule and intermittent uprisings, the constitution of the Irish Free State was adopted in December 1922. Northern Ireland with its Protestant majority remains part of the UK and the future of this province continues to be a dominant political issue in Ireland as well as in the UK. Successive Irish governments have favoured peaceful unification of all of Ireland, but negotiations between the two governments (and the nationalist and unionist communities in the North) have been hampered by disagreement over this border and its status. In 1985, the Anglo-Irish Agreement was signed, which gives the Republic a say in the affairs of Northern Ireland.

RELIGION, SPORT AND CULTURE

Although freedom of worship is practised in the Republic, 94 per cent of the people are Roman Catholic, with a small Protestant or Anglican minority. The Irish have a distinct predilection for rugby and soccer, but developed their own national sports in the nineteenth century as an alternative to these 'English' games. Hurling and Gaelic football (which has its counterpart in Australian Rules Football in Australia) are extremely popular.

Ireland has its own distinct cultural heritage, especially in its literature. Notable Irish writers include Jonathan Swift, Oliver Goldsmith, George Bernard Shaw, Oscar Wilde, James Joyce, W.B. Yeats, and Seamus Heaney, all of whom are united by their appreciation of the beauty of language. Ireland is a more relaxed and talkative country than Britain or the United States, and its plethora of pubs are the traditional place for meeting and socialising (as well as being another Irish export).

HOLIDAYS

There are nine national holidays: New Year's Day; St Patrick's Day (18 March); Good Friday; Easter Monday; June Bank Holiday; August Bank Holiday; October Bank Holiday; Christmas Day; and Boxing Day.

FACTORS INFLUENCING EMPLOYMENT

IMMIGRATION

Ireland is a full member of the EU and so EU nationals do not require a work permit. British citizens do not even require a passport to visit the country. US citizens and others who can prove Irish ancestry may be eligible for unrestricted entry to Ireland and even Irish nationality (which in turn confers full EU rights). Enquiries should be directed to the Irish Embassy in your home country.

Non-EEA nationals wishing to work in Ireland will require a work permit to be able to take up employment in Ireland. The prospective employer must apply on behalf of the would-be employee before the employee enters Ireland and there are strict eligibility criteria. There are exceptions to the working visa rules for professionals in IT, construction and nursing. Full information on visa restrictions can be obtained from the *Department of Foreign Affairs*, 80 St. Stephen's Green, Dublin 2; ☎ 1-478 0822; www.irlgov.ie/iveagh/.

The Irish authorities state that the need to protect employment opportunities for EU citizens is a key factor in determining whether or not a work permit will be issued.

LANGUAGE

Ireland is unique in having a first official language – Gaelic, which few people speak. English predominates almost everywhere, outside a few isolated areas in the west (the 'Gaeltacht').

HEALTH, WELFARE AND EDUCATION

The state social security system, funded partly by both employees' and employers' contributions and partly by general taxation, provides a comprehensive welfare system, including unemployment benefits. Those on low incomes and pensioners are entitled to a full range of hospital and medical treatment services, while those on higher earnings are liable to pay hospital consultant fees.

School attendance is compulsory for children between the ages of six and 15, and primary education is provided free in national schools. Free Secondary education only came into existence in the 1960s, which galvanised some of the economic and social change mentioned above, and today Ireland has one of the best-educated populations in Europe. More than 50 per cent go on to tertiary level education. There are seven universities in Ireland.

TRADE UNIONS

The Irish Trade Unions Congress was established in 1984. Freedom to form a trade association or union is guaranteed under the Constitution. More than half of the workforce belongs to unions and the Irish Congress of Trade Unions accounts for over 90 per cent of the total membership. There are also a small number of licensed employers' organisations.

EMBASSIES

British Embassy, 29 Merrion Road, Ballsbridge, Dublin 4; ☎1-205 3700; fax 1-205 3890; www.britishembassy.ie.
US Embassy, 42 Elgin Road, Ballsbridge, Dublin 4; ☎1-668 8777; http://dublin.usembassy.gov/.

TOURIST OFFICES

Irish Tourist Board (Bord Failte), Nations House, 103 Wigmore Street, London W1U 1QS; ☎0800-039 7000; www.discoverireland.com.
Irish Tourist Board, 345 Park Avenue, New York, NY 10154; ☎800-223 6470; www.discoverireland.com.

NEWSPAPERS

The national newspapers are the *Irish Independent* (90 Middle Abbey Street, Dublin 1; ☎1-705 5333; fax 1-872 0304; http://www.unison.ie/irish_independent/) which has job adverts on Thursdays and Sundays, and *The Irish Times* (4th Floor, Ballast House, Aston Quay, Dublin 2; ☎1-472 7103; e-mail services@irish-times.com; www.ireland.com), which has professional/executive level appointments on Fridays.

CONDITIONS OF WORK

The average employee in a small to medium sized firm in Ireland works between 37.5 and 39 hours per week and enjoys annual leave of 21 days. Four out of every five employees have an entitlement to sick pay and two-thirds of the workforce are in a company pension scheme. A recent survey conducted by the Irish Small Firms Association recorded that, on average, employees in Ireland earn 32% more than those working in similar positions in other EU countries.

A typical employee of a small firm earns between €20,000 and €30,000 per year. Levels of salary and benefits packages are influenced on the whole by the size of a company_the larger the company and turnover the better the remuneration package. Most wages and salaries in Ireland are paid monthly (12 times a year) or sometimes four-weekly (13 times a year), with payments generally being paid straight into an employee's bank or building society account.

A national minimum wage was first introduced in Ireland in 2000 and the rate has risen over the years. Unfortunately, the wage does not have to be paid to first time job entrants, those working as apprentices, or to a person employed by a close relative.

The standard working day for many of the Irish starts at 9am and finishes at 5.30pm, with an (unpaid) hour taken for lunch, usually sometime between noon and 2pm. European Directives govern the number of hours per week that an employee can work, which are at present set at an average of 48 hours in any four month period. Critically, this ruling does not mean that an employee cannot exceed the 48 hour limit, but that on average an employee may only work 48 hours in a week (not including breaks, annual leave, sick leave, maternity or adoptive leave, etc.). The ruling does not apply to the gardaí, the defence forces, those working at sea, trainee doctors, the self-employed, family employees, or transport employees.

Holiday entitlement for full-time employees in Ireland is for a minimum of 20 days annual leave though many companies include additional leave as part of their benefits packages. There are also nine public holidays in Ireland.

EMPLOYMENT PROSPECTS

GENERAL
Many large enterprises are foreign-owned and it may be worth approaching subsidiaries of UK- and US-owned companies. There is, however, a surplus of qualified professionals in many areas. Those looking for short-term work can usually find something, but wages may not be high.

SPECIFIC CONTACTS
British people interested in working in Ireland should ask their local Jobcentre for the publication *Working in the Republic of Ireland*. If already in Ireland, consult the vacancy boards at the nearest FAS (*Foras Aiscanna Saothair*) office. FAS (27-33 Upper Baggott Street, Dublin 4; ☎1-607 0500; fax 1-607 0600; e-mail info@fas.ie; www.fas.ie) is Ireland's Training and Employment Authority and has employment offices throughout the country which may be consulted by EU nationals. FAS also has a comprehensive jobsearch database at its Job-Bank website: http://jobbank.fas.ie.

Lists of recruitment agencies in various fields can be obtained by writing to the *Employment Agencies Section*, Department of Enterprise, Trade and Employment, 23 Kildare Street, Dublin 2; ☎1-631 2121; fax 1-631 2827; e-mail info@entemp.ie; www.entemp.ie). Private employment agencies are also listed in the Irish 'Golden Pages' (there is an excellent online version at www.goldenpages.ie).

The main source of seasonal work is the tourist industry and the largest demand is in the south-western counties of Cork and Kerry, especially the around the town of Killarney, which has more than 100 pubs, and Tralee. For a list of hotels contact the Irish Tourist Board (see above). Vacancies are sometimes registered with EURES; most commonly these will be hotel jobs which include accommodation and pay around €250 per week. *Cara International*, Chancery, Turlough, Castlebar, Co Mayo; ☎94-903 1720; fax 94-903 1723; e-mail info@carainternational.net; www.carainternational.net, places non-EU workers in hotels and bars in Ireland.

Try the following general recruitment websites in Ireland: www.jobsinireland.com; www.Ireland.com/jobs; www.monster.ie; www.recruitireland.com; www.nixers.com; www.irishjobs.ie.

Employment agencies worth trying include:

IRC: 11 Ely Place, Dublin 2; ☎1-661 0644; www.ircon.ie. Offers a wide range of permanent and temporary positions. Areas of employment covered include banking, accountancy, IT, sales and marketing, office personnel, insurance, call centre and multilingual work.

DB Recruitment: ☎1-278 0450; e-mail jobs@dbrecruitment.ie; www.debrecruitment.ie. A leading multilingual recruitment company. Its clients have constant requirements for multi-lingual candidates within customer service, telephone technical support and accounts positions in Dublin, Cork, Limerick and Belfast.

Reed: has branches in Cork (1st Floor, 91 Patrick Street, Cork; ☎021-427 5433) and

Dublin (47 Dawson Street, Dublin 2; ☎01-670 4466; www.reed.ie). Reed deals with general vacancies and also has dedicated consultants recruiting for the hospitality, computing and accountancy sectors.

AU PAIRS

Several of the au pair placement services in Ireland are offshoots of English-teaching centres in Dublin as is evident from their names: for example the *Swan Training Institute* (9-11 Grafton Street, Dublin 2, Ireland; ☎1-677 5252; fax 1-677 5254; e-mail admin@sti. ie; www.sti.ie).and the *Linguaviva Centre* (45 Lower Leeson Street, Dublin 2, Ireland; ☎1-678 9384/661 2106; fax 1-676 5687; e-mail enquiries@linguaviva.com). These schools are only secondarily au pair referral services, run for the benefit of students enrolled in their own English courses. By contrast, *CARA International* (Chancery, Turlough, Castlebar, Co. Mayo, Ireland; ☎94-903 1720; fax: 94-903 1723; e-mail: info@carainternational.net; www.carainternational.net.in) and the *Job Options Bureau* (Tourist House, 40-41 Grand Parade, Cork, Ireland; ☎21-427 5369; fax 21-427 4829; e-mail: info@joboptionsbureau. ie; www.joboptionsbureau.ie) are primarily au pair and nanny placement agencies, which can place young women in families all over Ireland. Try the following agencies:

The European Au Pair Agency, 554 South Circular Road, Dublin 8, Ireland; ☎1-453 4092; fax 1-454 5926; e-mail: eapa@indigo.ie.

Kidz Au Pair Agency, Upper Pembroke Rd, Passage West, Cork, Ireland; ☎21-485 9738; fax 21-484 1905; e-mail info@kidzaupair.com; www.kidzaupair.com.

The preferred minimum stay is six months, but most of the agencies undertake to make three-month summer placements. The recommended pocket money is on a par with that in Britain, no less than €80 a week for 30 hours of duties. There is also a strong demand for au pairs plus willing to work 40+ hours a week, and their weekly wage is about €115 in Dublin. One important difference between Irish and English agencies is that the ones in Dublin can charge a placement fee to incoming au pairs, though this may be waived in the case of girls applying through a European agent or subsumed in the cost of the compulsory language course. Experienced nannies placed through agencies like *Cara International* and *Job Options Bureau* usually earn at least €250 a week, while less experienced mother's helps earn wages based on the Irish minimum wage of €7.65 an hour (less allowable deductions for board and lodging).

The organisation MEI ('Marketing English in Ireland') has a web page that lists 16 language schools that offer au pair programmes (www.mei.ie/mei/Main/AuPair.htm). Many European young people are more drawn to Ireland than England as a venue for learning English because of the reputation of the Irish for being hospitable and family-oriented (not to mention Roman Catholic which is a factor for many girls from Spain, Italy, etc.).

MEDICAL STAFF

There are few positions for doctors at the higher levels of the profession in Ireland. However, there are opportunities at the lower end, for senior house officers and registrars for example, as many Irish graduates leave the country at this stage to gain experience abroad.

Information on medical (and other) agencies can be obtained by writing to the Employment Agencies Section, *Department of Enterprise*, Trade and Employment, Davitt House, 65a Adelaide Rd, Dublin 2; www.entemp.ie. The *Department of Health and Children* (Hawkins House, Hawkins Street, Dublin 2, ☎1-635 4000; fax 1-635 4001; www.dohc.ie) can advise on current prospects for employment in your profession.

VOLUNTARY WORK

Volunteering Ireland, Carmichael Centre for Voluntary Groups, Coleraine House, Coleraine Street, Dublin 7; ☎1-872 2622; fax 1-872 2623; e-mail info@volunteeringireland.com;

www.volunteeringireland.com, was set up in 1998 to provide information on voluntary work in the Republic of Ireland.

Conservation Volunteers Ireland, The Steward's House, Rathfarnham Castle, Dublin 14; ☎1-495 2878; e-mail cvi@cvi.ie; www.cvi.ie, arranges and co-ordinates environmental working holidays. No previous experience is needed but a knowledge of English is essential. Unpaid volunteers work eight hours per day on projects to conserve Ireland's national and cultural heritage. Membership costs €25 (€18 unwaged, €35 for a family) and volunteers pay a nominal charge for food, accommodation and transport.

Corrymeela Community, 5 Drumaroan Road, Ballycastle, Northern Ireland BT54 6QU; ☎028-2076 2626; www.corrymeela.org, is a Christian organisation committed to reconciliation in Northern Ireland and around the world. They need around 15 volunteers per week in the summer to work in arts and crafts, recreation, housekeeping, and other areas, as well as some longer-term volunteers for up to one year. All volunteers receive free board and lodging. Long-term volunteers also receive a stipend of £25 per week if they stay for six months or more. Contact the volunteer coordinator for further details.

INTERNATIONAL COMPANIES IN IRELAND

Accident and General International 23
34 Lower Abbey St
Dublin 1

Barclays Bank plc 4
47/48 St Stephen's Green
Dublin 2

Bioglan (Irl) Ltd 8
151 Baldoyle Industrial Estate
Dublin 13

Cadbury (Irl) Ltd 16
Coolock Dr
Dublin 5

Churchill Insurance Group 23
Block 6, Ballybrit Business Park
Co. Galway

Computer Associates Limited 10
Embassy House
Ballsbridge, Dublin 4

Dolphin Packaging Ltd 31
Greenore
Dundalk
Co Louth

Eagle Star Life Assurance 4
Eagle Star House
Frascati Rd
Blackrock, Co Dublin

Evode Industries Ltd 8
Newtown Swords
Co Dublin

Fujitsu Siemens Computers 10
Beckett Way Park West Business Campus
Nangor Road
Dublin 12

Gilbeys of Ireland Ltd 16
St. James Gate
Dublin 8

GlaxoSmithKline 8
Grange Road
Rathfarnham
Dublin 16

Grants of Ireland 22
St Laurence Road
Chapelizod
Dublin 20

Guinness Ireland Group 3
St James's Gate
Dublin 8

Kerridge Computer Systems 10
Anglesey House
Carysfort Avenue
Blackrock
Co Dublin

Laura Ashley (Ir) Ltd 60 Grafton St Dublin 2	9	TNT International Express Corballis Park Dublin Airport Cloghran Co Dublin	17
Reckitts (Ireland) Ltd Castlebellingham Co Louth	18		
		Trebor (Ireland) Ltd Coolock Dublin 5	16
Reliance Precision Ltd Parnell Street Bandon Co Cork	2	Turner Grain (Irl.) Ltd U8 Western Parkway Bus Ctr. Walkinstown Dublin 12	27
Smith & Nephew Ltd Kill o'the Grange Dun Laoghaire Co Dublin	12	Ulster Bank Ltd Ulster Bank Group Centre George's Quay Dublin 2	4
Thomson Financial Services (Ir.) Park House 195 North Circular Road Dublin 7	2	Wiggins Teape (Stationery) Ltd Gateway House East Wall Road Dublin 3	33

The Investment and Development Agency of Ireland publishes a list of *UK Companies in Ireland*, available free from *IDA*, Ireland House, 150 New Bond Street, London W1Y 2ZX; ☏ 020-7629 5941; fax 020-7629 4270; e-mail idaireland@ida.ie; www.ida.ie. (They also hold a useful list of American subsidiaries).

Italy

- **Year of EU Accession:** 1952
- **Italian Embassy,** 14 Three Kings' Yard, Davies Street, London W1K 4EH; ☎020-7312 2200; fax 020-7312 2230; www.amblondra.esteri.it
- **Italian Embassy,** 3000 Whitehaven Street NW, Washington DC 20008; ☎202-612 4400; fax 202-518 2154; www.italyemb.org
- **Currency:** 1 Euro (€) = 100 cents
- **Rate of Exchange:** £1 = €1.44; $1 = €0.78
- **Country Code:** +39

Italy's culture and climate, together with a race of people who are usually warmer and friendlier than those of northern European countries, has for many years attracted large British and American expatriate communities. Historical ties between Italy and Britain and the USA (where there are large communities of expatriate Italians) mean that Italian food, and art, and cinema, is already familiar to many. The major cultural difference lies in the unbridled expression of emotion, which is a virtue in Italy and may not come so easily to Britons and North Americans. Italy is a Catholic country with strong secular (and republican) traditions. Eating well is a great Italian pastime and there are many regional dishes, as well as more than 200 major wine regions. In Italy, there is an emphasis on consumption, and consumer goods – cars and clothes – are likely to account for a large proportion of the average Italian's budget. Housing is a relatively less important item of expenditure.

Work in Italy is hard to find unless you speak the language. Engineers are sometimes required for large-scale projects. Growth areas are in electronics, telecommunications, aviation and computing; there is an emphasis in Italian industry on design. The smaller companies, of which there are many in Italy, are more likely to recruit someone they know. However, there is a steady demand for au pairs, secretaries and teachers of English, as well as for workers in the hospitality industry. A 'creative approach' to the jobsearch is called for if you want to live and work in Italy.

GENERAL FACTS

POPULATION AND GEOGRAPHY

Italy has a population of approximately 58 million (500 per square mile/200 per sq km). The country extends over 117,578 square miles (304,525 sq km) and includes the islands of Sicily, Sardinia, Elba and others. The Vatican City, like San Marino, is an independent state (once memorably described as 'a country with a roof'). The average population density throughout the country is 190 per square km, but this is unevenly distributed; the industrial North being the most populated. The predominantly agricultural South has the highest birth rate and lowest death rate but overall the population has increased little. Many move north or emigrate in search of greater prosperity and employment. *Meridionale* is the name given to the south of Italy, which comprises 40 per cent of the land area, 35 per cent of the population, but only 20 per cent of the wealth.

There are about 1.5 million immigrants in the country – mainly from North and sub-Saharan Africa, but also from the Philippines, China, South America, Albania and former Yugoslavia.

CLIMATE

There is a great difference in climate between the north and south of the country. Winter is much drier and warmer in the south than in the northern and central areas. The hottest and driest month is July while the rainiest is November.

GOVERNMENT

Italy is a democratic republic. The President is elected by an electoral college and serves for seven years. The Chamber of Deputies and the Senate are elected to legislate and to advise the Council of Ministers by a combination of proportional representation and the British 'first-past-the-post system'. This body has administrative powers and is headed by the Prime Minister. Regional rivalries, and a fragmentation of Italian politics in recent years, mean that governments are often an unstable coalition. There is a doubt about the legitimacy of the State in Italian political life, which explains the traditional strength of the now reformed communist party (PDS), and the rise of neo-fascist groupings like the National Alliance (which now describes itself as democratic). In recent years the national identity itself has been challenged by strong regional political movements – a remnant of the days when Italy was a patchwork of different states.

Provincial interests are represented by 20 regions, with their own administrative structures, and supervised by a government commission. Regions are divided into Provinces, responsible for health and similar matters, and managed by elected councils. The unit of administration at local level is the *Commune*.

The Italian judiciary also deserves comment, in that suspects may be held for months or years without trial. This is not a country to be arrested in.

CITIES

Rome, the capital city, has about 2.7 million inhabitants, and there are in all 48 cities with populations above 100,000. Milan (1.3m), Turin (1.1m) and Genoa (700,000) form the 'industrial triangle' of the North. Florence, Venice, Bologna and Naples, (the third largest Italian city, with a population of 1.1 million) and many other smaller towns such as Cremona and Pisa, are famous around the world for their cultural or historical attractions.

RURAL LIFE

The Italian population is more evenly distributed between town and country than in most European countries. About 50 per cent of Italians live in small towns and villages, the majority of these being in the South. Rapid industrialisation has meant that just seven per cent of the population is now directly engaged in agriculture. The principal crops are sugar beet, wheat, maize, tomatoes and grapes. Italy is a world leader in wine production.

RELIGION, SPORT AND CULTURE

The vast majority of Italians are baptised into the Roman Catholic faith. Catholicism has a great influence on Italian life, but not all Italians are observant Catholics. The secular constitution guarantees freedom of religion, and there are Protestant and other minorities in the country.

Popular sports in Italy include football (which is a national obsession – Italy have won the World Cup four times in 1934, 1938, 1982 and 2006), fishing, golf, shooting, horse racing, motor racing, bowls (*bocce* – the only truly indigenous sport), cycling and yachting. Rugby has grown in popularity in recent years. All winter sports are popular in the Alpine regions and there are no less than three daily newspapers devoted to sport.

The annual number of visits made by Italians to the cinema is second only to the United States and opera, theatre and music flourish in all forms. Italy has played a major role in the history of art and architecture, and has many galleries, particularly in Rome, Florence and Venice displaying the country's art treasures.

FACTORS INFLUENCING EMPLOYMENT

IMMIGRATION

The *Italian Consulate General,* 38 Eaton Place, London SW1X 8AN; ☎020-7235 9371, or the Embassy and the various consulates in the USA (see below) will advise on entry requirements for nationals who require a visa to enter Italy. US citizens and EU nationals do not require a visa for stays of up to three months. EU and EEA citizens do not require a work permit.

All visitors who are not tourists are required to register with the police within three days of arrival. Registration entitles you to a stay of the same validity as your visa or, in the case of EU nationals, three months in which to look for work. For a longer stay a residence permit is required, available from the *questura* (police station) of the area of intended residence. Work permits for US citizens must be arranged from abroad.

LANGUAGE

Dialects, which may differ markedly from standard Italian, are spoken in the different regions of Italy. German, French and Slovenian are also spoken in border regions. German and French are the main second languages spoken, along with English. Prospective workers here are strongly advised to learn Italian as English is not widely spoken by older people, although the young are enthusiastic learners.

COST AND STANDARD OF LIVING

Italy has both very poor and very wealthy areas. The industrial region of Lombardy around Milan is reckoned to be the wealthiest in the EU. It should be remembered that Italy has overtaken Britain in terms of its Gross Domestic Product and the standard of living is noticeably higher in Lombardy or Tuscany than in Britain. Travel by road and rail is relatively cheap and easy. Tolls are payable on Italy's motorway (or *autostrada*) network..

HOUSING AND ACCOMMODATION

Recent building programmes have concentrated on erecting blocks of flats, of which there is now a surplus in Rome, but Naples and the South are generally still short of accommodation. Rents are highest in cities, and higher in the North than in the South.

HEALTH AND WELFARE

Contributory medical insurance (administered by the *Unità Sanitaria Locali*) now covers the whole of the working population, including foreigners. However, private medical services continue. The number of state hospitals is widely reckoned to be insufficient and some are run by the Church. Healthcare costs and contributions are a matter of intense public debate in Italy. A system of prescription charges (known as tickets) was instituted for doctors several years ago, although the chronically ill and some other groups are exempt from such charges. The Italian state social assurance scheme, which covers all other benefits, is run by the INPS (*Istituto Nazionale di Previdenza Soziale*) and employers pay the larger share of the contributions.

EDUCATION

Schooling is compulsory and free (apart from registration fees) for all children aged between six and 14 and lessons are usually held in the morning. From the age of three, a child can go to a crèche or nursery school. Elementary schools take pupils aged between six and 11. The next step for most is a middle school (*scuola media*), providing a three-year general course, and the possibility to stay on to take the final school leaving certificate (*maturità*). The more specialist *liceo* schools lead more directly to this certificate, which grants entry to university; or students may choose one of the many technical institutes for a diploma in subjects ranging from agriculture to zoology. The diploma is in itself a professional qualification, while the *liceo* merely prepares for university entrance. There are both State and private universities in Italy; however, the country has far fewer non-university higher education courses available than in France and Germany. The many private schools in Italy are incorporated into the state system so far as the curriculum and exams are concerned.

There are also English-medium and international schools in those areas where there are English-speaking expatriate communities.

NATIONAL SERVICE

Military service of 12-18 months is compulsory for all Italian males. Because conscientious objection is a civil crime many Italians emigrate to avoid it. Foreigners are exempt. People of Italian ancestry living abroad may hold dual citizenship without realising it, however, and they become subject to National Service obligations the minute they set foot in the country. If you have an Italian parent, even if you hold an Australian or US passport, for example, and have never been out of your country of birth, you would be well advised to check your position with the Italian Embassy before leaving home. Unsuspecting tourists have been jailed on arrival in Italy for failing to do their national service.

EMBASSIES AND CONSULATES

British Embassy, Via XX Settembre 80a (Porta Pia), 00187 Rome; ☎6-4220 0001; fax 6-487 2334 (8am-1pm and 2-4pm); www.britain.it.
There are consulates in Bari, Cagliari, Catania, Florence, Genoa, Milan, Naples, Palermo, Trieste, Turin and Venice.
US Embassy, Via Vittorio Venetto 121-00187 Rome; ☎06-46741; fax 06-488 2672; www.usembassy.it.
There are US consulates in Florence, Milan and Naples.
American Embassy to the Holy See, Via delle Terme Deciane 26, 00153 Rome; ☎06-4674 3428; fax 06-575 8346.

TOURIST OFFICES

Italian State Tourist Board (ENIT), 1 Princes Street, London W1B 2AY; ☎020-7399 3562; fax 020-7399 3564; www.enit.it.
Italian State Tourist Board (ENIT), Suite 1565, 630 5th Avenue, New York, NY 10111; ☎212-245 4822; fax 212-586 9249; www.italiantourism.com.

CONDITIONS OF WORK

WAGES

Salaries for professional and managerial staff are considerably higher than in Britain, but less skilled workers are worse off. For certain types of work a minimum wage is set by law. When evaluating the income of Italians as a whole, it is necessary to bear in mind that there remains a sizeable black economy and many, in particular the self-employed, manage to evade paying taxes altogether. It is also common for low-paid workers to have two or three jobs.

Women are paid more or less the same rate as men for the same work. There is still some prejudice against career women however, and relatively few have made it into the higher ranks of business and government. All employees receive an extra month's wages in December.

HOURS

The statutory working week is 40 hours, except for public sector employment where it is 36 hours. Firms can ask employees to work more than 40 hours per week but the hours will be subject to higher social security contributions and will be paid at premium overtime rates. The two-hour lunch break for siesta is common practice in the South, so the working day may last until 7pm. In the North, nine-to-five working is usual.

HOLIDAYS

Most employees receive between 25 and 30 days' holiday a year. In addition, there are the following public holidays: New Year's Day; Epiphany (6 January); Easter Monday; Liberation Day (25 April); Labour Day (1 May); Ascension Day (15 August); All Saints' Day (1 November); National Unity Day (5 November); Conception Day (8 December); Christmas Day; and Boxing Day.

TRADE UNIONS

The four major unions are organised according to their political affiliations and not by trade or sector. They are grouped together under the *General Conference of Labour*, along with several smaller unions. Total union membership is large but declining.

TAXATION

Taxes are imposed by the Treasury, the Ministry of Finance, the Minister of the Budget and by the regions, provinces and communes. Income tax is progressive and relatively low compared to other European countries. Those intending to work should go to the local tax office, the *Intendenza di Finanza*, and obtain a tax number (*codice fiscale*).

EMPLOYMENT PROSPECTS

GENERAL

The northern third of the country is wealthy while the South (*Meridionale*) is relatively underdeveloped. A number of Britons now live or have second homes in the central rural regions of Tuscany and Umbria, while Americans tend to find Rome and the cities of the North more congenial. There are many regional industries, such as wool textiles in Prato, silk in Como, or shoes in Verona. The large companies, like Fiat, Benetton, and Pirelli, are located in the North. Italian language skills are a must for anyone seeking employment in Italy. Job applicants should note that the postal service is sometimes slow and enquiries are best made by telephone or fax. *CESOP Communication* (Via San Felice 13 – Galleria Buriani, 40122 Bologna BO; ☎051-272441; fax 051-272265; e-mail info@recruitaly.it; www.recruitaly.it, provides comprehensive information on the working world in Italy, and a window for Italian companies interested in recruiting staff from abroad on its website. The site allows a direct approach to recent graduates interested in working in Italy, helping companies that have difficulties in finding qualified personnel in Italy, especially in the ICT sector.

NEWSPAPERS

Italian newspapers include *Il Giornale*, *Il Corriere della Sera* and *La Republica*. *The Informer* (c/o Buroservice snc, Via dei Tigli 2, 20020 Arese-MI; ☎02-9358 1477; fax 02-9358 0280; e-mail informer@informer.it; www.informer.it) provides useful business, cultural and community information to expats living in Italy. Its website is a mine of information and highly recommended. There are two fortnightly English-language newspapers published in Rome – *Wanted in Rome* (www.wantedinrome.com) sold on newsstands and in some bookshops, and the *Metropolitan*. The *English Yellow Pages* (www.intoitaly.it) updated annually, will be invaluable to any new arrival in Italy. The directory contains listings for English-speaking professionals, businesses and services in Rome, Florence, Bologna, Naples, Genoa and Milan. It is available at international bookshops and from newsstands. The online version also has listings for Palermo and Catania. Free classified ads can also be posted on the website. Also from the same publisher is the English White Pages, an alphabetical directory of English-speakers living in Italy.

SPECIFIC CONTACTS

EMPLOYMENT SERVICE
The state-run *Ufficio di Collocaménto Manodòpera* has lost its monopoly in employment and recruitment and private agencies are now permitted. A complete list of authorised Italian agencies can be found at www.italialavoro.it, the Italian *Ministero del Welfare* website. For those interested in temporary employment, there are also agencies listed in the Italian *Yellow Pages*. Unfortunately, few of these agencies will be likely to be able to help non-Italian speakers. Italy has 22 Euroadvisors (*euroconsiglieri*) who mainly help Italians wanting to work abroad. Vacancies in Italy are registered on the EURES website, www.eures-jobs.com/jobs/en/jobs.jsp.

ONLINE JOB RESOURCES
Online recruitment agencies are becoming increasingly common and many traditional recruitment agencies now have a web presence where their vacancy lists can be accessed and CVs submitted for consideration. A search using the main search engines such as Yahoo, Google and Lycos or meta engines such as www.mamma.com and www.dogpile.com will generate many such agencies. There are agencies that recruit for the whole of Europe and also some that specialise in Italy, e.g. www.monster.it, where you will find thousands of job offers (Italian version available only).

Alternatively, www.recruitaly.it gives access to job postings in English and provides further information on living and working in Italy and the site *Jobs in Italy* also provides useful links and resources, as does the website www.payaway.co.uk which lists agencies offering work in most areas covered in the *Temporary Work* section below, i.e. Agriculture, Au Pair and Tourism. Finally, *Job Partners* provide a recruitment service for employers around the world and local contact details can be found via their website, www.jobpartners.com.

Try the following websites:
www.adecco.it (temporary jobs agency)
www.alispa.it (temporary work agency)
www.assioma.org (IT specialist)
www.bestjob.it (portal of teleworking opportunities)
www.cambiolavoro.com (prepares and sends CVs to headhunters)
www.cercolavoro.com (claims to have over 30,000 job offers)
www.cliccalavoro.it (also has a newsletter about the job market)
www.corriere.it/lavoro/index.jhtml (newspaper jobs listings)
www.coopquadrifoglio.it (all kinds of jobs)
www.easyjob.it (temporary jobs agency)
www.eurointerim.it (temporary jobs agency)
www.eurometis.it (agency recruiting for banks, industry, IT etc)
www.ideallavoro.it (temporary jobs agency for service sector)
www.infojobs.it (claims 30,000 firms advertise on the website)

www.intoitaly.it (English-speaking jobs)
www.italialavoro.it (informative official Ministry of Welfare portal)
www.jobonline.it (useful general job site with newsletter)
www.jobsintourism.it/job/ (Italian tourist industry jobs)
www.manpower.it (temporary jobs agency)
www.maw.it (temporary work)
www.jobpilot.it (part of the worldwide Monster jobs network)
www.kangaroo.it (jobs in the IT sector)
www.lavoroeweb.com (very useful portal to everything to do with work)
www.lavoro.tiscali.it (Italian jobs portal)

TEACHERS

Italy has many English, American and international schools and colleges, which have a steady demand for teachers and there are good opportunities for English language teachers in Italy, mainly because the standard of language teaching in primary and secondary schools is generally poor. Most jobs will require some basic TEFL qualification, without which it will be an uphill struggle to find work. The *British Council* (Palazzo del Drago, Via 4 Fontane 20, 00184 Rome; ☎06-478141; fax 06-487 1070; e-mail studyandcultureUK@britishcouncil. it; www.britishcouncil.it) can offer useful advice. Offices in Bologna, Milan, and Naples. Addresses of schools are given under *Scuole de Lingua* in the Italian Yellow Pages. Some language schools include:

British Institute of Florence, Palazzo Strozzino, Piazza Strozzi 2, 50123 Florence; ☎055-2677 8200; fax 055-2677 8222; e-mail info@britishinstitute.it; www.britishinstitute. it. Hires teachers on two-year contracts, who must have RSA Diploma and two years' experience (preferably ESP – English for Specialised Purposes). Interviews are usually held in Florence. There are 50 other schools affiliated to the British Institute.

Posts in Italian state schools are not open to foreigners, except in conjunction with the British Council Education and Training Group (see the section on *Working Exchanges* in the chapter *Getting the Job*). However, there are a number of one-year posts for assistants in English faculties of Italian universities. Applications should be made direct to the university.

SHORT TERM WORK

English-speakers should look for temporary jobs where their language skills are a positive advantage, such as in hotels or offices, public and international relations (with the many companies which depend on trade), bilingual secretarial and English teaching work.

SEASONAL WORK

Over the summer Italy's tourist industry can offer employment both in the cities (such as Rome, Florence and Venice) and in the resorts along the Italian Riviera, the Adriatic and to the south of Naples. Many of the camping holiday organisers in the chapter on tourism operate in Italy. Details of specific vacancies in Italian hotels can be found in *Summer Jobs Abroad* (Vacation Work Publications, www.vacationwork.co.uk). Jobs can also be found in ski resorts in the Alps of Lombardy, the Dolomites, the Apennines north of Florence, and in the region to the northeast of Turin.

Italy is the world's largest producer of wine, but work on the grape harvest is traditionally done by locals and, more recently, by immigrants from east of the Adriatic. The comparatively high wages (sometimes 50 per cent more than for the equivalent job in France) and a welcome reportedly more hospitable, still make this sort of work worthwhile and September or early October is the best time to look for grape picking work. Vineyards can be found all over Italy, but chances of employment are greater in the North.

AU PAIRS

A considerable number of European au pair and nanny agencies deal with Italy, so British and other European au pairs should have little trouble arranging a job. There can sometimes be substantial delays between submitting your application and receiving details of a family, but on the other hand you may be given as little as a fortnight to get yourself organised for departure once the family's details are sent.

An agency in the UK that specialises in Italy is the *English-Italian Agency* (69 Woodside, Wimbledon, London SW19 7AF; ☎020-8906 3116; fax 020-8906 3461; email office@ childint.co.uk; www.childint.co.uk) though, like so many British agencies, it is now more active in bringing au pairs to Britain rather than sending them abroad. An agency with a consistently high number of vacancies in Italy is *Totalnannies.com* which publicises many of its choice jobs on the free monthly electronic newsletter *Jobs Abroad Bulletin* (www. jobsabroadbulletin.co.uk).

You can of course work directly with an Italian agency, since most of them will speak English, but make sure first that you won't be liable to pay a hefty registration fee. *ARCE* is a long established agency which makes placements free of charge throughout the country. Two agencies to try in Florence are:

Au Pair Florence, Via di Valiano 2/a Molino del Piano, 50065 Florence (tel/fax +39 055 8364663; aupairflorence@virgilio.it; www.aupairflorence.com). IAPA member.

Euro Au Pair, Via Ghibellina 96/R, 50122 Florence (☎055-242181; tel/fax 055-241722). Contact Laura Pini.

If you are already in Italy you can check the classified adverts in English language journals many of which are published online such as *Wanted in Rome* (www.wantedinrome.com) aimed at the expatriate community. Try notice boards in English language bookshops, for example the Lion Bookshop at Via dei Greci 33/36 in Rome, churches for expats like the Church of England on Rome's Via del Babuino and the student travel agency CTS (Centro Turistico Studentesco e Giovanile) where the staff may be able to advise. CTS is the main student travel agency in Italy which does far more than arrange flights and travel, e.g. its website www.cts.it has links to language courses *(corsi di lingua)* as well as to its offices *(sedi)* throughout Italy.

Language school notice boards are always worth checking. For instance at the Centro di Lingua & Cultura Italiana per Stranieri where Dustie Hickie took cheap Italian lessons in Milan, there was a good notice board with adverts for au pairs, dog-walkers, etc. Every region has a Youth Information Office *(Centro Informazione Giovani)* which is in a position to advise on holiday work, for example in Bologna the Informagiovani is at Piazza Maggiore n°6 (informagiovani@comune.bologna.it). Links to all the youth information centres throughout Italy can be found at www.comune.torino.it/infogio/cig/ecr.htm.

Alternative summer employment is available with tour operators. Mark Warner employ nannies at their Mediterranean Beach Club Hotels in Italy and Sardinia; further details from the Resorts Recruitment department on ☎0870 033 0760 (www.markwarner.co.uk/ recruitment).

OTHER WORK

Most types of casual work can only be found by people who are already in the country, and who can visit employment agencies and follow up newspaper advertisements. Many Italian organisations arrange summer work projects ranging from restoring old convents to preventing forest fires. In some cases it is necessary to apply through a partner organisation in your home country. *CTS-Centro Turistico Studentesco e Giovanile* (www.cts.it) is the largest Italian youth association and organises research activities and expeditions which use paying volunteers to work in the field and fund different projects carried out by scientists. Some of the projects are in Italy in the Alps, Apennines and National Parks.

Membership is required to join the expeditions. Further details can be obtained from the above address. The French-based organisation, *La Sabranenque* (www.sabranenque.com) uses voluntary labour to restore villages and monuments in Altamura (inland from Bari in Southern Italy) and Gnallo (Northern Italy). The cost of participation is £180 for three weeks in July/August.

INTERNATIONAL COMPANIES IN ITALY

Abbey National Mutui Spa   4
Via Nizza 48
00198 Rome

Andersen Spa   14
Via della Moscova 3
I-20121 Milan

Ashurst Morris Crisp Studio Legale Associato 24
Via Finocchiaro Aprile 14
20124 Milano

BP Italia Spa   35
Milano Fiori
Palazzo E/5-Strada 6
20090 Assago

Barclays Bank Spa   4
Via Moscova 18
20121 Milan

British Airways   3
Corso Italia 8
20122 Milan

British Gas Italia SpA   35
Piazza Cavour 2
20121 Milan

Cable & Wireless Italia   45
V. Ferrante Aporti
20125 Milano

CB Richard Ellis Spa   40
Via dei Giardini 4
20121 Milano

Christie's of London   15
Piazza Navona 114
00186 Rome

Commercial Union Italia SpA   23
Viale Abruzzi 94
20131 Milan

Coopers & Lybrand SpA   1
Via delle Quattre Fontane 15
00184 Rome

Deloitte SpA   1
Palazzo Caducci
Via Olona 2
20123 Milan

Enterprise Oil Italiana Spa   35
Via dei Due Macelli 66
00187 Roma

Fiat Spa   25
Via Nizza 250
10126 Torino

Generali Assicurazioni Spa   23
Piazza Duca degli Abruzzi 2
34132 Trieste

Glaxo Wellcome SpA   8
Via A. Fleming 2
37135 Verona

Grimaldi e Clifford Chance   24
Via Clerici 7
20121 Milano

HSBC Bank Plc   4
Via Santa Maria alla Porta 2
20123 Milano

Healey & Baker   40
Via Turati 25
20121 Milano

Human Technology Srl Viale Masini 4 40100 Bologna	10	Reuters Italia SpA V.le Fulvio Testi 280 20126 Milan	38
ING Barings (Italia) Srl Via Brera 3 20121 Milano	4	Royal & Sun Alliance Assicurazioni Via Martin Piaggio 1 16122 Genova	23
JCB Spa Via Enrico Fermi, 16 20090 Assago, Milan	25	Siemens SpA Viale P & A Pirelli 10 20126 Milan	10
KPMG Peat Marwick Fides Via Vittor Pisani 25 20129 Milan	1	Simmons & Simmons Grippo C.so Vittorio Emanuele 1 20122 Milano	24
Lloyd's of London Via Sigieri 14 20135 Milano	23	Smithkline Beecham SpA Via Zambeletti 20021 Baranzate Milan	8
National Westminster Bank plc Via F Turati 16-18 20121 Milan	4	Thomas Cook Italia Ltd. Viale Marche 54 00187 Rome	48
P & O Container Europe Srl Strada 4, Palazzo A, Scala 7 20090 Assago, Milano	17	Unilever Italia SpA Via Nino Bonnet 10 20154 Milan	8
PriceWaterhouseCoopers Corso Europa 2 20122 Milan	1	Woolwich Building Society Via Dante 16 20122 Milan	4
Reconta Ernst & Young SaS di Bruno Gimpel Via Torino 68 20123 Milan	1		

The *British Chamber of Commerce for Italy,* Via Dante 12, 20121 Milan; ☎02-877798; fax 02-8646 1885; www.britchamitaly.com, publishes a trade directory which contains not only a list of members but also a list of British firms present in Italy. The *American Chamber of Commerce in Italy,* Via Cantu, 20123 Milano, Italy; ☎02-869 0661; fax 02-805 7737; e-mail amcham@amcham.it; www.amcham.it on its website lists job vacancies for those with Italian-US experience and Italian language skills.

Luxembourg

- **Year of EU Accession:** 1952
- **Luxembourg Embassy,** 27 Wilton Crescent, London SW1X 8SD; ☎020-7235 6961; fax 020-7235 9734; e-mail embassy@luxembourg.co.uk
- **Luxembourg Embassy for USA and Canada,** 2200 Massachusetts Ave. NW, Washington DC 20008; ☎202-265 4171; fax 202-328 8270; www.luxembourg-usa.org
- **Currency:** 1 Euro (€) = 100 cents
- **Rate of Exchange:** £1 = €1.44; $1 = €0.78
- **Country Code:** +352

Luxembourg covers just under 1,000 square miles – on most maps even the abbreviation, LUX, scarcely fits within its borders. The total population is around 474,413, which means that the Grand Duchy does not offer unlimited job opportunities. It has an unemployment rate of two per cent. One quarter of Luxembourg's population is foreign; the highest proportion of foreigners in a European country, and two thirds of salaried workers are non-nationals.

Luxembourg is a member of the European Union and as such is subject to EU regulations concerning free movement of labour. EU citizens intending to stay for more than three months should visit the police at the *Info-Accueil des Etrangers – Service Municipal,* Bâtiment 'Petit Passage', 30 pl. Guillaume, 9 rue Chimay, 2090 Luxembourg; ☎4796-2751, to complete all the formalities and obtain an Identity Card for Foreign Nationals. Others must obtain from the employer a work permit (*Délaration Patronale*) which has been approved by the Administration de l'Emploi and by the Ministère de la Justice, Police des Etrangers, 16 Bvd. Royal, 1333 Luxembourg. General information including a list of Useful Addresses for New Residents is available from the Luxembourg Embassy.

LANGUAGE

The native tongue is *Letzeburgesch* (or 'Luxembourgeois' or 'Luxembourgish'). Luxemburgers usually also speak French and German, and English is widely understood. In fact, in a recent survey, Luxemburgers were found to be Europe's most accomplished language learners. The Embassy advises that a good knowledge of French and German is needed to work in Luxembourg. Work is most often obtained through personal contacts or commercial relationships. French is the official government and administrative language, while German is the language of the press and the church.

EMBASSIES

British Embassy, 5 Boulevard Joseph II, L-1840 Luxembourg; ☎229864; www.britain.lu.
US Embassy, 22 Boulevard Emmanuel Servais, L-2535 Luxembourg; ☎460123; fax 4614 01; http://luxembourg.usembassy.gov.

TOURIST OFFICES

Luxembourg Tourist Office, 122 Regent Street, London W1B 5SA; ☎020-7434 2800; fax 020-7734 1205; www.luxembourg.co.uk.
Luxembourg National Tourist Office, 17 Beekman Place, New York, NY 10022; ☎212-935 8888; fax 212-935 5896; www.visitluxembourg.com.

NEWSPAPERS

Adverts can be placed direct in the *Luxembourger Wort* (2 rue Christophe Plantin, 2988 Luxembourg; ☎4993-1; fax 499 3384; www.wort.lu); or via *The Powers Turner Group,*

Gordon House, Greencoat Lane, London SW1P 1PH; ☎020-7592 8300; fax 020-7592 8301; e-mail ppn-london@publicitas.com; www.publicitas.com.

EMPLOYMENT PROSPECTS

Luxembourg has a highly developed economy, a high standard of living and the lowest unemployment rate in the EU, currently 2 per cent. Its most important industries are banking and finance, manufacturing, media and communications. Jobs in these sectors, and in international organisations and tourism (Luxembourg has 250+ hotels) are most accessible to British and North American jobseekers (especially if they speak French and German). The major sector of employment is not agriculture or industry, but services. Luxembourg is famous for its discreet banking services and permits the operation of numbered accounts as in Switzerland, with the result that it is a powerful player in high-level finance. The best prospects for professionals are in IT for banking or administration. Additionally, the European Parliament is based in Luxembourg and has a recruitment service (see the *International Organisations* chapter).

EMPLOYMENT SERVICES

The national employment service, *Administration de l'Emploi,* 10 rue Bender, 1229 Luxembourg-Ville; ☎478 5300; fax 40 61 40; e-mail info@adem.public.lu; www.etat.lu/ adem/adem.htm. There are also branches at Esch-sur-Alzette (541054), Diekirch (802929) and Wiltz (958384). This service has a department, *Service Vacances*, which looks after students looking for summer jobs in warehouses, restaurants. You will need to visit the service in person to make use of its facilities.

SHORT TERM WORK

Luxembourg does offer some opportunities for short-term work. An employment agency that deals with temporary work is *Manpower-Aide Temporaire*, 42 Rue Glesener, 1630 Luxembourg; ☎48 23 23; www.manpower.lu. The Luxembourg Embassy in London holds a list of the 20 or so employment agencies in Luxembourg.

More than a million tourists visit Luxembourg each year, most for business or for short-stays and hotels and conference work provide many job openings. There is no central agency for this, but you may be able to get a temporary job by writing to hotels directly. The Luxembourg Embassy in London will supply a leaflet, *Hotels, Auberges, Restaurants, Pensions*, on receipt of an A4 SAE and 54p stamp.

There is some grape-picking work in the 25 miles (40 km) of vineyards along the Moselle around the town of Remich. The harvest begins in mid-September and lasts for two weeks or more. Jobs can only be obtained by approaching farmers directly. It is also worth contacting the *Centre Information Jeunes (CIJ)*, 26 Place de la Gare, Galeria Kons, 1616 Luxembourg; ☎26293-201; fax 26293-215; www.cij.lu, which runs a holiday-job service between January and August for students from the EU.

Further information on opportunities in Luxembourg can be found in *Live and Work in Belgium, the Netherlands and Luxembourg* (www.vacationwork.co.uk).

INTERNATIONAL COMPANIES IN LUXEMBOURG

A comprehensive list of UK and American companies with Luxembourg connections can be obtained from Luxembourg Embassies. Please enclose a large SAE. The *British Chamber of Commerce for Luxembourg,* 6 rue Antoine de Saint Exapéry, 1432 Luxembourg-Kirchberg; ☎465466; fax 220384; e-mail info@bcc.lu; www.bcc.lu. The *Belgium-Luxembourg Chamber of Commerce in Great Britain* can be contacted at Riverside House, 27/29 Vauxhall Grove, London SW8 1SY; ☎0870-246 1610; fax 0870-429 2148; www.blcc.co.uk.

The Netherlands

- Year of EU Accession: 1952
- Royal Netherlands Embassy, 38 Hyde Park Gate, London SW7 5DP; ☎020-7590 3200; fax 020-7225 0947; www.netherlands-embassy.org.uk
- Royal Netherlands Embassy, 4200 Linnean Avenue NW, Washington DC, 20008; ☎202-244 5300; fax 202-362 3430; www.netherlands-embassy.org
- Currency: 1 Euro (€) = 100 cents
- Rate of Exchange: £1 = €1.44; $1 = €0.78
- Country Code: +31

The prospects for work and residence in the Netherlands (Holland – meaning 'wooded land') are good for those who are qualified and willing to adapt to this liberal and fast-moving society. The Dutch authorities stress that immigration is not encouraged and permanent residence is only granted to non-EU citizens in rare cases in view of the very high population density and shortage of housing and work. This view is contradicted somewhat by the many British and US citizens who do actually live in the country. Culturally, the Netherlands can seem like home to many English-speaking people. The widespread use of English in everyday life contributes to this impression and the Dutch are famously multilingual. Economically, the Netherlands is still highly dependent on its international trade. More than any other country in this book, Holland could be described as truly cosmopolitan. However, some Dutch people are uneasy about this international identity and are less tolerant of foreigners. The Netherlands is a racially mixed society in which the children of immigrants have full Dutch citizenship.

GENERAL FACTS

POPULATION

The Netherlands has a population of 16.5 million and the population density is approximately 457 per sq km (compared to 232 per sq km in the UK), one of the highest in the world. The country covers 15,770 square miles/40,844 sq km (about half the size of Scotland, or twice the size of New Jersey), more than half of which is below sea level.

CLIMATE

The Netherlands' climate is very similar to that of England, but noticeably windier. Winters are mild and summers cool. The average highest temperature in Amsterdam in January is 41 deg F (5 deg C); in July 70 deg F (21 deg C). There are approximately 65 days of frost in an average year.

GOVERNMENT

The Netherlands is a constitutional monarchy. The head of state is Queen Beatrix. Legislative power rests with Parliament, which comprises two chambers. The Prime Minister exercises executive power through a Council of Ministers, drawn from the 150-strong Lower Chamber (similar to the UK's House of Commons) elected every four years on a basis of proportional representation. The upper chamber has 75 members who are elected by the Provincial Councils. Suffrage extends to all citizens aged 18 and over.

The Netherlands is divided into 625 municipalities, which are governed by councils whose members are elected every four years, except for the mayor who is appointed by the Crown. Between the local and national government are the provincial assemblies, whose members are also elected every four years.

CITIES

The Hague, also known as Den Haag and 's Gravenhage, is the seat of government and has a population of 680,000. Amsterdam, the capital, has a population of 700,000 or more while Rotterdam, the world's largest port, more than one million inhabitants. There are 17 other towns with over 100,000 inhabitants.

RURAL LIFE

Flowers and dairy products form part of a world-famous agricultural/horticultural industry, which accounts for roughly a quarter of all Dutch exports. Holland is highly urbanised and just two per cent of the population live in villages of less than 5,000 inhabitants. The Dutch value their leisure time and Groningen, Friesland and Flevoland have developed many outdoor recreational facilities. The Dutch government has also taken steps to clean up the environment, which has suffered severely from the recent expansion of agriculture and industry.

RELIGION, SPORT AND CULTURE

The Dutch constitution guarantees freedom of religion and that all sections of society, whether religious or secular, are represented in national institutions. One-third of the population are Roman Catholics (mostly concentrated in the south) and one-fifth belongs to the Dutch Reformed Church.

Sport plays an important part in Dutch life and one third of the population belongs to a sports club of one sort or another. Angling and cycling are the two most popular pastimes, and tennis is second only to football in terms of the number of official participants in the sport. In the winter, especially in Friesland to the north of the country, skating is a popular pastime. Weather permitting, 17,000 competitors participate in the annual *Elfstedentocht* ('Tour of the Eleven Towns') – a 124-mile (200km) skate along frozen canals between 11 towns in Friesland. One of the lesser-known consequences of global warming and mild winters has been to reduce the number of occasions on which this race can take place – last century it was only possible on 15 occasions, and the last race was in 1997.

The Netherlands has a wealth of museums (more than 1,000 at the last count) and art galleries. The larger towns all have a full programme of concerts, opera, ballet and theatre, and there is a flourishing cultural and nightlife. Amsterdam has acquired the reputation of being not only one of Europe's top tourist attractions but also a popular destination for young, alternative travellers.

FACTORS INFLUENCING EMPLOYMENT

IMMIGRATION

The Netherlands is a member of the EU and as such UK citizens have the right to work there. If you enter the Netherlands with the intention of staying for over three months, you should report to the Aliens' Police (*vreemdelingenpolitie*) within eight days of arrival. Although it is no longer necessary to obtain a residence permit (*verblijfsvergunning*), it is a good idea, as certain procedures, such as opening a bank account, will be much easier. Permits will normally be granted to persons with a definite job offer or adequate funds to support themselves.

The situation is more complicated for non-EU nationals. North Americans, Australians and others who require no visa to travel to the Netherlands are permitted to work for less than three months, provided that they report to the Aliens Police within three days of arrival and their employer has obtained a *tewerkstellingsvergunning* (employment permit) for them. In practice, however, this permit is unlikely to be issued for casual work. A leaflet called *Working in the Netherlands: New Rules for Aliens*, and a booklet called *Working in the Netherlands* are available from Dutch embassies. Once in the Netherlands the British Consulate can supply the leaflet *Living & Working in the Netherlands*. For US citizens, the American Consulate General issues the *General Information Guide for American Citizens Residing in the Netherlands*. For detailed information contact the Dutch immigration service, *Immigratie-en Naturalisatiedienst, afdeling Communicatie*, Postbus 3211, 2280 HE Rijswijk; ☎0900-1234561 or from outside the Netherlands: ☎+31-20889 3045; www.ind.nl.

LANGUAGE

The Dutch have an education system that places a great value on foreign languages, and English is understood almost everywhere. In fact, the language skills of the Dutch are so good that the average bus driver is likely to be far more articulate *in English* than many less well-educated native speakers. German is the second most commonly spoken language, followed closely by French. It is possible to get by with only a knowledge of English, but if you intend to stay for any length of time it is essential to try to learn Dutch, which has something in common with both English and German. Frisian, the country's second language, is spoken by 250,000 people in the northern province of Friesland, and is the European language closest to English.

COST AND STANDARD OF LIVING

Consumer prices for food and other goods are slightly higher than those in Britain. Wages tend to be quite a lot higher (30 per cent is one estimate) and this is a relatively egalitarian society, although there are pockets of poverty in the cities.

HOUSING AND ACCOMMODATION

The Netherlands has a fairly permanent housing shortage owing to the growing in population. The cost of rented property, especially in the Randstad area (the almost continuous conurbation which includes Amsterdam, Rotterdam and The Hague), is higher than in the UK, although house prices are comparable. More than half of all Dutch homes are of post-war constructions and about half are owner-occupied. You can be sure that rented property will always be immaculate, and you will be expected to keep it at that standard. The Dutch are very particular housekeepers.

HEALTH AND WELFARE

Payment for medical treatment is arranged through a number of health insurance schemes, both public and private. Taxpayers make no fewer than eight social security payments, including contributions totalling nearly 40 per cent towards unemployment and disability benefits, pensions and family allowances. These contributions are mostly withheld at source by employers. UK citizens need their EHIC card to get free health treatment. US citizens should take out insurance. For further information on your health rights in the Netherlands you can contact the Public Relations Department, Ministry of Health, Welfare, and Sports, Parnassusplein 5, 2511 VX The Hague; ☎70-340 7911 fax 70-340 7834; www.minvws.nl.

EDUCATION

Education is for the most part free and compulsory from five to 16; part-time education is also compulsory for a further two years. Nursery and childcare provisions are also widely available. Nearly two-thirds of children attend private schools (subsidised by the state), which are mostly denominational. There are three types of secondary school: the *gymnasium* (grammar school) which leads to university; vocational schools which give special technical or trade training; and general schools which tread a line between the two. There are five state universities, including two in Amsterdam; an agricultural university at Wageningen; and a Catholic university at Nijmegen.

NATIONAL SERVICE
All Dutch men between the ages of 18 and 25 must do military service for 14-17 months. Foreign nationals are not liable.

EMBASSIES AND CONSULATES
British Embassy, Lange Voorhout 10, 2514 ED The Hague; ☎70-427 0427; fax 020-427 0348; www.britain.nl.
British Consulate-General, Koningslaan 44, 1075 AE Amsterdam; ☎20-676 4343; fax 20-676 1069.
US Embassy, Lange Voorhout 102, 2514 EJ The Hague; ☎70-310 2209; fax 70-361 4688; http://thehague.usembassy.gov.
US Consulate, Museumplein 19, 1071 DJ Amsterdam; ☎20-575 5309; fax 20-575 5310.

TOURIST OFFICES
Netherlands Board of Tourism, PO Box 523, London SW1E 6NT; ☎0906-871 7777; fax 020-7828 7941; e-mail information@nbt.org.uk; www.holland.com/uk.
Netherlands Board of Tourism, 355 Lexington Avenue, 19th Floor, New York, NY 10017; ☎1-8884646552; www.holland.com/us.

CONDITIONS OF WORK

WAGES
There is a statutory minimum monthly wage for all workers aged 23-65 (approx. €1,264). All wage contracts are reviewed at six-month intervals and adjusted in accordance with the cost of living index. The Minister of Social Affairs is empowered to disallow wage agreements deemed to be contrary to the national interest. Wages are competitive with those anywhere in Western Europe.

WORKING CONDITIONS
The average working week in the Netherlands is the shortest in the EU, at 37.9 hours per week. The official working week is approximately 39 hours, although in reality it can be longer. The maximum working hours are restricted by law to nine hours a day and 45 hours per week. Employers must obtain a permit for overtime from the Labour Inspection Board. The usual holiday entitlement is 23 working days, though it can vary from 20-30 days. In addition, there are public holidays on: New Year's Day; Good Friday; Easter Monday; Queen's Day (30 April); National Liberation Day (5 May); Ascension Day; Whit Monday; Christmas Day; and Boxing Day.

TRADE UNIONS
Trade union membership is not compulsory (except in the printing industry) but 29 per cent of the Dutch workforce still belongs to a recognised organisation. There are three main unions, as well as a number of groups covering agricultural and retail trades. Dutch trade unions are not regarded as militant and do not normally strike to achieve their goals.

TAXATION
To encourage foreign investment the Dutch government has set up what is known as the '30 per cent rule', which allows foreigners to qualify for taxation on only 68 per cent of

their gross salary. There are five separate tariff bands and after allowances have been made there is a progressive scale of taxation that ranges from 34.40 per cent to 52 per cent on the excess. Further information about tax can be obtained from the local tax authority in the Netherlands or the *Ministerie van Financiën (Ministry of Finance)*, Central Information Directorate, Prinses Beatrixlaan 512, Postbus 20201, 2500 EE Den Haag; ☎70-342 8000; fax 70-342 7900; www.minfin.nl. Self-employed people should obtain form E101 in Britain before moving to The Netherlands (see *Rules and Regulations*).

EMPLOYMENT PROSPECTS

GENERAL

The Netherlands has a highly developed and diverse economy. Its major industries include petrochemicals, engineering, agriculture, information technology, transportation and publishing. The Dutch are the largest foreign investors in the USA, ahead of the British. The discovery of huge natural gas reserves, and to a lesser extent oil, in the provinces of Groningen and Drenthe has also greatly improved the Netherlands' already excellent economic prospects. Most British and American people will find temporary work through employment agencies, and the local and national press and word of mouth are also useful sources of information. Unemployment is highest in the south and northwest, so these areas are better avoided if you are looking for casual work. There is much less competition for work outside the summer season.

SPECIFIC CONTACTS

Dutch job centres (*gewestelijk arbeidsbureaux*) are found in every major city and town, and can offer job placements and advice on employment in the Netherlands. A full list of centres is available from the *Centra voor Werk en Inkomen (CWI)* on their website, www. cwi.nl. In Amsterdam the CWI can be found at: Kruislaan 413, NL-1098 SJ Amsterdam; ☎020-592 9333.

Most employers in Holland turn to private employment agencies for temporary workers to avoid the complicated paperwork involved in hiring a foreigner directly; these are, therefore, a very good source of work in large towns. You will find employment agencies listed under *Uitzendbureau* in the *Gouden Gids* (Yellow Pages). However, not all will accept non Dutch-speaking applicants. Most of the work on the books of such agencies will be unskilled work such as stocking shelves, production line work, cleaning, hotel work, roof repairing.

Try the following online recruitment agencies in the Netherlands.

www.abc-uitzendbureau.nl/
www.accord.nl
www.adecco.nl
www.allure-online.nl
www.arto.nl
www.creyfs.nl
www.content.nl
www.dactylo.nl
www.freeforce.nl
www.highline.nl/
www.horecauitzend.nl
www.jmwbeheer.nl
www.linvite.nl

www.oudstanding.nl
www.pagejobs.nl
www.partner.nl
www.starjob.nl
www.start.nl
www.studentalent.nl
www.studentenwerk.nl
www.tempo-team.nl
www.totaljobs.n
www.ubn-uitzendburo.nl/
www.unique.nl
www.vedior.nl
www.zoekbijbaan.nl

NEWSPAPERS

There are several national newspapers. *De Telegraaf* (www.telegraaf.nl), the highest circulation daily, is represented by *The Powers Turner Group*, Gordon House, Greencoat Place, London SW1P 1PH; ☎020-7592 8300; fax 020-7592 8301; email ppn-london@ publicitas.com; www.publicitas.com, as are *Het Parool* (www.parool.nl), *Trouw* and *De Volkskrant* (www.volkskrant.nl). There are also several English-language publications: *Roundabout* with listings of meetings and events, *Day by Day*, with listings for Amsterdam, and the *Dutch News Digest* (www.dnd.nl) appears daily and weekly, and on the internet.

MEDICINE AND NURSING

Information on existing vacancies in Dutch hospitals can be obtained from *Geneeskundige Vereniging tot Bevordering van het Ziekenhuiswezen*, Postbus 3140, 3502 GC Utrecht. On obtaining an appointment, a licence must be secured. Applications should be made to the *Ministry of Health, Welfare, and Sports*, Bureau Buitenlandse Diplomahouders, Postbus 20350, 2500 EJ The Hague; ☎70-340 7890; fax 70-340 6251. *Worldwide Healthcare Exchange,* The Colonnades, Beaconsfield Close, Hatfield, Herts AL10 8YD; ☎01707-259233; fax 01707-259223, recruits nurses for hospitals in the Netherlands.

SHORT TERM WORK

Dutch employers are accustomed to taking on the British and Irish for temporary jobs and to using the services of employment agencies like Randstad, ASB, Vedior, and Manpower. Language is not normally a problem, but some knowledge of Dutch could pay dividends in currying favour with potential employers. An on-the-spot job search is a good idea. Young people in Britain (18-28) with two years relevant experience in agriculture/horticulture who are looking for three to 12-month placements in the Netherlands can contact *Agriventure*, Speedwell Farm Bungalow, Nettle Bank, Wisbech, Cambridgeshire PE14 0SA; ☎01945-450999; www.agriventure.com.

The *JoHo Company* (*Jobs and Holidays*), 8-9, Stille Rijn, 2312 DE Leiden; ☎071-516 1277; fax 071-514 5003; e-mail info@joho.nl; www.carrierebank.nl, offers careers advice services to jobseekers with a degree, as well as information on travel and study. Offices in Amsterdam, Rotterdam, Leiden and Groningen.

SEASONAL WORK

The Netherlands has a comparatively long tourist season as the bulb fields attract tourists and workers from April to September. The most important region for bulbs is between Leiden and Haarlem. The centre has shifted from Hillegom to Noordwijk, and if you are looking for work in the bulb fields you will need a tent and a bicycle. Working conditions can be poor – the work is also very demanding physically – but food, accommodation and even beer is often provided free. It is possible to earn very good money picking bulbs, as overtime is paid at premium rates. The Dutch tourist office (PO Box 523, London SW1E 6NT; ☎0891-200277) produces a free map of the Netherlands showing the bulb growing areas.

An alternative to working on the bulbs is tomato picking, centred in Westland around the villages of Naaldwijk, Westerlee, De Lier and Maasdijk. The tomato harvest begins in early April, although work is available all year round if you are prepared to stay for at least one month.

Tourism attracts more than five million visitors to Holland every year. The best areas for finding work in tourism are Amsterdam, the coastal resorts of Scheveningen and Zandvoort, and the island of Texel. Vacancies are sometimes advertised on the EURES system (ask your employment centre to look) or if you are already in Holland contact the nearest Centra voor Werk en Inkomen (jobcentre).

TEACHING

The Dutch place such a high value on fluency in English that some have suggested that English should be the main language of instruction in schools. It is already widely used in Dutch universities, and Holland actually sends its own English teachers abroad. The implication is clear – this is not a country where you can easily find TEFL jobs. In general, the demand is for high-level university and college teachers. Dutch schools do not need to recruit abroad and they generally rely on local expatriates who often work part-time. *The British Council in The Netherlands*, Weteringschans 85a, 1017 RZ Amsterdam; ☎20-550 6060; fax 20-620 7389; e-mail information@britishcouncil.nl; www.britishcouncil.nl, can provide information on schools and work prospects in Amsterdam.

AU PAIRS

Despite the fact that the state provides excellent day care facilities for working mothers, the demand for au pairs seems to be growing, so that an increasing number of agencies make placements in the Netherlands.

Au pairs in Holland usually enjoy favourable working conditions, especially now that the Netherlands Au Pair Organisation or NAPO (www.napoweb.nl) has been established. As the Dutch chapter of IAPA, NAPO members strive to implement uniform standards, in conjunction with the government. For example the maximum number of hours an au pair can work is 30 per week. More than that, the person counts as a paid employee who has to pay taxes and social security contributions.

In 1999 the major au pair organisation Au Pair Discover Holland merged with *Travel Active Au Pair* (PO Box 107, 5800 AC Venray, Netherlands; ☎478-551900; fax 478-511911; e-mail info@travelactive.nl; www.travelactive.nl) which now runs a large inbound au pair programme as well as an international Work, Study Language and Exchange programmes. Another major agency is *S-Au Pair Intermediate* (Hinthamerstraat 34, 5211 MP 's-Hertogenbosch; ☎(0)73-614 9483; fax (0)73-691 0889; e-mail info@saupair.com; www.saupair.com).

Two good sources of links for au pairs are the webpages http://aupair.pagina.nl and 'Aussies in Holland' at www.coolabah.com/oz/hollandsite/employment.html. Among other agencies to try are:

Activity International, PO Box 694, 7500 Enschede, Netherlands; ☎53-483 10 40; fax 53-483 10 49; e-mail info@activity.aupair.nl; www.activity.aupair.nl.

Au Pair Interactive, Frans Halslaan 5, 1412 HS Naarden, Netherlands; ☎35-632 1190; fax 35-632 1191; e-mail info@aupairinteractive.com; www.aupairinteractive.com.

Happy Family Aupairs, Rotterdamse Rijweg 9, 3043 BE Rotterdam, Netherlands; ☎10-478 1470; fax 10-476 0186; e-mail: info@happyfamilyaupairs.nl; www.happyfamilyaupairs.nl.

House-O-Orange Au Pairs, Oostduinlaan 115, 2596 JJ The Hague, Netherlands; ☎70-324 5903; fax: 70-324 5913; e-mail house-o-orange@planet.nl; www.house-o-orange.nl.

Mondial/Kryspol Aupair Agencies, van Neijenrodeweg 731, 1082 JE Amsterdam, Netherlands; ☎20-645 8780; fax 84-213 7435; e-mail: info@aupair-agency.nl; www.aupair-agency.nl.

VOLUNTARY WORK

Archaeological and building restoration camps are arranged by *Nederalndse Jeugdbond voor Geschiedenis (NJBG)* (Prins Willem Alexanderhof 5, 2595 BE The Hague; ☎70-347 6598; fax 70-335 2536; www.njbg.nl. There are also numerous work camps affiliated to SCI-IVS (see *Voluntary Work* chapter); the registration fee for most Dutch work camps is about 100 guilders.

INTERNATIONAL COMPANIES IN THE NETHERLANDS

AT&T Network Systems   10
Postbus 1168
1200 BD Hilversum

Bank of America NA   4
Herengracht 469
1017 BS Amsterdam

Barclays Bank plc   4
Strawinskylaan 1353
1077 Amsterdam

BP Nederland BV   35
Westblaak 163
3012 KJ Rotterdam

Deloitte   1
Postbus 58110
1040 HC Amsterdam

Delta Lloyd Levensverzekering   23
Spaklerweg 4
Postbus 1000
BA Amsterdam

Dow Benelux   8
Herbert Dowweg 5
4542 NM Hoek

Ernst & Young Consulting   1
Drentestraat 20
1083 HK Amsterdam

Glaxo Smithkline BV   16
Postbus 780
3700 AT Zeist

Hamworthy Marine   39
Aploniastraat 33,
3084 CC Rotterdam

Hewlett-Packard Nederland   10
Postbus 667
1180 AR Amstelveen

Honeywell BV   10
Postbus 12683
1100 AR Amsterdam

ICL Nederland BV   10
Postbus 4000
NI-3600 KA Maarssen

Interbrew Nederland   16
Ceresstraat 13
Postbus 3212
4800 MA Breda

KPMG Management Services BV   4
Churchillplein 6
2517 JW Den Haag

Kvaerner John Brown Engineering   6
Houtsingel 5
2719 EA Zoetermeer

Lloyds Bank-TSB Bank plc   4
Gatwickstraat 17-19,
1043 GL Amsterdam

Logica BV   10
Wijnhaven 69
Postbus 22067
3003 DB Rotterdam

McCain Foods Holland   16
Postbus 43
2130 AA Hoofddorp

Mobil Oil BV   35
Graaf Engelbertlaan 75
4837 DS Breda

Oracle Nederland   10
Postbus 147
3453 ZJ De Meern

PA Consulting Group   34
Postbus 1043
3430 BA Nieuwegein

Pfizer BV   8
Postbus 37
2900 Capelle a/d Ijssel

Price Waterhouse Coopers NV   1
Prins Bernhardplein 200
1097 JB Amsterdam

Reuters Nederland BV Drentestraat 11 1083 HK Amsterdam	38	Smiths Foods Group Postbus 4 4940 AA Raamsdonksveer	16
Siemens Nederland Postbus 16068 2500 BB Den Haag	45	Sun Microsystems Postbus 1270 3800 BG Amersfoort	10
Shell International Petroleum Carel van Bylandtlaan 30 PO Box 162 2501 AN The Hague	35	Unilever NV Postbus 760 3000 DK Rotterdam	8

The Netherlands-American Trade Directory offers a complete picture of the American presence in the Netherlands and the Dutch presence in the United States. It is available from the *American Chamber of Commerce in the Netherlands*, WTC D-Tower, 6th Floor, Schiphol Boulevard 171, 1118 BG Luchthaven Schiphol; ☎020-795 1840; fax 020-795 1850; www.amcham.nl. *The Delft-The Hague Chamber of Commerce and Industry*, Postbus 29718, 2502 LS The Hague; ☎70-328 71 00, can also provide information about international companies in the Netherlands.

The Netherlands-British Chamber of Commerce publishes a detailed list of its members, the *Members Register* and *Anglo-Dutch Trade Directory* including British subsidiaries operating in the Netherlands, obtainable from the NBCC (☎020-7539 7960; www.nbcc. co.uk) for £25 including postage.

Norway

- **Royal Norwegian Embassy,** 25 Belgrave Square, London SW1X 8QD; ☎020-7591 5500; fax 020-7245 6993; www.norway.org.uk
- **Royal Norwegian Embassy,** 2720 34th Street NW, Washington DC 20008; ☎202-333 6000; fax 202-337 0870; www.norway.org/embassy
- **Currency:** 1 Norwegian Krone (NKr) = 100 øre
- **Rate of Exchange:** £1 = NKr 11.6; $1 = NKr 6.3; €1 = NKr 8
- **Country Code:** +47

Norway has one of the highest per capita incomes in Europe, and a correspondingly high standard of living. The nation's wealth largely stems from the vast oil and gas reserves beneath the continental shelf in the North Sea (which it shares to a large extent with Britain). It is a country of high mountains and fjords, which extend far into the Arctic Circle. Norway covers a total area of 324,000 square miles (839,156 sq km) and is 69 per cent mountain and wasteland, 27 per cent forest, and three per cent cultivated. Its population is only 4.3 million and 480,000 or so live in its largest city, and capital, Oslo. Fishing is on the decline but there are a large number of fish farms, making Norway the world's largest exporter of salmon and the country maintains a large merchant fleet. Recent years have seen the establishment of advanced technological industries.

Norway is cold in winter and can be hot in summer. The climate of coastal areas is moderated by the Gulf Stream. The people can appear to be rather reserved and tend to dress formally in a work or business environment. Punctuality is an important Norwegian virtue. There are restaurants, discotheques and clubs where folk music is played in Oslo and cities like Bergen, Stavanger and Trondheim. Fishing and skiing are popular pastimes; swimming is possible in the summer months in its coastal and inland waters. English is widely spoken. Norway is a member of the European Economic Area (EEA) but not the EU; what this means in practice is that EU jobseekers have much the same rights as in other European Union countries.

FACTORS INFLUENCING EMPLOYMENT

IMMIGRATION

Canadian and US citizens, and EU nationals, may remain in Scandinavia (including Norway) for up to 90 days without a visa. If they wish to stay longer EU nationals must apply to the police for a residence permit (*oppholdstillatelse*) but they do not require a work permit. North Americans must obtain work permits in all cases. Generally, workers from outside the EEA are subject to the following conditions: initial work permits will only be granted for a specific job with a specific employer at a specific place; applications for work permits must be filed in the applicant's native country or country of permanent residence; the employer must file a definite job offer on the approved form; and the employer must provide or arrange suitable accommodation for at least a year; applicants must be physically fit and literate in their native language and in Norwegian, for certain types of work. The Norwegian Embassy in your home country can provide more detailed information.

LANGUAGE

There are two official forms of Norwegian in use: the older *Bokmaal*, which is the principal language, and the newer *Nynorsk* (Neo-Norwegian), based on Norwegian dialects and developed following Norwegian independence from Denmark in 1814. Lappish is spoken by the Sami people in the north.

EMBASSIES AND CONSULATES

British Embassy, Thomas Heftyesgate 8, 0264 Oslo; ☎23-132700; fax 23-132727; www. britain.no.
There are also consulates in Alesund, Bergen, Bodes, Kristiansand, Stavanger, Tromsø and Trondheim.
US Embassy, Henrik Ibsens Gate 48, 0244 Oslo; ☎22-448550; www.usa.no.

TOURIST OFFICES

Norwegian Tourist Board, Charles House, 5-11 Lower Regent Street, London SW1Y 4LR; ☎020-7839 6255; www.visitnorway.com.
Scandinavian Tourist Board, 18th Floor, 655 Third Avenue, New York, NY 10017; ☎212-949 2333; www.visitnorway.com.

NEWSPAPERS

Oslo's leading daily is *Verdens Gang*. *Dagbladet*, the second most popular, is represented by Crane Media Partners, 20-28 Dalling Road, London W6 0JB; ☎020-8237 8601.
Vacancies for teachers, engineers, lawyers, are advertised daily in *Norsk Lysingblad*, Postboks 177, 8501 Narvik, which can be ordered by international subscription.
Engineers and other technical staff can place advertisements in *Teknisk Ukeblad*, Postboks 2476 Solli, N-0202 Oslo 2.

SPECIFIC CONTACTS

EMPLOYMENT SERVICE

The Europa Service of the *Arbeidsformidlingen* (Employment Service), Euroadviser, Øvre Slottsgate 11, Postboks 360 Sentrum, 0101 Oslo; ☎22-728800; fax 22-862301; e-mail aetat.jobservice.oslo@aetat.no; www.aetat.no, provides free advice on regulations for EEA nationals seeking work – working and living conditions in Norway, job vacancies and unemployment benefit. The Employment Service operates a Green Line, or free telephone service (☎800 33 166) providing information on vacancies throughout Norway. Other Employment Service offices can be found in the Yellow Pages. Oslo has a Use It office (Ungdomsinformasjonen), which can help with finding accommodation and work for young visitors. *Use It* is located at Møllergata 3, 0179, Oslo; ☎24-149820; fax 24-149821; e-mail mail@ung.info; www.unginfo.oslo.no.
Private temping and recruitment agencies can be found at www.gulesider.no (search for "vikarbyra").
There are more contacts and addresses, and information about living and working in Norway, in *Live and Work in Scandinavia* published by Vacation Work Publications.

NURSES

Under the ICN (International Council of Nurses) Nursing Abroad Scheme, the *Royal College of Nursing*, 20 Cavendish Square, London W1G 0RN; ☎0845-772 6100; www. rcn.org.uk, can arrange employment in Norway for RCN members only.
There is a general shortage of nurses in Norway, as many Norwegian nurses prefer

to work part-time. Other medical professionals currently in demand are anaesthetists, radiologists, paediatricians and psychiatrists. The Norwegian Medical Association (*Den norske laegeforening*) is at Postboks 1152 Sentrum, 0107 Oslo; ☎2310 9000; fax 2310 9010; e-mail legeforeningen@legeforeningen.no; www.legeforeningen.no.

OIL AND GAS EXPLORATION

Norway is among the world's top half-dozen oil and gas producers and there is a high demand for skilled personnel in the Norwegian oil industry, centred on Stavanger. Applications may be made through recruitment agencies listed in the *Oil and Gas, Mining and Engineering* chapter. The Norwegian state oil company, *Statoil*, has an office at Statoil House, 11a Regent Street, London SW1Y 4ST; ☎020-7766 7777; fax 020-7766 7862; e-mail statuk@statoil.com; www.statoil.co.uk. Addresses of other oil companies are given below under *Opportunities for US citizens* and *British Companies in Norway*.

TEACHING

The need for English teachers is limited because most Norwegians are taught the language very well at school. Most language schools rely on a pool of native speakers already resident in Norway and any jobs that are available are for part-time work and do not offer accommodation. Occasional TEFL work can be found through word of mouth or notice board adverts, but it would be asking for trouble to go to Norway planning to support yourself by this means alone.

SHORT TERM WORK

Paid temporary work has become difficult to obtain in recent years. The decline of the Norwegian fishing industry means that there is no likelihood of finding work in fish factories. Nonetheless, people who plan ahead may still be able to obtain well-paid casual work. When accepting a job, remember that the cost of living is very high, and check whether food and accommodation are provided.

There are many private employment agencies (like Manpower, Top Temp, and Norsk Personnel) in the main cities; look up *vikartjenester* or *vikarbyråer* in the Yellow Pages for contacts. Classifieds also appear for all kinds of temporary work in the daily newspaper *Aften Posten*.

THE WORKING GUEST PROGRAMME

Altantis Youth Exchange (Radhusgt 4, 0151 Oslo; tel/fax 2247 7179; e-mail atlantis@ atlantis.no; www.atlantis-u.no) runs a Working Guest Programme which allows people aged between 18 and 30 of any nationality to spend one to six months in rural Norway. Americans are limited to a maximum stay of three months. Applicants must speak English. Farm guests receive full board and lodging plus pocket money of at least kr825 per week for a maximum of 35 hours work. There is a registration fee of kr1,300 for stays of up to three months, and kr2,500 for longer stays. Atlantis was established in 1987 by the Norwegian Youth Council to promote international understanding and youth exchanges.

SEASONAL WORK

Norway's tourist hotels need a number of English-speaking staff over the summer. The greatest concentration of hotels can be found along the south coast around Kristiansand, and inland along the fjords north of Bergen. *The Directory of Summer Jobs Abroad* (Vacation Work Publications) lists many hotels which recruit English-speaking staff.

In the winter months, work is sometimes available in resorts like Lillehammer, Nordseter, Susjoen, Gausdal or Voss. A few UK tour operators, such as Inghams, hire staff for the holiday season in Norway.

OPPORTUNITIES FOR US CITIZENS

It is worth knowing that workers on oil rigs and those looking for summer work can apply for a work permit from within Norway. You could try contacting the companies listed below:

BP Amoco Norge, PB 197, Forus, 4065 Stavanger.
Enterprise Oil Norge, Løkkev. 103, 4007 Stavanger.
Esso Norge AS, Drammensveien 149, 0277 Oslo.
Exxon Mobil, PO Box 66 Forus, 4064 Stavanger.
Jotun AS, Hystadveien 167, 3235 Sandefjord.
Kvaerner Oil & Gas Field Development, Professor Kohtsvei 5, 1326 Lysaker.
Norsk Hydro ASA, Bygdøy Allé 2, 0257 Oslo.
A/S Norske Shell, Risavikvegen 180, 4098 Tananger.
Statoil ASA, 4025 Stavanger.

INTERNATIONAL COMPANIES IN NORWAY

Aker Offshore Construction 35
Postboks 589
4001 Stavanger

Avesta Sheffield 39
Postboks 6305
Etterstad
0604 Oslo

British Airways 3
PB 1293
0111 Oslo

Castrol Norge A/S 35
Drammensveien 167
0212 Oslo 2

Corus Norge A/S 28
PO Box 13
Skøyen
0212 Oslo

Deloitte Touche Tohmatsu 14
Postboks 347
0213 Oslo

DHL International A/S 17
Strømsviein 195
0668 Oslo

Gillette Group Norge A/S 11
Postboks 79
0611 Oslo

Glaxo Wellcome A/S 8
Sandakerv. 114A
0484 Oslo

ICL Norge A/S 10
Postboks 4285
0401 Oslo

International Lighting Systems 10
Drammensveien 130
0277 Oslo

KPMG A/S 14
Postboks 150
Bryn
0611 Oslo

Mobil Exploration Norway Inc 35
Postboks 510
4001 Stavanger

Portugal

- **Year of EU Accession:** 1986
- **Portuguese Embassy,** 11 Belgrave Square, London SW1X 8PP; ☎020-7235 5331; fax 020-7245 1287; e-mail london@portembassy.co.uk
- **Portuguese Embassy,** 2125 Kalorama Road, NW, Washington, D.C. 20008; ☎202-328 8610; fax 202-462 3726
- **Currency:** 1 Euro (€) = 100 cents
- **Exchange Rate:** £1 = €1.44; $1 = €0.78
- **Country Code:** +351

Portugal, with a population of 10.6 million, has been an independent state since the 12th century when the first King of Portugal fought his way down the coast and extended his tiny kingdom of Portuçale. It covers an area of 36,390 square miles (94,249 sq km) and includes two archipelagos in the Atlantic Ocean: the Azores and Madeira. Portugal is divided into several provinces and has a traditionally agrarian economy that has industrialised extensively in recent years, but remains less developed in the south. There are major infrastructure projects in place to improve the road network, and the metro in the capital Lisbon. Portugal has friendly ties and links with Britain that go back to the Middle Ages. Port wine is named after the country, and Madeira (from the island) is another of its famous varieties. Wine production continues to be important today – as is agriculture – but there is a much bigger industrial sector which is dominated by textiles. English is not widely spoken except among those who have dealings with English-speaking people. The Portuguese are Roman Catholics and religion plays an important part in national life, especially in rural areas. The southern coast, the Algarve, is a prime tourist destination, and has a large, mainly British, expatriate community.

Throughout the 1990s, Portugal's economy was one of the fastest growing in Europe, with a rate of employment lower than the EU average. The best chances of finding work are in the tourism and hospitality industries.

FACTORS INFLUENCING EMPLOYMENT

IMMIGRATION

Portugal is a full member of the EU, and EU citizens do not require work permits. If you intend to work for more than three months you should apply for a residence permit, an *Autorizacâõ de Residência* and will also need to apply for an identity card (*Bilhete de identidad*). Application forms are available at British consulates (see below). A leaflet entitled *Some Hints on Taking Up Residence and Living Conditions in Portugal* is available from The British Embassy in Lisbon (see below).

US citizens may remain in Portugal for up to 60 days without a visa. Work permits must be obtained before entering the country; and after arrival the contract of employment and documents, including a medical certificate, must be taken to the *Servicô de Estrangeiros e Fronteiras,* Rua Conselheiro Jose Silvestre Ribeiro 4, 1549-007 Lisbon; ☎217-115000; fax 217-140332; e-mail sef@sef.pt; www.sef.pt. Other offices are located in Coimbra, Faro, Madeira, the Azores and Porto. For a full list of local offices visit www.sef.pt/contactos.htm.

HEALTH AND WELFARE

The national health system is run by the *Ministério de Saúde*. UK visitors are advised to take their EHIC and E101 forms and others not paying national insurance contributions in the country are advised to take out private medical insurance. Social security benefits cover healthcare, pensions, sickness, unemployment, and maternity/paternity benefits. The local offices for such matters are the regional social security offices, *Centros Regionais de Segurancâ Social (CRSS)*.

TAXES

If you pay income tax you will need a fiscal number (*Cartaõ de Contribuinte*) obtainable at the local tax office on presentation of your passport. In addition to income tax, there is also a local municipal tax (*IMI*) – details of which are available at the town hall (*câmera municipal*).

EMBASSIES AND CONSULATES

British Embassy, 33 Rua de Saõ Bernardo, 1249-082 Lisbon; ☎21-392-4000; fax 21-392 4185; www.uk-embassy.pt.
There are also British Consulates in Oporto, Madeira, the Azores and Portimaõ.
US Embassy, Avenida das Forças Armadas, 1600-081 Lisbon; ☎21-727 3300; fax 21-726 9109; www.american-embassy.pt.
There is also a US Consulate in the Azores.

TOURIST OFFICES

ICEP Portuguese Trade and Tourism, 2nd Floor, 22 Sackville Street, London W1S 3LY; ☎020-7494 1517; www.visitportugal.com.
Portuguese Tourist Office, 590 Fifth Ave, 4th Floor, New York, NY 10036; ☎212-354-4403; www.portugal.org

SPECIFIC CONTACTS

The major industries in the Portuguese economy are textiles, pottery, shipbuilding, oil products, paper, glassware and tourism. Portugal is also the world leader in cork production (in Alentejo). The Portuguese economy has grown rapidly since EU accession, although salaries are comparatively low. TEFL teachers are paid more than the locals. Portuguese enterprises traditionally do not hire foreign workers and the most likely job openings are in tourism and teaching, or in infrastructure projects.

All state-run employment centres in Portugal are administered by the *Ministerio do Emprego e Sugurança Social*, (Rua das Picoas 14, 1069-003 Lisbon; ☎213-307400). There are *Centros Emprego* in Faro, Lisbon, Porto, Evora and Coimbra; about 84 nationwide.

Employment agencies are listed in the *Paginas Amarelas* under *Pessoal Temporário* (Temporary Personnel) and *Pessoal – Recrutamento e Selecção* (Personnel Recruitment and Selection). The majority are based in Lisbon and Porto although some of the larger chains have offices all over Portugal. For example, *Manpower* (head office: Rua Jose Fontana 9C, 1050 Lisbon; ☎213-129830; fax 213-129849; www.manpower.pt), Adecco (head office: Av. Duque de Loulé, 47A, 1069-154 Lisboa; ☎213-117700; fax 213-117749; www. adecco.pt), and Randstad (head office: Rua Joshua Benoliel 6, Edificio Alto das Amoreiras, 9ºB/10ºB, 1250-133 Lisboa; ☎213-715250; fax 213-715252; www.randstad.pt) all have offices throughout Portugal. The individual office addresses can be found on their websites.

Other useful websites to try are:
www.iefp.pt: The website of Portugal's national employment institute (*Instituto do Emprego e Formação Profissional*). Website in English currently under construction.

www.jobpilot.co.uk: More than 56,000 vacancies worldwide, searchable by sector, country and language.

www.anyworkanywhere.com: Mostly jobs with tour operators in Portugal.

www.eurojobs.com: Pan-European job-search facility.

www.hays.pt: Portuguese page of Hays recruitment specialists, specialising in jobs in accountancy, IT, telecoms, engineering, construction, logistics, and sales & marketing. English translation available.

http://empregos.online.pt: Portuguese language site claiming to display the most recent job offers in Portugal gathered from numerous recruitment websites.

www.net-empregos.com: Portuguese language site. Allows you to upload your CV and apply for vacancies online.

http://superemprego.sapo.pt: Portuguese language site listing jobs throughout Portugal.

NEWSPAPERS

Job vacancies (e.g. au pair, private English tutors) often appear in the weekly *Anglo-Portuguese News* published on Thursdays in Lisbon (Apartado 113, 2766-902 Estoril; ☎214-661423; fax 214-660358). In the Algarve, these are also to be found in *The News* (Apartado 13, 84021 Lagoa, Algarve; ☎282-341100; fax 282-341201; www.the-news. net). These are both on sale at most news-stands where foreign newspapers are to be found. You can also place job-wanted advertisements in either of these papers.

Portugal has a surprisingly large selection of situations vacant in its national newspapers, e.g. *Diário de Notícias, Público, Journal de Notícias,* and the weekly business and politics magazine *Expresso* (Jobs are listed under *Emprego* – employment). *Expresso,* published on Saturdays, is the most important newspaper for specialist and management vacancies – the job supplement, *Expresso Emprego,* contains up to twenty pages of quality jobs. Amongst the daily newspapers, the Lisbon-based daily, *Diário de Notícias,* carries the most vacancies, especially on Sundays. The more popular morning daily, *Correio da Manhã,* which is widely read in the south, also carries job advertisements, mainly for skilled and unskilled staff in the services. The *Jornal de Notícias* carries jobs primarily for Porto and the northern region. The monthly publication, *Exame,* is also a useful resource as it provides employer information and a good background to business in Portugal.

Portuguese newspapers will probably have to be consulted on the spot as they are not easily obtainable outside Portugal but may be available in some London newsagents, in specialised libraries, e.g. university and business libraries, and in the Canning House library in London (2 Belgrave Square, London SW1X 8PJ). Alternatively you may consult their online editions: www.correiomanha.ot; www.dn.pt; www.diárioeconomico.com; http://online.expresso.pt; www.jnotícias.pt; www.publico.pt.

TOURISM

Tourism in Portugal employs around 6.5% of the active population and produces 8% of the country's GDP. Chances of finding work are best with tour operators or in hotels, restaurants and clubs along the Algarve coast. Portugal had a bonanza year in 2004, mainly due to Euro 2004, which took place across eight cities and created a range of employment opportunities for job-seekers. The resulting boost to the economy and to Portugal's prestige as a tourist destination, has meant that many of these opportunities did not end when the tournament did. However, the Portuguese are protective of their tourist industry and this has been formalised in law. For example foreign tour managers in charge of a coach must ensure that they pick up an official Portuguese guide at major tourist venues.

The mass-market beach resort operators (e.g. *Thomson, MyTravel, CT2* and *First Choice)* employ reps in Portugal. *Style Holidays* and *Open Holidays* both employ resort reps every year to work between April and October. Part-season short-term contracts may also be available. First Choice have about 100 staff in place who speak another language (not necessarily Portuguese). Apart from these and some of the Europe-wide tour operators like *Driveline Europe, Erna Low, Headwater* and *Solo's,* many of the tour operators that feature Portugal are specialists. The founders of the well-known Travel Club of Upminster (54 Station Road, Upminster, Essex RM14 2TT; ☎01708-225000; www.travelclubofupminster.co.uk) virtually started tourism to Portugal from the UK when they fell in love with the country after the war. Occasionally they may need staff, but only if they can speak Portuguese. For links to UK tour operators to Portugal see the website of the Portuguese Trade & Tourism Office (www.portugalinsite.com).

Try the following tour operators:

Bonaventure Holidays, 6 Putney Common, London SW15 1HL (www.bonaventure-holidays.com).

Casas Cantabricas, 31 Arbury Road, Cambridge CB4 2JB (☎01223-328721; www.casas.co.uk).

CV Travel's Mediterranean World, The Manor Stables, West St, Great Somerford, Chippenham, Wilts. SN15 5EH (☎020-7581 0851; www.cvtravel.net).

Individual Travellers (Spain & Portugal), Manor Courtyard, Bignor, Pulborough, West Sussex RH20 1QD (☎01798-869485; e-mail portugal@indiv-travellers.com).

North Portugal Travel, Foxhill, Gambles Lane, Woodmancote, Cheltenham, Glos. GL52 4PU (☎01242-679867; www.northportugal.com).

Bike Riders: PO Box 130254, Boston, MA 02113, USA; ☎617-723-2354; fax 617-723-2355; e-mail info@bikeriderstours.com; www.bikeriderstours.com. Bicycle tour holidays in Portugal. Recruit 20 tour guides for April to October.

CV Travel: 43 Cadogan St., London SW3 2PR; ☎020-7591 2800; fax 020-7591 2802; e-mail cv@cvtravel.net; www.cvtravel.net. Upmarket villa holiday company. Require overseas reps for the summer season.

Open Holidays: The Guildbourne Centre, Chapel Road, Worthing BN11 1LZ; ☎01903-201864; fax 01903-201225; e-mail recruitment@openholidays.co.uk; www.openholidays.co.uk. Villa and apartment holidays. Reps required March to October.

Scott Dunn: Fovant Mews, 12 Noyna Road, London SW17 7PH; ☎020-8682 5005; fax 020-8682 5090; e-mail recruitment@scottdunn.com; www.scottdunn.com. Require summer resort managers, chefs, hosts, nannies etc.

Style Holidays: Coomb House, 7 St. John's Road, Isleworth, Middlesex TW7 6NH; ☎0870-442 3653; www.style-holidays.co.uk. Resort holidays in the Algarve and Madeira. Reps required April to October.

Travelsphere Ltd.: Compass House, Rockingham Road, Market Harborough, Leics LE16 7QD; ☎01858-410456; www.travelspehere.co.uk. Major coach tour operator. Require tour managers.

TEACHING

The vast majority of British tourists flock to the Algarve along the southern coast of Portugal, which means that many Portuguese in the south who aspire to work in the tourist industry want to learn English. Schools like the *Centro de Linguas* in Lagos and *Interlingua* in Portimao cater for just that market. But the demand for English teachers is greatest in the north. Apart from in the main cities of Lisbon and Porto, both of which have British Council offices, jobs crop up in historic provincial centres such as Coimbra (where there is also a British Council) and Braga and in small seaside towns like Aveiro and Póvoa do Varzim. These can be a very welcome destination for teachers burned out from teaching in big cities or first-time teachers who want to avoid the rat-race. The British Council (www.britishcouncil.org/portugal) has English language centres in a number of towns,: Almada, Alverca, Cascais (the prosperous seaside suburb of Lisbon), Coimbra, Foz do Douro, Maia, Miraflores and Parede.

Most teachers in Portugal have either answered adverts in the educational press or are working for International House which has nine affiliated schools in Portugal. About three-quarters of all IH students in Portugal are children, so expertise with young learners is a definite asset. Outside the cities where there have traditionally been large expatriate communities, schools cannot depend on English speakers just showing up and so must recruit well in advance of the academic year (late September to the end of June).

The *Bristol School Group* offers the only possibility for working in the Azores, so if you want to work in the most isolated islands in the Atlantic Ocean – over 1,000km west of Portugal – this is your chance. Small groups of schools, say six schools in a single region, is the norm in Portugal. A number of the schools listed below belong to such mini-chains. One of the most well-established is the *Cambridge Schools* group which every year imports up to 100 teachers.

As is true anywhere, you might be lucky and fix up something on the spot. In addition to calling at the British Council, check the English language weekly newspaper *Anglo-Portuguese News* which occasionally carries adverts for private tutors.

The Cambridge CELTA is widely requested by schools and can be obtained at International House in Lisbon (or part-time in Porto).

The consensus seems to be that wages are low, but have been improving at a favourable rate in view of the cost of living which is also low. Working conditions are generally relaxed. The normal salary range is €700-€1,000 net per month. Full-time contract workers are entitled to an extra month's pay after 12 months, which is partly why most teachers are employed on 9/10 month contracts. Some schools pay lower rates but subsidise or pay for flights and accommodation. Teachers being paid on an hourly basis should expect to earn €10-€15, but they will of course not be eligible for the thirteenth month bonus or paid holidays.

Below is a list of schools worth approaching:

American Language Institute Lisbon: Av. Duque de Loulé 22-1°, 1050-090 Lisbon; ☎213-152535; fax: 213-524848; e-mail ali@netcabo.pt; www.americanlanguageinstitute. com.

Bristol Schools Group: Instituto de Línguas da Maia, Trav. Dr. Carlos Pires Felgueiras, 12-3°, 4470-158 Maia; ☎229-488803; fax: 229-486460; e-mail bsmaia@bristolschool.pt; www.bristolschool.pt. Group of 9 small schools in Porto, inland and in the Azores.

Cambridge School: Avenida da Liberdade 173, 1250-141 Lisbon; ☎213-124600; fax: 213-534729; e-mail info@cambridge.pt; www.cambridge.pt. Portugal's largest private language school with 8 centres in Lisbon and other major cities.

CIAL – Centro De Linguas: Avenida Republica 14-2, 1050-191 Lisbon; ☎213-533733; fax: 213-523096; e-mail linguas.estrangeiras@cial.pt; www.cial.pt.

Instituto Britanico de Braga: Rua Conselheiro Januario 119-123, Apartado 2682, 4701-908 Braga; ☎253-263298; fax 253-619355; e-mail efl.IBB@mail.telepac.pt; www.alb-minho.pt.

International House (Lisbon): Rua Marquês Sá da Bandeira 16, 1050-148 Lisbon; ☎213-151493/4/6; fax 213-530081; e-mail info@ihlisbon.com; www.international-house. com.

International House (Porto): Rua Marechal Saldanha 145-1°, 4150-655 Porto; ☎226-177641; e-mail info@ihporto.org; www.ihporto.org. Also Leça da Pal , Rua Oliveira Lessa 350, 4450 Matosinhos; ☎229-959087.

Lancaster College: Praceta 25 de Abril 35-1°, 4430 Vila Nova de Gaia; ☎223-772030; fax 223-772039; e-mail info@lancastercollege.pt; www.lancastercollege.pt. Also at Covilhã, Estarrega, Santa Maria da Feira, Fafe, Oeiras, Arcozelo, Vizela and Estoril.

Novo Instituto de Linguas: Rua Cordeiro Ferreira, 19C 1°Dto, 1750-071 Lisbon; tel/fax 217-590770; e-mail admin@nil.edu.pt; www.nil.edu.pt.

Oxford School: Rua D. Estefania, 165-1°, 1000-154 Lisbon; ☎213-546586; fax 213-141152. Also: Av. Marques Tomar 104-4°dto, 1050-157 Lisbon. ☎217-966660; fax

217-951293; e-mail oxford-school@mail.telepac.pt. Also Av. Bons Amigos, 37-1° Dto, 2735-077 Cacém; ☎219-146343; www.oxford-school.pt.
Royal School Of Languages – Escolas de Linguas, Lda.: Rua José Rabumba 2, 3810-125 Aveiro. ☎234-429156/425104; fax 234-382870; e-mail rsl@royalschooloflanguages. pt; www.royalschooloflanguages.pt. Schools also in Porto, Agueda, Guarda, Ovar, Viseu, Mirandela, Macedo de Cavaleiros, Iihavo and Albergaria-a-Velha.
Speakwell Escola de Linguas: Praça Mário Azevedo Gomes, N° 421, 2775-240 Parede. ☎214-561771; fax 214-561775; e-mail speakwell@speakwell.pt; www.speakwell.pt.

VOLUNTARY WORK

Portugal's voluntary movement is still in its infancy – its development stunted by the fact that Portugal spent most of the twentieth century under a fascist dictatorship. However the voluntary sector is growing and widening in scope, finally moving away from a reliance on parochial and inward-looking organisations. Recent years have seen a definite increase in the number of associations and voluntary work organisations, especially those involved in youth work. This is at least in part thanks to the state-supported *Instituto Portugues da Juventud - IPJ*, (Av. da Liberdade No. 194, 1269-051 Lisbon; ☎213-179200; http://juventude.gov.pt) which was established in the 1990s in order to promote voluntary work amongst young people, and which overseas a programme of heritage protection and other short-term voluntary projects. Information detailing IPJ voluntary programmes can be found at www.voluntariadojovem.pt. EU programmes such as the European Voluntary Service have also played a role in stimulating Portugal's development in this area.

There is certainly a need for voluntary programmes within Portugal – one in five people still lives beneath the EU's poverty line. Those who have the resources to involve themselves in voluntary projects will find that they are welcomed, especially if they can offer a particular skill, and speak adequate Portuguese. Bear in mind however that many of these organisations remain under-funded and often unprofessional. Nevertheless, big business has started to become involved in donating money to help fund solidarity programmes and some well-known NGOs such as Amnesty International run programmes in Portugal. Those interested in Portuguese NGOs should visit the website of *Plataforma Portuguesa das Organizações Não Governamentais para o Desenvolvimento* (www. plataformaongd.pt) which lists around fifty NGOs, mainly based in Lisbon. Unfortunately the website is only available in Portuguese.

The following organisations are worth a try:
Associação Abraço: Rua da Rosa 243, 1°, 1200-385 Lisbon; ☎213-425929; http://abraco. esoterica.pt. A non-profit, charitable association involved with HIV/AIDS. Always recruiting volunteers for fund-raising, information dissemination, and personal care.
Aldeias Internacionais de Crianças: Rua Anchieta 29-4°, 1200 Lisbon; ☎213-477647. Charitable organisation offering a home for disadvantaged and abandoned children.
Amnistia Internacional: 13, 1° Andar, 1070-128 Lisbon; ☎213-861664; fax 213-861782; www.amnistia-internacional.pt. Worldwide campaigners for human rights. May well need volunteers.
Banco Alimentar Contra o Fome: Estação de CP de Alcântara Terra/Armazem 1, Avenida de Cueta, 1300-125 Lisbon; ☎213-649655 (Lisbon); ☎229-983140 (Porto). Institution devoted to redistributing food to the needy. Often looking for volunteers.
Fundação AMI: R. José do Patrocínio 49, 1949-008 Lisbon; ☎218-362100; fax 218-362199; www.fundacao-ami.org. Non-governmental international medical assistance organisation based in Portugal that runs a number of volunteer programmes.
OIKOS – Cooperação e Desenvolvimento: Rua de Santiago n°9, 1100-493 Lisbon; ☎218-823630; fax 218-823635; www.oikos.pt. NGO that runs voluntary projects fighting poverty and inequality.

Portuguese Association for Victim Support (APAV): Rua do Comércio 65-5°, 1100-150 Lisbon; ☎218-854090; fax 218-876351; www.apav.pt. Charity that provides confidential and free services and social support to victims of crime throughout Portugal.

Quinta das Abelhas: e-mail abelhas@pureportugal.co.uk; www.pureportugal.co.uk/abelhas. Alternative lifestyle/organic farming/low-impact living. Offer free camping and food in return for work.

Rotajovem: Largo do Mercado, 2750-431 Cascais; ☎214-862005; www.rotajovem.com. Youth projects.

OTHER CONTACTS

Chambers of Commerce in Portugal, and the *Portuguese-British Chamber of Commerce*, Rua da Estrela 8, 1200-669 Lisbon; ☎213-942020; fax 213-942029; e-mail info@bpcc.pt; www.bilateral.biz, will not act as employment agencies but may offer general advice on job prospects. They may also know which companies currently have vacancies. Try also the *Portuguese-UK Business Network* (4th Floor, 11 Belgrave Square, London SW1X 8PP; ☎020-7201 6638; fax 020-7201 6637; www.Portuguese-chamber.org.uk).

The *Hispanic and Luso Brazilian Council*, Canning House, 2 Belgrave Square, London SW1X 8PJ; ☎020-7235 2303; fax 020-7235 3587; e-mail enquiries@canninghouse.com; www.canninghouse.com, publishes a well-researched leaflet called *Portugal: A Guide to Employment and Opportunities for Young People* aimed primarily at the younger worker/traveller. The leaflet costs £4 from the above address. Embassies in the UK and US can supply other useful information.

The Vacation Work publication *Live & Work in Portugal* contains detailed information on all aspects of employment in Portugal.

INTERNATIONAL COMPANIES IN PORTUGAL

Agriter, Consultores e Gesto, Agricola Lda 1
Apartado 106
8600 Lagos

Barclays Bank International Ltd 4
Avenida da Republica 50-2nd Floor
1000 Lisbon

Beecham Portoguesa Produtos 11
Rua Sebstio e Silva 56
2745 Queluz

Berec Portoguesa Lda 7
Rua Gonçalves Zarco 6 6/J
1400 Lisbon

Bovis International Ltd. 40
Qta do Lago-Almansil
8100 Loulé
Algarve

BP Portoguesa 8
Praça Marqués de Pombal 13
1200 Lisbon

Cockburn Smithes & Cia Lda 16
Rua Corados 13
4400 Vila Nova de Gaia

Commercial Union Assurance Co Ltd 23
Av da Liberdade 38-4
1200 Lisbon

Companhia de Seguros (Eagle Star) 23
Rua de Outubro 70-6°/8°
1000 Lisbon

De La Rue Systems SA 38
Rua Prof. Fernando Fonseca 26
1600 Lisbon

Deloitte Touche Ross 1
Rua Silva Carvalho 234-4°
1200 Lisbon

DHL International 17
Aeroporto de Lisboa
Rua de Edificio 121 R/C
1700 Lisbon

Ernst & Young 1
Av António Augusto de Aguiar 31-3°
1000 Lisbon

Fastécnica Electrónica e Técnica Ltd 41
(Cable & Wireless)
Praça Prof Santos Andra 5
1500 Lisbon

Glaxo Wellcome Lda 8
Rua Dr. Antonia L. Borges 3
Arquiparque
Algés
1495 Lisbon

Hoover Eléctrica Portuguesa Lda 10
Rua D Estefania 90 A
1000 Lisbon

ICL Computadores Lda 10
Av Duque d'Avila 120
1050 Lisbon

Industrias de Alimentaçao (Heinz) 16
Av da Republica 52-7°
1000 Lisbon

James Rawes & Cia Lda 4
Rua Bernardino Costa 47
1200 Lisbon

Lloyds Bank plc 4
Avenida da Liberdade 222
1200 Lisbon

Lloyd's Register of Shipping 23
Av D Carlos 1, 44-6°
1200 Lisbon

Rank Xerox Portugal Lda 20
Rua Pedro Nunes 16
1058 Lisbon

Reckitt Portuguesa Lda 16
Rua S Sebastio da Pedreira 122-1°
1000 Lisbon

Rover Group Portugal 7
Rua Vasco da Gama
2685 Sacavém

Royal Exchange Assurance 23
Avenida Marquês de Tomar
Apartado 1234
1000 Lisbon

Shell Portuguesa SA 35
Av da Liberdade 249
1250 Lisbon

Taylor Fladgate & Yeatman 16
Rua Choupelo 250
4400 Vila Nova de Gaia

Unilever/Fima Lda 35
Largo Monterroio Mascarenhas 1
1000 Lisbon

Zeneca-Agro 8
Av. D. Carlos I 42-3°
1200 Lisbon

Spain

- o **Year of EU Accession:** 1986
- o **Spanish Embassy,** 39 Chesham Place, London SW1X 8SB; ☎020-7235 5555; fax 020-7259 5392
- o **Spanish Embassy,** 2375 Pennsylvania Avenue NW, Washington, DC 20037; ☎202-452 0100; www.spainemb.org
- o **Currency:** 1 Euro (€) = 100 cents
- o **Exchange Rate:** £1 = €1.44; $1 = €0.78
- o **Country Code:** +34

Spain is a major industrialised country with a strong agricultural sector. Since joining the EU in 1986 it has undergone rapid economic expansion and social change. Unemployment (at about 10 per cent) is high, although inflation is down. The economy and administration have also been reformed in recent years.

Spain used to be a centralised country, but power is being devolved to the regions, among which are Catalonia, the Basque Country and the Canary Islands. Spanish people are welcoming, and are generally international in their outlook. Agriculture remains important, and food and drink, especially wine, are enjoyed and understood. There are many regional delicacies. The evening, as in Italy, often starts with a leisurely stroll (the 'paseo') through the main streets, and dinner is not eaten until around 10pm. Cafés and restaurants are plentiful and cheap. The nightlife in towns, especially in Madrid, Barcelona and the Balearic Islands (Ibiza, Mallorca, and Menorca), is lively for both locals and tourists. Festivals and a general *joie de vivre* are an important part of the Spanish way of life.

Tourism is the biggest employment sector for foreigners, along with English teaching, however, a programme of privatisation means there are also new opportunities for consultants in finance and restructuring. There is expansion in the fields of electronics, information technology and industrial design, but traditional heavy industries (along with agriculture and fishing) are in general decline. The transition to democracy and away from a highly centralised economy has brought prosperity to many.

Spanish is universally spoken, although six regions use and teach their own languages besides Spanish. These languages are Catalan, Galician and Basque. English is widely spoken at a basic level, but a knowledge of Spanish is needed if you intend to do much more than just visit the country.

GENERAL FACTS

POPULATION AND GEOGRAPHY

Spain has an area of 189,950 square miles (491,968 sq km) and a population of around 40 million. Its capital, Madrid, has three million inhabitants. The other major cities are Barcelona (capital of Catalonia, 1.5 million), Valencia (740,000) and Seville (685,000). With the exception of Switzerland, this is the most mountainous country in Europe, with a vast central plateau – on which Madrid is located. The Mediterranean coastal area runs from the French frontier in the northeast down to the Straits of Gibraltar in the south. There are two Spanish enclaves, Ceuta and Melilla, on the North African mainland across the Strait of Gibraltar. Gibraltar is a British enclave in the far south of Spain.

CLIMATE

The climate varies from temperate in the north and the Mediterranean islands to dry and hot in the south, and sub-tropical in the Canary Islands off the west coast of North Africa. Madrid can be very cold in winter.

GOVERNMENT

Spain is a constitutional monarchy with 17 autonomous regions each of which have their own parliaments and presidents (and account for a quarter of all public spending). The Basque country and Catalonia have their own police and tax-raising powers, as well as nationalist movements seeking independence from the rest of Spain.

FACTORS INFLUENCING EMPLOYMENT

IMMIGRATION

EU citizens wishing to work in Spain do not require a work permit or a residence permit (*residencia*). They will however need a foreigner's identification number (NIE) issued by the *Oficina de Extranjeros*, and a social security card in order to work legally.

US citizens can stay in Spain for 90 days without a visa. Work permits must be obtained while outside Spain, and you will need to submit a copy of your contract, medical certificates and authenticated copies of your qualifications in duplicate. Anyone intending to live in Spain needs to acquire this Residence Entry Visa (*visado especial*) from the nearest Spanish consulate-general.

The *Spanish Education, Labour and Social Affairs Office* in London (20 Peel Street, London W8 7PD; ☎020-7727 2462; www.sgci.mec.es/uk) has information on working and health care in Spain.

EMBASSIES AND CONSULATES

British Embassy, Calle de Fernando el Santo 16, 28010 Madrid; ☎91-700 8200; fax 91-700 8272; www.ukinspain.com.
There are consulates in Seville, Alicante, Barcelona, Cadiz, Bilbao, Las Palmas de Gran Canaria, Santa Cruz de Tenerife, Málaga, Ibiza, Palma de Mallorca, Menorca and Vigo.
US Embassy, Serrano 75, 28006 Madrid; ☎91-587 2200; fax 91-587 2303; www.embusa.es. Consulate in Barcelona.

TOURIST OFFICES

Spanish Tourist Office, 22-23 Manchester Square, London W1U 3PX; ☎020-7486 8077; www.tourspain.co.uk.
Spanish Tourist Office, 666 Fifth Avenue, New York, NY 10103; ☎212-265 8822; www.tourspain.es.

EMPLOYMENT PROSPECTS

Career prospects are good for those who are willing to learn Spanish and are prepared to remain in Spain for some time. It has never been easier to set up your own business in Spain; most popular are language schools and enterprises catering for English-speaking expatriates working in tourism. Spain's tourist industry absorbs thousands of foreign workers in temporary and part-time jobs every year, however, there is not a lot of job mobility as employees are required by law to pay compensation to their employer if they break a contract.

Increasingly the trend for job-hunters is to use the internet. Indeed, according to www.jobtoasterspain.com, 124,000 people look for work in Spain via the internet every month.

A wealth of online databases and resources exists, but as is often the case with the internet, some resources are very useful, whereas others are out-of-date or poorly maintained. Some of the best websites are listed below, but it is a necessary evil to trawl the net for new and specialised sites which may be of greater use to your specific circumstances.

www.inem.es: The website of Spain's National Employment Institute (*Instituto Nacional de Empleo*).

www.monster.es: Spanish section of Monster.com with jobs all over Spain.

www.jobpilot.co.uk: More than 56,000 vacancies worldwide, searchable by sector, country and language.

www.jobtoasterspain.com: Site catering specifically for expats. Most jobs are on the Costa del Sol.

www.eurojobs.com: Pan-European job-search facility.

www.infojobs.net: Spanish language site with a range of jobs.

www.trabajo.org: Spanish language site with a range of jobs.

www.bolsadetrabajo.org: Spanish language site with a range of jobs.

www.laboris.net: Spanish language site with a range of jobs.

www.tecnoempleo.com: Spanish language site specialising in IT and telecommunications jobs.

www.excoge.com: Launched by the national Spanish newspaper *El Pais*, - helpful guide for career development.

www.oficinaempleo.com: Spanish language site with a range of jobs.

www.exposure-eu.com: Specialists in searching, selecting and recruiting key business personnel for jobs in Spain and Gibraltar.

www.recruitspain.com: Recruitment consultancy on the Costa del Sol for English-speaking candidates.

www.wemploy.com: Recruitment specialists on the Costa del Sol for English-speaking candidates.

www.balearic-jobs.com: Vacancies for English speaking seasonal workers in the Balearic Islands.

www.britishchamberspain.com: Website of the British Chamber of Commerce in Spain. British companies in Spain often register jobs here and for €25 it is possible to register as a potential candidate.

NEWSPAPERS

There are more than a hundred newspapers published both locally and nationally in Spain and the majority of these carry job advertisements. The most important newspapers, which have distribution throughout Spain and overseas are *El Pais* (www.elpais.es) and *ABC* (www.abc.es), *El Mundo* (www.elmundo.es) in Madrid, and *El Periodico* (www. elperiodico.es) and *La Vanguardia* in Barcelona. All of these newspapers are distributed throughout Spain and may be found in the larger cities and in public libraries in the UK. Job advertisements are usually published in the Sunday supplements, although these papers have a daily section dedicated to positions vacant.

A number of specialist jobseekers publications are also distributed nationally in Spain. These include *El Mercado de Trabajo* (www.mercadodetrabajo.com), which offers over 1,000 temporary and permanent jobs per week plus information on job fairs and training opportunities. It also offers an extensive *demandas de trabajo* or situations wanted column covering everything from lawyers to translators. Another weekly tabloid including many job advertisements is *Laboris*. Finally the Exchange and Mart-style publication *Segundamano* also offers a wide variety of jobs and has the added advantage of being published three times a week.

A job wanted ad can be placed in many Spanish newspapers through the London-based publishers representative, *Powers Turner Group* (Gordon House, Greencoat Place, London

SW1 1PH; ☎020-7592 8300; fax 020-7592 8301; www.publicitas.com/uk) who deal with many Spanish newspapers ranging from the nationally-read *El País* and *La Vanguardia* published in Barcelona to the more obscure regional publications. But they do not deal with any English-language newspapers in Spain, and these will have to be purchased while on a reconnaissance trip or directly from the publishers (or again you can request an inspection copy).

SPECIFIC CONTACTS

EMPLOYMENT SERVICES
The state-run *Instituto Nacional de Empleo (INEM)* is the Spanish equivalent of the UK Jobcentre and it used to be the only employment and recruitment agency which was allowed to operate officially in Spain. Branch offices are pretty evenly distributed throughout Spain and can be found online at www.inem.es or in the telephone directory. The INEM advertises mostly local positions but there are often a few national posts displayed. The offices generally have a good resource library and it is possible to obtain advice on job-hunting from a work counsellor.

Any newly arrived EU citizen has the right to sign on as a jobseeker (*demandante de empleo*) with the INEM. It is no longer necessary to produce a residence card in order to sign on, just a passport.

An *Agencia Privada de Colocación* is a non-profit making organisation and may only charge fees relating to expenses arising from the services provided. These agencies act as an intermediary in the job market. Currently they are highly restricted and kept subordinate to the INEM, although it is likely that the next few years will see a greater liberalisation of private agencies. The INEM keeps a record of all authorised work placement agencies. The majority of them are based in Madrid and – for English speakers – in Málaga and are listed in the Spanish Yellow Pages *(Paginas Amarillas)*. Bear in mind, however, that there is little point in applying for most jobs unless you are bilingual or have specialist skills needed for the job.

Short-term work is available in Spain from numerous *Empresas de Trabajo Temporal*, or ETTs. These are private companies that facilitate temporary employment by contracting workers themselves and then transferring or lending their services to other companies. ETTs often specialise in certain areas such as the hospitality and construction industries. Usually workers are only hired out during periods of great demand, so this kind of work is far from stable. ETTs can be found in the Spanish Yellow Pages or online at www.mtas. es/empleo/ett-OIA/inicio.htm. The Manpower temporary employment agency (www. manpower.co.uk in the UK and www.manpower.com in the US) has twenty or so branch offices in Spain but specifies the following conditions to potential applicants: their Spanish offices deal only in temporary work, they will accept enquiries from within Spain only, and all applicants must have references with them and be able to speak fluent Spanish as their service largely provides office, catering and industrial jobs where communication skills are essential. Other major ETTs in Spain are Adecco (www.adecco.es) and Randstad (www.randstad.es).

TEACHING
Candidates who know that they want to teach in Spain should consider doing their TEFL training with an organisation with strong Spanish links. Better still, do a TEFL training course in Spain. There are many training centres in Spain who can offer positions after the course has finished to their better students, take for example the Advanced Institute (address below), which has centres in Madrid and Barcelona.

For a listing of English language schools in Spain, a good place to start is the Education

Department of the Spanish Embassy (39 Chesham Place, London SW1X 8SB; ☎020-7235 5555; fax 020-7235 9905). As well as sending an outline of Spanish immigration regulations and a one-page handout 'Teaching English as a Foreign Language', it can send a list of the 350 members of FECEI, the national federation of English language schools *(Federación Española de Centros de Enseñanza de Idiomas)*, though they may not always have the most up-to-date list available. FECEI is concerned with maintaining high standards, so its members are committed to providing a high quality of teaching and fair working conditions for teachers. In order to become a member, a school has to undergo a thorough inspection. Therefore FECEI schools represent the elite end of the market and are normally looking for well qualified teachers. FECEI comprises 16 regional associations integrated in ACADE *(Asociación de Centros Autónomos de Enseñanza Privada*, Calle Ferraz 85, 28008 Madrid; ☎902-104080; fax 915-500122; www.acade.es).

Check the TEFL advertisements in the Education section of the *Guardian* every Tuesday, especially in the spring and early summer. Also try the *Independent* on Thursdays and the *Times Educational Supplement* on Fridays, though don't expect more than a sprinkling of international job ads. The monthly *EL Gazette* is also a good source of news and developments in the ELT industry, though it is pitched at the professional end of the market. An employment section, *EL Prospects*, comes free with the gazette, although there are far less advertisements than there used to be. An annual subscription costs £33 in the UK and £44 worldwide. Contact *El Gazette*, Unit 3, Constantine Court, 6 Fairclough Street, London E1 1PW (☎020-7481 6700).

Searching for *Escuela de Idiomas* on www.paginasamarillas.es (Spanish Yellow Pages) will produce lists of schools in the places you search, some with email and internet addresses. Most of the regional British Council offices in Spain maintain lists of language schools in their region apart from Madrid which does not keep a register of schools. The offices in Valencia, Bilbao, Barcelona and Palma de Mallorca also produce useful lists.

Most teaching jobs in Spain are found on the spot. With increasing competition from candidates with the Cambridge or Trinity Certificate (now considered by many language school owners a minimum requirement), it is more and more difficult for the under-qualified to succeed. The best time to look is between the end of the summer holidays and the start of term, normally 1 October. November is also promising, since that is when teachers hand in their notice for a Christmas departure. Since a considerable number of teachers do not return to their jobs after the Christmas break and schools are often left in the lurch, early January is also possible.

Salaries are not high in Spain and have not increased significantly over the past decade. A further problem for teachers in Madrid and Barcelona is that there is not much difference between salaries in the big cities where the cost of living has escalated enormously and salaries in the small towns. The minimum net salary is about €800 per month, though most schools offer €850-€950 after deductions for 25 hours of teaching a week. A standard hourly wage would be €10. The very best paid hourly wages, say €20, are paid by centres specialising in sending teachers out to firms or those teaching short courses which are funded by the European Union.

Try the following schools:

Advanced Institute: Fernandez de Los Rios 75, 28015 Madrid; ☎915-431992; fax 915-431992; e-mail tefljobs@terra.es.

British Council: Pº General Martínez Campos 31, 28010 Madrid; ☎913-373500; fax 913-373573; e-mail madrid@britishcouncil.es; www.britishcouncil.es.

EF Education: C/Balmes 150, 2º-6a, 08008 Barcelona; ☎934-159424; fax 934-154411; www.ef.com.

Escuelas de Idiomas Berlitz de España: Gran Via 80-4º, 28013 Madrid; ☎915-425466; fax 915-590998; e-mail milagros.santos@berlitz.es; www.berlitz.es.

English Educational Services: Alcalá 20-2º, 28014 Madrid; ☎915-329734; fax 915-

315298; e-mail movingparts@wanadoo.es.
Inlingua: P° General Martinez Campos 20, 28010 Madrid; ☎914-451984; e-mail madrid@inlingua.es; www.inlingua.es.
Linguarama Iberica: Orense 34, 28020 Madrid; ☎915-550485; fax 915-550959; e-mail madrid@linguarama.com; www.linguarama.com.

SECRETARIAL WORK

Opportunities are both widely available and lucrative for bilingual secretaries in Spain. According to the P.A. and secretarial recruitment specialists – the *Angela Mortimer Agency* (www.angelamortimer.com) in a recent article in *The Times*, it is now far more common for both P.A.s and secretaries to move to jobs all over Europe. They estimate that around 12% of their clients move regularly from country to country, sampling different lifestyles in exchange for their office skills. In Spain the most popular destinations for this type of work are Barcelona and Madrid. Whilst the salaries may not quite live up to those encountered in the UK (the average P.A. earning £20,000 in the UK, can expect to earn about £16,500 in Madrid), most agree that the lifestyle more than makes up for it. However, the agency also points out that the market has become far more competitive, with 38% of their clients being fluent in a second language, compared to 5%-10% ten years ago. Many speak three or even four languages, though fluent English and Spanish will be sufficient for the majority of jobs in Spain.

For anyone thinking of doing this kind of work it is often worth trying the Spanish Tourist Authority (www.spain.info) which employs a multitude of linguistically-able secretaries. Additionally a few London agencies place bi-lingual secretaries abroad such as Merrow Language Recruitment (100 New Kings Road, London SW6 4LX; ☎0845-226 4748; fax 020-7348 6038; e-mail recruit@merrow.co.uk; www.merrow.co.uk) and Appointments BiLanguage (143 Long Acre, London WC2E 9AD; ☎020-7836 7878; fax 020-7836 7615; e-mail info@appoitnmentsbilanguage.co.uk; www.appointmentsbilanguage.co.uk).

TOURISM

Tourism is undoubtedly one of Spain's largest industries, employing around 11% of the Spanish workforce. Large British tour operators like *TUI UK* and *First Choice* employ hundreds of representatives to work abroad as managers, sports instructors, chefs, bar and chamber staff, etc. each summer. First-time reps working for major tour operators, whether British, German or Scandinavian, have a 60% chance of being sent to a Spanish resort. Although it is sometimes easier to arrange a job with an organisation if you have a proven commitment to a career in tourism, this is not essential. Although you won't make a fortune (and will have to work hard), and although you may see decidedly little of real Spanish culture and life while working very long hours, these kinds of openings provide some potential for getting a job later on in tourism or related areas; and if for nothing else, then for a long, hot and enjoyable Spanish summer. The Spanish infrastructure is generally well organised which makes your work much easier.

Most of the British camping tour companies such as *Canvas Holidays, Club Cantabrica, Keycamp Holidays* and *Eurocamp* have sites in Spain. *Haven Europe* needs Spanish-speaking couriers and children's staff to work at mobile home and tent parks from early May to the end of September. There are also a number of smaller family businesses who employ in Spain such as *Harry Shaw City Cruiser Holidays*, *Solaire Holidays* and *Bolero International Holidays*. *My Travel* run self-catering holidays on Spain's foremost holiday islands and provide an extensive children's programme, employing nannies and animators. In some cases a knowledge of German can be more useful than Spanish as many holiday villages cater primarily for the 13.5 million Germans who visit Spain annually.

In addition to the cheap packages, a vast array of special interest tours and upmarket villa holidays is available in Spain. Companies like the following are sometimes looking for staff who speak good Spanish and know the country:

Headwater: The Old School House, Chester Road, Castle, Northwich, Cheshire CW8 1LE; ☎01606-720033; fax 01606-720001; e-mail info@headwater.com; www.headwater.com. Activity holidays.

Individual Travellers (Spain and Portual): Manor Courtyard, Bignor, Pulboroush, West Sussex RH20 1QD; ☎01798-869485; www.indiv-travellers.com.

Mundi Color: 276 Vauxhall Bridge Road, London SW1V 1BE; ☎020-7828 6021; www.mundicolor.co.uk.

A major employer near to Barcelona is the Universal Studios theme park, *Port Aventura*. This enormous theme park employs around 3,000 people annually and is certainly worth contacting for seasonal work (Universal Studios, Port Aventura, Dpto RR.HH., Avda Alcalde Pere Molas, Km. 2, 43480 Vila-Seca, Tarragona (Ap 90), fax 977-779097; e-mail recursos.humanos@portaventura.es; www.portaventura.es).

Those with relevant sports instruction qualifications may find work with one of the many companies offering activity holidays in Spain. For example *Acorn Adventure* (address below) need seasonal staff for their two water sports and multi-activity centres on the Costa Brava. RYA qualified windsurfing and sailing instructors, BCU qualified kayak instructors and SPSA qualified climbing instructors are especially in demand for the season April/May to September. *PGL* also needs staff for Spanish holiday centres and *TJM Travel* hire qualified instructors and ancillary staff for hotels and activity centres in Spain.

Sailors from around the world congregate in the hundreds of marinas along the Spanish coast and create some opportunities for employment on yachts. *Minorca Sailing Holidays* (www.minorcasailing.co.uk) hire nannies and other staff for their sailing centre in the Bay of Fornells, Menorca.

There are also opportunities for ski instructors in the winter season, especially at resorts such as Cerler, La Molina or El Formigal in the Pyrenees. The ski industry is flourishing in Spain and a few British tour operators such as *TUI UK* and *First Choice* require qualified instructors, as does the UK company *Ski Miquel* (☎01457-821200; www.miquelhols.co.uk) which has ski chalets in the Spanish resort of Baqueira.

Try the following tour operators for vacancies:

Acorn Adventure: 22 Worcester St, Stourbridge, West Midlands DY8 1AN; ☎01384-446057; www.acorn-jobs.co.uk. Staff needed for a water sports and multi activity centre near the resort of Tossa de Mar on the Costa Brava. Activity instructors and support staff required.

ATG-Oxford: 69-71 Banbury Road, Oxford OX2 6PJ; ☎01865-315679; fax 01865-315697; www.atg-oxford.co.uk/working.php. Walking and cycling tours. Seasonal workers required.

Canvas Holidays: East Port House, 12 East Port, Dunfermline, Fife KY12 7JG; ☎01383-629018; fax 01383-629071; www.canvasholidays.com. Season lasts from March to October. Recruitment takes place from October to March.

Club Cantabrica Holidays Ltd: 146/148 London Road, St Albans, Herts. AL1 1PQ; ☎01717-866177; fax 01727-843766; www.cantabrica.co.uk. Couriers and resort managers required from May to October.

Eurocamp: Overseas Recruitment Department, ☎01606-787522; www.holidaybreakjobs.com. Part of the Holidaybreak Group which includes Keycamp Holidays. Recruit up to 1,500 seasonal staff.

Haven Europe: 1 Park Lane, Hemel Hempstead, Herts. HP2 4YL; ☎01442-203967; recruitment hotline 01442-203970; fax 01442-241473; www.haveneurope.com. 300 seasonal staff required March to September.

MyTravel UK: Holiday House, Sandbrook Park, Sandbrook way, Rochdale, Lancs. OL11 1SA; ☎0870-241 2642; fax 01706-742328; www.mytravelcareers.co.uk. Giant UK tour operator. Brands include Airtours Holidays, Direct Holidays, Panorama and Manos

Holidays. Require huge numbers of staff from April to October.

Open Holidays: Guildbourne Centre, Chapel Road, Worthing, W. Sussex BN11 1LZ; ☎01903-201864; fax 01903-201225; e-mail recruitment@openholidays.co.uk; www. openholidays.co.uk. Overseas reps required from March to October.

Tall Stories: Brassey House, New Zealand Avenue, Walton on Thames, Surrey KT12 1QD; ☎01932-252002; fax 01932-252970; e-mail tina@tallstories.co.uk; www.tallstories. co.uk/jobs.shtm. Adventure sports holiday operators in Spain and Mallorca.

TUI UK: Human Resources Overseas, Greater London House, Hampstead Road, London NW1 7SD; ☎020-7387 9321; www.tui-uk.co.uk/jobopps. Giant tour operator including Thomson Holidays, Crystal Holidays and Simply Travel.

OTHER OPPORTUNITIES

Detailed information on all aspects of employment in Spain can be found in the Vacation Work book, *Live and Work in Spain*. Another source of information dealing with job opportunities in Spain is the *Hispanic and Luso-Brazilian Council*, Canning House, 2 Belgrave Square, London SW1X 8PJ; ☎020-7235 2303; www.canninghouse.com.

SHORT TERM WORK

Although Spain has a high rate of unemployment, especially among the young (which means that many young Spanish people go abroad to work), opportunities do exist for Britons, Americans and Australians who can get a work permit. Tourism is still a major area of employment for foreigners; however, these jobs generally do not pay well. As usual, the 'grapevine' is one of the best ways of finding work in the tourist industries, and the many British expatriates living and working in Spain may be able to offer help and advice. Around eight million people from the UK alone go on holiday to Spain every year, which gives an idea of the scale of the industry and the opportunities that exist in everything from casual hotel and bar work through to working for a travel agency. There are also huge numbers of visitors from Germany, Holland, France and other countries; knowledge of these languages will put you one step ahead of the competition in the job search.

AU PAIRS

Spain's demand for au pairs and mother's helps is booming. The number of agencies inside Spain and of European agencies which have added Spain to their list of destination countries continues to increase. At the beginning of the 21st century, the popularity of Spanish studies continues to increase in Britain and beyond. The last two decades have seen unprecedented economic growth in Spain, which has fuelled a huge demand for the English language. Many Spanish families want more than an au pair; they want a young English speaker to interact with their children on a daily basis. The emphasis on conversational English means that a certain number of families are happy to consider young men for live-in positions.

The chances of being able to arrange an au pair placement in Spain, even at short notice, are good. In many cases requirements are minimal, e.g. a knowledge of Spanish or experience of childcare may not be necessary. The majority of jobs are in the cities and environs of Madrid and Barcelona, though jobs do crop up in glamorous resorts like Marbella, Majorca, Tenerife and elsewhere.

The minimum pay for a standard au pair at present is €55/€60 per week, though agencies urge families who live in suburbs some distance from the city centre to pay a little more. No perks are built into the arrangement, so au pairs can't count on getting any paid holidays, subsidised fares or a contribution towards their tuition fees except at the discretion of their employers.

Au pair placement is undertaken by many English language schools in Spain. Placing an English speaker in the household of a young Spaniard learning English benefits everyone. One of the biggest and longest established agencies in the field with partner agencies around the world is *Club de Relaciones Culturales Internacionales* (Ferraz 82, 28008 Madrid; ☎915-417103; fax 915-591181; e-mail spain@clubrci.es; www.clubrci.es) which is a non-profit club allied to the Ministry of Culture and the Ministry of Education and member of IAPA.

Try the following agencies:

ABB Au-Pair Family Service, Via Alemania 2, 5°A, 07003 Palma de Mallorca, Spain; ☎971-752027; fax 971-900153; e-mail abbaupair@ono.com.

Actividad Au-Pair Internacional, Paseo de Gracia 78-Atic 2°, 08008 Barcelona, Spain; ☎932-157247; e-mail ainteraupair@jazzfree.com or bcnaupair@ya.com.

Agencia Intercambios Culturales Y Au Pair, San Joaquin No. 17, 07003 Palma de Mallorca, Baleares, Spain; tel/fax 971-755124; e-mail aicap@onon.com; www.aicap.es.vg.

Centros Europeos Galve S.A.., Calle Principe, 12-6°A, Madrid 28012, Spain; ☎915-327230; fax 915-216076; e-mail centros-principe@telefonica.net.

Crossing Limits S.L, Av. República Argentina n° 22, Bis 8F (Los Remedios), 41011 Seville, Spain; tel/fax 954-083931; e-mail info@crossinglimits.com; www.crossinglimits.com.

GIC Educational Consultants, Centro Comercial Arenal, Avda. del Pla 126, 2.22, 03730 Jávea (Alicante), Spain; ☎966-460410; fax 966-462015; e-mail ecsl@telefonica.net; www.gic-spain.com.

Interclass, c/ Bori i Fontestá 14, 6° 4°, 08021 Barcelona, Spain. ☎934-142921; fax 934-142931; e-mail info@interclass.es; www.interclass.es.

Interlink, Breton 17, Pral. Izda, 50005 Zaragoza, Spain; ☎976-569358; fax 976-563745; e-mail info@interlink-idiomas.com; www.interlink-idiomas.com.

Kingsbrook Languages & Services, Travessera de Gracia 60, 08006 Barcelona, Spain; ☎932-093763; fax 932-021598; e-mail aupair@kingsbrookbcn.com; www.kingsbrookbcn.com.

Servihogar, Calle del Pelicano 10, El Puerto de Santa Maria, Cádiz, Spain. tel/fax 956-851744; e-mail aupair@servihogar.org; www.servihogar.org.

For links to other agencies, check the website www.azzoomi.com/eng_chldcare_home. htm which lists about 20 agencies in Spain. If you deal directly with a Spanish agency, you may have to pay a placement fee though mostly the agencies charge large fees for outgoing placements.

CASUAL WORK

Tourism in Spain is such a vast industry that simply by turning up to the right place at the right time it is usually possible to find casual positions made available by the influx of 50 million or more visitors per year. The types of positions where there are always openings during the tourist season include, hotel and restaurant work, couriers and representatives, bar, club and disco work, PR, work in holiday camps, shop assistants and so on. Fluent English is an advantage for such jobs and explains why foreigners are often able to find work in areas of high Spanish unemployment.

If you can arrange to visit the Spanish coast in March before most of the budget travellers arrive, you should have a good chance of fixing up a job for the season. The resorts then go dead until late May and there may be jobs available.

The hotel and restaurant trade employs the majority of casual workers. Kitchen hands, chefs, hotel managers, waiters, maids, receptionists, cleaners etc. are required and although experience, qualifications and language skills are required for the better paid positions, there are numerous positions open to the inexperienced. Unfortunately, with this kind of work, long hours and low pay are fairly standard. Also many casual workers are employed illegally and therefore have no job protection and very few rights.

In the Canary Islands the season runs from November to March and Lanzarote and Tenerife offer the best chances for employment. Along the beachfront at Puerto del Carmen in Lanzarote and Playa de las Americas in Tenerife, almost every building is a bar, pizzeria, hamburgeria etc. Just walk along the front until you come to a place whose client language you speak and go in and ask. There are ample opportunities in the year round resorts of the Canary Islands for bar staff, DJs, beach party ticket sellers, timeshare salesmen etc. Many young people make ends meet by working as a 'PR' or 'prop', i.e. someone who stands outside trying to entice customers to come in.

A good starting point for finding out about seasonal job vacancies in Ibiza is the website of the Queen Victoria Pub in Santa Eulalia (www.ibizaqueenvictoria.com) which posts jobs and accommodation both on its site and on the pub notice board which anyone can drop by and consult. The Queen Vic itself employs a large number of European fun seekers. Two other websites worth checking are www.balearic-jobs.com and www.gapwork.com.

Seasonal and casual work in Spain can also be found in the Vacation Work Publications books: *Summer Jobs Abroad* (David Woodworth and Victoria Pybus) and *Work Your Way Around the World* (Susan Griffith).

VOLUNTARY WORK

There is great demand for volunteers in Spain in a variety of projects ranging from rural regeneration, to archaeological and conservation projects. International work camp organisations recruit for environmental and other projects in Spain for programmes as various as carrying out an archaeological dig of a Roman settlement in Tarragona to traditional stone quarrying in Menorca. The co-ordinating work camp organisation in Spain is the Instituto de la Juventud's *Servico Voluntario Internacional* (José Ortega y Gasset 71, 28006 Madrid; ☎913-637700; www.mtas.es/injuve) which oversees 150 camps every year. You can approach them independently as well as through a partner organisation in your own country (see below). International work camps usually operate from April to October and offer voluntary placements for two to three weeks.

Those looking for work in the Madrid region should contact the *Dirección General de Cooperación al Desarollo y Voluntariado* run by Madrid's regional government (Comunidad de Madrid; C/ Espartinas n° 10, 28001 Madrid; ☎900-444555; e-mail dgvoluntariado@madrid.org; www.madrid.org/voluntarios). This organisation co-ordinates voluntary projects in the area involving working with the disabled, the elderly, and working in conservation projects. They may also be able to help you to find projects in other parts of the country and have a useful on-line directory of NGOs.

An interesting opportunity for young volunteers with an interest in languages is the relatively new Englishtown project (Eduardo Dato 3, 1ˢᵗ Floor, 28010 Madrid; ☎915-914840; fax 914-458782; www.vaughanvillage.com). Englishtown is an abandoned Spanish village that has been transformed into a village 'stocked' with native English-speaking volunteers who live together with an equal number of Spanish people for an intensive week of activities, sports, games and group dynamics. The English native volunteers exchange conversation for room and board.

Two very different projects of particular interest to those concerned with sustainable environments are Sunseed Desert Technology and Ecoforest Education for Sustainability. Ecoforest (Apdo. 29, Coin, 29100 Málaga; ☎661-079950; e-mail info@ecoforest.org; www.ecoforest.org) is a charitable organisation set up to provide education about living and working in simple, natural and sustainable ways. The community of voluntary residents aims to demonstrate ecologically sound and self-reliant methods of food production. The Sunseed Desert Technology project (Apdo. 9, 04270 Sorbas, Almería; ☎950-525770; www.sunseed.org.uk) is located in the tiny village of Los Molinos in Southern Spain and aims to develop low-tech methods of sustainable agriculture in a semi-arid environment. Both projects rely heavily on volunteers.

INTERNATIONAL COMPANIES IN SPAIN

BDO Binder   1
Calle Serrano 85
28006 Madrid

Beecham Laboratorios SA   8
Travera de Gradia 9
08021 Barcelona

British Airways SA   3
Serrano 60-5°
28001 Madrid

Bufete Bano Léon   24
Pintor Lorenzo Casanova 66, 1st Floor
Alicante

British Tourist Authority   48
Torre de Madrid, Planta 6a
Plaza de España
28008 Madrid

Cadbury Schweppes España SA   16
Sor Angela de la Cruz 3
28020 Madrid

Commercial Union Assurance Co Ltd   23
Via Augusta 281-285
08017 Barcelona

Cory Hermanosos SA   17
León Castillo 421
35008 Las Palmas
Canary Islands

DeloitteSA   1
Torre Picasso, Planta 38
Plaza Pablo Ruiz Picasso
28020 Madrid

Ernst & Young SA   1
Plaza Pablo Ruiz Picasso
Torre Picasso 38°
E28020 Madrid

Flexibox de España SA   25
Ronda de los Tejares 19
14008 Cordoba

Formica Espanõla SA   18
Txomin Egileor 54
48960 Galdakao

Glaxo Wellcome SA   8
Apartado de Correos 37
28800 Alcala de Henares
Madrid

Guardian Assurance   23
Numero 158, Piso 1A
28002, Madrid

HSBC   4
Torre Picasso 33, Plaza Pablo,
Ruiz, Madrid

ICI España SA   8
Ctra Hostalric-Tosa
08490 Fogars de Tordera

Jones Lang Lasal Espãna   40
Paseo de la Castellana
Numero 33, Planta 14
28046, Madrid

Knight Frank & Rutley   40
Valázquez 24
28001 Madrid

KPMG Peat Marwick   1
Edificio Torre Europa
Paseo de la Castellana 95
26046 Madrid

Lloyds TSB Bank   4
Calle Serrano 90
28006 Madrid

Plessey Semiconductors   10
Plaza de Colon 2
Torres de Colon
Torre 18b
28046 Madrid

PriceWaterhouseCoopers   1
Edificio PriceWaterhouseCoopers
Paseo de la Castellana 43
26046 Madrid

Rank Video Services Iberia   36
Poligono Industriel
El Rasol
San Agustin
28750 Madrid

Rover España SA   7
Mar Mediterráneo 2
San Fernando de Henares
28850 Madrid

Royal Insurance España   23
Po. de la Castellana 60
28046 Madrid

Shell Espanõla SA   35
Rio Bullaque 2
28034 Madrid

Unilever España   16
Apartado 36156
28080 Madrid

United Biscuits   16
Productos Ortiz
Calle Alberto
Albocer 46-5B
28016 Madrid

The *British Chamber of Commerce*, C/ Bruc 21 1° 4°, 08010 Barcelona; www. britishchamberspain.com, publishes a *List of British Companies in Spain*. The *Spanish Chamber of Commerce in Great Britain* is at 126 Wigmore Street, London W1U 3RZ; ☎ 020-7009 9070; fax 020-7009 9088; e-mail info@spanishchamber.co.uk; www.spanishchamber. co.uk and publishes a number of Anglo-Spanish trade directories.

Sweden

- **Year of EU Accession:** 1995
- **Swedish Embassy,** 11 Montagu Place, London W1H 2AL; ☎ 020-7917 6400; fax 020-7724 4174; e-mail ambassaden.london@foreign.ministry.se; www.swedenabroad.com/london
- **Swedish Embassy,** 1501 M Street NW, Suite 900, Washington, DC 20005; ☎ 202-467 2600; fax 202-467 2699; e-mail ambassaden.washington@foreign.ministry.se; www.swedenabroad.com/washington
- **Currency:** 1 Swedish krona (plural kronor) Kr = 100 öre
- **Rate of Exchange:** £1 = Kr 13.3; $1 = Kr 7.2; €1 = Kr 9.2
- **Country Code:** +46

Sweden shares land borders with Finland and Norway, with a long Baltic Coast to the east. Half of the country is forested, and most of the many thousands of lakes are situated in the southern central area. It covers 174,000 square miles (450,659 sq km) and has a population of 8.9 million, of which 700,000 live in Stockholm, the capital. Other large cities are Göteborg (known in English as Gothenburg), Malmö and Uppsala. Sweden is a constitutional monarchy and government is exercised by a Council of State, composed of the Prime Minister and 13 ministries.

Sweden is now a member both of the European Economic Area (EEA) and the European Union (Sweden held the presidency of the EU for the first half of 2001). It has one of Europe's most advanced economies with a highly developed health care and social security system, and unemployment is traditionally low. The economy did well between 1997 and 2000, however, a global economic slowdown from 2001 has seen unemployment rising again (5 per cent in 2002). Immigration, at least from the non-Nordic countries, is not encouraged, although Sweden has a liberal policy in relation to refugees.

The extensive forests contribute to the production of wood-based products like paper and furniture, which account for 20 per cent of exports. Many industries have recently been privatised. Engineering, motor vehicle manufacture, mining, steel and chemical industries, as well as agriculture, are all important. The fastest growing manufacturing sector is the pharmaceutical industry, although this remains small in terms of total numbers employed.

Equal opportunities are important in Sweden, and more than 77 per cent of women are in employment; employers are required to take measures to promote equality at work. The standard working week is 40 hours by law, with five weeks' statutory paid vacation. Almost 90 per cent of all employees are members of a trade union.

While at work a smart dress sense is expected, and punctuality is important. Outside work Swedes are more relaxed, both in their dress and behaviour. English is quite widely spoken; and there is a lively nightlife, with pubs, cafés and discos in Stockholm. There are strict licensing laws, and smoking in prohibited on public transport and in most public buildings. In food, the emphasis is on healthy, simple eating (Sweden's most famous culinary concept is the *Smörgasbord*). The liqueur traditionally drunk with meals is *snapps*.

In October 1991, for the first time since the 1930s, Sweden elected a conservative-led government, but in 1994 the Social Democratic Party was returned to power. A coalition of the Social Democrats, with the Left Party and the Green Party as junior coalition partners, has been in power for the last four years. The current government is pursuing a policy of cutting taxes, while spending more on health and education.

The Swedish Government has a general information website at www.swednet.org.uk.

FACTORS AFFECTING EMPLOYMENT

IMMIGRATION

EU and EEA citizens must apply for a residence permit if they intend to stay in the country for more than three months, although they have the right to work in Sweden. Application can be made through embassies and immigration offices and the *Swedish Migration Board* (Invandrarverk, Box 601 70, Norrköping; ☎11-156000; fax 11-108155; e-mail migrationsverket@ migrationsverket.se; www.migrationsverket.se) can supply a list of addresses.

Non-EU nationals wishing to work in Sweden will need a work permit and these are generally only granted in cases of acute labour shortage of specifically qualified personnel. Work permits are issued for a specific job, which means that you may not change occupations or workplace without renewed assessment of labour market need. They are also time-limited and cannot be extended beyond the period stated in your application. It can take up to three months to process an application for a work permit.

Au pairs from non-EU countries will also require work permits and should follow the same procedures above; you will also require a residence permit. Americans can obtain information from the *Consulate General of Sweden* (Work Permit Section), 1 Dag Hammarskjold Plaza, 885 Second Avenue, 45th Floor, New York, NY 10017; ☎212-583 2550; fax 212-755 2732; e-mail generalkonsulat.newyork@foreign.ministry.se; www. swedenabroad.com. The *American-Scandinavian Foundation*, Scandinavia House, 58 Park Avenue, New York, NY 10016; ☎212-879 9779; e-mail info@amscan.org; www. amscan.org, can also assist with work permits for US residents.

TAXATION

Workers in Sweden pay both local and national income tax. However, national income tax is only payable if you are earning over SEK 298,600 (£21,860/$41,409). National income tax rates are currently 20-25% of the amount in excess of the threshold. The average local income tax rate is around 31%. VAT on goods and services is between six and 25 per cent. An additional 4.95 per cent is deducted from wages to pay for social security contributions, and this is topped up by a further 33 per cent paid by the employer. Employers also contribute towards pension funds under collective agreements.

SOCIAL WELFARE

All residents in Sweden are covered by national health insurance, which also pays an allowance to parents who need to stay home to care for sick children. Patients are charged a fee for medical consultations and drugs. However, hospitalisation costs and laboratory fees are met by the county council. A national occupational injury insurance system pays all healthcare costs arising from work-related accidents.

EMBASSIES AND CONSULATES

British Embassy, Skarpögatan 6-8, Box 27819, 115 93 Stockholm; ☎8-671 3000; fax 8-661 9766; e-mail info@britishembassy.se; www.britishembassy.se.
Consulates also in Göteborg and Sundsvall.
US Embassy, Dag Hammarskjölds Väg 31, 115 89 Stockholm; ☎8-783 5300; www. usemb.se.

TOURIST OFFICES

Swedish Travel & Tourism Council, 11 Montagu Place, London W1H 2AL; ☎020-7870 5600; www.visit-sweden.com.
Swedish Travel and Tourism Council, 18th Floor, 655 Third Avenue, New York, NY 10017; ☎212-885 9700; www.visit-sweden.com.

EMPLOYMENT PROSPECTS

GENERAL

Sweden's industries have traditionally been based on its natural resources, notably its forests and iron ore (for engineering, the automotive industries and aircraft and weapons manufacture). More recently, high-tech industries like electronics, pharmaceuticals and telecommunications have gained in importance. Work permits (for non-EU/EEA citizens) are short-term and specific, and the chances of working in Sweden on a long-term basis are limited. Swedish workers themselves are highly trained, and English is widely spoken. The best opportunities are in international companies, of which the country has a disproportionately large number: some 2,700 or so have their headquarters in Sweden.

NEWSPAPERS

In the UK, advertisements in the leading dailies *Sydsvenska Dagbladet* and *Göteborgs Posten* can be placed through Crane Media Partners, 20-28 Dalling Road, London W6 0JB; ☎020-8237 8601.

SPECIFIC CONTACTS

EMPLOYMENT SERVICES

The Swedish labour market comes under the aegis of the *Arbedsmarknadsstyrelse*, (www. ams.se) or Employment Service, which carries out government labour policies. About 90 per cent of all job vacancies in Sweden are reported to the Employment Service. The Labour Market Administration (*Arbetsmarknadsverket*) has about 380 employment offices (*Arbetsförmedlingar*) throughout Sweden which deal with about 35 per cent of all vacancies. The *Arbetsformedlingar* offer placements and job counselling services. Every employment office has access to a computer terminal with a list of vacancies (*platsautomaten*) and up-to-date information about jobs.

The main employment office is in Stockholm (*Arbetsförmedlingen*, Nybrogatan 15, Box 5855, 102 40 Stockholm; ☎8-5280 7900; fax 8-5280 7901; e-mailarbetsformedlingen-ostermalm@lanab.amv.se;), but for regional employment office details look under *arbetsförmedlingen* in the telephone directory. The office at Sveavägen has English-speaking staff; on Thursday afternoons there is an international jobs office open upstairs.

Private job agencies have been allowed to operate in Sweden since July 1993, and are becoming increasingly common. There are two types of agencies apart: private agencies which supply mostly office staff; and union agencies which deal mainly with salaried personnel such as engineers. To find an agency look under *arbetsförmedlingar* in the yellow pages of the local telephone directory. Manpower has 44 branches, Adecco 23.

You can also contact UK employment centres for information and advice on working in Sweden. Vacancies are listed on the EURES network: http://europa.eu.. A couple of useful websites for those seeking work in Sweden are: www.monster.se and www.stepstone.se.

MEDICAL STAFF

Information on registration requirements for foreign doctors and nurses is available from the *Socialstyrelsen (National Board of Health and Welfare)*, 106 30 Stockholm; ☎8-5555 3000; e-mail socialstyrelsen@sos.se.; www.sos.se. The Board advises, however, that the opportunities for foreign medical personnel to work in Sweden are extremely limited due to the lack of resources to provide the necessary complementary training. Vacancies are advertised in *Läkartidningen (Swedish Medical Journal)*, PO Box 5603, 114 86 Stockholm; ☎8-790 3300; fax 8-207619; www.lakartidningen.se/

TEACHERS

Casual work teaching English is rarely available. The Folk University (Eriksbergsgatan 14, PO Box 26152, 10041 Stockholm; ☎8-679 2950; fax 8-678 1544; e-mail info@ folkuniversitetet.se; www.folkuniversitetet.se) runs an adult English language programme in towns throughout the country and it is possible to gain a nine-month placement at one of a network of adult education centres. A TEFL qualification is essential.

OTHER OPPORTUNITIES

Reference to other opportunities in Sweden will be found in the *Getting the Job* chapter, especially the section *Agencies and Consultants*, and in the various chapters of the section on *Specific Careers*. *Live and Work in Scandinavia* (Vacation Work Publications) provides detailed information on employment opportunities in Sweden.

SHORT-TERM WORK

SEASONAL WORK

Opportunities for seasonal work are limited. People who are already in Sweden may be able to find work picking fruit and vegetables in market gardens, especially in the agricultural area of Skane in the South. Swedish employers are generally reluctant to apply for work permits since the authorities do not often grant them. Work is also available in hotels and bars, although this is usually poorly paid.

VOLUNTARY WORK

The main work camps organiser in Sweden is *IAL*, Barnängsgatan 23, 11 641 Stockholm, which is the Swedish branch of SCI. You will need to apply for their camps (which are mostly ecological) through your local branch of Service Civil International (IVS in Britain). Addresses are given in the chapter *Voluntary Work*.

INTERNATIONAL COMPANIES IN SWEDEN

Albany International AB Box 510 301 80 Halmstad	46	Castrol AB Box 49104 100 28 Stockholm	35
Atlantic Container Line AB Box 2531 403 36 Göteborg	17	DHL International AB Box 23260 104 35 Stockholm	17
Bonnier AB Torsgatan 21 113 90 Stockholm	38	Ernst & Young AB Box 3143 103 62 Stockholm	1
Bristol-Myers Squibb AB Box 152 00 167 15 Bromma	8	First Hospitality AB Box 24104 104 51 Stockholm	20
Calor AB Armégatan 40, Box 1810 171 22 Solna	35	GlaxoSmithKline AB Aminog. 27 431 23 Mölndal	8

ICL Sweden AB Box 40 164 93 Krista	10	Pilkington Floatglas AB Box 530 301 80 Halmstad	19
IBM Svenska Oddeg. 5 164 40 Kista.	10	Saab AB 581 88 Linköping	43
Ikea AB Box 700 343 81 Älmhult	18	Scandinavian Leisure Group AB 105 20 Stockholm	48
International Färg AB Box 44 424 21 Angered	32	Schenker-BTL AB 412 97 Göteborg	17
KPMG Box 16106 103 23 Stockholm	1	Siemens AB 194 87 Uppland Väsby	45
Lloyds Register of Shipping Första Langgatan 28B 32 Göteborg	23	Securitas AB Box 12307 102 Stockholm	43
Microsoft Finlandsg. 30, 164 93 Kista	10	Thorn Svenska AB Box 1362 171 26 Solna	10
Modern Times Group MTG AB Box 2094 103 13 Stockholm	38	Xerox AB Domnarvsgatan 11 163 87 Stockholm	30
		Zanda & Ingström AB Box 502 1169 29 Solna	6

The *Swedish Chamber of Commerce for the UK*, Sweden House, 5 Upper Montagu Street, London W1H 2AG; ☎020-7224 8001; fax 020-7224 8884; www.swedish-chamber.org. uk, publishes *LINK* magazine which contains details of the many British and foreign companies trading in Sweden.

Switzerland

- **Swiss Embassy**, 16-18 Montagu Place, London W1H 2BQ; ☎020-7616 6000; fax 020-7724 7001; www.eda.admin.ch/london
- **Swiss Embassy**, 2900 Cathedral Avenue, NW, Washington DC 20008; ☎202-745 7900; fax 202-387 2564; www.swissemb.org
- **Currency:** 1 Swiss Franc (SFr) = 100 rappen or centimes
- **Rate of Exchange**: £1 = SFr 2.26; $1 = SFr 1.23; €1 = SFr 1.57
- **Country Code:** +41

Switzerland is a confederation of 26 cantons, which have some degree of autonomy, including the right to levy taxes. Legislative power is exercised by the bicameral Federal Assembly, a Council of State representing the cantons, and the National Council which is elected every four years. Referendums are another important part of lawmaking, and are held, it seems, every five minutes on any issue that comes to mind. The abbreviation CH seen on mail and car registration number plates stands for Confederatio Helvetica (Swiss Confederation in Latin).

Switzerland has been internationally recognised as a neutral state since 1815 and, therefore, does not enter into military alliances with other states. It is not a member of the EU or EEA, and the Swiss are reluctant to give up what they see as their constitutional rights in order to enter into this larger political unit. It is, however, a member of the organisation that was the forerunner of the EEA, the European Free Trade Association (EFTA).

Switzerland has the highest mountains in Europe, green mountain pastures (alps) and many waterfalls and lakes. 7.5 million inhabitants live in this country of 15,940 square miles (41,284 sq km), with the population divided between religion (Roman Catholic and Protestant) and by language. Switzerland has a mixed economy, with many small craft industries (of which watchmaking is probably the most famous). There is a substantial chemical industry, and agriculture remains important (although half of Switzerland's food is imported). Banking dominates the service sector and Swiss banks are known for their discretion. Wages are high, as is the cost of living. With a per capita gross national product ranking the second highest in the world, Switzerland is a prominent player in the world economy.

Tourism plays an increasingly important role in the economy, and it is in this sector where most job opportunities lie. There are also openings in information technology and in some of the country's international organisations.

The weather systems produced due to the Alps cause the climate to be varied and rather unpredictable. Mountaineering, hiking, and winter sports are all popular, as is soccer. Food varies from canton to canton, and so does the way of life. Cheeses, meat dishes and cakes and pastries are some of the specialities that can be enjoyed in Swiss villages, towns and cities (chief among which are Bern, Zurich, and Basel). Restaurants and the nightlife are cosmopolitan. Switzerland is a country whose inhabitants dress well at work, and where business cards are important. Bern is the capital.

The national public holidays are: New Year's Day (1, 2 Jan); Good Friday; Easter Monday; Labour Day (1 May); Ascension Day; Whit Monday; National Day (1 Aug); Christmas Day; and Boxing Day.

FACTORS AFFECTING EMPLOYMENT

IMMIGRATION

Although Switzerland in not a member of the EU or the EEA, a bilateral treaty on free movement of labour for EU and EEA citizens has been concluded and came into force in June 2002. However, it is advisable for anyone seeking work in Switzerland to check with a Swiss embassy or the *Federal Office forMigration* (Quellenweg 9115, 3003 Bern-Wabern; ☎31-325 1111; e-mail info@imes.admin.ch; www.auslaender.ch) for current rulings on immigration. Canadian and US citizens and EU nationals may at present remain in Switzerland for up to three months without a visa.

It is very difficult to obtain a residence permit, as the current policy of the Swiss authorities is to limit the number of foreigners settling in their country. There is an annual quota based on skills and qualifications. As a rule only persons who have been offered jobs which cannot be filled by Swiss nationals have a chance of obtaining a resident permit. All foreigners must have a residence permit in order to enter Switzerland to take up employment, as there is no separate document that imparts the right to work. It is necessary to have a definite job offer in order to obtain the permit, known as an *autorisation de séjour* or *Aufenthaltsbewilligung*.

Temporary work permits are available in limited numbers for seasonal work, mainly in the hotel and catering trades (see below). Australians and New Zealanders are not eligible even for temporary work permits, and most resorts have several police keeping an eye on visas, so you take a significant risk if you choose to work illegally. Students on exchange schemes or wishing to train (for a maximum of six months) in a Swiss enterprise, or gain experience with machines and production procedures used in Swiss firms, are also subject to quota restrictions.

Swiss embassies and consulates can offer no information on the subject of employment. There is no consular involvement in the issuing of work and residence permits. A free booklet, *Living and Working in Switzerland* contains general information regarding entry and residence and the labour market. It can be obtained from Swiss Embassies.

EMBASSIES AND CONSULATES

British Embassy, Thunstrasse 50, 3005 Bern 15; ☎31-359 7700; fax 31-359 7701; www.britishembassy.ch.
There are consulates in Geneva, Basle, Lugano, Montreux/Vevey, Valais and Zurich.
US Embassy, Jubiläeumstrasse 93, CH-3005 Bern; ☎31-357 7011; fax 31-357 7344; http://bern.usembassy.gov/.

TOURIST OFFICES

Switzerland Tourism, 30 Bedford Street, London WC2E 9ED; ☎00800-100 200 30 or ☎020-7420 4900; e-mail info.uk@myswitzerland.com; www.myswitzerland.com.
Switzerland Tourism, Swiss Center, 608 Fifth Avenue, New York, NY 10020; ☎1-877 794 8037; fax 212-262 6116; www.myswitzerland.com.

LANGUAGES

Switzerland has a variety of languages within its small area and most educated people speak two or three fluently. Sixty-five per cent of the population speak Swiss German (Schweizer Tytsch) as their first language (which is almost incomprehensible to most German speakers, although the Swiss can also speak and write standard German without difficulty); 18.4 per cent speak French; and 9.8 per cent Italian. A further one per cent of the population speak dialects of a local language, Romansch, which bears some resemblance to Latin but little to German, French or Italian. Many Swiss speak excellent English.

EMPLOYMENT PROSPECTS

Switzerland is well-known for its banking and financial services. Other major employers of foreign workers include the many international organisations and multinational companies based in Geneva and those multinationals with headquarters in the country. Immigrant workers are to be found in most types of employment, and many unskilled workers come from Spain, Portugal and the former Yugoslavia.

NEWSPAPERS

The Powers Turner Group, Gordon House, Greencoat Lane, London SW1P 1PH; ☎020-7592 8300; ☎020-7592 8301; e-mail ppn-london@publicitas.com; www.publicitas.com, are agents for the most important Swiss newspapers, including *Tages Anzeiger, Basler-Zeitung, Le Temps,* and *Tribune de Genève.*

LABOUR FORCE

The Swiss labour force includes around a million foreign workers, 200,000 of whom are 'frontier commuters' living in neighbouring countries and commuting to Switzerland. Currently the unemployment rate is 2.7 per cent – extremely low for Europe.

SPECIFIC CONTACTS

INTERNATIONAL ORGANISATIONS

United Nations organisations like UNCTAD (UN Conference on Trade and Development); UNITAR (UN Institute for Training and Research); and UNHCR (UN High Commissioner for Refugees) are based in Geneva. Further details of these are given in the *United Nations* chapter. Administration, information technology, finance, language, legal and other skills will be required.

TEACHING

The *Swiss Federation of Private Schools*, Hotelgasse 1, Postfach 316, CH-3000 Bern 7; ☎31-328 4050; fax 31-328 4055; e-mail info@swiss-schools.ch; www.swiss-schools.ch, has lists of the addresses of Swiss private schools as well as information on language courses and holiday camps. The information is primarily produced for those looking to place their offspring in the schools and not for the benefit of jobseekers but details can still be found on the Swiss Federation of Private Schools webpages.

The main language schools in Switzerland are listed in *Teaching English Abroad*, published by Vacation Work Publications; www.vacationwork.co.uk, £12.95.

SHORT TERM WORK

The Swiss authorities recognise the need for temporary workers and therefore issue a work permit known as *Permis A* or *Saisonbewilligung* which is valid for nine months in one year. Each canton has a strict quota of nine-month permits. Once you have a work permit you enjoy similar rights to Swiss workers including a minimum wage set at around £1,000 per month, the possibility of obtaining unemployment benefit after six months – assuming that you have paid contributions, and accident insurance (although foreign workers should take out their own health insurance).

AGRICULTURE

Swiss farms offer temporary jobs over the summer, and it is reported that as many as a third of farmhands employed in the summer months are foreigners (mainly Portuguese).

Informal jobs can be found picking anything from cherries to hazelnuts; the area along the Rhône between Martigny and Saxon is especially recommended.

The grape harvest (*vendange*) in the French-speaking cantons of Vaud and Valais usually starts in mid-October, somewhat later than in France. Work should be arranged well in advance by contacting vineyard owners, who will then deal with the red tape for you.

Young people with some French or German who are interested in gaining experience of farm work can visit the *Landdienst-Zentralstelle (Central Office for Voluntary Farm Work)* (Postfach 2826, Mühlegasse 13, 8021 Zurich; ☎1-261 4488; fax 1-261 4432; e-mail admin@landdienst.ch; www.landdienst.ch) which can arrange a place on a farm between March and October. There is a registration fee but board and lodging are provided as well as pocket money. Applicants must be aged between 17 and 30 years.

AU PAIRS

The enthusiastic literature from Karin Schatzmann, proprietor of the *Perfect Way Au Pair Agency*, is probably not far off the mark when she says Switzerland is the best country in which to be an au pair. The 'pocket money' is strictly controlled by government directives and differs between the French and German areas. The pocket money in German cantons starts at SFr590 net for 30 hours of work up to SFr740 for 40 hours; in the Geneva area the monthly minimum is SFr760 (€500). The gross salary starts much higher than this (i.e. SFr1340, SFr1415 and SFr1490) but the allowable deductions for full room and lodging is SFr900 a month plus monthly earnings are further reduced by compulsory deductions (see section below).

Other perks for Swiss au pairs are unheard of elsewhere. For example you are entitled to five weeks paid holiday during your year if you are 20 years old or less, and four weeks if you are over 20. When on holiday you get not only your weekly net salary but also financial compensation for the meals which you are not eating with the family.

Pro Filia (Nationalsekretariat, Beckenhofstr. 16, Postfach, 8035 Zurich; tel/fax 1-361 5331; e-mail info@profilia.ch; www.profilia.ch) is a long-established Catholic au pair agency with branches throughout Switzerland. It charges incoming au pairs a fee of SFr300 which may be prohibitive for some, though it can be paid out of the first month's salary. Petite Pumpkin/Petite Fourni (125 bis route de Saconnex d'Arve, 1228 Plan-les-Ouates, Geneva; ☎22-771 1302; e-mail christine.breiteneder@lapetitefourni. com; www.lapetitefourni.com) works with its British counterpart Petite Pumpkin (www. petitepumpkin.co.uk). The au pair traffic is in both directions.

Two agencies that have strong links with Canada may be able to assist other English-speaking nationalities:

Can Au Pair, Geissbuelstrasse, CH-8704 Herrliberg (+41 1-915 26 81; fax +41 1-915 26 56; office@canaupair.ch; www.canaupair.ch). Arranges au pair contracts in Switzerland for Canadian women aged 18-28.

Wind Connections, Erlenbach (+41 44-915 4104, fax: +41 44-915 4105; info@ windconnections.ch; www.canadalink.ch). Specialises in placing au pairs from Canada, Australia and the UK with Swiss families. All candidates must be interviewed.

TOURISM

Switzerland has a healthy tourism industry over both the summer and winter seasons and needs to import many temporary workers from abroad, as the many vacancies for hotel work in *Summer Jobs Abroad* attest. This work is normally more than adequately paid, but the hours can be long and the work arduous.

Hotel work in the summer and winter seasons can be found in the many hotels listed in *Summer Jobs Abroad* (published by Vacation Work Publications). Other opportunities are listed in the *Transport and Tourism* and *Hospitality and Catering* chapters. The *Swiss Hotel Guide* (www.swisshotels.ch) provides detailed entries in English on thousands of hotels.

The Swiss organisation *Village Camps* organises American-style camps for children from the international and business communities, and requires all types of staff; priority is given to those who also speak German, French or Italian. An application and information pack is available from Village Camps, rue de la Morache, 1260 Nyon; ☎22-990 9400; fax 22-990 9494; e-mail camps@villagecamps.ch; www.villagecamps.com.

WORK EXCHANGES

Under an agreement between the UK and Switzerland, 400 British trainees can work in Switzerland each year and vice versa. Under this agreement, persons aged 18-35 who have completed their studies or occupational training and who wish to broaden their professional and linguistic skills will be granted a work and residence permit for one year, which may be extended for a further six months in special cases. Employment may only be taken within the occupation for which the applicant has been trained. Initial enquiries in the UK should be made to the *Immigration and Nationality Directorate* (Lunar House, 40 Wellesley Road, Croydon CR9 2BY; ☎0870-606 7766; e-mail indpublicenquiries@ind. homeoffice.gsi.gov.uk; www.ind.homeoffice.gov.uk), or the local Jobcentre.

A similar agreement exists with the USA, for 150 American trainees (age 21-30) to go to Switzerland each year. The relevant agency in the USA is AIPT (see *Working Exchanges* in the chapter *Getting the Job*).

OTHER WORK

Other opportunities are largely limited to voluntary work. Enquiries in the UK should be made to IVS. US residents can contact SCI (see *Voluntary Work*) for information on work camps. Also see *Working in Tourism* and *Working in Ski Resorts* published by Vacation Work Publications.

INTERNATIONAL COMPANIES IN SWITZERLAND

Many international companies are registered in Switzerland only for tax purposes and are not actively engaged in business there. The *British-Swiss Chamber of Commerce* in Switzerland, Freiestrasse 155, CH-8032 Zurich; ☎044-422 3131; fax 044-422 3244; and 12 York Gate, London NW1 4QS; ☎020-7544 4850; fax 020-7544 4851; e-mail info-uk@bscc.co.uk; www.bscc.co.uk can provide a list of member companies.

United Kingdom

- **Year of EU Accession:** 1973
- **British Embassy,** 3100 Massachusetts Avenue, Washington DC, 20008; ☎202-588 7800; fax 202-588 7850; www.britainusa.com
- **British High Commission,** 80 Elgin Street, Ottawa, K1P 5K7; ☎613-237 1530; fax 613-237 7980; www.britainincanada.org
- **Currency:** £1 (Pound Sterling) = 100 pence (p)
- **Rate of Exchange:** £1 = US$1.84 = €1.44
- **Country Code:** +44

The United Kingdom has long attracted workers from other countries, from the Commonwealth in particular, and more recently from other EU countries. There has been a growth in foreign investment in recent years, particularly by Japanese and US companies who see low labour costs, a skilled workforce, and Britain's participation in the larger market of the EU as advantages. The economy has become one of the most stable in Europe and is now enjoying the longest period of sustained economic growth. Unemployment (4.7%), though high, is lower than in many other European countries. The UK, with its diverse regions and cultural heritage, is a fascinating place to visit and to live in and is popular with visitors from many parts of the world.

Britain is a country still coming to terms with its diminished world role and its political destiny in Europe. These tensions, and other historical ones, have led to a rise in nationalist sentiments in Scotland and Wales and, in their more complicated manifestations, in Northern Ireland (where the Protestant community still regards itself as British). Britons may prefer to be identified depending on where they are born and bred as English, Scots, Welsh, or Northern Irish, and in many cases this is where the deepest national affiliations lie. Irish citizens may serve in Britain's armed forces. The British are traditionally patriotic, and there is strong feeling against the prospect of participation in EMU and the possibility of the replacement of the pound by the euro.

Language will not be a problem for the North American readers of this book but the culture may be. The British are considerably more reserved than North Americans and Australians, although at work they are nonetheless relatively informal (especially in European terms). Service 'with a smile' isn't as common as in the USA or Canada, and the bureaucracy can often be infuriating. Nightlife and socialising centres around the many pubs, which are focused inwards, rather like the British national character, instead of outwards, as in continental café culture. There are many international restaurants in the major towns and cities, and Britain's reputation for appalling cuisine is gradually giving way to an interest in food.

Tourism in the UK is a huge industry, but manufacturing industries and agriculture are in decline. It is in the large service sector and new technologies that employment opportunities are to be most often found; with a wide variety of other openings at all levels for those who speak the language.

GENERAL FACTS

POPULATION

The UK's population of 60.6 million increases annually by 0.28 per cent. There are sizeable minorities from the Commonwealth countries, in particular India, Pakistan, and the West Indies. The average population density throughout the country is 620 per square mile. Population distribution is relatively even if the sparsely populated mountainous areas of Scotland and Wales, and the disproportionately large population of London, are excluded.

CLIMATE

The climate is temperate, with some variation between north and south. The average winter temperature in the south is 40 deg F (4 deg C), and in summer 65 deg F (18 deg C); in summer temperatures may reach 86 deg F (30 deg C) or more. The North of England and Scotland are somewhat cooler. Rainfall is higher in the west and north.

GOVERNMENT

The UK is a constitutional monarchy. The monarch is Head of State and the temporal head of the Church of England, both of which are today largely symbolic roles. The two Houses of Parliament are the House of Lords and the elected House of Commons. The House of Lords is an upper chamber the composition of which is currently under review. Traditionally, hereditary peers had an automatic right to a seat in the Lords, however, in 1999, this right was rescinded leaving only a residual number of hereditary Lords selected by the House on the basis of their record of contribution. The other Lords are life peers, an honour bestowed by the Prime Minister of the day on the 'great and good'. The future of the House of Lords is uncertain as constitutional alternatives have not yet been either proposed or put in place.

The United Kingdom is made up of four separate countries – England, Scotland, Wales and Northern Ireland. The term 'England' and 'English' are strictly only applicable to England, and should not be used for the entire United Kingdom. The term Great Britain or Britain includes England, Scotland and Wales. Power is gradually being decentralised through a process of devolution to Scotland and Wales, and in 1999 both a Scottish Parliament and a Welsh National Assembly were convened. The constitutional arrangements for Northern Ireland, the Isle of Man, and the Channel Islands (which are geographically closer to France), are separate from those for the rest of the country.

CITIES

London, the capital, has about seven million inhabitants; other major cities include Birmingham (one million); Manchester (900,000), Leeds (700,000), Glasgow (700,000), Sheffield (500,000), Bradford (450,000), Liverpool (450,000), Edinburgh (capital of Scotland, 430,000) and Bristol (370,000).

RURAL LIFE

The UK is highly urbanised; just eight per cent of the population live in the countryside, although three-quarters of the land area is either cultivated or used for pasture. Farming is highly mechanised and only one per cent of the labour force is engaged in agriculture.

RELIGION, SPORT AND CULTURE

Religion does not play a major part in the lives of most people in the British Isles – 86 per cent of the population are nominally Christian, with 15 per cent belonging to the Roman Catholic faith, 57 per cent to the established Anglican Church, and the rest to various reformed churches. There are also Muslim, Jewish, Hindu and Sikh minorities. Catholics are the most observant of the Christian groups, although there has been a large-scale growth in the number and activity of evangelical churches in recent years.

Britons have a well-known obsession with sport, and invented many popular varieties, such as football, cricket and rugby. Unfortunately, the sporting inventiveness of their forefathers no longer extends to success in the international sporting arena. Other popular sports include fishing, golf, horse racing, athletics, bowls and sailing. Skiing is only possible in the Scottish Highlands when weather permits; otherwise British people travel abroad. Gardening is also very popular.

Britons are great readers – of newspapers if not of books. There is an increasingly cosmopolitan atmosphere in the major urban centres; theatre and music are particularly well supported, and there has been a recent renaissance in the cinema industry. Britain is also famous for its youth culture, and the country is regularly promoted throughout the world as 'Cool Britannia'.

FACTORS INFLUENCING EMPLOYMENT

IMMIGRATION

All those who are not British or EEA nationals will need a visa or entry clearance for all stays in the UK over six months.

Since November 2003, nationals of 10 "phase one" countries require entry clearance for stays of over 6 months. These countries are Australia, Canada, Hong Kong SAR, Japan, Malaysia, New Zealand, Singapore, South Africa, South Korea, and the USA. From November 2006, nationals of a further 55 "phase two" countries also require the same entry clearance. These include much of South America, the Caribbean island states and some African nations. For the full list of "phase two" countries and for the latest information on visa requirements, it is advisable to check the UK visa website at www.ukvisas.gov.uk.

WORK PERMITS

Nationals of the European Economic Area are free to enter the United Kingdom to seek employment without a work permit. At present this applies to citizens of EU countries, EEA member states of Norway, Iceland and Liechtenstein, and the European Free Trade Agreement (EFTA) member state of Switzerland. However EEA nationals still require a permit for the Channel Islands and the Isle of Man. The EU itself expanded in May 2004, increasing the number of countries by ten. These new countries are: Estonia, Latvia, Lithuania, Poland, Czech Republic, Slovakia, Hungary, Slovenia, Malta and Cyprus. However, nationals from eight of these states – Czech Republic, Estonia, Hungary, Latvia, Lithuania, Poland, Slovakia, and Slovenia – who find a job in the UK are required to register with the Home Office under the new Worker Registration Scheme as soon as they find work. This currently carries an initial charge of £70 (fees are reviewed regularly). This scheme was set up so that the government could monitor the impact of EU accession on the UK labour market and restrict access to benefits. Nationals from Malta and Cyprus have free movement rights and are not required to obtain a workers registration certificate.

For non-EEA citizens, the primary route for entry into the UK for the purpose of employment was previously the work permit system. Work permits were issued only where a genuine vacancy existed and where particular qualifications or skills were required that were in short supply from the resident and EEA labour force. In 2005, the government announced its intention to implement a Five Year Strategy for Immigration and Asylum. This represented a major overhaul of the work permit arrangements, as well as rules on immigration and asylum. Consequently, a new points-based system, designed to enable the UK to control immigration more effectively was introduced in March 2006 to replace the 80 different entry routes by which a non-EEA national could come to the UK to work.

The new points-based system of migration to the UK is still in the early stages of implementation. It is designed to control migration more effectively, tackle abuse and identify the most talented workers by consolidating entry clearance and work permit applications into one single-step application. The plan is to ensure that only those who benefit Britain can come here to work. These criteria are only for those workers from outside the EEA who wish to work or train in the UK. The system is based on 5 tiers:

o   Tier 1: Highly skilled workers, e.g. scientists or entrepreneurs;
o   Tier 2: Skilled workers with a job to offer, e.g. nurses, teachers or engineers;
o   Tier 3: Low skilled workers filling specific temporary labour shortages, e.g. construction workers for a particular building project;
o   Tier 4: Students;
o   Tier 5: Youth mobility workers and temporary workers, e.g. working holiday makers.

For each tier, applicants will need sufficient points to gain entry clearance to the UK. Points can be scored for skills or attributes which predict a worker's success in the labour market. For Tiers 3-5, under which most summer employment falls, points will be awarded depending on whether the applicant has: a valid certificate of sponsorship from an approved sponsor; adequate funds to live in the UK; proven compliance with previous immigration conditions and in some cases English language ability. A web-based self-assessment programme, which allows applicants to understand whether they meet the UK's criteria for entry can be found on the Home Office website.

Further details about the PBS are available at www.workingintheuk.gov.uk and the Home Office Immigration and Nationality Directorate (www.ind.homeoffice.gov.uk). Queries should be directed to Work Permits (UK)'s Customer Contacts Centre on (☎0114-207 4074).

LANGUAGES

English is spoken universally throughout the United Kingdom, with regional variations. Differences are mainly a matter of pronunciation. In addition, some Celtic languages are still spoken in the UK. About 20 per cent of the population of Wales is bilingual in Welsh and English and 32,000 speak Welsh only. In remote areas of Scotland Gaelic is spoken by about 90,000 people. A number of Asian languages such as Hindi, Urdu, Punjabi, Bengali, Gujarati, and Cantonese are spoken in the United Kingdom by immigrants and their children.

COST AND STANDARD OF LIVING

US citizens usually find the cost of living high in the UK, depending on the current exchange rate with the dollar. Basic items, such as food, public transport and gasoline (known in the UK as 'petrol') are far more expensive. House buying, which is a national preoccupation, is a major item of expenditure. The cost of living in the UK compares unfavourably with that elsewhere in Europe, and there is public clamour for the government to examine trading practices which, it is felt, are pushing prices up unfairly.

HEALTH AND WELFARE

Most workers are obliged to pay a fixed proportion of their earnings in National Insurance (NI) contributions. If you come to Britain to work, you should apply for a National Insurance number as soon as possible from a Social Security Office in your town (look in the Yellow Pages for address). You will need to give this number to employers, or at least have applied for one. Once you have paid enough of the right type of NI contributions you can claim Sickness Benefit, Maternity Allowance, Job Seeker's Allowance (unemployment benefit), State Retirement Pension. EU citizens will generally already be entitled to these, either directly or through reciprocal arrangements with their home countries; and there are agreements with Australia, Canada, New Zealand and the USA, which make it possible for citizens of those countries to qualify for a limited pension after paying one year's NI contributions. A complete list of these countries with reciprocal social security agreements is given in the *Rules and Regulations* chapter.

EDUCATION

Free schooling is available to all children aged between five and 18; it is compulsory from six to 16. Only 50 per cent of three to five year olds go to nursery school in the UK, one of the lowest figures in Europe, and efforts are currently being made to increase nursery provision. From the age of five onwards a variety of possibilities are available, including state-funded Primary Schools (age 5-11), or private Preparatory Schools (up to age 13)'. The majority (90 per cent) of children then go on to centrally funded state schools (11-16 or 11-18). At age 16, children can either leave school, with or without qualifications (GCSEs – General Certificate of Secondary Education); or go on to specialise in three subjects or more, taking 'A' (Advanced) Level examinations at 17 or 18. The minimum entrance qualification for university is two A levels. An alternative to the academically orientated 'A' levels are National Vocational Qualifications (NVQs) and Access courses. Alongside the under-funded state schools there are many partially state-aided or entirely independent private schools, many of which offer both boarding and day school facilities.

There are a number of international schools, an increasing number of which offer the International Baccalaureate, providing a more rounded education than the British 'A' Level system (which calls for early specialisation in three subjects).

British institutions of higher learning attract a growing number of foreign students every year. In spite of difficult economic circumstances, the UK has some of the most respected universities in the world, including its élite institutions, the Universities of Oxford and Cambridge. A relatively low percentage of the population goes on to higher education in comparison with other developed countries.

NATIONAL SERVICE

There is no compulsory military service in the United Kingdom.

EMBASSIES AND CONSULATES

US Embassy, 24 Grosvenor Square, London W1A 1AE; ☎020-7499 9000; www.usembassy.org.uk.
Canadian High Commission, Macdonald House, 1 Grosvenor Square, London W1K 4AB; ☎020-7258 6600; fax 020-7258 6333; www.canada.org.uk.

HOURS AND WAGES

A particular feature of the United Kingdom economy is the large number of low-paid, part-time jobs available. These at least leave some opportunities open to foreign workers willing to accept a subsistence wage. There is a legal minimum wage of £5.35 (aged 22+) or £4.45 (aged 18-21). Britons work more overtime than any other EU workers.

HOLIDAYS

Most workers receive four weeks' paid holiday per year. The public holidays are known as bank holidays. These are: 1 January; 2 January (Scotland only); Good Friday; Easter Monday; May Bank Holiday (1st Monday in May); Spring Bank Holiday (last Monday in May); Summer Bank Holiday (last Monday in August); Christmas Day; and Boxing Day.

SAFETY AND COMPENSATION

All businesses are obliged to have accident insurance to cover liability for an accident to one of their employees. They also have to report accidents to the authorities. The precise details of the rules and regulations can be obtained from the *Health & Safety Executive* (Infoline ☎ 0870-154 5500; www.hse.gov.uk).

TRADE UNIONS

In the 1980s legislation severely curtailed the power of the trade unions and there is a declining membership, which now stands at around 7.4 million. Unions represent different sectors or trades, and are generally members of the Trades Union Congress (TUC). Most union activity is concentrated in traditional heavy-industry sectors, such as mining and manufacturing, as well as in a few white collar areas like teaching and nursing (where poor conditions mean that there are regular threats of union action).

TAXATION

Foreigners who work in the United Kingdom are usually liable for UK income tax. Those from countries that have double taxation treaties with the UK may not be liable if they remain for less than six months in any tax year (April 6 to April 5) and are paying taxes abroad.

Unless you are self-employed or have your own company, tax will be deducted from your salary on a Pay As You Earn (PAYE) basis. There is a tax-free allowance (which is revised annually), and a progressive system of tax increments according to the level of income. PAYE means you will sometimes find that you are entitled to a tax rebate at the end of the tax year. In 1997, a tax self-assessment system was introduced, which means it is advisable to keep all pay-slips and details of your income throughout the year. Even those on PAYE will have to keep records, as they may be asked at random to fill out a self-assessment form. A local tax inquiry office will advise you on the necessary procedure (see *Inland Revenue – Inspector of Taxes* in the Yellow Pages). If you submit to self-assessment there is a penalty of £100 for late lodgement.

Value Added Tax (VAT) is payable on goods and services, with some exceptions, including food. Non-EU residents can reclaim VAT paid on goods (but not services) by presenting their passport and having VAT form 407 filled in by the retailer. This is presented to Customs & Excise for stamping on leaving the UK. The form is then returned to the retailer for your refund. Further information on this scheme is available from the VAT section of the UK Customs and Excise website (www.hmrc.gov.uk).

EMPLOYMENT PROSPECTS

There is no shortage of jobs for professionals in Britain, provided that they can obtain a work permit. The best opportunities lie in areas where a high level of training is required, such as medicine, the oil industry, management consultancy, scientific research, the IT and Telecommunications sector, social work and higher education.

The option of being transferred to the UK by a company based abroad is generally restricted to senior staff coming to the UK for career development, on the understanding that they will be transferred to another country in due course. The British Home Office expects junior staff to be hired in the UK. Marrying an EU citizen, claiming (and substantiating) UK ancestry, or participating in a recognised work exchange or working holiday scheme, are the only ways round such restrictions.

The future of the British economy will depend on the future of British science and the government has announced substantial new funding to support science teaching in schools, improve salaries and stipends for graduate scientists and engineers, and support technology transfer and university-business link ups.

NEWSPAPERS

The quality press, namely *The Times*, *The Guardian*, *The Independent* and *The Daily Telegraph* are some of the most respected newspapers in the world, and are the best source of job vacancies. Their addresses are given in the chapter, *Journalism*. All these newspapers now have electronic editions available on the internet and which include their current classified advertisements.

Local and free newspapers are a good source of job advertisements and accommodation. In London, the free magazines *TNT* and *Southern Cross*, which appear on Mondays, carries advertisements for accountants, au pairs and nannies, computer programmers, nurses, as well as for temporary employment agencies, travel agencies and firms which will deal with your tax affairs. These are aimed at its mainly Australasian readership. The address of *TNT Magazine* is 14-15 Child's Place, Earls Court, London SW5 9RX; ☎020-7373 3377; fax 020-7341 6600; e-mail enquiries@tntmag.co.uk; www.tntmagazine.com/uk/.

SPECIFIC CONTACTS

EMPLOYMENT SERVICE

Job vacancies are advertised on notice boards and computerised job banks at Jobcentres, which are to be found in most British towns. Anyone is free to look at these and enquire about the jobs on offer. Jobcentres have specific leaflets for EU and non-EU citizens looking for work, explaining work permit regulations, in particular WP1/5 for non-EU citizens. The addresses and telephone numbers of Jobcentres can be found under 'Employment Service' in telephone directories or online at www.jobcentreplus.gov.uk.

EMPLOYMENT AGENCIES

In addition to the government employment service, there are many temporary and permanent employment agencies. There is no legal restriction, as there is in much of Europe, on so-called 'temping' agencies arranging permanent posts. Some of the biggest, with branches in most major cities, are Reed, Brook Street Bureau, Adecco, and Manpower. The names and details of many UK management consultants are given in the chapter, *Getting the Job* and under *Specific Careers*. While recruitment consultants in the UK are happy to receive speculative applications from North Americans or Australasians, the regulations on work permits mean that only those who have suitable specialised qualifications are likely to attract the attention of these consultants, agencies, or potential employers.

MEDICAL STAFF

Jobs in medicine and nursing are available on both short and long term contracts. There is a shortage of doctors and, especially, nurses, and nursing is one field in which the Home Office is currently more than willing to grant work permits. Pharmacists are also in short supply and increasing numbers of Poles are being recruited to work in pharmacies in the UK. There is an active international recruitment campaign to bring Australian nurses to Britain to work for the NHS on one year and longer contracts. Nurses already in Britain will find agencies in *TNT Magazine* (address under *Newspapers*). Doctors may find current vacancies in the *British Medical Journal* (www.bmjpg.com), and employment agencies are increasingly used to fill these vacancies in National Health Service hospitals. The *Medicine and Nursing* chapter provides a summary of useful information.

TEACHERS

There is a shortage of teachers in certain subjects at secondary school level (mainly in mathematics and the sciences), British Local Education Authorities are often keen to recruit trained teachers from abroad who speak English, for either temporary 'supply' teaching or permanent work. Agencies dealing with this kind of work advertise regularly in *TNT Magazine* (see above). Work permit restrictions tend to exclude Americans. *Capita Education Resourcing* has offices throughout the UK (London office: Meridian House, Royal Hill, Greenwich, SE10 8RG; ☎020-8293 6318; fax 020-8858 8885; e-mail info.ers@capita.co.uk; www.capitaers.co.uk) and can find work in any subject area at primary or secondary level for teachers with work permits.

Exceptions to work permit restrictions can be made where a teacher is required for a school where a foreign curriculum is taught, such as the US curriculum. These 'American' schools in the UK fall into different categories: those that are run by the US Department of Defense; those which were started by Americans and take American pupils, but are not controlled by the US government; and international schools which follow a largely US curriculum. The following organisations will give information on these three categories:

Department of Defense Education Activity, 4040 North Fairfax Drive, Arlington, VA 22203; ☎703-696 3067; fax 703-696 2699; www.dodea.edu.
Office of Overseas Schools, US Department of State, Room H328, SA-1, Washington DC 20522; ☎202-261 8200; fax 202-261 8224; e-mail OverseasSchools@state.gov; www. state.gov/m/a/os/.
International Schools Services, 15 Roszel Road, PO Box 5910, Princeton, NJ 08543; ☎609-452 0990; fax 609-452 2690; e-mail edustaffing@iss.edu; www.iss.edu.

Work Exchange programmes for US teachers can be arranged by the *Fulbright Teacher Exchange Program*, 600 Maryland Avenue SW, Rm 235, Washington, DC 20024; ☎800-7260479; www.grad.usda.gov/International/. The *British Information Services* office at 845 3rd Ave., New York, NY 10022; ☎212-7450277; www.britain-info.org, issues a free leaflet, *Teaching in Britain*.

During the summer there are numerous English-language summer schools that will employ English-speakers with (or sometimes without) teaching experience. In some cases the courses are residential. Some contact addresses are listed below.

EF Language Travel, 114A Cromwell Road, London SW7 4ES; ☎020-7341 8612; fax 020-7341 8501; www.ef.com. Centres in Hastings, Brighton, London, Cambridge and Oxford.
Embassy CES, Recruitment Department, Lorna House, 103 Lorna Road, Hove BN3 3EL; ☎01273-322353; www.embassyces.com. Embassy CES is one of the largest British Council accredited summer school providers in the UK with more than 25 locations in the summer months all over the south of England, Wales, and in Ireland.
TASIS England American School, Coldharbour Lane, Thorpe, Surrey TW20 8TE; ☎01932-565252; fax 01932-564644; www.tasis.com. Counsellors as well as teaching aides needed. American applicants must have permission to work.

SHORT TERM WORK

The numerous temping agencies are the best sources for this kind of work but you can also consult Jobcentre job banks (see above).

AGRICULTURAL

Between May and October thousands of casual workers are recruited by farms in England and Scotland to pick fruit (strawberries, raspberries, apples, pears), vegetables (tomatoes, courgettes, potatoes, lettuces) and hops (used for making beer). Seven of the largest fruit growers in the UK are permitted to recruit fruit pickers from outside the EU. Applicants must be students aged 18-25, and can only stay in the UK until 30 November. Instead of having to obtain work permits, such foreign 'volunteers' are issued with Entrance Authorisation Cards under the Seasonal Agricultural Workers Scheme, provided they are used only for working on the issuing farm camp. Farm camps are international affairs, with workers mainly from eastern European countries. Due to the enlargement of the EU in May 2004, the Seasonal Agricultural Workers Scheme, which had been increasing annually to meet farmers' needs, has actually been reduced. This was because those who benefited most from this scheme were those who lived in the new EU members states and thus were able to work in the UK anyway. However, SAWS will remain in use until 2010, when it will be incorporated into the new points based system of entry.

The main recruitment organisation for this scheme is *Concordia*, 2nd Floor, Heversham House, 20/22 Boundary Road, Hove, Sussex BN3 4ET; ☎01273-422218; fax 01273-421182; e-mail info@concordia-iye.org.uk; www.concordia-iye.org.uk, which recruits pickers for over 160 camps between May and October. The following are some of the Home Office recognised farms:

Friday Bridge Agricultural Camp, March Road, Wisbech, Cambridgeshire PE14 0LR; ☎01945-860255.

International Farm Camp, Hall Road, Tiptree, Colchester, Essex CO5 0QS; ☎01621-815496.

R & JM Place, International Farm Camp, Church Farm, Tunstead, Norwich NR12 8RQ; ☎01692-536225/337.

The Australian-linked temping agency, *Bligh* (70 North End Road, London W14 9EP; ☎020-7603 6123; fax 020-7371 6898; www.bligh.co.uk), has an agricultural section which places people on farms throughout Britain, as well as operating placement services for nannies, and secretaries.

AU PAIRS AND NANNIES

Strictly speaking, North Americans and Australians, Kiwis and South Africans cannot be au pairs in the UK since they do not need to learn English. Nevertheless, there are a few organisations that will arrange au pair or mothers' help positions in the UK for English-speakers (see below). It should be noted that the UK only recognised the existence of male au pairs in 1992. Further information can be found in the *Au Pair and Domestic* chapter.

Au Pair USA/InterExchange, 161 Sixth Avenue, New York 10013, New York; ☎212-924 0446; fax 212-924 0575; e-mail info@interexchange.org; www.interexcahnge.org; places au pairs from the USA in the UK and worldwide. Full board, private room, weekly stipend, two weeks' paid vacation a year. Placements from nine to 12 months.

Australian Nanny and Au Pair Connection, 404 Glenferrie Road, Kooyong, Melbourne, 3144 Victoria, Australia; ☎3-9824 8857; e-mail rosemary@australiannannies.info; www.nannyconnection.com.au, can place nannies, au pairs, mothers' helps and housekeepers in the UK for six months or more. Summer placements are also possible.

TOURISM

It has been estimated that one worker in 10 is involved in the tourist and hospitality industry in Britain and there is always a demand for staff, such as waiters, dishwashers, chambermaids, bar staff, maids. In some cases, employers are willing to hire foreigners 'off the books'. Wages in the hotels and catering industry are often low. Board and lodging may be included in the terms of employment.

If you are applying from abroad, it is advisable to send a detailed CV and photo to the hotel of your choice several months in advance. Addresses can be found in the Vacation Work publication, *Summer Jobs in Britain*, or by asking for lists of hotels from British Tourist Boards abroad (see above). If you are in London, contact the *Jobcentre*, 1-3 Denmark Street, London W1, which deals exclusively with hotel and catering staff, or specialised private employment agencies (see *TNT Magazine* or the Yellow Pages). Another agency specialising in hotel work in the UK is *Montpelier Employment*, 34 Montpelier Rd, Brighton, Sussex BN1 2LQ; ☎01273-778686; www.montpelieremploymentagency.co.uk.

VOLUNTARY WORK

Foreign visitors may be surprised to learn that there is widespread poverty and deprivation in the UK, particularly in the inner cities and an estimated 17 per cent of the population live below the poverty line. There is both a need for voluntary workers, and a ready supply of local volunteers, so it is advisable to make arrangements in advance. A number of organisations and opportunities are listed in the *Voluntary Work* chapter of this book, but the most detailed reference guide available is the *International Directory of Voluntary Work* (Vacation Work Publications; www.vacationwork.co.uk).

Overseas nationals seeking voluntary work in the UK will fall under Tier 5 of the new points based system. Overseas nationals may be admitted for up to 12 months for the purpose of voluntary work providing their sponsor is a charity or non-charitable philanthropic organisation and the applicant is receiving no remuneration other than pocket money, board and accommodation. The work which they do must be closely related to the aims of the charity i.e. working with people, and they must not be engaged in purely clerical, administrative or maintenance work. Volunteers are expected to leave the United Kingdom at the end of their visit.

WORKING EXCHANGES

As the UK is a member of most international work exchange organisations, there is a good likelihood of finding a placement. Organisations to contact include IAESTE and AIESEC. *Future Farmers of America* (www.ffa.org) runs a work experience programme in the UK for young agriculturalists (19-24) with a strong background in production agriculture. Placements last from three-12 months and the programme fee is a minimum of $2400. See *Working Exchanges* (in *Getting the Job*) and the *Agriculture, Fisheries and the Environment* section for further information.

WORKING HOLIDAYS

US students seeking temporary work in the UK will fall under Tier 5 of the new points based entry system (previously known as the 'Work in Britain Program'). This allows full-time US college students and recent graduates over the age of 18 to look for work in Britain, finding jobs through BUNAC listings or through personal contacts. Jobs may be pre-arranged, though most participants wait until arrival in Britain to job hunt. US students on study abroad programmes through an American University overseas are also eligible for the programme. When students apply to BUNAC they will receive a'Blue Card.' The Blue Card must be presented to immigration on arrival in the UK. It is valid for six months and cannot be extended, although it is possible to obtain a second Blue Card in another calendar year if they again fulfil the eligibility requirements. The Blue Card costs $290 from BUNAC, PO Box 430, Southbury, CT 06488 (☎1-800 GO BUNAC; e-mail wib@bunacusa.org; www.bunac.org).

Nationals of Commonwealth countries (including Australia, New Zealand, Canada and South Africa) between the ages of 17 and 30 are permitted to visit the UK under Tier 5 of the new system (previously known as the 'Working Holiday Maker' scheme). This allows them to take up casual employment which will be incidental to their holiday, but not to engage in business or to pursue a career. The period which can be spent in the UK is two years and of that time, 52 weeks may be spent working full-time or part-time at no more than 20 hours per week.

Commonwealth citizens with at least one British-born grandparent may wish to apply for 'UK Ancestry employment entry clearance' from the British High Commission: this altogether eliminates the need for a work permit. Married couples must apply for separate entry clearance before travelling.

Canadian students, graduates and young people should contact the Student Work Abroad Programme (SWAP), which provides support to those wishing to work in Britain. It is administered by the Canadian Universities Travel Service, which has over 40 offices in Canada. For details see www.swap.ca.

Australians and New Zealanders should contact International Exchange Programmes (IEP), a non-profit organisation specialising in sending young Australians and New Zealanders on working holidays overseas. For more details visit www.iep.org.au or www. iep.co.nz.

INTERNATIONAL COMPANIES IN BRITAIN

The *American Chamber of Commerce (UK)*, 75 Brook Street, London W1Y 2EB, ☎020-7493 0381, publishes the *Anglo-American Trade Directory* which contains the names of 20,000 companies with trans-Atlantic links.

CENTRAL & EASTERN EUROPE

The 1990s saw a major realignment in the map of Europe and there is no longer a simple division between East and West. Instead countries such as Poland, the Czech and Slovak Republics, and Hungary perceive themselves once again as Central European. The three Baltic States to the north are keen to identify themselves with the West. The former Yugoslavian countries, Serbia and Montenegro, Kosovo, Croatia, Bosnia-Herzegovina and Macedonia, along with Albania, see themselves as belonging to the South East. Slovenia has close historical ties with Austria and Italy. There are states that come more directly under Russian influence, like Belarus and Ukraine (although the latter is independent from Russia). The Russian Federation itself stretches far into Central Asia, and to the Pacific coast.

The former Soviet Union was an artificial state; and its disappearance has seen the rise of competing nationalisms (not least in Russia itself). These tensions are expressed less acutely in the Central European countries, which have moved more easily to a market economy and aspire to membership of the European Union in the near future. The history of Eastern Europe is one of shifting borders. Each state has its own minority communities (like the Russians of the Trans-Dneister Republic who seceded from Moldova, which seceded in its turn from the part of the former Soviet Union which is now Ukraine). Some of these divisions will not last. Others are more stable. Poland, for example, has post-war borders that reach much further westwards than the historical Polish state but still has no claims on its lost territories in Lithuania, Belarus or the Ukraine. There is a desire in these countries simply for economic (and social) development and to avoid the conflicts that could arise between the patchwork of ethnic communities and nationalisms left behind by the collapse of the Soviet Union and Yugoslavia. In Russia itself, economic reform and reconstruction is a greater priority than nationalism, although there is a kind of nostalgia for communism and for the influence that the Soviet Union and its Tsarist forerunner used to wield in neighbouring countries. There are Russian minorities, too, in many countries in Eastern Europe and Central Asia. Russia is still the most influential country in the region.

As far as democracy and economic development are concerned, there is also a gradation from east to west (as there is in the kinds of nationalism which are expressed). Poland, the Czech Republic, Hungary, and Slovenia became members of the European Union in 2004; and Croatia and the Baltic States are developing closer economic ties. Direct investment from abroad is likely to increase as western European companies take advantage of an educated workforce that is cheap and flexible. A fragile prosperity has come to Russia itself, at least to certain sections of the population, although democracy is not so firmly established. Less successful have been Serbia, the Slovak Republic, Macedonia, Bulgaria, and Romania, as evidence by the recent war between Serbia and Kosovo. The Ukraine and Belarus are relatively poor and underdeveloped, as are the countries of Central Asia – namely Kazakhstan, Turkmenistan, Kyrgyzstan, and Tajikistan. Along with Uzbekistan, Armenia and Georgia, south of the Caucasus Mountains, they have found the transition from the centralised Soviet system to a diverse market economy most difficult (although there are substantial natural resources like minerals and oil in many of these). Political conflict continues in pockets throughout these areas.

It should be emphasised that all these countries now regard themselves as independent and sovereign states. The process of economic development and reconstruction is the background against which employment in these countries should be seen. There are many new opportunities for international workers – in everything from consultancy to volunteer work – as well as the challenge of living in a country whose history and way of life are often very different from the experience of most western Europeans or North Americans. Once again, there is an alignment from west to east: the countries of central Europe are those where there is the broadest range of job opportunities, and a less pronounced economic and cultural difference.

From the point of view of those interested in working in the region, these countries have certain features in common. Expatriate workers can be roughly divided into those who are sent there by large companies, and are therefore paid at international rates and those who work for local organisations, and are paid at the local rate. There are some areas of work – such as English teaching – which fall between these two categories.

Many foreigners who work in these countries are volunteers; some will even pay for the privilege. Others do valuable work in training and consultancy, in helping to put the local economy back on its feet; or in looking after the casualties of social change – the poor and underprivileged – where provision is often inadequate. As these economies develop, the growth in employment opportunities is likely to be in the 'middle' range of jobs – teaching, secretarial, retail, technical, and managerial positions.

In the wider jobs market, the main infrastructure opportunities lie in development: roads, railways, airports; telecommunications; financial services; and administration. Manufacturing industry and distribution are being developed, often in collaboration with foreign companies, as are service industries like food distribution and retailing. There are opportunities in oil, mining, gas, and engineering, airlines and road transport, and all the other areas where there are partnerships between 'Western' and local firms.

Challenging conditions (where accommodation is often cramped and bureaucracy a major problem) mean that volunteers, as well as other workers, will often be of a more adventurous nature. Professionals with real experience and understanding of their field, as well as the right qualifications are needed in consultancy and development. There are openings too for those who are more entrepreneurial; who know how to make new contacts and develop new ideas; and who can start a business and make it grow.

These countries of Central and Eastern Europe – and the territory covered by the Commonwealth of Independent States (CIS), which replaced the Soviet Union, and has now been succeeded by the Russian Federation – are all open for business, and to a wide variety of international jobseekers. Preparation, perseverance and practical knowledge, will all be required.

IMMIGRATION

The procedures for immigration and visas are subject to frequent change and you are advised to check with the embassy concerned. There may be restrictions on the import and export of local and international currency and the embassy or consulate will also advise on procedures for this. Companies which offer a visa service and travel and trade services in the region are *Asla Travel Group,* Riverside House, 160 High Street, Huntingdon, Cambs. PE29 3TF; ☎01480-433800; fax 01480-433799; e-mail visas@asla-select.co.uk; www.asla.co.uk; and in the USA *G3 Visas & Passports*, 3240 Wilson Boulevard, Suite 150. Arlington, VA 22201; ☎888-883 8472; fax 703-524 3374; e-mail info@g3visas.com; www.g3visas.com.

LANGUAGE

English is often spoken in the business community and by young people, but some knowledge of the local language will be an asset. A rival to English as a second language is German, and French can sometimes be used. Russian is universally spoken in the countries of the former Soviet Union, or CIS, and is widely spoken elsewhere, although it is no longer generally taught in Central and Eastern Europe or in the Baltic States.

NEWSPAPERS

The Powers Turner Group, Gordon House, Greencoat Lane, London SW1P 1PH; ☎020-7592 8300; fax 020-7592 8301; e-mail ppn-london@publicitas.com; www.publicitas. com, represents a wide variety of newspapers and other publications. There are English-language publications such as *The Warsaw Voice* and *The Budapest Sun* in many countries, aimed at local business and expatriate communities. The Russian newspaper *Pravda* can be found online at http://english.pravda.ru/.

OTHER CONTACTS

Other contacts may be found in the *Voluntary Work, Teaching*, and other chapters in the *Specific Careers* section of this book. The Commercial Department of your embassy in that country, or embassies and tourist offices in your own, are useful sources of up-to-date information. *UK Trade and Investment* (Kingsgate House, 66-74 Victoria Street, London, SW1E 6SW; ☎020-7215 8000; www.uktradeinvest.gov.uk), attached to the Department of Trade and Industry, offers business advice and background information on Eastern Europe as well as other countries.

The Baltic States

Estonia, Latvia and Lithuania are situated between Russia and the Baltic Sea. Their recent history was marked by Russian occupation in the 19th century and again in 1944. Each is now keen to assert its own national identity and culturally they are very different, although each one has a Russian minority population and still lives in the shadow of its larger neighbour. All three countries joined the European Union in 2004 and have since reaped the benefits of outside investment as companies fall over one another to take advantage of cheap labour and production costs and property investors race in to grab a bargain.

These are, in a sense, the most European of the states formerly part of the Soviet Union. Russian is spoken by all except the very young, but the locals prefer to speak English or German to foreigners. The Estonian language belongs, like Finnish, to the Finno-Ugric family of languages (and has even more case endings – fourteen). Latvian and Lithuanian belong to the Baltic group of languages and bear some relation to the Slavic and Germanic families. Language is a political issue and is seen as an expression of national identity. Increasingly, many Russian settlers now have to master the local tongue to find employment or get a work permit.

Other cultural influences have come from Denmark, Sweden, Poland, and especially Hanseatic Germany; the architecture in the coastal towns can be reminiscent of Germany or Holland. The Baltic States are similar to these countries in their weather too, with a mix of continental and maritime climates and prevailing westerly winds. The mean average temperature is 42 deg F (6 deg C) – the average being 41 deg F (5 deg C) in January and 62 deg F (17 deg C) in July.

There are also religious as well as cultural and linguistic differences between the countries. Estonians and Latvians are predominately Lutheran, whereas Lithuanians are mainly Roman Catholic. There are many Protestant, Russian Orthodox and Evangelical Reform churches, as well as a number of synagogues.

Estonia

○   **Year of EU Accession:** 2004
○   **Estonian Embassy,** 16 Hyde Park Gate, London SW7 5DG; ☎020-7589 3428; fax 020-7589 3430; www.estonia.gov.uk
○   **Estonian Embassy,** 2131 Massachusetts Avenue, Washington DC 20008; ☎202-588 0101; fax 202-588 0108; www.estemb.org
○   **Currency:** 1 Kroon (EEK) = 100 sents
○   **Exchange Rate:** £1 = EEK 22.61; $1 = EEK 12.27; €1 = EEK 15.65
○   **Country Code:** +372

Estonia is the most northerly of the Baltic States, with linguistic and cultural ties to Finland, its neighbour to the north. The population is 1.3 million, and nearly a third of the inhabitants live in the capital, Tallinn. Other big towns are Pärnu, Tartu and Narva, which straddles the border with Russia. The landscape, which covers 16,683 square miles (43,211 sq km), is not unlike that of Finland, with forests, lakes and islands. Estonians are a musical people and their departure from the Soviet Bloc was brought about by what was called the 'Singing Revolution'. Through the simple expedient of singing folk songs in harmony and *en masse* the Estonian people forced their demands for freedom. There are few raw materials, and the country relies mostly on imported commodities to produce finished goods. Agriculture and, increasingly, tourism are important. Privatisation was quite a rapid process in Estonia, and the cost of living is high. It became a member of the EU in May 2004 and it is widely hoped that many businesses from the west will set up in the country to take advantage of its zero rate of corporation tax. Sectors such as computer assembly, telecomunicationss, and genetics are the fastest growing and ports and shipping, forestry, and chemical products have attracted the interest of British companies.

IMMIGRATION

A work and residence permit are needed, but visas are not required by UK and US citizens to enter the country. These permits may be applied for in advance or on arrival at the *National Department of Immigration* (Kodakonsus ja Migratsiooniamet), Endla 13, Tallinn 15179; ☎612 6967; www.mig.ee/eng/. However, there is a limit on the number of permits granted each year. Currently this is just 0.05% of the permanent population of Estonia. Work permits will only be granted if they are approved by the Labour Market Board (www.tta.ee/).

EMBASSIES

British Embassy, Wismari 6, Tallinn 10136; ☎2-667 4700; fax 2-667 4725; www. britishembassy.ee.
US Embassy, Kentmanni 20, 15099 Tallinn; ☎2-668 8100; fax 2-668 8134; www.usemb.ee. Estonia has an online tourist board website at http://visitestonia.com.

SPECIFIC CONTACTS

For managers and businesses the immediate opportunities are in retail and the re-equipment and management assistance for the core Estonian industries of wood and textiles. The British Embassy Commercial Section provides information services for business travellers and others interested in Estonia.

TEACHING

There are many private language schools in Estonia with more being established all the time. The Estonian Embassy has details of these. The *British Council* (Vana-Posti 7, 10146 Tallinn; ☎2-625 7788; fax 2-625 7799; www.britishcouncil.ee) can provide details of English language schools, and local school and university contacts. They also have a useful resource centre.

Latvia

- **Year of EU Accession:** 2004
- **Latvian Embassy,** 45 Nottingham Place, London W1U 5LY; ☎020-7312 0040; fax 020-7312 0042; www.london.am.gov.lv/en/
- **Latvian Embassy,** 2306 Massachusetts Avenue, NW, Washington DC 20008; ☎202-328 2840; fax 202-328 2860; e-mail embassy@latvia-usa.org; www.latvia-usa.org
- **Currency:** 1 Lat (LVL) = 100 santims
- **Exchange Rate:** £1 = Ls 1.01; $1 = Ls 0.55; €1 = Ls 0.70
- **Country Code:** +371

Latvia covers 24,938 square miles (64,589 sq km) and has a population totalling 2.4 million. It borders Estonia to the north, Lithuania to the south, the Russian Federation to the east, and Belarus to the southeast. The capital is Riga, with 850,000 inhabitants. Other towns are Liepaja, Daugavpils, Rezekne, Valmiera, Jurmala and Jelgava. The coastal plain is flat, but inland the landscape is hilly with forests, lakes and rivers. Pollution is a problem along the Baltic coast, but there are also conservation areas. Key industries include the manufacture of railway rolling stock and light machinery, fertilisers, chemicals and electronics. A number of joint ventures have been established between Latvian and UK companies and the import/export business between the two countries is expanding.

IMMIGRATION

UK and US passport holders do not require a visa to visit the country for up to 90 days in any one year. Residence and work payments may be arranged in the country or before departure. For further information contact the Office of Citizenship and Migration Affairs (Raina Blvd. 5, Riga, LV1050; ☎800 7657; fax 733 1211; www.ocma.gov.lv) or the Latvian Embassy in your own country.

EMBASSIES

British Embassy, 5 J.Alunana Street, 1010 Riga; ☎777 4700; fax 777 4707; www.britain.lv.
US Embassy, 7 Raina Blvd, LV-1510 Riga; ☎703 6200; http://riga.usembassy.gov

SPECIFIC CONTACTS

The *Latvian Development Agency*, Perses iela 2, LV-1442, Latvia; ☎703 9400; www.liaa. gov.lv, has published a report on *Development Potential* which summarises areas where Latvia needs inward investment. The *British Chamber of Commerce in Latvia*, Room 605, Kr.Valdemara 21, LV-1010 Riga; ☎703 5202 fax 703 5318; e-mail info@bccl.lv; www.bccl.lv, has a database of contacts within Latvia and works closely with the Latvian Development Agency.

VOLUNTARY WORK

Latvian Student Volunteers (LSV), Laeplesa 75/III-32, 1011 Riga, arranges work camps in Latvia. Applications can also be sent through partner volunteer organisations in your own country (see chapter on *Voluntary Work*).

Lithuania

- ○ **Year of EU Accession:** 2004
- ○ **Lithuanian Embassy,** 84 Gloucester Place, London W1U 6AU; ☎020-7486 6401; fax 020-7486 6403; http://amb.urm.lt/jk/
- ○ **Lithuanian Embassy,** 2622 16th Street, NW, Washington DC 20009; ☎202-234 5860; fax 202-328 0466; www.ltembassyus.org
- ○ **Currency:** 1 Litas = 100 centas
- ○ **Exchange rate:** £1 = 5 Litas; $1 = 2.71 Litas; €1 = 3.45 Litas
- ○ **Country Code:** +370

Lithuania is the largest of the Baltic States, with a population of 3.6 million. Vilnius, the capital, has a population of 600,000. Other cities include Klaipeda, Palanga and Kaunas. It borders Latvia to the north, Poland and the Russian enclave of Kaliningrad to the southwest, and Belarus to the southeast. The landscape features plains and low hills with over 2,800 lakes, most of which are in the east. There is a great dependence on agriculture and the food industry is dominated by the production of milk, meat and fish. Textiles and knitwear, electrical, electronic and optical goods are also produced. Light rather than heavy industry predominates and the economy relies extensively on imported raw materials.

Other than the Russian Federation and the Ukraine, Germany is its main trading partner. The Lithuanian language features many dialects, and German and Polish are also widely spoken. English is used for international commerce, and by those who work in tourism.

IMMIGRATION

UK and US passport holders do not require a visa to visit for up to 90 days. Those who are looking for work may stay an extra three months on top of the 90 days without applying for a residence permit. Further information on applying for residence and work permits can be obtained from the Migration Department of the Ministry of the Interior (Sventaragio 2, LT-01122 Vilnius, Lithuania, ☎5-271 7112, fax: 5-2718210, www.migracija.lt.

EMBASSIES AND TOURIST OFFICE

British Embassy, Antakalnio 2, 10308 Vilnius; ☎5-246 2900; fax 5-246 2901; www.britain.lt.

US Embassy, Akmenř gatvë 6, Vilnius, Lithuania LT-03106; ☎5-266 5500; fax 370 5-266 5510; www.usembassy.lt.

Lithuanian State Department of Tourism, A Juozapaviciaus 13, 09311 Vilnius; ☎5-210 8796; fax 5-210 8753; www.tourism.lt.

SPECIFIC CONTACTS

The privatisation of industry has resulted in opportunities in re-equipping, and management consultancy. The *Lithuanian Development Agency* (Sv.Jono st. 3, 01123 Vilnius; ☎5-262 7438; fax 5-212 0160; e-mail info@lda.lt; www.businesslithuania.com) can supply information on privatisation. *The Association of Lithuanian Chambers of Commerce and Industry* (J.Tumo-Vaizganto g. 9/1-63a, 01108 Vilnius; ☎5-261 2102; fax 5-261 2112; e-mail info@chambers.lt; www.chambers.lt), can supply information on foreign companies investing in Lithuania.

TEACHING

The *British Council* in Vilnius (Jogailos 4, 01116 Vilnius; ☎5-264 4890; fax 5-264 4893; e-mail mail@britishcouncil.lt; www.britishcouncil.org/lithuania) advises that information concerning the employment of English language teachers is provided by the *Ministry of Education and Science* (A. Volano str. 2/7, 2600 Vilnius, ☎5-2622483; fax 52-612077; e-mail smmin@smm.lt; www.smm.lt).

Bulgaria

o **Likely date of EU Accession:** January 2007
o **Bulgarian Embassy,** 186-188 Queen's Gate, London SW7 5HL; ☎020-7584 9400; fax 020-7584 4948; www.bulgarianembassy.org.uk
o **Bulgarian Embassy,** 1621 22nd Street, NW, Washington, DC 20008; ☎202-387 0174; fax 202-234 7973; www.bulgaria-embassy.org
o **Currency:** 1 Lev (BGL) = 100 stotinki
o **Exchange Rate:** £1 = BGL 2.83; $1 = BGL 1.53; €1 = 1.95 BGL
o **Country Code:** +359

Bulgaria is located on the Black Sea Coast, between Romania to the north and Greece and Turkey to the South. Serbia and FYR Macedonia are its western neighbours. The population is 7.4 million in an area of 43,000 square miles. The capital Sofia in the west has 1.2 million inhabitants. The Balkan and the Rhodope Mountains stretch across the country to the Black Sea coast with its sandy beaches. The climate is never extreme, with warm summers and snow on the mountains in winter. The economy is traditionally agricultural and Bulgaria is known for its exported wine (an improving product). Food processing and packaging are important and there are heavy industries like engineering as well as newer ones such as biotechnology. The transition to a market economy has been slow, however. There is high inflation and increasingly high levels of unemployment.

A handshake is the common form of greeting and as in much of the region small gifts from one's own country are appreciated. There is one social convention of Bulgaria that may not come so easily to the Westerner – a nod of the head means 'no', a shaking of the head means 'yes'.

IMMIGRATION

British and North America passport holders require a visa to enter Bulgaria for more than 30 days. Longer-term residents require a residence and work permit, and those working or looking for work in Bulgaria should register at the local police station. Enquiries about work and residence permits should be made to a Bulgarian consulate or embassy abroad. If Bulgaria are granted accession to the EU in January 2007, the authorities will have to relax the regulations for EU residents entering the country to look for work. How quickly this will happen remains unclear at the time of writing.

EMBASSIES

British Embassy, 9 Moskovska Street, Sofia 1000; ☎2-933 9222; fax 2-933 9263; www. british-embassy.bg.
British Honorary Consul, 40 Graf Igantiev Street, Varna; ☎52-665 5555; fax 52-665 5755.
US Embassy, 16 Kozyak Street, Sofia 1407; ☎2-937 5100; fax 2-937 5320; http://sofia. usembassy.gov/.

TOURIST OFFICES

Bulgarian Tourism Office, 186-188 Queen's Gate, London SW7 5HL; ☎020-7589 8402; www.bulgariantourism.com.
Bulgarian Tourist Center, 317 Madison Ave., Suite 508, New York, NY 10017; ☎212-573 5530.

SPECIFIC CONTACTS

The Bulgaria Desk of UK Trade and Investment, Kingsgate House, 66-74 Victoria Street, London SW1E 6SW; www.uktradeinvest.gov.uk, can provide an information pack (for commercial or business purposes) containing a list of UK companies with Bulgarian links. The *British Bulgarian Chamber of Commerce* can be contacted at PO Box 123, Bromley BR1 4ZX; ☎020-8464 5007; e-mail info@bbcc.bg; www.bbcc.bg. The *Bulgarian Chamber of Commerce and Industry*, 42 Parchevich Street, 1058 Sofia; ☎2-987 2631; fax 2-987 3209; e-mail bcci@bbci.bg; www.bcci.bg can provide commercial advice and information.

TEACHING

The British Council in London (see the *Teaching* chapter) recruits a number of teachers for foreign language secondary schools in Bulgaria in a programme run by the Bulgarian Ministry of Science, Education and Technology.

TOURISM

SHG Recruitment, Specialist Holidays Group and Tui UK (www.shgjobs.co.uk), recruits a small number of representatives for skiing holidays in Borovets and Pamperova. Previous experience and fluent Bulgarian are desirable.

For voluntary work contacts see the *Voluntary Work* chapter in the *Specific Careers* section of this book.

Czech Republic

- o   **Year of EU Accession:** 2004
- o   **Czech Embassy,** 26-30 Kensington Palace Gardens, London W8 4QY; ☎020-7243 1115; fax 020-7727 9654; www.mzv.cz/london
- o   **Czech Embassy,** 3900 Spring of Freedom Street NW, Washington DC 20008; ☎202-274 9100; fax 202-966 8540; www.mzv.cz/washington
- o   **Currency:** 1 Koruna (Kc) = 100 hellers
- o   **Exchange Rate:** £1 = Kcs 41.23; $1 = Kcs 22.36; €1 = Kcs 28.47
- o   **Country Code:** +420

The Czech Republic covers 31,000 square miles (80,289 sq km). The population is 10.2 million, including German, Slovak, Hungarian, Ukrainian and Polish minorities. Bohemia to the west of the country is mountainous, and there are hills and a rich agricultural plain in Moravia to the east. One third of the territory is covered with forests, which are popular places for hiking or climbing. South Bohemia is picturesque, with castles, palaces and medieval towns. The climate is colder in winter and warmer in summer than in Britain, the average temperature in January being 32 def F (0 deg C) and in July 68 deg F (20 deg C). Prague, the capital, is an historic city on the banks of the River Vltava. Other major towns are Brno, Ostrava and Plzen. The official language is Czech, but German and English are also spoken.

The Republic of Czechoslovakia was declared in October 1918, and comprised the former Austro-Hungarian possessions of Bohemia, Moravia and Slovakia. In 1938, following the Munich Agreement, the country was occupied by Nazi Germany. After World War II, the communists seized power and remained in control of the country up until the bloodless 'Velvet Revolution' of November 1989. In 1992, it was decided that the country would split into independent Czech and Slovak Republics.

Czechoslovakia had one of the healthiest economies of the former Warsaw Pact countries. Production fell and inflation rose from 1991 onwards, but there has been a return to prosperity and stability in the new Czech Republic, which is less hampered by a dependence on heavy engineering than its Slovak neighbour. Unemployment currently runs at around eight per cent. Germany is now its main trading partner.

For those who wish to look for work in the Czech Republic, there are opportunities in English teaching and voluntary work. Workers who are posted there from abroad include lawyers, bankers, economists, diplomats and journalists (see the relevant career chapters).

IMMIGRATION

EU citizens do not need a residence permit to stay for up to three months. For longer stays, they should apply either to the embassy or consulate in their country of origin, or at the local police station in the Czech Republic. Those who intend to stay longer than thirty days should register their place of residence with the aliens department of the police upon arrival in the country. Work permits are not required by EU citizens, although the employer is obliged to notify the labour office.

US passport holders do not require a visa to enter the Czech Republic and may remain for up to three months before they need to apply for a residence permit. Work permits are arranged by the employer at local employment offices, and a photocopy of your passport and qualifications/diplomas are required. Long-term Czech residence applications must include this work permit and should be made to a Czech embassy abroad. Enquiries about work and residence permits should be made to a Czech consulate or embassy abroad.

EMBASSIES

British Embassy, Thunovská 14, 118 00 Prague 1; ☎2-5740 2111; fax 2-5740 2296; www.britain.cz.
US Embassy, Trziste 15, 118 01 Prague 1; ☎2-5702 2000; fax 2-5702 2809; www. usembassy.cz.

SPECIFIC CONTACTS

TEACHING

The English-language teaching industry is booming in the Czech Republic, with many private schools opening up. There is also some demand for teachers in other subjects –

from primary school level up to universities and other institutions of higher education. Salaries are usually only adequate to cover local living expenses, but it is usually possible to supplement a salary by teaching private classes. Free accommodation and medical insurance are sometimes provided. The following organisations can be contacted for work (and see under *Jazykové Skoly* in the telephone directory):

The Boland School T.E.F.L. Training Centre, Stefanikova 1, 60200 Brno, Czech Rep.; tel/fax: +420 541 241 674; e-mail: info@boland-czech.com; www.boland-czech.com. The Boland School was founded in 1992 and has T.E.F.L. teacher training centres in both the Czech Republic and Asia offering the International T.E.F.L. Diploma on a 4 and a half-week residential programme. Courses are held every month, all year round. Job placement service is available to all program graduates. The Boland School also provides Czech language courses and consultation services to those wishing to work or do business in the Czech Republic. For further details see www. boland-czech.com.

The Academic Information Agency (AIA) at the Ministry of Education, Youth and Sports, Dém zahraninich sluzeb MSMT, Senovázé námestí 26, PO Box 8, 111 06 Prague 1; ☎224-398 111; fax 224-229 697; e-mail aia@dzs.cz; www.dzs.cz, recruits qualified staff for primary and secondary schools. Applicants are sent a questionnaire that is then circulated among schools, which contact teachers directly when they are needed. Qualifications are necessary. Contracts are usually for one year and include free accommodation.

VOLUNTARY WORK

There is a great demand for voluntary workers, particularly for environmental projects. Prospective volunteers should take note of the escalating cost of living when considering their allowance. Free accommodation is a minimum requirement. For organisations arranging voluntary work see the *Voluntary Work* chapter.

INEX, Senovázné námestí 24, 116 47 Prague 1; ☎2-3462 1527; fax 2-3462 1390; e-mail inexsda@inexsda.cz; www.inexsda.cz, needs volunteers to take part in international work camps contributing to the environment and historical conservation in July and August. Volunteers pay for their own travel and insurance.

OTHER CONTACTS

The Commercial Department of the British Embassy, Prague, has prepared a list of British companies in the Czech Republic which can be obtained from the Embassy address above.

Hungary

o **Year of EU Accession:** 2004
o **Hungarian Embassy,** 35 Eaton Place, London SW1X 8BY; ☎020-7235 5218; fax 020-7823 1348; www.huemblon.org.uk
o **Hungarian Embassy,** 3910 Shoemaker St, NW, Washington DC 20008; ☎202-362-6730; www.hungaryemb.org
o **Currency:** 1 Forint (Ft) = 100 fillér
o **Exchange Rate:** £1 = Ft 401.36; $1 = Ft 217.79; €1 = Ft 277.22
o **Country Code:** +36

Hungary occupies an area of 36,000 square miles (93,239 sq km). The population of around 10.5 million is largely made up of Hungarian-speaking Magyars (92 per cent) with small

German and Gypsy minorities. The language belongs, like Finnish, to the Finno-Ugric family. German is also widely spoken. Most of the country is flat, and there are several ranges of hills, chiefly in the north and west. The country forms part of the catchment area of the River Danube on whose banks the capital Budapest is situated. Budapest has two million inhabitants. Other cities are Gyór, Pécs, Szeged, Debrecen and Miskolc. Summers can be very hot, with the temperature frequently reaching 86 deg F (30 deg C), while during winter the average is around 32 deg F (0 deg C).

Hungary's recent history is not dissimilar to that of most of Eastern Europe – domination by the Soviet Union followed by democratic reforms post-1989. The last Soviet troops left Hungary in June 1991. A striking feature of the Hungarian economy was the early adoption, in 1968, of some free market reforms, which provided much of the inspiration for change in other Warsaw Pact countries. Integration with the world economy has gone further than in some of its neighbours and foreign investment is high. It is a member of the Organisation for Economic Cooperation and Development (OECD), and in 2004 joined the EU. Agriculture is still a major activity, accounting for six per cent of Gross Domestic Product (GDP); and food products are currently 20 per cent of exports. Industrial production started to grow again in 1992, following a severe contraction in 1989-1991. Opportunities for foreigners seeking work are in English teaching, and in construction and investment projects. There are also opportunities for experts in industrial restructuring and finance. Pharmaceuticals, IT and telecommunications, and mining are important industries.

IMMIGRATION

British, US and EU citizens do not require a visa to enter Hungary and can remain in the country for 90 days (for UK citizens, six months). Work and residence permits must be arranged in advance by the Hungarian employer with the local authorities in Hungary. Foreigners wishing to stay for more than a year must obtain a residence permit from the police force in the town of residence within six months. In the case of Budapest this is BRFK Igazgatásrendészeti Fóosztály Kélföldieket Ellenórzó Osztály, 6th District Varosligeti fasor. Addresses must be registered within 30 days of arrival. The form requesting a residence permit, two passport photos, a letter from the employer (in Hungarian) and medical certificate will be required. Another form needs to be completed in duplicate to register your address, including the signature of the landlord/landlady, a copy of the contract, and details of rent paid. Certain high-level teachers and researchers, as well as executives and technical consultants sent to perform essential work for foreign companies with subsidiaries in Hungary, are exempted from work permit requirements.

EMBASSIES

British Embassy, Harmincad Utca 6, 1051 Budapest; ☎1-266 2888; fax 1-429 6360; www. britishembassy.hu.
US Embassy, Unit 1320, Szabadság tér 12, 1054 Budapest; ☎1-475 4400; fax 1-475 4764; http://budapest.usembassy.gov/.

TOURIST OFFICES

Hungarian Tourist Board, 46 Eaton Place, London SW1X 8AL; ☎020-78231032; www. hungarytourism.hu; www.gotohungary.co.uk.
Hungarian Tourist Board, 150 East 58th Street, New York, NY 10155; ☎212-3550240; www. hungarytourism.hu; www.gotohungary.com.

SPECIFIC CONTACTS

There is a great demand for English teachers and voluntary workers in Hungary. Other types of work are mostly available to those who are posted to Hungary by international companies or organisations. Some knowledge of German, or making an effort to learn some Hungarian before starting work, will make life considerably easier on arrival.

TEACHING

Most people who go to teach English in Hungary find it an excellent place to work and report that students are eager to learn. The work is not always well paid, however, and you should bear in mind that the cost of living is high, with rents in Budapest approaching those of London. Teaching posts can be found through the following organisations:

Central European Teaching Program (CETP), Beloit College, 700 College Street, Beloit, Wisconsin 53511; ☎1-608 363 2000; www.beloit.edu/, places teachers in 90 schools throughout Hungary (as well as Poland, Romania, and Latvia). A degree is required, TEFL/TESOL qualifications preferred; the ability to teach German as well as English is in great demand.

International House Language School, 1276 Budapest Pf 92; ☎1-316 2491; e-mail bp@ih.hu; www.ih.hu, employs 35 language instructors. Contracts are usually for one year. Minimum qualification: RSA/CELTA. Enquiries must be made to the London office in the first instance (see the *Teaching* chapter).

In addition, Hungarian embassies can provide useful information on job prospects and work permits for language teachers in Hungary.

Poland

o   **Year of EU Accession:** 2004
o   **Polish Embassy,** 47 Portland Place, London W1B 1JH; ☎0870-774 2700; fax 0870-744 2755, 020-7291 3573; e-mail polishembassy@polishembassy.org.uk; www.london.polemb.net
o   **Polish Embassy,** 2640 16th Street, N.W., Washington, DC 20009, USA; ☎+1 202-234 3800; e-mail polemb.info@earthlink.net; www.polandembassy.org
o   **Currency:** Zloty (Zl) = 100 groszy
o   **Exchange Rate:** £1 = Zl 5.83; $1 = Zl 3.18; €1 = Zl 4.04
o   **Country Code:** +48

Poland occupies an area of 124,500 square miles (322,500 sq km), equivalent to 90 per cent of that of Germany. Thirty-five per cent of the population of 38.5 million live in the countryside. There are lakes and islands in Mazuria, forests to the east and along the border with Belarus; and the River Vistula flows through the centre of the country to the Baltic Coast in the north. The climate can be termed moderate with both continental and maritime elements, with long winters (when average temperatures are usually below 32 def F (0 deg C) and mild summers (when the average is 64 def F/18 deg C or more). Poland's borders have shifted westwards during the course of its history and the capital Warsaw (with an estimated 1,700,000 residents) is now in the east of the country. Poland is the superpower of the 10 nations which became members sates of the EU in 2004. Its economy is only an eighth the size of Britian's. The greatest economic growth has taken place in the west and along the German border. Kraków in the south is the historic and cultural capital of Poland and is an international tourist destination. The nearby Tatra Mountains (part of the Carpathian Arc) are popular with hikers and skiers. Basketball and soccer are other popular sports; as are fishing, horseracing and boating. Other cities include Szczecin, Poznan, Wroclaw, Katowice, Lódz, Lublin, and Gdansk. Ninety five per cent of Poles are

Roman Catholic; there are also Orthodox, Jewish and Muslim minorities in the country. English is the most commonly taught second language. German, French and Russian are also spoken, but some knowledge of Polish will be useful for those staying for a longer time. Poles are relaxed and easy-going. Dress should be formal in the workplace. A short lunch break is common. Historical ties between Poland and Britain and the USA mean that nationals of these countries are made welcome and feel at home. Accommodation, as in other central and eastern European countries, is often cramped, and is getting more expensive.

Poland has had frequent boundary changes throughout its history. For a time it was divided between Prussia, Russia and the Austro-Hungarian Empire, and present-day Poland incorporates part of what was Germany. Poland has lost territory in Belarus, the Ukraine, and Lithuania (with which for a time it formed one kingdom). Forty-five years of Russian domination came to an end in 1991. In economic and cultural terms, Poland now looks to the west and is one of the pillars of NATO in the region. In the 1980s and 90s, Poland suffered much greater economic disruption than Hungary or the Czech Republic, but industrial production has recovered. Foreign investment is high, and many industries have now been privatised. Poland is on course for membership of the European Union, although with increased prosperity the cost of living is also rising.

Agriculture is of primary importance, and still employs around one in four workers. Much of Polish industry still needs to be modernised if it is to have any hope of competing with more developed economies; and the first wave of foreign workers living in the country, as elsewhere in the region, were often businessmen and consultants, developing trade or partnership links between Polish and international companies. Some parts of the country, like Gdansk and Silesia, are heavily industrialised, but Poland also has some largely unspoilt natural landscapes, including the last tract of primeval forest in Europe, the beautiful Bialowieza National Park – home to the rare European bison.

IMMIGRATION

British and US passport holders may enter and remain in Poland for up to 90 days without a visa. Those staying longer than three months need to obtain residence permits or temporary residence permits. Since 1st May 2004, when Poland joined the EU, EU citizens can take up employment without possessing a work permit. For details contact Consulate General of the Republic of Poland (73 New Cavendish Street, London W1W 6LS; ☎0870-774 2800; e-mail konsulat@polishconsulate.co.uk; www.polishconsulate.co.uk) or visit the website of Polish Ministry of Foreign Affairs (www.msz.gov.pl).

NEWSPAPERS

The English-language newspaper, *The Warsaw Voice* can be found on the Internet at www.warsawvoice.pl.

EMBASSIES

British Embassy, Aleje Róz 1, 00-556 Warsaw; ☎022-311 0000; fax 022-311 0250; e-mail info@britishembassy.pl; www.britishembassy.pl.
Consulates in Poznan, Szczecin, Wroclaw, Lodz, Katowice, Gdansk, Karaków, and Lublin.
US Embassy, Aleje Ujazdowskie 29/31, 00-540 Warsaw; ☎022-504 2000; www.warsaw.usembassy.gov.

TOURIST OFFICES

Polish National Tourist Office,Level 3, Westgate House, West Gate, London W5 1YY; ☎08700-675011; fax 08700-675011; e-mail info@visitpoland.org; www.visitpoland.org.
Polish National Tourist Office, 5 Marine View Plaza, Hoboken, NJ 07030, USA; ☎+1 201-420 9910; fax +1 201-584 9153; e-mail pntonyc@polandtour.org; www.polandtour.org.

SPECIFIC CONTACTS

Work opportunities in Poland are similar to those in Hungary and the Czech Republic, with openings for consultants and specialists, and in English teaching and voluntary work. The ability to speak Polish and other languages will be necessary for jobs at other levels such as secretarial work. Pay scales are low and the cost of living is rising. It is advisable to obtain up-to-date information on exchange rates and the cost of living in order to ensure that you are being paid a living wage. Some international companies will pay an additional allowance to their expatriate workers.

PRIVATE SCHOOLS

The following privately funded international schools in Warsaw recruit English speaking teachers for a variety of subjects:

American School of Warsaw, Bielawa, ul. Warszawska 202, 05-520 Konstancin-Jeziorna, Warsaw; ☎022-702-8500; e-mail schoolboard@asw.waw.pl; www.asw.waw. pl. Has 840 students in elementary, middle and high school. Its academic programme follows International Baccalaureate. Employs 100 teachers and specialists. Employment application form available online.

The British School, ul. Limanowskiego 15, 02-943 Warsaw; ☎022-842 3281; fax 022-842 3265; e-mail british@thebritishschool.pl; www.thebritishschool.pl. The school includes nursery, primary and secondary school, catering for over 500 pupils. Its programme follows the English National Curriculum, GCSE and IGCSE, and the International Baccalaureate Diploma.

International American School, ul. Dembego 18, 02-796 Warsaw; ☎022-649 1440, 022-649 1442; fax 022-649 1445; e-mail secretary@ias.edu.pl; www.ias.edu.pl, for grades pre-K to grade 12, with about 200 students overall. Offers dual diploma system: the Polish Diploma and the International Diploma.

LANGUAGE SCHOOLS

Enthusiasm for learning English and about life in Britain or the United States is intense. Demand for English teachers is such that almost anyone who can speak the language will find work. Indeed, it is fair to say that prospects for TEFL in Poland are the best in the world. In recent years, some travellers have taken advantage of this and have exploited their students and language schools through a certain lack of diligence. Schools now are aware of this, however, and standards tend to be higher. The main limitation is the salary, and appropriate qualifications will give you the edge in negotiating a reasonable wage. There is also scope for private tuition. Some useful contacts are given below:

American Academy of English, ul. Slowackiego 16, Katowice 40 094; tel/fax 032253 0272; www.ameracad.com, employs more than 40 North American teachers with a university degree in branches throughout Poland. Apartment provided plus medical insurance and other benefits.

Berlitz Poland, ul. Towarowa 22, 00-847 Warsaw; ☎022 652 0848; e-mail instructors@ berlitz.pl; www.berlitz.pl, around 140 teachers in nine centres across Poland. British, Irish, Americans, Canadians and Australians preferred with a college education. No assistance with accommodation.

Cambridge School of English, ul. Konwiktorska 7, 00-216 Warsaw; ☎022-635 2466; fax 022-635 1184; e-mail cambridge@cambridge.com.pl; www.cambridge.com.pl. Cambridge School of English employs 20 teachers for 1,000 students at all levels and ages. It recruits English native speakers with CELTA or TESOL qualifications and university degree. Contracts are for 9 months (from September to June). Working hours are from Monday to Thursday, and either Friday or Saturday; up to 22 hours per week. Teachers should be prepared to teach children (aged 6 and upwards) and adolescents, carry out exam preparation courses (FCE, CAE, CPE) and give lessons to individuals and companies. Facilities include professional development seminars, one senior staff member per four teachers for advice and support. An established course syllabus is used. Applications should be made directly through the school, adverts in established newspapers, TEFL.com or via agency.

ELS-Bell School of English, ul. Nowy Swiat 2, 00-495 Warsaw; ☎022-621 3836; fax 022-625 7734; e-mail recruitment@elsbell.com; www.bellschools.pl, associated with Bell Educational Trust of Cambridge. Centres in Gdansk, Gdynia, Bydgoszcz, Szczecin, and Warsaw. CELTA plus university degree required.

English School of Communication and Skills, ESCS Personnel Department, ul. Walowa 2, 33-100 Tarnów; ☎014-627 0153; e-mail personnel@escs.pl; www.escs.pl. Recruits English native speakers from the UK, Ireland, Canada, the US and Australia. It offers general language courses and business English courses, as well as TEFL courses for teachers. Branch offices mainly in the South.

The Orange School, Al. Solidarnosci 117, Warsaw; fax 022-429 0603; e-mail vomeni@orangeschool.pl; www.orangeschool.pl. A Warsaw-based school with branches in other cities in Poland. Recruits English native speakers with university degree. Candidates with previous experience in teaching preferred. Details can be found on its website.

Szkola Jezykowa British School, ul. Powsinska 34, Warsaw; ☎022-858 3600; e-mail warszawasadyba@britishschool.pl; with 60 schools around Poland, it offers general language courses.

The *Anglo-Polish Universities Association* (93 Victoria Road, Leeds LS6 1DR; ☎0113-275 8121) organises 'The Spirit of Adventure Teaching Holiday in Poland'. These enable British-educated native speakers to spend between three and seven weeks in the summer at holiday camps sponsored by Polish colleges. A detailed information pack is available from APASS at a cost of £3 plus SAE.

For other organisations which recruit language teachers see the *Teaching* chapter. The British Council in Warsaw (Al. Jerozolimskie 59, 00-697 Warsaw; ☎022-695 5900; fax 022-621 9955; e-mail info@britishcouncil.pl; www.britishcouncil.org/poland) can provide a list of local language schools.

VOLUNTARY WORK

Christian Charity Service, ul. Foksal 8, 00-366 Warsaw; ☎022-313 1425; fax 022-313 1500; e-mail chsch@chsch.org.pl; www.adra.pl. A Christian charity organisation operating both in Poland and abroad, including Ukraine and Kosovo.

Global Volunteers, 375 East Little Canada Road, St. Paul, MN 55117-1628, USA; ☎+1 800 487 1074; fax +1 651 482 0915; e-mail email@globalvolunteers.org; www. globalvolunteers.org, offers international volunteer programmes including projects in Poland. Volunteers are needed to teach conversational English and to work in after-school shelters where they would provide care and companionship for children from dysfunctional families. Discounts available for students, families and groups. No special skills are required. Inquiries for additional information may be submitted through their website. For more information about Global Volunteers see the chapter on *Volutnary Work.*

Youth Voluntary Projects, www.volunt.net, lists over 1,200 international volunteer opportunities, including projects in Poland. Service projects last from 2 weeks to one year and the programme includes environmental, cultural, construction, educational and cultural types of work. Most programmes have age an requirement of 18-25 years.

OTHER OPPORTUNITIES

Google Poland, www.google.pl/jobs/, recruits experienced specialists for managerial positions and sales coordinators. Positions located mainly in Warsaw. Résumés should be sent to jobs@google.com with the job title in the subject.

Tele2 Polska Ltd., ul. Marynarska 21, 32-674 Warsaw; ☎022-607 0605; fax 022-607 0651; www.tele2.pl; a Swedish communications company operating in Poland since 1999. It offers international trainee positions. Applications should be submitted online.

Romania

o **Likely date of EU Accession:** January 2007
o **Romanian Embassy,** Arundel House, 4 Palace Green, London W8 4QD; ☎020-7937 9666; fax 020-7937 8069; e-mail roemb@ roemb.co.uk; www.roemb.co.uk
o **Romanian Embassy,** 1607 23rd Street NW, Washington, DC 20008; ☎202-332 4846; fax 202-232 4748; www.roembus.org
o **Currency:** 1 Leu (BGL) = 100 bani
o **Exchange Rate:** £1 = 51,559 Lei; $1 = 28,135 Lei; €1 = 35,706 Lei
o **Country Code:** +40

Romania lies between the Black Sea in the southeast, and Montenegro, Serbia and Hungary in the west. Moldova and Ukraine lie to the north and Bulgaria to the south. Romania covers an area of 92,000 square miles (238,279 sq km), has a total population is 22.3 million (and a population density of 247 per square mile). It is divided into four parts. The Carpathian Mountains separate the mountainous and forested Transylvania and Moldavia in the north from the flat Danube plain of Wallachia in the south and east and the Black Sea coast and Danube delta. The capital, Bucharest, has two million inhabitants. The majority religion is Romanian Orthodox, and there are Roman Catholic, Protestant, Muslim and Jewish minorities. Some Hungarian and German is spoken in the border areas of the country in addition to Romanian. Agriculture supports a third of the population; and oil, natural gas and their products are important in the industrial sector. The state of the economy remains fragile, with high inflation and unemployment. Romania is scheduled to join the EU on 1 January 2007, provided it can address the outstanding issues identified in the European Commission's May 2006 Comprehensive Monitoring Report.

IMMIGRATION

British passport holders and Americans may stay for up to 30 days without a visa. Business visa applications should include the name of the sponsoring Romanian company. Those working or looking for work should register at the local police station; they require a residence and work permit. Enquiries about these should be made to a Romanian consulate or embassy abroad. It is likely that the residence regulations will change for EU citizens, assuming that Romania is granted accession to the European Union in January 2007.

EMBASSIES

British Embassy, Strada Jules Michelet 24, 010463 Bucharest; ☎1-201 7300; fax 1-201 7317; www.britishembassy.gov.uk/romania.

US Embassy, Strada Tudor Arghezi 7-9, Bucharest; ☎21-200 3300 4042; fax 21-200 3442; www.usembassy.ro.

TOURIST OFFICES

Romanian National Tourist Office, 22 New Cavendish Street, London WIM 7LH; ☎020-7224 3692; www.romaniatourism.com.
Romanian National Tourist Office, 355 Lexington Avenue, 19th Floor, New York, NY 10017; ☎212-545 8484; www.romaniatourism.com.

SPECIFIC CONTACTS

The British Embassy in Bucharest publishes a quarterly 'Commercial Newsletter', which details UK companies investing in Romania. The *Ministry of Industry and Commerce*, 152 Victoria Ave., Bucharest, Sector 1; ☎1-659 2321, or the *Chamber of Commerce and Industry*, 2 Octavian Goga Ave., Bucharest, Sector 3; ☎1-322 9500, may also offer advice and commercial information. The Romania Desk of *UK Trade and Investment*, Kingsgate House, 66-74 Victoria Street, London SW1E 6SW; www.uktradeinvest.gov.uk, can provide an information pack for commercial or business purposes; and holds lists of foreign trade organisations and UK business representatives and companies in Romania.

TOURISM

SHG Recruitment, Specialist Holidays Group and Tui UK, (www.shgjobs.co.uk) requires experienced reps who speak Romanian to meet and look after skiers in Poiana Brasov and Sinaia.

Russian Federation

o   **Russian Embassy,** 13 Kensington Palace Gardens, London W8 4QX; ☎020-7229 2666; fax 020-7229 5804; www.great-britain.mid.ru
o   **Russian Embassy,** 2650 Wisconsin Avenue NW, Washington DC 20007; ☎202-298 5700; fax 202-298 5735; www.russianembassy.org
o   **Currency:** 1 Rouble (Rub) = 100 kopeks
o   **Exchange Rate:** £1 = Rub 49.36; $1 = Rub 26.94; €1 = Rub 34.18
o   **Country Code:** +7

The Russian Federation stretches from its borders with Finland, the Baltic States, Belarus and the Ukraine in the west, across the Ural Mountains and through Siberia to the port of Vladivostok in the east. It is about twice the size of the United States in land area (nearly seven million square miles/18 million sq km) and has a low population density (22 per square mile). The capital, Moscow, has nine million inhabitants. Other major cities are St. Petersburg, Arkhangelsk, Nizhny Novgorod, Volgograd, Vorkuta, Yekaterinburg, Omsk, Novosibirsk, Irkutsk, Yakutsk, Khabarovsk, and Vladivostok. There is a patchwork of different republics which are all regarded as part of Russia: Adygheya; Bashkortostan; Buryatia; Chechnya; Chuvashia; Daghestan; Gorno-Altai; Ingushetia; Kabardino-Balkaria; Kalmykia; Karachayevo-Cherkess; Karelia; Khakassia; Komi; Mari El; Mordovia; Northern Ossetia; Sakha (Yakutia); Tatarstan; Tuva; and Udmurtia. European Russia extends from the North Polar Sea to the Black Sea in the south, and is bordered by the Ural Mountains in the east. Russian is universally spoken, along with some English, French and German.

Russian Orthodox is the main religion of Russia, with minorities of Muslims, Buddhists and Jews. Russia ended 2005 with its seventh straight year of growth, averaging 6.4%

annually since the financial crisis of 1998. There is a range of natural resources, and rich farming land where private ownership is becoming more common. Oil and gas, which accounts for about 70 per cent of the stock market, are major export earners, as well as coal and minerals including diamonds and gold, nickel, copper, and iron ore. Serious problems persist in Russia and the country remains heavily dependent on exports of commodities, leaving the country vulnerable to swings in world prices. Other problems include widespread corruption, capital flight, and brain drain. Businesses are closing, there are extensive shortages, and the infrastructure of road and telephone communications is deteriorating. There is an extensive rail network, and air-routes which connect the more distant centres, but these are all unreliable. Developing modern distribution and transport networks, and modernising manufacturing and the service industries, are some of the sectors in which international consultants are required.

Many western companies have developed joint ventures with Russian partners. Business and work relations are often developed through personal contacts and trust, rather than in more formal ways. Deficiencies in the legal system mean that investment is often a risk; and there are rules for personal safety which should be followed, as in all the countries of the former Soviet Union, such as keeping expensive valuables out of sight and not calling too much attention to yourself as a foreigner.

Knowledge of the Russian language is a great advantage. Public transport, like the famous Moscow metro, is relatively cheap, if crowded. Theatre, concert and variety performances are plentiful and there is a lively nightlife in Moscow and St. Petersburg. There is also a big difference between life in these two cities and the provinces, where the pace of life is slower and where there are not so many visitors from abroad.

IMMIGRATION

British and US passport-holders need a visa, and a letter of invitation from a business or other organisation in Russia is required. Those working there should register with the local police and obtain a residence and work permit. Note that in Russia these days, rules are subject to change at a moment's notice, and frequently do. Enquiries should be made to your nearest Russian embassy or consulate.

EMBASSIES

British Embassy, 10 Smolenskaya Naberezhnaya, Moscow 121099; ☎095-956 7200; fax 095-956 7201; www.britaininrussia.ru.
British Consulate General in Ekaterinburg and St Petersburg.
US Embassy, Bolshoy Devyatinskiy Pereulok 8, Moscow 121099; ☎495-728 5000; fax 495-728 5090; http://moscow.usembassy.gov/
US Consulate General, Ulista Furshtadskaya, 15, St Petersburg 191028; ☎812-331 2600; fax 812-331 2852.
Consulate in Ekateringburg and Vladivostok.

SPECIFIC CONTACTS

The Commercial Department of the British Embassy in Moscow produces a *Business Directory* with British commercial representations in Russia and the former Soviet Union, and British companies operating in Russia. Some UK recruitment consultants have vacancies in Russia, particularly for accountants (see *Management Recruitment Consultants* in the chapter *Getting the Job*).

The Russia Desk of *UK Trade and Investment*, Kingsgate House, 66-74 Victoria Street, London SW1E 6SW; www.uktradeinvest.gov.uk, can supply information for commercial or business purposes; and holds lists of UK business representatives and companies in Russia.

VOLUNTARY WORK

Work camps are co-ordinated by *Russian Youth Voluntary Service*, Novaia Ploshchadj 6, Office 7, 101970 Moscow. You should make initial enquiries through a partner organisation in your own country. *Russian Volunteers Association and Volunteer Center*, Moscow Charity House, Novyi Arbat 11, of. 1728-1735, Moscow 121099; ☎095-292-9127 is a partner organisation of the United Nations Volunteers organisation (see the *Voluntary Work* chapter).

Slovakia

o **Year of EU Accession:** 2004
o **Slovak Embassy,** 25 Kensington Palace Gardens, London W8 4QY; ☎020-7313 6470; fax 020-7313 6481; www.slovakembassy.co.uk
o **Slovak Embassy,** 3523 International Court NW, Washington DC 20008; ☎202-237 1054; fax 202-237 6438; e-mail information@slovakembassy-us.org; www.slovakembassy-us.org
o **Currency:** 1 Koruna (Sk) = 100 hellers
o **Exchange Rate:** £1 = Sk 55.61; $1 = Sk 30.34; €1 = Sk 38.51
o **Country Code:** +421

The Slovak Republic covers 17,000 square miles (44,029 sq km). The population is 5.4 million; and the capital, Bratislava, has 440,000 inhabitants. The other major city is Kosice with 240,000 inhabitants. The northern area is hilly, as it approaches the Carpathian Mountains; the southern and eastern parts of the country are low-lying and agricultural. The River Danube connects the country with Vienna, to the west, and the Black Sea to the east. There are cold winters and mild summers. There are some mineral and gas resources, and also a large chemical industry. Agriculture is particularly important for export earnings, as is the export of beer and timber. Slovakia is making efforts to develop its tourism, in particular winter sports, which, like hiking and hunting, are also popular with the locals.

Slovakia's main international vocation since independence in 1992 has become – like its central European neighbours – holding membership of organisations such as the EU and NATO that can confirm its independent status and help with economic development. Slovakia is developing new trading links with EU countries, especially Germany, as well as continuing to trade with traditional trading partners like Poland, the Ukraine and Hungary. Privatisation is the watchword in the Slovakian economy and experts are needed in the financial services field. It is also aiming to develop its traditional craft-based industries and to be less dependent on heavy industry. There are opportunities in trade and development, English-teaching and voluntary work.

IMMIGRATION

EU and North American passport holders do not require a visa to visit the Slovak Republic. Foreigners may work only after they have been granted residence and work permits. Enquiries about work and residence permits should be made to an embassy or consulate abroad. Applications should be submitted to an embassy in the country of origin, and accompanied by a provisional work permit from the local labour office in Slovakia along with a letter from the employer, a doctor's certificate, and five photographs. These documents must be in Slovak or with an authorised Slovak translation. The procedure can take up to 60 days. Further information is available from the Office of the Border and Aliens' Police (www.minv.sk/uhcp/new/drupob.htm).

EMBASSIES AND TOURIST OFFICE

British Embassy, Panská 16, 811 01 Bratislava; ☎2-5998 2000; fax 2-5998 2237; www. britishembassy.sk.

US Embassy, PO Box 309, 814 99 Bratislava; ☎2-5443-3338; fax 2-5443 0096; www. usis.sk.

Slovak Tourist Board, Namestie L.Stura 1, PO Box 35, 974 05 Banska Bystrica; ☎48-413 6146; fax 48-4136149; www.sacr.sk. The agency can supply a variety of brochures including *General Information: What you do not know about Slovakia'*.

SPECIFIC CONTACTS

TEACHING

There is a general shortage of English teachers in the Slovak Republic, although there are many language schools in the country. This makes hunting for TEFL work promising. *Language Link* (181 Earl's Court Road, London SW5 9RB; ☎020-7370 4755; fax 020-7370 1123; e-mail teacher.training@languagelink.co.uk; www.languagelink.co.uk) is affiliated with the *Akadémia Vzdelávania*, the largest semi-private language school in Slovakia, and actively recruits teachers from the UK. American TEFL teachers should try the *City University* (11900 N.E. First Street, Bellevue, Washington 98005; ☎425-637 1010; e-mail info@cityu.edu; www.cityu.edu) for placements in Slovak schools. The two campuses of the *City University* in Bratislava and Trencin cater mainly to Slovak students of business who receive intensive language training alongside their business administration studies.

VOLUNTARY WORK

INEX Slovakia, Prazská 11, 81413 Bratislava; ☎02- 5729 7304; fax 02-5729 7306; www.inex.sk – recruits volunteers for work camps aimed at promoting international understanding and co-operation mainly in environmental and historical conservation. The working language is English.

Slovenia

o   **Year of EU Accession:** 2004
o   **Slovenian Embassy,** 10 Little College Street, London SW1P 3SJ; ☎020-7222 5400; fax 020-7222 5277
o   **Slovenian Embassy,** 1525 New Hampshire Avenue NW, Washington DC 20036; ☎202-667 5363; fax 202-667 4563
o   **Currency:** 1 Slovenian Tolar (SIT) = 100 stotins
o   **Exchange Rate:** £1 = SIT 346.08; $1 = SIT 188.84; €1 = SIT 239.64
o   **Country Code:** +386

The Slovene lands were part of the Holy Roman Empire and Austria until 1918. In 1929, they were incorporated into Yugoslavia and remained part of this country until 1991, when the Slovenes established their independence after a 10-day war. The Slovenian Republic has a total area of 7,827 square miles (20,273 sq km) and lies in the eastern Alps bordering the Adriatic Sea, with Austria to the north and Croatia to the south. This alpine mountain region has a short coastal strip, mountains, and numerous rivers in the east. Its highest point is Triglav ("Three-Heads") at 9,396 ft (2,864 metres). Forests cover half the territory and it is the third most afforested country in Europe, following Finland and Sweden. Slovenia has a coastal Mediterranean climate, with mild to hot summers, and cold winters in the plateax and valleys to the east. Average temperature in January is 28 deg F (–2 deg C) and 70 deg F (21 deg C) in July. About eight per cent of Slovenia is environmentally protected, the largest area being the Triglav National Park. The Skocjan caves are on the World Heritage List, and the Secovlje saltpans are included on the Ramsar List of Wetlands of International Importance.

Slovenia has a population of two million, comprising 92 per cent Slovenians; Italians and Hungarians are indigenous minorities with rights protected under the Constitution. Other ethnic groups identify themselves as Croats, Serbs, Muslims, Yugoslavs, Macedonians, Montenegrins, and Albanians. The majority are Roman Catholic (72 per cent), followed by Eastern Orthodox, Christian, Muslim, and Protestant religions. The capital city is Ljubljana. Other major towns include Maribor, Celje, Kranj, Velenje, Ptuj, Koper, Novo Mesto, Jesenic, Trbovlje, Nova Gorica, and Murska Sobota. The official language is Slovene, one of the South Slavonic group of languages.

Slovenia is regarded as one of the most successful examples of a country in transition from socialism to a free market economy. It has a stable annual economic growth around 3.1 per cent, with an unemployment rate of about 6.3 per cent. Slovenia has excellent infrastructure, a well-educated work force, and an excellent central location. In March 2004 it became the first transition country to graduate from borrower status to donor partner at the World Bank. Slovenia plans to adopt the euro by 2007 and has met the EU's criteria for inflation. Major industries are agriculture, manufacturing, textiles, and timber products. The country has 14 wine-growing areas which produce many high-quality varieties. It is a parliamentary democratic republic with 182 municipalities and 11 urban municipalities.

IMMIGRATION

Citizens from the UK and USA do not require visas for stays of up to 90 days, nor do those from Australia, Canada, Israel, and Japan. A residence permit is required thereafter. Citizens of other countries can obtain visas from any Slovenian embassy or consulate.
There are no restrictions on working in Slovenia for EU citizens although nationals of these countries must register at the *Slovenian Employment Service,* Cesta v Rožno dolino 1X/6, 1000 Ljubljana; ☎61-479 0947; e-mail info@ess.gov.si; www.ess.gov.si.

EMBASSIES

British Embassy, Trg republike 3, 1000 Ljubljana; ☎1-200 3910; fax 1-425 0174; e-mail info@british-embassy.si; www.britishembassy.si.
US Embassy, Prešernova 31, 1000 Ljubljana; ☎1-200 5500; fax 1-200 5555; www.usembassy.si.

TOURIST OFFICES

Slovenian Tourist Office, 10 Little College Street, London SW1P 3SJ; ☎020-7222 5400; fax 020-7222 5277; www.slovenia-tourism.si.
Slovenian Tourist Office, 345 East 12th Street, New York, NY 10003; ☎212-358 9686; fax 212-358 9025; e-mail slotouristboard@sloveniatravel.com; www.slovenia-tourism.si.

SPECIFIC CONTACTS

Finding a job in Slovenia requires a range of strategies. Major employers are in the manufacturing (metal, electronics, textiles, automotive parts, chemicals, glass products, and food processing), tourism and transport sectors. The *Chamber of Commerce and Industry Slovenia* (www.gzs.si/eng/) provides valuable information for those seeking employment, while the *University of Ljubljana* (Kongresni trg 12, 1000 Ljubljana; ☎ 1-241 8500; www. uni-lj.si), and the *University of Maribor* (Slomskov trg 15, 2000 Maribor; ☎ 02-235 5280; www.uni-mb.si) should be able to help overseas graduates find jobs. National newspapers are a good source. *Delo* (www.delo.si) is the national newspaper and vacancies are listed in the Tuesday and Saturday editions. Online periodicals include *Slovenia News* (www. slonews.sta.si), which covers politics, commerce, culture, science, and sport; and *Slovenia Business Week* (www.gzs.si/eng/news/sbw/), an electronic business weekly including topics on the Slovenian economy. The main job opportunities are likely to be in teaching English, and voluntary work available through international agencies.

Useful Addresses

Ministry of Labour, Family and Social Affairs, Kotnikova 5, 1000 Ljubljana; ☎ 1-369 7700; 1-369 7832; www.mddsz.gov.si

Employment Services of Slovenia, Central Office, Cesta v Rožno dolino 1X/6, 1000 Ljubljana; ☎ 1-479 0947; e-mail info@ess.gov.si; www.ess.gov.si

Canada

- **Canadian High Commission,** 38 Grosvenor Street, London W1K 4AA; ☎020-7258 6600; fax 020-7258 6333; www.canada.org.uk
- **Canada Centre (Canada House),** 62-65 Trafalgar Square, London WC2N 5DT; ☎020-7930 8540
- **Canadian Embassy,** 501 Pennsylvania Avenue, NW, Washington DC 20001; ☎202-682 1740; fax 202-682 7701; www.canadianembassy.org
- **Currency:** $ (Canadian) 1 = 100 cents
- **Rate of Exchange:** £1 = CAN$2.11; US$1 = CAN$1.13; €1 = CAN$1.44
- **Country Code:** +1

Since World War II, Canada has accepted over five million immigrants, more than a million of whom have come from Britain and Ireland. The unacceptably high level of unemployment in recent years has necessitated strict controls, however, and the flow of incoming migrants is now limited to those possessing the skills and qualifications that are in major demand. The attractions of Canada are many. According to a United Nations ranking, taking into account factors such as life expectancy, education and adjusted real incomes, Canada ranks number one in the world as a place to live and work, and fourth out of 53 countries in technological sophistication. The country offers good prospects for those with a science and technology background.

GENERAL FACTS

POPULATION
Canada has a population of 33 million. It is bounded to the west by the Pacific Ocean, to the east by the Atlantic and to the south by the 'Lower 48' of the USA. With a land area of 3,851,809 square miles (9,976,146 sq km), it is the world's second largest country (after Russia). Overall population density is 7.5 per square mile, however, the population is unevenly distributed and all regions except the Maritime Provinces (Nova Scotia, New Brunswick and Prince Edward Island) have large, almost uninhabited areas. Eighty per cent of the total population is concentrated in the four provinces of Quebec, Ontario, Alberta and British Columbia. By contrast, the Yukon and Northwest Territories contain 0.3 per cent of the population yet cover one-third of Canada's total area.

CLIMATE
The climate varies widely: from severe Arctic conditions in the north to the more moderate climates of the temperate coastal regions, with extremes of heat and cold experienced in the central provinces. The Pacific coast has the highest rainfall while inland snow covers all regions during the three to five months of winter. In general, Canadian winters are cold but dry, springs are short but dramatic, and summers warm and sunny for two or three months, with clear and crisp autumns.

GOVERNMENT

Canada is a confederation of ten provinces (Ontario, Quebec, Nova Scotia, British Columbia, Alberta, Saskatchewan, Manitoba, New Brunswick, Prince Edward Island and Newfoundland) and two territories (Yukon and Northwest Territories). The Queen is the Head of State of Canada and is represented by a Governor-General, nominated by the Canadian Prime Minister.

The federal government legislates over matters of national and general concern, including defence, external affairs, trade, the postal services, navigation and shipping. Provinces have jurisdiction over matters of local interest, including municipal institutions, the law relating to property and civil rights, health care and education. Federal legislative power is vested in the Parliament of Canada, which consists of the Queen, an appointed upper house (the Senate), and a lower house (the House of Commons), elected by universal adult suffrage.

A consistent feature of Canadian politics is the strong separatist movement in the French-speaking province of Quebec. A referendum in October 1992 on the Charlottetown Accord, which would have enshrined Quebec's special status in the constitution, resulted in rejection by five of the ten provinces of Canada, including Quebec itself. The question of Quebec's remaining within the Canadian confederation is still an open one; with the electorate fairly evenly divided on the issue.

CITIES

The major cities are Toronto, with a population of 4.2 million; followed by Montreal (3.3 million); Vancouver (1.8 million); the capital Ottawa (1 million); Edmonton (860,000); Calgary (750,000); Quebec City (700,000); and Winnipeg (650,000). Altogether there are over 25 metropolitan areas with over 100,000 inhabitants.

RURAL LIFE

The post-war years have seen a continued drift to the cities; only 20 per cent of the population now lives in the countryside. Agriculture is still Canada's most important primary industry – farmed land exceeds 174 million acres and there are 260,000 farms, all highly commercialised, mechanised and specialised, producing mainly wheat, other field crops, dairy products, livestock, fruit, vegetables, tobacco, honey, maple syrup and furs.

Forestry is another major rural occupation – forests cover 800 million acres and pulp and paper manufacture are the most important related industries.

MINING AND PETROCHEMICALS

Canada is rich in mineral wealth with vast reserves of petroleum and natural gas, and is a major world producer of nickel, iron ore, copper and zinc. Exports of crude and fabricated mineral products account for nearly 25 per cent of Canada's total exports. Canada exports about $7 billion worth of crude petroleum annually.

RELIGION, SPORT AND CULTURE

According to the most recent census, 28 per cent of Canada's population is of British origin, 23 per cent of French extraction, and the remaining 49 per cent of other origins. The native peoples, Native Canadians and Inuit (Eskimos), are estimated to number just 2 per cent of the population. The indigenous population suffer from high levels of unemployment, poor health and a general disaffection, which has resulted in one of the world's highest suicide rates. There are 54 different Indian languages or dialects, plus Inuktitut, the language of the Inuit.

Around 42 per cent of Canadians are Catholics and 23 per cent Protestants; 1.5 per cent of the population is Jewish.

The USA exerts a strong cultural influence on Canada, especially in the provinces near the US border. The Arts in Canada have developed rapidly in recent decades and now exhibit a growing sense of Canadian identity. As well as theatre, ballet and music in the cities, there is a strong crafts movement in more isolated areas. In recent times, Canadian television programmes and films, and especially animated films, in English and French, have become more widely known internationally.

The multicultural nature of Canadian society is recognised and supported by government policy. A Multicultural Directorate was established in 1971 and provides assistance to a wide range of activities organised by various cultural groups.

Canadians spend a lot of their free time outdoors. Most provinces have set aside vast areas of the country for the conservation of the environment and the enjoyment of visitors. Most of the national and provincial parks provide camping facilities and hiking trails. Skiing, swimming, ice-skating, ice hockey, tennis and golf are amongst the most popular recreational activities, and sports facilities throughout the country are generally excellent.

FACTORS INFLUENCING EMPLOYMENT

IMMIGRATION

Most immigration since the war has been to the province of Ontario. Although British citizens do not require a visa to enter Canada, visitors cannot change their status from visitor to worker while remaining in the country. Persons who wish to work in Canada must obtain the appropriate documentation prior to entering Canada from their home country.

Under current regulations, the flow of migrants is tied closely to labour market demands. There are several categories of immigrants, and these categories are commensurate with the different aims of the immigration programme. The policies are designed to:

o   Attract qualified workers or investors who can strengthen the Canadian work force or economy;
o   Reunite families where one member or more is already resident in Canada;
o   Help those seeking refuge from persecution in their own country, or those who wish to retire to Canada.

Non-refugee immigrants to Canada will apply either as Family Class or Independent applicants. Applicants in the independent category are assessed according to several factors, including age, education, knowledge of English and French, training and occupation. Under current immigration regulations, persons in certain occupations are able to meet the selection criteria without arranged employment, although in practice this is highly unusual; others require a job offer that has been certified by employment officials in Canada to be a position for which no qualified Canadians are available. In some cases the presence of relatives – brother, sister, uncle or aunt – can assist a person's application. Canada operates a points system in assessing applications.

In addition to the Family and Independent Applicant categories, Canada is encouraging applications from those with proven business ability and substantial capital to invest. It is possible to apply to enter as an entrepreneur, self-employed immigrant, or as an investor.

The Canadian High Commission in London (address above) deals with all immigration matters for England, Scotland, Wales and Northern Ireland. For the province of Quebec the approval of the Quebec immigration office, *Le ministère des Relations avec les citoyens et de l'immigration* (MRCI) must be obtained before applying for a visa from the Canadian government. British citizens must contact the Service d'immigration du Quebec, Délégation générale du Quebec, 87-89 rue de la Boetie, 75008 Paris; ☎ 1-5393 4545; fax 1-5393 4546; www.cic.gc.ca; *Brownstein & Brownstein & Associates*, 6000 Cote Des Neiges, Suite 590, Montreal, Quebec, H3S 1Z8; ☎ 514-939 9559; fax 514-939 2289; e-mail immigrate@brownsteinlaw.com; www.brownsteinlaw.com, are attorneys specialising in immigration, with associated offices in many countries around the world.

The *Immigration Division (Visa Section)*, is at 38 Grosvenor Street, London W1X 4AA; ☎020-7258 6699 in Britain, and in the United States there is a *Canadian Consulate General*, at 1251 Avenue of the Americas, New York, NY 10020-1175; ☎212-596 1628; fax 212-596 8790. Offices in Detroit, Los Angeles, and Seattle.

REGULATIONS FOR US CITIZENS

US citizens do not require a passport to enter Canada, merely proof of US citizenship (e.g. driving licence), and they may stay for up to 90 days as tourists. Employment Authorizations (or Student Authorizations for students) must be arranged from outside Canada. The prospective employer first informs the nearest Canada Employment Centre (CEC) about the job offer. If the CEC agrees that there are no suitable Canadian residents available to fill the job you may then apply for an Employment Authorization from the nearest Canadian diplomatic representative office.

LANGUAGE

Canada is officially bilingual in French and English, and all federal government publications and federal court decisions are published in both languages. French- and English-language radio and television are available throughout the country, and it is the intention to make state financed schooling available in both languages wherever numbers warrant. In Quebec, French is the official language.

COST AND STANDARD OF LIVING

British visitors find the standard of living high in Canada and many articles, food and clothing in particular, are much cheaper than at home.

HOUSING AND ACCOMMODATION

Although there is no actual housing shortage in Canada, there is a shortage of low-cost housing and it is for this reason that the Immigration Department recommends immigrants to have accommodation pre-arranged if possible. Government loans are available for homebuilding and buying. Sixty-five per cent of homes are owner-occupied.

HEALTH AND WELFARE

Each provincial government has primary responsibility for health, and operates two insurance programmes – one for hospital treatment, one for medical care. There are also supplementary private insurance schemes, often operated through payroll deductions.

Family allowances are paid for all dependent children under 18 years of age. All persons aged 65 and over who have lived in Canada for at least ten years (regardless of citizenship) receive a monthly old age pension. If their income is limited, they receive an additional guaranteed income supplement. There is also a contributory pension scheme (EIC) whereby employees pay up to 1.4 per cent of their income while working.

Social assistance is provided for people in need by a shared-cost programme. The government provides 50 per cent of the cost to each province by agreement. There is also an unemployment insurance scheme, contributions for which are shared by workers and employers.

EDUCATION

Education is compulsory for all children for about ten years in every province and is free up to the end of secondary school. The starting age is six years old and the minimum leaving age is usually 16 years old. Most schools are co-educational and few people are privately educated. In some provinces, French-speaking pupils are entitled by law to receive instruction in French. In Quebec the policy is to register the children of immigrants in French schools.

Higher education is provided by 68 universities and some 200 colleges; students may receive financial aid in the form of federal or provincial loans, repayable over a period of up to ten years.

EMBASSIES AND TOURIST OFFICES

British High Commission, 80 Elgin St., Ottawa, Ontario K1P 5K7; ☎613-237 1530; fax 613-237 7980; www.britainincanada.org. There are British consulates in Montreal, Quebec City, Toronto, Vancouver, Halifax, Winnipeg, and St. John's.

US Embassy, 490 Sussex Drive, Ottawa, Ontario K1N 1G8; ☎613-238 5335; www. usembassycanada.gov. There are US consulates in Calgary, Halifax, Montreal, Quebec, Toronto, Winnipeg and Vancouver.

Canadian Tourism Commission, Canada House, Trafalgar Square, London SW1Y 5BJ; ☎020-7258 6322; www.canadatourism.com.

Canadian Tourism Commission, 11 Riverside Drive, Suite 8L West, New York, NY 10023; ☎212-874 6488.

CONDITIONS OF WORK

WAGES

The only federal law governing wages is the Canada Labour (Standards) Code, which covers only government employees and workers in industries under federal jurisdiction. This Code, which also prohibits unequal pay and discrimination based on sex, race, colour or religion, is the basis for the different provincial laws covering all professions and workers. However, there are wide variations from province to province. Minimum wages vary but at the time of writing stand between CAN$6.70 and CAN$8.50 in most provinces. The average yearly salary for a skilled worker is in the region of CAN$40,000.

Salaries are usually paid fortnightly and many companies have a bonus scheme in which a profit-related bonus is paid at the end of the year. This is usually referred to as the Christmas bonus, and can make a substantial difference to an annual salary.

HOURS

For government employees and workers in industries under federal jurisdiction the working week is five days of eight hours each. In general, any hours worked above eight in a day, or forty in a week, must be paid at time and a half, up to a maximum of 48 hours a week. The average working week in practice is 38 or 39 hours.

HOLIDAYS

Annual paid holidays vary from two to four weeks. There are also ten national public holidays: New Year's Day; Good Friday; Easter Monday; Victoria Day (25 May, or the Monday immediately preceding); Canada Day (1 July); Labour Day (first Monday in September); Thanksgiving (second Monday in October); Remembrance Day (11 November); Christmas Day; and Boxing Day. The different provinces also observe local holidays.

SAFETY AND COMPENSATION

Canadian industry is proud of its low injury rate, and is very safety-conscious. Many large firms conduct constant safety programmes, supplementing the minimum safety standards laid down in most provinces.

All employees in industries and workplaces covered by Workmen's Compensation Funds are entitled to free medical aid and payment of up to 75 per cent of regular earnings. Benefits are also provided for the spouses of workers killed while at work.

TRADE UNIONS

Union membership represents about a third of the labour force. The collective bargaining system between employers and unions functions under the federal Industrial Relations and Disputes Investigation Act, and under labour relations acts in all provinces. The government has the ultimate duty of conciliation when parties are unable to reach an agreement. In some provinces, legislation forbids strikes by workers in essential services, such as by firemen, policemen and hospital employees.

TAXATION

Income tax is deducted on a PAYE basis, with allowances for dependent children, pension contributions etc. Typically, a single man earning $25,000 would pay around $5,000 in tax. On the same salary, a married man with two children under 16 and a dependent wife would pay $4,000. Tax is paid in two parts – federal and provincial, so tax rates vary from province to province.

Municipal authorities also levy taxes, especially on corporate incomes. The federal government levies a seven per cent Goods and Services Tax that, unlike VAT, is not always included in the ticket price. All provinces except Alberta have a provincial sales tax (PST) ranging from four per cent to twelve per cent.

EMPLOYMENT PROSPECTS

Canada's economy is the seventh largest in the world, and prospects look good for continued growth. In 2005, the country had the world's ninth-highest GDP per capita and the ninth-highest overall GDP. The nation is heavily dependent on the United States economy; when the USA does well, Canada does almost as well. When the US economy dives, the Canadian economy follows.

The slide of the US dollar from 2003 to 2005 has had a major effect on the Canadian economy. On the plus side, the country has more spending power, but the relatively strong Canadian dollar has had a devastating effect on manufacturing, filmmaking and other businesses that provided goods or service to the US. US businesses that were happy to outsource jobs to Canada when it was thirty percent cheaper are less inclined to do so as the differential between the two currencies dwindles.

There were 13 million Canadians in the workforce in 2005, not including the self-employed, who number up to two million. The unemployment rate is typically 2% to 5% higher than the American rate, and it hovers between 6% and 10%. Much of the unemployment afflicts those in the fisheries industry and the dwindling manufacturing sector, areas which immigrants are unlikely to select.

Like the United States, Canada is quickly becoming an information society, with information industries predicted to employ as much as 50% of the future work force. Canada was 15th in the 2004-2005 World Economic Forum's Global Competitiveness Report, a rise from 16th place the year before but a considerable drop from its sixth-place finish in 1998. However Canada is a world leader in telecommunications, aerospace and nuclear technology, bioengineering and geographical exploration. These areas offer great potential for immigrants with a background in science and technology, though as the economy grows, so will job opportunities in the service sector.

NEWSPAPERS

Newspapers are available for reference at Canada Centre in Trafalgar Square, London, where the library can be used by prior appointment. Local city and regional newspapers can be consulted at the offices of the provincial government offices, where information will be given on subscriptions and advertising.

The *Globe and Mail*, Canada's only national newspaper, contains a daily employment and careers section, with a special supplement on Saturdays. It is represented in the UK by *The Powers Turner Group*, Gordon House, Greencoat Lane, London SW1P 1PH; ☎020-7592 8300; fax 020-7592 8301; e-mail ppn-london@publicitas.com; www.publicitas.com, and is available in many large newsagents around Britain. The *National Post* advertises vacancies in all areas of business and finance.

Copies of *Canada News*, a monthly newspaper for tourists and migrants, are available from Canada House, London, or by subscription from *Outbound Publishing*, 1 Commercial Road, Eastbourne, East Sussex BN21 3QX; ☎01323-726040; www.outboundpublishing.com.

Try also *Canada Employment Weekly* (21 New Street, Toronto, ON M5R 1P; ☎416-964-6069; www.mediacorp2.com/cew) and *Canadian Business Magazine* (One Mount Pleasant Rd., 11th Floor, Toronto, ON M4Y 2Y5; ☎416-764-1200; www.canadianbusiness.com).

SPECIFIC CONTACTS

EMPLOYMENT SERVICES
Once in Canada, immigrants can use the services of the Canada Human Resource Centres (HRCs), which display lists of vacancies in their 'job banks'. There are over 400 HRCs Centres across the country. Addresses are available from the High Commissions and in telephone directories. There are also hundreds of private recruitment agencies and executive search firms operating in Canada offering both permanent and temporary work. The following agencies are worth contacting:

Addecco Canada: 109 King Street East, Toronto, ON M5C 1G6;   ☎416-646-3322; fax 416-366-8035; www.addecco.ca.

The Association of Canadian Search, Employment and Staffing Services (ACSESS): 6835 Century Ave. Second Floor, Mississauga, ON L5N 2L2;   ☎905-826-6869; www.acsess.org.

Hunt Personnel: 760-789 West Pender Street, Vancouver, BC V6C 1H2; ☎604-688-2555; fax 604-688-6437; www.hunt.ca.

The Employment Solution: 40 Holly Street, Suite 500, Toronto, ON M4S 3C3;   ☎416-482-2420; fax 416-482-9282; www.tes.net.

Commercial and non-commercial websites valuable to job-hunters include: *Canada WorkInfoNet* (www.workinfonet.ca); *Canadian Jobs Catalogue* (www.kenevacorp.mb.ca); *HRDC Job Bank* (jb-ge.hrdc-drhc.gc.ca); and www.workopolis.com.

For more information about living and working in Canada, and specific addresses and contacts, see *Live and Work in the USA and Canada* (www.vacationwork.co.uk).

MEDICAL STAFF
For doctors, the Canadian Medical Association (1869 Alta Vista Drive, Ottawa, Ontario K1G 3Y6;   ☎800-457-4205; www.cma.ca) publishes the *Canadian Medical Association Journal, Canadian Journal of Surgery, Canadian Association of Radiologists Journal and the Canadian Journal of Respiratory Therapy*. Each of these has a jobs section. For information on qualifications and registration of foreign doctors, contact The Medical Council of Canada (PO Box 8234 Station T, Ottawa, ON K1G 3H7; ☎613-521-6012; www.mcc.ca). Pharmacists should contact the Canadian Pharmacists Association (1785 Alta Vista Dr., Ottawa, ON K1G 3Y6; ☎613-523-7877; www.pharmacists.ca). Nurses can contact the *Canadian Nurses' Association* (50 Driveway, Ste. 1, Ottawa, ON K2P 1E2; ☎613-237-2133; www.cna-nurses.ca).

ACCOUNTANTS
Canada is more accessible to British accountants than the USA. Nevertheless, it is advisable to gain Canadian qualifications. Contact the *Canadian Institute of Chartered*

Accountants (277 Wellington Street West, Toronto, Ontario M5V 3H2; ☎416-977 3222; fax 416-977 8585; www.cica.ca) for information on mutual recognition, or the acceptance of qualifications towards a Canadian qualification. One recruitment agency active in the financial field is *Robert Half*, PO Box 824, 181 Bay St Suite 820, Toronto M5J 2T3; ☎416-350 2330; fax 416-350 3573; e-mail toronto@roberthalffinance.com; www. roberthalf.com.

TEACHERS

Just a decade ago, the teaching profession in Canada was overcrowded at all levels. Now it looks like grade-school and high-school teachers will be in demand as older teachers retire. Scientists are still in demand at the university level, but in liberal arts it is much more difficult to find a university position in Canada than it is in Britain. In fact, aspiring Canadian academics now view Britain as the place where they are most likely to find work. For these reasons it is not advisable to go to Canada with the expectation of working as a teacher or professor. However, you may be able to find work through one of the following organisations:

British Council: Education and Training, 10 Spring Gardens, London, SW1A 2BN; ☎020 7930 8466; fax 020 7389 4426; www2.britishcouncil.org/learning.htm.

League for the Exchange of Commonwealth Teachers: LECT 7 Lion Yard, Tremadoc Road, Clapham, London SW4 7NQ; ☎0870 770 2636; fax 0870 770 2637; www.lect.org.uk.

Association of Heads of University Administration Canada Exchange: AUA National Office, University of Manchester, Oxford Road, Manchester M13 9PL; ☎0161 275 2063; fax 0161 275 2036; www.aua.ac.uk.

Association of Universities and Colleges of Canada: 350 Albert Street, Suite 600, Ottawa, ON K1R 1B1; ☎613-563-1236; fax 613-563-9745; www.aucc.ca.

Canadian Education Exchange Foundation: 250 Bayview Drive, Barrie, ON L4N 4Y8; ☎705-739-7596; fax 705-739-7764; www.ceef.ca.

Canadian Teacher's Federation: 2490 Don Reid Drive, Ottawa, ON K1H 1E1; ☎613-232-1505; fax 613-232-1886 www.ctf-fce.ca.

Council on International Exchange: 7 Custom House Street, 3rd Floor, Portland, ME 04101; ☎207-553-7600; fax 1-207-553-7699; www.ciee.org.

Society for Educational Visits and Exchanges in Canada: 57 Auriga Drive, Suite 201, Ottawa ON K2E 8B2; ☎613-998-3760; www.sevec.ca.

OTHER OPPORTUNITIES

Opportunities in Canada are also referred to throughout the *Specific Careers* section of this book, which covers a wide range of professions.

SHORT TERM WORK

Foreigners looking for legal temporary work in Canada must either apply for specific jobs before they arrive and then wait for the employer to arrange a work permit, or take part in an approved educational scheme such as that offered by BUNAC. People looking for casual (illegal) work when in Canada risk exposure because they will not be able to provide a prospective employer with a Canadian social insurance number (which is required by law).

LIVE-IN CAREGIVER

The immigration programme for foreign domestic workers is continually being tightened, making it more difficult for applicants to qualify for the programme. Nonetheless, coming to Canada as a nanny or a live-in caregiver for the elderly or disabled still offers a method of permanent entry to Canada. After just two years of employment as a live-in caretaker, you can bypass the point system and apply for permanent residency.

Families who wish to hire nannies must get job approval from a Human Resources Centre Canada (HRCC) before they are allowed to offer the position to a foreigner. You must have an approved job offer before coming to Canada; this can be arranged independently or through one of the agencies listed below. Prospective domestic carers must have the equivalent of a grade 12 education (A levels), at least six months training in the care-giving field or at least one year of relevant, paid, full-time employment, at least six months of it with the same employer. You must be competent in either English or French. You must state your intention to eventually apply for permanent residency when you apply for employment authorisation. Though the point system is not used, you will be evaluated carefully and only recommended for the programme if immigration officers think you are likely to contribute to the workforce when the nanny contract has expired. You must reapply for the permit after one year of employment.

After two years in Canada, during which you must live in your employer's home, you can apply for permanent residency; if accepted, you must continue working as a caregiver for an additional year. When you receive your permanent residency permit you will have the right to work in any field in Canada; your chances of being accepted will therefore increase if you can show that you have undergone an educational or vocational training programme while working as a caregiver.

There will be a $150 processing fee for the initial Employment Authorisation and a $475 fee for the permanent residency application. If you are fired or quit your job for any reason, you will have to locate another caregiving job and obtain another Employment Authorisation. You can also apply for a standard two-year employment authorisation if you have no intention of applying for permanent residency. It may be easier to get Employment Authorisation under these circumstances, but bear in mind that you will not be able to apply for permanent residency once in Canada. To get more information, send a self-addressed, stamped 10 x 15 envelope to the *Canadian High Commission:* (Immigration Section, 38 Grosvenor Street, W1K 4AA; ☎020-7258-6600; fax 020-7258-65330) or the *Canadian Consulate General Immigration Regional Programme Centre (3000 HSBC Center, Buffalo, NY 14203-2884; fax 716- 852-2477)*. Write 'LCP' clearly in the top left corner of the envelope.

Agencies that recruit nannies for positions abroad are listed below. Pay is usually quite low, but you will not have to pay for rent or food. Meeting other nannies and making friends should not be difficult and you may have the opportunity to travel or go on vacations with your host family. The publication, *The Au Pair and Nanny's Guide to Working Abroad* is a valuable source for those looking for au pair work abroad and is available at £12.95 (plus p&p) from Vacation Work (☎601865-241978; www.vacationwork.co.uk).

ABC Nannies Canada: 11420 95 A Ave., Delta, BC V4C 3V5; ☎604-581-1018; www. abcnannies.ca.

Canadian Nannies: Canadian Sitter Incorporated, P.O. Box 64015, Oakville, ON L6K 3X1; ☎905 465 2883; www.canadiannanny.ca.

GreatAuPair.Com: InteliMark Enterprises, LLC, 21001 San Ramon Valley Blvd., Suite A4-326, San Ramon, CA 94583; ☎925-478-4100; fax 925-551-8484; www.greataupair. com.

Select Nannies Inc.: 210 Glendale Avenue, Suite 107, St. Catharines, ON L2T 3Y6; ☎905-327-4000; www.selectnannies.ca.

TEACHING ENGLISH

The Canadian government offers permanent residents' free classes in English as a second language. Large numbers of immigrants and refugees from eastern Europe, Asia and Africa mean that there are many opportunities for teachers, either in public programs or in the numerous private ESL schools. These private schools cater to Asian immigrants or visitors and most can be found in Toronto or throughout British Columbia. *Teaching English Abroad* (Vacation Work, £12.95; www.vacationwork.co.uk) gives information on teaching English and how to find English-teaching jobs. Other listings may be found in the *Education* section of *The Guardian* on Tuesdays and the Times Educational Supplement on Fridays.

Teaching English as a Second Language in Canada (TESL): PO Box 44105, Burnaby, BC V5B 4Y2; ☎ or fax: 604-298-0312; www.tesl.ca.

International Language Schools of Canada: 555 Richards Street, Vancouver, B.C., V6B 2Z5; ☎604-689-9095, fax 604-683-0771.

WORK PROGRAMMES FOR STUDENTS AND OTHER YOUNG PEOPLE

Work exchange programmes are available for students who wish to work for 2-12 months in Canada. BUNAC (*British Universities North America Club*) (16 Bowling Green Lane, London EC1R 0QH; ☎020-7251 3472; www.bunac.org) organises a *Work Canada* programme. UK Students are issued a temporary visa by the agency, but will be responsible for finding their own accommodation and job once in Canada. Support services are provided on arrival through SWAP in Canada. The student Work Canada programme is open to UK and Irish passport holders studying at a UK University.

BUNAC also operate a non-student Work Canada programme for UK passport holders age 18-35. Applicants receive a 12 month open work authorisation enabling them to undertake virtually any job, any where in Canada. Applicants receive an arrival orientation and support whilst in Canada but are responsible for finding their own work and accommodation.

Places on both BUNAC programmes are subject to annual quota. Early application is recommended.

Programs for students with specific interests include:

International Association for the Exchange of Students for Technical Experience: British Council, 10 Spring Gardens, London, SW1A 2BN; ☎020 7389 4771; www.iaeste.org. uk.

Association for International Practical Training: 10400 Little Paxtuent Pkwy, Ste. 250, Columbia, MD 21044-3510; ☎410-997-2200.

Council on International Educational Exchange: 7 Custom House Street, 3rd Floor, Portland, ME 04101; ☎207-553-7600; www.ciee.org.

OTHER WORK

It is possible to take part in various construction projects in native Canadian communities around the year. These are arranged by *Frontiers Foundation* (2615 Danforth Avenue, Suite 203, Toronto, Ontario M4C 1L6; ☎416-690 3930; fax 416-690 3934; www. frontiersfoundation.org). Participants need to pay their own travel expenses as far as Toronto, and must be free to work for at least three months. Expenses are paid in Canada only. Frontiers Foundation organises construction projects and others in low-income rural communities across Canada.

INTERNATIONAL COMPANIES IN CANADA

The British High Commission in Ottawa (see above) can supply information about the many British companies operating in Canada. The *Canada-United Kingdom Chamber of Commerce*, 38 Grosvenor Street, London W1K 4DP; ☎020-7258 6578 fax 020-7258 6594; e-mail info@canada-uk.org; www.canada-uk.org, can also supply commercial information.

United States of America

- **US Embassy,** 24 Grosvenor Square, London W1A 1AE; ☎020-7499 9000; www. usembassy.org.uk
- **US Consulate General,** 3 Regent Terrace, Edinburgh, Scotland, EH7 5BW; ☎0131 556-8315; fax 0131 557 6023
- **US Consulate General,** Danesfort House, 223 Stranmillis Road, Belfast BT9 5GR; ☎028-9038 6100; fax 028 9068 1301
- **Currency:** (US) $1 = 100 cents
- **Rate of Exchange:** £1 = $1.86; €1 = $1.27
- **Country Code:** +1

The United States is still seen as the land of opportunity. Britons are no longer allowed to participate in the Green Card 'lottery' (see *Immigration* below) although people from Northern Ireland and Eire are. However, many thousands of Britons still emigrate or take up employment there through the conventional visa programme. If one of your parents was born in one of the qualifying countries you could still be able to participate in this annual lottery. There has been a strong economic upturn since the early-1990s and opportunities are very good for highly trained foreign workers, and are likely to remain so. In particular, the USA will need to import thousands of foreign scientists to make up for the shortfall at home. If you have 'exceptional ability' (which means a major and original achievement in science, academia, the Arts, athletics, or business) your chances of being accepted as a migrant are much improved.

Following the terrorist assaults of 2001, 100,000 people in the airline industry and a further 60,000 in the travel industry lost their jobs. However, the economy had officially already entered a recession, which is only the second US recession in 20 years, indicating how buoyant the US economy has been since the close of the 1970s and that decade's energy crises. The economy has now gained strength, with a five percent growth rate forecast. An increase in manufacturing output and a revival in consumer demand is also predicted.

GENERAL FACTS

POPULATION
The resident population of the USA is 298.4 million. The capital, Washington, has a population of 600,000, but 16 other cities have populations that are larger. The total land area is 3,536,855 square miles (9,160, 419 sq km) including Alaska and Hawaii, and the country spans seven time zones.

The population density is about 75 per square mile, but distribution is uneven, with areas of desert and mountains, and the great expanses of Alaska, almost uninhabited. The majority of the population live within 50 miles of a coastal shoreline.

CLIMATE
The climate can be classified as Continental, but varies from Arctic in Alaska to sub-tropical in Hawaii and Florida – the only two states that get no frost. Average January temperatures are below freezing in all but the southern states, and in the northern mid-west states the average is often below 32 deg F (0 deg C). Summer, on the other hand, can be

unbearably hot, with average July temperatures rising to 86 deg F (30 deg C) and up to 104 deg F (40 deg C).

Precipitation is on average about twice as high as in Britain, but intermittent heavy snowfalls, rainstorms and hurricanes, rather than constant drizzle, account for most of this. In the desert areas (New Mexico, Arizona and Nevada for example) annual rainfall is only two to three inches (five to eight cm).

GOVERNMENT

The United States is a federal republic led by a President, who is elected by all citizens aged 18 and over, for a four-year term of office. No president may serve for more than two terms. The President, and the cabinet he appoints, forms the executive branch of the government.

Congress is the seat of the legislature and consists of the Senate and the House of Representatives. Each State elects two senators, who serve a six-year term. One third of the membership is renewed every two years. There are only two major political parties: the Democrats and the Republicans.

The USA is a confederation of states, each of which has its own governor and legislature (which takes different forms in different states). These have considerable autonomy and legislative power; they run their own courts and police forces and levy their own taxes. They are further sub-divided into counties, which are responsible for local government.

CITIES

As the world's leading industrial power, the USA has built its economy on large industrial cities. Eighty per cent of the population live in urban areas, and there are 39 metropolitan areas with over a million inhabitants.

The major cities and conurbations are: New York (the world's second largest port after Rotterdam), Los Angeles, San Francisco, Chicago, Houston, Philadelphia, San Diego, and Detroit.

RURAL LIFE

Cultivated land covers 47 per cent of America's total land area; forests another 32 per cent. With a farming population of only six million, the USA still leads the world in both production and export of meat and agricultural produce. The size of some farms in the mid-west is enormous. About 50 per cent of the country's farms cover 2,000 acres (809 ha) or more.

RELIGION, SPORT AND CULTURE

All major religious faiths are represented. The many denominations of the Protestant or Episcopalian Church predominate but Catholicism is stronger in some areas such as the Mexican-influenced Southwest. Industrial regions settled by immigrants from southern and eastern Europe also have large Catholic populations.

The USA is one of the few countries in the world where soccer is not a major sport, however, interest in it is growing and the World Cup was held there in 1994. The main sports are baseball, American football, ice hockey and basketball. Tennis and skiing are also popular and there are facilities for golf, horseracing and almost every other sporting activity.

Cultural facilities are of the highest standard with cinemas, theatres, concert halls and galleries in all large towns and cities. America continues to successfully export its popular culture – movies, rock music, television programmes, baseball caps, jeans and fizzy drinks – around the world.

FACTORS INFLUENCING EMPLOYMENT

IMMIGRATION

Getting hold of anything more than a visitor's visa for the United States involves a long and complicated procedure, and quite a large financial outlay in application and other fees. Immigration quotas are limited, which allow the Immigration Service to be very selective. Those wishing to enter the country solely for the purpose of employment must have a definite job offer (petitions must be filed by the prospective employer) and must obtain a certification from the US Department of Labor that there are no able, willing and qualified workers in the USA for that particular type of employment. Only workers with really valuable skills will be considered for work permits.

US immigration laws were comprehensively reformed by the 1990 Immigration Act. The total number of immigrants entering the US annually rose as a result to about 650,000.

Three categories of immigrants are now recognised

o *Family-sponsored immigrants*: 226,000 visas are issued per year to relatives of US citizens. This includes spouses and children and sons and daughters of US citizens. It also includes brothers and sisters of US citizens and their spouses and children, provided the US citizens are aged over 21; also parents of US citizens over 21.

o *Employment-based immigrants*: A total of 140,000 immigrant visas are available; divided into five main categories. Preferences 1 to 3 include persons of extraordinary ability, exceptional ability and highly skilled workers, preference 4 covers ministers of religion, religious workers and employees of certain international organisations (10,000). Preference 5 is for those who can invest at least $500,000 into an enterprise.

o *Diversity Transition immigrants*: Reserved for persons with a definite job offer coming from countries considered to have been previously adversely affected by the provisions of the immigration law.

The Diversity Immigrant Visa Programme (commonly known as the Green Card Lottery) offers around 55,000 immigrant visas per year, and a percentage of these are reserved for citizens of Northern Ireland and the Irish Republic. Britons with a parent from an eligible country may apply, but should bear in mind that the chances of obtaining a place by this method are about 200:1 (and even then you will still need to find a job). Priority is given to applicants from countries with repressive regimes, and political refugees are given priority above many other categories.

There are also many types of 'non-immigrant' visa issued to people wishing to take up short-term work in the US. These are only issued for the following categories: lecturers and performing artists; trainees and exchange visitors on approved programmes; intra-company transferees on short-term transfers; and other temporary workers fulfilling limited term contracts. Non-immigrant and tourist visas cannot be changed to immigrant visas once you are in the US, except in special circumstances, such as marriage to an American. Holders of exchange visitor visas are normally required to spend at least two years outside the US before being considered for an immigrant visa.

When considering emigration to the United States, the first step is to contact the Visa Branch at the US Consulate General as rules have been tightened since the 9/11 attacks. Because of the strong possibility of an application being rejected or taking longer than expected, it is advisable not to make any definite plans until the visa is issued.

There is also a Visa Branch for Northern Irish citizens at Queen's House, 14 Queen Street, Belfast BT1 6EQ; ☎028-9032 8239.

COST AND STANDARD OF LIVING

British visitors find the USA cheaper than home in many respects. Retail food prices, for instance, compare very favourably with those in the UK because so much is home-produced. Gasoline (petrol) is less than half the price it is in Britain. Entertainment, apartment rental and certain luxury items tend to be more expensive, but because wages are two to three times higher, these things are well within the reach of most of the population.

HOUSING AND ACCOMMODATION

On average, rents are somewhat higher than in Britain, but so too is the average size and quality of property. Housing of all kinds is generally readily available in the United States. There is relatively little public housing (the equivalent of council housing in the UK), and most people either own their own homes or rent privately-owned houses or flats. Average house prices vary enormously across the country.

HEALTH AND WELFARE

While there is no equivalent to the British National Health Service in the USA, the Social Security Department provides, against contributions from employees and employers, benefits for old age, disability, unemployment and injury.

Personal medical insurance is the responsibility of the individual, who must insure him/ herself privately. Many employers give advisory and financial assistance in this. Because medical fees are so high, insurance premiums are also high, and can account for 5-10 per cent of the weekly pay packet. This is an inevitably necessary expense.

EDUCATION

State laws concerning the ages of compulsory school attendance vary, but the highest minimum age is seven years old and nearly all states set the upper age at 16, although obtaining a high school diploma usually requires attendance at school until the age of 18. Public schools are free but there are also a number of private, fee-paying schools.

With over 2,500 universities and specialised training colleges, gaining entrance to higher education is easier than in the UK. Each state controls at least one university, which gives preference to state residents. University courses are completed on the basis of credits, which offer students the chance to change courses, even colleges, or drop out for a year or two, without damaging their chance of obtaining a degree. On the whole, university courses last for a minimum period of four years. University tuition fees range from $5,000 to $20,000 a year, but government loans are available. Most parents start budgeting for a college education as soon as a child is born.

NATIONAL SERVICE

Although the draft was ended in 1973, the Selective Service System is still functioning and requires all men aged 18-26 to register for possible call-up in the case of a national emergency. This also applies to alien residents, who must register with their local Selective Service Board within 60 days of arrival or, if application for residence is granted after arrival, within 60 days of registration as a resident.

BRITISH EMBASSY AND CONSULATES

British Embassy, 3100 Massachusetts Ave. NW, Washington DC 20008; ☎202-588 6500; fax 202-588 7850; www.britainusa.com.

There are Consulates in Atlanta, Boston, Chicago, Houston, Los Angeles, San Francisco, Dallas, Denver, Miami, Orlando, New York and Seattle.

CONDITIONS OF WORK

WAGES

A minimum wage of not less than $5.15 per hour is required by State and Federal Law. Equality of pay for women is fast becoming a reality. In matters of employment, discriminating against an individual due to that person's sex, age, colour, creed or national origin, is illegal. An average salary for a data processing manager is $88,000, but for an accountant $46,000, and for senior executives $140,000. Graduates can expect a starting salary of at least $17,350.

HOURS

Americans are the most overworked people in the developed world and up to half of the workforce is estimated to be suffering from symptoms of work-related stress. On average Americans work fifty hours per week which is in stark contrast to the 35 hour working week in France. The standard is a 40-hour, five-day week. Banks and shops keep longer hours than in Britain, and all-night shops are common. Working on Sundays, and Sunday trading, is generally forbidden, but laws vary from state to state. Blue-collar workers are generally entitled to overtime pay or compensation, but this depends on the individual industry.

HOLIDAYS

Most employees are given at least two weeks' paid holiday a year. Holiday allowance is usually increased according to the time that the employee has spent with a company. There are also ten nationally observed public holidays: New Year's Day; Martin Luther Day (15 Jan); President's Day (third Monday in February); Memorial Day (last Monday in May); Independence Day (4 July); Labor Day (first Monday in September); Columbus Day (second Monday in October); Veterans' Day (fourth Monday in October); Thanksgiving (fourth Thursday in November); and Christmas Day. Other holidays vary from state to state but Lincoln's Birthday (12 February); St. Patrick's Day (17 March); and Arbor Day (26 April) are quite widely observed.

SAFETY AND COMPENSATION

Safety standards are set down by federal and state laws and are rigidly enforced. Compensations are paid for injury, accident, death and disability. Very few benefits, even in the cases of permanent disability, are payable for an indefinite period, but short-term payments are quite adequate.

TRADE UNIONS

Union membership in manufacturing has fallen dramatically in the last 10-15 years, although there has been a corresponding rise in membership of state and federal government unions. Most unions are affiliated to the American Federation of Labor and Congress of Industrial Organizations (AFL-CIO). Labor Courts exist to arbitrate between employers and employed.

TAXATION

Federal and state income tax is deducted on a PAYE basis at fixed rates, and adjusted at the end of the tax year. Total tax deductions are generally less than 25 per cent of the total income.

Sales tax (between two per cent and 7.5 per cent, varying from state to state) is payable on most goods and services. State variations make for big differences in the prices of many items, for instance, cigarettes, alcohol and cars.

EMPLOYMENT PROSPECTS

The latest figures show that the employment market in the USA is improving and during 2004/5 more than two million jobs were created. Currently, the unemployment rate stands at 5.4% albeit just slightly lower than the December 2001 rate of 5.8% which was the highest figure in six years. Manufacturing was the worst affected with greater job losses during President Bush's first term than in any other four-year period since World War II. The non-manufacturing economy, on the other hand, did quite well. Sectors like electronics, aviation, industrial machinery, and cars were badly hit by the economic downturn at the beginning of the new millennium and US exports remain troubled.

The Department of Commerce secretary, Carlos M Gutierrez, said in 2005 that: 'President Bush's tax relief has helped America create three million jobs since May 2003. To sustain our economic recovery, the Bush administration is pursuing pro-growth policies including making tax relief permanent, eliminating trade barriers, and reforming and strengthening entitlement programs. Under President Bush's leadership, more Americans are working than have ever worked before.'

According to the US Bureau of Economic Analysts, three sectors made notable contributions to faster US personal income growth in 2005 – professional services, finance, and construction. The top three states, North Dakota, Iowa, and South Dakota, benefited from record or near-record production of corn, soybeans, and other crops. The area of the US with lowest unemployment rate is the Great Plains region, which includes the Dakotas, Nebraska, Kansas, and Oklahoma. These states offer the greatest protection against the 'knock-on' effect whereby individual companies take down others in the same community in a chain reaction of bankruptcies. States most vulnerable to this effect are Hawaii, Alaska and Washington. Contrary to popular belief, high-growth companies exist in all sectors of the economy. Technology companies from computing to bio-technology are not necessarily going to be the most successful companies. A survey by the National Council on Entrepreneurship found that high growth companies exist in all areas of the US and span the spectrum of economic activity. Finding the right job also entails picking a well-managed company with good prospects for success and a contented workforce.

NEWSPAPERS

The only truly national newspapers in the USA are *USA Today* and the *Washington Post*. The former's London office, *USA Today International Corporation* (10 Wardour Street, London W1V 3HG; ☎020-7559 5859, www.usatoday.com) places adverts in the domestic edition. They advise that it is worth buying the domestic editions for jobs vacant ('Help Wanted') advertisements, and the international edition (available from most big London newsagents) for nationwide financial and industry news. The *New York Times*, has a large 'Help Wanted' section on Sundays, and is represented by *The Powers Turner Group*, Gordon House, Greencoat Lane, London SW1P 1PH; ☎020-7592 8300; fax 020-7592 8301; e-mail ppn-london@publicitas.com; www.publicitas.com.

Several newspapers in the UK carry advertisements for jobs in the USA. *The Guardian* has international job adverts in its various daily supplements and the *Financial Times* is a good source of jobs for senior business and executive positions. The *Times Educational Supplement* and the *Times Higher Educational Supplement* are fruitful sources of jobs in the teaching profession, and often carry international advertisements.

SPECIFIC CONTACTS

There are more specific addresses and contacts on all aspects of emigration to the United States in *Live and Work in the USA and Canada* published by Vacation Work Publications (www.vacationwork.co.uk). There are a number of US websites advertising vacancies:

America's Employers (www.americasemployers.com); *America's Job Bank* (www.ajb.dni.us); *CareerMart* (www.careermart.com); *CareerMosaic* (www.4work.com); *CareerBuilder.com* (www.careerbuilder.com); *Monster* (www.monster.com); *Net-Temps* (www.net-temps.com); and *Job Bank USA* (www.jobbankusa.com/jobs.html).

Job Services, the state operated employment service, operates a network of some 2,000 local offices in major cities around the country. These 'Employment Service Centers' provide free counselling, testing and job placements, and allow access to computerised listings of possible openings across the country. They are listed in the Yellow Pages under Employment Service or Job Service.

AU PAIRS

The only legitimate way for an au pair to work in the USA is on a J-1 visa obtainable through US government-designated agencies. The official au pair programme allows young women and men with childcare experience to work for an American family for a minimum of one year, with numerous other conditions of participation.

A separate programme exists for qualified child carers/nannies called variously the 'Au Pair Extraordinaire' or 'Au Pair Elite' programme depending on the agency. Candidates with the appropriate nanny or childcare qualification (NNEB, BTEC, Diploma in Nursing, NVQ3) can earn more than an au pair ($200 a week as compared to $139) but are still limited to a one-year stay. A programme called Educare America (www.educareamerica. co.uk) was introduced in 2002 in which the emphasis is more on study and cultural exchange than on childcare (described below).

The basic requirements for au pairs in the US are that participants be between 18 and 26, speak English to an acceptable standard, have a full clean driving licence and provide a criminal record check. They must also show that they have had at least 200 hours of recent childcare experience, which can consist of regular babysitting, helping at a summer playscheme or school. Anyone wanting to care for a child under two must have 200 hours of experience looking after children under two and must expect the programme interviewers to delve more deeply than they used to.

The fixed level of weekly pocket money paid on official au pair programmes to America has now been brought into line with the US minimum wage requirements. At the time of writing the weekly payment was $139.05 plus room and board in return for 45 hours of childcare (including babysitting) and domestic duties. Perks always include a free transatlantic flight plus one-way or return from New York to the family, compulsory four-day orientation in New York, ongoing support from a community counsellor, up to $500 from the family to cover fees for a course of study, and two weeks paid vacation. Au pairs are given at least 1½ days off per week plus one complete weekend off a month.

Prospective au pairs around the world must apply through a small number of sponsoring organisations (currently six) which must follow US government guidelines. Applicants are required to pay a good faith deposit of $400-$500 which is returned to them at the end of 12 months but which is forfeit if the terms of the programme are broken. *Au Pair in America* (part of the American Institute for Foreign Study) is the largest sender from the UK and worldwide.

The *Educare America* programme is overseen by *AIFS* and uses a network of agencies to recruit candidates, chief among them in the UK – *Childcare International Ltd* (Trafalgar House, Grenville Place, London NW7 3SA; ☎020-8906 3116; fax 020-8906 3461; e-mail office@childint.co.uk; www.childint.co.uk). Like the Au Pair Programme, Educare is a 12-month programme with departures in winter and summer, for which successful applicants must be interviewed and attend a four-day safety and childcare orientation on arrival. The families participating in the programme will have children at school and the work will involve supervising these children before and after school. The number of working hours is 30, the weekly pay is $105 and the programme fee is $850 which covers flights to the

US. Participants study six hours a week at an accredited US post-secondary college or university during term-time for which they receive a contribution of up to $1,000 from their host families.

The main agencies are:

American Institute for Foreign Study (AIFS), 37 Queen's Gate, London SW7 5HR; ☎020-7581 7300; e-mail info@aupairamerica.co.uk; www.aupairamerica.com. Runs the *Au Pair in America* Program. Appointed interviewers located throughout UK and Europe.

AuPairCare Cultural Exchange, 2226 Bush Street, San Francisco, CA 94115; ☎415-434 8788; e-mail info@aupaircare.com; and 5 Parklands, Blossomfield Road, Solihull B91 1NG; ☎07973-886979; fax 0121-233 9731; e-mail lorraine@au-pairs4u.com; www.au-pairs4u.com. Also offer Au Pair Elite Programme for qualified nannies.

Au Pair in America, River Plaza, 9 West Broad Street, Stamford, CT 06902; ☎203-399 5000; e-mail aupair.info@aifs.com; www.aupairamerica.com.

Cultural Care Au Pair, EF Center, One Education Street, Cambridge, MA 02141; ☎1-617-619 1100; www.culturalcare.com. Overseas offices in Australia, Austria, Brazil, Colombia, Germany, Mexico, Poland, Russia, and Sweden plus agents in countries such as South Africa, Czech Republic, Peru, Panama, Croatia, and Hungary. Also operate through an agent in London.

EurAupair, 250 North Coast Highway, Laguna Beach, CA 92651; ☎949-494 5500; fax 949-497 6235; e-mail info@euraupair.com; www.euraupair.com. UK partner is *EurAupair UK*, 17 Wheatfield Drive, Shifnal, Shropshire TF11 8HL; ☎01952-460733; e-mail maureen@asseuk.freeserve.co.uk.

Experiment in International Learning (EIL), World Learning, PO Box 676, Kipling Road, Brattleboro, VT 05302; ☎1-802-257 7751; fax 1-802-258 3248; e-mail info@worldlearning.org; www.experiment.org/aupair.htm; and 287 Worcester Road, Malvern, Worcestershire WR14 1AB; ☎0168-456 2577; fax 0168-456 2212; e-mail info@eiluk.org; www.eiluk.org. Offices in many countries worldwide.

go Au Pair, 111 East 12300 South Draper, UT 84020; ☎1-888-287 2471; fax 1-888-287 2470; e-mail inforequest@goaupair.com; www.goaupair.com.

InterExchange, 161 Sixth Avenue, New York, NY 10013; ☎212-924 0446, fax 212-924 0575; e-mail info@interexchange.org; www.interexchange.org.

COMPUTERS/IT

Prospects for work in the computer industry are still good but with one drawback: you can get the job easily enough, but you might have to wait four or five months for your H1-B visa.

Clear that hurdle and you should be welcomed with open arms by UK recruitment companies working for clients in the USA. The skills most in demand are database export orientated projects and knowledge of SAP, Java, and Oracle skills. Maintenance of derivative and data feeds are crucial for the financial sector. Technical support for both IT and non-IT companies is likely to remain in high demand too. Salaries are high for the most experienced: starting on around $75,000 a year it can be possible to triple that on a five-year placement. The magazine *Computerworld* is a useful source of jobs and can be accessed online at www.computerworld.com. Other helpful sites include www.itcareers.com, www.computerjobs.com or the Federal job site www.usajobs.opm.gov which has a section dedicated to information technology. Try also the established online IT hub www.zdnet.com for listings of tech jobs.

MEDICINE AND NURSING

The market for nurses in the USA is buoyant, especially for those with specialised knowledge such as pediatric intensive care nursing. America intends recruiting one million nurses by 2010 and has launched a recruitment drive in the UK. Perks include two months of rent-free accommodation, air fares, visas for family members, and the possibility of obtaining citizenship. By 2020 the shortfall of nurses may range between 300,000 to 650,000. The current and projected shortfall then provides plenty of opportunity for nurses trained outside the US. But those thinking of taking up nursing in the USA should be warned that good experience is vital. With no state health service to support you through training, you are regarded very much as an independent practitioner and as a result will have a higher professional status than nurses in the UK. The average annual salary of a registered nurse (RN) in the US is $45,000.

British qualifications are highly respected, and the USA is currently a favoured destination for nurses and midwives, as it is for doctors looking for locum posts. To practise professional nursing in the USA you must pass a state licensing examination. The *Commission on Graduates of Foreign Nursing Schools* (CGFNS, 3600 Market Street, Suite 400, Philadelphia, PA 19104; ☎215-349 8767; fax 215-662 0425; e-mail info@ cgfns.org; www.cgfns.org) has an exam which is necessary to pass in order to sit for the National Council of State Boards of Nursing Licensure Examination (NCLEX). Passing the CGFNS is a requirement of the H1-A (Registered Nurses) visa, and you must have an offer of full-time work from a US employer.

The Northeast has the highest doctor to patient ratio in the US, and medical practitioners are in shorter supply in southern states. With the most expensive healthcare in the world, the best equipped hospitals and R&D facilities, and salaries a good deal higher than in Europe, working as a doctor or medical researcher in the USA is still an extremely attractive prospect. There are also opportunities on the non-clinical side. Working for a pharmaceutical company researching and testing drugs pays up to $150,000 a year.

NMS and O'Grady Peyton (addresses below) are the two main UK organisations that sponsor nurses through NCLEX, guarantee them jobs at the end of the three- to four-month course, and also sponsor them for a green card.

O'Grady Peyton International, 1/3 Norton Folgate, London EC1 6DB; ☎0870-700 0141; fax 0870-700 0141; e-mail routeeurope@ogradypeyton.com; www.ogpinc.com.
PHP Health Professional, Central House, 1 Ballards Lane, Finchley, London N3 1QX; ☎0800-581917.
National Council of State Boards of Nursing, 111 East Wacker Drive, Suite 2900, Chicago, IL 60601; ☎312-525 3600, fax 312-279 1032; e-mail info@ncsbn.org; www.ncsbn. org. Can provide addresses of state boards of nursing.

TEACHING

One possibility for securing work as a teacher in the United States is to teach English as a foreign language to the thousands of immigrants who settle there every year. Just about every university and college in the major cities has an ESL programme, as do a range of government and charitable organisations. Commercial schools offer a wide variety of classes but tend to focus on survival ESL and EAP (English for Academic Purposes) with writing as a major component.

Although the demand for ESL teachers is enormous, it is very difficult for foreigners who do not have a 'green card' to obtain the necessary working visa. The standard required qualification is an MA in TESOL offered by many universities and colleges in the USA, many of which are listed in the annually updated *EL Guide* (see below). American organisations are beginning to recognise the Cambridge CELTA (Certificate in English Language Teaching to Adults) which can be obtained in four weeks at a large number of centres worldwide. *EL Prospects*, the monthly job supplement to the *EL Gazette,* carries some ads for openings in the US, though most of those are academic posts in universities where it might be possible for the employer to overcome the visa problem in the case of highly qualified candidates.

Bilingual/bicultural classes are run in thousands of high schools across the country. Many require staff who are not only state-certified teachers but also bilingual in exotic languages like Hmong or Gujarati. Most larger cities have at least one free or low-cost workplace literacy/vocational ESL programme which caters for immigrants needing assistance with the basics of English. Some of these programmes operate in outposts (e.g. churches, libraries) and many depend on local volunteers as tutors. Volunteer positions can conceivably lead to better things. Another way of getting your foot in the door is to make yourself available as a substitute (for which you will need a telephone and preferably an answering machine).

Even for qualified American teachers, part-time work is the norm, often referred to as being hired as an 'adjunct'. Many contracts are not renewed creating a transient English teaching population. Pay is hourly and varies according to region, $22-$32 in Chicago, $25-$40 in San Francisco. Part-timers almost never get benefits which means no health insurance or vacation pay. Even full-time teaching openings may be for just nine months with pay as little as $20,000 in the Midwest.

TESOL (Teachers of English to Speakers of Other Languages, 700 S Washington Street, Suite 200, Alexandria, VA 22314; ☎703-836 0774; fax 703-836 7864; e-mail info@ tesol.org; www.tesol.org) is a non-profit, professional association which offers various publications and services to members, who number around 14,000. The association offers an online job board, a job newsletter for TESOL members and an annual job fair, all of which may include English language teaching opportunities anywhere in the world.

In most states you need to be a US citizen in order to be employed in a public school; the same restrictions will seldom apply in private schools, where opportunities are better. Apply directly to the principal.

Applications for positions on the staff of a university are usually made direct. Several directories published by Petersons (www.petersons.com) in the US give details of schools and universities. Also see the *Directory of Postsecondary Institutions* (from www.amazon. com) a complete list of American universities and institutes of higher education; lists of vacancies in modern language departments and English departments are supplied by the *Modern Language Association's* Job Information Service (www.mla.org) A print subscription to the jobs list costs around $45 for a year and an online subscription costs $18.

EL Gazette (monthly) & *EL Guide* (annual), Unit 3, Constantine Court, 6 Fairclough Street, London E1 1PW; ☎020-7481 6700; fax 020-7488 9240; e-mail info@elgazette.com; and PO Box 61202, Oklahoma City, OK 73146; fax 405-557 2538; www.elgazette.com. News and developments in the industry pitched at the professional end of the market.

Eflweb, www.eflweb.com. A leading provider of job and recruitment services to the EFL industry. The place for new and prospective EFL/ESL teachers.

Fulbright Commission, Fulbright House, 62 Doughty Street, London WC1N 2JZ, ☎020-7404 6994; fax 020-7404 6834; e-mail education@fulbright.com; www.fulbright.co.uk/eas.

Modern Language Association, Job Information Service, 26 Broadway, 3rd Floor, New York, NY 10004; ☎646-576 5000; www.mla.org.

UNIVERSITY STAFF

Applications for university positions are usually made direct. The *Directory of Federal Postsecondary Institutions* is a complete list of American universities and institutes of higher education. It is available from the Office of Postsecondary Education, 1990 K Street, NW, Washington DC 20006; ☎202-502 7750; and online at www.ed.gov.

SHORT TERM WORK

America presents a number of obstacles for foreigners looking for work. Students have a definite advantage as they can obtain work visas as part of approved Exchange Visitor Programs with comparative ease, which enable them to look for work inside the country. Others wanting to work legally must first obtain an offer of a job, then wait several months while the employer applies for a *Temporary Worker Visa* for them. These temporary visas apply only to specific jobs and cannot be transferred if you come across a better job when in America. Below is a list of official 'program sponsors' for exchange visitors, organisations approved for the issue of the J-1 visas:

AIESEC/US, 127 West 26th Street 10th Floor, New York City, NY 10001; ☎212-757-3774; www.aiesecus.org.

American-Scandinavian Foundation, Scandinavia House, 58 Park Avenue, New York, NY 10016; ☎212-879-9779; www.amscan.org.

Association for International Practical Training (AIPT), 10400 Little Patuxent Parkway, Suite 250, Columbia, Maryland 21044-3519; ☎410-997 2200; www.aipt.org.

CDS International, 871 United Nations Plaza, New York, NY 10017-1814; ☎212-497 3500; fax 212-497 3535; e-mail info@cdsintl.org; www.cdsintl.org.

Council of International Programs USA, 1700 East 13th Street, Suite 4ME, Cleveland, Ohio 44114; ☎216-566 1088; fax 216-566 1490; e-mail info@cipusa.org; www.cipusa.org.

InterExchange, 161 Sixth Avenue, Suite 902, New York, NY 10013; ☎212- 924 0446; e-mail info@interexchange.org; www.interexchange.org.

SEASONAL WORK

An enormous range of summer jobs exists in America. Organisations which place young British people on children's summer camps in America are listed under *Camp Counsellors* below. The *British Universities North America Club (BUNAC)*, 16 Bowling Green Lane, London EC1R 0BD; ☎020-7251 3472; fax 020-7251 0215; e-mail enquiries@bunac. org.uk; www.bunac.org.uk, also operates the *Work America Programme* which enables students to look for and take up any temporary work they want in America between June and October. Qualifying for the programme and the J-1 work and travel visa depends on having a pre-arranged job, sponsorship, or proof of adequate funds. Programme brochures are available from October onwards.

Camp Counsellors

Looking after a camp full of schoolchildren during the summer vacation may not be everybody's idea of fun, but with hundreds of children in the USA spending at least part of their summer at a camp, staff needs are always high. Most summer camps are staffed on an international basis by male and female camp counsellors who provide leadership, assist in organisation and take part in the various activities. The programme of activities is usually varied and includes all kinds of sports, handicrafts, and artistic and educational pursuits. Sometimes counsellors are chosen for their special skills in these areas, particularly the ability to entertain and motivate children. Many organisations also offer opportunities for travel once the contract has been completed.

British Universities North America Club (BUNAC), 16 Bowling Green Lane, London EC1R 0BD; ☎020-7251 3472; fax 020-7251 0215; e-mail enquiries@bunac.org; www. bunac.org. BUNAC operates a variety of programmes in the USA, Canada and Australia for students and other young people. *BUNACAMP* is a low-cost, non-profit camp counsellor programme which places young people aged 19½-35 in US and Canadian summer camps from mid-June to the end of August. Applicants should have some kind of leadership experience with children and/or specialised creative or sporting skills. Nurses and those with secretarial skills are also invited to apply. Programmes provide a return flight, work and travel visa (through US sponsors ICCP), salary, board and lodging while at camp, and up to six weeks' travel afterwards. Interviews begin in November. BUNAC also operates programmes in New Zealand and South Africa.

Camp America, 37a Queen's Gate, London SW7 5HR; ☎020-7581 7373; fax 020-7581 7377; e-mail brochure@campamerica.co.uk; www.campamerica.co.uk. Camp America primarily places people from Europe, Asia, Africa, Australia, and New Zealand on American summer camps. They recruit skilled people for a variety of jobs, from Camp Counsellor, to Camp Power or Resort America positions, throughout the USA. Camp Counsellor applicants must be available for a minimum of nine weeks. Work consists of childcare and/or teaching sports activities, music, arts, drama, and dance. Camp Power applicants must be full time students available for a minimum of nine weeks. Typical job roles involve assisting in kitchen/laundry duties, administration and general camp maintenance. Experience in administrative roles, maintenance work, health care, and catering is preferable. Resort America applicants must also be full time students and available for a minimum of 12 weeks. Duties consist mainly of providing catering and administration support at holiday resorts and hotels. Experience in leisure and hospitality management, food and beverages supervision and entertainment is preferable. Applicants for all three positions must be able to leave the UK between 1 May and 27 June. Face-to-face interviews are conducted by locally appointed Camp America interviewers. All programmes offer free return flights from London and other selected international airports to New York, transfer to camp/resort, free accommodation and meals, up to 10 weeks of travel time after camp or resort duties. Pocket money ranges from $600 to $1100, dependent on age and experience.

Camp Counsellors USA, UK Office, Green Dragon House, Unit 4cc, 64-70 High Street, Croydon, Surrey CR0 9XN; ☎020-8688 9051; fax 020-8680 4539; e-mail info@ccusa.co.uk; www.ccusa.co.uk, has a high-quality programme placing young people (19-28) as counsellors at American summer camps. Each year CCUSA staff inspect the camps and interview counsellors so that improvements can be made where necessary. CCUSA require people with sports or nursing qualifications, or who are willing to assist the physically and mentally handicapped. Proficiency in the arts, outdoor pursuits, water sports, is also useful. Patience, a good sense of humour and a high degree of maturity are prerequisites. Counsellors receive a free return flight to the USA, pocket money and the chance to travel after the camp.

BRITISH COMPANIES IN THE USA

The Anglo-American Trade Directory, is published by *British-American Business Inc.*, 75 Brook Street, London W1K 4AD; ☎020-7467 7400; www.babinc.org and aims to list 'all British and American businesses having trade and/or investment relations with each other'.

Latin America

No one can deny that progress has been made in recent years towards greater political and economic stability in Latin America, but few countries in this region can offer their own citizens the employment or education prospects to which they aspire. Development is often hampered by high levels of debt and an uneven distribution of wealth. There is also a general under-utilisation of human resources so that on average only one-third of the population is economically active compared with 50 per cent in more advanced economies. The distribution of work shows a fundamental imbalance. On the one hand there is a large unskilled or semi-skilled workforce unable to find suitable employment while on the other, there is a constant demand for skilled technicians and managers.

Despite the efforts made by Latin American governments to combat illiteracy, and to expand the capacity of their education systems, many countries are not yet in a position to prepare a sufficient number of students for the various professions. Much of this is attributable to the fact that many children leave school at an early age with a minimal level of skills. In spite of the assistance of international organisations, vocational training and the training of higher-level personnel also lags behind other parts of the world. Training and development are areas where there is scope in Latin America for international jobseekers as skills still fall far short of requirements.

As with many other transitional regions, Latin America has to accept a considerable outflow of its own qualified personnel. In many cases, these engineers and scientists, doctors and skilled technicians pursue their training abroad, often in the United States, and are likely to pursue a career outside their country of origin as well. Confronted with this problem of an immediate need for a skilled, trained workforce, governments have pursued supplementary policies to attract the expertise required, often through multilateral and/or bilateral technical co-operation programmes. Organised by aid agencies, these place experts at the disposal of developing countries for a fixed period of time.

As far as permanent migration is concerned, it is clear that in the current economic climate Latin America can only accept a limited number of immigrants from wealthier countries, in certain specialised areas such as consultancy, English-language teaching, tourism, or voluntary and development work. Those who are interested should contact the relevant embassies or the *Intergovernmental Committee for Migration* (see below) which is active in promoting the transfer of foreign experts to Latin America.

LANGUAGES

Apart from the many Native American languages, the almost universal language of Latin America is Spanish. The main exceptions are Brazil where the official language is Portuguese – and the former colonies and possessions of other European countries, where French, English and Dutch are spoken. English is not widely spoken, except in the former British territories like Guyana and Belize, and among the middle classes. If you are going to study Spanish or Portuguese, it is worth noting that there are significant variations between the European dialects and their South American counterparts; this is something to take into consideration when choosing a language course.

POLITICS AND CULTURE

While Latin America has a great deal to offer in terms of cultural achievements in art and literature, and a lifestyle that is relaxed and friendly, there is a darker side – the ever-present problem of political instability and human rights violations. In the 1980s, many of the former military dictatorships gave way to freely elected governments, but these democracies are not always rooted in civil society and there is the possibility in many of these countries that the situation will deteriorate again. The eradication or persecution of indigenous populations and the widespread destruction of rainforests are also matters of concern to foreign workers.

Detailed information about political and environmental developments is available from pressure groups such as Amnesty International, Friends of the Earth, and Survival International (whose addresses can be found in your local telephone directory and are useful sources of supplementary information about Latin America).

IMMIGRATION AND WORK PERMITS

Employment in all Latin American countries is subject to obtaining work and/or residence permits. In general, the procedure is based on your finding a job first, while either in or outside the country, after which the employer applies for a work permit on your behalf. Residence permits will normally be issued on production of a valid work permit. For some countries, residence permits may be issued without a firm job offer provided certain other criteria are fulfilled, such as financial viability, character references, health certificates and political testimonies. In most cases, residence permits must be obtained before arriving in the country.

As a rule Latin American embassies and consulates abroad do not send out very detailed information. In compiling this book, Peru, Mexico and Brazil were exceptions to this; certainly none of them is in any way involved in finding or offering employment. If pressed, most will send at least a circular describing the procedures involved, and refer enquirers to other addresses for further information. National tourist agencies may be able to provide more relevant general information.

EMPLOYMENT PROSPECTS

Most Latin American countries are rich in raw materials and those in mainland South America generally maintain a trade surplus with the rest of the world. Certain countries have also made great progress in developing their industries, notably Brazil, Chile, Argentina and Mexico. Prospects for future development appear to be improving now that serious efforts are being made to reduce the crippling burden of debt. The general liberalisation of local economies should also increase demand for foreign workers.

There is a strong movement towards instituting free-trade areas on the lines of the European Union, which may eventually embrace the whole of North and South America. In 1992 Canada, the USA and Mexico negotiated the North American Free Trade Agreement (NAFTA), which has led to the abolition of many tariff and trade barriers between these countries. Trade barriers have been lifted between Venezuela, Colombia, Bolivia, Peru and Ecuador, to establish the Andean Common Market; as well as in Central America and the Caribbean.

Suitably qualified people with Spanish or Portuguese are in a good position to find translating or secretarial work in the more developed areas. Anyone with money to invest or a good track record in business will also generally be welcomed. For others, the most practical method of obtaining work in Latin America is through an overseas posting from an international company. Sectors where there is a regular demand for foreign workers include petrochemicals in countries such as Ecuador, Venezuela and Colombia, and banking and finance wherever there are large foreign banks. Many Japanese and Far Eastern companies are moving production facilities to Latin America because of its low labour costs, especially to Mexico and Panama. Further opportunities for work in Latin America can be found in most chapters of the *Specific Careers* section.

NEWSPAPERS

Argentina's principal English language daily, *The Buenos Aires Herald*, has a website at www.buenosairesherald.com. Many Brazilian newspapers, magazines and journals, including *O'Estado de Saõ Paulo* and *Jornal do Brasil* are also available online.

SPECIFIC CONTACTS

Apart from the addresses quoted under separate countries below, the following organisations are involved in migration and employment in Latin America:

International Organization for Migration (IOM), PO Box 71, 17 Route des Morillons, 1211 Geneva 19, Switzerland; ☎22-717 9111; fax 22-798 6150; e-mail info@iom.int; www.iom.int, runs a programme for assisting in the emigration of European technical and professional workers to Latin American countries. IOM has offices throughout Latin America, and issues free booklets and fact sheets on aspects of life and work in all these countries (see the *International Organisations* chapter).

LatPro, Inc., 8551 West Sunrise Blvd., suite 302, Plantation, FL 33322, USA; e-mail sales@latpro.com; www.latpro.com, is an executive search consultancy specialising in the selection and location of Spanish and Portuguese speakers for Latin American companies.

ENGLISH TEACHING AND TOURISM

For those without professional qualifications, opportunities are generally limited to teaching English or working in the travel industry. Unskilled or semi-skilled manual work is generally not open to foreign workers. There is a considerable demand for English teachers all over Latin America but wages are low by international standards. Trying to obtain a permit for this kind of work is often impractical and unnecessary, unless you wish to work for an established organisation such as the British Council or USIA (see *Teaching* chapter).

The chances of working for a tour operator are good if you have the right languages and skills. UK travel companies operating in Latin America are featured in the *Travel and Tourism* chapter.

VOLUNTARY WORK

If you are unwilling to risk a trip without pre-arranged work, volunteering is another possibility, but participation costs can be high. American residents have a range of opportunities open to them in this respect. Major organisations in this area for Britons and Americans are included in the *Voluntary Work* chapter.

WORK EXCHANGES

Major work exchange organisations such as IAESTE and AIPT can sometimes arrange positions in Latin America. CIEE arranges work projects in Ecuador and Mexico. See the *Working Exchanges* section of the *Getting The Job* chapter.

British students of Spanish in universities may apply for an assistantship in a Latin American school through the *British Council Education and Training Group* in London (see *Working Exchanges*).

USEFUL PUBLICATIONS

Further information on casual work in Latin America can be found in Susan Griffith's book, *Work Your Way Around the World* (Vacation Work Publications). A general source of information on work opportunities is available at the *Hispanic and Luso Brazilian Council*, Canning House, 2 Belgrave Square, London SW1X 8PJ; ☎020-7235 2303; fax

020-7235 3587; www.canninghouse.com. The Council publishes a series of information leaflets on courses and job opportunities in Latin America, as well as providing assistance with a wide variety of enquiries on educational and cultural matters. Extensive listings of voluntary work opportunities are to be found in *International Directory of Voluntary Work* published by Vacation Work.

COUNTRY INFORMATION

ARGENTINA

In spite of the war over the Falklands close links remain between Britain and Argentina, and there is a long-established British expatriate community in the country. At one time Argentina was the most prosperous and developed country in South America but due to corrupt governments Argentina's economic difficulties are pretty dire. Enquiries about visa requirements should be addressed to the *Argentine Embassy*, 65 Brook Street, London W1K 4AH; ☎020-7318 1300; fax 020-7318 1301; www.argentine-embassy-uk.org, or to the *Argentine Embassy*, 1600 New Hampshire Avenue NW, Washington DC 20009; ☎202-238-6401; www.embassyofargentina.us.

BOLIVIA

Teaching English is the best bet for those seeking employment in Bolivia, however, wages are likely to be very low. General enquiries about immigration can be made to the *Bolivian Embassy*, 106 Eaton Square, London SW1W 9AD; ☎020-7235 4248; fax 020-7235 1286; e-mail info@embassyofbolivia.co.uk; www.embassyofbolivia.co.uk; or the *Bolivian Embassy*, 3014 Massachusetts Avenue, NW Washington DC 20008; ☎202-483 4410; fax 202-328 3712; www.bolivia-usa.org.

BRAZIL

To take up employment in Brazil, an application for a temporary, or permanent, work permit in favour of the visa applicant must be made by a prospective Brazilian employer to the Ministry of Labour. Application for a permanent visa, based on the establishment of commercial or industrial activities, requires transference of US$200,000. Details are set out in a circular issued by the *Brazilian Embassy*, 32 Green Street, Mayfair, London W1K 7AT; ☎020-7399 9000; fax 020-7399 9100; e-mail info@brazil.org.uk; www.brazil.org. uk; or the *Brazilian Embassy*, 3009 Whitehaven Street, Washington DC 20008; ☎202-238 2828; www.brasilemb.org.

CHILE

Residence permits are required by all those who wish to work in Chile, or stay more than 90 days, for any purpose. Applications for residence permits will be considered individually by the *Chilean Embassy*, Consular Section, 12 Devonshire Street, London W1G 7DS; ☎020-7580 6392; fax 020-7436 5204; www.echileuk.demon.co.uk; or 1732 Massachusetts Ave., NW, Washington DC 20036; ☎202-785 1746; fax 202-887 5579; www.chile-usa.org. Enquiries about employment, accompanied by information on your qualifications, experience and type of employment being sought, should be addressed to the *Servicio Nacional de Empleo*, Avenida Independencia 2, 3er Pabellón, Santiago, Chile.

COLOMBIA

Enquiries about immigration and work permits should be addressed to the *Embassy of Colombia*, 3 Hans Crescent, London SW1X 0LN; ☎020-7589 9177; fax 020-7581 1829; www.colombianembassy.co.uk; or the *Embassy of Colombia*, 2118 Leroy Place, NW Washington DC 20008; ☎202-387 8338; fax 202-232 8643; www.colombiaemb.org.

COSTA RICA

Sandwiched between Panama and Nicaragua, Costa Rica has become a popular destination for teachers, environmentalists and voluntary workers, because of its progressive social policies and good human rights record. The management of its rainforests is seen as exemplary by many. The *Embassy of Costa Rica* is at 14 Lancaster Gate, London W2 3LH; ☎020-7706 8844; fax 020-7706 8655. In the US, the *Embassy of Costa Rica* is at 2114 'S' Street, NW Washington, DC 20008; ☎202-234 2945; fax 202-265 4795; www. costarica-embassy.org.

GUYANA

Information on immigration is obtainable from the Passport and Consular Section, *Guyana High Commission*, 3 Palace Court, Bayswater Road, London W2 4LP; ☎020-7229 7684; fax 020-7727 9809. *Guyana's Embassy* in the USA is at 2490 Tracey Place, NW, Washington DC 20008; ☎202-265-6900; fax 202-232 1297. Although preference in employment is given to Guyanese nationals, non-nationals who possess certain skills can secure employment on a contract basis.

MEXICO

Industry is expanding rapidly in Mexico, and some North American firms are relocating some of their activities there. Wages tend to be one-tenth of those in the USA. Casual work opportunities are limited to teaching English or crewing on yachts. The English-language newspaper *Mexico City News* is useful for finding work. Information on immigration can be obtained from the *Embassy of Mexico (Consular Section)*, 8 Halkin Street, London SW1X 7DW; ☎020-7235 6393; www.mexicanconsulate.org.uk; or 1911 Pennsylvania Avenue, NW, Washington DC 20006; ☎202-728 1600; www.embassyofmexico.org. The Embassy emphasises that it does not have information on firms or employment; and that immigration is not permitted except where firms require certain specialists and professionals, in which case the firm itself applies to the immigration authorities in Mexico City.

PARAGUAY

Opportunities for work and residence are good, and the requirements for establishing residence are minimal – a passport, health certificate and character references (an offer of work is not essential). Contact the *Embassy of Paraguay*, 344 High Street, Kensington, London W14 8NS; ☎020-7610 4180; fax 020-7371 4297; www.paraguayembassy.co.uk; or 2400 Massachusetts Avenue, NW, Washington DC 20008; ☎202-483 6960; www. embaparusa.gov.py.

PERU

An open market economy as well as other policies have stimulated foreign investment and thus created a demand for a wide variety of jobs for specialised foreign workers. A definite job offer is a pre-requisite to obtaining a work visa. Applications for work visas must be made by the employer through the *Ministry of the Interior*. Information and assistance can be obtained from the *Embassy of Peru*, 52 Sloane Street, London SW1X 9SP; ☎020-7235 1917; fax 020-7235 4463; www.peruembassy-uk.com; or 1700 Massachusetts Avenue, NW, Washington DC 20036; ☎202-833 9860; www.peruvianembassy.us.

URUGUAY

Residence permits are issued upon submission of a variety of documents testifying physical, mental, political and financial soundness. The details are set out in the circular *Formalities to be Complied with by Applicants for Permanent Residence in Uruguay*, available from either the *Embassy of Uruguay*, 2nd Floor, 140 Brompton Road, London

SW3 1HY; ☎020-7589 8835; fax 020-7581 9585; or 1913 I Street NW, Washington DC 20006; ☎202-331 1313; fax 202-331 8142; www.uruwashi.org.

VENEZUELA

Notwithstanding its substantial oil revenues, Venezuela is still a developing country in some respects. Immigration, even of high-level technical and managerial personnel, is subject to quotas. Application for a work permit must be made by the employer in Venezuela, who must also act as a sponsor for the individual obtaining a residence permit. *The Venezuelan Embassy*, Consular Section, 56 Grafton Way, London W1T 5DL; ☎020-7387 6727; fax 020-7583 3253; www.venezlon.co.uk, or 1099 30th Street, NW, Washington DC 20007; ☎202-342 2214; fax 202-342 6820; www.embavenez-us.org both may be able to offer advice regarding employment and investment prospects in Venezuela.

EMBASSIES AND CONSULATES

Argentina

British Embassy, Dr Luis Agote 2412, 1425 Buenos Aires, Argentina; ☎11-4808 2200; fax 11-4808 2274; www.britain.org.ar.

US Embassy, Avenida Colombia 4300, 1425 Buenos Aires, Argentina; ☎11-5777 4533; fax 11-5777 4240.; http://buenosaires.usembassy.gov/.

Bolivia

British Embassy, Avenida Arce 2732, Casilla 694, La Paz, Bolivia; ☎2-243 3424; www. britishembassy.gov.uk/bolivia.

US Embassy, Avenida Arce 2780, Casilla 425, La Paz, Bolivia; ☎2-216 8000; fax 2-216 8111; http://lapaz.usembassy.gov/.

Brazil

British Embassy, Sector de Embaixadas Quadra 801 Conjunto K, CEP 70200-010, Brasilia; ☎61-3329 2300; fax 61-3329 2369; www.uk.org.br.

British Consulate-General, Praia do Flamengo 284 2 andar, Caixa Postal 669, CEP 22210-030, Rio de Janeiro-RJ, Brazil; ☎21-2555 9600; fax 21-2555 9671. There are also consulates also in in Belém, Fortaleza, Mánáus, Recife, Salvador, Belo Horizonte, Rio Grande, Saõ Paulo, Santos and Curitiba.

US Embassy, Lote 3, Quadra 801, Avenida das Nacões, 70403-900, Brasilia, DF, Brasil; ☎61-3321 7000; fax 61-3225 9136; www.embaixada-americana.org.br. There are consulates in Rio de Janeiro and Saõ Paolo.

Chile

British Embassy, Avenida El Bosque Norte 0125, Las Condes, Santiago 9, Chile; ☎2-370 4100; fax 2-370 4170; www.britishembassy.gov.uk/chile. There are consulates also in Punta Arenas and Valparaíso.

US Embassy, Avenida Andrés Bello 2800, Las Condes, Santiago, Chile; ☎2-232 2600; fax 2-330 3710; www.usembassy.cl.

Colombia

British Embassy, Carrera 9, No. 76-49, Piso 8 y 9, Bogotá; ☎1-326 8300; fax 1-326 8303; www.britain.gov.co. There are Consulates in Cali and Medellín.

US Embassy, Calle 22D-Bis #47-51 (Postal address: Carrera 45 #22D-45), Bogotá DC., Colombia; ☎1-315-0811; http://bogota.usembassy.gov.

Costa Rica
British Embassy, Apartado 815-1007, Edificio Centro Colón, San José, Costa Rica; ☎258 2025; fax 233 9938; www.britishembassycr.com.
US Embassy, Calle 120 Avenida 0, Pavas, San José, Costa Rica; ☎519 2000; fax 519 2305; http://usembassy.or.cr/.

Ecuador
British Embassy, Citiplaza Building, Naciones Unidas Ave. and Republica de El Salvador, PO Box 17-17-830, Quito, Ecuador; ☎2-297 0800; fax2-297 0807. There are consulates in Guayaquil and Galápagos.
US Embassy, Av. Patria y Av. 12 de Octubre Avenues, Quito, Ecuador; ☎2-256 2890; fax 2-250 2052; www.usembassy.org.ec.

Guatemala
British Embassy, 16 Calle 0-55, Zona 10, Edificio Torre Internacional, Level 11, Guatemala City, Guatemala; ☎2-367 5425; fax 2-367 5430.
US Embassy, Avenida La Reforma 7-01, Zona 10, Guatemala City, Guatemala; ☎2-326 4000; http://guatemala.usembassy.gov.

Guyana
British High Commission, 44 Main Street, PO Box 10849, Georgetown, Guyana; ☎2-226 5881/4; fax 2-225 3555; www.britishhighcommission.gov.uk/guyana.
US Embassy, PO Box 10507, 100 Young and Duke Streets, Kingston, Georgetown, Guyana; ☎2-225 4900; fax 2-225 8497; http://georgetown.usembassy.gov/.

Honduras
British Embassy is the same as that for Guatemala City, Guatemala.
British Honorary Consul, San Pedro Sula, PO Box 20058, Honduras; ☎550 2337; fax 550 2486.
US Embassy, Avenida La Paz, Apartado Postal No. 3453, Tegugicalpa, Honduras; ☎236 9320; fax 236 9037; http://honduras.usembassy.gov/.

Mexico
British Embassy, Rio Lerma 71, Col Cuauhtémoc, 06500 Mexico City, Mexico; ☎5-5242 8500; fax 5-5242 8517; www.britishembassy.gov.uk/mexico. There are consulates in Acapulco, Cancún, Ciudad Juarez, Tijuana, Oaxaca, Monterrey, Guadalajara and Veracruz.
US Embassy, Paseo de la Reforma 305, Colonia Cuauhtámoc, 06500, Mexico City DF, Mexico; ☎5080 2000; www.usembassy-mexico.gov. There are consulates in Matamoros, Monterrey, Puerto Vallarta, Tijuana, Ciudad Juarez and Guadalajara.

Nicaragua
British Embassy is the same as that for Costa Rica.
US Embassy, PO Box 327, Km 4½, Carretera Sur, Managua, Nicaragua; ☎268 0123; fax 266 9943; http://usembassy.state.gov/managua/wwwhemba.html.

Panama
British Embassy, Swiss Tower, Calle 53, Apartado/PO Box Number 0816-07946, Panama City, Panama; ☎269 0866; fax 223 0730; www.britishembassy.gov.uk/panama.
US Embassy, Torre Miramar, Apartado 6959, Avenida Balboa, Entre Calle 37 y 38, Panama City 5, Panama; ☎207-7000; http://panama.usembassy.gov.

Paraguay
British Embassy is the same as that for Buenos Aires, Argentina.
British Honorary Consulate, Eulogio Estigarribia, 4846 C/ Monseñor Bogarin, Asunción, Paraguay; ☎21-210 405; fax 21-600 448.
US Embassy, Avenida Mariscal López 1776, Asunción, Paraguay; ☎21-213715; fax 21-213728; http://paraguay.usembassy.gov.

Peru
British Embassy, Torre Parque Mar (Piso 22), Avenida Jose Larco, 1301, Miraflores, Lima, Peru; ☎1-617 3000; fax 1-617 3100; www.britemb.org.pe. There are consulates in Arequipa, Trujillo and Cusco.
US Embassy, Avenida La Encalada Cuadra 17 s/n, Surco, Lima 33, Peru; ☎1-434 3000; fax 1-618 2397; http://peru.usembassy.gov.

Uruguay
British Embassy, Calle Marco Bruto 1073, 11300 Montevideo, PO Box 16024, Uruguay; ☎2-622 3630; fax 2-622 7815; www.britishembassy.org.uy.
US Embassy, Lauro Muller 1776, Montevideo 11200, Uruguay; ☎2-418 7777; fax 2-418 8611; http://uruguay.usembassy.gov.

Venezuela
British Embassy, Torre La Castellana, Piso 11 Avenida la Principal de la Castellana, La Castellana, Caracas 1061, Venezuela; ☎12-263 8411; fax 12-267 1275; www.britain. org.ve. Consulates in Maracaibo, Valencia, San Christobel, Margarita and Mérida.
US Embassy, Calle F con Colinas de Valle Arriba, Caracas 1080, Venezuela; ☎12-975 6411; http://embajadausa.org.ve/.

AUSTRALASIA

Australia

- o **Australian High Commission,** Australia House, Strand, London WC2B 4LA; ☎020-7379 4334; fax 020-7240 5333; www.uk.embassy.gov.au
- o **Australian Embassy,** 1601 Massachusetts Avenue, NW, Washington DC 20036-2273; ☎202-797 3000; fax 202-797 3168; www.austemb.org
- o **Currency:** 1 Australian Dollar (A$) = 100 cents
- o **Rate of Exchange:** £1 = A$2.43; US$1 = A$1.31; €1 = A$1.67
- o **Country Code:** +61

Although some five million migrants have settled in Australia in the post-war period, the number of newly admitted immigrants has been drastically reduced in recent years. A significant number of these – about 10,000 a year – are British; and the Australian government is still eager to encourage immigrants with useful skills and training. More than 840 international companies have established headquarters in Australia. One area of expansion guaranteed to generate jobs well into the future is Australia's very successful tourist industry.

GENERAL FACTS

Population
Australia's total population is 20.2 million with a yearly increase of 0.85 per cent, two-fifths of this through net migration. Spread over three million square miles (7.7 million sq km), the average population density is very low – six per square mile. Population distribution is very uneven, however, with only one person per square mile in Western Australia, and a mere 0.3 in the Northern Territory. More than 90 per cent of Australians are of European descent (75 per cent or so from Britain and Ireland). Of the indigenous inhabitants – the aborigines – only 100,000 remain. Australia has a large ethnic Asian population, made up mainly of Chinese, Vietnamese, and Indians. 94 per cent of the population is in employment.

CLIMATE
Because of its enormous area Australia's climate varies considerably, ranging from tropical and sub-tropical in Queensland and other northern areas to temperate, cooler weather in the south. In the western and central regions desert conditions prevail.

In general, Australia is warm and sunny (Perth has a daily average of almost eight hours of sunshine) and summer temperatures often exceed 101 deg F (38 deg C). Humidity is high in the northeast and snow falls in Tasmania and on the Australian Alps.

Annual rainfall varies from 160 inches (406 cm) along the tropical northeast coast to below five inches (13 cm) in the Lake Eyre region of northern South Australia. Annual rainfall in the capital cities is less extreme and varies between Darwin with 58.7 inches (149 cm) and Adelaide with 2.1 inches (5 cm).

GOVERNMENT

Australia is made up of six states and two self-governing territories – New South Wales, Victoria, Queensland, South Australia, Western Australia, the island of Tasmania, Northern Territory, and the Australia Capital Territory. It has both a Federal and a State system of government. Matters of national concern, such as defence, are the responsibility of the Federal Parliament and Government. Six State governments and legislatures have responsibilities within their own boundaries, which complement the activities of the Federal Government. About 900 local government bodies are concerned with matters of a local or regional nature.

Close institutional links are retained with Britain and the Commonwealth. Queen Elizabeth II is also the Head of State of Australia and is represented by a Governor-General and the six State Governors at national level. In November 1999, a referendum was held to decide whether Australia should become a republic, replacing the Queen with an elected Australian Head of State. Although there was overwhelming support for the republican concept (87 per cent indicated that they would vote for a republic were the question untangled from its constitutional issues), a 'NO' vote was returned in every state, due to the electoral model chosen to replace the current constitutional monarchy. In brief, it was proposed that the new Head of State be elected by Parliament rather than by direct election, and it was this the Australian people opposed. Nonetheless, there remains a very strong desire for Australia to become a republic.

CITIES

The majority (65 per cent) of the Australian population live in urban metropolitan areas, with a further 20 per cent in provincial towns. Australian cities cover a much larger area than those in Europe, as most Australians prefer to live in detached houses set in their own gardens, rather than in flats or terraced houses. The suburbs of Sydney for instance (the largest of Australia's cities, with 4.5 million inhabitants) cover a radius of more than 19 miles (30 km). Other capital cities have varying populations ranging from Melbourne's 3.1 million, to Darwin with 80,000. Canberra, the national capital, has 310,000 inhabitants.

Australia's cities are all located on the coast, and life revolves around the great outdoors. Sydney is currently enjoying massive growth and development and enjoying a vibrant economy boom since the Olympic Games were held there in August 2000. It can also now boast the world's finest sporting facilities.

RURAL LIFE

Only about 15 per cent of Australians live in rural areas. Some of these are farmers while others are engaged in mining or development projects. Most aborigines also live on the land, mostly in reserves or settlements. In recent years Aboriginal land rights campaigns, supported by a number of key High Court decisions, have seen significant tracts of rural and outback land, as well as various sacred sites, returned to Aboriginal ownership.

RELIGION, SPORT AND CULTURE

Australians are not, in general, very religious. Christianity is the majority faith, with 24 per cent of the faithful belonging to the Church of England; 26 per cent are practising Roman Catholics. Most other faiths have a minority representation among Australia's very diverse immigrant population. Religious freedom is an important tenet of Australian life; religious education is not a compulsory subject in schools.

Hot summers and a sandy coastline have made swimming Australia's favourite pastime, closely followed by other water sports such as yachting, powerboat racing and surfing.

British settlers introduced their traditional sports such as cricket, tennis, golf, rugby and athletics – and Australians have excelled in all of these. Australian Rules football (a mixture of rugby and Gaelic football) is the national sport. Swimming and sport are key elements in the Australian educational curriculum and Australians are generally 'sport-mad'.

Australia has a thriving arts scene, which derives much of its potency from its Australian rather than its European roots. A tradition of fine artists (Nolan, Drysdale, Boyd) and opera singers (Joan Sutherland), plus international success in literature (Patrick White's Nobel Prize, and Peter Carey's Booker Prizes for example) reveals vigour and originality in the arts. In particular, a new generation of Australian filmmakers have made their mark over recent years and Australia is now a world centre of film production, with the final part of the *Star Wars* prequel trilogy being produced in the country that gave birth to *Crocodile Dundee* and *Mad Max* two decades ago. Aboriginal art is now established in the mainstream and has become a cultural export. There are several international arts festivals, notably in Adelaide and Perth, both of which attract the cream of world talent. The Australian Broadcasting Commission supports symphony orchestras in six states and there are numerous national and state opera and ballet companies.

FACTORS INFLUENCING EMPLOYMENT

IMMIGRATION

British, American and Canadian citizens require visas in order to enter Australia as tourists, students or workers. Tourists require a Visitor's Visa, which has been pretty much superseded by the 'Electronic Travel Authority' (ETA), available to British and US citizens and EU nationals. ETAs can be obtained from any participating travel agent and are issued free of charge. Some travel agents charge an administration fee, which the Australian Embassy advises is, essentially, a 'rip-off'. Enquiries about the various visas available to suit your requirements should be made to the nearest high commission or embassy, as this is a complicated field.

Current Australian immigration policy stems from the basic principle that employment opportunities must be available as a first priority to Australian citizens and migrants admitted for permanent settlement. During periods of high unemployment the quota of migrants must inevitably be reduced, although there is always a separate quota for humanitarian entry.

Eligibility for permanent settlement falls into five categories: those with close family connections who must be sponsored by their relatives; people whose occupations are in the labour shortage category; those nominated by an Australian employer for a specific job under the Employment Nomination Scheme ENS; and experienced business people with definite proposals and sufficient capital (at least A$500,000) to establish viable enterprises which will aid Australia's economic development.

The labour market is very competitive but currently there are opportunities in accounting, health, and trades. Skilled migrants are required, especially in the wine industry. Few opportunities are available for unskilled or semi-skilled workers. Details of occupations in current demand are available, together with free leaflets on immigration and life in Australia from Australian High Commissions and Embassies.

Under the Government's Temporary Residence policy there is provision for those from overseas who are management, executive, professional, technical and specialist personnel to enter Australia for a specific employment period where it can be shown that the job cannot be filled by an existing resident. It is restricted to working for a sponsoring organisation, although you can change sponsors.

The Financial and Migrant Information Service of the *Commonwealth Bank of Australia*, Senator House, 85 Queen Victoria Street, London EC4V 4HA; ☎ 020-7710 3999; fax 020-

7710 3939; www.commbank.com.au, conducts special 'Information Days' for approved migrants at venues in London, Manchester, Edinburgh and Glasgow. To obtain further details of these promotions as well as information on such aspects as housing, the cost of living, taxation, health insurance, household expenses, transfer of capital and banking/investment facilities, contact the Bank at the above address.

Citizenship will normally only be granted after at least two years' residence in Australia.

The private company *The Emigration Group Ltd.* (7 Heritage Court, Lower Bridge Street, Chester, Cheshire CH1 1RD; ☎0845-230 2526; fax 01244-342288; e-mail info@TEGltd. co.uk; www.jobfastrack.co.nz) provides full assistance with applications for residence and/or work visas. Sister company *Taylor & Associates* (PO Box 1401, Chester CH1 1FF; www.jobfastrack.co.nz) matches job-seekers with employers to provide an effective and total emigration service.

WORKING HOLIDAY-MAKER SCHEME

The Working Holiday-Maker scheme aims to promote international understanding by giving young people the opportunity to experience the culture of another country. It allows working holiday-makers to enjoy an extended holiday by supplementing their travel funds through incidental employment, thus experiencing closer contact with local communities. Australia has reciprocal working holiday arrangements with Canada, Denmark, Germany, Hong Kong Special Administrative Region of the People's Republic of China, Norway, Ireland, Japan, Republic of Korea, Malta, the Netherlands, Sweden and the United Kingdom. Although there are specific arrangements with these countries, the Australian working holiday scheme is applied globally, and applicants from other countries are considered where there might be a benefit both to the applicant and to Australia.

The Working Holiday Visa is available to applicants between the ages of 18 and 30. Applicants may be either single or married, but must not have any dependent children. You must not have previously entered Australia on a working holiday visa and you will also need to meet health and character requirements and be outside Australia at the time of the visa being granted. The visa is valid for 12 months from the day of issue, and allows a stay of 12 months from date of entry into Australia.

When you apply for a Working Holiday visa, you must demonstrate that your main purpose in visiting Australia is to holiday, and that any work you expect to undertake will be solely to assist in supporting you while on vacation. You must have a good chance of finding temporary work, and may not enrol in formal studies of any kind. You must also have a return ticket or sufficient funds for a return airfare, in addition to being able to demonstrate $5,000 in funds for your travels (or a parental guarantee for the same amount). A Working Holiday visa usually allows for multiple entry, which means that you may leave and re-enter the country as many times as you like (within the time restriction of your visa). When a visa is granted, ensure that it has been stamped 'multiple entry'. You cannot get an extension on a Working Holiday Visa under any circumstances (though you can apply to change your visa status if you meet requirements), and must leave the country on or before the expiry date of your visa.

A limit (reviewed annually) may be imposed on the number of Australian Working Holiday visas granted. A number of factors influence the volume of applications for working holiday visas, such as the strength of various economies around the world, and the popularity of certain kinds of tourism. Some prospective working holiday-makers have suffered under the new 'capping' rules, and have had their application for a visa refused after paying for their travel. Travel agents who specialise in Australian travel suggest that one way of avoiding this is to plan to commence the working holiday shortly after the beginning of July, which is the beginning of the annual visa allocation period. Applications made at this time have a good chance of succeeding.

Once in Australia, surveys show that most working holidaymakers find temporary or casual employment in farming, clerical and hospitality industries. Fruit picking, bartending, secretarial and clerical work obtained through temp agencies, and labouring are all popular options for travellers, and this work tends to be widely available on a seasonal basis. Most travellers experience three or four different jobs over the period of their visit, holding each for six to eight weeks at a time. The Working Holiday Maker scheme permits you to work for a maximum of three months for any one employer. If you are found to be working beyond the approved time limit you may have your visa cancelled. At present, Working Holiday visas cost $155 and processing takes about four to five weeks. Form 1150 available from the Department of Immigration and Multicultural and Indigenous Affairs contains additional information on the scheme.

STANDARD OF LIVING

More than 60 per cent of the Australian population live in the five major cities of Brisbane, Sydney, Melbourne, Adelaide and Perth. Most of the rest also live in cities and towns along the coastal fringe. The cost of housing varies considerably from state to state and depends on such factors as proximity to facilities and the city centre. Prices for three-bedroom houses in Sydney's suburbs average around A$316,000. Housing is cheaper in Perth and Adelaide, while Melbourne and Brisbane are as expensive as Sydney. Rented accommodation is most expensive in city centres and a one-bedroom flat in a down-market area of Sydney will cost at least A$200 a week. The Financial and Migrant Service of the Commonwealth Bank of Australia, (address above), issues a comprehensive *Cost of Living and Housing Survey*, free to prospective migrants to Australia.

Australia has the highest level of home-ownership in the world, with over 75 per cent of Australian homes either mortgaged or owner-occupied. Most Australians live in single-storey houses with a garden at both the front and the back of the house. A basic family home is expected to comprise three bedrooms, an open-plan living and dining area, fitted kitchen, at least one bathroom, and a separate laundry (including a large sink, known as a trough, and fitted plumbing for a washing machine). Every home without exception (indeed, by law) has a laundry, and it is unheard of to install a washing machine in a kitchen. Four-bedroom houses are also very common, but there are very few recently built two bedroom houses. Most houses are likely to have a family room (informal living area) in addition to the usual two reception rooms, and will generally have two bathrooms, one of which is usually an en suite. The focus of the bathroom is always the shower, which is *never* located over the bath. Australian showers come on hot and strong from the mains, and electric showers and booster pumps are not required; bathrooms are always tiled, and a carpeted bathroom is a source of extreme amusement to Australians visiting Britain. Kitchens always include a cooker (known as a stove) and fitted cupboards, which in modern houses will include a large pantry cupboard. Carpets, curtains and light fittings are always included in the price unless stated otherwise. A very large number of homes in Australia have a swimming pool.

HEALTH

Persons who are approved to live in Australia for a period more than six months are entitled to enrol for, and receive, basic hospital and medical cover under the National Health Insurance scheme, Medicare. Funded by a 1.25 per cent income surcharge, Medicare covers hospital accommodation and treatment as well as 85 per cent of the scheduled fee charged by general practitioners. Supplementary insurance for services not covered by Medicare such as dental and optical treatment or treatment in hospital as a private patient, is available from private health organisations. The standard of health care in Australia is very high, and is not yet beset by the problems that bedevil the NHS. Nonetheless, private health insurance is popular and affordable and the government actively encourages people to subscribe to schemes, offering incentives and tax rebates.

EDUCATION

Education is a responsibility of the state governments and varies slightly in curriculum, examinations and age requirements from state to state. Education is free in both primary and secondary schools, however, there also many private, fee-paying schools – usually denominational – that are attended by one out of every four children. Schooling is compulsory from ages six to 16 in all states. The school year begins in February and is divided into either three or four terms, depending on the State. University entrance exams (HSC in NSW and Victoria, TEE in Western Australia, etc.) are taken at age 17.

There are 21 universities and more than 200 specialist or technical colleges. The Australian Government operates a number of student assistance schemes, and grants are subject to a means test. Tertiary education is no longer free in Australia but is paid for by the student through contributions known as HECS. These can be deferred and repaid through taxation after graduation.

EMBASSIES AND CONSULATES

British High Commission, Commonwealth Avenue, Yarralumla, Canberra, ACT 2600; ☎2-6270 6666; fax 2-6273 3236; www.britaus.net. There are consulates in Perth, Brisbane, Adelaide, Melbourne, and Sydney.
US Embassy, Moonah Place, Yarralumla, Canberra, ACT 2600; ☎2-6214 5600; http://canberra.usembassy.gov/.
There are consulates in Melbourne, Perth and Sydney.

TOURIST OFFICES

Australian Tourist Commission, Gemini House, 10-18 Putney Hill, London SW15 6AA; ☎020-8780 2229; www.australia.com.
Australian Tourist Commission, 2049 Century Park East, Suite 1920, Los Angeles, CA 90067, USA; ☎310 229 4870; www.australia.com .

CONDITIONS OF WORK

Hours

Hours of work are fixed by awards or legislation and are usually 35 or 38 hours per week, based on a five-day week, except for the retail trade (5½-day week) or those who work on a shift basis.

Holidays

Most employees receive four weeks' paid holiday per annum. In addition, there are eleven national public holidays – New Year's Day; Australia Day (26 Jan); Good Friday; Easter Monday; Anzac Day (25 April); May Day; Queen's Birthday (10 Jun); Labour Day (7 Oct); Christmas Day; Boxing Day.

Safety and Compensation

State and national laws protect workers by laying down strict conditions, applicable to all workplaces, concerning standards of safety, sanitation, heat and lighting. Frequent inspections are carried out by officers of a State's Department of Labour and Industry. All employers are required to insure their workers against industrial accidents; compensation is paid either in weekly amounts or as a lump sum, based on the worker's normal earnings. All workplaces have a health and safety representative.

TRADE UNIONS

The trade union movement in Australia has become much weakened over the past few decades, with fewer Australian employees joining unions than ever before. To offset loss of membership, many unions have amalgamated with others in related trades and professions, forming super-unions with increased negotiating power. The unions that have remained strongest are those representing industries in which there is continued unrest, particularly in teaching, nursing, policing, and wharfside occupations. 'Closed shops' are illegal, but the powerful BLF (Builders Labourers Federation) is occasionally known to operate union-only sites. Most workplaces have a union representative, and if you choose to join, dues can be automatically deducted from your salary. Union dues are a tax-deductible expense. The *Australian Council of Trade Unions* (Level 2, 393 Swanston Street, Melbourne VIC 3000; ☎3-9663 5266; fax 3-9663 4051; www.actu.asn.au) is the national trade union organisation and can provide advice on the union most appropriate to your circumstances and occupation.

Taxation
All people in employment in Australia are now obliged to have a tax file number. You can apply for this through the Australian Taxation Office in your State, or pick up a form in any post office. Income tax is deduced on Pay-As-You-Go (PAYG) basis, and adjusted at the end of the tax year (30 June). Deductions are allowed for dependants and private health insurance schemes. The first $6,000 is tax-free. There is a 17 per cent rate on the tax band between $6,001 to $20,000; followed by 30 per cent on the next band up to $50,000; and 42 per cent on the band up to $60,000. All additional income is taxed at 47 per cent. Every employed person must file a self-assessment tax return, issued to every home by post in the annual Tax Pack. Further details can be obtained from the Australian High Commission or from the Australian Taxation Office (ATO). The ATO has a very comprehensive website at www.ato.gov.au.

EMPLOYMENT PROSPECTS

Australia has traditionally derived its wealth from its vast agricultural and mineral resources, which has made the country vulnerable to fluctuations in commodity prices. All aspects of Australian industry and services are highly developed. The demand is now for highly skilled workers such as teachers, medical staff, computers specialists, and engineers. Requirements change constantly, so it is worth checking with Australian information offices.

Prospective migrants are advised to contact the Australian High Commission. The Immigration Department can supply a free fact sheet which contains details of minimum and basic wages, recent wage increases by geographical area and the latest information on job vacancies.

In many professions, eligibility for work in Australia depends on acceptance of British or US qualifications. Agreement has been reached on the mutual acceptance of many qualifications, but in some fields the membership of an Australian professional association, or the passing of additional examinations is a necessity.

Individual assessments of qualifications and employment prospects are referred back to the Commonwealth Department of Employment, Education and Training, whose National Office of Overseas Skills Recognition (NOOSR) decides what recommendation to make concerning would-be migrants or temporary residents. NOOSR stresses that would-be migrants should have their qualifications assessed (as far as possible) before travelling to Australia. Otherwise they may find that they cannot obtain work.

In principle, it is not possible to move to Australia without a pre-arranged job; and new migrants are not allowed to draw state benefits until they have been in Australia for six months.

The Agents General for individual Australian states can offer information on all aspects of life in their respective areas, but in general recruitment is confined to specific requests from employers. Their methods of recruitment usually centre on advertising campaigns in the national press.

NEWSPAPERS

Regional newspapers can be consulted in the Reading Room of Australia House in London (which also holds the Australian Yellow Pages). A useful source of information in the UK is the monthly newspaper, *Australian News*, available by subscription from *Outbound Publishing*, 1 Commercial Road, Eastbourne, East Sussex BN21 3XQ; ☎01323-726040; e-mail info@outbound-newspapers.com; www.outboundpublishing.com, which also supplies a number of other guides. *TNT Magazine* (14-15 Childs Place, London SW5 9RX; ☎020-7373 3377; fax 020-7341 6600; e-mail enquiries@tntmag.co.uk) publishes a useful *Australia and New Zealand Independent Traveller's Guide*, available in tourist offices and travel agents. TNT also publishes an Australian edition, *TNT Magazine Australia* (www. tntmagazine.com/au/).

Australia's two most important media conglomerates, Fairfax Holdings and Newscorp, both have electronically-published versions of their various newspapers available on the internet. This is probably the best way to keep up with classified jobs listings. The Fairfax site at www.mycareer.com.au carries around 10,000 advertisements per day. *The Australian* (Newscorp) jobs pages are online at www.careerone.com.au.

SPECIFIC CONTACTS

Listings of professional bodies and relevant State authorities can be supplied by the high commissions and embassies (see addresses above).

INFORMATION TECHNOLOGY

Information technology is a major growth sector in the Australian economy and is projected to continue to expand through to 2007. Job prospects are strong for well-qualified and experienced professionals, and there is a particular need for people with PowerBuilder, Unix, SAP, e-commerce. The government is keen to encourage the IT sector, particularly in areas where application of new technology will enhance Australia's competitiveness in the export market.

Michael Page International, Level 7, 1 Margaret Street, Sydney, NSW 2000; ☎2-8292 2000; fax 2-8292 2001; e-mail sydneyit@michaelpage.com.au; www.michaelpage.com. au. Temporary and contract work in finance & accounting, legal, sales & marketing, technology, human resources and engineering.

MEDICAL

Overseas-qualified doctors already granted permission to work in Australia are required to pass stringent registration examinations before they are permitted to practice.

Both State Registered and State Enrolled Nurses are in demand throughout Australia, particularly those qualified in specialist fields such as Accident and Emergency, Intensive Care and Psychiatry. You will need to have your qualifications ratified by the *Nurses Registration Board* in the state in which you live and then register with the Board before you are able to apply for work.

Information on nursing in Australia is provided by the *Australian Nursing and Midwifery Council Incorporated* (ANCI, First Floor, 20 Challis Street, Dickson, ACT 2602; Postal Address: PO Box 873, Dickson, ACT 2602; ☎02-6257 7960; fax 02-6257 7955; www. anmc.org.au). ANCI also has a list of all Nurses' Registration Boards in Australia.

PETROCHEMICALS

There has been massive investment in oil and gas exploration, particularly in the North West Shelf Natural Gas Project off the coast of Western Australia. Engineers of all types are in demand in this industry, and petrochemical engineering is identified by DEET as an area of particular employment shortage. Deep-sea divers are also required. Growth in the professional and para-professional occupations of the petrochemical industry currently stands at around 5.4 per cent.

Global Technical Recruitment, Level 8, 33 Berry Street, North Sydney, NSW 2060; ☎2-9957 1008; fax 2-9957 1329; e-mail resume@globaltr.com.au; www.globaltr.com.au, provide specialist engineering staff Australia-wide.

USEFUL CONTACTS

Adecco, Level 3, 9 Hunter Street, Sydney, NSW 2000; ☎2-9244 3400; fax 2-9223 4626; e-mail sydney@adecco.com.au, is the world's leading employment services company, with more than 5,000 offices in 58 countries. They have a dedicated Australia website at www.adecco.com.au, and can be contacted at their main Sydney office. For office locations in other areas call 132 993.

Bayside Group, Level 17, Town Hall House, 456 Kent Street, Sydney, NSW 2000; ☎02-9261 5100; fax 02-9261 5300; www.baysidegrp.com.au. Supply executive recruitment, temporary and contract placements of legal, IT and accountancy staff.

Crowe Associates, Level 17, Town Hall House, 456 Kent Street, Sydney, NSW 2000; ☎2-9261 5100; fax 2-9261 5300; www.crowe.com.au, Supply executive recruitment, temporary and contract placements of legal, IT and accountancy staff.

Goldstein and Martens Recruitment Consultants, Level 4, 285 George Street, Sydney, NSW 2000; ☎02-9262 3088; fax 02-9262 3409; e-mail enquiries@goldsteinmartens. com.au; www.goldsteinmartens.com.au. Pays $2-$3 above the average hourly wage.

Involvement Volunteers Association, PO Box 218, Port Melbourne, VIC 3207; ☎03-9646 9392; e-mail ivworldwide@volunteering.org.au; www.volunteering.org.au.

Metro Personnel, Level 6, Thakral House, 301 George Street, Sydney, NSW 2000; ☎02-9299 5477; fax 02-9299 5941; www.metropersonnel.com.au.

Select Appointments, Level 3, Select House, 109 Pitt Street, Sydney NSW 2000; ☎2-8258 9999; fax 2-8258 9988, specialise in placing professional, motivated travellers. They have positions for receptionists, data entry operators, secretaries, accounts clerks, medical and legal secretaries, WPOs, and warehousing staff. Select have offices in Adelaide, ☎8-8468 8000; Perth, ☎8-9321 3133; Brisbane, ☎7-3243 3900; Melbourne, ☎3-8663 4700; www.select-appointments.com.au

AAA Nannies, PO Box 157, Sanctuary Cove, Brisbane, Qld 4212; ☎7-5530 1123; www. nanny.net.au. Australia's leading au pair agency with offices Australia-wide.

Online employment sources:

Australian Job Network: www.jobsearch.gov.au.

Australian Government Information (www.nla.gov.au/oz/gov/). Entry point to all Australian government websites.

Australian Taxation Office (www.ato.gov.au). Information on Australian tax laws.

CareerOne Services Pty Ltd: www.careerone.com.au. This Interactive site carries more than 30,000 jobs listed daily.

Department of Employment and Workplace Relations (www.dewrsb.gov.au). Workplace relations in Australia, maritime transport, policy and legislation, government employment, and related sites.

Jobnet: www.jobnet.com.au. The largest IT jobsearch website in Australia. Thousands of permanent, contract and consulting positions available for IT Professionals

Office of Small Business, Department of Industry, Tourism and Resources (www.industry. gov.au). The small business sector has accounted for 70% of jobs growth over the past decade.

Melbourne City Council (www.melbourne.vic.gov.au). Includes information on products and services of Melbourne City Council as well as details of forthcoming events, maps and guides.

Monster.com: www.monster.com.au. Local portal for the leading online careers network.

MyCareer: www.mycareer.com.au. This Fairfax site lists daily advertisements carried in a range of national papers. It carries around 10,000 advertisements per day, and is searchable by job type and location.

NSW Department of State and Regional Development, (www.srd.nsw.gov.au). Information for potential investors and business migrants to Sydney and New South Wales.

New South Wales Government (www.nsw.gov.au). Includes information on doing business with the NSW government, rural information, reports and papers, related links.

Queensland Government Online (www qld.gov.au). Includes information on business in Queensland, and government departments and agencies.

Tasmania Online (www.tas.gov.au). Includes information on investing in Tasmania and migrating to Tasmania.

Government of Victoria (www.vic.gov.au). Includes information on state projects, arts, business, and education.

Australia White Pages (www.whitepages.com.au). Online access to eight million residential, business and government listings.

The Australian Yellow Pages Telephone Directory (www.yellowpages.com.au). National searchable database.

Willing Workers On Organic Farms Australia: www.wwoof.com.au. Willing Workers On Organic Farms (WWOOF) is a form of cultural exchange in which WWOOFers live and work as family with host farms, and learn about the skills of organic growing as well as the area they are visiting.

OTHER OPPORTUNITIES

Opportunities in Australia are also referred to in the *Specific Careers* chapters. *Live and Work in Australia and New Zealand* (Vacation Work Publications, www.vacationwork. co.uk) contains comprehensive details on employment contacts and information about living and working in Australia.

SHORT TERM WORK

There are several schemes that enable people to pre-arrange short term work in Australia, but many of the most interesting – and lucrative – jobs are available only for those who are prepared to make the journey to Australia and make an on the spot job search. Those aged between 18 and 30, and who are not deterred by the cost of a flight to Australia, can obtain the working holiday visa described above.

OFFICIAL SCHEMES

British Universities North America (BUNAC) (16 Bowling Green Lane, London EC1R 0BD; ☎020-7251 3472; fax 020-7251 0215; e-mail enquiries@bunac.org.uk; www. bunac.org.uk). The Work Australia programme is open to citizens of the UK, Ireland, the Netherlands and Canada between the ages of 18 and 30, and is especially suitable for gap- and final-year students. Participants can take any job, anywhere in Australia. The benefits of going with BUNAC include help with booking flights and obtaining insurance, pick-up from the airport on arrival, guaranteed accommodation for the first two nights and comprehensive orientation to help with jobs, tax, health. Participants on the BUNAC North American programme can continue westwards from Los Angeles with a Hawaiian stopover en route to Australia. Proof of £2,000 in personal funds is a requirement of the programme, but the cost of the airfare can be taken out of this and stopovers can be made on the return route.

VOLUNTARY WORK

Countless charitable organisations throughout Australia rely on volunteers to help run their many aid, development and conservation programmes. Becoming involved in such enterprises offers the working holiday-maker an opportunity to experience a different side of Australian life while gaining new skills and contributing to a worthwhile cause. If you are interested in volunteering in any capacity, contact the Charities' Commission in your state (listed under Government Organisations in the White Pages) who will be able to supply you with a list of all the charities registered with them. Visitors to Australia who are interested in the country's unique landscape are often particularly attracted to conservation work, and *Conservation Volunteers Australia* (National Head Office, PO Box 423, Ballarat, VIC 3353; ☎03-5330 2600; fax 03-5330 2292; e-mail info@conservationvolunteers.com.au; www.conservationvolunteers.com.au), can help with placements in this field. Volunteers contribute $30 per day to cover accommodation, meals, and projected travel expenses.

OTHER WORK

The Australian Government's *Job Network* can help those looking for work, when work is available. A national network of around 200 private, community and government organisations, its branches notify each other by computer of any vacancies and in some major cities there are branches that specialise in temporary work. These offices are most helpful to those looking for seasonal work on farms, and issue a booklet that gives the locations and dates of various harvests around the country. Two of the most important of these are the tobacco harvest, which begins in the Atherton Tablelands of Northern Queensland in late September and around Myrtleford in central Victoria in late January; and the grape harvest, which takes place in February and March. Two particular regions to head for are Griffith in New South Wales and the Barossa Valley in South Australia. There are also possibilities for working as ranch hands (roustabouts) in the outback, especially on sheep farms when shearing takes place in October and November, and February and March. *Live and Work in Australia and New Zealand* (see above) contains a harvest guide, including locations and times.

Temporary work is available in offices, shops, restaurants, bars, petrol stations. The Australian Job Network may be able to help people find such work, as may any of the many private agencies such as *Bligh*, Level 7, Dymocks Building, 428 George Street, Sydney NSW 2000; ☎2-9235 3699; fax 2-9221 3480; e-mail staff@blighappointments. com; www.blighappointments.com. The Department of Employment and Workplace Relations provides a very comprehensive website detailing available jobs, and with links to other employers at www.workplace.gov.au.

INTERNATIONAL COMPANIES IN AUSTRALIA

Many international companies have subsidiaries, and in many cases their regional headquarters for the Asia-Pacific area, in Australia. The *Australian British Chamber of Commerce*, Suite 2, Level 15, 3 Spring Street, Sydney, NSW 2000; ☎2-9247 6271; fax 2-9247 6671; e-mail abcc@britishchamber.com; www.britishchamber.com, can provide information on British companies operating in Australia.

New Zealand

o   **New Zealand High Commission,** New Zealand House, 80 Haymarket, London SW1Y 4TQ; ☎020-7930 8422; fax 020-7839 4580; www.nzembassy.com
o   **New Zealand Embassy,** 37 Observatory Circle, NW, Washington DC 20008; ☎202-328 4800; fax 202-667 5227; e-mail nz@nzemb.org; www.nzembassy.com
o   **Currency:** NZ$1 = 100 cents
o   **Rate of Exchange:** £1 = NZ$3.02; US1$ = NZ$1.62; €1 = NZ$2.07
o   **Country Code:** +64

New Zealand has some of the world's most beautiful scenery and, although the standard of living has fallen steadily since the late 1970s, still offers a quality of life that can hardly be matched by any other country. New Zealand's current immigration policy is meant to attract migrants with the skills and experience required for the country's economic development. These laws have been altered to bring them into line with the points system already operating in Australia and Canada (see below).

GENERAL FACTS

POPULATION

New Zealand comprises two large islands and some smaller islands covering 103,736 square miles (268,675 sq km). The total area is slightly larger than that of the UK, with average population density is 35 per square mile. The total population of 4.1 million includes those of European and Maori descent, and immigrants from East Asia and the Pacific islands.

CLIMATE

While generally similar to the climate in Britain, there is a greater range of weather from north to south and New Zealand's average temperatures throughout the year are 38 to 40 deg F (three to four deg C) higher. The North Island is considerably warmer. Rainfall is heavier than in the UK, but unevenly distributed, with the Southern Alps receiving 480 inches (1,219 cm) and Central Otago a mere 16 inches (41 cm). Unusual features of the landscape include geysers, volcanoes, glaciers and fjords, and there are occasional earthquakes.

GOVERNMENT

New Zealand is a parliamentary democracy; a Governor-General represents the Queen, but, politically, is not particularly significant. The House of Representatives has 97 members. The Parliament, headed by the Prime Minister, is elected by all citizens and permanent residents aged 18 and over. New Zealand is politically more conservative than Australia, and values its ties and links with Britain. Republicanism has not yet become a major issue.

CITIES

Eighty-four per cent of the population live in urban areas, and more than 1.6 million inhabit the four main cities. Auckland (910,600) is New Zealand's largest city – one-third of manufacturing employees in the developing secondary industries work there. Wellington (327,000), the capital, is famous for its fine harbour, and houses many national organisations. Christchurch (310,000), the largest city on South Island, is a beautiful, open city set in lush farmland and known for its parks, botanical gardens and sports grounds. Dunedin (110,000) was founded by Scotsmen and as well as being an important educational centre is also the port for the agricultural area of Otago.

RURAL LIFE

Pasture and arable land accounts for 53 per cent of New Zealand's land area; forests cover a further 27 per cent. Both are essential to the country's economy. Although farms are large, not much manpower is required due to the high level of mechanisation – a typical farm could be run by a farmer, his wife and an agricultural labourer only, with occasional extra help. Famously, there are more sheep than people in New Zealand.

RELIGION, SPORT AND CULTURE

There is complete religious freedom. The majority of the population (15 per cent) belong to the Anglican Church; the remainder include Presbyterians (11 per cent), Catholics (12 per cent) and Methodists (three per cent). New Zealand is a modern country with its own distinctive culture, which includes an appreciation of the outdoor life. New Zealand is ideal for all kinds of sport, with facilities for rugby (the national game), cricket, soccer, tennis, skiing, sailing.

FACTORS INFLUENCING EMPLOYMENT

IMMIGRATION

British citizens may enter New Zealand without a visa and can remain in the country for up to six months, if they are in possession of sufficient funds and a return ticket. New Zealand has working holiday schemes with the following countries: Canada,Chile, Denmark, France, Germany, Ireland, Italy, Japan, Korea, Malaysia, Netherlands, Singapore, Sweden, United Kingdom, Argentina, Uruguay, Taiwan, United States, Malta, Finland, Belgium, Czech Republic, Norway, Thailand. The schemes allow citizens of these countries who are aged 18-30 to take up temporary work while they holiday in New Zealand. All schemes, apart from the United Kingdom, allow travel for up to 12 months. The United Kingdom scheme allows travel up to 23 months; for more information on all working holidays please go to www.immigration.govt.nz/whs. US citizens may visit for up to 90 days without a visa. All visitors may extend their stays to 12 months by applying to Immigration New Zealand.

Immigration New Zealand (INZ) is the Government Department responsible for issuing temporary and permanent residence visas to New Zealand. They have a range of options to accommodate different types of workers and work closely with employers to grant visas to those who have the skills and work experience that New Zealand needs. INZ has a lot of information on jobs in New Zealand given to them by employers, recruiting companies and regional and economic development councils. They are available for consultation at one of the many events, details of which can be found on the 'Upcoming Events' page of the following website: www.immigration.govt.nz.

It is possible for visitors to New Zealand to obtain a temporary work permit from the Department of Labour if they find a job while in New Zealand, provided that they can show that they are not depriving a New Zealand resident or citizen of employment

People seeking to live permanently in New Zealand may apply for Residence under the Skilled Migrant stream. This is a structured, points based system. Points are awarded for qualifications, work experience and age. Points are also additionally awarded to those who have an offer of Skilled Employment of 12 months of more. Applicants who have an offer of employment are also prioritised.

For more details about the Skilled Migrant process and the details of recent selection marks go to the Immigration website (www.immigration.govt.nz). Here you can look at

Immigration policies and download application forms and guides. If it is your intention to apply for residence under the Skilled Migrant points based system you may also lodge your Expression of Interest online.

E-mails to the following address: jobsinfo@dol.govt.nz will provoke an automated response from the Department of Labour detailing websites and e-mail addresses of New Zealand employers and agents who are prepared to assist prospective migrants with finding employment in New Zealand.

**New Zealand
Working Holiday Scheme**

New Zealand has reciprocal agreements with more than twenty countries allowing people aged 18 to 30 years to work temporarily while on holiday in New Zealand.

If you meet the conditions of the United Kingdom Working Holiday Scheme, you can stay in New Zealand for up to 23 months, working for as long as 12 months in total. You can be flexible and have several jobs with different employers, or work 12 months in one position.

When you apply online your visa can be approved within days. You can also find links to employers on our website, helping you to organise a job before you get to New Zealand.

To check the conditions and apply online go to
www.immigration.govt.nz/whs

Immigration New Zealand
TE RATONGA MANENE

Another useful resource is the London branch website (www.immigration.govt.nz/London) which contains information about processing times and provides advice on how best to present your residence application. Here you will also find up-to-date information relating to upcoming immigration shows where INZ will have representation.

Applications for Residence, through the Skilled Migrant or Family streams should be addressed to *Immigration New Zealand* Mezzanine Floor, New Zealand House, 80 Haymarket, London SW1Y 4TE; fax 020-7973 0370. The contact centre for *Immigration New Zealand* is ☎09069 100 100. Calls cost £1 per minute.

HOUSING AND ACCOMMODATION

New Zealanders typically prefer to live in detached bungalows with large gardens. An average three-bedroom house in one of the larger cities will cost around NZ$180,000. Prices are highest in Auckland and Wellington. New Zealand has a very high rate of home-ownership. There is no shortage of accommodation, with rents starting at as little as $90 a week. Most rented accommodation is privately-owned and local authorities do not play a major role in supplying housing.

HEALTH AND WELFARE

New Zealand's social security system is financed by taxation, and no special contributions are required. With one in three of New Zealanders on welfare benefits of some kind, and a huge budget deficit, the Government decided in 1992 to reduce benefits. Hospital funding is currently in a state of upheaval, and visits to doctors and prescriptions have also become more expensive. You can expect to pay up to $40 to see a doctor and at least $80 for dental treatment. Private health insurance is popular and affordable, and about 60 per cent of New Zealanders have some kind of private cover.

EDUCATION

Education is compulsory between the ages of six and 16, and free from age three (kindergarten) to age 19 (except for those in private schools). Most children start co-educational primary school at age five, and at 12 or 13 years old go on to secondary school where a two-year general course is followed by one year's specialisation leading to the School Certificate examination.

University entrance is by examination or by a certificate of fitness issued by a recognised school. Most students remain at school for one extra year after qualifying to obtain the University Bursary, which entitles the holder to a university grant covering tuition fees and an annual allowance. There are universities in Auckland, Christchurch, Dunedin, Hamilton, Palmerston North and Wellington. There are also 13 technical institutes and six teacher-training colleges.

NATIONAL SERVICE

New Zealand has abolished compulsory military service, and maintains a purely voluntary defence system.

EMBASSIES AND CONSULATES

British High Commission, 44 Hill Street, Wellington 1; ☎4-924 2888; fax 4-924 2822; www.britain.org.nz.
British Consulate-General, Level 17, IAG House, 151 Queen Street, Auckland 1, ☎9-303 2973; fax 9-303 1836; www.uktradeinvest.co.nz.
US Embassy, 29 Fitzherbert Terrace, Thorndon, Wellington; ☎4-462 6000; fax 4-499 0490; http://wellington.usembassy.gov/.

CONDITIONS OF WORK

WAGES

Although there is a minimum wage fixed by national legislation, each profession or industry also has sets of minimum wages, which are usually higher than the national minimum of NZ$9.50. The average hourly wage in New Zealand is $19.81 for males and $16.75 for females. Salaries in New Zealand are lower than those for equivalent positions in the USA, the UK and Europe. However, living costs are considerably lower too.

HOURS

Wages are based universally on the 40-hour, five-day week. In some industries, overtime is paid at up to time and a half for the first three hours, and double time for every hour worked thereafter, depending on workplace agreements, however overtime rates are increasingly being reduced or disappearing completely. Flexitime (known as glidetime) is becoming more common, and there is generally more flexibility in working hours than previously.

HOLIDAYS

Employees are legally entitled to at least three weeks' paid holiday per annum. In addition, there are the following public holidays; New Year's Day; 2 January; Waitangi Day (6 February); Good Friday; Easter Monday; Anzac Day (25 April); Queen's Birthday (first Monday in June); Labour Day (fourth Monday in October); Christmas Day; and Boxing Day. Each province also celebrates its own Anniversary Day.

SAFETY AND COMPENSATION

Industrial awards lay down certain standards, but conditions are usually far above the minimum. Employers are obliged to insure their workers against industrial accidents resulting in temporary incapacity disablement or death.

TRADE UNIONS

Union membership is not obligatory under national legislation. Under the Labour Relations Act of 1987, only unions with at least 1,000 members can be legally registered, leading to the amalgamation of many smaller unions. All unions are represented by one collective organisation, the New Zealand Council of Trade Unions. Only about 20 per cent of the workforce now belongs to a trade union.

TAXATION

A direct tax on personal income is deducted on a PAYE basis and includes social security contributions. Allowances are made for dependants, life insurance premiums, school fees, charitable donations. The highest band personal tax rate is currently 33 per cent. There is a Goods and Services Tax (equivalent to VAT) of 12.5 per cent on most items.

EMPLOYMENT PROSPECTS

The major problem facing the New Zealand economy is the difficulty of establishing large-scale industries in a country with only 3.6 million inhabitants. Manufacturing industries have not grown at the rate that was expected in the 1980s, and the government hopes that following drastic free market reforms and the end of chronic inflation, New Zealand's international competitiveness can be quickly restored.

New Zealand is very anxious to encourage qualified immigrants and business people, in part to reverse a New Zealand brain and investment drain. Today, 65 per cent of jobs are in service industries, compared with 10 per cent in agriculture.

NEWSPAPERS

The Saturday editions of the major New Zealand dailies are available for inspection at the Migration Branch on the first floor of New Zealand House. *TNT Magazine* publishes a useful travel guide (see *Australia, Newspapers*). A number of New Zealand papers are available online. These include: *The New Zealand Herald* (www. nzherald.co.nz); *The Otago Daily Times* (www.odt.co.nz); *The Dominion Post* (www. dompost.co.nz); *The Waikato Times* (www.waikatotimes.co.nz; and *The Press* (www. press.co.nz).

SPECIFIC CONTACTS

The Department of Labour in New Zealand provides job-search assistance through WorkSite, a national network of offices advertising local vacancies. They carry a wide range of vacancies for casual, skilled and unskilled work, and offer advice and information on training for job seekers. It also provides a service specifically for linking the skills of

new migrants with the needs of New Zealand employers (e-mail newkiwis@chamber.
co.nz; www.newkiwis.co.nz), which allows you to enter your details and CV on a database
to be searched by potential employers. There is no fee to use WorkSite or NewKiwis,
but you have to be a New Zealand resident or citizen. Contact WorkSite (e-mail info@
worksite.govt.nz) for an office near you. The New Zealand Department of Labour website
may also prove useful (www.dol.govt.nz).

It is also worth contacting the following recruitment and job search agencies for
intending emigrants:

Adecco: Level 9, Qantas House, 191 Queen Street, Auckland; ☎(09) 309 7572; fax (09)
309 4197; e-mail auckland@adecco.co.nz; www.adecco.co.nz.

Geneva Health International: 40-42 Parker Street, London WC2B 5PQ; ☎020-7600
0859; fax 020-7600 0944; e-mail janec@genevahealth.co.uk; www.genevahealth.com.
NZ: PO Box 106 339, Auckland; ☎(09) 916 0200; fax (09) 916 0201; e-mail info@
genevahealth.com.

Global Career Link: International recruitment specialists in finance, accounting, banking,
IT, law, HR and sales and marketing. ☎Toll free in NZ: 0800 499 325 or Wellington:
+64 4 499 3250, Auckland: +64 9 370 1180; e-mail info@globalcareerlink.co.nz; www.
itfutures.co.nz.

JobCafé International: www.jobcafe.co.nz/.

NewJobz: www.newjobz.co.nz.. Attend the *Emigrate* and *Opportunities NZ* Expos in
London.

Parker Bridge Recruitment Ltd: UK Offices in London, Edinburgh and Reading; www.
parkerbridge.co.uk. London: ☎020-7464 1550; fax 020-7464 1999; e-mail info@
parkerbridge.co.uk. Edinburgh: ☎0131 718 6002; fax 011 718 6125; e-mail Edinburgh@
parkerbridge.co.uk. Reading: ☎ 0870 351 7170; fax 0870 351 7171; e-mail reading@
parkerbridge.co.uk. NZ offices in Auckland (☎(09) 377 3727; fax (09) 303 1496) and
Wellington (☎(04) 472 4380; fax (04) 472 4379); www.parkerbridge.co.nz or see the
Parker Bridge listings on www.seek.co.nz. Financial sector.

Prime Recruitment Contracts: 37 Locks Heath Centre, Locks Heath, Southampton, SO31
6DX; ☎01489-559 090; fax 01489-559995; e-mail contracts@prime-recruitment.
co.uk; www.prime-recruitment.co.uk.

Psych Recruitment: e-mail enquiry@psych-recruitment.com; www.psych-recruitment.
com. Psychologists recruitment agency.

Taylor & Associates: PO Box 1401, Chester CH1 1FF; e-mail nzjobs@jobfastrack.co.nz;
www.jobfastrack.co.nz. Initial enquiries are best addressed to the UK representative
office; ☎0845 230 2526; e-mail info@TEGltd.co.uk.

TMP Worldwide Inc: Visit the website to complete an online 'Contact' form; www.tmp.
com. Advertising and communications, and directional marketing. The website has
pages specifically for those from the USA, Australia, Belgium, France, Germany, Hong
Kong, Ireland, Italy, Malaysia, the Netherlands, New Zealand, Singapore, Spain and the
United Kingdom.

Other Useful Websites. For job listings try: www.job.co.nz, http://joblist.co.uk, www.
nzjobs.co.nz, www.kiwicareers.govt.nz; www.monster.com, www.netcheck.co.nz, www.
seek.co.nz and www.workingin-newzealand.com. Bear in mind though that these do not
necessarily represent the entire job market, particularly towards the senior executive
end. For the latest information about the employment scene, see: www.nzherald.co.nz/
employment/.

ACCOUNTING, FINANCE AND BANKING

An accountant wishing to practise in New Zealand must be a member of the New Zealand Society of Accountants. Under a reciprocal agreement, membership of the society is automatically granted to members of any of the main British Associations of Chartered Accountants; The Canadian Institute of Chartered Accountants (and Provincial Institutes) and the Institute of Chartered Accountants in Ireland.

There are good prospects for qualified accountants in New Zealand, both in public accountancy and in other fields. There are also excellent opportunities for young people (up to age 25) who are almost qualified and intend to complete their academic training in New Zealand.

Further information on prospects and eligibility for registration is available from the Executive Director, *Institute of Chartered Accountants of New Zealand*, Level 2, Cigna House, 40 Mercer Street, Box 11342, Wellington 6034; ☎4-474 7840; fax 4-473 6303; e-mail registry@icanz.co.nz; www.icanz.co.nz. Advertisements can also be placed in the *Chartered Accountants Journal of New Zealand* (available from the above address).

The following recruitment organisations deal specifically in this area:

Chandler Macleod Group (Recruitment Solutions): Ground Floor, Huddart Parker Building, 1 Post Office Square, Wellington; ☎(04) 473 7693; fax (04) 498 8969; Level 5, HSBC Building, 290 Queen St, Auckland; ☎(09) 379 8771; fax (09) 379 8772; www.recruitmentsolutions.co.nz.

Clayton Ford Recruitment: PO Box 10 083, Wellington; ☎(04) 473 6223; fax (04) 471 2100; e-mail wnweb@claytonford.co.nz; PO Box 7697, Auckland; ☎(09) 379 9924; fax (09) 379 7785; e-mail support.akl@claytonford.co.nz; www.claytonford.co.nz.

DG&A Recruitment Consultants: PO Box 4006, Auckland; ☎(09) 358 0888; fax (09) 303 0254; e-mail debbie.graham@dgal.co.nz; www.debbiegraham.co.nz.

DOCTORS AND MEDICAL STAFF

Doctors registered in the UK or Eire by virtue of a university degree obtained in either of these two countries are eligible for registration in New Zealand. Queries on eligibility should be addressed to the Secretary, *Medical Council of New Zealand*, Level 13, Mid City Tower, 139-143 Willis Street, PO Box 11-649, Wellington; ☎4-384 7635; fax 4-385 8902; e-mail info@mcnz.org.nz; www.mcnz.org.nz. To ascertain eligibility for registration as specialists, doctors should contact the *Medical Council of New Zealand*. Actual recruitment is carried out by local health boards, previously known as 'Crown Health Enterprises'. Agencies also recruiting medical staff include:

Auckland Medical Bureau: PO Box 37 753, Parnell, Auckland; ☎(09) 377 5903; fax (09) 377 5902; e-mail doctors-amb.nz@xtra.co.nz; www.doctorjobs.co.nz.

Eden Health Recruitment: Free phone from within NZ: 0800 445 999, or from the UK: 0800 0322 107. PO Box 3843, Wellington; ☎(04) 471 4876; fax (04) 471 2100. PO Box 7697, Auckland; ☎(09) 300 4315; fax (09) 918 2031. E-mail general@edenhealth. co.nz; www.edenhealth.co.nz.

eNZed Paramedical: 65 MacDonald Road, Glenview, Hamilton 2001; ☎(07) 843 0080; fax (07) 843 0081; e-mail enzedpa@wave.co.nz; www.enzedparamedical.co.nz.

Health.career.co.nz: http://health.career.co.nz. Adcorp New Zealand, Level 1, 21 Allen Street, Wellington; ☎0800 523 267; e-mail health.career@adcorp.co.nz.

Health Recruitment International: PO Box 205, Wellington; ☎(04) 499 1885 or 0800 188 688; fax (04) 499 1600; e-mail health@recruitment.com; www.healthrecruitment.com.

Medical Staffing International: 35 Kesteven Avenue, Glendowie, PO Box 25-172, St Heliers, Auckland; ☎(09) 575 4258; fax (09) 575 4259; e-mail info@medicalstaffing. co.nz; www.medicalstaffing.co.nz.

Medlink International Recruitment Centre Ltd: Recruit specialist physicians. PO Box 337, Wanganui; ☎(06) 348 7664; fax (06) 348 7665; e-mail info@medlink.co.nz; www. medlink.co.nz.

ENGINEERS

Intending migrants can advertise in *e.nz magazine*, the bi-monthly journal of the *Institution of Professional Engineers New Zealand* (158 The Terrace, PO Box 12241, Wellington; ☎ 4-473 9444; fax 4-474 8933; e-mail ipenz@ipenz.org.nz; www.ipenz.org.nz).

The following organisations recruit for the engineering sector:

Career Engineer: PO Box 331 330, Takapuna, Auckland; ☎ (09) 489 0820 or 021 666 821; e-mail enquiry@careerengineer.co.nz; www.careerengineer.co.nz.

Engineering and Technical Personnel: www.engineerjobs.co.nz.

Match 2 Recruit: PO Box 30-442, Lower Hutt; ☎ (04) 570 0179; fax (04) 570 0122; e-mail cv@match2.co.nz;.www.match2.co.nz

Rob Law Consulting Group: PO Box 10080, Wellington; ☎ (04) 499 8800; fax (04) 499 0955. PO Box 8934 Eden Terrace, Auckland; ☎ (09) 309 9555; fax (09) 309 0008, e-mail alans@roblaw.co.nz; www.roblaw.co.nz.

TAD Technical Careers and Contracts: Level 9, Qantas House, 191 Queen Street, PO Box 105-199, Wellesley Street, Auckland; ☎ (09) 309 9316; fax (09) 309 0212; e-mail auckland@tad.co.nz; www.tad.co.nz.

Technical Recruitment Solutions Ltd: www.trs.co.nz. Offices in Auckland, Wellington and Christchurch.

TEACHING

There are excellent work opportunities within the New Zealand education system. At the time of print, there is a particular demand for early childhood teachers and secondary school teachers of English, mathematics, physics, chemistry, ICT, technology, computing and physical education. Teachers of children with special needs are also needed in early childhood services, and primary and secondary schools. Qualified, experienced teachers of children with learning or behavioural issues, those working with children with physical disabilities and teachers of English to speakers of other languages are sought after at present. The majority of overseas-trained teachers appointed to New Zealand schools come from The UK, Ireland, Australia, Canada and South Africa. Across the board, there is such demand that registered teachers originally from New Zealand who have gone overseas to work are being offered a $5000 incentive to return home to work. Contact TeachNZ for more information (TeachNZ, Ministry of Education, PO Box 1666, Wellington; www.teachnz.govt.nz).

Immigrants intending to teach must have their qualifications verified and checked for comparability with New Zealand qualifications by the New Zealand Qualifications Authority. Teacher registration is compulsory for all teachers in the state sector in New Zealand. The TeachNZ website has details and you can electronically request the relevant forms. The *Education Gazette* is published fortnightly and advertises all permanent teaching positions in state and independent schools. You can read the *Gazette* online, where it is constantly updated (www.edgazette.govt.nz), or by subscribing directly to PO Box 249, Wellington (☎ (04) 917 3990; fax (04) 917 3991). Teaching positions in universities and polytechnics are usually advertised on the institutions' own websites.

SHORT TERM WORK

Opportunities for temporary work in New Zealand are very similar to those in Australia. For British citizens, there is a 'Working Holiday Scheme' enabling British citizens to travel to New Zealand for up to 12 months.

US students can spend up to six months working in New Zealand between 1 April and 31 October through the *Work in New Zealand* programme run by Council Exchanges in New York (see *Working Exchanges* in the *Getting the Job* chapter).

SEASONAL WORK

People already in the country may be able to get jobs during the season in hotels in New Zealand's expanding skiing resorts. Areas to head for include Mount Hutt and Coronet Peak in the Southern Alps on the South Island and Mount Ruapehu on the North Island. Jobs over the New Zealand summer may be found in Nelson and Christchurch on the South Island or Tauranga or the Bay of Islands on the North Island.

Casual fruit picking jobs may be found, from picking peaches and apricots around Kerikeri in December, to picking kiwi fruit in May around the Bay of Plenty. It is also possible to stay on farms while doing some work in exchange for board and lodging. Farmers often look for casual workers at local youth hostels. The dates and locations of different harvests are covered in detail in the book *Work Your Way Around the World* (Vacation Work Publications, www.vacationwork.co.uk).

INTERNATIONAL COMPANIES IN NEW ZEALAND

Australian Business, formerly the Australia and New Zealand Chamber of Commerce UK, (34-35 Southampton Street, London WC2E 7HE; ☎0870-890 0720; fax 0870-890 0721; www.australianbusiness.co.uk), can provide details of British companies active in New Zealand. The *American Chamber of Commerce in New Zealand Directory* is published annually by the *American Chamber of Commerce in New Zealand*, PO Box 106 002, Level 6, Affco House, 12-26 Swanson Street, Auckland Central 1001; ☎9-309 9140; fax 9-309 1090; e-mail amcham@amcham.co.nz; www.amcham.co.nz.

Antarctica

As well as the highly trained scientists and others needed to run an Antarctic research station such as McMurdo Station, a certain number of dogsbodies are needed. The Raytheon Technical Services Company is subcontracted by the US government's National Science Foundation to hire between 800 and 1,000 Americans to run the station, a third of whom are women. Of these, a certain number are general assistants (GAs) who, among many tasks, do quite a lot of snow shovelling. Openings also exist for chefs, electricians, computer programmers, typists, construction workers and so on. Contracts are for four, six or twelve months.

Raytheon begin considering applications in April though may not choose their summer season personnel (to work October to mid-February) until the last moment. Even though the work schedule is nine hours a day, six days a week, these jobs are massively oversubscribed, so perseverance will be needed, plus excellent health (physical, mental and dental) and a willingness to travel at short notice. The contact address is Human Resources Department, Raytheon Polar Services Company, 7400 South Tucson Way, Centennial, Colorado 80112-3938; ☎303-790 8606; www.rpsc.raytheon.com.

Britain's five research stations and two research vessels in Antarctica are overseen by the *British Antarctic Survey* (High Cross, Madingley Road, Cambridge CB3 0ET; ☎01223-221400; email employment@bas.ac.uk; www.antarctica.ac.uk/employment/index.html). All support staff hired by BAS must be suitable qualified and willing to sign an eight- or 33-month contract.

ASIA

China

o **Embassy of the People's Republic of China,** 49-51 Portland Place, London W1B
  4JL; ☎020-7299 4049; www.chinese-embassy.org.uk
o **Embassy of the People's Republic of China,** 2300 Connecticut Avenue, NW
  Washington DC 20008; ☎202-328 2500; www.china-embassy.org
o **Currency:** 1 Yuan (Y) or Renminbi = 10 jiao = 100 fen
o **Exchange Rate:** £1 = Y14.86; $1 = Y7.97; €1 = Y10.16
o **Country Code:** +86

The People's Republic of China underwent rapid economic expansion during the late 1980s. Excessive imports and high inflation forced the government to slow economic growth from 1989. There are moves towards liberalising the economy, allowing for greater foreign participation and co-operation. The suppression of the democracy movement in 1989 and the continued occupation of Tibet have done damage to China's prestige, but not to its international trade contacts. Overall economic growth is high (China now has the world's second largest GDP) but China is really a series of interlocking economies where some areas are developed and prosperous while other provinces lag behind. The growth rate in 2006 was 10 per cent, about four times the world's average growth, and is the fastest growing economy in the world. China's policy-makers are concentrating on infrastructure development, in building roads and other lines of communication and technology transfer, which means that larger UK and US companies setting up there often include consultancy and training for local staff as part of the deal. There are numerous opportunities in China for English teachers – an estimated 450 million people are currently learning English. Currently there about 440,000 foreigners working and living in China, mainly in manufacturing and social services.

GENERAL FACTS

Population
China is the world's most populous country, and the third most important in terms of land. It has an estimated population of over 1.3 billion spread over 3,696,100 square miles (9.5 million sq km) and the average population density is 325 per square mile; although 80 per cent of the population is concentrated in the east, especially the northeast.

CLIMATE
The climate varies greatly from region to region. While the whole of north China has harsh winters with cultivation only possible in the summer, the south is humid with mild winters and hot summers that last between five and eight months. In the very south of the country the climate is tropical and year-round cultivation is possible. Temperatures during winter vary from 50 deg F (10 deg C) in the Yangtse Valley, to freezing in inner Mongolia. During the summer the temperature reaches 95 or 104 deg F (35 or 40 deg C) in some areas. The

highest rainfall is recorded during the summer, except in the arid northwest of the country and in Tibet.

GOVERNMENT

Under the Constitution of 1982, the National People's Congress (NPC) became the most powerful organ in the state hierarchy. Its deputies are elected by each region for a five-year term. The NPC elects the Head of State – the President of the People's Republic of China – and the national Government – the State Council – to administer the country.

China is divided into 23 provinces (with Taiwan, which the government considers a province of China), four municipalities (Beijing, Shanghai, Tianjin, and Chongqing), five autonomous regions including Tibet, and two Special Administrative Regions. The latter two regions, which form 50-60 per cent of the total land, are home largely to minority nationalities including at least 55 different ethnic groups, compared to the Han Chinese group, which comprises 94 per cent of the rest of the population.

CITIES

Shanghai is the largest city, with a population of eight million, followed by Beijing with 7 million, Tientsin (six million), Shen-yang (4.5 million), Wuhan (four million) and Canton (3.5 million).

RURAL LIFE

China consists largely of high mountain ranges, deserts and steppes. Only 10.3 per cent of the country is under systematic cultivation, although a recent survey showed that the agricultural sector employed about 60 per cent of China's labour force. This is changing, however, and there is a drift to the cities and a more industrial pattern of development in the countryside. The main crops are cereals, rice, tea and cotton. Most agricultural production is carried out on self-administered fields. The administrative functions of the People's Communes were abolished by the new Constitution, leaving them as mainly economic enterprises.

RELIGION, SPORT AND CULTURE

Most Chinese are officially non-religious, or atheists. The indigenous religion is a combination of Confucianism, Taoism and Animism, mostly aimed at the preservation of traditional social values and the propitiation of numerous deities. Veneration of ancestors is an essential part of Chinese culture. There are also estimated to be 70 million Buddhists, 27 million Muslims and two million Christians. During the Cultural Revolution places of worship were ransacked; the 1982 Constitution granted the people freedom of religious activity, but under strict state control.

There is an ancient tradition of physical fitness in China, and every school and factory has sports facilities. Fitness also forms part of a general awareness of civil defence. The younger generations are mainly interested in Western sports in which China has had international success, especially in swimming, football, table tennis and badminton. Older people prefer the traditional martial arts (*wushu*) such as *taijiquan* for which China is famous. Beijing will host the 2008 Olympic Games.

China's cultural heritage is very rich, with a literature going back over 2,500 years. The 20th century saw a great spread of literacy; and modern works of a more popular nature have been added to the older literary tradition. Calligraphy and painting are the two most respected art forms, evidence of which can be seen wherever you go in China. Dancing, singing, theatre and opera are vibrant parts of Chinese culture, although not necessarily to Western tastes.

FACTORS INFLUENCING EMPLOYMENT

IMMIGRATION

Although procedures tend to be constantly changing, tourist visas are easy to obtain by requesting a visa application form from the nearest Chinese embassy. Tourist visas permit you to stay in China for the duration of your tour or visit; an extension may be granted within the country. It is usual to arrange a visa through the *China International Travel Service* (☎ 10-6522 2991; fax 10-6522 2862; e-mail shuyu@cits.com.cu; www.cits.net), which is the official state travel agency. Enquiries about visas should be made well in advance.

Foreign workers, once informed that they have a job in China, will be requested to apply for a visa. They will be supplied with an interim visa, which on arrival in China, they take to the Public Security Office where they will be given a residence permit. You should allow six months to a year to organise a job and the appropriate permit.

LANGUAGE

The official language of China is Mandarin (known as *putonghua* to the Chinese), a dialect originating in the north of the country. Although roughly 70 per cent of the population speak Mandarin, there are eight major dialects, of which Cantonese is the most important.

Chinese is a tonal language, which means that the intonation you use can change the meaning of a word; this makes learning the language exceptionally demanding for speakers of Western languages. The writing system is also extraordinarily complex, consisting of a system of some 60,000 characters or ideographs, of which about 7,000 are in current use. A system of Romanisation, known as *pinyin*, is also widely used, especially in areas frequented by foreigners.

CURRENCY

Renminbi (Rmb) is the local currency and produced in units of *Yuan*. Salaries are paid monthly, in cash. Sending money back home can be done through the Bank of China and some Units (see below) will arrange this directly for you. It is possible to open an account at the Bank of China, but this offers no advantages. Money can also be transferred to China fairly easily (at least in Beijing) by a bank draft to the Bank of China.

HOUSING AND ACCOMMODATION

There are two types of housing available for foreigners: at the place of work or in a hotel. Recent policy has been to try to house everyone at their place of work. Now 80 per cent of urban families own a house or flat.

At the place of work, flats are usually provided which are comfortable enough, if a little spartan. Obviously a good deal will depend on where you are working – flats in the provinces can be very basic indeed and hot water and electricity will certainly be rationed. The main benefits of such housing are the proximity to work and the full involvement with it that this implies. The disadvantages include never being able to get away from work – particularly important for teachers, who may be inundated with 'visitors'.

Hotels offer the advantages of a larger foreign community with the chance to meet workers in different fields. Although foreign workers live in a special area, with their own flats, they can use the facilities of the rest of the hotel. These can include tennis courts, swimming pools and so on. There are also courses available in Chinese, martial arts, calligraphy and various other traditional skills. Hotel life is undoubtedly more comfortable than in the place of work, but one can begin to feel cut off from the Chinese themselves.

THE UNIT

The Unit is the administrative division of any workplace. Its responsibilities go far beyond mere work, however, and cover just about every aspect of its employees' lives. It is the Unit that employs, arranges housing, and gives permission for marriages, study and travel. For foreign workers, almost as much as for Chinese colleagues, the Unit determines the quality of life.

Units vary from institute to institute, especially in their political colouring. While most welcome foreigners sincerely and openly, there are still some that resent the privileges given to foreigners and they make no secret of this. Try not to antagonise your Unit. If they take against you they can very easily make your life extremely difficult. Conversely, they can be very helpful in arranging extra visas, travel permits and even interpreters.

The Unit will assign you an interpreter to help with day-to-day problems. How useful an interpreter proves to be depends very much on the luck of the draw and it is worth complaining if an interpreter is of no use since the post is a coveted one, and can lead to study abroad. Most Units employing foreigners have a Foreign Affairs Office and it is through this that most things are arranged, and any problems should be directed there. In the case of finding yourself up against a truly hostile Unit it is possible to appeal direct to the Ministry of Education and to arrange a transfer.

EDUCATION

School in China begins at the age of seven. Six years in Primary School are followed by six years in Secondary School (three years at Junior Middle and three at Senior Middle). Higher education is open to students who can pass the strict Entrance Examination organised every year in July by the Ministry of Education.

Children of foreign workers, if of school age, would benefit by being in the one of the cities or Beijing itself. Only Shanghai and Beijing have English-speaking schools, run by diplomatic missions for the children of their staff and a few others. Space is limited and it is best to write to the embassy or consulate in advance. They take children up to 13 and charge at least $4,000 a year.

EMBASSIES AND TOURIST OFFICES

British Embassy, 11 Guang Hua Lu, Jianguomenwai, Beijing 100600; ☎10-5192 4000; fax 10-6532 1937; e-mail info@britishcentre.org.cn; www.britishembassy.org.cn.
There are consulates in Shanghai, Guangzhou and Chongqing.
US Embassy, 3 Xiu Shui Bei Jie, Chaoyang District, Beijing 100600; ☎10-6532 3831; http://beijing.usembassy-china.org.cn.
There are also US Consulates in Guangzhou, Chengdu, Shanghai and Shenyang.
China National Tourist Office, 4 Glentworth Street, London NW1 5PG; ☎020-7935 9787; www.cnto.org.uk.
China National Tourist Office, 350 Fifth Avenue, Suite 6413, Empire State Building, New York, NY 10118; ☎212-760 8218; fax 212-760 8809; www.cnto.org.

Holidays

Public Holidays are I January *New Year's Day*, 8 March *International Women's Day* (half day off for women),
1-3 May *Three days holiday for International Labour Day*, 4 May *Youth Day* (half day off for those aged 14-20),
1 June *International Children's Day* (half day off for ages 13 and under), 1 July *Birthday of the Chinese Communist Party*, 1 August *Anniversary of the founding of the People's Liberation Army* (for all armed forces personnel), and 1-3 October *Three days holiday for National Day*.

EMPLOYMENT PROSPECTS

Since the late 1970s, China has employed an increasing number of foreigners to aid its modernisation programme. Most of these have been in academic institutions, but recently they have been employed in other fields too, for example in the areas of trade and joint ventures. The policy on foreign consultants is administered by *The Foreign Experts Bureau* of the State Council (FEB) but actual recruitment and day-to-day affairs are handled by the *Bureau of Foreign Affairs* of the Ministry of Education (BFA). The BFA puts out a pamphlet outlining its requirements and policies entitled, *Information for the Recruitment of Foreign Experts*, that can be obtained from the BFA itself or local embassies. As a rule, they are interested in three types of personnel: genuine experts in particular fields, media people and teachers.

GENERAL

There are a number of jobs that do not involve teaching, although this can be a useful skill whatever field you happen to be working in. It is never a bad idea to pack a few TEFL books before you go.

Most non-teaching jobs are presently in the media, although the market is expanding. All these jobs confer Foreign Expert (FE) status, the status given to most foreigners who work for the Chinese government (see below, under *Teaching*) and therefore enjoy much the same terms and conditions. FEs are expected to work a full year with just one month's holiday and they also usually work a longer day, and a six-day week. The majority of jobs are in Beijing and can begin at any time of the year. Anyone who thinks their skills could be useful to the country's modernisation programme should write to the *Bureau of Foreign Affairs* (see below, under *Addresses*) enquiring about possible openings.

The *China Publishing Group*, 24 Baiwanzhuang Road, Beijing; ☎10-6899 6217; fax 10-6899 7796; e-mail wandi@china.org.cn; www.china.org.cn, employs a number of FEs to work on its various publications. These include *China Today, China Pictorial* and *Beijing Review* and are produced in English, German, Spanish and Japanese. The work consists of editing and polishing literally translated copy and making it read properly. While this is sometimes interesting, wading through almost incomprehensible 'Chinglish' can quickly become tedious.

Other potential employers include the daily English-language newspaper, the *China Daily*, the *Xinhua News Agency, Beijing Radio,* and *Central China Television (CCTV)*. All of these employ FEs as journalists and editors, but do not expect to become a roving reporter – the work is mainly correcting work written by Chinese staff.

Listed below are a number of recruitment agencies based in China or that recruit staff for positions in China.

Bole Associates, 11th Floor Unit 1101, The Exchange Beijing, No. 2 Dong Huan Nan Lu Chao Yang District, Beijing 100022; ☎(86) 010 6567 6678; fax (86) 010 6567 6538; e-mail bej@bo-le.com; www.bo-le.com. Has six core practices including internet, financial services, consumer products, pharmaceutical, industrial and China appointments.

Futurestep Corporate USA Headquarter, 1800 Century Park East, Suite 900, Los Angeles, CA 90067, USA; e-mail info@futurestep.com.hk; www.futurestep.com.hk.

Futurestep (UK Office), 123 Buckingham Palace Road, London, SW1W 9DZ, UK; ☎ (44) 0207 312 3200; e-mail info@futurestep.com.hk; www.futurestep.com.hk.

L&K Consultancy (Shanghai Office): ☎(86) 021 6466 4666; e-mail lkconsuc@online. sh.cn. This is a Singapore consulting firm specialising in Executive search in China. They advertise senior management positions such as General Manager, Deputy General Manager, Financial Controller, Marketing Manager, National Sales Manager etc.

Hudson (Shanghai Office), 11/F, Room 1104, Central Plaza, No.227 Huangpi Bei Lu,

Shanghai 200003; ☎(86) 021 6375 8922; fax (86) 021 6375 8211; www.hudson.com/us/.

Hudson (GuangzhouOffice), Room 735, The Garden Hotel, 368 Huanshi Dong Lu, Guangzhou, 510064; ☎(852) 2528 1191; www.hudson.com/us/.

Hudson (London Office), Chancery House, 53-64 Chancery Lane, London, WC2A 1QS; ☎ (44) 0207 187 6000; fax (44) 0207 187 6001; www.hudson.com/us/.

Stanton Chase International (Baltimore/Washington Office), 100 East Pratt Street, Suite 2530, Baltimore, Maryland 21202 U.S.A; ☎(1) 410 528 8400; fax (1) 410 528 8409; www.stantonchase.com.

Stanton Chase International (London Office), 56 Haymarket, London, SW 1Y 4RN, U.K.; ☎(44) 0207 930 6314; fax (44) 0207 930 9539; www.stantonchase.com.

Lynton John & Associates (Beijing Office), ☎(86) 010 66526 09614; www.ljaconsult.com.

PriceWaterHouseCoopers (Beijing) Limited, 18/F North Tower, Beijing Kerry Centre, 1 Guang Hua Road, Chaoyang District, Beijing 100020; ☎ (86) 010 6561 2233; fax (86) 010 8529 9000; www.pwcglobal.com.

PriceWaterHouseCoopers (Shanghai) Limited, 12/F Shui On Plaza, 333 Huai Hai Zhong Road, Shanghai 200021; ☎(86) 021 63(86) 3388/(86) 021 6386 6688; fax (86) 021 6386 3300/(86) 021 6386 2288; www.pwcglobal.com

Euro-group (Beijing), ☎(86) 010 6510 1789; e-mail szhang@euro-group.com.

TEACHING

There are literally thousands of higher education establishments in China, including universities, colleges, foreign language institutes, institutes of science and technology and so on. It is difficult to assess the relative status of these, but in general the universities are top of the pile. Nearly all of them hire foreigners, the majority of whom are taken on as language teachers. Each year there are nearly 700 posts, of which 400 are to teach English. Other disciplines include literature, history, law, economics, all the sciences and technology. There is also an increasing demand for management training and any discipline connected with business.

Non language-teaching posts are generally under the auspices of various agencies, such as the UN and the EU, but there are opportunities for the independent teacher too. To teach the hard sciences or the arts one really needs to be an expert with the appropriate qualifications, and to be perceived as such by the Chinese.

Most teachers in China end up teaching English, regardless of their original brief. Although some do teach their own subject, it is quite common to travel to China believing you are to teach one subject only to end up teaching another. The Ministry of Foreign Affairs of the Chinese government recruits Foreign Teachers (FTs) and Foreign Experts (FEs) through Chinese embassies every year. You need to hold a masters degree or above in the relevant areas, such as English and Linguistics, to be a FE. Moreover, you are also required to have some teaching experience at tertiary level. FTs are mainly university graduates and are not required to have teaching experience. FTs are placed in secondary schools or sometimes primary schools while FEs can choose to work in university level institutes. Applications should be made to the Chinese embassy in your home country including a covering letter, a CV/resumé, a copy of your passport (the page with your personal details), a copy of your education certificate and a passport-size photo to your application. There are also different short-term and long-term programmes held by the China Education Association for International Exchange (CEAIE) for foreigners.

There are plenty of other channels for foreigners to seek for teaching positions in China and one of the best routes is to join a work programme, such as Professional Placement in Chinese Schools organised by China Services International (CSI). CSI only arranges for foreign teachers or experts to go to schools which are assessed by local governments and have fulfilled all criteria. In another words, CSI works closely with local provincial authorities and local schools in order to assure a positive placement experience for potential foreign teachers. International talents who participate in the CSI teaching placement programme will receive a monthly salary based on contractual agreement.

Salaries for teaching jobs in China are about 2,200 *yuan* per month (US$268/£157), but the salary varies slightly amongst schools. An interesting point to note is that the salary is open for negotiation and you may ask for a higher salary. Educational level and teaching experience are important factors to determine your salary. The salary of a foreign teacher who has a Bachelor degree is not less than 2,200 *yuan* per month; a masters degree holder with five years teaching experience will earn 3,300 *yuan* (US$400/£235) or more per month; and the monthly salary of a doctorate degree holder or an Associate Professor from an overseas institution will be 4,600 *yuan* (US$560/£330) or above. At the end of each academic semester, every foreign teacher will receive 1,000 *yuan* (US$120/£70) as their end-of-term bonus. Other benefits include fully-paid furnished accommodation during the contractual period, and a one-way international travel ticket or an equivalent sum of money in *yuan*. The council on International Educational Exchange (CIEE) also organises a very similar programme to that of CSI. You should bear in mind that you should only apply to schools that have obtained provincial authorisations to hire foreigner teachers. Otherwise, you may find that the school cannot afford to provide the above salary payments and benefits.

The British Council also runs a programme arranging university graduates to be English teaching assistants in Chinese secondary schools (see below).

You can find teaching jobs in China through a number of recruitment websites, such as the China TEFL (Teaching English as a Foreign Language) Network, the Zhejiang Foreign Experts Service and China Education. There are more and more private institutes looking for foreigners to teach English and it is easy to find a huge number of these institutes through a Google or Yahoo search. There are several placement organisations, such as CIEE, who have links with these foreign language institutes and they will be able to arrange a teaching job in China for you.

Useful Addresses & Websites:

China Education Association for International Exchange (CEAIE), 160 Fuxingmen Nei Dajie, Beijing 100031 (mailing address: 37 Damucang Hutong, Beijing 100816; ☎(86) 010 6641 6582; fax (86) 010 6641 6156; e-mail ceaie@ceaie.edu.cn; www.ceaie.edu.cn.

China Services International (CSI), www.chinajob.com/En/.

Council on International Educational Exchange (CIEE), 52 Poland Street, London W1F 7AB, UK: ☎(44) 020 7478 2020; fax (44) 020 7734 7322; e-mail infoUK@ councilexchanges.org.uk; www.councilexchanges.org.uk.

The British Council, Language Assistants Team, Education and Training Group, British Council, 10 Spring Gardens, London SW1A 2BN; ☎(44) 020 7389 4596; e-mail assistants@britishcouncil.org; www.languageassistant.co.uk.

China TEFL network, http://www.chinatefl.com/vacancy.html. A China teaching job-listing site.

Zhejiang Foreign Experts Service, http://www.teach-in-zhejiang.com/ywrc/login.asp. It provides the latest ESL/EFL vacancies in schools in China.

China Education, http://www.chinatoday.com/edu/a00.htm. This provides information of vacancies in universities in China.

Language Link, 21 Harrington Road, London SW7 3EU; ☎(44) 020 7225 1065; fax (44) 020 7584 3518; e-mail info@languagelink.co.uk; www.languagelink.co.uk.

SPECIFIC CONTACTS

The Boland School T.E.F.L. Training Centre, 195 Fengmen Road, Suzhou, Jiangsu Province, 215006 China; tel/fax +86 512 6741 3422; e-mail info@boland-china.com; www.boland-china.com. The Boland School was founded in 1992 and has T.E.F.L. teacher training centres in both the Czech Republic and Asia offering the International T.E.F.L. Diploma on a four and a half-week residential programme. Courses are held every month, all year round. Comprehensive job placement assistance is provided to all programme graduates following training. The Boland School also has a Chinese cultural department where Chinese language, Kung Fu, Cooking and other cultural courses are offered, and also a Business Department which provides China business seminars and full-service business consultation services for those interested in doing business in China. Visit www.boland-business.com for details.

TheBritish Council recruits up to 50 English language specialists to work on their ELT development projects in China. Minimum qualifications are an MA in an appropriate subject and several years' teaching experience, preferably overseas. Project lecturers are employed by Chinese institutions on Foreign Expert conditions and receive a sterling subsidy. Advertisements are placed in the Education press each February/March for posts beginning the following September. Enquiries should be made direct to the Chinese Links Officer at the Education and Training Group, British Council, 10 Spring Gardens, London SW1A 2BN; ☎020-7930 8466; fax 020-7389 6347; e-mail generalenquiries@britishcouncil.org; www.britishcouncil.org. The British Council has also established links with Chinese teaching associations.

IST Plus, Rosedale House, Rosedale Road, Richmond, Surrey TW9 2SZ; ☎020-8939 9057; fax 020-8939 9090; e-mail info@istplus.com; www.istplus.com, has a Teach in China programme which offers an opportunity for graduates to spend five or 10 months teaching English in a university, college, or school in China. There is no age limit and teaching/TEFL qualifications are not required in order to apply. Successful applicants attend a one-week training course on arrival in Shanghai; focusing on learning Chinese, understanding Chinese culture, and giving an insight to TEFL. Host institutions in China provide private accommodation (usually a teacher's apartment on or near the campus), and a monthly salary, which is generous by Chinese standards. Participants are responsible for paying their outward airfare and programme fee to IST Plus to cover the costs of arranging the placement, processing all paperwork required for visas and work permits, visa fees, the training centre, and 24-hour emergency support while in China. The host institution on completion of a 10-month contract pays return fare. IST Plus sends participants on this programme in late August and early February in accordance with the Chinese semester system, and applicants are encouraged to return forms and application materials at least three months before in order to ensure that a suitable placement is found.

Teaching positions for UK residents are also available through VSO (see the *Voluntary Work* section).

SHORT TERM WORK

Many local and foreign organisations arrange for foreigners to go to China to lead summer programmes or participate as assistants every year. Most of these are English learning programmes for secondary school students or for English teachers in China. The China Education Association for International Exchange (CEAIE) organises such programmes every year and invites foreigners to teach English. The programme for secondary teachers lasts for six weeks while an English camp for students is two weeks shorter.

There are many organisations that recruit volunteers to teach in China. Educational Services International –ESI (444 E. Huntington Drive Suite 200, Arcadia, CA 91006, USA; ☎626 294 9400; fax 626 821 2022; e-mail teach@esimail.org; www.teachoverseas.org)

a US Christian group, also organises summer programmes in China but it only recruits English speakers who are Christians. Two-weeks of training will be provided before going into China and the whole programme lasts for about six weeks. You can make your application at anytime of the year but you have to pay about US$3,400 (£1,800) for joining the programme.

WorldTeach (c/o Center for International Development, Harvard University, 79 John F. Kennedy Street, Cambridge MA 02138 USA; ☎617 495 5527; fax 617 495 1599; e-mail info@worldteach.org; www.worldteach.org) is a non-profit organisation based at the Centre for International Development at Harvard University. They recruit voluntary English speakers to teach English in summer camps in China every year. The whole programme lasts for about two months (from late June to late August) and every volunteer participates in two to three camps in different areas in China. There is a cost of about US$3,900 (£2,160) for joining the programme.

Colorado China Council (4556 Apple Way, Boulder, CO 80301, USA; ☎303 443 1108; fax 303 443 1107; e-mail alice@asiacouncil.org; www.asiacouncil.org) includes a great deal of sightseeing out of the teaching time and it sometimes organises additional trips after the programme which you can join by paying extra. You need to hold at least a Bachelor degree to join the programmes of CCC. As with ESI and WorldTeach, participants need to pay for joining the programme.

TOURISM

Working in cafes in tourist areas can sometimes be undertaken without a working visa, but you are usually paid at a low rate. Hotels very often employ foreigners to teach their staff English, to write or translate menus, or as receptionists. You can approach a hotel directly and ask if it requires a foreign worker. You will have a greater chance of getting a job if you look into those in the tourist areas. Portfolio International (*www.portfoliointernational. com/sect1/*) are professional recruitment experts specialising in the hotel and catering industries. Positions are categorised into hotel general managers, hotel operations, leisure and golf, sales and marketing, corporate, food, drink and entertainment and chefs.

AGRICULTURE

Even though many cities are transforming into industrial and financial bases, agriculture in China is still a major supplier of food to many countries. If you want to experience life in rural areas and are interested in farming and horticulture, the International Farm Experience Programme can arrange a three-month placement on the outskirts of Beijing: *International Farm Experience Programme*, Young Farmers Centre, National Agriculture Centre, Stoneleigh, Warwickshire CV8 2LG; ☎(44) 024 7685 7204.

INTERNSHIPS

China joined IAESTE (International Association for the Exchange of Students with Technical Experience) in February 2000. IAESTE offers paid course-related work placements for students in science, engineering and technology to provide them with practical experience as well as theoretical knowledge. These placements normally last for 12 weeks in summer but longer placements can be arranged at other times of the year (www.iaeste.org).

The internship is open to students attending courses at universities, institutes of technology and similar institutions of higher education in science, engineering and technology. You must be studying at a university at the time of the internship, which means you cannot join the programme either before your school term starts in the university, or after you finish your studies. Exceptions can be made for fresh graduates doing their practical training immediately after final examinations. Post-doctorate trainees will normally not be accepted.

You must apply to the IAESTE office in your home country. The application period usually lasts from September to early or mid-January and you are required to pay an application fee of US$50 (£27). You will then be provided with a list of details of all international internships and you have to submit an application update, resumé, transcripts, etc. Successful candidates will be notified by mid-March but placement has to be confirmed by the employer.

Abroad China, based in the USA, organises both exchange studies and placements for university students. It helps to arrange placements in many fields, including accounting, design, business administration, management, communications, computer science, consulting, education, English as a second language, finance, human resources, information systems, international relations, marketing, advertising, public relations, public policy, government, social work, law, hotel/restaurant hospitality and tourism. Short-term interns are usually unpaid but people staying with the organisation for more than six months usually receive a stipend. *Abroad China* will arrange accommodation, usually in universities or host families, for participants.

IAESTE United States, 10400 Little Patuxent Parkway, Suite 250, Columbia, MD 21044-3519, USA; ☎(1) 410 997 3069; fax (1) 410 997 5186; e-mail iaeste@aipt.org; http://aipt.org/subpages/iaeste_us/index.php.
Abroad China, Inc., 11250 Roger Bacon Drive, The Atrium Business Center, Unit 6, Reston, VA 20190 USA; ☎(1) 703 834 1118; fax (1) 703 834 7277; e-mail info@abroadchina.net; www.abroadchina.net.

ADDRESSES

Great Britain China Centre, 15 Belgrave Square, London SW1X 8PS; ☎020-7235 6696; fax 020-7245 6885; e-mail contact@gbcc.org.uk; www.gbcc.org.uk.
Ministry of Foreign Affairs, No. 2 Chaoyangmen Nandajie, Chaoyang District, Beijing 100701; ☎10-6596 1114; www.fmprc.gov.cn/eng.

Hong Kong Special Administrative Region

(Part of the People's Republic of China)

CURRENCY

The unit of currency is the Hong Kong Dollar: HK$1 = 100 cents
Rate of Exchange: £1 = HK$14.49; $1 = HK$7.77; €1 = HK$9.91

As Hong Kong has a tradition that is different from the rest of China and is the most likely destination for British and US jobseekers, some specific information about this special administrative region of China is included here.

The success of Hong Kong as a leading manufacturing and commercial centre in Asia, and its strong links with the UK and other English-speaking countries, mean that opportunities for British and American citizens are likely to continue, despite its return to China on 1 July 1997. In some areas, such as construction, expatriates are likely to be replaced by local workers, and administration is no longer a route to employment in Hong Kong. Financial services, consultancy, IT and Telecommunications, and work for joint ventures and international companies, are the main areas of prospective employment. The expected downturn in foreign opportunities has not materialised and prospects remain good.

Hong Kong suffered fallout from Asia's economic crises in the late 1990s, and has experienced rising unemployment (8.3 per cent) as well as falling property prices. However, be that as it may, Hong Kong is currently the largest trading partner (and the largest source of foreign investment) for China due to its vibrant free market economy, dependent on international trade. Natural resources are limited and a large proportion of the food and raw materials are imported. Imports and exports exceed the GDP. Even before Hong Kong reverted to Chinese administration it had extensive trade and investment ties with China. Per capita Gross Domestic Product compares with that in the four big countries of Western Europe and the GDP growth averaged five per cent in 1989-97. The widespread Asian economic difficulties in 1998 hit the economy quite hard as did the SARS outbreak in 2003. Nevertheless a solid rise in exports, a boom in tourism from the mainland due to the Chinese easing travel restrictions, and a return of consumer confidence has resulted in the resumption of strong growth from late 2003 to 2006.

GENERAL FACTS

GEOGRAPHY
Hong Kong consists of 236 islands, and a part of the Chinese mainland east of the Pearl River estuary adjoining the Chinese province of Guandong (Kwangtung). Victoria, on Hong Kong Island, is the commercial centre. Topographically, Hong Kong is mostly steep hillside, and living conditions are crowded. Hong Kong is divided into four main areas - Kowloon, Hong Kong Island, the New Territories and the Outlying Islands. Kowloon and the New Territories are on a peninsula of the Chinese mainland. Hong Kong Island is on the southern side of the harbour facing Kowloon. The New Territories has a 12 miles (20 km) land border with China proper.

The climate is sub-tropical and subject to the monsoon. The winter is cool and dry, and the summer hot and humid. Most rain falls during the summer. Hong Kong is one of the most densely populated areas in the world, and the total population is about 6.94 million; 95 per cent of these are Chinese. Cantonese is spoken by the majority of people, but several other dialects are also spoken. The English language is widely spoken and plays an important part in business life.

HISTORY
The island of Hong Kong was ceded by China to Britain in 1841; Kowloon was acquired in 1860, and the New Territories were leased from China in 1898. Hong Kong was run by a British-appointed Governor for 100 years until its return to China in June 1997 under the terms of the original lease. Under the Sino-British Joint Declaration, signed in 1985 by the British and Chinese governments, China guaranteed 'to preserve Hong Kong's unique economic position and way of life for 50 years after 1997,' and to allow Hong Kong to exercise a degree of autonomy (except in such areas as defence and foreign affairs).

Although the situation is at present far from clear, developments in the rest of China such as its transition to a semi-market economy, mean that it is in China's interest to preserve this important trading and financial asset and many of its institutions. Hong Kong seems likely to continue as an important manufacturing and commercial centre.

Before the handover to China in 1997, many of the wealthy and educated moved to other countries creating openings for many foreign professionals. Hong Kong continues to enjoy a high degree of autonomy and retains its own currency, laws, and border controls.

The cost of living in Hong Kong is reasonably high, housing rental or purchase being the main expense, with food and entertainment less so. Getting about on public transport is cheap.

GOVERNMENT

Under the principle of 'One Country, Two Systems', the Hong Kong Special Administrative Region (SAR) has its own constitution – the Basic Law – and enjoys a high degree of autonomy from the rest of China. Fundamental rights and freedoms are guaranteed in Hong Kong through the commitments made in the Joint Declaration and enshrined in the Basic Law. The SAR is headed by a Chief Executive supported by an Executive Council and Legislative Council, and run by an impartial and professional civil service.
Religion, Sport and Culture

The dominant religions in Hong Kong are Buddhism and Taoism, although there are many other religions represented including Christianity and Catholicism.

Popular pursuits include horse racing, golf, water sports, and contact sports such as football and rugby. The nightlife in Hong Kong is lively, both for locals and expats. Horseracing takes place at the famous 'Happy Valley' racetrack and each Easter Hong Kong is host to the international Rugby Sevens tournament. The Hong Kong marathon takes place in January.

FACTORS INFLUENCING EMPLOYMENT

IMMIGRATION

UK citizens are allowed a six-month visa free stay in Hong Kong. US citizens do not require a visa for visits of up to 90 days. Extensions of stay may be granted upon application to the *Hong Kong SAR Immigration Department* (2nd Floor, Immigration Tower, 7 Gloucester Road, Wan Chai, Hong Kong; ☎2824 6111; fax 2877 7711; e-mail enquiry@immd.gov.hk; www.immd.gov.hk).

Hong Kong's policy on immigration allows foreigners to enter, live and work in the area if they possess a special skill or profession that is not available locally, and if their activity will significantly benefit the local economy. Applicants for an employment visa must first secure an offer of employment.

EMPLOYMENT PROSPECTS

CONDITIONS OF EMPLOYMENT

Most expats live in some considerable style in Hong Kong. There are a number of international schools in the area and wages for professionals are good and taxes low. Accommodation is expensive and apartment based and, not surprisingly due to the lack of space, the flats are small – around 800 square feet for a two or three bedroom apartment. Rents vary enormously according to the location, the condition, and facilities (such as swimming pool, gym and security). An apartment in Causeway Bay or Wanchai costs about $8,000 (£650/US$1,0000) a month for 500 square feet (47 sq metres). Expect to pay $10,000 (£800/US$1,300) for 800 square feet (75 sq metres) in these busy areas. Salaries are high in Hong Kong. The monthly average salary of all industries of HK$10,600 with low tax rates. Many expats work in investment banking and the financial services sector, law and IT recruitment.

EMBASSIES AND TOURIST OFFICES

British Consulate General, No 1 Supreme Court Road, PO Box 528, Central Hong Kong; ☎2901 3000; fax 2901 3066; e-mail consular@britishconsulate.org.hk; www.britishconsulate.org.hk.

US Consulate General, 26 Garden Road, Hong Kong; ☎2523 9011; fax 2845 1598; www.usconsulate.org.hk.

Hong Kong Tourism Board, 6 Grafton Street, London W1S 4EQ; ☎020-7533 7100; fax 020-7533 7111; e-mail info@discoverhongkong.com;www.discoverhongkong.com.
Hong Kong Tourism Board, 115 East 54th Street, 2nd Floor, New York, NY 10022; ☎212-421 3382; fax 212-421 8428; www.discoverhongkong.com/usa/.

NEWSPAPERS

Hong Kong occupies a leading position in Asia in terms of IT and telecommunications with sophisticated and varied media. Both Chinese (usually Cantonese) and English are widely used, and most official documents are printed in both. There are a number of English-language daily newspapers in circulation, including the *Asian Wall Street Journal* (www. awsj.com/), the *Eastern Express*, the *Hong Kong Standard*, and the *International Herald Tribune*. The world-famous *South China Morning Post* (www.scmp.com) has a very good classified section.

SPECIFIC CONTACTS

EMPLOYMENT SERVICES

Beyond Recruitment, www.staffservice.com/eng.
Gemini Personnel Limited, 15/F Silver Fortune Plaza, 1 Wellington Street, Central Hong Kong, ☎2525 7283; fax 2810 6467; www.gemini.com.hk.
Executive Access, 1308 Prince's Building, 10 Chater Road, Hong Kong; ☎852-2877 8772; fax 852-2877 8339; www.execaccess.com, is Asia's leading independent executive search firm with offices in Hong Kong, India, Singapore, and Tokyo. Market leaders within the banking and finance, consulting, telecom and IT industries. Also manages executive searches for sectors including media and entertainment, manufacturing, energy, luxury goods, insurance and natural resources.
TMP Worldwide Executive Search, Unit 1106, 11/F Vicwood Plaza, 199 Des Voeux Road Central, Hong Kong; ☎852-2114-5050; fax 852-2891-5018; www.tmp.com.

TEACHERS

Although it isn't as easy to get casual teaching work as it was before the handover in 1997 (employers who take on staff without work permits now face fines or the threat of jail sentences) there is still work to be had. The language of instruction in schools has (controversially) been switched from English to Chinese and this has led to a number of private English-language schools being established. A government scheme to recruit qualified English teachers is administered by the Hong Kong Education Department (Expatriate Teacher Exchange, 13F Wu Chung House, 213 Queen's Road East, Wanchai). The *British Council* (3 Supreme Court Road, Admiralty, Hong Kong; ☎2913 5100; fax 2913 5102; e-mail info@britishcouncil.org.hk; www.britishcouncil.org.hk) has its own teaching operation in Hong Kong and advertises vacancies at www.britishcouncil.org/ home-about-us-working-with-us.htm. Hong Kong TEFL institutes include:

Island School, 20 Borrett Road, Hong Kong; ☎2524-7135; email school@is.esf.edu.hk. Recruits in Hong Kong and the UK in January.
Venture Language Training, 1A 163 Hennessey Road, Wanchai; ☎2507-4985; fax 2511 3798. Recruits about 12 teachers (British) with TEFL qualifications and/or experience.
Ready to Learn, 1st Floor, 4W Ng Sing Lane, Yau Ma Tei, Kowloon; ☎2388 1318; fax 2388 3081; www.rtl.com.hk. Recruits about 30 teachers on one-year renewable contracts.

SHORT TERM WORK

There are hundreds of expat bars and restaurants in Hong Kong and it seems likely that there will always be a call for English-speaking bartenders and waiting staff – especially in the Western-style bars in Lan Kwai Fong on Hong Kong Island. The celebrated *Travellers Hotel* in Chung King Mansions (40 Nathan Road) has useful notice boards and, due to the high cost of accommodation elsewhere, remains a base for many long-term visitors. It is not unheard of for white westerners to find work as extras in films – the Hong Kong film industry nearly matched *Bollywood* in the number of films it manages to churn out. Modelling can also be a lucrative way to turn a shilling. Model booking agencies can be found in the local telephone directories.

There are plenty of secretarial and personnel agencies in Hong Kong but you will need to convince them that you intend to stay long-term. It isn't worth their while to apply for a work permit for transients. A couple of agencies to try are *Sara Beattie Appointments*, 8/F, Hennessy Centre, 500 Hennessy Road, Causeway Bay, Hong Kong; ☎2507 9333; fax 2827 2929; www.sarabeattie.com.hk, and *Owens Personnel Consultants Ltd*, 1201 Double Building, 22 Stanley Street, Central Hong Kong; ☎2845 6220; fax 2845 5621; e-mail resume@owens.com.hk; www.owens.com.hk.

OTHER OPPORTUNITIES

Trained nannies may find families willing to hire them and it is worth approaching agencies in the UK (see the *Au Pair and Domestic* chapter). However, the majority of expats hire Filipinas for their childcare needs.

The environmental pressure group and charity *EarthCare* (PO Box 11546, Hong Kong; ☎25780434; fax 25780522; www.earth.org.hk) recruits a number of volunteers each year to work on green campaigns. Basic accommodation is provided but volunteers must be self-funding.

INTERNATIONAL COMPANIES IN HONG KONG

The *Hong Kong Economic and Trade Office*, 6 Grafton Street, London W1S 4EQ; ☎020-7499 9821; fax 020-7495 5033; e-mail general@hketolondon.gov.hk; www.hketolondon. gov.hk, represents and promotes the Hong Kong government's interests in Europe and may be able to help with possible employment leads. It has a useful website with links to various related sites. Further information on British companies with offices in Hong Kong can be obtained from *UK Trade & Invesment*, Kingsgate House, 66-74 Victoria Street, London SW1E 6SW; ☎020-7215 5444/5; www.tradepartners.gov.uk. The *Hong Kong Government Information Centre* at www.info.gov.hk/eindex.htm, contains general information on Hong Kong with links to the Hong Kong Labour Department.

Japan

- **Japanese Embassy,** 101-104 Piccadilly, London W1J 7JT; ☎020-7465 6500; fax 020-7491 9348; e-mail info@embjapan.org.uk; www.uk.emb-japan.go.jp
- **Japanese Embassy,** 2520 Massachusetts Avenue NW, Washington DC 20008; ☎202-2386700; fax 202-328 2187; www.us.emb-japan.go.jp/english/html/index.htm
- **Currency:** the yen (¥)
- **Rate of Exchange:** £1 = ¥213; $1 = ¥114; €1 = ¥146
- **Country Code:** +81

Japan has undergone massive development over the last 50 years and is now the world's second most technologically powerful economy and third-largest economy. The economy has suffered a downturn and a continuing fall of stock market prices but it seems to have turned the corner. The estimated growth rate is 3.5 per cent and the business environment is predicted to improve throughout 2007. The unemployment rate is currently at 4.4 per cent and there are now many more opportunities for foreigners seeking to work in Japan. Japanese industry is based on engineering and high-tech industries, and nowadays a lot of the basic production industries have been moved to less expensive countries (Britain, for example) because of high labour costs in Japan itself.

Getting a job in Japan is not such an easy option now that more and more foreigners are based there, but it can be rewarding, especially for those who are willing to stay for some time and who get to know its remarkable culture and (most importantly) its language. Job opportunities range from teaching English to technical work. Although younger Japanese are less insular in outlook than their parents, they are far less Westernised than many might think. Certainly, it is important to understand a little of the Japanese way of life before you go. Japan is one of the safest countries in the world in which to live, and also one of the most conservative. The desire to find out more about European or US customs, which many Japanese people express, is matched by a belief that Westerners will never understand their culture. Etiquette and behaviour are very different in Japan, and you will need patience and tolerance if you are going to understand the country, its people and their culture. There are about 170,000 foreigners with work permits living in Japan.

GENERAL FACTS

POPULATION

Japan is one of the world's most crowded countries, with around 127.4 million inhabitants spread over 145,874 square miles (377,815 sq km). There are four large islands – Hokkaido, Honshu, Shikoku and Kyushu – and several hundred smaller ones. The average population density is high, varying from the sparsely populated island of Hokkaido in the north, to the crowded flat coastal strip of Honshu.

CLIMATE

Japan lies in the northeast corner of the Asian monsoon region, so the months of June and July are extremely wet and humid. Temperatures range from 23 deg F (–5 deg C) in Sapporo in winter to 95 deg F (35 deg C) in Kagoshima in summer. In the winter months, snowfall can be heavy on the island of Hokkaido and the north of Honshu, but is infrequent south of Tokyo.

GOVERNMENT

Under the new Constitution of 1947, Japan renounced war and the threat and use of force. The Constitution also withdrew the reins of power from the Emperor, who remains as a symbol of the State and the Unity of the People. Legislative power now lies in the hands of the *Diet*, composed of the House of Representatives and the House of Councillors. Representatives are elected for four years, councillors for six. The Prime Minister, who is nominated by the *Diet*, heads the 20-member Cabinet, which forms the executive branch of the government. The right-wing Liberal Democratic Party has governed Japan almost without interruption, although in the last several years there has been some political instability, with the LDP losing control of the government, and several changes of Prime Minister

Regional government is based on 47 prefectures, which are divided into 3,262 local administrations – 644 cities (*shi*), 1,974 towns (*machi*), and 644 villages (*mura*). In addition, there are 43 rural prefectures,.

CITIES

Eighty per cent of Japan's population live in cities, and well over half in the four metropolitan areas of Tokyo, Osaka, Nagoya and Kobe. The largest cities are Tokyo, the capital (11.8 million); Yokohama (3.3 million), Osaka (2.5 million), Nagoya (2.1 million); Sapporo (1.7 million); Kobe (1.5 million) and Kyoto (1.5 million). There are twelve other cities with over 500,000 inhabitants.

RURAL LIFE

Japan is a mountainous land, and only 13 per cent of it is cultivated. The farming population numbers about 20 million, living on some five million farms. The main crop is rice, of which 13 million tons are produced a year. Other crops include tea, tobacco, potatoes and wheat. Forests account for 67 per cent of the land area. The other major primary industry is fishing, with a catch of 12 million tons a year. Japan has the world's most lucrative fishing fleet.

LABOUR FORCE

The labour force numbers 64 million, or 63 per cent of the population aged 15 and over. The distribution is eight per cent in agriculture, 23.6 per cent in manufacturing, 22.2 per cent in trade, and 25.9 per cent in services. A severe shortage of workers developed during the late 1980s, but the slowdown of more recent times, which has resulted in Japanese companies no longer guaranteeing employees a job for life, has changed the situation somewhat. Large companies have an increasing demand for university graduates.

RELIGION, SPORT AND CULTURE

Shintoism, the worship of nature and ancestors, is the traditional Japanese faith. It is not really a religion in the Western sense, though, and most Japanese consider themselves to be adherents of both Shinto and Buddhism. All religions are tolerated; and Christianity is actively practised, but by just one per cent of the population. Festivals, many of them with a religious basis, are an important part of Japanese culture and daily life.

Most western sports are represented, including athletics, soccer, rugby, baseball, and skiing, with tennis and golf being the most popular as well as the most expensive in which to participate. The traditional Japanese sports are *sumo* (wrestling), *kendo* (fencing), *kyudo* (archery), as well as the more familiar martial arts of *judo, karate* and *aikido*.

Literature, theatre, art and music are heavily influenced by western traditions; but traditional Japanese forms are still alive – such as *noh* and *kabuki* drama, *bunraku* puppet theatre, *haiku* poetry, and music played on the *shakuhachi* (a bamboo flute), *koto* or *shamisen* (stringed instruments). Other major traditional art forms are flower arranging (*ikebana* or *kado*), the tea ceremony (*chanoyu*) and calligraphy (*shodo*).

FACTORS INFLUENCING EMPLOYMENT

IMMIGRATION

Britons and US citizens require no visa to enter Japan and can stay as tourists for up to six months (UK) or three months (US citizens). It may be possible to extend a tourist visa by applying to one of the immigration offices at least ten days before its expiry.

Japanese embassies do not issue work permits. When you have obtained a job, your employer will go to the local immigration bureau in Japan to apply for a 'certificate of eligibility', which is in effect a work permit. Once it has been processed, the original will be sent to the employee, who can then obtain a working visa from any local Japanese embassy or consulate. If you are already in Japan, your employer will have to go through the same procedure, and you will then have to make your application from outside Japan. The most popular places to apply from are Korea and Taiwan. The work visa has to be collected from the same place, but it is possible to return to Japan while waiting for your papers to be processed.

Because of the need for unskilled labour and a total ban on immigration, the Japanese authorities tend to tolerate a small number of illegal workers – most of them come from poorer Asian countries. However, the penalties for working illegally are severe for the employer and for the worker, who is certain to be deported. The Japanese police do not spend a great deal of time looking for illegal western workers, but one has to bear in mind the possibility of being exploited by unscrupulous employers. Since 2001 the governments of Japan and the United Kingdom have entered into a Working Holiday visa agreement. The scheme makes it possible for citizens of one country to enter the other primarily for a holiday over an extended period and to be able to take work incidental to their holiday in order to supplement their travel funds. This type of visa is also available to Australian, Canadian, French, German, and New Zealand nationals. In 2003, the government introduced the Volunteer Visa Scheme which allows British citizens to undertake voluntary work for a registered charitable organisation in Japan for up to one year. For information in the UK on visas and work permits, contact the *Japanese Embassy*, 101-104 Piccadilly, London W1J 7JT; ☎020-7465 6500; fax 020-7491 9348; www.uk.emb-japan.go.jp. General information about Japan is available from the *Japanese Information and Cultural Centre* at the same address.

LANGUAGE

Japanese syntax bears no resemblance to that of European languages, but the phonology (sound system) is not as difficult to master as it might at first appear, and there is no hierarchy of tones as in Chinese. The writing system has borrowed essentials from China, but uses far fewer symbols. Although most Japanese have studied English at school very few can speak it beyond an elementary level. The Japanese way of teaching English concentrates on grammar and writing rather than on speaking.

COST AND STANDARD OF LIVING

The cost of living, reportedly, is not as high as suggested in the West. It is not that different to the UK because of the much reduced value of the yen coupled with the high value of the pound but Americans will find it more expensive The major item of expenditure is likely to be on rent. A tiny unfurnished flat in a city is likely to cost at least ¥65,000 (£3,200/$5,855) per month. Food can be expensive. Public transport is relatively cheap. Looking for work can take time, and it would be unwise to go to Japan without a healthy wad of Yen to get by on. Due to the high living costs it may take some time before you can begin to save money once you have found work – the usual estimate is that working in Japan only starts to become worthwhile from a financial point of view after about six months.

HOUSING AND ACCOMMODATION

For newcomers, home ownership in a Japanese city is a virtual impossibility because of astronomical prices and the impossibility of arranging home loans. Rented accommodation is available, but very expensive. Heavy deposits (non-returnable) are almost always paid when moving into rented accommodation, and an agreed percentage is returned to you when you move out. As contracts are for a limited duration, a deposit will have to be paid every few years. This is known as 'key money' and you should budget four to six months rent as establishment costs. Unless you speak fluent Japanese, you will need to take a Japanese friend or interpreter along with you when meeting the landlord. Employers may help with finding accommodation, and some have apartment blocks solely for their employees, but otherwise estate agents' windows (*fudosan*) are the best place to look.

In big cities, many foreigners stay in *Gaijin Houses* (some of which advertise in the *Tokyo Journal, Kansai Time-Out*). While the cost may be reasonable (£20 a night) living conditions can be basic. They tend to get extremely full during the summer.

HEALTH AND WELFARE

Japan's social security system has made great progress since the war. The Social Insurance Act of 1961 laid down programmes for health insurance, pension insurance, unemployment insurance and industrial accident insurance. Resident aliens are required to enrol with the local health insurance office (*kokuho*), unless they are covered by some other insurance scheme. Medical expenses tend to be high, but facilities are very good in the cities. You will still have to pay a percentage of your treatment costs, depending on the scheme.

EDUCATION

Education is free and compulsory between the ages of six and 15, but 95 per cent of pupils stay on after the age of 15. Education is divided into five basic stages – kindergarten (up to the age of six), elementary school (for six years); junior high school (for three years); and senior high school. There are several technical colleges offering courses lasting up to four years. Japan has nine major universities – seven State-run (Tokyo, Kyoto, Sapporo, Sendai, Osaka, Kyushu and Nagoya), and two private (Keio and Waseda). Competition to enter prestigious universities is intense and often requires several attempts and a period in a *juku* or crammer.

NATIONAL SERVICE

In accordance with post-war treaties with the USA, Japan has been allowed to build up a self-defence force, which numbers around 250,000. Enlistment is purely voluntary, so aliens are not liable to conscription.

EMBASSIES AND CONSULATES

British Embassy, No 1, Ichiban-cho, Chiyoda-ku, Tokyo 102-8381; ☎3-5211 1100; fax 3-5275 3164; e-mail embassy.tokyo@fco.gov.uk; www.uknow.or.jp. There are consulates in Sapporo, Hiroshima, Nagoya and Osaka.

US Embassy, 1-10-5 Akasaka, Minato-ku, Tokyo 107-8420; ☎3-3224 5000; fax 3-3505-1862; http://tokyo.usembassy.gov/.

There are consulates in Fukuoka, Nagoya, Okinawa, Osaka, and Sapporo.

TOURIST OFFICES

Japan National Tourist Organisation, Heathcoat House, 20 Savile Row, London W1S
3PR; ☎020-7734 9638; www.seejapan.co.uk.
Japan National Tourist Organisation, One Rockefeller Plaza, Suite 1250, New York, NY
10020; ☎212-757 5640; fax 212-307 6754; e-mail visitjapan@jntonyc.org; www.jnto.
go.jp/eng/.

CONDITIONS OF WORK

WAGES

There is little legislative control over wages, which nevertheless manage to keep up
with the retail price index. The pattern of Japanese wage levels contains some unique
features, such as the generous fringe benefits, which amount to an average of 20 per
cent of a worker's actual wage. Regular bonuses at six-monthly intervals can boost
salary by a further 25 per cent. Salary scales rise steeply with age and seniority, and
skilled and qualified workers are highly paid, although wage differentials within
companies are not so great as in Britain or the United States. Unskilled work is,
however, not well paid.

HOURS

Since 1960, when the average working week was 44.7 hours, the five-day, 40-hour
week has been slowly phased in. Most industries and offices now open only five
days a week, and the average working week is already below 40 hours, in theory.
In practice, custom and company loyalty mean that many workers routinely put in a
60-hour week.

HOLIDAYS

As with wages, the allocation of annual paid holidays is often based on length of
service; but two weeks is usually the minimum period given. Very few Japanese will
take even the holidays allocated to them. Britons may find the length of holidays in a
Japanese company far too short. The following national public holidays are observed:
New Year's Day; Coming of Age Day (15 January); National Foundation Day (11
February); Spring Equinox (21 March); Greenery Day (29 April); Constitution
Memorial Day (3 May); Children's Day (5 May); Respect for the Aged Day (15
September); Autumnal Equinox (23 September); Health Sports Day (10 October);
Culture Day (3 November); Labour Thanksgiving Day (November 23); Emperor's
Birthday (23 December).

SAFETY AND COMPENSATION

Worker's accident insurance is covered in the broad welfare programme. Enterprises
with more than five employees are all compulsorily insured, with contributions shared by
employers and employees. Smaller enterprises are required to provide their own insurance
cover, with contributions paid entirely by the employers.

TRADE UNIONS

National unions are virtually unknown in Japan. The union structure is based on
individual enterprises, rather than on trades or professions. About 16 million workers
(about 25 per cent of the labour force) belong to unions. The main function of unions
is to take part in the annual collective bargaining negotiations held each spring, the so-
called 'spring offensive'.

TAXATION

Tax is deducted at source and, if necessary, adjusted at the end of the tax year. Basic taxes are very low – six to nine per cent – and include social security payments. Workers pay health insurance on an individual basis. Japanese citizens have to pay at least 10 per cent of their income in local municipal taxes, but unless you intend to stay in Japan for more than a year, you will probably not have to pay these.

EMPLOYMENT PROSPECTS

Looking for work in Japan from abroad can be a difficult process and the Japanese embassy does not offer help. Of course it is possible, however, to apply directly to companies and schools.

Work is easier to find once you are in Japan, and much recruitment activity (and business life in general) is based on personal links. Employment agencies are springing up, but on the whole the best method for seeking work is to read the English-language newspapers, or contact companies or schools in person or by telephone. In larger cities, *Gaijin Houses* have notice boards with advertisements, and they are often willing to allow you to use their phone number as a point of contact.

Given the international nature of Japanese business, there are opportunities for managerial, technical and professional staff as well as openings in the fields of finance and banking, among others. Japanese companies and international firms operating in Japan are increasingly willing to take on foreigners as regular employees, as long as they can speak the language, or are willing to learn how to do so.

There is also a lot of scope for editorial and translation work where English, other European and some Middle Eastern languages can all be useful to varying degrees. Advertising agencies, together with publishers of newspapers, magazines and books, require proofreaders, editors and so on. A specialist knowledge of legal or technical terminology, along with a high level of linguistic knowledge in one's own language are always useful assets.

Non-teaching jobs tend to be scarce outside the big cities and you may need to do some teaching while looking around. Teaching business people and others privately can be a possible source of useful contacts for other work.

NEWSPAPERS

Japanese language newspapers are not an especially good source of job vacancies, due to the Japanese custom of recruiting directly from high schools and colleges. If you have a command of written Japanese, it may, however, be worth consulting the *Asahi Shimbun, Yomiuri Shimbun, Mainichi Shimbun*, and the *Nihon Keizai Shimbun*, all of which carry some job advertisements. English language newspapers in Japan, on the other hand, are probably one of the best ways for English speakers to find employment. Most foreign companies seeking staff with competence in English will advertise in these publications, as do English language schools seeking teachers. The *Japan Times* is the best established of these newspapers and carries an excellent employment section in its Monday edition. It also has a website at www.japantimes.co.jp which includes its employment classifieds. The other major English language newspapers are the *Daily Yomiuri* and the *Mainichi Daily News*. Regionally, *Kansai Time Out* also has an employment section which can be viewed on its website at www.kto.co.jp.

If you can read Japanese you can also try the leading employment listings magazines sold on the newsstands called *Recruit Book, B-ing* and *Travaille*. The same company also runs a website called Recruit Navi (www.recruitnavi.com).

SPECIFIC CONTACTS

RECRUITMENT COMPANIES

Cannon Persona, 12 Nicholas Lane, London EC4N 7BN; ☎020-7621 0055; fax: 020-7621 1001; e-mail info@cpir.com ; www.cpir.com. UK based recruitment company specialising in working with European companies operating in Japan.

Alex Tsukada International Ltd., Rm 1309 Aoyama Bldg., 2-3 Kita Aoyama, Minato-ku, Tokyo 107, ☎03-3478 5477, fax +81 3-3408 6753.

East West Consulting, Chichibuya Bld., 7-4 Koji-machi 3-chome, Chiyoda-ku, Tokyo 102; ☎03-3222 5531; fax 03-3222 5535, e-mail eastwest@ewc.co.jp; www.ewc.co.jp.

Egon Zehnder International Co Ltd, 3rd Fl., Marunouchi Mitsui Bldg., 2-2 Marunouchi 2-chome, Chiyoda-ku, Tokyo 100; ☎03-5219 0450; fax 03-52190451; www.zehnder.com.

Ingenium Group, Plaza 246 Bldg., 3F, 3-1-1 Minami Aoyma, Minato-ku, Tokyo 107, ☎03-5775 1953; fax 03-5775-1952, e-mail clients@ingeniumgroup.com; www.ingeniumgroup.com.

Korn/Ferry International Japan, 18th Fl., Shin Nikko Bldg. East, 10-1 Toranomon 2-chome, Minato-ku, Tokyo 105; ☎03-3560 1400; fax 03-3560 1460; www.kornferry.com.

tmp.worldwide, 4F, Joire Hanzomon, 2-19, Hayabusa-cho, Chiyoda-ku, Tokyo 102, tel 03-3511 5668; fax 03-3511 5670; e-mail jpresume@tmp.com; www.jp.tmp.com.

Tokyo Executive Search Company Limited, 6th floor, Blancho HY Building, 11-5 Niban-cho, Chiyoda-Ku, Tokyo 102; ☎03-3230 1881; fax 03-3230 2860; e-mail info@tesco.co.jp; www.tesco.co.jp.

USEFUL WEBSITES

Escape Artist Japan, www.escapeartist.com/japan/japan.htm

Gaijinpot: jobs in Japan, www.gaijinpot. Comprehensive and searchable listings for jobs in business, entertainment, IT, media and education.

Jobs In Japan, www.jobsinjapan.com. Listings on bilingual, teaching, IT, modelling jobs etc.

Japan Jobs Guide, www.japanjobsguide. Very useful portal and directory of job-finding links, plus a search engine.

Tokyo Connections, www.tokyoconnections.com. Masses of listings, links and opportunities.

Career Cross Japan, www.careercrossjapan. Bilingual online recruitment.

Japanese Jobs, www.japanesejobs.com. Job opportunities in Japan for bilingual applicants.

Planet Recruit, www.planetrecruit.com, Searchable database of international opportunities in IT, Engineering and management, including Japan.

Asia Net, www.asia-net.com. Job opportunities in Japan for bilingual applicants.

Career Builder, www.careerbuilder.com. Seachable international database divided into professional categories.

Cannon Persona International Recruitment, www.cpir.com. UK-based Japanese recruitment agency; includes executive and IT jobs in Japan.

Access Japan, www.accesstech.com. A leading IT recruitment firm.

Jforce, www.jforcegroup.com. Computer software and IT jobs in Japan.

International Computer Professionals Association, www.icpa.com. IT, marketing, and finance recruitment for multinational companies operating in Asia and the US Pacific Coast.

Hall Kinion International, www.tkointl.com. High-tech career opportunities in Japan.

Yamasa, ww.yamasa.org/internships. Comprehensive resource for finding internships in Japan.

ENGLISH TEACHING

Teaching English is probably the most obvious type of full-time work to be found in Japan. There is a great demand for English teachers in universities, colleges and language schools, and in government departments and big businesses. Britons and Americans are at a slight disadvantage in seeking part-time or full-time work, as Canadians, Australians and New Zealanders aged 18-30 can use the 'working holiday scheme' which allows them to work in Japan for up to a year without a work permit. A further consideration is the fact that Japan has recently been flooded with highly qualified American English teachers, and it is now becoming difficult to find a good job without a Masters Degree in a relevant subject. It is therefore advisable to arrange a job before going out to Japan. If you find a job while in the country it is very helpful to carry your degree certificate with you as it is impossible to arrange a work permit without one. Note that you will need the *original*, copies will not be accepted by the immigration office.

There are over 500 English schools in Tokyo alone and thousands more in the rest of Japan. Some of the bigger schools have representatives abroad, who recruit teachers, but the majority do not. Those that do may pay less than the going rate. If you are looking for work on the spot while in Japan, the crucial point to remember is that you will need a sponsor in order to obtain a permit, which will only be granted if a school can offer a full-time contract.

For those looking for work once in Japan, most hiring is done in March and September. The school and university year begins in April, and other terms start in September and January. There are a limited number of openings in Japanese high schools as teachers' assistants (see the JET programme below), but these are highly sought after (as are the vacancies at Japanese universities and colleges) because of the high salaries and generous holidays offered.

Teaching can be very well paid – the basic monthly salary is about ¥220,000 to ¥320,000 per month. However, with the Yen weakened against the Pound, it is considerably less profitable than it was just a few years ago. Salaried teaching in a language school tends to bring in less money than freelance work but will usually involve less travel around town and most schools will pay for your season ticket. Teachers' pay varies, depending on the quality of the school and its staff. Private lessons are usually very lucrative (up to ¥6000 per hour), especially if you teach small groups of students who each contribute to the cost. The most effective way to make money is to organise a small school in your home, if you have enough space. It is possible to advertise by distributing leaflets in blocks of flats, but a more effective approach is to get to know people and offer to teach them. If you ask around, you may be able to inherit some private students from someone who is leaving the country.

Besides the language schools, companies also organise private classes for businessmen. These may take place within the company building, or on school premises. Lessons are either very early in the morning or in the evening to fit around working hours. Lessons tend to focus on conversation more than grammar since Japanese students receive very thorough English grammar instruction during their time at school. Enthusiasm and a friendly personality are more of an asset than an in-depth knowledge of English grammar.

Each year, about 700 qualified graduates are recruited in Britain by the Japanese Government to work as teaching assistants in Japanese schools under its Japan Exchange and Teaching (JET) Programme. Positions are available in secondary schools, technical schools and local education authorities, and private companies. Contracts are for one year.

The Programme is open to British citizens under the age of 40 who hold a degree from a university or college of higher education. Teaching qualifications and experience are an advantage, but not essential. Contracts begin in July. For recruitment, the period of application is usually from October to mid-December. For more information and application forms contact the *Japanese Embassy,* 101-104 Piccadilly, London W1J 7JT; ☎020-7465 6500; fax 020-7491 9348; e-mail info@embjapan.org.uk; www.embjapan.org.uk.

A large number of American and Canadian citizens, and smaller numbers of Australians and New Zealanders, are also recruited each year. US applicants should contact their nearest Japanese Consulate or the *JET Program Office,* Embassy of Japan, 2520 Massachusetts Avenue, NW, Washington DC 20008; ☎202-238 6772/3; e-mail jet@embjapan.org; www.mofa.go.jp/j_info/visit/jet/index.html.

Teachers are also needed to teach the resident British and American children in Japan, for whom a number of special international schools exist. The ELT Group of the British Council is notified of vacancies in Japanese state schools. For information on direct recruitment by the *British Council* in Japan contact the ELT Group, British Council, 10 Spring Gardens, London SW1A 2BN; ☎020-7930 8466; fax 020-7389 6347; e-mail general.enquiries@britishcouncil.org; www.britishcouncil.org. Vacancies in Japan are also advertised in the British press. The minimum requirement is a Certificate (or preferably a Diploma) in teaching English as a foreign language (see the *Teaching* chapter). Also see the *Teaching* chapter for organisations which recruit for language schools in Japan.

Japan Association of Language Teachers, Nishi-Uru, Shio-Jo, Karasuma, Shimogyo-Ku, Kyoto 600, Japan; ☎075-221-2376. Provides information on jobs to teachers with a TESL or similar teaching qualification.

AEON Inter-Cultural U.S.A, .1960 East Grand Avenue, #550 El Segundo, CA 90245, U.S.A.; ☎310-414-1515; fax 310-414-1616; email aeonla@aeonet.com; www.aeonet. com; AEON Japan, Shinjuku I-Land Tower Bldg. 12F, 6-5-1 Nishishinjuku, Shinjuku-ku, Tokyo 163, Japan; ☎03-5381 1500; fax 03-5381 1501; e-mail aeonetrec@corp. aeonet.co.jp. One of the largest chains of English conversation schools in Japan with 200 branches.

America Eigo Gakuin (American English Institute), USA Office: PO Box 1672, St George, UT 84771; ☎435-628 6301, e-mail rpurcell@infowest.com. Japan Office: 5-2-21 Misono-cho, Wakayama 640, ☎734-360581. 30 schools, mostly in rural areas.

ECC Foreign Language Institute, Osaka Office, ☎06-6636-0334. Tokyo Office, ☎03-5330 1585. Nagoya Office, ☎052-332 6156; www.ecc.co.jp. Over 120 schools.

GEOS Corporation, apply online at www.geoscareer.com or call the office in London ☎020-7397 8401 or in Toronto ☎416-777-0109.

Interac Co. Ltd., Fujibo Bldg. 2F, 2-10-28 Fujimi, Chiyoda-ku, Tokyo 102, ☎03-3234 7857, fax 03-3234 6055; e-mail recruit@interac.co.jp; www.interac.co.jp. Ten branches with over 250 teachers.

James English School, HQ 4-16-6, Teraoka, Izumi, Sendai 980, ☎022-772-0161; e-mail JesLiason@aol.com; www.jesjapan.com. 17 branches in northern Japan.

Nova Group, Carrington House, 126/130 Regent Street, London W1R 5FE, ☎020-7734 2727, fax 020-7734 3001, e-mail tefl@novagroup.demon.co.uk, website www. teachinjapan.com. Over 3,000 teachers in 300 schools throughout Japan.

Shane English School, c/- Saxoncourt Recruitment, 124 New Bond Street, London W1S 1DX, ☎020-7491 1911, fax 020-7493 3657. 100 schools in Tokyo area.

Useful Websites

TEFL.com, www.tefl.com. Giant database of English teaching jobs and many other resources.

ELT News, www.eltnews.com/jobs. The website for English teachers in Japan lists job openings.

English Job Maze, www.englishjobmaze.com. Guide to teaching English around the world with information on issues such as salaries and tax.

O-hayo Sensei, www.ohayosensei.com. Specialist TEFL site, including jobs in Japan.~

Safe Jobs in Japan, www.safejobsinjapan.com. Informative TEFL website, including jobs bulletin board for teaching in Japan.

ESL Job Centre, www.edunet.com/jobs/index.html. A general English language teaching job website with many jobs in Japan.

AEON – Teaching English in Japan, www.aeonet.com. Very comprehensive site, with jobs listings and other information.

Dave's ESL Café, www.eslcafe.com. Well-known site for EFL teachers and students around the world. Extensive information on all aspects of teaching English.

SHORT TERM WORK

The high cost of travelling to Japan prevents most from looking for temporary work there. Even if a job can be found beforehand, it might easily take two months for a work permit application to be processed. Once you are in Japan, however, it is quite easy to pick up casual part-time employment. The most popular jobs for Westerners are as models, movie extras, waiters/waitresses, hosts/hostesses, and translating and editing work. Hostessing involves chatting to and dancing with Japanese businessmen, whose English tends to be limited. Acting can be an attractive prospect, but does not pay well. Radio and television networks employ foreigners to help with language programmes. There are about 150 broadcasting companies in Japan, the most important being the *Nippon Television Network* (NTV), the *Tokyo Broadcasting System* (TBS) and *TV Asahi. Nippon Hoso Kyoukai* (NHK) is the only state network. Westerners with fluent Japanese who can speak entertainingly are in great demand for television chat shows, but few fall into this category.

There is no call for au pairs in Japan, as it is still unusual for Japanese women to work once they have a family. Some European families, such as diplomatic staff, make informal arrangements with young women from their home countries to do this type of work. Pocket money may be wholly inadequate as far as paying for leisure activities in Japan goes.

INTERNATIONAL COMPANIES IN JAPAN

The *British Chamber of Commerce in Japan*, 3F Kenkynsha Eigo Centre Building, 1-2 Kagurazaka Shinjuku-ku, Tokyo 162-0825; ☎3-3267 1901; fax 3-3267 1903; e-mail info@bccj.jp; www.uknow.or.jp, produces a list of members. The *Japanese Chamber of Commerce and Industry in the UK* is at Salisbury House, 29 Finsbury Circus, London EC2M 5QQ; ☎020-7628 0069.

The *American Chamber of Commerce in Japan (ACCJ)*, Masonic 39 Mori Building 10F, 2-4-5 Azabudai, Minato-ku, Tokyo 106-0041; ☎3-3433 5381; fax 33-3433 8454; www.accj. or.jp, publishes a directory of members and has a number of publications on living and working in Japan. The ACCJ also provides a résumé listing service for job hunters. Many ACCJ companies hire staff through this service.

Singapore

- Singapore High Commission, 9 Wilton Crescent, Belgravia, London SW1X 8SP; ☎ 020-7235 8315; fax 020-7245 6583; www.mfa.gov.sg/london/
- Singapore Embassy, 3501 International Place, Washington DC 20008; ☎ 202-537 3100; fax 202-537 0876; www.mfa.gov.sg/washington/
- Currency: Singapore S$1 = 100 cents
- Rate of Exchange: £1 = S$2.94; US$1 = S$1.58; €1 = S$2.01
- Country Code: +65

Singapore's economy has expanded rapidly in recent decades, and now rivals that of Japan in terms of efficiency. The Singapore government actively encourages the recruitment of highly skilled workers from English-speaking countries through various special employment and residence schemes to relieve the local labour shortage.

GENERAL FACTS

Singapore's territory consists of the island of Singapore, at the tip of the Malay Peninsula, and 57 islets inside its territorial waters. Singapore's total land area is about 247,644 square miles (641.4 square kilometres), 90 per cent of which is occupied by the main island. Half of the land is built-up, with a further 3.3 per cent farmland, and some five per cent of forest. The island can be divided into three regions: the central hilly region, the relatively flat eastern region, and the western area of hills and valleys.

Singapore has a fairly uniform temperature, high humidity and abundant rainfall. The average daily temperature is 80 deg F (26.7 deg C).

The population of around 4 million is made up of 76.3 per cent Chinese, 15 per cent Malay, 6.4 per cent Indians and 2.3 per cent from other ethnic groups. Fifty-five per cent of the population is under 30.

The main faiths of the Singaporeans are Buddhism, Christianity, Islam, Taoism and Hinduism. The official languages are Malay, Chinese (Mandarin), Tamil and English. Malay is the national language; English the language of administration.

Singapore was acquired for Britain in 1819 by Sir Stamford Raffles. It was accorded British Crown Colony status after the Second World War and was declared an independent Republic in December 1965. It has been ruled by the People's Action Party since 1959 as a virtual one-party state. All foreign publications, cassettes, films, and now the internet, are subject to censorship. There are also draconian laws against any form of anti-social behaviour (up to S$1,000 fine for littering), with the result that this is one of the cleanest and safest cities in Asia. Drug traffickers are commonly sentenced to death.

FACTORS INFLUENCING EMPLOYMENT

American and British citizens may remain in Singapore for up to 90 days without a visa. Aliens who come to Singapore on Social Visit Passes (as tourists) may take up work there provided they first obtain either a Work Permit issued by the Ministry of Manpower, or an Employment Pass or Professional Visit Pass issued by the Immigration Department. An Employment Pass is issued to any foreign worker with a sponsoring employer and who is not a permanent resident and who holds a university degree or has a basic salary of more than S$2,000 per month. Employment Passes are usually valid for a three-year period.

Useful information about all aspects of working in Singapore is available from Contact Singapore (www.contactsingapore.org.sg).

Employment Pass holders who wish to reside permanently in Singapore may apply for an Entry Permit. There are a number of schemes whereby foreigners can obtain permanent resident status (Entry Permit). Under the Professional/Technical Personnel and Skilled Workers Scheme, any person working in Singapore who is below 50 years of age, and who has professional, specialist or technical skills enabling him or her to pursue a trade or profession in Singapore, may apply for permanent residence.

TRADE UNIONS

There are numerous employee trade unions, a few employer unions and a federation of employee trade unions – the National Trades Union Congress (NTUC).

EMBASSIES

British High Commission, 100 Tanglin Road, Singapore 247919; ☎6424 4200; fax 6424 4264; e-mail commercial.singapore@fco.gov.uk; www.britain.org.sg.

US Embassy, 27 Napier Road, Singapore 258508; ☎6476 9100; fax 6476 9340; http://singapore.usembassy.gov.

TOURIST OFFICES

Singapore Tourism Board, 1st Floor, Carrington House, 126-130 Regent Street, London W1B 5JX; ☎020-7437 0033; fax 020-7734 2191; e-mail info@stb.org.uk; www.visitsingapore.com.

Singapore Tourism, 1156 Avenue of the Americas, Suite 702, New York, NY 10036; ☎212-302 4861; fax 212-302 4801; e-mail newyork@stb.gov.sg; www.visitingsingapore.com.

EMPLOYMENT PROSPECTS

Singapore's economy has progressively diversified over the years. Singapore has the fifth highest per capita GDP in the world and is positioning itself as the region's financial and high-tech hub. Trade and manufacturing (especially electronics) are the traditional mainstays of the economy. Financial and business services also play an increasingly important role in Singapore's prosperity. High-tech industries are expanding rapidly, while much basic manufacturing is being transferred to the neighbouring countries of Malaysia and Indonesia.

NEWSPAPERS

Advertisements can be placed direct in the English language paper, *The Straits Times*, 390 Kim Seng Road, Singapore 0923; www.asia1.com.sg/straitstimes.

SPECIFIC CONTACTS

EMPLOYMENT SERVICE

The Ministry of Manpower (18 Havelock Road, Singapore 059764) runs an online employment service at https://pes.wda.gov.sg/jbs, to assist employers to securing workers and to help jobseekers obtain work. Further useful information is available from the Ministry of Manpower website: www.mom.gov.sg.

EMPLOYMENT AGENCIES

Worldwide recruitment agencies, such as *Ecco* and *Drake International* also have branches in Singapore, as do most major players in the finance and IT sectors.

Adecco, 10 Anson Road, #35-14 International Plaza, Singapore 079903; ☎6227 7882; fax 6227 7712l; www.adecco-asia.com. Temping agency.

JAC Property & Employment Pte. Ltd., 14-10 Hong Leong Centre, 138 Robinson Road, Singapore 0104; ☎2246864 – recruits qualified management, marketing and financial personnel.

Technilink Manpower Services Pte Ltd., 20 Raffles Pl #09-01 Ocean Towers, Singapore 048620; ☎635 8 4336 – can place experienced and qualified personnel in industry, design, construction, petrochemicals.

Jobsite Singapore, www.jobsite.com.sg. Popular Singapore-based recruitment website.

TEACHING

Qualified and experienced teachers (of all levels) are in demand in Singapore, mainly for expatriate schools and in higher education. Agencies in the UK which can help find work in Singapore can be found in the *Teaching* chapter.

The Recruitment Unit of the *Ministry of Education* in Singapore (1 North Buona Vista Drive, Singapore 138675; ☎6872 1110) is responsible for recruiting teachers of English on two-year contracts in secondary schools. Candidates must have a degree in English and relevant teaching qualifications; no prior experience is necessary.

The *British Council* (Napier Road Centre, 30 Napier Road, Singapore 258509; ☎6473 1111; fax 6472 1010; e-mail enquiries@britishcouncil.org.sg; www.britishcouncil.org.sg) has a teaching operation which hires qualified teachers locally and can also provide a list of 72 language schools. The schools recruit a high proportion of Australian teachers.

USEFUL CONTACTS

The Singapore *Economic Development Board,* 250 North Bridge Road #28-00, Raffles City Tower, Singapore 179101; ☎6832 6832; fax 6832 6565; www.edb.gov.sg, can be approached direct for information about job opportunities and have a good website.

INTERNATIONAL COMPANIES IN SINGAPORE

Kompass South East Asia Ltd, 36 Robinson Road, #19-01 City House, Singapore 068877; ☎6827 8750; fax 6827 8751; www.kompass.com.sg, publishes the *Directory of British Business in Singapore*. The *Singapore International Chamber of Commerce*, 10-001 John Hancock Tower, 6 Raffles Quay, Singapore 048580; ☎62241255; www.sicc.com.sg, may also be contacted for commercial information.

South Korea

- Embassy of the Republic of Korea, 60 Buckingham Gate, London SW1E 6AJ; ☎ 020-7227 5500; fax 020-7227 5503; www.koreanembassy.org.uk
- Embassy of Korea (Consular Section), 2320 Massachusetts Avenue, NW, Washington DC 20008; ☎ 202-939 5653; fax 202-342 1597; www.dynamic-korea. com
- Currency: Won (KRW)
- Rate of Exchange: £1 = 1,781 Won; $1 = 955 Won; €1 = 1,218 Won
- Country Code: +82

Korea is a country split into two. It was a Japanese colony from 1910 until 1945, which was later divided between Soviet and American zones of occupation. The communist North's attempt to conquer the South in 1950 was halted by United Nations intervention; after which the country was partitioned. The economy of the North today is on the verge of collapse and remains one of the last outposts of the communist world. South Korea became a free market and, in recent years, a democratic country. Its economy grew at a remarkable rate from the 1950s, but had started to run into difficulties by the late 1980s. High inflation rates, a problem of overstaffing, and high labour costs are all clouds on the horizon of Korea's new-found prosperity. These factors play against South Korea in competing with some of the more stable Asian economies. South Korea's GDP per capita is seven times that of India, 16 times North Korea's, and comparable to the lesser economies of the European Union.

In 1988, Korea successfully hosted the Olympic Games and in 2002 co-hosted (with Japan) the FIFA World cup. These events, together with the establishment of democracy (President Roh Tae Woo was elected through direct elections in December 1987), have focused world attention on the country. At the time of writing, the problem of reunification with North Korea is no closer to resolution, however, and the integration of Korea with its northern neighbour continues to dominate political discussion.

Korea's unique culture is relatively unknown to outsiders, and is well worth discovering. In spite of the tragic history of their country, Koreans are generally friendly and helpful towards foreigners. The main stumbling block is language – English is not widely understood outside the capital, Seoul.

GENERAL FACTS

The Republic of Korea (South Korea) has a population of roughly 48.8 million people, some 27 per cent of whom are under 15. The country has a population density of 1,143 people per square mile; 75 per cent live in urban areas, the largest of which is the capital Seoul, with 11 million inhabitants, followed by Pusan with 3.9 million, and Taegu with 2.3 million.

The Republic covers a land area of 38,211 square miles (98,966 sq km) and is mostly mountainous, with a rugged east coast. The climate is extreme with long, cold winters and a short, very hot and humid summer.

The main language and ethnic group is Korean. The major faiths are Buddhism, Confucianism, Christianity (mainly reformed) and the indigenous Korean religions of Wonbulgyo and Chondokyo.

FACTORS INFLUENCING EMPLOYMENT

IMMIGRATION

American citizens may visit Korea for up to 30 days without a visa, provided they have confirmed return tickets. For longer stays a visa is required. British, Canadian and Irish citizens do not require visas to enter Korea as tourists or for business purposes, and may remain for up to 90 days. The length of your intended stay should be made clear to the immigration authorities on arrival, otherwise you will only receive a 30-day transit visa. Any foreigner who wishes to stay for more than 60 days for whatever purpose is required to apply for a residence certificate at the District Immigration Office in Korea (addresses available from Korean embassies).

Any alien wishing to work in Korea must have a definite job offer before applying for a work permit. Applications should be addressed to the Korean Embassy (see above).

EMBASSIES AND CONSULATES

British Embassy, Taepyeongno 40, 4 Jeong-dong, Jung-gu, Seoul 100-120; ☎2-3210 5500; fax 2-725 1738; e-mail bembassy@britain.or.uk; www.britishembassy.or.kr.
US Embassy, 32 Sejong-no, Jongno-gu, Seoul 110-710; ☎2-397 4114; http://seoul. usembassy.gov/.

TRADE UNIONS

Trade union activity is strictly controlled by the Government. Regional union organisation is banned, strikes are almost impossible and unions are only allowed to operate individually on a single company basis.

EMPLOYMENT PROSPECTS

Korea's major industries are textiles, electronics, shipbuilding and motor manufacture. The agrarian sector is very important, with 22 per cent of the land under permanent cultivation. The main crops are rice, barley and vegetables (especially cabbages and garlic).

What concerns the economic planners at the moment is diversification in Korea's export-orientated economy. This requires the exploration and opening-up of more European markets (in particular those of Eastern Europe) and the introduction of more foreign technology, to move the Republic towards a position where it is as much a supplier of parts as of finished products.

Korean industry is dominated by huge, family-owned corporations, known as *chaebol*, some of which are now household names in the West, for example, Daewoo, Hyundai and Samsung. Prospects for foreign workers are not especially good, since Korean workers are well educated and very few foreigners can speak Korean. In addition, wages are considerably lower than in Japan or the West.

NEWSPAPERS

The two English language daily papers take advertisements direct. These are: *The Korea Herald*, 1-12, 3-ga, Hoehyon-dong, Jung-gu, Seoul; ☎2-7270205, (www.koreaherald. co.kr) and *The Korea Times* (http://times.hankooki.com). Advertisements are also handled by *Bel-Air*, Bel-Air House, 10 Gainsborough Road, Woodford Bridge, Woodford Green, Essex IG8 8EE.

SPECIFIC CONTACTS

The British Embassy in Seoul cannot assist those looking for employment in Korea, and suggests contacting the Korean Embassy. Lists of Korean firms trading abroad may be obtained from the *Korea Trade Centre*, 5th Floor, 39 St James's Street, London SW1A 1JD; ☎020-7491 8057; www.investkorea.org.

TEACHING

There is a considerable demand for English teachers in South Korea, mainly in Seoul and Pusan. Much of the teaching is done by travellers on tourist visas, who risk fines and deportation if caught. One possibility is to enter Korea on a tourist visa, find for a job, and then fly out to Japan while your work permit is being processed (this works the other way round, when looking for work in Japan). Full-time jobs are sometimes advertised in the UK press or through agencies (see *Teaching* chapter). Salaries are somewhat lower than in neighbouring Japan, but there is also less competition for jobs.

Both *ILC* in the UK, and *TESOL Placement Bulletin* in the US have openings in Korea from time to time. If you have good qualifications it is worth contacting a Korean university or college (there are more than 100) direct. Addresses can be obtained from a Korean embassy. For US citizens the US Embassy in Seoul can provide a comprehensive handout, *Teaching English in Korea: Opportunities and Pitfalls*. Some of the well-known language schools are:

ELS International/YBM , 649-1 Yeoksam-dong, Kangnam-gu, Seoul 135-081; ☎2-552 1492; e-mail teach@ybmsisa.co.kr; www.ybmhr.com/index.asp – offers one-year contracts with a competitive salary and return air fare. Interviews are held in the UK and USA. Contact the head office in Culver City, USA (see *Teaching* chapter).

Berlitz Korea, 3rd Floor, Kyungam Building, 157-27 Samsung-dong, Kangnam-gu, Seoul; ☎2-3453 4266; 2-3453 4733; e-mail study@berlitz.com.sg; www.berlitz.com.sg, employs between 30 and 50 teachers in two franchised schools in Seoul. American, Canadian, and British preferred for one-year contracts.

THE MIDDLE EAST
& NORTH AFRICA

In terms of the international jobs market, the oil-producing countries of the Middle East and North Africa occupy a position that is not unlike the now developed economies of East Asia. Sixty years ago, these regions were struggling economically and there were few opportunities for development. The discovery and exploitation of oil, and the price rises in this essential commodity instituted by OPEC in the 1970s, changed everything as revenues have been ploughed back into development, hospitals, universities and industry. Oil revenue has provided the money to pay wages that are still relatively high, and sometimes among the highest in the world, while taxes are generally low (and most expatriates earn tax-free salaries). A recent downturn in the price of oil has led, however, to a contraction in Middle East development and prospects are not at present as good as they have been in the past. Salaries are also relatively lower, and the region is not necessarily a financial goldmine for expatriates any longer. Countries are trying to broaden the base of their economy and to create more long-term industries. However, while there is still money available to invest in infrastructure like roads, airports, defence systems, irrigation and so on, there is still a time lag in the training of local personnel to fill labour needs, particularly in managerial and skilled positions. The demand for foreign workers in the Middle East is continuing, but there are fewer opportunities in the petrochemical and construction industries than previously.

The highest demand remains in the Gulf States. Past diplomatic incidents have limited contacts with Iran and Iraq, while Jordan continues to struggle with its own economic problems. Israel is dealing with an influx of new citizens from Russia, many of whom are highly qualified and experienced. The countries that belong to the Organisation of Petroleum Exporting Countries (OPEC), like Saudi Arabia, Bahrain, and the United Arab Emirates, are the traditional destinations for expatriate workers in the region.

The potential for political instability in the Middle East is one drawback to life in the region, although Gulf Arabs are hospitable and the Gulf is the most stable region in the Middle East. Some find the expat lifestyle enjoyable, despite the strict rules on alcohol and anti-social behaviour, and women, whether as employees or spouses, will have to cope with severe restrictions on their dress and activities. Some states are more liberal than others in this respect, although all ban alcohol and require the external observance of Ramadan (no eating in public before sundown). Gulf Arabs themselves may not all be as highly moral or pious as they appear, however, and there are many who live a less observant life behind closed doors (and even some who know how to smuggle in the odd bottle of whisky).

Conditions in the workplace – office buildings, hotels, and hospitals, tend to be up-to-date, with the latest technology widely available. Ways of working and doing business may be less modern, though, and foreign workers will have to get used to a more relaxed approach to getting things done. It is important to be careful when negotiating contractual terms and conditions. The Gulf States are outwardly modern and advanced societies, but they retain a deeply-rooted value system and this cosmopolitan appearance is often only surface deep. To understand these countries you will have to find some sympathy and understanding for their Islamic inheritance and traditional values. Foreign travel and the widespread use of English in business circles have done little to change more enduring attitudes to human relations that, as in every country, have positive and negative sides. Expats who are attracted by high wages and low or non-existent income taxes sometimes fail to consider this aspect of Middle Eastern life and are affected by boredom and loneliness. Some local customs (such as the 4am call to prayer) come as an unwelcome surprise; many others find they cannot get used to the climate, or to living under a rather controlling regime.

The main recruitment needs are for professional and technical staff, especially in engineering and medicine. The range of vacancies is wide: accountants, IT professionals, doctors, nurses, marketing professionals and conference managers, all types of engineers, technicians and fitters, and anyone with qualifications relating to the petrochemical or construction industries may be able to find work in the Middle East. Many contracts are offered for single men, especially on oilrigs, and the number of jobs open to women is correspondingly limited. In the Gulf States, men are often preferred to women – even in jobs that are dominated by females, such as nursing, back home.

Most contractors recruit for large-scale projects rather than for individual positions. International recruitment agencies, large companies and contract consortiums advertise in the national and international press or specialist magazines in the particular field of work. In many countries most expats are housed in compounds on or near work sites, which are in some ways isolated from the society in which they are based. They provide a support network, and often include medical facilities and a school, as well as entertainment or sports facilities, but may also contribute to a sense of isolation and boredom.

LANGUAGES

The languages of the Middle East all belong to the Semitic group (except for Persian and Turkish) and are therefore related to each other. Arabic is the most common, and is spoken in Saudi Arabia, the Gulf States, Syria, Iraq, Lebanon, Jordan and North Africa. Within this area there are major dialect variations in both the written and spoken language. The most noticeable dividing line is that between the Maghreb area (Morocco, Algeria, Tunisia and the western part of Libya) and countries to the east. The other major languages are Farsi (or Persian) and Hebrew (spoken only in Israel). A knowledge of the local language is useful, although most educated Arabs are bilingual in either English or French (or Italian in Libya).

CUSTOMS AND CULTURE

In the Arab world more than in most countries, expatriate western workers are forced to accept that they are outsiders (see above). While no one expects foreign workers to become Muslims, it is necessary not to offend against codes of social behaviour or dress.

Many Arab countries were European colonies in the past, and in these cases the tolerance of European lifestyles is greater. Lebanon, Jordan and Oman fall into this category. The greatest difficulties arise in Saudi Arabia and some of the Gulf States where Islamic laws are applied to foreigners and locals alike. Needless to say, it is essential to know what is acceptable and what is not. In general, consuming alcohol, intimacy with others, even if unmarried, and certainly same-sex relationships, or even aggression towards local people, can be grounds for imprisonment, deportation, or worse.

Cultural traditions rest on the Arabic language and its literature – in particular the Koran. Arab classical music and dance thrive in Egypt and are enjoyed everywhere. The previously lively cultural scene in Lebanon, with its large French-speaking Christian population, suffered greatly during the years of civil war, but is now in the process of reconstruction and a new flowering. As far as the Gulf States are concerned, freedom of expression is very limited, and all films, books and other media are subject to strict censorship.

Saudi Arabia

o   **Royal Saudi Arabian Embassy,** 30 Charles Street, Mayfair, London W1J 5DZ; ☎020-7917 3000; e-mail ukemb@mofa.gov.sa; www.saudiembassy.org.uk
o   **Royal Saudi Arabian Embassy,** 601 New Hampshire Avenue, NW, Washington DC 20037; ☎202-3374076; e-mail info@saudiembassy.net; www.saudiembassy.net
o   **Currency:** 1 Saudi Riyal (SRl) = 100 halalah
o   **Exchange rate:** £1 = SRls 7; $1 = SRls 3.75; €1 = SRls 4.79
o   **Country Code:** +966

There are a number of opportunities for citizens of English-speaking countries interested in professional, skilled and semi-skilled work in Saudi Arabia.

The USA and the UK are both traditionally seen as an ideal source of talented staff for recruitment to the Kingdom. English is the main language of commerce and professional qualifications from English-speaking countries are highly respected. The country has close historical ties with Britain, which helped it gain independence during World War I, and with the USA, on which it relies for military support.

Saudi Arabia's economic development began with the discovery of the first oilfield in Dammam in 1938. Initially, the Saudis had little control over the exploitation of their greatest natural resource, but with the formation of the Organisation of Petroleum Exporting Countries (OPEC) in 1973, and the consequent huge rises in the price of crude oil, the country began the process of turning itself into a modern, industrialised State. In addition to oil, Saudi Arabia has also started to mine and produce gold, silver and copper.

The ruling al-Saud family retains tight control over all affairs and steps towards a more open political regime are being taken only cautiously. The country is, however, relatively stable. The government has begun to permit private sector and foreign investor participation in the power generation and telecom sectors. As part of its effort to attract foreign investment and diversify the economy, Saudi Arabia acceded to the WTO in 2005. High oil revenues have enabled the government to substantially increase spending on job training, education and infrastructure development.

Foreigners seeking work in the Kingdom must first obtain a work permit, which has to be applied for by the employer or sponsor in the Saudi. When this has been obtained it is forwarded to the Saudi Arabian Embassy in your home country, who will then issue you with a visa. As soon as you arrive in Saudi Arabia you should register with your local embassy or consulate.

Riyadh is the royal capital of Saudi Arabia, and Jeddah the administrative capital. Both have populations slightly over 500,000.

EMPLOYMENT PROSPECTS

Saudi Arabia's continued development requires the presence of qualified and experienced foreign personnel, although government policy aims to reduce the requirement for large numbers of expatriates in the long term. As the mainstay of the Kingdom's national economy, oil accounts for some 70 per cent of Gross National Product and 90 per cent of its exports. These days about 50 per cent is exported in crude form, while the rest is refined or processed into other products.

Saudi Arabia has for a number of years been building up basic industries, including refining, steel and fertiliser plants. Most of this heavy industry is concentrated in Jubail, Jeddah and Yanbu. Other types of industry, such as the production of building materials, chemicals, cement, electrical equipment, rubber and plastics are also expanding. Great emphasis is also placed on developing agriculture, which now accounts for six per cent of GNP.

The job prospects for expats depend almost entirely on government spending on new projects. The greatest source of international employment is construction, which employs nearly 20 per cent of the entire Saudi workforce. One recent project has been the £10 billion Al-Yamamah airbase, which covers an area the size of London. Companies such as British Aerospace had as many as 4,000 workers on site during construction, and this is the general pattern in large infrastructure projects. Other areas where large contracts are currently being secured include road construction and drainage, school and office construction, hospitals, air-conditioning, telecommunications systems, and street networks and water reservoirs. Jobseekers should note that attacks on expats have increased over the last few years and this should be borne in mind when weighing up the pros and cons of taking a job in Saudi.

A useful list of current tenders is published in the *Middle East Economic Digest*, available on subscription from *MEED*, 151 Rosebery Avenue, London EC1R 4GB; ☎ 020-7505 6600; fax 020-7505 6969; www.meed.com. Other titles include *MEEDmoney, The Advertisers' Guide to the Middle East*, and the *Finance Guide to the Middle East*. The *British Embassy's* Commercial Department, PO Box 94351, Riyadh 11693; ☎ 1-488 0077, may be able to offer general advice on working opportunities in Saudi Arabia; and the *Council of Saudi Chambers of Commerce and Industry*, PO Box 16683 Riyadh 11474; ☎ 1-405 3200; fax 1-402 4747; e-mail council@saudichambers.org.sa, can offer commercial information and advice.

Saudi Arabian Information Resource, in the UK is at 18 Cavendish Square, London W1M 0AQ; ☎ 020-7629 8803; www.saudinf.com; and Nasseriya Street, Riyadh 11161; ☎ 1-401 4440; fax 1-402 3570; e-mail sair@saudinf.com.

EMBASSIES AND CONSULATES

British Embassy, Al Hamra, PO Box 94351, Riyadh 11693; ☎ 1-488 0077; www. britishhembassy.gov.uk/saudiarabia.
There is a consulate in Jeddah.

US Embassy, PO Box 94309, Collector Road M, Diplomatic Quarter, Riyadh 11693; ☎ 1-488 3800; http://riyadh.usembassy.gov/. There are consulates in Jeddah and Dhahran.

NEWSPAPERS

Advertisements may be placed in the English language daily, *Arab News*, SRP Building, Madinah Road, PO Box 10452, Jeddah 21433; ☎ 2-639 1888; fax 2-639 3223; e-mail arabnews@arabnews.com; www.arabnews.com. There is also a weekly English-language business magazine, *Saudi Economic Survey*, PO Box 1989 Jeddah; ☎ 2-651 4952; e-mail info@saudieconomicsurvey.com; www.saudieconomicsurvey.com.

SPECIFIC CONTACTS

CONSULTANTS AND AGENCIES

Many of the agencies mentioned in the *Getting the Job* chapter deal with posts in Saudi Arabia and other Middle Eastern countries. Agencies under *Computer Services* and *Oil, Mining and Engineering* are particularly likely to be involved in recruitment for the Middle East.

MEDICINE AND NURSING

There is always a demand for medical personnel in Saudi hospitals. The following recruitment agencies specialise in the region:

Arabian Careers Ltd., Berkeley Square House, 7th floor, Berkeley Square, London W1X 5LB; ☎020-7495 3285; fax 020-7355 2562; email recruiter@arabiancareers.com; www.arabiancareers.com. Wide range of medical and nursing appointments in the Middle East.

Business Aid Centre (BAC), PO Box 8743, Dubai, UAE; ☎4-337 5747; fax 4-337 6467; e-mail recruit@bacme.com; www.bacdubai.com. Medical and hospital administration personnel for the United Arab Emirates.

CCM Recruitment International, 258 Belsize Road, London NW6 4BT; ☎020-7316 1859; fax 020-7316 1895; www.ccmrecruitment.com. Specialises in the recruitment of Medical, Engineering, Teaching, Administration and IT professionals for the Middle East.

HCCA International, Mountainview House, 151 High Street, Southgate, London N14 6PQ; ☎020-8882 6363; fax 020-8882 5266; e-mail london@hccaintl.com;; and 103 Powell Court, Tennessee 37027; ☎615-255 7187; fax 615-255 7093; e-mail usa@hccaintl.com; www.hccaintl.com. International healthcare management and recruitment company specialising in the Middle East.

Bridgewater International Recruitment Direct, 109 Bodmin Road, Astley, Tyldesley, Manchester M29 7PE; ☎01942-873158; fax 01942-896946; e-mail birdrecruit@blueyonder.co.uk; www.bridgewaterinternational.co.uk, recruits healthcare personnel for in the Middle East.

OIL AND GAS ENGINEERING

Possibly the best opportunities lie in the hydrocarbon and petrochemical industries. The following agencies specialise in the field:

Contracts Consultancy Ltd (CCL), 162-164 Upper Richmond Road, Putney, London SW15 2SL; ☎020-8333 4141; fax 020-8333 4151; e-mail ccl@ccl.uk.com; www.ccl. uk.com, recruits high calibre, well-qualified engineers and professionals with recent experience of offshore and onshore oil, gas, power, and infrastructure projects in the UK, Europe, Africa, the Middle and Far East.

Umm Al-Jawaby Oil Service Company, Recruitment Department, 15-17 Lodge Road, London NW8 7JA; ☎020-7314 6000; fax 020-7314 6001; e-mail jobs@jawaby.co.uk; www.jawaby.co.uk. Overseas recruitment for the oil and petrochemical industries.

Other Countries

IMMIGRATION AND WORK PERMITS

Methods of obtaining the necessary work and residence permits vary, but in most cases the consulate rather than embassy will be responsible for paperwork. In every country in this part of the world, expats will have to overcome bureaucratic procedures and time-consuming paperwork that has to be filled out (usually in triplicate) at each stage of the application. Most of the forms are printed in several languages and in some cases they must also be completed in Arabic, or accompanied by an official translation into Arabic. In most instances, your employer will assist in obtaining a work permit.

Information is given below for each of the countries offering a significant number of employment openings to international workers, along with the addresses of their embassies.

BAHRAIN

Generally considered the most cosmopolitan of the Gulf States, many expatriates based in Saudi Arabia come here for relaxing weekends. This is a small country with only 699,000 people. Nevertheless, of these, 235,000 are non-nationals and the country is home to numerous multinational firms with business in the Gulf. Petroleum production and refining account for 30% of its GDP. Non-oil sectors of the economy include aluminium smelting, ship repair, building materials, iron and steel pelletising and light engineering, as well as food processing and banking. In 2005 Bahrain and the USA ratified a Free Trade Agreement, the first of its kind between the US and a Gulf State. Application for a work permit is made by the employer in Bahrain. The *Embassy of Bahrain* is at 30 Belgrave Square, London SW1X 8QB; ☎020-7201 9170; fax 020-7201 9183; www. bahrainembassy.co.uk and 3502 International Drive, NW, Washington DC 20008; ☎202-342 1111; www.bahrainembassy.org.

JORDAN

The Hashemite Kingdom of Jordan, now ruled by King Abdullah II following the death of the internationally respected ruler of Jordan King Hussein, in 1999, is hoping to become the centre of IT in the Middle East. The country doesn't yet offer many employment opportunities, however, and still relies heavily on foreign aid. There is a *British Council* office at First Circle, Jebel Amman, PO Box 634, Amman 11118 (☎6-4636147/8 www. britishcouncil.org/jordan.htm), which can advise on current English-teaching prospects. The *Embassy of Jordan* is at 6 Upper Phillimore Gardens, London W8 7HA; ☎020-7937 3685; fax 020-7937 8795; e-mail info@jordanembassyuk.org; www.jordanembassyuk. org, and 3504 International Drive, NW, Washington, DC 20008; ☎202-9662664; www. jordanembassyus.org.

KUWAIT

The number of jobs available in Kuwait following the Gulf War has not increased, partly because the Sheikhdom is endeavouring to reduce its dependence on foreign workers. Enquiries should be made to agencies or contractors, rather than embassies. As in other countries of the Middle East there is always a demand for teachers both of EFL and at international schools. Work permits must be by the employer in Kuwait obtained in advance. The *Embassy of the State of Kuwait* can be contacted at 2 Albert Gate, Knightsbridge, London SW1X 7JU; ☎020-7590 3400, fax 020-7823 1712; www.kuwaitinfo.org.uk. The *Kuwait Information Office* in the USA is at 2600 Virginia Avenue, Suite 404, NW, Washington DC 20037; ☎202-338 0211; fax 202-228 0957. There is a useful website detailing all thing Kuwaiti at www.kuwait-info.org.

MOROCCO

Work permits are necessary for employment in Morocco. They are generally only given to people who speak French and/or Arabic, for positions where no Moroccan is available to fill the post. Applications should be addressed to the *Ministère de l'Emploi*, Quartier Administratif, Rabat, Morocco.

Because of high urban unemployment among local professionals and graduates (currently running at over 20 per cent), the main opportunities are in English teaching (see the *Teaching* chapter) or with tour operators (see *Transport, Tourism and Hospitality*). Note that these positions are not usually well paid. The *Moroccan Embassy* is at 49 Queen's Gate Gardens, London SW7 5NE; ☎020-7581 5001; fax 020-7225 3862; e-mail mail@ sifamaldn.org (the Consulate telephone number is 020-7724 0719); 1601 21st Street, NW, Washington DC 20009; ☎202-462 7979; fax 202-265 0161.

OMAN

The Gulf State of Oman has close historical links with Britain, which gave military assistance when the country was threatened by an internal rebellion in the early 1970s. It offers a comparatively good quality of life for expatriates. Advertisements for workers sometimes appear in the national and international recruitment press. The Embassy of Oman is sometimes involved in recruitment of workers from abroad. As with most Gulf States, it is economically reliant on its oil industry. There are, however, also particularly good opportunities for teachers.

A prospective employer must first obtain a Labour Clearance from the Directorate General of Labour, *Ministry of Social Affairs & Labour*, PO Box 560, Muscat and a 'No Objection Certificate' from the Directorate General of Immigration, Oman. Upon arrival, a residence permit (valid for two years, renewable) must be obtained. Further details from the *Embassy of the Sultanate of Oman*, 167 Queen's Gate, London SW7 5HE; ☎020-7225 0001, and 2535 Belmont Road, NW, Washington DC 20008; ☎202-387 1980; fax 202-745 4933.

UNITED ARAB EMIRATES

A union of seven small sheikhdoms, most of the United Arab Emirates' wealth is generated by Abu Dhabi and Dubai. Without their extensive oil and gas reserves, the Emirates' might otherwise still be economically dependent on pearl diving, fishing and dates. Dubai is also a significant trading centre and fast developing its non-petroleum industries. In Abu Dhabi, employment opportunities are mainly in petrochemicals. The economy of the UAE is currently experiencing contraction as its oil exports are highly reliant on the Asian market, which is in significant recession. The UK is the United Arab Emirates' second largest supplier of imports, and a number of British firms have subsidiaries or agents there.

The *Embassy of the United Arab Emirates*, 30 Princes Gate, London SW7 1PT; ☎020-7581 1281; fax 020-7581 9616; e-mail information@uaeembassyuk.net; and 3522 International Court NW, Suite 400, Washington DC 20008; ☎202-243-2400, fax 202-243 2432 suggests that those considering employment in the UAE should write to the *Ministry of Labour*, PO Box 809, Abu Dhabi, but is otherwise unable to help.

OTHER COUNTRIES

There is far less demand for foreign workers in the other countries of the Middle East and North Africa, but the embassies listed below may be able to provide information on procedures if necessary.

Algerian Embassy, 54 Holland Park, London W11 3RS; ☎020-7221 7800; fax 020-7221 0448.
Algerian Embassy, 2118 Kalorama Road, NW, Washington, DC 20008; ☎202-265 2800; fax 202-667 2174; www.algeria-us.org.

Egyptian Embassy, 26 South Street, London W1K 1DW; ☎020-7499 2401; fax 020-7491 1542; e-mail etembuk@hotmail.com.
Egyptian Embassy, 3521 International Court, NW, Washington, DC 20008; ☎202-8955400; fax 202-244 5131; www.egyptembassy.us

Israeli Embassy, 2 Palace Green, London W8 4QB; ☎020-7957 9500; fax 020-7957 9555.
Israeli Embassy, 3514 International Drive, NW, Washington, DC 20008; ☎202-364 5500; www.israelemb.org.

Lebanese Embassy, 21 Palace Garden Mews, London W8 4RA; ☎020-7229 7265; fax 020-7243 1699; e-mail emb.leb@btinternet.com.
Lebanese Embassy, 2560 28th Street, NW, Washington, DC 20008; ☎202-939 6300; fax 202-939 6324; www.lebanonembassyus.org.

Syrian Embassy, 8 Belgrave Square, London SW1X 8PH; ☎020-7245 9012; fax 020-7235 4621; www.syrianembassy.co.uk.
Syrian Embassy, 2215 Wyoming Avenue, NW, Washington, DC 20008; ☎202-2326313; fax 202-265 4585; www.syrianembassy.us.

Tunisian Embassy, 29 Prince's Gate, London SW7 1QG; ☎020-7584 8117; fax 020-7225 2884.
Tunisian Embassy, 1515 Massachusetts Avenue, NW, Washington DC 20005; ☎202-8621850; fax 202-862 1858; http://tunisiaembassy.org/.

Yemeni Embassy, 57 Cromwell Road, London SW7 2ED; ☎020-7584 6607; fax 020-7589 3350; e-mail info@yemenembassy.org.uk; www.yemenembassy.org.uk.
Yemeni Embassy, 2319 Wyoming Avenue, NW, Washington, DC 20008; ☎202-965 4760; fax 202-337 2017; www.yemenembassy.org/.

AFRICA

Work prospects (paying) for semi-skilled foreigners are limited in most of Africa. Much of the continent is in serious financial debt and civil wars, droughts and disease have left their mark on economies that have generally been mismanaged since most if the African countries achieved independence. Corruption is endemic and the economic situation has led to political instability, although democracy is making a tentative reappearance in some countries. On Independence, the former colonial powers left behind their own democratic institutions, but these have often failed to take root, and the map of Africa does not really correspond to the various ethnic and national affiliations. The colonial past of much of Africa has meant there are many cultural links with Western Europe and North America. Africans often speak English or French and have a greater understanding than in some Asian countries of Britain and other European countries. Emigration has meant that many are familiar with life in Europe or the USA – at first, second or third hand. While the formal job market may be unpromising for Western jobseekers (and dependent on 'primary' areas of development and infrastructure) there are informal opportunities for those with the right skills, or for the more adventurous who are willing to fund their own trip and living costs.

Macroeconomic structures – to lay the foundation for industrial and commercial development and the long process of nation building – are the lynchpin of international work in sub-Saharan Africa. Environmentalists and agriculturalists, and those working in related industries such as food processing and distribution, as well as health-care workers, engineers, and those who can train and act as advisers in these fields, are most in demand. The difficulties must not be overlooked, but there are also opportunities for work, in tourism for example, or in the exploitation of mineral and energy resources – which are already sources of employment for international jobseekers in countries like the Gambia, Nigeria, Senegal and Zimbabwe. There are likely to be jobs for many of those experienced enough in the local conditions and who are looking for work while living or travelling in Africa. Otherwise, the international recruitment press, and publications like *African Business* (IC Publications, 7 Coldbath Square, London EC1R 4LQ; ☎020-7713 7711; fax 020-7713 7898; e-mail icpubs@africasia.com; www.africasia.com), can be sources of direct and indirect job opportunities in this region.

Skillshare Africa (126 New Walk, Leicester LE1 7JA; ☎0116-254 1862; fax 0116-254 2614; e-mail info@skillshare.org; www.skillshare.org) is a charity which recruits qualified volunteers and workers in construction, civil engineering, auto mechanics and other technical areas, in Botswana, Lesotho, Mozambique and Swaziland. Offices in Botswana, Kenya, Lesotho, Mozambique, Namibia, Swaziland, and Tanzania. (There is more about voluntary and development work in Africa in the *Voluntary Work* chapter). Other jobs and careers which involve working in Africa can be found in the chapters on the *United Nations, International Organisations, Teaching* and *Transport and Tourism.*

A knowledge of French will in many cases be an advantage. There are vacancies in the often more affluent French-speaking parts of West Africa, for instance, which are generally advertised in the French press. The recruitment pages of the major French newspapers like *Le Monde* (www.mondediplo.com/) and *Le Figaro* (www.lefigaro.fr/) can be a useful way of finding jobs in countries which have strong French connections. Portuguese is also spoken in Angola and Mozambique. English is, however, the most widely known and fastest growing medium of communication in the domains of business and international trade throughout Africa.

South Africa, with its greater expat population, and more developed economy, is a separate case and is dealt with below.

South Africa

o   **South African High Commission,** South Africa House, Trafalgar Square, London WC2N 5DP; ☎020-7451 7299;   fax 020-7451 7283; e-mail general@ southafricahouse.com; www.southafricahouse.com
o   **South African Embassy,** 3051 Massachusetts Avenue NW, Washington DC 20008; ☎202-232-4400; www.saembassy.org
o   **Currency:** 1 Rand = 100 cents (R or ZAR)
o   **Rate of Exchange:** £1 = R12; $1 = R7; €1 = R8.88
o   **Country Code:** +27

South Africa has made a successful transition to a majority elected democratic government, which at present includes all sections of the population. This has led to the raising of sanctions, and increased trade and employment opportunities (although unemployment is a problem, especially at the unskilled end of the job market, across all sections of its ethnically and culturally diverse communities). At the southern end of the African continent, South Africa has the largest economy in the region. Agriculture is strong enough to make it self-sufficient in most food products and an exporter of some, such as fruit and wine. The foundation of its economy is the mining of valuable metals like chromium, manganese, vanadium and platinum, as well as gold and diamonds. There was a slowdown in the 1980s, in part due to sanctions (which were a factor in the transition to a democratic majority government) and the country's priority is currently to ease its considerable foreign debt. A Reconstruction and Development Programme (RDP) was aimed at reducing some of its social inequalities. Manufacturing contributes 32 per cent to its Gross National Product, agriculture four per cent, and service industries 64 per cent.

The underlying strengths of the South African economy can be gauged from its relatively successful survival in the troubled global environment of 1998. In that year depressed commodity prices, including gold, and problems in world markets from Asia to Russia, provided a difficult trading background. Much has changed since then, however, growth has not been strong enough to cut into the 27 per cent unemployment, and daunting economic problems remain from the apartheid era, especially the problems of poverty and lack of economic empowerment among the disadvantaged groups. Existing levels of unemployment, lack of meaningful job creation, and a very serious crime problem are fundamental problems facing the government today. The spectre of AIDS, as in other countries in Africa, is also a major area of concern both in social and economic terms.

Britons still represent the largest group of immigrants to South Africa, with about 1,000 settling there every year. These range, according to the South African High Commission, from pensioners wishing to spend their retirement there to 'young professionals seeking to advance their careers.' A larger number of white South Africans are emigrating every year to countries like Australia, Britain and New Zealand.

GENERAL FACTS

POPULATION

South Africa has a population of 44.1 million. In terms of migration, the majority of newcomers come from the UK, Europe and Zimbabwe. Some of its own citizens have emigrated to Britain and the USA more recently, though. The Republic covers 450,000 square miles (1.2 million sq. km or one-eighth the size of the USA) and is divided into nine regions: Gauteng, Mpumalanga, Northern Province, North West Province, Northern Cape, Free State, KwaZulu Natal, Eastern Cape, and Western Cape.

CLIMATE AND GEOGRAPHY

The country is divided into three main geographical regions: plateau, mountains, and the coastal belt. The vegetation is generally grassland, changing to bush in the Northern Province, and approaching dry, desert conditions in the northwest. The climate is broadly temperate, but the summer heat can be oppressive and often exceeds 86 deg F (30 deg C). Winter temperatures average 62 to 66 deg F (17 to 19 deg C) and during these months the interior is renowned for its clear, sunny skies. The average daily sunshine varies from 7.5 to 9.5 hours.

RELIGION, SPORT & CULTURE

South Africa is a predominantly Christian country (68 per cent). The largest grouping is the Black Independent Church movement, while the largest of the established churches is the Dutch Reformed Church (*Nederduitse Gereformeerde Kerk*). An estimated five million people follow traditional religions to a greater or lesser extent. The other major religions are Hinduism, Islam and Judaism.

Sport is a driving force in South African life. One major factor in bringing about political change in the 1970s and 80s was the severing of international sporting links, in cricket, rugby, and athletics in particular, which are especially popular among the white population. Soccer is mainly popular in the townships, and is the most widely played game in terms of number of participants. Other pastimes include tennis, golf and a host of water sports – in all of which South Africans have excelled.

South Africa possesses as rich a cultural mix as anywhere in the world. The major cities can offer theatres, cinemas, music and other arts, and a cultural life that is a mixture of European and African influences.

FACTORS INFLUENCING EMPLOYMENT

IMMIGRATION

EU, US, Canadian and Australian citizens do not require a visa for holiday and business visits to South Africa. Anyone considering studying or working must, however, obtain the appropriate residence or work permit, and the South African Consular Section (15 Whitehall, London SW1A 2DD; ☎020-7925 8910) can advise on this. Work permits are only issued to individuals who are in possession of a firm written offer or contract of employment from a South African employer. The number of visas is limited, and applicants must meet strict criteria, the most important of which is whether or not a person already in South Africa can fill the position offered. If they can, then you will be refused a work permit.

Citizenship: A migrant can apply for citizenship after a five-year period of permanent residence. No requirement exists for individuals to relinquish their original nationality or citizenship. New migrants are allowed to change their occupation within the first three years of residence only with permission from the Department of Home Affairs. A holder of a permanent residence visa who does not wish to become a South African citizen after the designated five-year period relinquishes the right to both residence and citizenship.

LANGUAGES

There are 11 official languages existing side by side in South Africa: Afrikaans, English, isiNdebele, Sesotho sa Leboa, Sesotho siSwati, Xitsonga, Setswana, Tshivenda, isiXhosa and isiZulu. The majority of South Africans speak English, and signposts, government literature and telephone directories are printed in this language. In general, newspapers and the broadcasting media operate in separate languages, the main ones being English and Afrikaans.

COST AND STANDARD OF LIVING

Although prices are lower than in the UK or USA, so are the salaries. Costs vary from region to region and in the case of fresh foodstuffs, also differ according to the season. The previously disproportionately high standard of living of the white population of mainly Dutch and British descent has diminished somewhat, and there is a new black middle class. All sections of society have suffered from an incomplete recovery from the recession of the 1980s, however. Housing for expats, which typically have swimming pools and tennis courts, is still luxurious by most standards. The excellent climate and superb scenery are major attractions for prospective expats.

HEALTH

The system of healthcare is presently under strain; and private insurance is recommended. One of the first priorities of the national Reconstruction and Development Programme (RDP) has been to bring together the various services as one national health system.

EMBASSIES AND CONSULATES

British High Commission, 255 Hill Street, Arcadia, Pretoria, 0002; ☎12-421 7500; fax 12-421 7555; www.britain.org.za.
There are consulates also in Cape Town, Port Elizabeth, East London, and Durban.
US Embassy, PO Box 9536, 877 Pretorius Street, Pretoria; ☎12-431 4000; fax 12-342 2299; http://pretoria.usembassy.gov/.
Consulates in Cape Town, Durban, and Johannesburg.

TOURIST OFFICES

South African Tourism (SATOUR), 6 Alt Grove, London SW19 4DZ; ☎020-8971 9364; fax 020-8944 6705; www.southafrica.net.
South African Tourist Board (SATOUR), Suite 2040, 20th Floor, 500 Fifth Avenue, New York, NY 10110; ☎212-730 2929; fax 212-764 1980; www.southafrica.net.

CONDITIONS OF WORK

WAGES

A system of industrial councils oversees collective bargaining. Minimum wage levels differ from industry to industry and from region to region. By law, a minimum of two weeks' sick leave is payable. Wages are generally lower than in the UK or the USA.

HOURS

The normal working week is 40 hours, and does not exceed 46 hours. Some industries shut down annually for three weeks from the middle of December.

EMPLOYMENT PROSPECTS

South Africa generally requires migrants with certain specific skills, in particular in computers, medicine, engineering (including petrochemicals), financial management, business consultancy, accountancy and sales.

NEWSPAPERS

The monthly newspaper for potential migrants, *South Africa News*, is available from some travel agents in the UK, or by subscription from Outbound Publishing, 1 Commercial Road, Eastbourne, East Sussex BN21 3XQ; ☎01323-726040; e-mail info@outbound-newspapers.com; www.outboundpublishing.com. *The Powers Turner Group*, Gordon House, Greencoat Lane, London SW1P 1PH; ☎020-7592 8300; fax 020-7592 8301; e-mail ppn-london@publicitas.com; www.publicitas.com, represents the largest circulation newspaper, the *Sunday Times*. Advertisements in South African newspapers can also be placed through their offices in South Africa. One of the major South African newspaper groups is *Independent Newspapers* (☎21-481 6200; www.iol.co.za), who publish the *Cape Argus, Cape Times, Daily News, Pretoria News, The Star, The Mercury, Sunday Independent, Sunday Tribune*, and *The Independent on Saturday* among others.

SPECIFIC CONTACTS

EMPLOYMENT AGENCIES

A selection of agencies is given below:
Kelly Staffing Experts: Gauteng; ☎11-722 8300; fax 11-722 8194; e-mail headoffice@kelly.co.za; www.kelly.co.za. Branches throughout South Africa.
Drake International: 1st Floor, Silver Oaks Centre, 14-36 Si, Durban 4001, KwaZulu Natal; ☎31-2013156; fax 31-201 6013; www.drakeintl.com.
Prostaff: 5 Morris Street, Rivonia, Fourways, Gauteng; ☎11-807 6066; www.prostaff.co.za.
Equity Personnel: 63 Craighall Estates, Alexandra Road, Waterfall Avenue, Craighall, Gauteng; tel/fax 11-442 6871; e-mail equitypersonnel@netactive.co.za.

PROFESSIONAL ORGANISATIONS

Professional organisations are quick to point out they do not act as employment agencies. However, they can often prove a useful source of general information on career prospects and offer possible contacts to job hunters. A selection is given below:

The South African Institute of Architects, Bouhof (ground floor), 31 Robin Hood Road, Robindale, Randburg; ☎11-782 1315; fax 11-782 8771; e-mail admin.gifa@saia.org.za; www.saia.org.za.
The South African Medical Association, PO Box 74789, Lynnwood Ridge, Pretoria 0040; ☎12-481 2000; fax 12-481 2100; www.samedical.org.
The South African Dental Association, 31 Princess of Wales Terrace, Houghton 2193, Gauteng; ☎12-345 4307; www.sada.co.za.
The South African Nursing Council, PO Box 1123, Pretoria 0001, Gauteng; ☎12-420 1000; fax 12-343 5400; e-mail resgistrar@sanc.co.za; www.sanc.co.za.
The South African Pharmacy Council, PO Box 40040, Arcadia 0007, Gauteng; ☎12-319 8500; ☎12-321 1492; www.pharmcouncil.co.za.

OTHER OPPORTUNITIES

General Information on South Africa, listings of companies, commercial and development projects, trade fairs, can be obtained from *UK Trade and Investment*, Kingsgate House, 66-

74 Victoria Street, London SW1E 6SW; ☎020-7215 8000; www.uktradeinvest.gov.uk.

The *United Nations Development Programme* (see the chapter *International Organisations*) has a field office in South Africa, mail address: PO Box 6541, Pretoria 0001; ☎12-338 5063; www.unctad.org.

Other Countries in Africa

IMMIGRATION AND WORK PERMITS

The procedures for immigration vary from one African country to another. The respective embassies in London (with the exception of those listed under *Government Agencies* in the *Getting the Job* chapter) are unlikely to assist in either issuing/processing work permits or arranging work. Tourist offices may be able to offer useful information and advice about the country in question, for medical and travel purposes for example. Applications generally involve a great deal of paperwork, and may take months to process.

NAMIBIA

For those who really want to get away from it all, Namibia could be an ideal destination, with a population of 1.4 million spread out over an area four times the size of Great Britain. This very scenic and unspoilt land only gained its independence from South Africa in March 1990, after years of bitter struggle. The main economic activities are mining and agriculture, as well as tourism. Tourists from Britain and the USA do not require an entry visa for stays of up to three months; business visitors should provide a letter of introduction. Because of very high unemployment, the government has had to clamp down on foreign workers and it is now necessary for potential employers to look for local workers first. Residence and work permits must be arranged in advance with the Ministry of Home Affairs. For further information contact: *Namibian High Commission* at 6 Chandos Street, London W1G 9LU; ☎020-7636 6244; fax 020-7637 5694; e-mail Namibia.hicom@btconnect.com; and the *Namibian Embassy*, 1605 New Hampshire Avenue, NW, Washington DC 20009; ☎202-986-0540; fax 202-986 0443; www.namibianembassyusa.org.

NIGERIA

A brief circular from the Nigerian High Commission in London states bluntly: 'There are no employment opportunities in Nigeria'. The majority of jobs in Nigeria are for skilled personnel who are recruited by multinational companies or the government. These are usually in connection with the oil industry, which accounts for up to 90 per cent of Nigeria's export earnings. English language teachers are often in short supply and jobs are usually available on the spot rather than through UK adverts. GDP rose strongly in 2005, based largely on increased oil exports and high global crude prices. Enquiries to the *Nigerian High Commission* which is at 9 Northumberland Avenue, London WC2 5BX; ☎020-7839 1244; fax 020-7839 8746; www.nigeriahc.org.uk; and at 3519 International Court NW, Washington DC 20008; ☎202-986 8400; fax 202-775 1385; www.nigeriaembassyusa.org.

The rest of Africa offers very few employment opportunities. The positions that are available tend to be with aid agencies and multinational organisations (see chapters on *Voluntary Work, United Nations* and *International Organisations* in particular). The Embassies and High Commissions listed below can provide information on immigration, but are unlikely to offer much advice on work prospects.

Botswana High Commission, 6 Stratford Place, London W1C 1AY; ☎020-7499 0031; fax 020-7495 8595.
Botswana Embassy,1531-3 New Hampshire Avenue, NW Washington 20036, ☎202-244 4990; www.botswanaembassy.org.

Ethiopian Embassy, 17 Prince's Gate, London SW7 1PZ; ☎020-7589 7212; fax 020-7584 7054; e-mail info@ethioembassy.org.uk; www.ethioembassy.org.uk.
Ethiopian Embassy, 3506 International Drive NW, Washington, DC 20008; ☎202-364 1200; e-mail info@ethiopianembassy.org; www.ethiopianembassy.org.

The Gambia High Commission, 57 Kensington Court, London W8 5DG; ☎020-7937 6316-8; fax 020-7937 9095; e-mail gambia@gamhighcom.wanadoo.co.uk.
The Gambia Embassy, Suite 1000, 1155 15th Street, NW, Washington, DC 20005; ☎202-785 1399; www.gambiaembassy.us.

Ghana High Commission, 13 Belgrave Square, London SW1X 8PN; ☎020-7235 4142; fax 020-7245 9552; www.ghana-com.co.uk.
Ghanaian Embassy, 3512 International Drive, NW, Washington, DC 20008; ☎202-686 4520; fax 202-686 4527; www.ghana-embassy.org.

Kenya High Commission, 45 Portland Place, London W1N 4AS; ☎020-7636 2371; fax 020-7323 6717.
Kenya Embassy, 2249 R Street, NW, Washington, DC 20008; ☎202-387 6101; fax 202-462 3829; www.kenyaembassy.com.

Senegal Embassy, 39 Marloes Road, London W8 6LA; ☎020-7937 7237; fax 020-7938 2546; e-mail mail@senegalembassy.co.uk; www.senegalembassy.co.uk.
Senegal Embassy, 2112 Wyoming Avenue, NW, Washington, DC 20008; ☎202-234 0540; www.senegalembassy-us.org.

Sudan Embassy, 3 Cleveland Row, St James's, London SW1A 1DD; ☎020-7839 8080; fax 020-7839 7560; e-mail admin@sudanembassy.co.uk; www.sudan-embassy.co.uk.
Sudan Embassy, 2210 Massachusetts Avenue, NW, Washington, DC 20008; ☎202-338 8565; fax 202-667 2406; www.sudanembassy.org.

Tanzania High Commission, 3 Stratford Place, London WIC 1AS; ☎020-7569 1470; fax 020-7491 3710; www.tanzania-online.gov.uk.
Tanzanian Embassy, 2139 R Street, NW, Washington, DC 20008; ☎202-884 1080; fax 202-797 7408; www.tanzaniaembassy-us.org.

Zambian High Commission, 2 Palace Gate, Kensington, London W8 5NG; ☎020-7589 6655; fax 020-7581 1353; www.zhcl.org.uk.
Zambian Embassy, 2419 Massachusetts Avenue, NW, Washington, DC 20008; ☎202-265 9717; www.zambiaembassy.org.

Embassy of the Republic of Zimbabwe, Zimbabwe House, 429 Strand, London WC2R 0JR, ☎020-7836 7755; fax 020-7379 1167.
Zimbabwe Embassy, 1608 New Hampshire Avenue, NW, Washington, DC 20009; ☎202-3327100; fax 202-483 9326.

Appendix One

Further Reading

In addition to the titles listed below, a number of Vacation Work publications also provide useful further reading and contact details. A catalogue is available from Vacation Work, 9 Park End Street, Oxford OX1 1HH, England; ☎ 01865-241978; fax 01865-790885; www.vacationwork.co.uk.

A Mouthful of Air, Language and Languages, Especially English, Anthony Burgess, Hutchinson, 20 Vauxhall Bridge Road, London SW1V 2SA (1992).

AGCAS Careers Information Booklets, CSU (Publications) Ltd., Prospects House, Booths Street East, Manchester M13 9EP.

And A Good Job Too, David Mackintosh, Orion Publishing Group Ltd., Orion House, 5 Upper St Martin's Lane, London WC2H 9EA (1993).

Build Your own Rainbow, a Workbook for Career and Life Management, Barrie Hopson and Mike Scally, Mercury Books, 125A The Broadway, Didcot, Oxfordshire OX11 8AW.

Career Opportunities in the European Commission, European Commission (UK address: 8 Storey's Gate, London SW1P 3AT).

Careers Encyclopaedia, Audrey Segal and Katherine Lea (eds.), Cassell, Wellington House, 125 Strand, London WC2R 0BB; 387 Park Avenue South, New York, NY 10016-8810.

CEPEC Recruitment Guide, CEPEC Ltd., Princes House, 36 Jermyn Street, London SW1Y 6DN.

Changing Your Job After 35: The Daily Telegraph Guide, Godfrey Golzen and Philip Plumbley, 7th edition, Kogan Page.

The EARLS Guide to Language Schools in Europe, Cassell, Wellington House, 125 Strand, London WC2R 0BB; 387 Park Avenue South, New York, NY 10016-8810.

Great Answers to Tough Interview Questions, by Martin John Yate, Kogan Page.

Guide to Careers in World Affairs, Foreign Policy Association, 729 Seventh Avenue, New York, NY 10019.

How to Complete a Job Application Form, University of London Careers Service (ULCS), 50 Gordon Square, London WC1H 0PQ.

How to Get a Job in the Pacific Rim, Robert Sanborn and Anderson Brandao, Surrey Books, 230 East Ohio Street, Suite 120, Chicago, Illinois 60611.

How to Pass Graduate Recruitment Tests, Mike Bryon, Kogan Page.

How to Write a Curriculum Vitae, University of London Careers Service (ULCS).

International Guide to Qualifications in Education, Cassell.

Job Hunting Made Easy, John Bramham and David Cox, Kogan Page.

Opportunities to Work in the European Community's Institutions, J. Goodman and C. Tobin, CSU (Publications) Ltd., Armstrong House, Oxford Road, Manchester M1 7ED.

The Penguin Careers Guide, Anna Alston and Anne Daniel, Penguin Books, 27 Wrights Lane, London W8 5TZ.

Summer Jobs Abroad, Vacation Work Publications.

Teaching English Abroad, Vacation Work Publications.

What Color Is Your Parachute?, Richard Nelson Bolles, Ten Speed Press, PO Box 7123, Berkeley, California 94707.

Work, Study, Travel Abroad, Council on International Educational Exchange, 205 East 42nd Street, New York, NY 10017.

Work Your Way Around the World, Vacation Work Publications.

Working in the European Union, W.H. Archer and A.J. Raban, CSU (Publications) Ltd.

Working in Tourism, Vacation Work Publications.

Working on Cruise Ships, Vacation Work Publications.

Writers' & Artists' Yearbook 2007, A&C. Black Ltd., 35 Bedford Row, London WC1R 4JH.

Yearbook of Recruitment and Employment Services, Federation of Recruitment and Employment Services Ltd. (FRES), 36-38 Mortimer Street, London W1N 7RB.

Appendix Two

Worldwide Living Standards

The following table represents the average Gross National Income per capita in thirty-nine of the countries cited in this book.

	US Dollars
Australia	27,070
Austria	32,280
Belgium	31,280
Bulgaria	2,750
Canada	28,310
China	1,500
Czech Republic	9,130
Denmark	40,750
Estonia	7,080
Finland	32,880
France	30,370
Germany	30,690
Greece	16,730
Hungary	8,370
Ireland	34,310
Israel	17,360
Italy	26,280
Japan	37,050
Jordan	2,190
Latvia	5,580
Lithuania	5,740
Netherlands	32,130
New Zealand	19,990
Norway	51,810
Poland	6,100
Portugal	14,220
Romania	2,960
Russian Federation	3,400
Saudi Arabia	10,140
Singapore	24,760
Slovak Republic	6,480
Slovenia	14,770
South Africa	3,630
South Korea	16,960
Spain	21,530
Sweden	35,840
Switzerland	49,600
United Kingdom	33,630
USA	41,440

Source: *World Development Indicator, The World Bank,* 2004

Appendix Three

Key to Company Classifications

1 Accounting and Auditing

2 Advertising and Public Relations

3 Airlines and Aerospace Products

4 Banking, Finance and Investment

5 Boats

6 Building Materials

7 Cars & Other Vehicles

8 Chemicals and Pharmaceuticals

9 Clothing

10 Computers and Electronics

11 Cosmetics and Toiletries

12 Dental, Medical and Optical Supplies

13 Department Stores

14 Executive and Management Consultants

15 Export and Import Trading

16 Foodstuffs and Beverages

17 Freight Storage and Transport

18 Furnishings and Domestic Appliances

19 Glassware and Tiles

20 Hotels and Restaurants

21 Hotel Supplies

22 Industrial Instruments and Precision Engineering

23 Insurance

24 Lawyers

25 Machinery and Industrial Equipment

26 Machine Tools

27 Mechanical Handling Equipment

28 Metal Products

29 Music and Musical Instruments

30 Office Equipment

31 Packaging

32 Paints

33 Paper Products

34 Personnel Agencies

35 Petrochemicals

36 Photographic Equipment

37 Plastics

38 Printing, Publishing and Graphics

39 Pumps and Hydraulic Equipment

40 Real Estate

41 Ropes and Cables

42 Rubber Goods

43 Security

44 Shoes

45 Telecommunications

46 Textiles

47 Tobacco and Tobacco Machinery

48 Tourist Agencies and Travel Services

49 Toy Manufacture

50 Watches and Jewellery

Index to Organisations

Vacation Work Publications

**Vacation Work Publications, 9 Park End Street, Oxford OX1 1HH
Tel 01865-241978 Fax 01865-790885**

Visit us online for more information on our unrivalled range of titles for work,
travel and gap years, readers' feedback and regular updates:
www.vacationwork.co.uk

Books are available in the USA from
The Globe Pequot Press, Guilford, Connecticut
www.globepequot.com